The Great Calming and Contemplation

Kuroda Institute
Classics in East Asian Buddhism

The Record of Tung-shan
Translated by William F. Powell

Tracing Back the Radiance:
Chinul's Korean Way of Zen
Translated with an Introduction by Robert E. Buswell, Jr.

The Great Calming and Contemplation

A Study and Annotated Translation of the First Chapter of Chih-i's Mo-ho chih-kuan

Neal Donner and Daniel B. Stevenson

A Kuroda Institute Book
University of Hawaii Press
Honolulu

Printed in the United States of America
93 94 95 96 97 98 5 4 3 2 1

Library of Congress Cataloging-in-Publication Data
Donner, Neal Arvid.
The great calming and contemplation : a study and annotated translation of the first chapter of Chih-i's Mo-ho chih-kuan / Neal Donner and Daniel B. Stevenson.
p. cm. — (Classics in East Asian Buddhism)
"A Kuroda Institute book."
Includes bibliographical references and index.
ISBN 0-8248-1514-9 (alk. paper)
1. Chih-i, 538–597. Mo ho chih kuan. 2. Meditation—T'ien-t'ai Buddhism. 3. T'ien-t'ai Buddhism—Doctrines. I. Stevenson, Daniel B., 1952– II. Chih-i, 538–597. Mo ho chih kuan. English. Selections. f1993. III. Title. IV. Series.
BQ9149.C454M6433 1993
294.3'443—dc20 92-41546
CIP

The Kuroda Institute for the Study of Buddhism and Human Values is a non-profit, educational corporation, founded in 1976. One of its primary objectives is to promote scholarship on Buddhism in its historical, philosophical, and cultural ramifications. The Institute thus attempts to serve the scholarly community by providing a forum in which scholars can gather at conferences and colloquia. Conference volumes, as well as individual monographs, are published in the Institute's Studies in East Asian Buddhism series. To complement these scholarly studies, the Institute also makes available reliable translations of some of the major classics of East Asian Buddhism in the present series.

University of Hawaii Press Books are printed on acid-free paper and meet the guidelines for permanence and durability of the Council on Library Resources

Contents

Foreword

Buddhism is the religious teaching of Śākyamuni Buddha, who lived in northern India nearly two and one half millennia ago. It was introduced to the world when Śākyamuni achieved supreme perfect enlightenment and first began to expound the nature of ultimate reality and the methods of religious practice through which it could be achieved. According to Buddhist teaching, all people intrinsically possess the same capacity as Śākyamuni to become Buddhas or "fully enlightened beings." It is my wish that everyone would embrace religious practice and become Buddhas. When the world becomes a world of Buddhas or bodhisattvas who aspire to become Buddhas, then for the first time our cherished hope for the achievement of human happiness and world peace will be realized.

Buddhism consists of the Buddha dharma and the Buddhist path. The Buddha dharma expresses the content and nature of the Buddha's enlightenment. We are all driven by our preoccupation with the narrow and fictitious self and thereby ignore the natural law of the interdependence of causes and conditions. For this we are always in conflict with others and the world around us and must endure a life of needless suffering. The Buddha dharma instructs us to rid ourselves of suffering and find the intrinsic joy of Buddhahood by abandoning our ignorant preoccupation with self and abiding in the realm where there is no self. The Buddhist path offers concrete guidance for cultivating body and mind in order to grasp ultimate reality and achieve freedom from the afflictions of the illusory self. Developing wisdom and awakening to the real is the Buddha dharma. Actualizing enlightenment within ourselves and living in accordance with reality is the Buddhist path.

The Great Calming and Contemplation (*Mo-ho chih-kuan*) was expounded by the Chinese meditation master Chih-i (538–597), the Grand Master of

Translated by Francis Cook and Neal Donner.

Mount T'ien-t'ai, and taken down by his disciple, master Kuan-ting (561–632) of Chang-an. It is a manual offering comprehensive instruction on how to perfect these twin aspects of the Buddhist teaching—the Buddha dharma and the Buddhist path. Central to the text is the concept of "calming and contemplation, tranquility and luminosity" (*chih-kuan ming-ching*) as a religious practice.[1] This concept was esteemed by nearly every Buddhist movement in China. It was transmitted to Japan when Saichō or Dengyō Daishi (766–822) established the Tendai teachings on Mount Hiei, and from there it became the foundation of Japanese Buddhism.

The Buddha dharma and the Buddhist path represent the doctrinal theory and practice of Buddhism, respectively. When these two aspects of the teaching interpenetrate fully, all afflictions and karma will be extinguished and a knowledge of undefiled reality equal to that of the Buddhas themselves will stand revealed. The *Mo-ho chih-kuan* explains in theory and practice how, when Buddha nature is manifested and all things converge spontaneously in the one mind, there is the possibility of abiding in the realm of perfect freedom. It teaches that sitting in meditation (*zazen*) is the principal means for simultaneous cultivation of calming and contemplation, stillness and illumination. Of all the methods for acquiring samādhi or insight into ultimate reality, seated meditation is the easiest to practice. For this reason, in summarizing the various methods for cultivating samādhi mentioned in Buddhist scriptures, the *Mo-ho chih-kuan* makes a special point of demonstrating how the entire path to realization may be subsumed in the single practice of seated meditation. This instruction is an important and distinctive feature of the text.

Chih-i believed that the many different teachings expounded by the Buddha Śākyamuni and preserved in the Buddhist tradition were devised according to the principle of expedient means (upāya). That is to say, since the inconceivable reality of Buddhahood was far too sublime for most people to grasp directly, the Buddha devised provisional teachings to match the different capacities of his followers and lead them in graduated fashion to the singular goal of Buddhahood. With the preaching of the *Lotus Sūtra* toward the end of his career, Śākyamuni brought all of these expedients together, elucidated their design, and revealed their ultimate end. Thus the *Lotus Sūtra* was preached as the consummate statement of Buddhist teaching that would serve as a guide to all people for ages to come.

For Chih-i, the *Lotus Sūtra* itself is the essence of Buddhism, the eternal teaching that informs all other Buddhist scriptures and promises tranquility of mind and hope for all people in all times. On the basis of this

1. Kuan-ting's preface to the *Mo-ho chih-kuan* opens with these four words. They have come to be regarded as the essence of the text and of T'ien-t'ai practice.

belief, he taught the *Mo-ho chih-kuan,* which he presented as a method of practice that encompasses the spiritual vision of this sūtra. In other words, the *Mo-ho chih-kuan* is the guide for putting the sublime doctrine of the *Lotus Sūtra* into practice—a guide to realizing the true spirit of the *Lotus.*

The marvelous doctrine of the *Lotus Sūtra* itself is spelled out in two other works of Chih-i: the *Fa-hua hsüan-i,* which discusses the profound import of the *Lotus Sūtra,* and the *Fa-hua wen-chü,* which is a phrase-by-phrase explanation of the contents of the scripture. These three treatises—known as the "three great texts of T'ien-t'ai"—together explain the essence of the Buddha dharma and Buddhist path, Buddhist doctrine and Buddhist practice, as set forth in the *Lotus Sūtra* and as understood by Chih-i and the T'ien-t'ai tradition.

The *Mo-ho chih-kuan* is composed of ten chapters, which are organized according to a sequence of five basic topics: (1) arousing the thought of enlightenment, (2) practice, (3) manifesting the results, (4) rending the net (of confusion over the diversity of Buddhist teachings), and (5) returning to the great abode. Chapters 1 to 5—concerned with arousing the thought of enlightenment—offer an overview of the path of calming and contemplation, define the terminology of calming and contemplation, expound the conceptual essence of calming and contemplation, demonstrate how the totality of Buddhist practice is accomplished through the single method of calming and contemplation, and so on, all in order to give the practitioner a clear understanding of the technique of calming and contemplation (*chih-kuan*) and to awaken in him or her a keen determination to practice it. This is because one must arouse the thought of enlightenment properly in order to practice Buddhism effectively. The sixth and seventh chapters of the *Mo-ho chih-kuan* deal with specific details of practice. Chapter 6 discusses the concrete preparations and preliminary conditions necessary for the successful practice of calming and contemplation. Chapter 7, which is by far the longest, describes in great detail the technique of calming and contemplation proper. Regrettably, Chih-i never delivered his lectures on the remaining three of the proposed ten chapters and five topics.

Calming and contemplation represents the most suitable method of discipline for achieving human perfection. "Calming" (*chih*) allows the mind to enter samādhi and dwell peacefully in its originally enlightened nature. "Contemplation" (*kuan*) involves using this mind that is dwelling peacefully in its original nature as a basis for contemplating the identity of all things with ultimate reality. This is the practice of simultaneously combining the "tranquility" of samādhi, which renders the mind selfless, with the "luminosity" of wisdom, which sees all things universally just as they are, displaying their true value. This basic concept has been taught in scriptures and treatises for a long time, and the *Mo-ho chih-kuan* is esteemed because of the profound and detailed instruction it provides on its actual practice.

Altogether there are three different approaches to the practice of calming and contemplation: the gradual, the variable, and the perfect and sudden. In the gradual, which is designed for persons of lesser ability, one progresses in sequence from shallow techniques to deep. In the variable, one practices in varying ways, depending on one's particular capacity and the circumstances at hand. The perfect and sudden approach is the loftiest of the three, intended for persons of the keenest ability. In this practice one develops the virtues of samādhi by conforming directly to ultimate reality from the very beginning. All three approaches are teachings of Mahāyāna Buddhism and will ultimately lead to Buddhahood, but the *Mo-ho chih-kuan* mentions the first two approaches only briefly and focuses mainly on the perfect and sudden calming and contemplation. Hence the text is called "The Great (*Mo-ho*) Calming and Contemplation." The heart of the *Mo-ho chih-kuan*'s teaching on the perfect and sudden calming and contemplation is found in the discussion of the four forms of samādhi in the first chapter (the Synopsis, whose translation follows), the twenty-five preliminary expedients in the sixth chapter (on Preparatory Expedients), and the ten modes for practicing calming and contemplation in the seventh chapter (on Contemplation Proper). The text has been greatly revered for the comprehensive way in which these three sections systematize the essentials of Buddhist practice.

All people are endowed with a supreme, universal nobility. If, through truly understanding this nobility individuals realize that they are inalienable members of a single community, and if these self-awakened individuals truly create a community of self and others who help each other, then for the first time a balance of self and society will appear that will afford genuine peace and happiness for all. In the wake of scientific advancement, however, humans have lately displayed a tendency to make results the primary consideration. When this preoccupation with result turns into gross materialism, there is a danger that it will destroy the cooperative bond between self and others. It is important that the nobility of the self stands at the center of society. If we do not have a society in which self and others coexist satisfactorily, real peace and happiness will also not appear. We must grasp reality on the basis of the truth of interrelationship, of mutual dependence of causes and conditions, and create a society of selfless individuals who think and act out of spontaneous concern for and gratitude toward other people. Therefore, the time has come when people everywhere in the world need to understand the *Mo-ho chih-kuan* and actually practice it in order to perfect themselves.

Indeed, this English translation of the first chapter (or Synopsis) may turn out to be our best guide to human happiness. Having a deep interest in the translation of this crucial Chinese text, with all its profound meaning, I would like to conclude by paying my respects to the labor that went into it.

THE REVEREND YAMADA ETAI

Preface

In the centuries following its founding by the Buddha Śākyamuni around the fifth century B.C.E., the Buddhist tradition gradually spread from its homeland in India throughout the vast reaches of the Asian continent. In response to the diverse cultures it encountered there, new forms of Buddhist thought, practice, and institution were produced, many of which became vital and self-sustaining traditions in their own right. When we speak of Buddhism today, we generally do so in terms of three broad regional legacies, each of which is identified by a common written language, canonical literature, and institutional culture. They include the Buddhism of East Asia (i.e., China, Korea, Japan, and Vietnam), the Thervāda tradition of Southeast Asia, and the Vajrayāna or "tantric" Buddhism of the Himalayas.

The work at hand is a translation and study of a major section of the *Mo-ho chih-kuan* or "[Treatise on] the Great Calming and Contemplation" by the Chinese monk Chih-i (538–597). Chih-i himself is revered as the principal founder of the T'ien-t'ai school, one of the most influential and enduring traditions of East Asian Buddhism.[1] As the terms "calming" (*chih* or *śamatha*) and "contemplation" (*kuan* or *vipaśyanā*) in the title indicate, his *Great Calming and Contemplation* is primarily a treatise on meditation or religious practice. It is styled the "great" (*mo-ho* or *mahā*) calming and contemplation because it sets forth the "perfect and sudden" (*yüan-tun*) approach to Buddhahood, a distinctively East Asian conception of the Buddhist path regarded by Chih-i and his contemporaries as the epitome of the Buddha's teaching.[2] This fact, together with the text's

1. The tradition takes its name after Mount T'ien-t'ai in southeast China, the mountain on which Chih-i established the school's first major monastic center. In Korea the Chinese name is read "Chŏntae," and in Japan, "Tendai."

2. The earliest editions of the *Mo-ho chih-kuan* circulated by Chih-i's disciple

extraordinary comprehensiveness, has not only made the *Mo-ho chih-kuan* the foremost treatise of the T'ien-t'ai school but has also earned it the respect of virtually every school of East Asian Buddhism. Such an illustrious history and catholicity of appeal secures it a place alongside of Buddhagosa's *Visuddhimagga* and Tsong-kha-pa's *Lam-rim chen-mo* as one of the great classics of Buddhist spirituality.

The original text of the *Mo-ho chih-kuan* consists of ten main chapters distributed over a total of ten fascicles—the equivalent of some four or five volumes in English. The present book contains a translation of the first chapter of the *Mo-ho chih-kuan*, together with the influential preface composed and attached to the text by Chih-i's disciple, Kuan-ting (561–632), the man originally responsible for recording and editing the work. This opening chapter is itself known as the Synopsis (*ta-i*), for the simple fact that it rehearses in condensed form the basic structure and thematic content of the *Mo-ho chih-kuan* as a whole, with certain variations. Because of its self-contained character, T'ien-t'ai exegetes have treated it almost as a work unto itself. We are thus not without precedent in choosing to publish the Synopsis chapter as a separate translation.

The work that follows is based on a 1976 dissertation written by Neal Donner for his doctorate at the University of British Columbia. In 1989, Peter N. Gregory proposed adding it, as revised by Dan Stevenson, to the Kuroda Institute's Classics in East Asian Buddhism series, which is published in conjunction with the University of Hawaii Press.

Our translation relies on the *Taishō shinshū daizōkyō* edition of the *Mo-ho chih-kuan*,[3] together with a collection of four major interlineal commentaries—one Chinese, three Japanese—issued under the title *Makashikan*, 5 vols., Bukkyō taikei series nos. 22–26.[4] The four include (1) *Chih-kuan fu-hsing ch'uan-hung chüeh*, by the ninth Chinese T'ien-t'ai patriarch, Chan-jan (711–782);[5] (2) *Shikan bugyō shiki*, by the eminent twelfth-century Tendai exegete Shōshin; (3) *Makashikan bugyō kōgi*, by the late Tokugawa-period Tendai monk Chikū (1780–1862); and (4) the

---

and editor, Kuan-ting, were actually titled "The Perfect and Sudden Calming and Contemplation" (*Yüan-tun chih-kuan*). It was not until the third and final edition that Kuan-ting settled on the current title.

3. T no. 1911. The *Taishō* text is based on a Ming-dynasty printed canonical edition, with alternate readings provided through collation with Sung- and Tokugawa-period printed texts.

4. Bukkyō taikei kanseikai (Iwada Kyōen, chief ed.) *Makashikan*, 5 vols., Bukkyō taikei series no. 22–26 (Tokyo: Bukkyō taikei kanseikai, 1912, 1919, 1932, 1933; reprinted by Nakayama shobō busshorin, 1978). The same four commentaries, with the original text, have been republished together in Tada Kōryū, ed., *Tendai daishi zenshū: Makashikan*, 5 vols. (Tokyo: Nippon bussho kankōkai, d.u.).

5. Also found in T no. 1912.

Makashikan bugyō kōjutsu, by the nineteenth-century Tendai priest Shudatsu (1804–1884).[6]

Various modern Japanese renderings of the *Mo-ho chih-kuan* have also proved helpful. Donner originally had at his disposal Sekiguchi Shindai's two-volume *Makashikan* published in the popular Iwanami bunko series (1966).[7] Since then, several additional translations have become available, including those by Muranaka Yūjō[8] and Nitta Masa'aki.[9] Two other recently published reference tools indispensable to the study of the *Mo-ho chih-kuan* also deserve mention. One is the *Makashikan ichiji sakuin*,[10] a massive single-character concordance to the text; the other, a comprehensive listing of scriptural citations in the *Mo-ho chih-kuan*.[11]

With Peter Gregory's encouragement and coordination, Donner in 1989 went back through his dissertation and made numerous corrections and improvements. Over the next year, Stevenson compared the translation line by line with the original text, consulting along with it T'ien-t'ai commentaries and modern Japanese translations. Various minor adjustments to wording and phrasing were made throughout the translation, but substantial revisions were limited only to select sections—a point testifying to the durability of Donner's original work. The most significant changes introduced by Stevenson occur in the chapter on the four samādhis, which deals with the ritual practices that are his specialty.

Stevenson also revised the footnotes, with the aim to place the content of the *Mo-ho chih-kuan* more within its traditional exegetical framework. Hence, where Donner had previously paraphrased or explained, Stevenson introduced extensive citations from Chan-jan's commentary (*Chih-kuan fu-hsing ch'uan-hung chüeh*) and other T'ien-t'ai sources.[12]

6. Chikū and Shudatsu were both influential figures associated with the Anraku-ha, a late Tokugawa-period movement on Mount Hiei that sought to curb the influence of esoteric *hongaku* thought and to revive the "classical" traditions of Tendai monastic discipline and exegesis.

7. Sekiguchi Shindai, *Makashikan*, 2 vols., Iwanami bunko series, 33-309-2 (Tokyo: Iwanami shoten, 1966).

8. Muranaka Yūjō, *Makashikan*, Daijō butten no. 6 (Tokyo: Chūō kōronsha, 1988).

9. Nitta Masa'aki, *Makashikan*, Butten kōza no. 25 (Tokyo: Daizō shuppansha, 1989).

10. Yamada Kazuo, ed., *Makashikan ichiji sakuin* (Tokyo: Daisan bunmeisha, 1985).

11. Chūgoku bukkyō kenkyūkai, ed., *Makashikan inyō tenkyo sōran* (Tokyo: Nakayama shobō busshorin, 1987), previously published in serial form in *Tendai* 2–6 (1981–1983). This list of references is derived almost verbatim from the four commentaries contained in Iwada, ed., *Makashikan*, Bukkyō taikei series nos. 22–26. Certain attributions remain tenuous.

12. Citations from the *Chih-kuan fu-hsing ch'uan-hung chüeh* are introduced by

Diverse technical terms are generally rendered literally. Some superfluous distinctions may thereby be retained, where a single English equivalent could possibly have communicated the meaning more efficiently. But the careful reader will not be misled. On the other hand, a one-to-one correspondence between Chinese and English technical terms simply cannot be preserved for such a common term as *fa* ("dharma," "teaching," "psycho-physical constituent," or simply "thing"), where range of meaning and/or frequent repetition make it difficult to stick to a single equivalent. In instances when a knowledge of the original Chinese term is useful it has been transliterated in parentheses. A glossary of these terms (with character equivalents) is provided following the translation.

The *Mo-ho chih-kuan* is a notoriously terse and uneven text—a condition that probably reflects the fact that it began as a set of lecture notes taken down by Chih-i's disciple Kuan-ting. Around many of the work's internal rifts have grown exegetical systems and controversies that have occupied T'ien-t'ai readers for centuries. For us as translators to gloss over or resolve these difficulties without due attention to interpretive tradition would be to obscure many of the very features that have contributed to the work's ongoing vitality. Hence, significant inconsistencies and ambiguities in the text (especially when they have proved problematic for later T'ien-t'ai tradition) are deliberately preserved in the translation and highlighted in the footnotes. Major intrusions in the translation are signaled by the use of brackets.

The translation of obscure T'ien-t'ai technical terms or expressions has been based, where possible, on definitions within the writings of Chih-i or within the particular body of sūtras and treatises that he and his contemporaries are known to have used. Otherwise Chan-jan was taken as the authority. There are two reasons for relying so heavily on the latter in the text and the notes. First, it is at best tenuous to attempt any systematic reconstruction of the *Mo-ho chih-kuan* apart from Chan-jan's commentary, given the lack of early materials as well as the enormous impact that Chan-jan's work has had on shaping the current text.[13] And second, since Chan-jan's version of the text and commentary became the normative one for virtually all of East Asia, adopting his reading at least puts us within the mainstream of later T'ien-t'ai exegetical discourse. Chapter subheadings in the translation follow Chan-jan, as do most (but not all) decisions on variant textual readings.

---

the words, "Chan-jan says (or states, etc.)," followed by the respective *Taishō* reference. Additional sources consulted include works of Hui-ssu (515–577), Chih-i (538–597), Kuan-ting (561–632), and Chan-jan (711–782), as well as Sung-period figures such as Chih-li (960–1028) and Tsun-shih (963–1032).

13. See Satō Tetsuei's work on the development of the *Mo-ho chih-kuan* as summarized in his *Tendai daishi no kenkyū*.

The main body of this work is preceded by a foreword and three introductory chapters. The foreword is composed by the Reverend Yamada Etai, the current archbishop of the Japanese Tendai school. The first of the three introductory chapters, by both Donner and Stevenson, provides background for certain key T'ien-t'ai concepts as well as for the design of the Synopsis Chapter and its relationship to the *Mo-ho chih-kuan* as a whole. The second and third chapters, by Stevenson, provide an overview of the cultural history of the *Mo-ho chih-kuan* and reflect on issues concerning its role as a sacred text in the T'ien-t'ai tradition.

In the course of completing this project we have benefited from the support of numerous sponsors, friends, and colleagues. Special gratitude goes to Yamada Etai, archbishop of the Tendai school on Mount Hiei, for his generous support in the form of a subvention to help defray the publication costs of this project (as well as for kindly supplying the calligraphy of the title that graces the cover and frontispiece of the book); and to Maezumi Roshi, President of the Kuroda Institute, for his continued interest and moral support.

Peter N. Gregory, Executive Director of the Kuroda Institute and Professor of Religious Studies at the University of Illinois at Champaign-Urbana, has given generously of his time to offer editorial guidance, to proofread successive drafts, and to help produce the final manuscript. Without his kindness and encouragement (not to mention his patience) the work would never have seen completion. Our thanks also go to Barbara E. Cohen for her labor in copyediting the manuscript and in compiling the index.

Much of Stevenson's work on this project was completed while in residence at the University of Michigan under the combined support of the University of Michigan Institute for the Study of Buddhist Literature and the Chung-Hwa Institute of Buddhist Studies, Taipei. The stimulating company of Professors Luis O. Gomez, Donald S. Lopez, Jr., and T. Griffith Foulk of the University of Michigan Buddhist Studies program has contributed to his effort in numerous untold ways.

I (Dan Stevenson) wish to thank two persons for their very special roles in this enterprise. One is the Venerable Sheng-yen, President of the Chung-Hwa Institute of Buddhist Studies, who has steadily encouraged my studies over the years and without whom I would have no real inkling of the depth and vitality of the Chinese Buddhist tradition. The other is my wife, Miwa. Her loving support and her willingness to put up with the extraordinary pressures that a project like this brings have been unfailing. My personal labors are above all dedicated to them.

And I (Neal Donner) would like to thank the family that has helped make me me: my late father Otto Donner, who loved me too much to protest my aberrant career choices; his second wife Maria Donner, who so much enriched his latter years; my former wife Carol Linnell, who has never forgotten her co-parenting role; my children Erich Donner and Rebecca Donner, who taught me as much as Buddhism has; my brother Michael Donner, who never stopped loving me despite our differences; and my mother Jane Donner Sweeney and her second husband Vince Sweeney, who have blended the search for enlightenment with the honoring of family connections better than any human beings I have ever known.

DANIEL B. STEVENSON
NEAL DONNER

Abbreviations and Conventions

Chan-jan	Unless otherwise specified, refers to Chan-jan, *Chih-kuan fu-hsing ch'uan-hung chüeh*
Great Treatise	*Ta-chih-tu lun* (**Mahāprajñāpāramitā Śāstra*), attributed to Nāgārjuna
Hsiao chih-kuan	*Hsiu-hsi chih-kuan tso-ch'an fa-yao*
HTC	*Wan-tzu hsü-tsang ching* (Hong Kong reprint edition of *Dai-Nihon zokuzōkyō*)
Hurvitz	Unless otherwise specified, refers to Leon Hurvitz, trans., *Scripture of the Lotus Blossom of the Fine Dharma*
Kōgi	*Makashikan bugyō kōgi*, by Echō Chikū (1780–1862)
Kōjutsu	*Shikan bugyō kōjutsu*, by Daihō Shudatsu (1804–1884)
Lotus Sūtra	*Miao-fa lien-hua ching* (*Saddharmapuṇḍarīka Sūtra*)
MHCK	*Mo-ho chih-kuan*
Middle Treatise	*Chung-lun* (*Mūlamadhyamakakārikā*), by Nāgārjuna
Muranaka	Muranaka Yūjō, *Makashikan*
Nitta	Nitta Masa'aki, *Makashikan*
Shiki	*Shikan bugyō shiki*, by Hōjibō Shōshin (fl. late twelfth century)
T	*Taishō shinshū daizōkyō*
TCTL	*Ta-chih-tu lun*
Tz'u-ti ch'an-men	*Shih ch'an p'o-lo-mi tz'u-ti fa-men*

Citations from the Taishō canon are given according to the following conventions. Entire works are cited by author (where appropriate), title, and Taishō serial number (e.g., *Miao-fa lien-hua ching*, T no. 261). Specific passages are cited by author (where appropriate), title, Taishō volume number, page number(s), column(s) (a, b, or c), and, if appropriate, line number(s) (e.g., *Chung-lun,* T 30.2b6–7). In the case of texts contained in the *Hsü tsang ching*, entire works are cited by author (where appropriate), title and HTC volume number (e.g., Tao-sheng, *Fa-hua ching shu,* HTC 150). Specific passages are cited by author (where appropriate), title, volume number, page number(s), column(s) (a or b), and line number(s) (e.g., Tsung-chien, *Shih-men cheng-t'ung,* HTC 130.763a6).

Transliterations of Chinese terms are given according to the Wade-Giles system; Japanese, revised Hepburn. As a rule, Sanskrit is used in the translation only when a Chinese term is itself a transcription of Sanskrit, or when the Chinese renders a Buddhist technical term that now sees common English usage (e.g., dharma). Buddhist Sanskrit terminology that is considered to have entered the English language (see *Webster's Third New International Dictionary*) is not italicized.

Titles of Buddhist sūtras and exegetical works are reproduced in various ways. For scriptures that are well known to Western audiences, we have adopted the most commonly used English, Sanskrit, or Chinese equivalent: e.g., *Lotus Sūtra, Middle Treatise, Vimalakīrti Sūtra, Avataṃsaka Sūtra, Nirvāṇa Sūtra, Ying-lo ching.* Titles that are extant in Sanskrit or that represent Chinese transcriptions of Sanskrit are generally given in Sanskrit. Where the title is reconstructed from a Chinese transcription (without an extant Sanskrit counterpart) an asterisk (*) is placed before it (e.g., **Daśabhūmika-vibhāṣa Śāstra*). Chinese titles are either translated into English or transcribed in romanized form, the deciding factor being the relative frequency with which the text appears. All titles and their Chinese equivalents are cross-referenced in the bibliography.

For easy reference, page, column, and line numbers for the Taishō edition of the *Mo-ho chih-kuan* are given at the beginning of each paragraph of the translation in part II.

Part I

The *Mo-ho chih-kuan* and the T'ien-t'ai Tradition

CHAPTER 1

The Text of the *Mo-ho chih-kuan*

Neal Donner and Daniel B. Stevenson

Background of the *Mo-ho chih-kuan*

This book presents an annotated translation of the first chapter of the meditation text *Mo-ho chih-kuan* (The Great Calming and Contemplation)[1] by Chih-i (538–597). As the principal founder of the T'ien-t'ai tradition, Chih-i produced one of the most successful syntheses of the disparate fragments of teaching that Chinese Buddhism had become in the 400 years since the last decades of the Han dynasty, when Indian sūtras were first made available to the Chinese in a language they could understand. Not that there were in his day no other men devoted to this vast eclectic enterprise; already by the late fifth and early sixth centuries broad systematizations of Buddhist doctrine—known as *p'an-chiao* or "classification of teachings"—had become the standard tool for sorting out the complexities of Buddhist tradition and establishing its most sublime principles. It is well known that Chih-i borrowed heavily from a number of such theories popular among his contemporaries, notably the "three southern and seven northern" systems of *p'an-chiao* that he mentions in his works.[2] Not only did his own scheme of doctrinal classification turn out to be more comprehensive and enduring than those of his predecessors, but he also brought religious practice (*kuan*) into his great synthesis so firmly that the T'ien-t'ai tradition—alongside of the better-known Ch'an or Zen tradition—has remained one of the great well-springs and theoretical arbiters of East Asian Buddhist practice down to modern times. In short, Chih-i—surveying the totality of the received scriptural tradition—united practice (*kuan*) with doctrine (*chiao*), and doctrine with practice, producing an integrated systematization of the two,

1. T no. 1911. *Mo-ho* is a Chinese transcription of the Sanskrit *mahā*, meaning "great." *Chih-kuan* represents the Chinese translation of *śamatha-vipaśyanā*.
2. These theories and their impact on Chih-i are discussed in Hurvitz, "Chih-i."

where his predecessors had attempted only to arrange the various doctrines in the sūtras into an understandable and consistent whole. The terminologies and categories of classification around which Chih-i organized this broad-reaching synthesis introduced vital new ways of looking at Buddhist thought and practice and opened the door to developments in Buddhist thought and practice hitherto unseen in Indian tradition.

His role in producing a unified vision of Chinese Buddhism has often been compared to the role of his patron, the first emperor of the Sui dynasty (581–618), in reuniting the north and south of China after a period of three and one-half centuries of geopolitical division. Indeed, the analogy is closer yet: before the Sui the north of China is said to have been oriented toward the practical side of Buddhism, just as its leaders were men of action, often barbarian in ancestry, whereas the south tended toward the theoretical, the doctrinal, just as its leaders were aristocrats and scholar officials. Whatever the legitimacy of such historical metaphors or the nature of the relationship between Chih-i and his imperial patron,[3] the only points that need emphasis are the remarkable comprehensiveness of Chih-i's synthesis of Buddhist teaching and the deliberate emphasis that this synthesis places on the integration of doctrinal learning and religious practice. In Chih-i's own words, doctrine and practice are like "the two wings of a bird" or "the two wheels of a cart."[4] Should either one of the two be impaired, spiritual progress would falter.

Most of Chih-i's works fall easily into the category of either doctrine or practice. What little is known about his thought in the West derives mostly from the doctrinal side, and within that it is primarily his system of doctrinal classification that is expounded in outline in Western sources,[5] especially the so-called five periods and eight teachings (*wu-shih pa-chiao*), a matter that will not be dealt with here other than to note that Sekiguchi Shindai has thrown serious doubt on the received opinion that this rubric accurately represents the thought of Chih-i.[6] Less known is

3. The most thorough biography of Chih-i in English remains that of Leon Hurvitz in his "Chih-i," pp. 100–182. Stanley Weinstein has discussed the effect of imperial patronage on Chih-i's doctrinal system in "Imperial Patronage in the Formation of T'ang Buddhism." For the political background, see Wright, "The Formation of Sui Ideology, 581–604."

4. The complementarity of doctrine and practice as a central theme in Chih-i's teaching is discussed in Donner, "Sudden and Gradual Intimately Conjoined."

5. The work of Daniel Stevenson has begun to rectify this situation; see, for example, his 1987 Columbia University dissertation, "The T'ien-t'ai Four Forms of Samādhi and Late North-South Dynasties, Sui, and Early T'ang Buddhist Devotionalism."

6. Sekiguchi's seminal articles on this subject (penned over a period from 1965 to the mid-1970s), together with selections from his most significant opponents, have been conveniently collected and republished in Sekiguchi, ed., *Tendai kyō-*

the side of his system dealing with religious practice. About half of the thirty-five of Chih-i's works still extant[7] deal with practice, as can be immediately seen from their titles, which all contain words like "dhyāna" *(ch'an)*, "calming and contemplating" (*chih-kuan*), "samādhi" (*san-mei*), and "repentance" (*ch'an*).

The three best-known works of Chih-i are the *Fa-hua hsüan-i* (Profound Meaning of the *Lotus Sūtra*),[8] the *Fa-hua wen-chü* (Words and Phrases of the *Lotus Sūtra*),[9] and the *Mo-ho chih-kuan* (The Great Calming and Contemplation). These are revered as the very heart of T'ien-t'ai tradition, for which they are commonly referred to as the "three great texts of T'ien-t'ai," or alternatively as the "three great texts of the *Lotus*." The first two belong to the doctrinal part of Chih-i's works, as they are both commentaries to the *Lotus Sūtra*[10] in their different ways. The third of the three great texts, the *Mo-ho chih-kuan*, is the only one of the three that deals with the religious practice "wing of the bird." By its inclusion with the *Fa-hua hsüan-i* and *Fa-hua wen-chü*, T'ien-t'ai tradition asserts that the *Mo-ho chih-kuan*, like the other two, is primarily based on the *Lotus Sūtra*. In fact, the *Mo-ho chih-kuan* has very little to do with that scripture, beyond an occasional vagrant quotation and the specific rite of the lotus samādhi, one among a group of ritual meditations expounded in the section on the four forms of samādhi.

Sekiguchi Shindai has taken special note of this fact in his criticism of the "five periods and eight teachings" scheme of T'ien-t'ai doctrinal classification, thereby challenging the long-held belief that Chih-i identified T'ien-t'ai teaching exclusively with the *Lotus Sūtra*. For if we accept, as

---

gaku no kenkyū. For an excellent restatement of Sekiguchi's arguments, see Chappell, "Introduction to T'ien-t'ai Ssu-chiao-i of Chegwan" (a revised version of which is included in Chappell, ed., *T'ien-t'ai Buddhism: An Outline of the Fourfold Teachings*).

7. There is a convenient listing of these as well as his lost works in Hurvitz, "Chih-i," p. 332.

8. T no. 1716. For critical discussion of the composition, date, and editions of Chih-i's works, the best single source remains Satō, *Tendai daishi no kenkyū*. A significant portion of the *Fa-hua hsüan-i* has been translated by Paul Swanson in his *Foundations of T'ien-t'ai Philosophy: The Flowering of the Two Truths Theory in Chinese Buddhism*.

9. T no. 1718. Hirai Shun'ei has recently thrown the status and date of composition of the *Fa-hua wen-chü* into question by showing that large portions of it are lifted from the *Lotus Sūtra* commentaries of the San-lun scholar Chi-tsang (549–623); see Hirai, *Hokke mongu no seiritsu ni kansuru kenkyū*.

10. *Saddharmapuṇḍarīka Sūtra*; Chih-i used Kumārajīva's translation, *Miao-fa lien-hua ching*, T no. 262. Several translations are available in English. Unless otherwise specified, all references herein are to Leon Hurvitz's translation, *Scripture of the Lotus Blossom of the Fine Dharma* (hereafter cited as "Hurvitz").

later T'ien-t'ai advocates of the "five periods and eight teachings" claim,[11] that the *Lotus* is supreme among Buddhist sūtras and that T'ien-t'ai teaching represents that sūtra's purest expression, and if we also accept that doctrine and practice must be congruent (as Chih-i states so often and so forcefully), then how is it that the *Lotus* plays such a small part in Chih-i's single most important text on religious practice?[12] In fact, it seems that for Chih-i the perfect teaching (*yüan-chiao*)—the most sublime of the Buddha's doctrinal teachings and the teaching that informs the *Mo-ho chih-kuan*—is not the monopoly of any one sūtra but can be found in a great variety of scriptures, including all those (and they are many) drawn on in the *Mo-ho chih-kuan*.[13] It would seem, then, that Chih-i was less partisan in his view of Buddhist scripture than later tradition would lead us to believe. If Chih-i exalted the *Lotus Sūtra* at all, it was not for its exclusivity but for its comprehensiveness and finality: according to it, every animate being, without exception, will achieve supreme, perfect enlightenment, not even excepting Devadatta, the Buddhist Judas, nor even women (although they have to change into men on the way).[14] No animate being is outside the Buddhist fold, nor a fortiori does any form of Buddhist teaching—Hīnayāna included—fail to achieve the final goal, for all are the word of the Buddha, and their teachings ultimately participate in a unified salvific design. The later sectarian emphasis of the T'ien-t'ai and particularly the Japanese Nichiren tradition on the *Lotus* as superior to all other scriptures has veiled the catholicity of Chih-i's original thought.

At its most basic level, religious practice (*kuan*) in the T'ien-t'ai tradition is organized according to the ancient Buddhist concept of calming (*śamatha*) and contemplation (*vipaśyanā*), although in its T'ien-t'ai adaptation this concept is considerably altered and enlarged. Within the category of Chih-i's works on practice there is a group of three texts, each of which is regarded as the theoretical statement for one of three different approaches to the cultivation of calming and contemplation (*chih-kuan*).[15] The *Shih ch'an po-lo-mi tz'u-ti fa-men* (Elucidation of the Graduated Ap-

11. See, for example, the close association of this scheme with the *Lotus* in Chegwan's influential *T'ien-t'ai ssu-chiao i* (T no. 1931), as translated by David Chappell in Chappell, ed., *T'ien-t'ai Buddhism*, pp. 62–66.

12. For Sekiguchi's arguments, see his "Shishu-zammai ron," reprinted in *Tendai kyōgaku no kenkyū*, pp. 115–126.

13. One of the most important and oft-cited sources for the perfect teaching in Chih-i's works is the *Avataṃsaka Sūtra*, a point that made for a great deal of controversy when the Hua-yen school became popular and T'ien-t'ai exegetes began to focus ever more narrowly on the scriptural primacy of the *Lotus*.

14. For an interesting discussion of this theme, see Schuster, "Changing the Female Body."

15. Kuan-ting mentions this trio in his introduction to the Synopsis (T 46.3a 3–10).

proach of the Perfection of Dhyāna),[16] also known as the *Tz'u-ti ch'an-men* (Graduated Approach of Dhyāna), represents Chih-i's systematization of the gradual-and-sequential (*chien-tz'u*) calming and contemplation. This work was delivered in lecture form in 571; it was taken down by his disciple Fa-shen (d.u.) and afterwards edited by his greatest disciple Kuan-ting (561–632). The *Liu-miao fa-men* (Six Wondrous Teachings),[17] a short work of only one fascicle, outlines the system (though it is questionable whether it is an independent system at all) of the variable (*pu-ting*) calming and contemplation. And the *Mo-ho chih-kuan* itself, compiled from a series of lectures Chih-i delivered in 594, is the summation of the perfect and sudden (*yüan-tun*) calming and contemplation. This work was taken down by Kuan-ting and edited several times after Chih-i's death before it reached the form in which it is known to us today in the Taishō canon.

The variable calming and contemplation merely involves a fluid alternation between the different stages and practices of the gradual approach, as occasions demand and conditions permit. Because the *Liu-miao fa-men* is no more than a brief work on *ānāpāna* or "contemplation of the breath," it does not occupy a large place in the corpus of Chih-i's works. Thus there remain the *Tz'u-ti ch'an-men* and the *Mo-ho chih-kuan* as Chih-i's principal works on meditative theory and practice.

Aside from these three, another of Chih-i's works on meditative theory that deserves mention is the two-fascicle *Hsiao chih-kuan* (Small Calming and Contemplation), known more formally as the *Hsiu-hsi chih-kuan tso-ch'an fa-yao* (Essentials for Sitting in Meditation and Cultivating Calming and Contemplation).[18] Because of its title, the *Hsiao chih-kuan* is often mistakenly regarded as a synopsis of the *Mo-ho chih-kuan* (since the names of the two works mean, respectively, the "small" and "great" calming and contemplation). In fact this work lies midway between the *Tz'u-ti ch'an-men* and the *Mo-ho chih-kuan* in both form and date. It borrows heavily from the former work, while broadly anticipating certain structures of the latter. Of the two, it is probably closer in character to the *Tz'u-ti ch'an-men* and, thus, only indirectly related to the *Mo-ho chih-kuan* itself.[19]

The ten-fascicle *Tz'u-ti ch'an-men* was by far the most comprehensive systematization of Buddhist practice of its day. It stands near the beginning of Chih-i's career (as possibly his earliest work), whereas the *Mo-ho chih-kuan* stands near the end, yet it remains comparable to the later work in many ways. The structure of the two works is very similar, down to the

16. T no. 1916.

17. T no. 1917.

18. T no. 1915. This work is available in two English translations: one by Wai-tao in Goddard, ed., *A Buddhist Bible*, pp. 437–496; the other by Charles Luk (Lu K'uan-yü) in his *Secrets of Chinese Meditation*, pp. 111–156.

19. For dating and analysis of the *Hsiao chih-kuan*, see Sekiguchi's study of the text (with critical edition) in *Tendai Shōshikan no kenkyū*. See also Satō, *Tendai daishi no kenkyū*, pp. 241–265.

number of the chapters and even their names. It is of great interest, however, that whereas Chih-i used the word *ch'an* (dhyāna) to sum up religious practice in the earlier work, this was replaced by the compound *chih-kuan* (*śamatha-vipaśyana*) in the *Mo-ho chih-kuan* and other later opera of the master. Since that time it has been *chih-kuan* (i.e., calming and contemplation) that has served as the overarching term for religious practice in the T'ien-t'ai tradition, whereas the Ch'an tradition appropriated for itself the term which Chih-i had already discarded as not comprehensive enough.

It is well known that *ch'an* represents the Indic word *dhyāna* and *chih-kuan* translates *śamatha-vipaśyanā*, but as Chih-i used the two terms, they have several levels of meaning not included in the Indian originals. Each denotes for him the whole of religious practice, not merely the concentrative aspect, which is traditionally regarded as but one of three foundational disciplines of Buddhism (śīla, samādhi, and prajñā). For Chih-i, morality (śīla) and wisdom (prajñā) are also included in the meaning of both *ch'an* and *chih-kuan*. But in his later years Chih-i grew to regard religious practice and religious perfection as fundamentally composed of two elements: the static and the dynamic, the quiescent and the luminous, the cessation of delusion (nirvāṇa) and the intuiting of ultimate reality (bodhi). To express this quality the dyad *chih-kuan* became a more suitable term for him than *ch'an*, which in its role of *dhyāna-pāramitā* is often set against *prajñā-pāramitā* and is thereby skewed toward the static or quietistic side of the duality.

Altogether, Chih-i's use of the binome *chih-kuan* may be understood at three levels. In its causal sense—as the traditional twofold methodology of religious practice of *śamatha* and *vipaśyanā*—it means calming and contemplation. Calming (*chih*) is like a closed and windless room; contemplation (*kuan*) is like the lamp that burns brightest when the air is still. Calming is the soap that loosens the dirt; contemplation is the clear water that rinses it away. Calming is the hand that holds the clump of grass; contemplation is the sickle that cuts it down. Calming loosens or works the roots of the tree; contemplation pulls it out.[20] Then again, *chih-kuan* may also refer to the effect of religious practice. In that case the English "tranquility and insight" or "stillness and clarity" is more appropriate, as the depths of a pond become clear when the ripples on its surface are stilled and the sediment in its waters settles.[21] Finally, *chih-kuan* may be understood as a description not of the practitioner but of the nature of ultimate reality itself. With this latter sense in mind Chih-i regularly glosses *chih-kuan* as "quiescence and illumination" (*chi-chao*).[22]

20. Originally from the *Nirvāṇa Sūtra* (T 12.793c24–794a10), these similes are invoked by Chih-i in the MHCK.

21. For Chih-i's use of this metaphor, see MHCK T 46.19b29–c30.

22. For example, Chih-i states in the MHCK (T 46.18c5–6): "The dharma-

The Perfect and Sudden Approach

The Three Truths and Three Discernments

What exactly is the perfect and sudden calming and contemplation, and why, as an expression of this path, is the *Mo-ho chih-kuan* regarded as the *summa* among T'ien-t'ai treatises on religious practice? In order to orient ourselves properly to the text and its teaching, a review of some of the main features of T'ien-t'ai thought is in order. Throughout his later works, including the *Mo-ho chih-kuan*, Chih-i frequently resorts to the T'ien-t'ai system of three truths (*san-ti*) and three discernments or contemplations (*san-kuan*)—emptiness (*k'ung*), provisionality (*chia*), and the middle (*chung*)—as a basis for distinguishing different forms of Buddhist doctrine and practice. This three truths system introduces the middle truth as a third, absolute truth that transcends and unifies the conventional ([*loka*]*saṃvṛti-satya*) and ultimate (*paramārtha-satya*) truths. In this respect, it represents a uniquely Chinese expansion of the two truths theory of classical Indian Madhyamaka.[23]

The three truths present emptiness, provisionality, and the middle from a quasi-ontological perspective, as the principle (*li*) or cardinal truth (*ti*) inherent to the nature of things. The three discernments are methods of contemplation that actualize these truths from within phenomenal experience. Chih-i himself cites the *Ying-lo ching* and *Jen-wang ching*, two influential Chinese apocryphal scriptures, as the principal sources for this threefold formula, as well as its differentiation into subjective and objective perspectives.[24] To these he matched yet a third and fourth set of distinctions: a system of three forms of wisdom (*san-chih*) from the *Ta-chih-tu lun*, the lengthy commentary to the *Mahāprajñāpāramitā Sūtra* attributed to Nāgārjuna,[25] and three forms of delusion or affliction (*san-*

nature is eternally quiescent (*chi*); this is the meaning of *chih*. But while eternally quiescent, it is ever luminous (*chao*). This is the meaning of *kuan*."

23. For a recent, in-depth discussion of the development of the T'ien-t'ai three truths theory, see Swanson, *Foundations of T'ien-t'ai Philosophy*.

24. The *P'u-sa ying-lo pen-yeh ching* (T no. 1485) and *Jen-wang pan-jo p'o-lo-mi ching* (T no. 246) will be referred to by these abbreviated titles throughout. For a summation of the origins of these scriptures and their impact on Chih-i, see Swanson, *Foundations of T'ien-t'ai Philosophy*, pp. 38–56. Chih-i cites these two scriptures as sources for the three discernments/truths in nearly every major discussion of this formula that appears in his later works. See, for example, *Fa-hua hsüan-i*, T 33.704c17; *San kuan i*, HTC 98.76a; *Ssu chiao i*, T 46.727c3; and *Wei-mo ching hsüan-shu*, T 38.525b22, 534c19–25. An excellent introduction to the entire issue of Chinese Buddhist apocrypha is available in Buswell, ed., *Chinese Buddhist Apocrypha*.

25. See TCTL, T 25.257c–260c. For translation and discussion of this section, see Lamotte, *Traité*, 4:1735ff. The TCTL, T no. 1509, was one of the most important texts from which Chih-i drew scriptural authority. For a discussion of the text, see Ramanan, *Nāgārjuna's Philosophy as Presented in the Mahā-Prajñāpāramitā-*

huo) systematized by Chih-i himself from such sources as the *Śrīmālā Sūtra*.

Taken together, the three discernments contemplate the dharmas of phenomenal experience in order to eradicate the delusions and reveal the three truths. As the latter emerge, their respective wisdoms are generated simultaneously. Chih-i equates the terminologies of these systems as follows:[26]

The three discernments of the *Ying-lo ching*

1. entering emptiness from provisionality
2. [re]entering provisionality from emptiness
3. entering the middle [through integration of the two]

remove the three delusions of

1. intellectual view (*chien*) and emotive attachment (*ssu*)
2. delusion that obscures multiplicity (*ch'en-sha huo*)
3. root nescience or ignorance (*wu-ming*)[27]

manifest the three truths of

Ying-lo ching	or	*Jen-wang ching*
1. inexistence (*wu-ti*)		1. true (*chen*)
2. existence (*yu-ti*)		2. conventional (*su/shih*)
3. absolute truth of the middle way (*chung-tao ti-i-i ti*)		3. absolute (*ti-i-i*)

and produce the three wisdoms (from the *Ta-chih-tu lun*) of

1. omniscient wisdom (*sarvajñatā*; *i-ch'ieh chih*)
2. modes of the path (*mārgajñatā*; *tao-chung chih*)[28]
3. omniscient wisdom of all modes (*sarvākarajñatā*; *i-ch'ieh chung chih*).

Śāstra. Most scholars now believe that the work was originally composed in Chinese by Kumārajīva; Richard Robinson summarizes the arguments in his *Early Mādhyamika in India and China*, pp. 34–39.

26. *Ying-lo ching*, T 24.1014b12–23; see also Swanson, *Foundations of T'ien-t'ai Philosophy*, pp. 45–56.

27. The delusions of intellectual view and cultivation literally mean afflictions "removed in the path of view or vision" (*darśana-[mārga]-prahātavya-kleśa*) and "removed in the path of cultivation" (*bhāvanā-[mārga]-prahātavya-kleśa*). They describe, respectively, false views of self and various emotive attachments that obscure the truth of emptiness and, according to Chih-i, are removed specifically in the Hīnayāna path or the lower stages of the Mahāyāna. The "delusion that obscures multiplicity"—literally, the "delusion that conceals particulars as numerous as the dust and sands of the Ganges"—represents attachment to emptiness, which obscures the infinite variety of provisionality and hence impedes the bodhisattva's power of expediency. Nescience obscures the middle truth.

28. That is, modes of the various realms and destinies of (provisional) existence.

One of the most celebrated scriptural passages associated with the T'ien-t'ai three truths (at least in Western literature on the subject) is verse eighteen from the twenty-fourth chapter of the *Middle Treatise* (*Chung-lun*), Kumārajīva's translation of Nāgārjuna's *Mūlamadhyamakakārikā* (with commentary): "Whatever dharma arises on the basis of the myriad causes and conditions, that I declare to be identical to inexistence (*wu*) [or, emptiness (*k'ung*)].[29] It is also provisional designation (*chia-ming*). This, furthermore, is the meaning of the middle way (*chung-tao*)."[30]

Modern scholars agree that in this verse Nāgārjuna had in mind no other truth besides the two truths that permeate the Madhyamaka dialectic—the ultimate and conventional truths of *paramārtha-satya* and [*loka*]*saṃvṛti-satya*. But Chih-i and the T'ien-t'ai tradition, reading it in light of such sources as the *Ying-lo ching*, accept that this verse expounds not two truths but three. Hence from contemplation of the single object of conditioned dharmas one may elicit, in their respective order or all at once, the three truths or principles of emptiness, provisionality, and the middle.[31]

The terminologies of these different sources (the *Ying-lo ching*, *Jen-wang ching*, *Ta-chih-tu lun*, *Chung-lun*, and others) are used interchangeably by Chih-i in discussions involving the three truths doctrine, although the familiar triad of emptiness, provisionality, and the middle from the *Ying-lo ching* and *Chung-lun* is used most often. Nāgārjuna's verse holds an unusually conspicuous place in the *Mo-ho chih-kuan* itself. Kuan-ting cites it in his introduction to substantiate the claim that Chih-i's teaching of calming and contemplation looks to Nāgārjuna as its founding patriarch (*kao-tsu*). Over the sections of the Synopsis that follow—especially the first lesser chapter on Arousing the Great Thought [of Enlightenment]—it is invoked repeatedly to illustrate perspectives on the three truths taken by different doctrinal systems.

In form, the three truths actually describe a tetralemma—a set of four possible propositions—constructed on the basis of the two initial alter-

29. Chih-i's citations of the passage (as well as the Sanskrit) both use the term "emptiness" (*k'ung; śūnyatā*). The Taishō edition of the *Chung-lun* has "inexistence" (*wu*); see T 30.33b11.

30. *Chung-lun*, T 30.33b11–12. The verse appears as number eighteen in current editions of both the Sanskrit *Kārikā* and (Taishō) *Chung-lun*.

31. See Swanson, *Foundations of T'ien-t'ai Philosophy*, pp. 1–17, for the translations of the Sanskrit verse by Kalupahana, Sprung, Lamotte, Nagao, and Robinson, as well as further discussion of its place in Chih-i's works. The form of the Chinese does suggest that three names are being given to the same dharmas. In the Sanskrit version of this passage, however, there is no suggestion at all of three rather than two truths: *Yaḥ pratītya-samutpādaḥ śūnyatāṃ tām pracakṣmahe/Sā prajñaptir upādāya pratipat saiva madhyamā*: "We call dependent origination 'emptiness.' In association it is (conventional) designation. This is the middle way."

natives of (1) provisional or conventional existence and (2) emptiness. For the middle truth, as its name suggests, designates a synthesis achieved through the (3) simultaneous affirmation (*shuang shih/chao*) and (4) simultaneous negation (*shuang fei/wang*) of the two poles of existence and emptiness.

The three discernments, in turn, present this same tetralemma as a sequence of theses/antitheses that lead dialectically to the middle truth (i.e., the vision of Buddhahood). For example, by contemplating the dharmas of mundane existence as dependently originated (*pratītya-samutpāda*), devoid of self-existence (*niḥsvabhāva*), and hence utterly inapprehensible (*anupalabdha*), one "enters emptiness from provisionality." The delusions of view and cultivation that bind one to saṃsāra are severed, and one achieves the liberation of nirvāṇa. By applying the same critique to the truth of emptiness itself, one severs biased attachment to emptiness (i.e., the delusion that eclipses the infinite sandlike features of existence) and reaffirms its fundamental identity with provisional existence. In effect, one fearlessly "reenters" or "comes forth into" provisional existence from emptiness but this time as the self-sovereign master of saṃsāric existence rather than as its naïve victim.[32] From this point on both extremes of existence and emptiness are "simultaneously illumined and simultaneously eradicated" (*shuang-chao shuang-wang*). When all vestiges of dualism (i.e., root nescience) vanish, the transcendent and unalloyed middle—the third and absolute truth—is revealed.

Both schemes pose something of a conceptual problem, because the middle truth is unavoidably bound up with (even contingent on) its two extremes, when in fact T'ien-t'ai theology seeks to establish just the opposite. For T'ien-t'ai thinkers, it is the middle that is ultimately real (*shih*) and fundamental. The two truths of emptiness and provisionality are secondary derivations—false or, at best, provisional constructs (*ch'üan*) devised to convey the ultimate reality of the middle in a language consistent with the conventions of deluded experience.

The task of clarifying the relationship between a monistically conceived middle and a plurality of defining extremes pushes Chih-i to develop various paradoxical qualifications of the middle truth. But despite his efforts, ambiguities remain and continue as a major source of controversy throughout subsequent T'ien-t'ai history.[33] As an ultimate reality (*shih*)

32. Chih-i, borrowing a distinction from the *Śrīmālā Sūtra* (T 12.219c), refers to this as an expedient "birth and death produced through spiritual transformation" (*shen-pien sheng-ssu*), as opposed to the afflictive "birth and death of fixed [karmic] allotments" (*fen-tuan sheng-ssu*) characteristic of ordinary saṃsāra.

33. The "home-mountain" (shan-chia) and "off-mountain" (shan-wai) controversies of the Sung period (960–1279) in part entailed a debate over whether the phenomenal distinctions of "provisional" existence are the product of delusion and hence dissolved into an undifferentiated unity when the perfect middle is

that synthesizes and utterly transcends the two provisionally devised (*ch'üan*) truths, Chih-i describes the middle as an unalloyed and singular truth (*i-ti*). By the same token, however, the very relativity implicit in the notion of a singular, transcendent middle undermines the middle's monistic inclusiveness. To counter this sort of fragmentation, Chih-i disabuses the middle of any hint of ontological integrity and characterizes it as utterly decentered. Thus it becomes a non-middle, an inconceivable (*pu-k'o-ssu-i*) middle that effaces itself in a simultaneous "identity with emptiness, identity with provisionality, and identity with the middle" (*chi k'ung chi chia chi chung*), where "any one [perspective] interfuses with all three, and the three, one" (*i chi san san chi i*). Pushing this line of reasoning to its extreme, the very distinctions that establish an ultimate reality must vanish altogether. "The path of speech is cut off, the reach of discursive thought is annihilated,"[34] and absolute truth itself reverts to "no truth" (*wu-ti*).

Lest one become lost in abstraction, it is important to stress the point that the middle, as a sacred fundament and supreme religious goal, is real and concrete for Chih-i. In this regard, the most effective of all the didactic formulations devised by Chih-i is the metaphor of the rounded (*yüan*) versus the one-sided (*p'ien*). The rounded or perfect (as it is often rendered) describes the inconceivable totality of the middle—the a priori and universal middle that holistically subsumes, yet transcends, the very extremes that define it. The one-sided or biased, by contrast, represents any partial or dualistic view, such as existence and inexistence, provisionality and emptiness, saṃsāra and nirvāṇa, and even the view of the middle, if improperly conceived. The power of the image, of course, lies in its monistic inclusiveness and its elimination of any sense of subordination of the middle to dualistic extremes.

The Four Teachings and the Perfect and Sudden Path

Expressed in terms of the three truths, the supreme task of the Buddhist dharma is to reinstate beings who have become mired in the biased views of existence and inexistence to the perfect holism of the middle—the intrinsic and all-embracing reality of Buddahood. Even so, the ability to

---

realized or whether they possess ontological reality and are retained in a multiperspectival interfusion of universal and particular or particular and particular. The latter view, espoused by Ssu-ming Chih-li (960–1028) as "encompassment based on the essential nature" (*hsing-chü*) and later elaborated by his followers into a full theory of "encompassment of individual marks" (*hsiang-chü*), was accepted as the orthodox line. For a general discussion of this controversy, see the works of Andō Toshio, *Tendai-gaku*, pp. 329–384; *Tendai shisō-shi*, pp. 15–64; and *Tendai shōgu shisō ron*, pp. 160–265; see also Hibi Nobumasa, *Tōdai Tendai-gaku kenkyū*, pp. 315–407.

34. MHCK, T 46.21b7.

fathom the rounded middle must differ according to the nature and degree of the individual's afflictive biases. From this it follows that approaches to the middle will likewise vary—some subtle, others crude, some direct, others roundabout.

The notion of different paths for persons of different capacities (*ken*) is fundamental to the entire medieval enterprise of classification of the teachings (*p'an-chiao*) and one of the linchpins of Chih-i's own systematization of Buddhist doctrine and practice. Throughout his works Chih-i professes an absolute faith in the cohesiveness of the Buddha's word. Since it is unthinkable—even heretical—to assume that doctrinal conflicts in the Buddhist sūtras reflect rifts in the Buddha's salvific vision itself, the only feasible explanation for Chih-i is that they are there by design. The operative concept behind this design is the notion of skillful use of expedient devices (*upāya*)—the idea that the Buddha, out of unconditional compassion for others, devised different doctrines and strategems of discourse to accommodate the diverse capacities and circumstances of his audience. In his effort to reveal the logic behind the received word—to reclaim the "original intent of the Buddha" (*fo-i*), so to speak—Chih-i produced the foundations of T'ien-t'ai thought (*chiao*) and practice (*kuan*): in essence, the three approaches to calming and contemplation and the rudiments of the five periods and eight teachings.

It would take us too far afield to venture with any depth into Chih-i's theories of *p'an-chiao* here. But in the interest of placing the *Mo-ho chih-kuan* and its perfect and sudden contemplation properly within the framework of T'ien-t'ai doctrine, a brief review of the four teachings (*ssu chiao*) is necessary. Inspired by such distinctions as the three vehicles and one vehicle expounded in the *Lotus Sūtra*,[35] Chih-i extracted a total of four distinct doctrinal schemes from Buddhist scripture, all embracing varying degrees of provisionality and truth. They include the tripiṭaka teaching, the shared teaching, the separate teaching (*pieh-chiao*), and the perfect or rounded teaching.

The tripiṭaka teaching (*tsang-chiao*),[36] the Hīnayāna teaching of the śrāvaka, is designed for beings of dull capacity who are deeply entrenched in mundane existence. By characterizing existence as suffering, they are induced to renounce saṃsāra, remove the delusions of view and cultivation, and attain the nirvāṇa of the arhat. This goal is achieved through

35. In chapter 2 on "Expedient Devices" the *Lotus* presents the three vehicles—śrāvaka, pratyekabuddha, and bodhisattva—as expedient teachings utilized by the Buddha to reveal the one true Buddha vehicle; see Hurvitz, pp. 22–47. For a thorough discussion of the issue of one versus three vehicles in the *Lotus*, see Fujita, "One Vehicle or Three?"

36. So named, according to Chih-i, because it is primarily set forth in the tripiṭaka collection of the *Āgamas, Vinaya,* and *Abhidharma*. See his explanations of the term offered in *Ssu chiao i*, T 46.721b, and *Wei-mo ching hsüan-shu*, T 46.532b.

an analytic reduction of existence to its dharmic components (*fen-hsi k'ung*) and, ultimately, the featureless quiescence of emptiness. Although the tripiṭaka teaching affords liberation from saṃsāra, it remains caught up in the duality of existence and emptiness and so falls short of the middle way. Hence it remains a biased and merely provisional doctrine—one that must wait for the more profound teaching of the Mahāyāna to be completed.

The shared teaching (*t'ung-chiao*) receives its particular name for two reasons: first, because it advocates an immediate or intuitive understanding of emptiness (*t'i-k'ung*) that is foundational to all Buddhist teachings, Hīnayāna as well as Mahāyāna; and second, because it incorporates the alternative soteriological ends of all three vehicles (i.e., śrāvaka, pratyekabuddha, and bodhisattva) within its scheme of the path.[37] Both features—its emphasis on emptiness and its salvific ambiguity—make the shared teaching a purely transitional and therefore incomplete doctrine.

The separate teaching (*pieh-chiao*) is the exclusive domain of the bodhisattva: its principles, its language, its practices, its professed goals are purely Mahāyāna, unshared (*pu-kung*) by any of the lesser two vehicles or teachings. For the first time the middle truth of Buddhahood is openly established as the supreme goal, and the two truths of emptiness and provisionality demoted to the status of expediency. Nevertheless, spiritual progress in the separate teaching is decidedly gradualistic (*chien-tz'u*) in character. Over a course of fifty-two levels—drawn again from the *Ying-lo ching*—the bodhisattva proceeds in dialectical sequence (*tz'u-ti*) through the three truths, passing first from mundane or provisional existence to emptiness, back to provisionality (with simultaneous discernment of emptiness), and finally to the middle. Only with the last twelve levels of the fifty-two—the ten bhūmi or bodhisattva stages, plus penultimate enlightenment (*teng-chüeh*) and wondrous enlightenment (*miao-chüeh*)—are the two biased views of emptiness and provisionality shed, root nescience penetrated, and the middle truth of Buddhahood revealed. In this respect, even though the separate teaching ultimately reaches the middle, its approach is roundabout and crude, for it lends excessive concreteness to the dualism of existence and emptiness and its attendant delusions and requires a string of biased expedients to redress these imbalances and achieve its final goal.

The perfect teaching (*yüan-chiao*), as its name suggests, is the only teaching among the four that conforms directly to the nature of ultimate reality. Hence it is equivalent to the genuine (*shih*) one Buddha vehicle mentioned in the *Lotus Sūtra*. Here the perfect (*yüan*) vision of the inconceivable middle truth is presented "all at once" (*tun*), without the media-

37. The last four of the ten stages of the shared teaching are arhat, pratyekabuddha, bodhisattva, and Buddha. See Chappell, *T'ien-t'ai Buddhism*, p. 121.

tion of the provisional (*ch'üan*) and gradualistic (*chien-tz'u*) expedients that characterize the tripiṭaka, shared, and separate doctrines. Being the most marvelous and profound of paths, it is intended only for bodhisattvas of keenest ability (*li-ken*).

As in the separate teaching, a set of fifty-two stages[38] is used to mark progress on the perfect path. However, unlike the former, these stages describe only quantitative and not qualitative changes in perspective or insight, for at each stage the rounded vision of Buddhahood itself—i.e., the inconceivably interfused middle—is perfectly replete (*yüan*). Thus in the perfect path all formal distinctions with regard to the three delusions, three levels of wisdom, three truths, and even the notions of stage and path, saint (*ārya*) and ordinary being (*pṛtagjana*), collapse. Severance of one affliction is severance of all afflictions; one wisdom or truth is all wisdoms and truths; the initial thought of enlightenment is itself the final goal of Buddhahood.

This concept of the perfect teaching as a pathless path is most succinctly expressed in a second scheme known as the six identities (*liu-chi*)—a condensation of the fifty-two stages devised by Chih-i.[39] The term "identity" (*chi*) stresses that every dharma or defilement at every moment is seen to be fully identical with the middle way. The number "six" distinguishes six experiential stages in the process of actualizing this identity.

The gradual and sequential calming and contemplation of the *Tz'u-ti ch'an-men* represents the step-by-step approach to Buddhahood of the separate teaching, with certain features included that are common to the shared and tripiṭaka doctrines. As the perfect and sudden (*yüan-tun*) approach to calming and contemplation, the *Mo-ho chih-kuan* describes the meditative practice of the perfect teaching (*yüan-chiao*). Drawing on the metaphor of holism so fundamental to the middle view, it takes a perspective on the contemplative process different from that of the sequential dialectic suggested in our earlier discussion of the three truths. In the perfect or rounded approach, any and every condition—wholesome or unwholesome, defiled or pure, saintly or afflicted—serves equally as a basis for discernment. Not only is nothing excluded, but also nothing is altered, nothing added, and nothing rejected, for everything, just as it is, affirms the totality of the middle way. Rather than invoke the shibboleths of emptiness and existence and struggle gradually through the refutations of the three discernments, the perfect calming and contemplation reduces the meditative dialectic to a simple process of expansion of horizon. No bias is removed or middle apprehended. Instead, the intrinsic participation (*chü*) and mutual identity (*chi*) of all biases within the

38. Fifty-seven, if one includes the five grades of discipleship invented by Chih-i.

39. See Donner, "Sudden and Gradual Intimately Conjoined."

rounded totality are revealed effortlessly and directly: one is all and all is one. This is the point of Kuan-ting's core statement in the preface to the *Mo-ho chih-kuan*, which proclaims: "There is not a single sight or smell that is not the middle way." And it is the thrust of Chih-i's famous dictum of "three-thousand world-realms [replete] within an instant of thought" (*i-nien san-ch'ien*) or "three discernments in one mind" (*i-hsin san-kuan*), which serves as the basic model for sudden and perfect contemplation in the *Mo-ho chih-kuan*.[40]

The Structure of the *Mo-ho chih-kuan*

The text of the *Mo-ho chih-kuan* as we have it today is the third of three different editions produced by Chih-i's disciple Kuan-ting. If we count Kuan-ting's original lecture notes as well, we are four times removed from the original words of Chih-i. Both the first and second editions of the text were entitled *Yüan-tun chih-kuan* (The Perfect and Sudden Calming and Contemplation), but they differed considerably in that the first was twenty fascicles in length and the second reduced to ten. The third and final edition is also a work of ten fascicles, although various changes appear to have been made in its contents. The most noticeable difference between it and earlier versions, of course, is the new title *Mo-ho chih-kuan* or *The Great Calming and Contemplation*.[41]

The Ten Chapters

In concept the *Mo-ho chih-kuan* consists of a total of ten chapters, of which the first, the *Ta-i* or Synopsis, is presented in translation here. This Synopsis occupies two of the ten fascicles of the *Mo-ho chih-kuan* or, in terms of total pages, about one-seventh of the whole. Although the present translation is the longest segment of Chih-i's works yet to appear in a Western language,[42] it is a mere fragment of the whole corpus that he has left behind—less than ten percent of his work on practice and about two percent of his entire body of lectures and writings.

As its name implies, the Synopsis is an outline or compendium of the

40. Explanations of the "three-thousand worlds in an instant of thought" are available in Hurvitz, "Chih-i," pp. 271–318; and de Bary, ed. *The Buddhist Tradition*, pp. 165–166.

41. For details concerning these different editions, see Satō, *Tendai daishi no kenkyū*, pp. 370–379. We know that all three versions continued to circulate in China at least well into the eighth century, since they were consulted by Chan-jan when he composed his commentary to the MHCK. The twelfth-century exegete Shōshin cites an old edition of the MHCK in his *Shikan bugyō shiki*, indicating that one of the two earlier versions also reached Japan.

42. As noted earlier, Swanson has recently published a translation of an extended portion of Chih-i's *Fa-hua hsüan-i* in his *Foundations of T'ien-t'ai Philosophy*.

whole of the *Mo-ho chih-kuan,* which as such makes it virtually a self-contained work. In fact, in form it is less truncated than the *Mo-ho chih-kuan* itself, since the last three of the projected ten chapters of the overall work were never delivered, nor were the last three of the ten sections in chapter 7. As the text itself explains,[43] the five subsections of the Synopsis (which we shall call the lesser chapters) are correlated with the ten chapters of the whole (which we shall call the greater chapters), according to the following scheme:

	Ten Greater Chapters		Five Lesser Chapters
1.	Synopsis	1.	Arousing the Great Thought
2.	Explanation of Terms		Arousing the Great Thought
3.	Characteristics of the Essence of the Teaching		Arousing the Great Thought
4.	Inclusion of All Dharmas		Arousing the Great Thought
5.	One-sided versus Perfect Calming and Contemplation		Arousing the Great Thought
6.	Preparatory Expedients	2.	Engaging in the Great Practice
7.	Contemplation Proper*		Engaging in the Great Practice
8.	Result and Recompense**	3.	Manifesting the Great Results
9.	Generation of the Teachings**	4.	Rending the Great Net
10.	Returning of the Purport**	5.	Returning to the Great Abode*

* incomplete
** title alone exists

As we see from the chart, the first five greater chapters correspond to lesser chapter 1 of the Synopsis; greater chapters 6 and 7 correspond to lesser chapter 2; and the last three chapters of each list correspond one-to-one. It is clearer from the list of lesser chapters than the list of greater chapters, yet true of them both, that their sequence contains an inner logic. That is to say, they trace the progress of the religious practitioner from (1) the first arousing of the thought of enlightenment (*bodhicitta*)—when he realizes the possibility of Buddhahood within himself and awakens the aspiration to achieve it—to (10) the full and final attainment of this indescribable goal, beyond all teaching, beyond all thought. Between the two events lies religious practice itself. In its broadest sense, practice is construed as two differently directed but complementary activities: the "upward seeking" (*shang-ch'iu*) of personal liberation and illumination and "downward transformation" (*hsia-hua*) of others out of the vow of compassion. This upward seeking and downward transforming, at least in spirit, are present at every stage of the path, from beginning to end. Nevertheless, there is also a cause and effect relationship between them,

43. See T 46.5b.

for the power to transform naturally increases as the practice of calming and contemplation bears fruit. This idea is expressed by the chapter sequence of (7) Contemplation Proper, (8) Result and Recompense, and (9) Generation of the Teachings, where the ability to generate expedients to guide others is itself activated by the fruition of calming and contemplation.

Greater chapter 1, as an overview of the entire path of calming and contemplation (and the *Mo-ho chih-kuan* itself), aims to foster a correct understanding of and aspiration for enlightenment. Greater chapters 2 through 5 continue to deepen this understanding through progressively refined discussion of the doctrinal bases of calming and contemplation. Greater chapter 2 explains the basic terminology of calming and contemplation; chapter 3 elucidates the conceptual fundaments (*t'i*) or principles (*li*) that define the use of calming and contemplation in different doctrinal systems; chapter 4 demonstrates how all teachings or doctrinal perspectives are subsumed within the single practice of calming and contemplation; and chapter 5 clarifies the crucial distinction between one-sided (*p'ien*) and perfect (*yüan*) applications of calming and contemplation. Thus by the fifth chapter the principles of the perfect and sudden calming and contemplation (*yüan-tun chih-kuan*)—that is, calming and contemplation as applied specifically within the context of the perfect teaching (*yüan-chiao*)—are clearly understood.

Chapters 6 ("Preparatory Expedients") and ("Contemplation Proper") are concerned with meditative practice per se. Whereas chapter 6 is short (one fascicle in length), chapter 7, incomplete though it is, takes up all the rest of the *Mo-ho chih-kuan*, amounting to more than half the work.

The subject of chapter 6 is the twenty-five preparatory expedients (*fang-pien*). These represent five groups of five members each, which together describe the requisite conditions for effective practice of calming and contemplation. The five basic groups include: (1) fulfilling the five conditions of purity in observing the disciplinary code, having proper clothing and food, situating oneself in a quiet place, halting all involvement in worldly affairs, and acquiring worthy spiritual friends (i.e., a teacher or compatriots in the practice); (2) suppressing the desires for the five objects of the five senses; (3) discarding the five hindrances or coverings (*nivāraṇa*) of craving, anger, sleepiness, restlessness, and doubt; (4) regulating the five factors of diet, sleep, body, breath, and mind; and (5) practice of the five dharmas of aspiration, perseverance, mindfulness, discrimination (between the lesser joys of the mundane world and the greater joys of samādhi and prajñā), and single-mindedness.

Derived primarily from the *Ta-chih-tu lun*,[44] these twenty-five prepara-

44. They are taken mainly from the seventeenth fascicle (on *dhyāna-pāramitā*)

tory conditions for the practice first appear in the *Tz'u-ti ch'an-men*, where the explanation of them is considerably more detailed than in the *Mo-ho chih-kuan*. They also constitute roughly half of the *Hsiao chih-kuan*. They thus appear regularly in Chih-i's works, from early to late, and form an indispensable part of both the perfect and sudden and gradual and successive approaches to practice.

Chapter 7 of the *Mo-ho chih-kuan* expounds the famous ten modes of discernment (*shih sheng kuan-fa*) and ten spheres (or objects) of discernment (*shih kuan-ching*), which together define the practice of calming and contemplation proper.[45] Their counterpart in the Synopsis is the four forms of samādhi (*ssu-chung san-mei*) in lesser chapter 2. The two systems present very different angles on practice, the main point of distinction being that the classification in chapter 7 primarily involves mental technique, whereas that of the four samādhis emphasizes the ritual and physical regimen through which mental discernment is carried out.

The ten spheres or objects of contemplation describe various experiential fields or conditions—ranging in character from abnormal, through normal, to supernormal—to which the method of sudden and perfect contemplation itself may be applied. These include: (1) the sphere of the *skandhas/āyatanas/dhātus* (i.e., the normal psycho-physical process of sense experience and cognition), (2) conditions of affliction (*kleśa*), (3) conditions of illness, (4) eruptions of karmic influence from past lives, (5) conditions of demonic influence (i.e., the māras), (6) states of meditative concentration (dhyāna and samādhi), (7) (wrong) views, (8) overweening arrogance, (9) stages of the two vehicles, and (10) stages of the bodhisattva path.

The ten modes of discernment describe the perfect and sudden method of calming and contemplation proper. Thus to whichever of the ten spheres is manifest at the moment, one applies the ten modes of discernment as a meditative technique. The ten modes themselves are arranged in a sequence from subtle to coarse, primary to ancillary. The first mode is generally considered to be the crucial one; it is here that Chih-i expounds the famous vision of three-thousand worlds in an instant of thought (*i-nien san-ch'ien*). As circumstances require, the meditator may go on to employ anywhere from one (i.e., the second) to all of the remaining nine modes to assist his practice. Altogether the ten include: (1)

---

of the TCTL, T 25.180b–190a. For a brief discussion of their origins and character, see Andō, *Tendai-gaku*, pp. 209–216.

45. The term *kuan*, otherwise commonly rendered as "contemplation," is translated as "discernment" here in order to reflect the more generic sense that it carries in this context and to avoid the confusion that may arise from thinking that it stands in contrast to calming. The twin aspects of calming and contemplation are both comprehended by the ten modes of discernment.

contemplating [the object or sphere at hand as identical with] the realm of the inconceivable [truth] (*kuan pu-k'o-ssu-i ching*), or identifying the object as simultaneously identical with emptiness, provisionality, and the middle; (2) arousing the true and proper thought of enlightenment; (3) skillfully settling the mind (*an-hsin*) through calming and contemplation; (4) eradicating dharmas completely ; (5) distinguishing between blockage (*she*) and penetration (*t'ung*); (6) cultivating the [thirty-seven] factors of enlightenment (*bodhipakṣadharma*); (7) employing auxiliary methods to assist the way; (8) knowing the stages of spiritual progress; (9) forbearing in the face of fame or disgrace; and (10) avoiding attachment to the dharma. There is a definite logic to the sequential arrangement of both the ten modes and the ten realms of contemplation, but it would take us too far afield to discuss it in detail here.[46]

The fifth, sixth, and seventh fascicles of the ten-fascicle *Mo-ho chih-kuan* are entirely taken up by the exposition of the ten modes as directed toward the first sphere of discernment—the sphere of the *skandhas*, *āyatanas*, and *dhātus*. In fascicles eight, nine, and ten the second through the seventh spheres of discernment are discussed, with the ten modes applied respectively to each. The text of the *Mo-ho chih-kuan* ends with the seventh sphere. The last three spheres of discernment and, following them, the last three projected chapters of the work were never expounded at all by Chih-i, a fact that has created a great deal of discomfort among Buddhists in East Asia for a thousand or so years.

Why should this *summa* have been left incomplete? Chan-jan's explanation has become the traditional one: the end of the summer *varṣa* retreat caused the termination of the lectures.[47] In other words the lecturer ran out of time. Noting a strikingly similar textual ellipsis in the *Tz'u-ti ch'an-men*, Sekiguchi has suggested that these lacunae were intentional rather than accidental. The explanation is, Sekiguchi contends, that Chih-i wanted to direct his teaching to the beginner on the path and did not want to waste words describing its furthest reaches.[48] In his *Ssu-chiao i* (The Meaning of the Four Teachings) Chih-i states clearly that "what is necessary is to make the doctrine and the practice clear to beginners; it is futile and meaningless to expound about saints, bodhisattvas, and Buddhas,"[49] while elsewhere in the same work he says he will "only indicate

46. Among the many Japanese sources on this subject, Andō's *Tendai-gaku*, pp. 217–264, contains one of the best treatments. Also see Sekiguchi, *Tendai shikan no kenkyū*, pp. 8–20.

47. See T 46.143a14–19.

48. Sekiguchi, *Tendai shikan no kenkyū*, pp. 54–64.

49. Chih-i, *Ssu-chiao i*, T 46.752b. This work, one of the few works actually written by Chih-i, was originally part of a commentary to the *Vimalakīrti Sūtra* (*Wei-mo ching hsüan-i*) that Chih-i produced at the behest of Prince Yang Kuang in 595 and later retracted in order to rework. It should not be confused with

the chapter [headings] for the upper stages."[50] Having no false illusions that he was a highly realized being, Chih-i, it seems, thought it futile to expound to beginners on stages that he himself had yet to reach.

Despite the silence of the greater chapters of the *Mo-ho chih-kuan*, the Synopsis does contain comments on these upper reaches in outline, since the last three lesser chapters correspond to the last three greater chapters. Yet of the three it is only lesser chapter 5 that has anything of substance to say that has not already been said elsewhere in the Synopsis: lesser chapters 3 and 4 are so short as to be practically nonexistent.

The Introductions of Kuan-ting and Chih-i

The *Mo-ho chih-kuan* as a whole is preceded by two introductions, the first by Kuan-ting and the second one by Chih-i himself. Strictly speaking these both fall outside the Synopsis proper. But in a broader sense they may be included, since the *Mo-ho chih-kuan* is traditionally regarded as an integral work, and these introductions strive to present an overview of the text much in keeping with the spirit of the Synopsis itself.

The *Mo-ho chih-kuan* is famous for its opening line: "Calming and contemplation, luminosity and tranquility" (*chih-kuan ming-ching*). These are the words of Kuan-ting, not of Chih-i. Nevertheless, for anyone at all conversant with the T'ien-t'ai (or Tendai) tradition, these words immediately call to mind the metaphor of simultaneous quiescence and illumination that stands as the cardinal expression of the perfect and sudden path and the essence of the *Mo-ho chih-kuan* as a whole. Kuan-ting's introduction is keenly concerned with establishing the legitimacy of this equation—not just as a concept but as a text (i.e., the *Mo-ho chih-kuan*) as well as a tradition (i.e., T'ien-t'ai). This task he approaches in three ways: historically, through a rehearsal of the origins and lineage of the *Mo-ho chih-kuan*'s teaching of calming and contemplation; theoretically, through a core statement of the differences between the three forms of calming and contemplation and the centrality of the perfect and sudden approach; and scripturally, through citation of passages from the Buddhist sūtras that verify these approaches as the authentic teaching of the Buddha.

Kuan-ting's rehearsal of the lineage of the teaching begins with the dharma, itself eternal, and proceeds through twenty-four western patriarchs, extending from the Buddha Śākyamuni through Nāgārjuna and Vasubandhu to Siṃha. With Siṃha's violent death the continuous succession terminates forever. This lineage he refers to as the "golden-mouthed transmission," for the reason that it extends from the golden tongue of

---

Chegwan's *T'ien-t'ai ssu-chiao-i* (Outline of the T'ien-t'ai Fourfold Teachings), T no. 1931. For an English translation of the first two fascicles of Chih-i's *Ssu-chiao i*, see Rhodes, "Annotated Translation of the *Ssu-chiao-i*."

50. Chih-i, *Ssu-chiao i*, T 46.739a.

the Buddha himself. Kuan-ting then presents a second, separate genealogy, which traces the specific teaching of the *Mo-ho chih-kuan* backwards from Chih-i, through Hui-ssu (515–577),[51] to the latter's teacher Hui-wen (d.u.). He singles out Nāgārjuna as the connecting link between the two otherwise unrelated lines. For although Nāgārjuna himself was long deceased, Hui-wen is said to have devised his method for cultivating the mind on the basis of Nāgārjuna's *Ta-chih-tu lun*.[52]

This brief genealogical account by Kuan-ting represents the only systematic statement of T'ien-t'ai origins to be found in early T'ien-t'ai works, a feature that has made it the *locus classicus* for virtually all later discussions of T'ien-t'ai patriarchal history. Equally famous is Kuan-ting's core description of the three approaches to calming and contemplation that immediately follows. Here, especially, we find the eloquent statement that represents for T'ien-t'ai tradition the very essence of the *Mo-ho chih-kuan* and the sudden method of calming and contemplation: "There is nothing that is not true reality. When one fixes the mind on the dharmadhātu as object and unifies mindfulness itself with the dharmadhātu [just as it is], then there is not a single sight nor smell that is not the middle way."[53]

Kuan-ting's current introduction to the *Mo-ho chih-kuan* is known to be a good deal longer than those attached to his two earlier editions of the work. According to Satō Tetsuei, whose text-critical work on the different redactions of the *Mo-ho chih-kuan* we have noted earlier, the first edition contained no preface (or lineage account) but commenced directly with a summation of the three forms of calming and contemplation.[54] To the second edition Kuan-ting added scriptural citations, a lineage statement, and an account of the date and location of the lectures whence the text originated, all of which were placed before the statement on calming

51. For a study of Hui-ssu's life and thought, see Magnin, *La vie et l'œuvre de Huisi (515–577)*.

52. The tenuous connection between Hui-wen and Nāgārjuna was worked out in more detail by later T'ien-t'ai historians. Hui-wen came to be portrayed as a person of "saintly" or "sagely" (*sheng*) endowments who "achieved enlightenment on his own" (*tu-wu*) through the auspices of the TCTL and/or Nāgārjuna's celebrated verse on the "three truths" in the *Middle Treatise*. "Although he never knew Nāgārjuna in person," it is claimed that "he saw Nāgārjuna's mind." See the two thirteenth-century treatises, *Shih-men cheng-t'ung* (HTC 130.730b17–18) and *Fo-tsu t'ung-chi* (T 49.178b–c).

53. T 46.1c23–2a2.

54. Satō, *Tendai daishi no kenkyū*, pp. 370–382. Satō draws his data primarily from Chan-jan (T 46.141b–142a) and Shōshin, *Shikan bugyō shiki*. Satō (and Chan-jan) fail to note whether the core statement on the three forms of calming and contemplation (the only part of the introduction from the first edition of the text) was originally by Chih-i or the later addition of Kuan-ting.

and contemplation. This material, however, was not distinguished as a separate introduction but integrated directly into the text, inseparable from the prefatory remarks of Chih-i himself. In the third and final edition, Kuan-ting redistributed the contents of his prefatory remarks and extricated them from the body of the *Mo-ho chih-kuan* to form the introduction that we have today.

The introduction by Kuan-ting is followed by Chih-i's own brief introductory remarks on the overall concept and structure of the *Mo-ho chih-kuan,* containing an explanation of the ten greater chapters of the text and their relationship to the five lesser chapters of the Synopsis. Following these remarks, the Synopsis proper—the first of the ten greater chapters of the *Mo-ho chih-kuan*—begins.

Greater Chapter 1: The Synopsis

As its title "Arousing the Great Thought [of Enlightenment]" suggests, the first of the five lesser chapters of the Synopsis is devoted to the initial awakening of the thought of enlightenment (*bodhicitta*), which for a bodhisattva signals the beginning of the religious quest. After a brief review of the Chinese and Sanskritic terminology bearing on the concept of the thought of bodhi (*p'u-t'i hsin*) or thought of the way (*tao-hsin*), the rest of the chapter proceeds to distinguish between wrong (*fei*) and right (*shih*) views of bodhi or the way.

As is well known, the Chinese word *tao* or "way," although equated with "bodhi," can mean enlightenment as well as an ordinary path. Playing on this polyvalence, Chih-i extends the expression "thought of the way" (*tao-hsin* for *bodhicitta)* to include virtually any objective or any outlook around which a person might organize daily existence. In an initial effort to distinguish broadly the right from the wrong, Chih-i reduces erroneous mentalities or paths to a generic set of ten. These include six mentalities that correlate to the six destinies of deluded rebirth (*gati*) and keep one bound to the wheel of saṃsāra, three misguided notions of religious quest that lead to rebirth among the māras (demonic beings) or the Brahma-heavens and, finally, the liberating but flawed religious goals of the two Buddhist vehicles of śrāvaka and pratyekabuddha. Thus in one swoop all mundane paths, paths of heterodox religions or philosophies, and the Hīnayāna are dismissed as erroneous aspirations having nothing to do with true bodhi.

Chih-i next turns to the topic of the right arousing of the thought of enlightenment. His discussion falls into three sections: an analysis of the four levels of interpretation of the four noble truths (*ssu-chung ssu-ti*), the four extensive vows (*ssu hung-yüan*), and the six identities (*liu chi*).

The fourfold four noble truths function as a system of doctrinal classification developed by Chih-i on the basis of four different levels of interpretation of the four noble truths suggested in the Saintly Practices chapter of the *Nirvāṇa Sūtra*.[55] They include: (1) the arising-and-perishing four noble truths, (2) the nonarising-and-nonperishing four noble truths, (3) the innumerable four noble truths, and (4) the unconstructed four noble truths. The fourfold four noble truths find an immediate counterpart in the T'ien-t'ai four teachings (*ssu chiao*)—the tripiṭaka, shared, separate, and perfect, respectively—with which they are often deliberately matched in Chih-i's later works (including the subsequent chapters of the *Mo-ho chih-kuan*). In the Synopsis, however, it is the system of the fourfold four noble truths rather than the four teachings that is employed to sort out hierarchically the different levels of Buddhist truth. (In his commentary, Chan-jan equates them with their specific counterparts among the four teachings.)

According to Chih-i, all four presentations of Buddhist doctrine contained in the fourfold four noble truths can lead to the supreme goal of Buddhahood, even that of the Hīnayānist arising-and-perishing noble truths or the tripiṭaka teaching.[56] In this respect all are correct. However, only the unconstructed four noble truths—the equivalent of the perfect teaching (*yüan-chiao*)—reveal the true and unmediated vision of the Buddha. The other three are expedient and hence only real in part. Thus setting one's aspirations on the unconstructed four noble truths is the truly correct arousing of the thought of enlightenment.

Chih-i's initial exposition of the fourfold four noble truths follows with a discussion of ten basic means by which the right forms of bodhicitta may be awakened in the practitioner—by inferring from truth itself, by hearing the dharma expounded, by seeing the different forms of the Buddha and their characteristic marks, by the salvific influence of the magical powers of the Buddha, and so forth. The last six of these ten ways of arousing bodhicitta he leaves unexplained, although in his commentary Chan-jan fills in some of the gaps. Taken together, each of the ten forms of arousing bodhicitta can entail the presentation of any one among the doctrines of the fourfold four noble truths, each of which may be understood by the listener in one of four ways. So there are theoretically a total of 160 possible modalities for generating the thought of enlightenment that are implied by the analysis in lesser chapter 1.

Doctrinal understanding (*chieh*) generates a vow (*yüan*), and the vow seeks its fulfillment in the practice of the path (*hsing*). In this respect, arousing the thought of enlightenment ultimately entails a process of

55. T12.676b–683a. See Swanson, *Foundations of T'ien-t'ai Philosophy*, pp. 226–234, for translation of an important discussion of the fourfold four noble truths in Chih-i's *Fa-hua hsüan-i*.

56. According to Chih-i, the Hīnayānist perspective is correct only insofar as it is understood not as a scheme unto itself but as an expedient precursor to the Mahāyāna, as the *Lotus Sūtra* itself urges.

three phases, and its overall correctness hinges on correctness in all three. According to Chan-jan,[57] this is Chih-i's reason for completing his discussion of arousing the thought of enlightenment with a treatment of the four extensive bodhisattva vows (*ssu hung-yüan*) and the six identities (*liu chi*). The four vows are none other than the familiar set of four stanzas from the *Ying-lo ching* cited regularly in Chinese and Japanese Buddhist monasteries today: "Beings without limit I vow to deliver; afflictions without end I vow to sever; approaches to dharma incalculable I vow to practice; unexcelled Buddhahood I vow to attain."

Chih-i explains the meaning of the four extensive vows from the perspective of each of the fourfold noble truths but singles out that of the unconstructed (i.e., the perfect teaching) as the truly correct one. The six identities, with which lesser chapter 1 concludes, describe the six basic stages of the perfect teaching, thereby outlining the course of practice through which the four vows seek fulfillment.

Lesser chapter 2, "Engaging in the Great Practice or the Four Samādhis," contains the exposition of the four forms of samādhi (*ssu-chung san-mei*), for which it has become the most famous of the five chapters of the Synopsis. The term "samādhi" as it is used here means "method of religious discipline" in addition to its usual sense of meditative concentration or experience of religious insight. The number "four" describes a tetralemma constructed on the basis of the two alternatives of walking and sitting. Together they yield a scheme for classifying methods of samādhi practice according to four possible modes of physical activity: constantly sitting, constantly walking, part walking/part sitting, and neither walking nor sitting. In theory the rubric of the four samādhis is comprehensive and open-ended, capable of accommodating any form of religious practice. In fact, however, the four modalities themselves are closely identified with a set of six specific ritual meditations known as one-practice samādhi, pratyutpanna samādhi, lotus samādhi, vaipulya repentance, invocation of Avalokiteśvara (Kuan-yin) repentance, and the samādhi of freely following one's thought (*sui-tzu-i*).[58] The chapter on the four forms of samādhi itself is simply a description of these various rites.

Each of the six ritual meditations presented under the rubric of the four samādhis, with the exception of freely following one's thought, is treated from the two perspectives of its procedure for practice and an exhortation to practice. "Procedure" (*fang-fa*) refers to the ritual and meditative content of the given practice, which it organizes according to the three perspectives of body, speech, and mind. Here mental proce-

57. T 46.181a16–20.

58. For an authoritative discussion of the four samādhis and their respective practices in early T'ien-t'ai, see Stevenson, "The Four Kinds of Samādhi in Early T'ien-t'ai Buddhism."

dure itself is identified with the practice of calming and contemplation; it is therefore inaccurate to say that the four samādhis deal only with the physical aspects of the practice, and that the exposition of the mental discipline is reserved exclusively for greater chapter 7. In fact, the seamless integration of mental contemplation with the ritual gestures of body and voice is precisely the feature that has earned the lesser chapter on the four samādhis such high esteem among East Asian Buddhists. The concluding exhortation to practice encourages the practitioner to take up the rite by describing the benefits derived from it.

The constantly sitting samādhi, also known as the one-practice samādhi (*i-hsing san-mei*), is based on two "Mañjuśrī sūtras," the *Wen-shu shuo ching* (*Saptaśatika-prajñāpāramitā Sūtra*)[59] and the *Wen-shu wen ching* (*Mañjuśrī-paripṛcchā Sūtra*).[60] It entails constant, seated meditation for a fixed period of ninety days, during which time the meditator strives to identify the mind directly with the dharmadhātu. Invocation of a Buddha's name and confession (in this case the identity of the Buddha is not specified) are permitted when contemplation becomes impaired by drowsiness or other mental obstructions.[61]

The constantly walking samādhi is identified with the practice of pratyutpanna samādhi, as outlined in the three-fascicle *Pan-chou san-mei ching* (*Pratyutpanna-samādhi Sūtra*)[62] and the *Shih-chu p'i-po-sha-lun* (**Daśabhūmika-vibhāṣa Śāstra*).[63] While concurrently reciting the name and visualizing the form of Amitābha Buddha, the practitioner must

59. T no. 232, whose full title is *Wen-shu-shih-li so-shuo pan-jo po-lo-mi ching*, was translated by Mandrasena in 503.

60. T no. 468, whose full title is *Wen-shu-shih-li wen ching*, was translated by Saṅghbhadra in 518.

61. See Faure, "The Concept of One-Practice Samādhi in Early Ch'an."

62. T no. 418, translated into Chinese by Lokakṣema toward the end of the second century. For an annotated translation of the Tibetan version, see Harrison, *The Samādhi of Direct Encounter with the Buddhas of the Present*. The first appendix discusses in detail the Lokakṣema translation and its divergence from the Tibetan text. See also Harrison, "*Buddhānusmṛti* in the *Pratyutpanna-Buddha-Saṃmukhāvasthita-Samādhi Sūtra*."

63. T no. 1521. Like the TCTL, the *Shih-chu p'i-p'o-sha lun* is said to be a work of Nāgārjuna translated by Kumārajīva. The text consists of a prose commentary (itself incomplete) to a set of root verses taken from the *Daśabhūmika Sūtra*. Takemura Shōhō has suggested that the prose commentary may have been based on the recitation and oral commentary of Buddhayaśas, whom Kumārajīva sought out in order to gain a clearer understanding of the meaning of the ten bhūmi and to facilitate his translation of the *Daśabhūmika Sūtra* (see Takemura, *Jūjūbibasharon no kenkyū*, pp. 15–16, 21–22). Discussion of the *Pratyutpanna-samādhi Sūtra* and its practice takes up the greater part of six chapters of the *Shih-chu p'i-p'o-sha lun* (T 26.68c–88c).

continually circumambulate an altar to Amitābha for a fixed period of ninety days. It is thus called "constantly walking."

Under the part walking/part sitting samādhi Chih-i includes two rites, the vaipulya repentance and the lotus samādhi. "Part walking and part sitting" here means an alternation between the two ritual activities of walking meditation and seated meditation. The vaipulya repentance, which is based on a quasi-esoteric Buddhist sūtra known as the *Ta-fang-teng t'o-lo-ni ching* (**Mahā-vaipulya-dhāraṇi Sūtra*),[64] centers around ritual circumambulation and recitation of dhāraṇī incantations, interspersed with extended periods of seated meditation. The period of the practice is only seven days, and laypersons are permitted to participate. The concept of the lotus samādhi derives from chapters 14 (Comfortable Conduct) and 28 (Encouragements of Universal Worthy) of the *Lotus Sūtra*, but its ritual form is inspired mainly by the *Kuan P'u-hsien ching* (Sūtra on the Visualization of Samantabhadra).[65] The rite itself, which extends for twenty-one days, entails a ritual cycle of confession before the visualized image of Samantabhadra, circumambulation accompanied by recitation of the *Lotus Sūtra*, and seated meditation. It is said that Chih-i was initially enlightened through practice of the lotus samādhi.

Last of the four forms of samādhi is the neither walking nor sitting samādhi. Unlike the previous three samādhis, Chih-i divides his discussion of this topic into four parts: cultivation on the basis of the sūtras, contemplation amid good or wholesome dharmas, contemplation amid evil dharmas, and contemplation amid neutral dharmas. Together these describe two distinctly separate concepts of samādhi cultivation.

The heading of cultivation on the basis of the sūtras serves as a repository for any ritual meditations based on the Buddhist scriptures that do not fit neatly into the established categories of sitting, walking, or part sitting/part walking. In this capacity, it simply completes the tetralemma in a manner consistent with the parameters of ritual structure that characterize the previous three samādhis. As his example of such a rite, Chih-i cites the repentance for the invocation of Avalokiteśvara, a quasi-esoteric rite based on the *Ch'ing Kuan-shih-yin ching*[66] that lasts from twenty-one to forty-nine days and involves a miscellany of activities, in-

64. T no. 1339.

65. The *Kuan p'u-hsien p'u-sa hsing-fa ching* (T no. 277), translated by Dharmamitra during the early fifth century, is commonly regarded as an extension of the last chapter ("Encouragements of Universal Worthy or Samantabhadra") of the *Lotus Sūtra*, because it elaborates on cult guidelines for the worship of Samantabhadra initially set forth in that chapter.

66. The full title is *Ch'ing Kuan-shih-yin hsiao-fu tu-hai t'o-lo-ni ching* (Scripture of the Dhāraṇī for Invoking Avalokiteśvara to Dissipate Poison and Harm), T no. 1043. It was translated by Nan-t'i (Nandin) during the last years of the Eastern Chin dynasty (317–420).

cluding ritual offerings, confession, invocation of dhāraṇī, sitting, and recitation of sūtras.

The remaining three sections on contemplation amid good, evil, and neutral dharmas describe an entirely different approach to practice known formally as the "samādhi of freely following one's thoughts" (*sui-tzu-i san-mei*) or "samādhi of maintaining wakeful awareness of mind" (*chüeh-i san-mei*).[67] Freely following one's thoughts (*sui-tzu-i*), as its name implies, represents a free-style approach to meditation where any and all forms of physical activity and any and all forms of sense perception—regardless of whether they are morally good, evil, non-valent, ritually structured, or ritually unstructured—are used indiscriminately as a basis for cultivating samādhi.

Contemplation amid evil activities, itself an alarming concept, is perhaps the most interesting of all the sections expounded in this lesser chapter 2 on the four samādhis.[68] Significantly, most of the ten spheres that serve as the objects of contemplation in greater chapter 7 are also evil, so that it is possible to say that this samādhi most closely summarizes the contemplations in chapter 7. The guiding principle here is "Do not try to suppress the evil thought but dispassionately watch it arise." The practice is compared to landing a large fish: one must play out the line and let it surface and submerge freely until it is worn out and can be pulled in by the slender, weak line (of meditation). Since this practice carries a certain potential for abuse, Chih-i ends his discussion not with the usual encouragements to practice but with words of caution.

Because of the striking way in which several of the four samādhis anticipate developments in other Buddhist movements such as Ch'an and Pure Land, much interest has centered on the question of which rite among the four samādhis was most important to Chih-i. From the late T'ang on, Buddhist historians have tended to view the pratyutpanna or constantly walking samādhi as the most central of T'ien-t'ai practices, especially in Japan. But it is clear that this is a distortion that arose with the growing Pure Land influence within T'ien-t'ai itself, for this walking samādhi takes as its chief practice the contemplation and recitation of the name of the Buddha Amitābha. Andō Toshio, seeking to revise the picture, claims that it was rather the one-practice or constantly sitting samādhi and the neither walking nor sitting samādhi that had the highest place in Chih-i's mind, inasmuch as they represent the fundamental practice of seated meditation, on the one hand, and meditation practiced in

67. The names as well as the format of Chih-i's description are based on two earlier T'ien-t'ai works on this practice, Hui-ssu's *Sui-tzu-i san-mei* (HTC vol. 98) and Chih-i's *Mo-ho pan-jo p'o-lo-mi ching chüeh-i san-mei* (T no. 1922). Chih-i (or Kuan-ting) cites liberally from Hui-ssu.

68. See Donner, "Chih-i's Meditation on Evil."

all aspects of daily life, on the other.[69] Here Chih-i would have had no quarrel with the Ch'an school.

In Japanese Tendai Buddhism, the pratyutpanna or constantly walking samādhi and lotus samādhi are the only two among the original practices that have seen continual usage down to modern times. A recent effort on Mount Hiei to reclaim the ancient forms of T'ien-t'ai practice, however, has resulted in a reconstruction of the one-practice or constantly seated samādhi from literary sources. Others may yet follow. As one of the most detailed and authoritative texts on the four samādhis, lesser chapter 2 of the Synopsis continues to shape T'ien-t'ai practice today as it has for thousands of years.

Lesser chapters 3 and 4 are so short that no more needs to be said about them. But the discussion in lesser chapter 5 on the final return of the practitioner, and of the purport of all the teachings, to the secret treasury (*pi-mi chih tsang*), the great abode (*ta-ch'u*), is of quite some interest. The entire chapter centers around an important passage in the *Nirvāṇa Sūtra,* where the "secret treasury" of the Buddhas is identified with three eternal and unchanging meritorious qualities (*san-te*) of the dharma-body, prajñā, and liberation.[70] These three qualities describe the unchanging enlightened condition that is the foundation of all the Buddhas and their salvific activities as well as the true legacy of all living beings. Moreover, they represent "the great abode" to which Buddha, sentient beings, and salvific effort together "return." When impeded, the properties of the three qualities themselves transmute into the bases of deluded existence in the form of the three obstacles (*san-chang*): nescience, biased attachment to aspects of the teaching (i.e., mistaken outlook or opinion), and (doltish) incognizance (of one's bound condition).[71] Purified or redelineated according to the middle, these very obstacles are themselves the three qualities. Between obstacle and meritorious quality there is no difference; nor can any distinction be made between before or after, fundamental or derived. Thus in full keeping with the vision of the perfect path, defilement and enlightenment, beginning of the path and end of the path, are utterly identical and interpenetrating.

69. See Andō, *Tendai shisō-shi,* pp. 380–387.

70. T 12.616b8–17. These also correlate with the three dharmas of true nature (*chen-hsing*), illumination (*kuan-chao*), and assistance to attainment (*tzu-ch'eng*) in *Fa-hua hsüan-i.*

71. This listing of three obstacles (*san-chang*) is an unusual one, and its origins are unclear. *Fa-hua hsüan-i* (T 33.742b28–c18)—in a similar discussion of the three meritorious qualities and their correlative obstacles—gives the three obstacles as the three delusions of (1) view and cultivation/attachment, (2) obscuration of multiplicity, and (3) nescience.

CHAPTER 2

The Status of the *Mo-ho chih-kuan* in the T'ien-t'ai Tradition

Daniel B. Stevenson

From the time the Buddhist sūtras and śātras first made their way to the East their teachings have always been replete with the elixir of truth. The [dharma] masters of this land, lamenting the fact that their contemporaries were unable to distinguish its principles, concentrated their efforts on scriptural exegesis as the means to penetrate [the essential vision of] the tradition (*tsung*). Yet, occupying themselves with minor points, they obscured the major, and, clinging to the one-sided (*p'ien*), they neglected the whole (*yüan*). As such, the means to reveal the wonder of living realization [lit. "mind-transmission"] were never made available, and those who would tread the path [to enlightenment] were left yearning for the birth of a sage.

Purely through his own endowments and without recourse to transmission [from a teacher], the venerable [Hui-wen] of the Northern Ch'i awakened spontaneously to Nāgārjuna's truth of the identity of emptiness, provisionality, and the middle. He fashioned a method of meditation on the basis of it and taught it to Nan-yüeh [Hui-ssu], . . . who in turn taught it to Chih-i. Relying on this practice Chih-i became enlightened to [the profound import of] the *Lotus Sūtra* and went on to reclaim anew the grand enterprise. . . . He is said to have once remarked, "Transmission of the way lies in practice, and practice is founded on preaching." Thus he sketched out the five periods [of the Buddha's career] and elaborated in detail the eight teachings. [On the basis of these] he synthesized the miscellaneous writings [of the Buddhist canon] and grounded their essential design (*tsung*) in the *Lotus Sūtra*. . . . With [the Buddha's] discourses on doctrinal teaching (*chiao*) thus explained, the concept of religious practice (*kuan*) also required clarification. This Chih-i set forth in the single treatise of the *[Great] Calming and Contempla-*

> *tion* (*Mo-ho chih-kuan*), . . . [in which he] refuted the hundred theories [of his age] and transcended both ancient and recent [understandings]. Thus it became the foundation from which [Buddhist] teachings are illuminated for the entire world.[1]

Like their counterparts within the Confucian tradition, Chinese Buddhists developed a particularly keen interest in charting the history of their tradition and bringing that history to bear on the spiritual and moral life of the present. As a consequence, the maintenance of lineage histories, which trace the genealogical descent of a given school from its quasi-mythical inauguration down through successive generations of patriarchs, became as central to the articulation of Chinese Buddhist sectarian identity as doctrinal teaching and cult were. This phenomenon has proved to be both a blessing and a bane for the study of Chinese Buddhism. For while these sectarian histories provide an invaluable record of earlier periods from which all too few sources survive, they typically construct that record in terms of the historiographical conventions and ideological agendae of religious historians writing centuries after the events in question. The extent to which these conventions have been replicated in modern scholarship and inadvertently pattern some of our most basic assumptions about Chinese Buddhist history and culture has become a growing concern in the field of Chinese Buddhist studies today.[2]

The previous chapter briefly reviewed the content of the *Mo-ho chih-kuan* and indicated the place that it has traditionally held within the systematic framework of T'ien-t'ai doctrine (*chiao*) and practice (*kuan*). The aim of this chapter is to look beyond the narrow confines of the text itself and take up the broader issue of the cultural history of the *Mo-ho chih-kuan*—specifically, the role that the *Mo-ho chih-kuan* played as sacred scripture within the lives of the individual and the community. The issues of genre, the historicity of sources, and historiographic models are especially acute. Not only must one rely heavily on T'ien-t'ai sectarian histories to reconstruct this scenario, one must also answer to a tradition of secondary scholarship that until recently has tended to reproduce the normative views of later T'ien-t'ai tradition to an unusual degree.

As a case in point one need only look to the quasi-mythological account of T'ien-t'ai origins and the *Mo-ho chih-kuan* cited at the beginning of this chapter. The passage in question comes from the *Fo-tsu t'ung-chi* (Record of the Lineal Transmission of the Buddhas and Patriarchs), the cele-

1. Chih-p'an, *Fo-tsu t'ung-chi,* T 49.177c11–178a8.

2. Zen Studies, fueled by discoveries of lost texts in the Tun-huang manuscript collections, has especially contributed to this revision. Several Western studies of note include John McRae, *The Northern School and the Formation of Early Ch'an Buddhism*; Bernard Faure, *The Rhetoric of Immediacy*; Peter N. Gregory, *Tsung-mi and the Sinificiation of Buddhism*; and T. Griffith Foulk's "The 'Ch'an School' and its Place in the Buddhist Monastic Tradition."

brated T'ien-t'ai sectarian history compiled by the thirteenth-century cleric Chih-p'an (ca. 1269). As the most articulated description of the T'ien-t'ai sectarian genealogy, the *Fo-tsu t'ung-chi* became the chief literary source for later T'ien-t'ai historical ideology. In this capacity, it has exerted a powerful influence on modern scholarship, as comparison of the preceding passage with virtually any recent summary of the highlights of T'ien-t'ai history and their contribution to Chinese Buddhism will reveal.[3]

Such considerations of genre and historical context bear on the cultural history of the *Mo-ho chih-kuan* in several ways. To begin with, given the confusing overlay of historical event and historiographic myth that surrounds the *Mo-ho chih-kuan*, it is essential that we place sources in their proper contexts and part the veil of mytho-historical trope in an effort to reveal the complex process and historical nuances that contributed to the text's "preeminence" within T'ien-t'ai tradition. At the same time, we must allow ourselves to enter the world of mytho-historical paradigm itself and explore the way in which its discursive structures defined the presence of the *Mo-ho chih-kuan* within the lives of its followers, for no study of the *Mo-ho chih-kuan* as a sacred text would be complete without the effort to appreciate what it meant for a thirteenth-century T'ien-t'ai follower to engage the *Mo-ho chih-kuan* as the vision of the patriarchs and "the foundation from which [Buddhist] teachings are illuminated for the entire world."

In the pages that follow I hope to accomplish something of both. This chapter traces the development of the basic mythic structures and hermeneutical conventions that defined the *Mo-ho chih-kuan* as one of the central sacred texts of the T'ien-t'ai order and concludes with a brief description of the form that these conventions came to take in the routines of Sung period T'ien-t'ai monasteries. The following chapter discusses issues concerned more directly with the reading and interpretation of the *Mo-ho chih-kuan* within this hermeneutical framework. Here we will look at the treatment that certain textual (and intertextual) ambiguities—notably the cultic complex of the four samādhis—receive at the hands of T'ien-t'ai exegetes and modern scholars and the implications that such treatment has for understanding the historical and cultural dynamic of T'ien-t'ai tradition.

The *Mo-ho chih-kuan* and the T'ien-t'ai Revelation

The sectarian lineal history that we see fully developed in later sources finds its *locus classicus* in the genealogy of "western patriarchs" and "eastern masters" set forth in Kuan-ting's (561–632) introduction to the

3. See, for example, the preface to Ikeda Rosan's recent *Makashikan kenkyū josetsu*, pp. 1–6, or Leo Pruden's entry on "T'ien-t'ai" in *The Encyclopedia of Religion*.

Mo-ho chih-kuan. As the most substantial of the early accounts of T'ien-t'ai origins, sectarian historians have gravitated to this introduction as a basis for organizing the bits of patriarchal lore that appear scattered throughout early T'ien-t'ai sources. Modern scholars, following their example, have likewise sought in it clues to understanding the historical circumstances in which T'ien-t'ai ideology and "sinitic" Buddhism as a whole took shape. Thus Kuan-ting's summary of T'ien-t'ai origins—and, by implication, the origin of the text of the *Mo-ho chih-kuan* that it introduces—is deeply bound up with some of the most consequential distinctions of Chinese Buddhist history.

It has long been noted, for instance, that the "golden-mouthed transmission" of the western patriarchs includes the authors of most of the great Indian treatises and exegetical traditions that dominated early medieval Chinese discussions of Buddhist doctrine—Nāgārjuna, Aśvaghoṣa, and Vasubandhu being three illustrious examples.[4] In contrast to this foreign and textually oriented legacy of the western patriarchy, the enigmatic Hui-wen (n.d.) and Hui-ssu (515–577) present an altogether different image—that of a "self-enlightened" (*tu-wu*) charismatic, who draws his authority not from received text and tradition but from transhistorical inspiration. Noting the presence of this same polarity throughout any number of late North-South Dynasties (317–589) and early T'ang (ca. 618) Buddhist documents, scholars have posited the existence of two distinctive regional traditions operating in fifth- and sixth-century Buddhism: a sophisticated exegetical Buddhism fostered among the educated Chinese aristocracy of the South and a highly pragmatic Buddhism among the "barbarian" rulers of the North.[5] Again drawing on conventions of T'ien-t'ai patriarchal history, the emergence of the T'ien-t'ai school is represented as a watershed synthesis of these two regional religious traditions realized contemporaneously with the Sui (581–618) political reunification of China.

This theory has much to commend itself, especially when we recall the long-standing cultural and political differences that beset northern and southern China, as well as the powerful connection that Chih-i forged

4. Nāgārjuna's works were the focus of various Madhyamaka-oriented *San-lun* and *Ssu-lun* lines (so-named for their emphasis on the "three" or "four treatises" of his translated into Chinese). Writings of Aśvaghoṣa (the reputed author of the influential *Ta-sheng ch'i-hsin lun* or "Awakening of Faith"), Asaṅga, and Vasubandhu were central to the Tathāgatagarbha- and Yogācāra-based *Ti-lun* and *She-lun* lines. For their contributions to Chinese Buddhist exegesis all of these figures were revered as great bodhisattvas.

5. The distinction is widely held but has been most thoroughly developed by T'ang Yung-t'ung in his classic *Han Wei liang-Chin Nan-pei ch'ao Fo-chiao shih,* and Ōchō Enichi in his *Chūgoku bukkyō no kenkyū,* pp. 256–289. Both are summarized in Hurvitz, "Chih-i," pp. 74–86.

with the Sui ruling house. But my interest here is not so much historical facticity as it is the significance that this cluster of images holds for T'ien-t'ai believers as discursive paradigm. Indeed, given the close connection that developed in later T'ien-t'ai between patriarchal genealogical narrative and the construction of religious identity and soteriological purpose, I believe that we come closer to both the spirit and function of sectarian historiography if we think of it in terms of the role that myth plays in religion. Viewed from this perspective, the provocative question with which Kuan-ting introduces the T'ien-t'ai lineage or "creation story"—"Does [the Buddhist dharma] shine of itself with the heavenly light of truth or is it [secondarily] derived like the blue [that is refined] from the indigo [plant]?"—raises an issue that we might ordinarily think of as historically specific to the level of a fundamental problematic of T'ien-t'ai spirituality. The synthesis achieved by the patriarchal visionaries Hui-ssu and Chih-i, in turn, becomes a deed of *illo tempore*—a primal struggle to bring the light of revelation into the world—that, simply by the act of remembrance or retelling, stands as the timeless model and task of every T'ien-t'ai practitioner.

One need not look far to appreciate the mythic resonances of Kuan-ting's patriarchal narrative. For, indeed, the parallels between Kuan-ting's twofold genealogy and the T'ien-t'ai ideological linchpin of "doctrinal learning" (*chiao*) and "meditative praxis" (*kuan*) are already unmistakable. However, I would like to draw attention to another quasi-historical trope, similar in form, that figures more directly in Chih-i's writings themselves and is thus even more elemental than Kuan-ting's patriarchal structure. It is Chih-i's penchant for constructing the T'ien-t'ai ideal of "integrated learning and practice" against a backdrop of two specific personifications of excess or abuse: the "dhyāna master of benighted realization" (*an-cheng ch'an-shih*) and the "dharma master [given to pedantic] memorization and recitation of texts" (*sung-wen fa-shih*).

Both figures are endowed with a tangible historicity in Chih-i's works. He rails against their excesses as though they were self-evident (at times appearing to address these individuals directly) and on several key occasions holds their depravities specifically responsible for inciting the traumatic Northern Chou persecutions of the Buddhist saṅgha (574–577). At no time, however, does Chih-i ever affix an actual name or face to these figures. This anonymity seems to have enhanced their power as mythic paradigms, ultimately allowing them to be invoked freely by later T'ien-t'ai reformers in their continuing efforts to identify and defend a T'ien-t'ai orthodoxy.

The pedantic dharma master is characterized by Chih-i as one whose words (*yü*) do not match his deeds (*hsing*)—the individual who, caught up in the exigencies of the written text, sacrifices spiritual substance for an empty intellectualism. In fact, the trope resonates closely with the image of the corpulent exegete so roundly criticized in contemporary apocryphal scriptures for his lowly addiction to the fortunes of the metropolitan monastery and aristocratic support.[6] The benighted dhyāna practitioner is his polar opposite. Due to his indifference or even animosity toward scriptural exegesis, he promotes an ignorant asceticism and subjective intuition over deference to the wisdom of received tradition. The lot of both is spiritual stasis, if not wholesale destruction. The untutored meditator, inflating or grossly misconstruing the nature of his visions, is prone to sink into the oblivion of his own private madness. The scriptural pedant ends up dismissing religious practice altogether, either because he sees it as the domain of the spiritually obtuse or becomes so cowed by the complexities of the path that he cannot bring himself to settle on the first step. In this respect, they represent for early T'ien-t'ai the living image of spiritual obstruction—the "failed/fallen" Buddhist.

At the same time, however, the subjective flaws of these dhyāna and dharma masters extend beyond mere personal defeat and contribute ultimately to an evil of a far more insidious sort. Chih-i finds behind both extremes a common overbearing pride, the primary fault of which lies in its inability—both affectively and intellectually—to affirm the universal inclusiveness and harmony of design of the Buddha, dharma, and saṅgha. When confronted with different points of view this vanity turns to spite. The saṅgha becomes fragmented with dispute; base cynicism abounds; and the Buddha's tradition, losing all credibility in the eyes of the populace and court, is brought to destruction. Such were the errors, according to Chih-i, that lead to events like the Northern Chou persecution.[7] Thus the sin of the pedantic dharma master and benighted dhyāna master lies not so much in the loss they bring upon themselves as in the damage that they inflict on the tradition at large. In this latter capacity, especially, Chih-i finds an analogue for them in the "legions of māra,"[8] the archetypal demon who is the enemy of the Buddha dharma and "destroyer of the good roots of others."[9]

Against this backdrop T'ien-t'ai developed its particular vision of reli-

6. See, for example, the *Hsiang-fa chüeh-i ching* (Sūtra of Resolving Doubts During the Semblance Dharma Age) (T no. 2870) and *Tsui miao-sheng-ting ching* (Sūtra of the Marvelous and Sublime Samādhi). The former is the subject of a Master's thesis by Kyoko Tokuno, "A Case Study of Chinese Buddhist Apocrypha: The *Hsiang-fa chüeh-i ching*"; the latter is discussed and published in Sekiguchi Shindai, *Tendai shikan no kenkyū*, pp. 379–402. Both were influential in early T'ien-t'ai as well as in the Three Stages (San-chieh chiao) movement.

7. See MHCK, T 46.18c20–21a2; see also, *Kuan-hsin lun shu*, T 46.587c–588a.

8. *Kuan-hsin lun*, T 46.575a; and Kuan-ting's *Kuan-hsin lun shu*, T 46.587c–588a.

9. Chih-i's most lucid discussion of the various māras appears in *Shih ch'an-p'o-lo-mi tz'u-ti fa-men*, T 46.507a1–4.

gious practice and perfection, a vision that incorporates two essential dimensions: one is the quest for personal salvation; the other, a sense of corporate responsibility for Buddhist tradition as a whole. Both ideals are realized through the twofold discipline of comprehensive study of the Buddhist teachings (*chiao*) coupled with meditative cultivation (*kuan*). Working together like the two complementary "wheels of the cart" or "wings of the bird," doctrinal study "illumines" and "guides" meditative insight, and insight "enriches" and "actualizes" doctrinal study, until the two meld seamlessly in a mastery of both the inspired and received domains of Buddhist tradition. As represented in the formal soteriology of the T'ien-t'ai path, sainthood is tantamount to "reclaiming the Buddha's intent" (*te fo-i*) both in its transhistorical aspect as an eternally abiding reality (the "heavenly light of truth," as Kuan-ting would put it) and also as it is historically constituted in the pedagogic design of his recorded discourses (the "secondarily derived blue of the indigo"). As Chih-i states in one of the most celebrated T'ien-t'ai descriptions of perfection from the *Mo-ho chih-kuan*:

> Understanding [i.e., learning] purifies practice, and practice promotes understanding. Illuminating and enriching, guiding and penetrating, they reciprocally beautify and embellish one another.[10] They are like the two hands of a single body, which, working together, keep it clean. [Yet this synthesis of learning and practice] is not just a matter of clearing away impediments and overcoming obstacles in order to inwardly advance one's own enlightenment. One must also achieve a thorough comprehension of the sūtras and treatises so that one can outwardly reveal to others what they have not heard before. When one combines one's own training with the training of others, benefit is then complete. If one such as this is not the teacher of all humankind and the jewel of the nation, then who is?[11]

10. Chan-jan says in his *Chih-kuan fu-hsing ch'uan-hung chüeh* (T 46.278c21–27): " 'Wisdom' means an understanding of calming and contemplation. 'Practice' refers to the actual practice of calming and contemplation. When practice is endowed with understanding, practice will not go astray. When understanding is endowed with practice, understanding will have power and direction. Understanding is like the 'illumination' of the sun; practice is like the 'enriching or moistening' of the rain. When light and moisture are in proper proportion, the myriad things reach completion. When practice and understanding are not one-sided, the myriad virtues are brought to fulfillment. Understanding is analogous to the 'guidance' of a caravan chief; practice is analogous to his fellow merchants 'progressing toward' [their destination]."

11. MHCK, T 46.49a. The passage in question is also the *locus classicus* for Saichō's famous concept of training the Tendai priest as the servant of the state and "jewel of the nation"; see Groner, Saichō, pp. 143–144.

Even in the earliest T'ien-t'ai sources, the ideal of "learning and practice" (*chiao-kuan*) and its demonic antithesis are organized into an infrastructure that systematically draws together all aspects of T'ien-t'ai lore—patriarchal hagiography, formal soteriology, classification of the teachings (*p'an-chiao*), and even the program of the *Mo-ho chih-kuan* itself. According to the scheme of the six identities, for example, the T'ien-t'ai path begins with "hearing the doctrine" and "acquiring verbal comprehension" of the perfect teaching (*yüan-chiao*). Meditative prowess (*kuan-hsing*), developed in the third identity, brings living insight to the word, such that "actions . . . match words, and words match actions" and "mind and mouth are in perfect correspondence." As scripture and practice increasingly confirm one another, unshakable faith (*hsin-chieh*) arises. With unshakable faith one enters the state of "worthy" (*hsien*), a condition that reaches its culmination in the fourth identity—the identity of resemblance. Thereupon one achieves full mastery of the received tradition, embodying its totality so perfectly that "all of one's ruminations and speculations turn out to be [in perfect accord with] what has been expounded previously in the scriptures."[12] "Just as if one were to break open a single mote of dust to reveal a billion rolls of sūtras," Chih-i tells us, "Buddhist teachings as extensive as sands of the Ganges will be realized within a single instant of thought."[13]

Upon entering the fifth identity, that of increments of truth or realization, one passes from the condition of "worthy" (*hsien*) to that of full "saint" or "sage" (*sheng*). Rather than a guarantor of tradition, one at this point becomes a veritable creator of tradition—a self-sustaining fount of dharma capable of spontaneously generating teachings (*ch'i-chiao*) as though one were a Buddha oneself. Indeed, being fully endowed with the vision of the inconceivable middle truth, the "saint" is referred to as a true "son" of the Buddha, distinguishable from the latter only by the relative "maturity" of his powers. Thus for all practical purposes the fifth identity represents the fulfillment of the path, and the sixth identity—the marvelous enlightenment of Buddhahood itself—all but loses its distinctiveness as a religious goal.

Early T'ien-t'ai patriarchal hagiography is quite deliberate in its effort to homologize the spiritual attainments of Hui-ssu and Chih-i with the generalized pattern of the T'ien-t'ai path. The biographies of both figures center around dramatic descriptions of enlightenment experiences, the characteristics of which are easily (and often explicitly) identified with specific stages of the path. Hui-ssu, for instance, is said to have attained the identity of resemblance—the stage of "worthy." As Kuan-ting states in his introduction to the *Mo-ho chih-kuan*: "In a flash of thought he ex-

12. MHCK, T 46.10b20–10c5.
13. MHCK, T 46.20b4–7.

perienced total realization, and dharma-accesses of both the Lesser and Greater Vehicles brilliantly opened forth [for him]."[14] Chan-jan goes on to comment: "From this moment on [Hui-ssu's] eloquence and awakening were so extensive that when he encountered scriptures that he had never heard before he experienced no doubts whatsoever about their content and could understand them perfectly without the explanation of others."[15]

Chih-i, by his own profession, is said to have realized the level of the five grades of disciplehood, a grade of "worthy" slightly lower than that of his master, Hui-ssu. The circumstances of his awakening are too involved to recount here. But in what is perhaps the most celebrated encounter between Hui-ssu and Chih-i, the latter is recorded as saying of Chih-i's insight and abilities: "Even should an assembly of one-thousand masters of written scripture (*wen-tzu shih*) seek to get the better of your eloquence they could never exhaust it. Among preachers of the dharma you are foremost."[16]

Such detailed attention to religious experience is itself an unusual phenomenon when it comes to conventions of medieval Buddhist biography. When one considers as well the centrality that these experiences play in the extended drama of the two patriarchal careers—i.e., the way in which their character and accomplishments build directly on these merits—the integral connection between patriarchal hagiography, the doctrinal formalities of the T'ien-t'ai path, and such mytho-historical paradigms as the evil dhyāna and dharma masters becomes all the more apparent.

The *Mo-ho chih-kuan* and Historical Paradigm

The *Mo-ho chih-kuan* is Chih-i's most comprehensive and systematic statement of the T'ien-t'ai path of "learning" (*chiao*) and "practice" (*kuan*). This fact together with Kuan-ting's representation of the *Mo-ho chih-kuan* as the quintessence of the patriarchal revelation—i.e., "the approach to dharma that Chih-i himself practiced in his own mind"—establishes a powerful precedent for organizing T'ien-t'ai tradition and its history in terms of a patriarchal transmission centered chiefly around the *Mo-ho chih-kuan*. Indeed, as is evident in the passage from the *Fo-tsu t'ung-chi* cited at the beginning of this chapter, later sectarian histories uniformly build their accounts around the genealogical structures outlined in Kuan-ting's introduction. Extending this lineage from Chih-i down to the Sung period, the *Fo-tsu t'ung-chi* traces a T'ien-t'ai "orthodox line of transmission" (*cheng-t'ung*) through a succession of nine patriarchs (*tsu*) ranging

14. MHCK, T 46.1b22.
15. *Chih-kuan fu-hsing ch'uan-hung chüeh*, T 46.149a15–16.
16. Kuan-ting, *Sui T'ien-t'ai Chih-che ta-shih pieh-chuan*, T 46.192a8–9.

from Nāgārjuna and Hui-wen to Chan-jan (711–782), followed by an additional eight patriarchs from Chan-jan's disciple Tao-sui through the Sung reviver Chih-li (960–1028). At the heart of this so-called orthodox line (*cheng-t'ung*) stand the twin disciplines of "doctrinal learning" (*chiao*)[17] and "meditation" (*kuan*), which are epitomized scripturally by Chih-i's two *Lotus Sūtra* commentaries and, above all, by the *Mo-ho chih-kuan*. Among these various elements the discipline of "calming and contemplation" (*chih-kuan*) is highlighted in individual biographies as the main thread of sectarian continuity.

This strict lineal representation is responsible for the tendency among modern scholars to construe T'ien-t'ai history primarily as the evolution of a fixed body of ideas and treatises at the hands of a select group of patriarchal figures. Its discursive significance notwithstanding, there is no evidence that the notion of a central patriarchal prelacy ever became an institutional reality for Chinese T'ien-t'ai followers (although, at the regional level, attempts may have been made in this direction from time to time). Nor do we find that Mount T'ien-t'ai—the peak from which the school takes its name—ever exerted unchallenged authority as the geographical center for T'ien-t'ai tradition at large. Even during the Sung period—the heyday of patriarchal genealogies such as the *Fo-tsu t'ung-chi*—T'ien-t'ai remained a dispersed tradition organized around a plurality of semiautonomous master-disciple dharma successions (*ssu-fa*). As best as we can tell, this state of affairs was typical of earlier periods as well.

More importantly, the *Fo-tsu t'ung-chi* itself acknowledges that its concept of patriarchy is in large measure arbitrary and ahistorical, thereby belying the idea that the construct was anything more than a mytho-historical trope. Not only is the designation of patriarch (*tsu*) reserved exclusively for figures of the distant past (the list of patriarchs in the *Fo-tsu t'ung-chi* stops with Chih-li; earlier Five Dynasties and Sung formulations apparently ended with Chan-jan), but the succession that links them itself remains a tenuous reconstruction. Chih-p'an makes it patently clear that Chih-i, Kuan-ting, Chan-jan, and Chih-li are the true luminaries of the patriarchal saga, with the figures who fall between them added mainly to "connect the dots." Hence the *Fo-tsu t'ung-chi* singles out this particular dharma-succession (*ssu-fa*) as the orthodox line (*cheng-t'ung*) not because it held any historical primacy per se but for the simple reason that Chan-jan and Chih-li were retrospectively perceived to have made substantial contributions to the tradition. In point of fact, for both figures that contribution is described in suggestively similar ways—i.e., as the "reclaiming" (*chung-hsing*) of T'ien-t'ai teaching from the brink of extinction

17. Principally understood to mean the T'ien-t'ai system of *p'an-chiao* or "doctrinal classification"—i.e., the "five periods and eight teachings" (*wu-shih pa-chiao*).

through the compiling of exegetical works that bear significantly on later tradition.[18]

The qualifications that the *Fo-tsu t'ung-chi* places on its own concept of the orthodox line of transmission (*cheng-t'ung*) underscore the fact that its patriarchy is primarily a historiographical convention whose thrust is paradigmatic and ideological in nature—itself the product and agent of history rather than a verbatim record of it. Considerations of this sort suggest that we treat its subsidiary elements—especially the exalted status of the *Mo-ho chih-kuan*—not as unconditionally given facts but as an outgrowth of a lengthy and at times fierce competition between a number of different ways of discursively organizing T'ien-t'ai teaching.

Despite the importance that Kuan-ting's introduction to the *Mo-ho chih-kuan* assumed in the eyes of later historiographers, it is not the only account of T'ien-t'ai origins found in early writings of the school. Nor was it necessarily always the axis around which the tradition organized its history over the centuries that followed. Kuan-ting introduces Chih-i's famous discourse on doctrinal classification (*p'an-chiao*) in the *Fa-hua hsüan-i* ("[Discourse on] the Profound Import of the *Lotus Sūtra*") with a genealogical statement that is as compelling as that of the *Mo-ho chih-kuan*.[19] In addition, various early T'ien-t'ai documents recount a legend that presents Hui-ssu and Chih-i as incarnated bodhisattvas who originally received the *Lotus Sūtra*—and by implication, the T'ien-t'ai revelation—directly from Śākyamuni Buddha on Mount Gṛdhrakūta. Each holds the potential of developing a somewhat different take on the origin and nature of T'ien-t'ai tradition, a potential that was from time to time realized in the form of distinctive cultic or regional traditions.[20]

The two poles of "doctrinal learning" (*chiao*) and "meditation" (*kuan*)

18. See *Fo-tsu t'ung-chi*, T 49.130a26–b7, 178a, and 194a–b. Both Chan-jan and Chih-li are said to have revived T'ien-t'ai after an extended period of eclipse. Chan-jan is credited by Chih-p'an with having arrested the decline of T'ien-t'ai exegesis and having purified T'ien-t-ai teachings of compromising and erroneous elements from other schools. Chih-li reclaimed T'ien-t'ai "orthodoxy" after its scriptures had been lost and its traditions all but disrupted by the Hui-ch'ang persecution in the mid-ninth century.

19. *Fa-hua hsüan-i*, T 33.800a19–26.

20. The earliest extant sources for this legend are Kuan-ting's *Chih-che ta-shih pieh-chuan*, T 50.191c21–23, and Tao-hsüan's *Hsü kao-seng chuan*, T 50.564b18–22. Accounts from *Fa-hua chuan-chi* (see T 51.56c–57a) and *Hung-tsan fa-hua chuan* (T 51.22c)—two ninth-century collections of biographies of *Lotus* devotees centered around the region of Ch'ang-an—give the most developed version of the tale. There are suggestions that it was closely connected with a regional cult of the lotus samādhi popularized by Hui-chao and Fa-ch'eng, two spiritual descendants of Chih-i and Hui-ssu who settled at Wu-chen Monastery south of Ch'ang-an. See also Taira Ryōshō, "Ryōzen dōchō ni tsuite."

likewise permitted a host of cultic and scriptural associations other than the narrow identification with the *Lotus Sūtra* suggested by later exegetes. As we have already noted in the previous chapter, there is nothing in the *Mo-ho chih-kuan* or its early history to substantiate any direct connection with the *Lotus Sūtra*. Moreover, the textual history of the *Fa-hua hsüan-i*, *Fa-hua wen-chü*, and *Mo-ho chih-kuan* as a whole indicates that they were not brought together and ensconced at the heart of T'ien-t'ai tradition as the "three great texts of the *Lotus*" until sometime around the eighth century—more than one hundred years after Chih-i's death.[21]

When we examine the early T'ien-t'ai exegetical and textual record, we find that Chih-i and his successors compiled treatises of the "profound import" (*hsüan-i*) and "interlinear" (*wen-chü* or *shu*) genre for any number of sūtras other than the *Lotus*, including such long-standing Chinese favorites as the *Vimalakīrti*, *Nirvāṇa*, *Suvarṇaprabhāsa*, and various Pure Land sūtras. Not only is there no evidence that one particular scripture was consistently promoted over others, but T'ang-period sources indicate that the spiritual descendants of Chih-i realigned T'ien-t'ai doctrine freely in order to accommodate whatever sūtra or ideology caught their fancy. A perfect example is the synthesis of T'ien-t'ai doctrine and the esoteric Buddhism of the *Mahāvairocana Sūtra* developed by I-hsing (682–727) and his circle. This same tendency continues right into the Sung period with the "off-mountain" (*shan-wai*) T'ien-t'ai interest in the apocryphal *Śūraṅgama Sūtra*.[22] Then again, differences could also arise over which of the two disciplines—doctrinal learning (*chiao*) or meditative insight (*kuan*)—takes precedence in religious training, as we see from the "home-mountain" (*shan-chia*) and "off-mountain" (*shan-wai*) controversies over the nature of spiritual development. Finally, the inherent catholicity of the meditative system of the *Mo-ho chih-kuan* also allowed T'ien-t'ai praxis (*kuan*) to conform itself to a diversity of cultic and soteriological forms, from the "wordless" subitism of Ch'an, to the elaborate rites of esoteric Buddhism, to the quest for rebirth in the Pure Land of Amitābha. This flexibility is reflected in the steady expansion of the cultic repertoire of the four samādhis over the course of the T'ang and Sung.

Any and all of these factors could—and to varying degrees did—generate divergent perspectives within the T'ien-t'ai tradition. Indeed, a

21. The most solid evidence to this effect has been developed by Hirai Shun'ei in his studies of the *Fa-hua wen-chü*; see his *Hokke mongu no seiritsu ni kansuru kenkyū*, pp. 143–163.

22. The term "off-mountain" (*shan-wai*) refers to a loose-knit group of T'ien-t'ai masters who were opposed by Chih-li and subsequently "excluded" from the "home-mountain" T'ien-t'ai camp due to their unorthodox doctrinal views. They espoused a tathāgatagarbha-oriented interpretation of T'ien-t'ai teaching that drew strongly on the apocryphal *Śūraṅgama Sūtra* and late-T'ang Ch'an/Hua-yen thought. See the third section of the following chapter for more information.

closer look at T'ang-period T'ien-t'ai documents reveals a far more fluid and complex situation than the narrow lineal reconstructions of the Sung historians admit. In addition to the well-known revival of T'ien-t'ai learning fostered around Mount T'ien-t'ai in southeast China by Chan-jan, and his mentor Hsüan-lang (673–754), we know of at least two other long-standing and vital centers of T'ien-t'ai teaching. One was Yü-ch'üan Monastery in Hupei, a major T'ien-t'ai institution originally founded by Chih-i himself and the site where he subsequently preached both the *Mo-ho chih-kuan* and *Fa-hua hsüan-i*. The other was the T'ang capital of Ch'ang-an and its surrounding environs, including Mount Wu-t'ai to the north. Both regions sponsored traditions of considerable antiquity and uniqueness, whose differences were no doubt exacerbated by rapprochements with other powerful localized movements such as Northern Ch'an, Hua-yen, the Pure Land teachings of the Shansi masters Tao-ch'o (562–645) and Shan-tao (613–681), and the esoteric Buddhism of Śubhākarasiṃha and Amoghavajra.[23] Such diversity suggests that we should speak in the plural when we speak of eighth-century T'ien-t'ai "tradition," with Chan-jan's particular camp constituting but one among a number of semiautonomous lines.

Of the various regional T'ien-t'ai movements that populated the Chinese landscape during the mid-T'ang, it is only from Chan-jan's line that an appreciable literary record has survived. Naturally, this lack of corroborating evidence makes it difficult to determine just how Chan-jan's views compared with or fared in relation to his T'ien-t'ai contemporaries. Whatever the broader picture may have been, one of the most distinctive features of Chan-jan's works is the systematic effort to identify the "three great texts" of the *Mo-ho chih-kuan*, the *Fa-hua hsüan-i*, and the *Fa-hua wen-chü* as the core of T'ien-t'ai tradition. Apparently following the initiative of his master, Hsüan-lang,[24] Chan-jan explicitly equated T'ien-t'ai doctrinal learning (*chiao*) with "marvelous understanding" (*miao-chüeh*) of the profound tenets of the *Lotus Sūtra* as set forth in Chih-i's two commentarial treatises on that scripture. T'ien-t'ai contemplation (*kuan*)—as set forth specifically in the *Mo-ho chih-kuan*—he defined as the "marvelous practice" (*miao-hsing*) of the *Lotus Sūtra*, thereby setting the precedent for regarding the *Mo-ho chih-kuan* as a *Lotus*-oriented text. Thus the soteriological vision of the T'ien-t'ai path became nothing less than realization

23. For an overview of the evidence pertaining to these regional traditions, see Sekiguchi Shindai, *Tendai shikan no kenkyū*, pp. 185–205; and Ōkubo Ryōjun, "Tōdai ni okeru Tendai no denshō ni tsuite."

24. See Hirai Shun'ei, *Hokke mongu no seiritsu ni kansuru kenkyū*, pp. 143–163. Chih-i's interlinear commentary to the *Lotus Sūtra*, the *Fa-hua wen-chü*, appears to have been little more than a jumbled—and generally neglected—collection of jottings before Chan-jan's teacher, Hsüan-lang, reedited the work and began to lecture on it in conjunction with the *Fa-hua hsüan-i* and *Mo-ho chih-kuan*.

of the "lotus samādhi" (*fa-hua san-mei*), and the tradition itself the "school or doctrine of the *Lotus [Sūtra]*" (*fa-hua tsung*).[25] In the opening lines of his synoptic digest of the *Mo-ho chih-kuan*, the *Chih-kuan ta-i*, Chan-jan states: "This scripture [of the *Lotus*] alone deserves to be called 'wondrous.' Hence only it is suitable for establishing the aims of religious practice (*kuan*). The course of discipline known as the five [sets of] expedients and ten modes [of discernment] itself constitutes the perfect and sudden calming and contemplation, and it is based wholly on the *Lotus*. Therefore, the perfect and sudden calming and contemplation is just another name for the lotus samādhi."[26]

To set this program on a solid foundation, Chan-jan penned a number of treatises on the "three great texts," including massive interlinear commentaries for each of Chih-i's treatises, together with various shorter expository tracts. In the case of the *Mo-ho chih-kuan*, three of Chan-jan's works in particular came to be held as definitive by later T'ien-t'ai exegetes: his lengthy interlinear commentary, the *Chih-kuan fu-hsing ch'uan-hung chüeh* (Delineations for Supporting Practice and Broadly Disseminating [the Great] Calming and Contemplation), and his much shorter *Chih-kuan i-li* (Selected Topics from [the Great] Calming and Contemplation), and *Chih-kuan ta-i* (Synoptic Digest of [the Great] Calming and Contemplation).[27]

Chan-jan is remembered by Sung T'ien-t'ai historians as a great reformer of T'ien-t'ai teaching—the "lord of the exegetical record" (*chi-chu*)[28] or "master of the received teachings" (*chiao-chu*),[29] whose massive commentaries to Chih-i's three treatises "clarified the orthodox line (*cheng-tsung*) for generations to come."[30] Such an assessment, of course, dates from some two hundred years after the fact and carries with it the particular investment that Sung-period T'ien-t'ai monks placed in Chan-jan and his writings. On the whole, the sparseness of the T'ang record affords us little information about Chan-jan's impact on his contempo-

25. See Chan-jan, *Chih-kuan i-li*, T 46.447b3–4, and *Chih-kuan ta-i*, T 46.459b 10–14.

26. *Chih-kuan ta-i*, T 46.459a–b.

27. *Chih-kuan fu-hsing ch'uan-hung chüeh* (T no. 1912); *Chih-kuan i-li* (T no. 1913); and *Chih-kuan ta-i* (T no. 1914). Toward the end of his career Chan-jan compiled yet a fourth work, the *Mo-ho chih-kuan fu-hsing sou-yao chi* (Record of Selected Essentials of the [Great Calming and Contemplation]) (HTC 99), which represents a condensed, interlinear "selection of essential points" from the *Chih-kuan fu-hsing ch'uan-hung chüeh*. For discussion of the date and circumstances of compilation of these works, see Hibi Nobumasa, *Tōdai Tendai-gaku kenkyū josetsu*, pp. 135–235 and 257–289.

28. *Shih-men cheng-t'ung*, HTC 130.753b; *Fo-tsu t'ung-chi*, T 49.177c16.

29. *Shih-men cheng-t'ung*, HTC 130.753b.

30. *Fo-tsu t'ung-chi*, T 49.178a22–23.

raries. Apparently he taught widely (mainly in Chekiang and Kiangsu, with a journey at one point to Mount Wu-t'ai in North China) and attracted the notice of the T'ang imperial court as well as of several eminent literati.[31] Moreover, his spiritual descendants seem to have found their way into most of the major regional centers of T'ien-t'ai learning. Ultimately, however, we find little evidence that either Chan-jan or his works ever achieved any uniform authority during his day; and the record provided us by Japanese pilgrims such as Saichō and Ennin further suggests that the pattern of an eclectic and regionally diversified T'ien-t'ai tradition continued to be the norm despite Chan-jan's self-appointed mission to tighten up the school.

Whatever the actual case may have been, the Hui-ch'ang persecution (842–846) and Huang Ch'ao uprising during the mid-ninth century dealt a devastating blow to southern and northern traditions alike.[32] The effort to reconstitute T'ien-t'ai teachings a century later—fortuitously centered in Chan-jan's home territory of Chekiang and organized primarily as a drive to recover T'ien-t'ai scripture—brought Chan-jan and his works to the fore.[33] Thus, almost by historical default, Chan-jan's exegetical and historiographical program became the authoritative medium for understanding the teachings and tradition of Chih-i. To understand the foundations of later T'ien-t'ai thought and practice—especially as they concern the *Mo-ho chih-kuan*—we must therefore turn to the example set in the works and hagiography of Chan-jan.

Chan-jan, by his own profession as well as that of his disciples,[34] saw himself as a reformer whose mission it was to rescue T'ien-t'ai teaching

31. For an overview of Chan-jan's career, see Hibi Nobumasa, *Tōdai Tendaigaku kenkyū josetsu*, pp. 7–81; for his connections with eminent literati, see Pulleyblank, "Neo-Confucianism and Neo-Legalism in T'ang Intellectual Life, 755–805."

32. For an account of these events and their impact on Chinese Buddhism, especially the "doctrinal" schools, see Weinstein's *Buddhism under the T'ang*, pp. 114–150.

33. See Chappell, *T'ien-t'ai Buddhism*, pp. 25–30.

34. See, for instance, the characterizations employed by Chan-jan's disciple P'u-men in the latter's preface to the *Chih-kuan fu-hsing ch'uan-hung chüeh*, T 46.141a–b. The preface was compiled when the work was published in 765, some fifteen years before Chan-jan's death. See also the various inscriptions and documents of Chan-jan's lay disciple Liang Su: *T'ien-t'ai ch'an-lin ssu pei* (*Fo-tsu t'ung-chi*, T 49.438a–b); *Chih-che ta-shih chuan lun* (*Fo-tsu t'ung-chi*, T 49.440a–c); *Shan-ting chih-kuan* (HTC 99.206–207 and 118–120); and, especially, *T'ien-t'ai chih-kuan t'ung-li* (*Fo-tsu t'ung-chi*, T 49.438c–440a). It is recorded that Chan-jan once claimed to his disciples, "If you wish to get hold of the true [teaching], then whom can you turn to if you abandon me?" (See *Shih-men cheng-t'ung*, HTC 130.754a3–4; and *Fo-tsu t'ung-chi*, T 49.188c21).

from growing stultification, hybridization, and error. To this extent he was a staunch traditionalist. Clothing himself in the rhetoric of patriarchal tradition, he envisioned T'ien-t'ai teaching as the embodiment of a founding sagely genius and himself as one called to rectify and reclaim (but not alter) that original vision. Indeed, the very imagery by which Chan-jan defines his cause—such as the trope of archetypal struggle against the excesses of demonic dhyāna and dharma masters—harks directly back to the T'ien-t'ai inaugural drama, thereby linking Chan-jan paradigmatically to the tradition's founders. However, the world in which he functioned and the issues that he addressed are those of mid-T'ang period China. As a consequence the tradition that he "recovers" takes on distinctly new parameters and introduces postures toward T'ien-t'ai teaching, tradition, and the text of the *Mo-ho chih-kuan* not seen in earlier works.

One of the clearest and most eloquent statements of Chan-jan's novel stance on T'ien-t'ai tradition is to be found in the list of ten reasons for composing a commentary to the *Mo-ho chih-kuan* with which he opens his *Chih-kuan fu-hsing ch'uan-hung chüeh*. A quick review of its contents should suffice to convey the salient features of Chan-jan's program. Five of the ten points (i.e., items 5 and 7–10) set forth the familiar concept of the T'ien-t'ai path of doctrinal learning (*chiao*) and meditative contemplation (*kuan*) against the traditional demonic motif of the benighted dhyāna practitioner and scriptural pedant.[35] The remaining five points, however, cast the *Mo-ho chih-kuan* in a distinctly new light and are especially pertinent for understanding the ideological shift introduced by Chan-jan.

The first reason that Chan-jan gives for writing his commentary is "to show that [the text of the *Mo-ho chih-kuan*] itself represents the transmission of the [patriarchal] master [Chih-i] and that it is not a mere [exercise in] intellectualization that stands apart from the master's [true] intent."[36] The second and third reasons are to rectify erroneous interpretations of the patriarchal teachings (i.e., the *Mo-ho chih-kuan*) that have arisen in the course of their transmission and to prevent these errors from becoming compounded in the future. The fourth is to guide persons of distant regions who esteem the practice of the T'ien-t'ai teaching of calming and contemplation but lack a master within the tradition to guide them. The sixth reason is to help students of the *Mo-ho chih-kuan* to avoid the diffi-

35. For Chan-jan's most concise statement of the principles of T'ien-t'ai learning and practice see his opening summary in the *Chih-kuan ta-i*, T 46.459a–b. In essence, Chan-jan's approach to the T'ien-t'ai path proceeds in emulation of Chih-i, who himself "comprehensively elucidated the sūtras (and most notably the *Lotus*) by means of the 'five profundities' and 'ten points of explication' [set forth in the *Fa-hua hsüan-i*] and synthesized (*jung-t'ung*) all forms of contemplation by means of the five sets of expedients and ten modes [of the *Mo-ho chih-kuan*]."

36. *Chih-kuan fu-hsing ch'uan-hung chüeh*, T 46.141b20–21.

culties (and potential misinterpretations) posed by the terseness of the text's language and the unevenness of its presentation (literally, the inconsistent and ambiguous use of "expanded" [*kuang*] and "abbreviated" [*lüeh*] forms of discourse in the *Mo-ho chih-kuan*).

Chan-jan's identification of the text of the *Mo-ho chih-kuan* with the transmission of the "patriarchal mind" may at first glance seem unremarkable, especially given the close connection established between the two in Kuan-ting's introduction and in later Sung sectarian histories. In fact, however, it is a point of considerable import, which represents for Chan-jan a deliberate and significant reassessment of both text and tradition. To appreciate this shift we must say a word or two about the polemical context within which it seems to have taken shape. Throughout his writings on the *Mo-ho chih-kuan*, Chan-jan repeatedly criticizes a tradition within T'ien-t'ai that espoused the notion of an "oral teaching" (*k'ou-chüeh*) or "transmission of the essentials of mind" (*hsin-yao*) separate from and more fundamental than Chih-i's literary legacy. This he describes as the teaching of "a separate or special single [essence of calming and contemplation] outside of the three [written treatises on calming and contemplation]" (*san wai pieh i*). The parallels with the Ch'an teaching of a "wordless transmission apart from the scriptures" are unmistakable, enough so that one is tempted to see this development as a product of the rapprochements between T'ien-t'ai and Ch'an that were forged at such regional centers as Yü-ch'üan Monastery and Ch'ang-an. Chan-jan, however, does not identify it as an alien intrusion from Ch'an or as a matter of intersectarian polemic but treats it as a deviation endemic to T'ien-t'ai tradition. In his effort to rectify it he makes the unequivocal—and striking—claim that the repository of the "patriarchal mind" is to be found precisely within the written text of the *Mo-ho chih-kuan*, not elsewhere. Commenting on the key line in Kuan-ting's introduction where the *Mo-ho chih-kuan* is identified as the "practice that Chih-i used in his own mind,"[37] Chan-jan says in the *Chih-kuan fu-hsing ch'uan-hung chüeh*:

> This [statement by Kuan-ting] is also intended to prevent later generations from practicing in ways that go against [what has been taught], for this one text is thereby established as containing all the basic features of practice. Some say that there is a special transmission of the essentials of mind (*hsin-yao*) apart from the three [basic treatises and systems of calming and contemplation] and, therefore, that the three works are useless. But even if there were an oral transmission given face to face, it could not amount to anything more than a verification of one's own private realizations before the master. The techniques for contemplating and settling the mind

37. MHCK, T 46.1b.

> presented in this text would still stand as sufficient unto themselves. How much the more so if later practitioners do not have a personal transmission to rely on. Apart from this text what else is there to speak of? Thus one should have faith in the fact that this [text and teaching itself] represents the [patriarchal] transmission.[38]

As the first and foremost of his ten points, Chan-jan's deliberate identification of the patriarchal tradition with the text of the *Mo-ho chih-kuan* firmly establishes the primacy of text over intuitive insight or charisma and makes the issue of textual hermeneutics central to both religious practice and the concept of authoritative voice within T'ien-t'ai tradition. The implications of this shift in perspective become apparent when we explore the remainder of Chan-jan's points in light of this basic assertion.

Chan-jan's emphasis on the patriarchal vision and his identification of that vision with the *Mo-ho chih-kuan* recast the T'ien-t'ai spiritual enterprise in profoundly new ways. Most important, of course, is the fact that the twin disciplines of learning (*chiao*) and practice (*kuan*) and the concept of spiritual progress come to devolve closely around the engagement and mastery of canonical text. At the same time, however, it is misleading to think that they go no further than a formal acquisition of written lore. For mastery of the text is understood to be nothing less than a quest for the authorial mind (i.e., the patriarchal genius) behind the written word—a quest that is intentionalist to the highest degree. Hence, to fathom the seamless design that informs the *Mo-ho chih-kuan* is to return to *illo tempore* and reveal the mind of the founding patriarchs themselves; and to know this living vision of the patriarchs is not only to become a "worthy" (*hsien*) of the Third or Fourth Identity but to take one's place among these figures and appropriate their ancestral charisma for oneself. Thus, as text and patriarch come to the fore, the traditional norms of T'ien-t'ai soteriology—formally described in terms of the stages of the Six Identities—are increasingly subordinated to the mytho-historical rhetoric of patriarchal ancestry and lineage sanction.

Chan-jan, however, characterizes the *Mo-ho chih-kuan* as a work that is problematic by nature. And these difficulties—i.e., its incompleteness and unevenness—at once pose a unique set of impediments to salvation and call for more comprehensive principles of textual praxis.

In effect, casual interpretation represents an improper and potentially flawed interpretation of scriptural text, the errors of which even the eye of meditative insight fail to redress. The full design of the work—the cohesive patriarchal vision that informs it—reveals itself only through an exhaustive erudition that goes beyond the confines of the immediate text and, ultimately, draws in the entire received tradition. Thus, according

38. *Chih-kuan fu-hsing ch'uan-hung chüeh*, T 46.147b19–29.

to his disciples Liang Su and P'u-men, the outstanding contribution of Chan-jan's commentary to the *Mo-ho chih-kuan*—the feature that places him and his work among the ranks of the patriarchal "worthies" (*hsien*)—is the fact that it "[comprehensively] weaves together the net of received teachings"[39] and "extrapolates fully (*pei*) the meaning of the former sage's expanded (*kuang*) and abbreviated (*lüeh*) [discourse], so that it covers the range of superior and inferior capacities."[40]

Such an emphasis on cross-textual analysis would seem to occasion a heightened concern for sectarian canon and textual hermeneutics as well. For the ideological thrust of the "patriarchal vision" could vary considerably depending on which texts are consulted and how they are prioritized, not to mention the strategies by which they are interpreted.

Finally, we must note Chan-jan's intriguing suggestion (in the fourth of his ten reasons) that his commentary alone, judiciously used, is sufficient to reveal the patriarchal vision and retrieve tradition from the *Mo-ho chih-kuan* in the absence of a person to person transmission. Here we find grounds for a discontinuous concept of tradition or lineage—one that would seem to permit breaks to occur in time and space without foreclosing on its integrity or the possibility of its future rejuvenation.

One would expect all of these considerations to have an impact, in some form or another, on the patriarchal historiographies that sanction them. And, indeed, Chan-jan's general emphasis on text—together with the possibility of a historically discontinuous tradition—seems to resonate closely with the orthodox line (*cheng-t'ung*) of nine patriarchs that began to take shape around him shortly after his death and reached full maturity with the T'ien-t'ai revival in the eleventh century. As a case in point let us take the discussion of patriarchal lineage that introduces the *T'ien-t'ai chiao sui-han mu-lu* (ca. 1030) by the Northern Sung master Tsun-shih (963–1032).[41]

In 1024 Tsun-shih succeeded in prevailing on the imperial court to sanction and officially admit a collection of T'ien-t'ai works into the Buddhist tripiṭaka. The *T'ien-t'ai chiao sui-han mu-lu*—along with its rehearsal of the nine-membered lineage—was compiled shortly thereafter as a catalogue and guide to this select T'ien-t'ai canon. Although it is only one among a number of early Sung narrations of T'ien-t'ai patriarchy, it is not only a seminal account but one that is fully representative of the genre at that time.

The nine patriarchs listed by Tsun-shih extend from Nāgārjuna and Hui-wen through Chan-jan, with the events surrounding the tradition's inauguration based principally on Kuan-ting's preface to the *Mo-ho*

39. Liang Su, *Chih-kuan t'ung li* (in *Fo-tsu t'ung-chi*), T 49.440a6–7.
40. P'u-men, *Chih-kuan fu-hsing ch'uan-hung chüeh hsü*, T 46.141a27–28.
41. *T'ien-t'ai chiao sui-han mu-lu* (in *T'ien-chu pieh-chi*), HTC101:263b.

chih-kuan. Separated from Nāgārjuna by more than a millennium, the Chinese patriarch Hui-wen is said to have awakened to the way and established the basics of T'ien-t'ai calming and contemplation solely through contact with a Chinese translation of Nāgārjuna's works. ("He never knew Nāgārjuna's face but he knew Nāgārjuna's mind," as the thirteenth-century *Shih-men cheng-t'ung* puts it.)[42] Thus, at the headwaters of T'ien-t'ai tradition stands the archetypal example of discontinuity. A second hiatus, however, occurs between Kuan-ting and Chan-jan. During this period "when the teachings were in eclipse,"[43] Tsun-shih tells us, "the *Mo-ho chih-kuan* was handed down without ever being unrolled" and its tenets never put into practice. With Chan-jan and his mentor Hsüan-lang, the tradition was put back on track, mainly through Chan-jan's "authoring of detailed commentaries that assist learning (*chiao*) and meditative practice (*kuan*)."[44] Hence, of the nine generations enumerated by Tsun-shih, the transmission of teachings between Hui-wen and Chih-i was purely oral and, at best, rudimentary; that between Kuan-ting and Chan-jan was both oral and attenuated.

Chih-i, Kuan-ting, Chan-jan, and (to some extent) Hsüan-lang are singled out from the other so-called patriarchs precisely because of their emphasis on textual exegesis, systematization, and the compilation of written treatises.

Significantly, many of the tropes employed by Tsun-shih and his contemporaries can be traced directly to works of Liang Su, a lay disciple of Chan-jan who lived some two centuries earlier. Liang Su himself, in fact, is the author of the oft-cited statement that, between Kuan-ting and Hsüan-lang, "[the *Mo-ho chih-kuan*] was handed down without ever being unrolled and its stated teaching never put into actual practice," as well as the image of Chan-jan as one who, "expanded in detail [on Chih-i's text] in his commentary of some tens of thousands of words, thereby systematically laying out the net of the received teaching."[45] Thus, in the patriarchal persona developing around the living figure of Chan-jan we see the same emphasis on text and textual tradition that characterizes his own writings. These conventions, in turn, set the pattern for early Sung formulations of the nine-membered patriarchy and the monumental historical reconstructions of such later works as the *Fo-tsu t'ung-chi*.

The massive effort in the tenth century to retrieve from abroad T'ien-t'ai works that had been lost during the Hui-ch'ang persecution and the

42. *Shih-men cheng-t'ung*, HTC 130.730b.

43. From Tsun-shih, *T'ien-t'ai tsu-ch'eng chi* (in *T'ien-chu pieh-chi*), HTC 101.263a6.

44. *T'ien-t'ai chiao sui-han mu-lu*, HTC 101.264a5–7.

45. See Liang Su's *T'ien-t'ai chih-kuan t'ung-li* in *Shan-ting chih-kuan* (HTC 99.118–120) and his *Chih-che ta-shih chuan lun* in *Fo-tsu t'ung-chi* (T 49.440a5–7).

rebellion of Huang Ch'ao brought together an imposing body of scripture, some of which had disappeared from China long before the fateful events of the ninth century. The sudden infusion of this material into a severely weakened exegetical tradition confronted the T'ien-t'ai revivers with daunting questions about canonicity, interpretation, and the ideological contours of T'ien-t'ai tradition. These internal difficulties were further exacerbated by the growing challenge of Ch'an, whose efforts to consolidate its own mythic history, ideology, and monastic system during the early tenth century had already attracted the attention of the royal house of Wu-yüeh and made it the leading Buddhist school in southeast China.

The controversy that grew out of this situation was both far-reaching and sustained, ultimately defining a set of issues that occupied T'ien-t'ai thinkers for the next 300 years. For the most part it devolved around two main exegetical camps. The first, which centered on the figure of Chih-li, stuck closely to the hermeneutical principles and view of tradition set forth in Chan-jan's commentaries to the "three great texts on the *Lotus*." The second camp, more dispersed in character, was nonetheless typified by a common tendency to appropriate T'ien-t'ai doctrine through a system based on the tathāgatagarbha thought of works such as the *Śūraṅgama* and *Nirvāṇa* sūtras and of the Hua-yen/Ch'an thinker Kuei-feng Tsung-mi (780–841). As the tradition sorted itself out over the two centuries that followed, Chih-li's line secured its claim to orthodoxy as the "home-mountain" (*shan-chia*) branch of T'ien-t'ai and marginalized its rivals as heterodox or "off-mountain" (*shan-wai*). In the interim, Chih-li himself (like Chan-jan before him) was given the historical distinction of having "revived [T'ien-t'ai tradition] in midstream" (*chung-hsing*). Thus the hermeneutical principles and the view of text, canon, and tradition laid down by Chan-jan—epitomized above all in his monumental commentaries to Chih-i's "three great texts on the *Lotus*"—came to serve as the basis of later T'ien-t'ai orthodoxy.

The *Mo-ho chih-kuan* and Sung T'ien-t'ai Monastic Life

The growing sectarianism of the Sung period, as well as new developments in the relationship between the saṅgha and the state, brought with it various changes in the Buddhist monastic system, changes that proved definitive for later T'ien-t'ai institutions as well as for the life of the *Mo-ho chih-kuan*. During the tenth century, Ch'an and T'ien-t'ai leaders of the Chekiang area began to petition the government to have certain monasteries permanently attached to their schools as model centers of sectarian training. For the Ch'an and T'ien-t'ai schools this affiliation promised a secure basis from which to spread their doctrines, not to mention enormous prestige and a host of other perquisites traditionally associated with imperial support. The court in turn saw in it a powerful means to establish centralized control over the Buddhist church. The cooperation that subsequently developed between church and state led to an increasing parochialization of the monastic system itself. Entire monasteries for the first time began to be classified according to a uniform distinction between "meditation" (*ch'an*) and "teachings" (*chiao*) institutions, a distinction that for all intents and purposes became (and remained) synonymous with the two schools of Ch'an and T'ien-t'ai, respectively.[46]

Initially these designations were applied to the handful of Ch'an and T'ien-t'ai monasteries duly recognized by the court as model centers of training, but as time went on they were extended to an ever-increasing number of institutions. This growing polarization of the monastic system generated a corresponding desire to standardize (and, in certain respects, differentiate) *ch'an* and *chiao* monastic procedure. The formal guidelines for institutional organization and routine that were produced in response to this demand—known in their literary form as *ch'ing-kuei* or "pure rules"—not only became normative for the Sung period but set the basic pattern that has governed Ch'an and T'ien-t'ai monasteries down to the present day. Given the fact that these changes mark such a significant watershed in T'ien-t'ai institutional history, no introduction to the *Mo-ho chih-kuan* would be complete without touching on the various ways in which the text and its study figured into the routine established in Sung T'ien-t'ai monasteries.

A good place to begin our discussion is the distinction between "meditative" (*ch'an*) and "teaching" (*chiao*) institutions itself. At the hands of later historians these labels have led to a number of unfortunate misconceptions, mainly due to their having been taken as descriptions of practical rather than ideological differences. For instance, because of its associations with "meditation," the so-called *ch'an* monastery is often thought of as a place dedicated especially to religious practice and experience, and by contrast the *chiao* or "teachings" monastery is seen as an institution geared solely to doctrinal study. When invested with the additional pejorative twist of "spiritual substance" versus "dead-letter

46. A third category is generally added to this list: "vinaya" (*lü*) monasteries. The latter appear to have developed more slowly than the other two designations, and their nature remains somewhat ambiguous. This entire process seems to have been initiated by the Ch'an school during the tenth century. Following the precedent set by Ch'an, Chih-li (of Yen-ch'ing yüan) and Tsun-shih (of T'ien-chu ssu) followed suit and petitioned to have their monasteries designated as "public abbacy *teachings* cloisters" during the early eleventh century. See Takao Giken's work on Sung Buddhism collected in Takao, *Sōdai bukkyō-shi no kenkyū*, especially his "Sōdai ji'in no jūjisei" (pp. 57–74). For a more recent summary of these developments see Foulk, "Myth, Ritual, and Monastic Practice in Sung Ch'an Buddhism."

pedantics," the resulting image of T'ien-t'ai tradition and the "teachings" monastery is a dry and negative one indeed.

The terms *ch'an* and *chiao* do not so much refer to the actual routines that characterize monastic life as they do to the ideology of religious tradition and authority that operates there. The former, as such, simply describes an institution organized around the "special transmission [of the enlightened mind-dharma] outside of received scripture" (*chiao-wai pieh-ch'uan*) that is the representative ideological claim of the Ch'an or "meditation" school; and the latter, a system based on the T'ien-t'ai notion that the received word/tradition of the Buddhist sūtras and their commentaries is the primary ground of religious authority. The two terms might signal certain differences in semiotic and ritual procedure, even concepts of practice, but in no way can they be taken as a unilateral distinction between meditative practice and textual study per se. *Ch'an* and *chiao* institutions alike housed libraries, lecture halls, meditation halls, and programs of religious training that entailed both the study of the written word and meditative practice. In fact the T'ien-t'ai monastic system paid more formal attention to meditative cultivation than did the so-called Ch'an or Meditation School itself. Furthermore, when one actually examines the use of the term *chiao* in early Sung sources, there is no indication that it was considered a demeaning label or that it was originally foisted on T'ien-t'ai followers as a result of Ch'an hegemony. On the contrary, as early as the beginning of the eleventh century the expression was actively and enthusiastically used by T'ien-t'ai monks themselves to refer to both their monasteries and their school.[47]

What might we say of the similarities and differences that attended the *ch'an* and *chiao* institutions themselves? Sung-period Ch'an sources maintain that the Ch'an monastic system was a unique institution devised personally by the T'ang patriarch Pai-chang Huai-hai (749–814) to meet the special dictates of Ch'an practice.[48] Although they are not so brazenly self-promoting in their historical claims as their Ch'an brethren, Sung T'ien-t'ai masters traced their concept of monastic organization to an equally venerable source—the writings of Chih-i himself.[49] Thus sectar-

47. See Takao, *Sōdai bukkyō-shi no kenkyū*, pp. 61–62. See also Tsun-shih, *T'ien-chu ssu shih-fang chu-ch'ih i* in *T'ien-chu pieh-chi*, HTC 101.307a–b; and documents composed by Chih-li in *Ssu-ming tsun-che chiao-hsing lu* (T 46.908b–910a) relating to the investiture of Pao-en (or Yen-ch'ing) yüan as a public *chiao* monastery.

48. The earliest substantial description of the system attributed to Pai-chang appears in the eleventh century *Ching-te ch'uan-teng lu* (1004), incorporated in the form of a brief tract known as the *Ch'an-men kuei-shih* (Rules for Ch'an Followers); for details see Martin Colcutt, "Early Ch'an Monastic Rule," and Foulk, " 'The Ch'an School' and Its Place in the Buddhist Monastic Tradition."

49. See Tsun-shih, *T'ien-chu ssu shih-fang chu-ch'ih i* in *T'ien-chu pieh chi* (HTC 101.307a). See also Shunjō, *Seishukishiki narabi ni jūrokukandōki* in Ishida Shūshi,

ian historiography would lead one to expect substantial (and long-standing) differences between *ch'an* and *chiao* monasteries. Such differences, however, are not to be found. Aside from certain minor institutional variations, T'ien-t'ai and Ch'an monastic documents show the two systems to be strikingly close, so that we are compelled to regard their claims to historical uniqueness with skepticism.[50] Rather than look for cross-influences or some prototypal structure linked with one tradition or the other, a more plausible explanation might be that the Ch'an and T'ien-t'ai movements of the Sung drew on a common monastic culture, which they subsequently reshaped to their own individual ideology and design. Before we take up the peculiarities of the T'ien-t'ai monastic system and their significance for the *Mo-ho chih-kuan*, let us describe briefly the common denominators of Sung monastic culture on which they were grounded.

Ch'an and T'ien-t'ai monasteries were typically laid out according to a central north-south axis, along which stood the most important ceremonial halls, such as the Triple Gate (*san-men*), the Buddha Hall (*fo-tien*), the Dharma or Lecture Hall (*fa/chiang t'ang*), and clustered together at the north end, the Abbot's Quarters (*fang-chang*) and Patriarchs' Hall (*tsu-t'ang*). This axis in turn split the monastery precincts into two distinct lateral quadrants. The western quadrant housed the Saṅgha Hall (*seng-t'ang*)—namely, the large communal structure lined with raised platforms on which the assembly of actively practicing monks slept, took their meals, and spent several hours a day seated in meditation (*tso-ch'an*). Nearby stood various other buildings essential to the Saṅgha Hall routine, including the lavatories, the quarters for Saṅgha Hall officers, and the monastery library. The eastern quadrant housed the storehouses, kitchens, and quarters and offices of the staff responsible for daily administration of the monastery and its estates (including dormitories for postulants and temple menials).

This division in ground plan itself reflected a fundamental distinction in monastic routine and personnel. The regimen of the western quadrant—i.e., the Saṅgha Hall—described a self-contained life of study and practice which, in effect, segregated its residents from other sectors of the monastery and identified them as a specialized community unto themselves. Known formally as the "monks who practice with the assembly" (*i-chung hsüeh-hsi seng*), this community represented the active em-

ed., *Shunjō risshi*, p. 391. Both are clearly based on Chih-i's *Li chih-fa* in *Kuo-ch'ing pai-lu* (T 46.793c).

50. The problems inherent in the *Ch'an-men kuei-shih* and the Pai-chang attribution are discussed at length in Foulk, "The 'Ch'an School' and Its Place in the Buddhist Monastic Tradition"; see also Foulk, "Myth, Ritual, and Monastic Practice in Sung Ch'an Buddhism."

bodiment of T'ien-t'ai and Ch'an ideals of religious training and, as such, the very heart of the monastic institution itself. By contrast the residents of the eastern quadrant addressed an entirely different set of concerns. They were collectively referred to as the "monks who attend to practical affairs" (*chih-shih seng*). As their name suggests, their responsibilities mainly centered on the everyday operation of the monastery and its estates. They thus served as the support staff for the Saṅgha Hall and the institution at large.

The monastery as a whole moved according to a common schedule. Within this framework the Saṅgha Hall and managerial sectors pursued their independent (yet complementary) routines, coming together as a single community only on the occasion of religious services and convocations in the halls of the central axis. The liturgical year was organized around winter and summer training semesters, each of which lasted approximately three months. The summer semester corresponded to the traditional three-month "rains retreat" (*varṣa*) set forth in the Buddhist Vinaya. Life in the Saṅgha Hall revolved at the daily level around a uniform schedule of morning and noon meals (served in the Saṅgha Hall), two or three fixed intervals of worship in the Buddha Hall,[51] two to four periods of seated meditation in the Saṅgha Hall,[52] and regular morning and evening discourses or debates in the Dharma Hall.

The T'ien-t'ai tradition lent its unique stamp to these basic building blocks of Sung monastic culture in a number of different ways.[53] One such strategy was simply to imbue the daily cycle of meditations, ritual worship, and dharma discourses with a liturgical and curricular content particular to T'ien-t'ai. Thus rather than dramatize the lore or "Recorded Sayings" (*yü-lu*) of the Ch'an patriarchs as a Ch'an master might do, the dharma convocation of a T'ien-t'ai master might involve systematic "lectures" (*chiang*) on the treatises of Chih-i and Chan-jan. The most conspicuous deviation from the Ch'an monastic system, however, was the accommodation of the cults of the four forms of samādhi as a third mode

51. Sung T'ien-t'ai monasteries, according to Tsun-shih and Shunjō, held a dawn or morning service, service before the noon meal, and dusk or evening service.

52. In T'ien-t'ai monasteries, periods of seated meditation were held in the early night and before dawn. Ch'an monastic codes mention four periods for meditation.

53. The description of T'ien-t'ai monastic procedure offered here is based on three main sources: Tsun-shih (964–1032), *T'ien-chu ssu shih-fang chu-ch'ih i* and *Pieh li chung-chih* (in *T'ien-chu pieh-chi*, HTC 101.306b–311a); descriptions of the Sung T'ien-t'ai monastic system by the Japanese pilgrim Shunjō (1166–1227), *Seishukishiki narabi ni jūrokukandōki*, in Ishida, ed., *Shunjō risshi*, pp. 391–404; and a revised T'ien-t'ai monastic rule (dated 1347) by the Yüan-period monk Tzu-ch'ing, *Tseng-hsiu chiao-yüan ch'ing-kuei*, HTC 101.687a–792b.

of religious activity distinct from the routines of the eastern and western quadrants. This tripartite model—i.e., (1) practice on the basis of the community hall, (2) attendance to practical affairs of the monastery, and (3) repentance (or performance of the four samādhis) in separate sanctuaries—found a specific antecedent in a short monastic code compiled by Chih-i and allegedly implemented on Mount T'ien-t'ai at the end of the sixth century.[54] On the basis of this connection Sung T'ien-t'ai authors deliberately advanced the institution of the four samādhis as a hallmark of the T'ien-t'ai monastic system. From what we can see in the records of Japanese pilgrims such as Jōjin and Dōgen, separate halls or cloisters for the specialized cultivation of repentance and samādhi were indeed a regular feature of T'ien-t'ai institutions during the Sung.[55]

Such was the basic setting within which T'ien-t'ai "learning and practice" (*chiao-kuan*) was actualized during the Sung. What implications might it have had for the role of the *Mo-ho chih-kuan* as sacred scripture? In principle meditative practice (*kuan*) was to be carried out uninterruptedly throughout all daily activities, regardless of the sector or routine in which one was enrolled. Indeed, one can find any number of short tracts by Sung authors—some of them incorporated directly into the monastic codes—that apply the *Mo-ho chih-kuan*'s central contemplation of "three-thousand realms in an instant of thought" (*i-nien san-ch'ien*) to such activities as eating, reciting scripture, and ritual prostration.[56] In terms of the monastic institution, however, contemplation found more formal expression in the two daily periods of seated meditation (*tso-ch'an*) in the Saṅgha Hall and, especially, the practice of the four samādhis. The T'ien-t'ai luminaries Tsun-shih and Chih-li were both avid practitioners and advocates of the rites of the four samādhis, with Chih-li himself having spent more than ten years in cloisters dedicated to their practice.[57] In addition, manuals for these rites dating from the Sung period state quite clearly that a theoretical grasp of the *Mo-ho chih-kuan* was a mandatory prereq-

54. Chih-i, *Li chih-fa* (in Kuan-ting, *Kuo-ch'ing pai-lu*), T 46.793b–794a.

55. For Jōjin, see Hirabayashi Fumio, *San-tendai-godai-zan-ki kōhon narabi ni kenkyū*, p. 17 (Hsing-chiao ssu), p. 28 (Ta-tz'u ssu), pp. 43–50 (Kuo-ch'ing ssu), p. 62 (Chih-ch'eng ssu). See also Takashi James Kodera, *Dōgen's Formative Years in China*, p. 131.

56. Tzu-ch'ing, *Tseng-hsiu chiao-yüan ch'ing-kuei*, HTC.770b–776a.

57. As recorded by Chih-li's disciple Tse-ch'üan, in *Ssu-min Fa-chih tsun-che shih-lu*, Chih-li undertook two extended three-year retreats for the lotus samādhi and repentance of [the dhāranī] of great compassion (*ta-pei ch'an-fa*), eight retreats for the forty-nine day invocation of Avalokiteśvāra (Kuan-yin) repentance, five retreats for the month-long lotus samādhi repentance, twenty performances of the ten-day repentance based on the *Sūtra of Golden Light* (*Suvarṇaprabhāsa Sūtra*), fifty performances of the seven-day Amitābha repentance, and ten retreats for the three-week repentance of great compassion (T 46.919c17–920a2).

uisite for practice of the four samādhis. We can thus say with fair confidence that the discipline of meditative praxis (*kuan*) and, indeed, the path outlined in the *Mo-ho chih-kuan* found its most immediate practical counterpart in the institution of the four samādhis.

Textual study and doctrinal learning (*chiao*) were likewise built into the formal routine of T'ien-t'ai monasteries in various distinctive ways. On a daily basis, monks of the Saṅgha Hall would gather in the Dharma Hall after morning gruel to hear lectures on sūtras or T'ien-t'ai treatises by the abbot or a designated senior monk. On the bimonthly *uposatha* days these convocations in the Dharma Hall were led by the abbot and took on a particularly solemn character. In the evening they again convened in the Dharma Hall, presumably under the guidance of senior monks, where they "drew lots and polished [their learning] by engaging one another in lively debate."[58] The period after the noon meal was designated a free time for monks to read and study on their own.

During the biannual fall and summer training semesters, the entire program of study and practice was intensified, with extended lecture series organized around a particular work or topic.[59] It is recorded of Chih-li, for instance, that over the course of his career he lectured on the *Mo-ho chih-kuan* and Chih-i's two *Lotus* commentaries in their entirety no fewer than seven or eight times each. Such shorter works as the Chan-jan's *Chih-kuan ta-i* or *Chih-kuan i-li* were apparently discussed with enough frequency that a record of their number was not kept.[60] Given the length of the texts, the lectures on the "three great texts" were almost certain to have been given during autumn and summer lecture series.

Contact with the *Mo-ho chih-kuan*, as with any treatise of the sectarian canon, was hedged about on all sides by ritual procedure and protocol. Private reading and study were certainly encouraged; but this activity was limited to designated times and locations and followed strict procedures. Texts were generally borrowed from the monastery library and studied either in a special reading room or the Dharma Hall. "When 'reciting' a

58. Shunjō, *Seishukishiki narabi ni jūrokukandōki*, in Ishida, ed., *Shunjō risshi*, p. 394b.

59. Tzu-ch'ing in the *Tseng-hsiu chiao-yüan ch'ing-kuei* (HTC 101.741a) cites as the classic example Chih-i's summer lecture series at Yü-ch'uan monastery that formed the basis of the *Mo-ho chih-kuan*.

60. From Tse-ch'üan's *Ssu-ming Fa-chih tsun-che shih-lu* (in *Ssu-ming tsun-che chiao-hsing lu*, T 46.919c1–6). Other treatises (somewhat shorter in length) on which Chih-li lectured include: *Chin-kuang-ming hsüan-shu* (ten times), *Kuan-yin pieh-hsing hsüan-shu* (seven times), and *Kuan wu-liang-shou ching shu* (seven times)—all three are works legendarily attributed to Chih-i that were "rediscovered" in the Sung. Chan-jan's *Shih-pu-erh men* and *Shih-chung hsin-yao* were also a frequent topic. Chih-li wrote subcommentaries for all of these except the *Shih-chung hsin-yao*.

text," Tzu-ch'ing's monastic manual tells us, "it is not permitted to sit with one's robe hanging in disarray. Nor may one lean on the forearm or on a pillow, whisper or laugh with others, or salute and beckon others with one hand (while tending the book with the other). . . . When reading a sūtra, one should not do so in a loud voice. Nor should one unroll the entire text, leave its cover and clasp in disorder, or walk about reading with the text in hand."[61] In short, one approached the task with the sobriety and decorum that was properly due sacred scripture.

By and large, however, contact with T'ien-t'ai texts and teachings came mainly through the medium of formal lectures, classes, or debate under the tutelage of the abbot and senior monks. Symbolically as well as in fact, access to the sectarian canon and the authority to interpret it was contingent on a strict system of hierarchy.

At the most basic level only fully ordained monks were allowed to enroll in the Saṅgha Hall. As a rule, postulants, laborers, and lay guests or functionaries were housed in special dormitories in the eastern quadrant and excluded from all but the most public services and convocations. Among the registered monks of the monastic community differences in status were determined by one's rank in the monastic bureaucracy or, when that did not apply, seniority in ordination. Rank in the monastic hierarchy devolved from one's relative proximity to the central authority of the monastery, the all-powerful figure of the abbot (*chu-ch'ih*).

Much as in the Ch'an system, in Sung-period T'ien-t'ai monasteries monks were differentiated into three broad groups on the basis of their professed relationship to the abbot: (1) those who were full residents of the monastery but who, for whatever reason, did not formalize a master-student relationship with the abbot, (2) those who did formalize such a relationship and were given the privilege of "entering the abbot's quarters" (*ju-shih*) to seek personalized instruction, and (3) "true room-entering disciples" (*chen ju-shih ti-tzu*)[62] who showed sufficient promise to be admitted to the abbot's inner circle and designated as "dharma heirs" (*fa-ssu*).[63]

The privilege of "entering the abbot's quarters" appears in theory to have been open to any fully enrolled member of the community. Nonetheless, it was clearly a solemn commitment that was not requested or

61. Tzu-ch'ing, *Tseng-hsiu chiao-yüan ch'ing-kuei*, HTC 101.774a.

62. Ibid., HTC 101.720a.

63. Ibid., HTC 101.718b–720a, and 740a. These distinctions appear in documents pertaining to Chih-li as well. He is said, for example, to have had some thirty "disciples who received the charge of dharma" (eight of whom became eminent abbots in their own right), some 500 students who "ascended the gate and entered his chambers," and countless numbers of monks who at one time or another took up residence in his monastery. *Fo-tsu t'ung-chi* finds parallels to this structure in biographical records of Chih-i and Chan-jan as well.

granted casually. In this respect it marked a key watershed in both the life of the individual monk and the monastic system at large. Candidates for the top training and administrative posts in the eastern and western quadrants were generally selected from the more promising of this group, although there might be exceptions to this rule. The most exalted of these positions—such as personal acolyte to the abbot (*tai-che*), chief-seat (*shou-tso*), or the penance-prior responsible for the halls of the four samādhis (*ch'an-shou*)—were clearly the domain of dharma-heirs who were on the track to becoming abbots themselves.[64]

Precisely how abbots became abbots and what kinds of abbacies prevailed in Sung China is an issue that is far too complex to take up here. In principle and in fact, however, status as a dharma-heir was a minimum requirement for the position. Given the fact that an abbot is defined chiefly by the specific position he holds or the institution in which he serves (both of which may change), the concept of dharma-heir takes center stage as the main emblem of authority that corporately united the T'ien-t'ai school.

In simplest terms, a dharma-heir is a disciple duly sanctioned by a previous dharma-holder as one who has received "transmission of the T'ien-t'ai teaching" (*ch'uan fa*) in a continuous line of succession that in theory extends back to the founding patriarchs themselves. As we noted previously in our discussion of the *Fo-tsu t'ung-chi*, the notion of dharma succession should not be confused with that of patriarchy (*tsu*). For the designation of patriarch was an honorific title reserved primarily for the nine (or thirteen) deceased figures renowned for their historical contributions to T'ien-t'ai tradition.

The exact qualifications necessary to become a dharma-heir are not certain. Most likely there was a fair amount of variation from one master to the next. Chih-li and Tsun-shih, in their remarks on the virtues of the ideal abbot, suggest that it was one who was "rich and broadly accomplished in both meritorious practice and learning" (*te hsüeh po fu*).[65] Or, as Chih-li puts it, "a monk who has achieved mastery of both [doctrinal] understanding and [meditative] practice and is genuinely [capable of] transmitting the T'ien-t'ai teaching."[66] Writing approximately two and one half centuries later, Chih-p'an in the prefatory remarks to his *Fo-tsu t'ung-chi* outlines three basic criteria by which transmission was construed among contemporary masters: (1) attainment of illumination in medita-

64. Tzu-ch'ing, *Tseng-hsiu chiao-yüan ch'ing-kuei*, HTC 101.718–720.

65. Tsun-shih, *T'ien-chu ssu shih-fang chu-ch'ih i*, in *T'ien-chu pieh-chi*, HTC 101.307a.

66. Chih-li, *Shih t'ieh yen-ch'ing ssu*, in *Ssu-ming tsun-che chiao-hsing lu*, T 46.909b8.

tive practice,[67] (2) the ability to grasp the cardinal meaning in lecturing to and training others, (3) the ability to clarify and preserve the patriarchal legacy (*tsung*) through written works.[68] From references such as these it is clear that the dharma-heir was considered to be one who had realized the golden-mean between doctrinal learning (*chiao*) and practice (*kuan*) and was thus fit to become the living embodiment of T'ien-t'ai tradition. His recognition as such placed him within the distinctive genealogy that traced its descent from the trunk-line ancestry of the T'ien-t'ai patriarchs.

This pedigree of the dharma-heir *qua* abbot was actively maintained through any number of ritual forms and institutions of the T'ien-t'ai monastery, thereby establishing him as the supreme spokesperson for the teaching. By way of example, let us consider the most public and solemn of the ritual contexts within which a work such as the *Mo-ho chih-kuan* would have been encountered—namely, the bimonthly lectures given by the abbot in the Dharma Hall. According to the fourteenth-century *Tseng-hsiu chiao-yüan ch'ing-kuei*, when the abbot chose to observe the bimonthly dharma convocation, official notice was posted and the Dharma Hall duly equipped with a high seat or "dharma-throne" (*fa-tso*), incense altar, candles, and other ritual implements. Following the cues of bell and drum, the monks of the eastern and western quarters filed in by order of monastic rank, bowed in obeisance to the high seat (still empty at this point), and took their respective places on either side of the hall. The abbot himself then entered, ascended before the high seat, prostrated, made formal offering of incense, and took his seat on the dharma-throne. Thereupon the abbot's personal acolytes would formally petition him to preach the dharma. The lecture would then begin. If it concerned the *Mo-ho chih-kuan*, Chan-jan's commentary would surely be used. When the discourse finished, obeisance was again offered—this time to the abbot as well as the seat—and the assembly filed out in due order.[69]

The hierarchical placement of the community around the central image of the abbot and the high seat dramatizes effectively the circumstances under which text and its meaning were imparted in T'ien-t'ai institutions. The high seat or dharma-throne (*fa-tso*), as it is known, was an extraordinarily ornate pedestal, the very image of the "lion's throne"

67. Chih-i in his *Kuan-hsin lun* (the last work) suggests that the authority to interpret T'ien-t'ai teachings was contingent upon attainment of the meditative insight that comes with the third identity—the identity in meditative praxis. See T 46.586a, to which Sung authors often allude.

68. *Fo-tsu t'ung-chi*, T 49.131a20–21. It is not certain whether Chih-p'an is referring to a method for construing transmission that prevailed among masters of his day or a method that he himself adopts in order to determine who would be included in his list of Chinese dharma-heirs descended from the patriarchs.

69. *Tseng-hsiu chiao-yüan ch'ing-kuei*, HTC 101.713b–714a.

or "Mount Sumeru throne" (*hsü-mi tso*) on which images of the Buddha were themselves enshrined. In T'ien-t'ai ritual literature the two are synonymous, the terms "dharma-throne" (*fa-tso*) or "high seat" (*kao-tso*) being used interchangeably for both the seat of the Buddha and the seat from which the abbot preaches dharma. Death anniversary observances for the major T'ien-t'ai patriarchs took place in the Dharma Hall as well, the high seat serving as the altar on which the patriarch's portrait was enshrined and his "spirit" invoked. Thus in this symbolic setting there coalesced the presence of the Buddha, the T'ien-t'ai patriarchy, and the abbot, thereby making the latter the living analogue of the other two.

That the rite itself was a veritable reenactment of the Buddha's preaching of dharma is not only obvious from the imagery but also patently acknowledged in the T'ien-t'ai ritual literature itself. The acolytes of the abbot are identified with Ānanda and Kuan-ting, the famous attendants of the Buddha Śākyamuni and the patriarch Chih-i, respectively.[70] When they petition the abbot to preach, it is tantamount to requesting the Buddha himself to turn the wheel of dharma. The offering of incense is a standard—and highly solemn—gesture that begins virtually every major Buddhist rite. It was accompanied by a hymn and visualization through which the eternally abiding Buddhas and their retinues throughout the universe are summoned and made present in the assembly.[71] Thus the abbot offering incense before the empty dais establishes the seat (and himself) as the archetypal center of a timeless and universal saṅgha.

One can find numerous other ways in which these symbolic motifs are reinforced in monastic procedure. What this meant for the *Mo-ho chih-kuan* and other works of the sectarian canon was that access and interpretation were tightly controlled by the monastic elite. Hence, while a text like the *Mo-ho chih-kuan* might be studied by virtually anyone in private, the right to expound it authoritatively in public was contingent on admission to this inner circle. By implication this involved a lengthy tenure at the feet of an acknowledged master and was earned only through demonstrated mastery of the exegetical norms and attendant ethos of normative tradition. While this did not necessarily obviate individual growth and creativity, it did ensure that that innovation remained carefully ensconced within certain prescribed social and cultural contexts.

70. See Shunjō, *Seishukishiki narabi ni jūrokukandōki*, in Ishida, ed., *Shunjō risshi*, p. 396. See also *Tseng-hsiu chiao-yüan ch'ing-kuei*, HTC 101.720a.

71. See Stevenson, "The T'ien-t'ai Four Forms of Samādhi."

CHAPTER 3

The Problematic of the *Mo-ho chih-kuan* and T'ien-t'ai History

Daniel B. Stevenson

The *Mo-ho chih-kuan* has a long-standing reputation among East Asian Buddhists as a vexatious text. Quite apart from the work's immense length and scope, its terse style and technical complexity raise problems of interpretion at nearly every turn. Chan-jan drew deliberate attention to these difficulties in his commentaries to the *Mo-ho chih-kuan*. And with the subsequent acceptance of his identification of patriarchal tradition with patriarchal canon, the "unevenness" and "density" of the *Mo-ho chih-kuan* itself became a defining parameter of T'ien-t'ai soteriology as well as ecclesiastical authority.

The *Mo-ho chih-kuan* was not approached casually in the T'ien-t'ai establishment of the Sung. Access to sacred text and the privilege to voice one's understanding of it were hedged about by a host of institutional and cultural norms, the very same norms, in fact, that defined the T'ien-t'ai monastic hierarchy and the investiture of T'ien-t'ai abbots. Hence, regardless of any claim one might have to private or autonomous insight, the sanction to read *qua* interpret the *Mo-ho chih-kuan* publicly rested with the fulfillment of a wide range of formal expectations and, ultimately, the endorsement of the inner circle of the T'ien-t'ai community. While charismatic presence and other such affective criteria may have been one of these expectations, equally if not more significant was the acknowleged mastery of sectarian canon and the systematic "vision" lurking within its pages.

One might imagine that such a formal deference to text and the strictures of a hierarchically controlled orthodoxy would prove deadening to individual voice and creative change within the T'ien-t'ai community. Indeed, precisely this line of thinking has led some Buddhist scholars to decry the sectarian retrenchment of Sung-period T'ien-t'ai and Ch'an as a mark of religious ossification and "decline."[1] Even the most cursory look at Sung T'ien-t'ai materials, however, belies the inadequacy of such a picture. Not only was innovation in T'ien-t'ai cult and institution extensive during the Sung (the emergence of Pure Land spirituality into the T'ien-t'ai mainstream and liaisons with Ch'an being two examples), but interest in canonical criticism and doctrinal theory also flourished as never before, resulting in protracted debates that animated the T'ien-t'ai community well into the fourteenth century.

Many of the controversies that occupied the T'ien-t'ai community during the Sung were generated from the *Mo-ho chih-kuan* itself; and those that did not originate there soon localized around the text. It was precisely those points of ambiguity that received the most attention. Hence the centrifugal tendency of the *Mo-ho chih-kuan* to fly apart at the seams required continual effort at containment in new syntheses and itself became a fundamental dynamic in shaping the T'ien-t'ai tradition. No study of the *Mo-ho chih-kuan* can afford to ignore the text's elusiveness and the vital way in which that elusiveness has impacted historically on the T'ien-t'ai community.

One of the most significant ambiguities in the *Mo-ho chih-kuan* centers around the role of the ritual meditations described in the four samādhis section of the Synopsis. In its most basic terms the central issue devolves around the status of ritual form within the general scheme of T'ien-t'ai spiritual praxis. The *Mo-ho chih-kuan* contains two potentially divergent discourses on religious cultivation. One places primary emphasis on an interiorized contemplation of mind or religious truth and reduces ritual to an ancillary or even metaphoric role. The other stresses the incantatory potency of ritual itself, thereby subordinating contemplation to the service of ritual invocation. Both exist in simultaneous tension with one another, and together they constitute the basic discursive framework around which discussions of religious practice have been organized throughout T'ien-t'ai history, including such broad-ranging and controversial issues as the control of "vulgar" religious cults or Pure Land and Ch'an polemics. Indeed, the tension between these interpretive poles was one of those "fertile antimonies" that "serve in their very irresolvability to keep the tradition alive, to foster its growth, and to prevent its closure or ossification."[2]

The various interpretive positions that developed represent an ongoing oscillation between a range of paradigmatic possibilities rather than a strict linear evolution of T'ien-t'ai orthodoxy. Under such circumstances,

1. To date this has been the prevailing view of Sung Buddhism—i.e., a period when we witness, to use the words of Kenneth Ch'en, a "decline in the creative impulse within the saṅgha" (*Buddhism in China*, p. 389).

2. Buswell and Gimello, eds., Introduction, *Paths to Liberation*, p. 24.

to emphasize one mode of discourse over the other or to substitute a pat solution for the *Mo-ho chih-kuan*'s inherent inconsistencies—as modern Tendai scholarship has tended to do—is to overlook the complexity and richness of the text and, even worse, to misrepresent altogether the real vitality of its tradition.

The Two Discourses of the *Mo-ho chih-kuan*

The concern of the *Mo-ho chih-kuan* as a whole is the perfect and sudden path. Thus the text begins with the "arousing of the intention to seek perfect enlightenment" and aspires to chart this process all the way through to the crowning achievement of Buddhahood. Discussion of the perfect and sudden practice of calming and contemplation per se occurs at two key places in the text: in the Synopsis chapter, where it is presented in the guise of the four forms of samādhi, and in the elaborate scheme of the twenty-five preliminary expedients and the ten modes and ten spheres of discernment of greater chapters 6 and 7. Identified respectively as the "abbreviated" (*lüeh*) and "expanded" (*kuang*) discussions, the *Mo-ho chih-kuan* itself suggests that an implicit thematic unity pertains between these two sections and their systems.[3] Thus from the time the *Mo-ho chih-kuan* first began to circulate, there were definite precedents for regarding the four samādhis and ten modes as a single integrated program of practice.

Precisely how these sections and their systems relate to one another, however, remains problematic. The four samādhis chapter of the Synopsis focuses on the performative content of specific repentance and samādhi rites, which it organizes according to the simple denominator of physical posture or activity. Greater chapters 6 and 7 deal more in theoretical abstraction (the twenty-five expedients) or interiorized reflection (the ten modes of discernment) and have virtually nothing to say about specifics of time, place, and circumstance, much less the exigencies of ritual cult. Indeed, aside from isolated references suggesting that the ten modes of discernment of chapter 7 were to be applied within the context of the four samādhis, at no point does the *Mo-ho chih-kuan* spell out in systematic detail the relationship of one system or section to the other.[4]

3. See Chih-i's introduction to MHCK, T 46.3b10–4a18. For Kuan-ting's views on the relationship between the four samādhis of the Synopsis and greater chapters 6 and 7 see *Kuan-hsin lun shu*, T 46.607c29–b2. See also *Ssu nien-ch'u*, T no. 1918 (especially 46.574b26–27 and 574c25–29).

4. See, for example, MHCK, T 46.110a and 114c. The most substantial reference, which appears at the conclusion of Chih-i's discussion of the ten modes of discernment (T 46.100b16–21), strongly implies that the four samādhis simply describe the "phenomenal" (*shih*) or outward setting within which an interiorized "contemplation" (*kuan*) of the ten modes is cultivated.

Thus the elaborate ritual programs of the four samādhis and the abstract contemplations of the ten modes stand in disembodied tension with one another, leaving the reader to determine their respective contributions to religious practice.

The ambiguity that pertains between the contemplative programs of the Synopsis and greater chapters 6 and 7 is replicated and, in certain respects, amplified in the four samādhis section itself. For instance, under the rubric of the four samādhis the Synopsis chapter gives detailed attention to some six different ritual meditations. With the exception of *sui-tzu-i* ("freely following one's thoughts"),[5] each is circumscribed from the others by a unique cult orientation and ritual cycle. Whatever common structures pertain among them—such as "contemplation of principle (*li*)" or "calming and contemplation of the mind" (*i chih-kuan*)—they are always cast in the guise of the specific rite. Hence, in the final analysis, cultic content is exalted as the nonnegotiable ground of religious praxis.

Yet the very organization of this miscellany of rites into a cohesive system of four forms of samādhi intimates the existence of universal principles that at once transcend and take precedence over considerations of specific ritualized content. Chih-i, for example, in the opening lines of the section on the four samādhis remarks, "The four activities are the objective basis (*yüan*) [for meditative discernment]. In contemplation (lit., *kuan-hsin*) one resorts to this basis in order to tame and rectify [the wayward mind]."[6] In so doing, he establishes mode of physical activity and interiorized contemplation as an essential dyad operating uniformly throughout each of the different samādhi rites. This polarity resonates with another taxonomic dyad that Chih-i routinely uses to organize religious practice: "phenomenal activity" (*shih*) or "phenomenal [ritual] procedure" (*[shih] fang-fa*) and "application of calming and contemplation to the mind" (*i chih-kuan*) or "contemplation of principle" (*li-kuan*).[7]

In this simple descriptive strategy we find a rationale for linking the rites of the four samādhis not only with one another but also with the abstract systems of chapters 6 and 7. In its very universality, however, the dyad of "phenomenal activity" and "contemplation of principle or mind" also harbors a potential for reification and reduction that threatens to eclipse cultic particularity. Thus it is but a short step from the "taxo-

5. The designation *sui-tzu-i* ("freely following one's thoughts") originates with Hui-ssu (*Sui-tzu-i san-mei*, HTC 98.687a) but is given the alternate name of *chüeh-i san-mei* ("samādhi of wakeful awareness of mind") by Chih-i and discussed extensively in an independent work of that title (*Shih Mo-ho po-jo p'o-lo-mi ching chüeh-i san-mei*, T no. 1922).

6. MHCK, T 46.11a27–28. Similar statements appear in other works of Chih-i and Kuan-ting: *Kuan-hsin lun shu*, T 46.601a11–13.

7. See, especially, MHCK, T 46.18c10–18; see also the parallel account of the four samādhis in Kuan-ting's *Kuan-hsin lun shu*, T 46.600b–603c.

nomic" to the "essential"—namely, a view of the four samādhis that derogates the specifics of cult ritual to a merely figurative role and exalts in their stead a generic contemplation of mind applied to an equally generic physical routine of sitting or walking. Indeed, this possibility becomes especially pronounced when one notes the close parallels between Chih-i's dyadic opposition of "phenomenal activity" (*shih*) and "discernment of principle" (*li*) and the view of religious practice set forth in *sui-tzu-i*, the one practice among the four samādhis that does not fit within their highly ritualized program.

Sui-tzu-i or the practice of "freely following one's thoughts" espouses a free-form approach to religious practice where all forms of sensory experience (*ch'en* or *ching*) or physical activity (*shih*)—good as well as evil—provide an equally viable ground for contemplation of the mind (*kuan-hsin*) and realization of samādhi.[8] Because it "extends universally through all forms of activity, walking as well as sitting,"[9] Chih-i classifies it under the fourth of the four samādhis—the "neither-walking-nor-sitting samādhi." But in its indiscriminate approach to the doings of body, speech, and mind, *sui-tzu-i* tends to level all distinctions of valency between ritually structured and unstructured action. This subversion of the very priorities on which the cult-oriented system of the four samādhis as a whole is based sets *sui-tzu-i* in a category by itself and suggests a tension in T'ien-t'ai praxis that goes far deeper than a mere difference in taxonomical or descriptive perspective.[10] Should one specifically enlist the similarities between *sui-tzu-i* and Chih-i's generic dyad of "phenomenal activity" (*shih*) and "discernment of mind" (*kuan-hsin*), it becomes especially easy to subsume the entire scheme of the four samādhis under the aegis of *sui-tzu-i*.

The ambiguities in the *Mo-ho chih-kuan* generated diversity and contention within T'ien-t'ai tradition relatively early in the school's history. Chan-jan's writings together with various other mid-T'ang period sources suggest the existence of a range of different positions on the *Mo-ho chih-kuan* and T'ien-t'ai practice. Some (in anticipation of the "off-mountain" [*shan-wai*] masters of the Sung) espoused a "structureless" approach to contemplation reminiscent of *sui-tzu-i* and downplayed the ritual lore of the four samādhis as mere scriptural example or apologetic. Others took the opposite stance, choosing to emphasize specific cults (such as the lotus or pratyutpanna samādhis) over the generic view of

8. According to the MHCK, in *sui-tzu-i*, contemplation is applied fluidly and indiscriminately to the six activities (walking, standing, sitting, reclining, talking, miscellaneous actions) and the six sense perceptions, regardless of whether those activities are good, evil, or neutral in valency.

9. MHCK, T 46.14b27–28.

10. This is exemplified most clearly in Chih-i's cautions against the abuse of *sui-tzu-i* and, especially, its meditation on evil dharmas; see MHCK, T 46.18c10–20a24. See also Ikeda, *Makashikan kenkyū josetsu*, p. 264.

contemplation suggested by *sui-tzu-i* and such formulae as the four activities and ten modes. Others yet chose to dismiss the text of the *Mo-ho chih-kuan* in its entirety in favor of an "immediate" approach to calming and contemplation reminiscent of the "wordless" transmission of Ch'an.

Chan-jan made a deliberate effort to salvage the systemic integrity of the text of the *Mo-ho chih-kuan* (and Chih-i's overall vision of Buddhist practice) by treating its internal discrepancies as topical rather than substantive issues. Elaborating on the familiar notion of "abbreviated" (*lüeh*) and "expanded" (*kuang*) modes of discourse, Chan-jan insisted that the four samādhis section of the Synopsis is "abbreviated" with regard to the details of "calming and contemplation of the mind" (*i chih-kuan*) but "expanded" in its treatment of "phenomenal [ritual] setting and activity" (*shih*). Conversely, chapters 6 and 7 are "abbreviated" with respect to phenomenal ritual procedure and "expanded" with regard to calming and contemplation of mind. Hence the two sections of the *Mo-ho chih-kuan* purport to describe a single integrated system of religious practice from two separate perspectives.[11]

In many respects, however, Chan-jan's strategy is more a sleight of hand than it is a tangible solution. Not only does he fail to spell out the rationale that governs these different perspectives as modalities of a single discourse of praxis, but he also leaves unclarified the details of their functional relationship within the context of actual ritual performance. Therefore, far from settling matters, Chan-jan's insistence on the conterminal unity of the *Mo-ho chih-kuan* and Chih-i's vision of religious practice had the obverse effect of bringing their disparities more acutely into focus. As a consequence the entire issue of their synthesis became a problematic that occupied T'ien-t'ai posterity for centuries to follow.

Like their T'ien-t'ai predecessors, modern scholars have themselves felt considerable discomfort over the loose ends of the *Mo-ho chih-kuan*. Thus around the ambiguities of the four samādhis and the ten modes of discernment has developed one of the fundamental concerns of T'ien-t'ai studies, a concern that is typically represented as an effort to "recover" Chih-i's original vision of the perfect and sudden practice from the inadequacies of his own writings and the distortions of later tradition.[12] As a rule, attention has been focused primarily on the infrastructure of the *Mo-ho chih-kuan*, the idea being that the principles of taxonomy are more likely to hold the key to Chih-i's approach to religious practice than biography or the specifics of cult performance. This preference for the explicative and systematic has led to the peripherali-

11. See Chan-jan, *Chih-kuan fu-hsing ch'uan-hung chüeh*, T 46.183a26–b5, and elsewhere; see also *Chih-kuan ta-i*, T 46.459c18.

12. See Ikeda, *Makashikan kenkyū josetsu*, pp. v–vii and 1–6. See also Andō, *Tendai-gaku*, pp. 3–6, 187, and Sekiguchi, *Makashikan*, 1:9–14.

zation of ritual and cult and resulted in a representation of T'ien-t'ai religious practice that is cast closely in the reductive language and image of *sui-tzu-i*.

For instance, noting the similarities between Chih-i's accounts of *sui-tzu-i* and the taxonomical categories used in the section on the four samādhis and Greater Chapters 6 and 7 of the *Mo-ho chih-kuan*, Sekiguchi Shindai and Andō Toshio both concluded that Chih-i's entire program of religious practice boiled down to two simple forms: contemplation of mind while seated in traditional cross-legged (i.e., *zazen*) posture and contemplation of mind while engaged in a *sui-tzu-i*-style "meditation amidst all activities."[13] More recently Ikeda Rosan has reiterated this thesis, adding to it the suspiciously Sōtō Zen twist that Chih-i's doctrine of the four samādhis "decries all distinctions of value or priority among the four activities" and advocates the simple view that "the activities of everyday life are themselves the primary ground of religious practice."[14]

Aside from the most perfunctory rehearsal of the material in the Synopsis, these scholars make little mention of the specific lore and independent literature on the rites of the four samādhis, much less consider its significance seriously. Where such references do occur, the tone is for the most part derogatory. Ritual content is typically characterized as "external ceremony" (*gai naru keitai*), "ritual formalism" (*keishiki*), "external physical gesture" (*gaigi, shingi*), or at best a "preliminary expedient" (*zen no hōben*) within which an essential "interior contemplation" (*naikan*) is applied.[15] Hence, "inner contemplation" is singled out as the principal power that "animates" or "effects realization" (*shushō*), whereas ritual setting and gesture are seen as mere external mechanics with little intrinsic spiritual value. This distinction likewise finds its way into text-critical evaluations of early T'ien-t'ai documents, such that works that promote elements of ritual lore (such as Chih-i's *Fa-hua san-mei ch'an-i* or *Tz'u-ti ch'an-men*) are often dismissed as either a gratuitous concession to the religiously inept or relics of a less "enlightened" phase of Chih-i's career. Thus in a rather remarkable example of insular thinking, Chih-i's lectures on the *Mo-ho chih-kuan* (represented variously as the triumph of the

13. Sekiguchi, *Tendai shikan no kenkyū*, pp. 143–154; and Sekiguchi, *Makashikan*, 2:362–366. See also Andō, *Tendai shisō-shi*, pp. 380–387, and Andō, "Tendai Chigi no jōdokyo."

14. A teaching which, according to Ikeda, later was displaced by emphasis on the practice of Buddha-mindfulness; Ikeda Rosan, *Makashikan kenkyū josetsu*, p. 317. See also his "Tendai shishu-zammai no shūyō," p. 133.

15. See Shioiri, "Shishu-zammai ni atsukawareta Chigi no sembō," pp. 272–273; Hurvitz, "Chih-i," pp. 319–320; Hayashi, "Makashikan ni okeru shishu-zammai no ichi kōsatsu," pp. 208–210; Sekiguchi, *Makashikan*, 2:366; Sekiguchi, *Tendai shikan no kenkyū*, p. 143; Sekiguchi, *Tendai kyōgaku no kenkyū* ("Shishu-zammai ron"), p. 125; Ikeda, *Makashikan kenkyū josetsu*, p. 316.

systematic over the unsystematic, the rational over the affective, the sudden over the gradual, the pristine contemplation of mind over the materialistic designs of religious cult, Chinese intuitivism over Indian scholasticism) are reaffirmed as both the epitome of Chih-i's career and a watershed in the emergence of a "mature" sinitic Buddhist tradition.[16]

For all of the exhaustive and, at times, insightful analysis that Sekiguchi and others have marshaled from Chih-i, there are two problems that seriously challenge the conventions for thinking about T'ien-t'ai religious practice that have grown out of their efforts. The first (and certainly the most damaging) is a simple matter of historical evidence. Contrary to the eminently "rational" image of religious practice that they profess to find in early T'ien-t'ai—i.e., the pristine emphasis on "contemplation of principle" (*li kuan*)—the historical record gives every indication that the cults of the four samādhis (in all their ritual splendor) were in fact *the* primary ground of T'ien-t'ai religious life. Indeed, not only were they institutionally central to the T'ien-t'ai community throughout its emergent period, but they also continued to develop and thrive in this capacity for at least a millennium or more.[17] This point is underscored by the literary record as well, which—apart from the brief description in the Synopsis chapter of the *Mo-ho chih-kuan*—counts no fewer than ten separate manuals on the rites of the four samādhis among the works of Hui-ssu and Chih-i and points to a continuous production of literature on this subject in T'ien-t'ai circles well into the Ming.[18] Simply stated, the ritual dimension of the four samādhis cannot be so easily dismissed.

The second problem concerns the more fundamental issue of the discursive agendae that we as modern scholars bring to the study of T'ien-t'ai practice. Sekiguchi Shindai himself is very much heir to a legacy of scholarship that is deeply bound up with the normative Japanese Buddhist tradition and shaped against the background of late Tokugawa- and Meiji-period modernization and religious reform. Not unlike D. T. Suzuki, the great popularizer of Zen Buddhism and its study in Japan and the West, Sekiguchi has achieved a certain renown in the world of Buddhist studies for his efforts to commend T'ien-t'ai as a "modern" or "enlightened" tradition untainted by trappings of "medieval" religious

16. Ōno Eijin, "Tendai Chigi no zammai shisō kō," pp. 124–125 and 132–134. Although his concern is mainly text-critical, Satō Tetsuei also suggests this position with respect to the four samādhis in his "Tendai daishi ni okeru shishu-zammai no keisei katei." See also, Shioiri, "Shishu-zammai ni atsukawareta Chigi no senbō," and more recently, Rhodes, "*Hokke-zammai-zangi* kenkyū josetsu."

17. See Stevenson, "Four Kinds of Samādhi in Early T'ien-t'ai," and idem, "The T'ien-t'ai Four Forms of Samādhi."

18. Sung T'ien-t'ai masters Tsun-shih and Chih-li composed at least ten works between them, several of which expound newly developed rites centering on Avalokiteśvara and the Pure Land contemplations of Amitābha.

institution and culture.[19] This agenda is stated most boldly in Sekiguchi's writings on T'ien-t'ai *p'an-chiao* (doctrinal classification), which he himself describes as an effort to demystify and modernize a tradition that has "lost all credibility in the face of modern critical scholarship on Buddhism and, hence, [lost] the authority to guide the Buddhist world."[20] But it takes no leap of the imagination to see Sekiguchi's denigration of ritual as proceeding from a similar desire to shed T'ien-t'ai of its embarrassingly "medieval" or "pre-Reformation" past, especially when considered in light of his well-known interest in reclaiming the culture of *zazen* (which he refers to as "the distinctive contribution and foundation of Buddhist as well as East Asian thought") for the T'ien-t'ai school.[21]

This point suggests that Sekiguchi's dichotomization of T'ien-t'ai praxis can ultimately be laid at the door of the post-Reformation intellectual tradition of the West.[22] Doubtless this is in part the case. At the same time we must not lose sight of the fact that the East Asian Buddhist tradition itself boasts a number of well-hewn discursive oppositions of a strikingly similar nature, including such distinctions as elite or monastic versus vulgar or popular, the approach of principle (*li-kuan*) versus that of phenomenal ritual and devotion (*shih-kuan*), insight versus action, Zen versus Pure Land, sudden (*tun*) versus gradual (*chien*), direct or real (*shih*) versus expedient (*fang-pien* or *ch'üan*).[23] In point of fact, Sekiguchi's "protestant" reading of T'ien-t'ai praxis not only has a very credible basis in the *Mo-ho chih-kuan* itself but actually finds its historical equivalent in one pole of the extended Sung-dynasty (960–1279) controversies on the subject of T'ien-t'ai meditation and ritual praxis—that of the so-called

19. The strategies of D. T. Suzuki have been examined thoroughly by Robert Sharf in "Occidentalism and the Zen of Japanese Nationalism." See also Faure, *The Rhetoric of Immediacy*, pp. 3–31.

20. This point is made openly by Sekiguchi in a series of key articles directed toward the Tendai organization and Buddhist scholars, notably, "Goji hakkyō ron" and "Goji hakkyō wa Tendai kyōhan ni arazu," and *Tendai kyōgaku no kenkyū*, esp. pp. 21, 36, 85, 647–689.

21. Sekiguchi, *Tendai shikan no kenkyū*, p. 1. Sekiguchi's highly polemical—albeit informative—attempts to rewrite the history of Chinese T'ien-t'ai and Ch'an/Zen in an effort to reassign credit for the culture of *zazen* to Chih-i are legendary in Buddhist studies circles. For a brief review of Sekiguchi's scholarship on this subject, see Bielefeldt, *Dōgen's Manuals of Zen Meditation*, pp. 62–63. Sekiguchi's general thesis is recapitulated in Sekiguchi, *Tendai shikan no kenkyū*, pp. 271–281.

22. On this subject, see Smith, "The Bare Facts of Ritual," in *Imagining Religion*. Also see the more recent, Bell, *Ritual Theory, Ritual Practice*, pp. 1–46.

23. For a discussion of this rift and its paradigmatic significance in Ch'an or Zen Buddhism (and its parallels in Western intellectual traditions), see Faure, *The Rhetoric of Immediacy*, pp. 1–95, 284–320; see also Bielefeldt, *Dōgen's Manuals of Zen Meditation*, pp. 55–70.

shan-wai or "off-mountain" partisans. Hence despite its unmistakable resonances with Western critical traditions newly imported to Japan, Sekiguchi's take on the *Mo-ho chih-kuan* also stands well within the discursive and hermeneutical legacy of his T'ien-t'ai forebears.

Our task, then, entails becoming aware of our own categorical assumptions about relgious practice while concurrently trying to illuminate the complex nuances that attend their deceptively similar counterparts in the Chinese Buddhist tradition. In the pages that follow, we will briefly examine the paradigmatic ambiguity between ritual and contemplation in T'ien-t'ai religious culture, investigate some of the ways in which it played itself out historically, and draw out some of the general implications these findings may have for various prevailing models that we bring to the study of Chinese Buddhism.

Ritual "Work" and Contemplative "Insight"

The summary descriptions of the four samādhis offered in the *Mo-ho chih-kuan* and Kuan-ting's *Kuan-hsin lun shu* cite regularly from the independent ritual manuals composed by Hui-ssu and Chih-i, thereby suggesting an implicit connection between the two bodies of material. Whether Chih-i intended these materials to be used together or not, virtually all subsequent speculations on the four samādhis and the contemplative system of the *Mo-ho chih-kuan*—whether we are speaking of Chan-jan and such eminent Sung thinkers as Chih-li, or the self-appointed Ming T'ien-t'ai reviver Ou-i Chih-hsü (1599–1655)—have drawn these ritual manuals indistinguishably into their fold. Although this intertextual connection has been largely overlooked in modern scholarship, it implies that any serious effort to sketch out the discursive topography of T'ien-t'ai ritual and contemplative discourse must necessarily look beyond the confines of the *Mo-ho chih-kuan* and take into account this peripheral body of literature. Let us now take up some of the more basic conventions of ritual structure and terminology that are commonly employed both in the individual manuals of Hui-ssu and Chih-i as well as in more synthetic works such as the *Mo-ho chih-kuan* and Kuan-ting's *Kuan-hsin lun shu*.

The ritual meditations outlined in the independent manuals are presented as perfectly circumscribed programs of religious practice, each drawing from its root scripture(s) a particular semiotic universe, which in turn gives its unique stamp to ritual form as well as to soteriological expectation. At the most basic level of performance, this autonomy translates into a highly formalized program of symbol and gesture, which is at once binding and closed to arbitrary substitution or innovation. It would be inconceivable, for instance, for someone intent on performing pratyutpanna samādhi to replace the cult image of Amitābha with that of the *Lotus Sūtra*, substitute a twenty-one-day period for the specified ninety, or choose to simply sit down rather than walk. For any such alteration—at least if done without due justification—would entail a fundamental violation of the rite. Yet despite their exclusivity at the level of cult and performance, the various rites of the four samādhis clearly draw on a common repertoire of liturgical form and structure, one that involves certain elemental principles of ritual procedure, efficacy, and soteriology that extend beyond the confines of the immediate cult.

Virtually every rite begins with a standardized procedure for purification of the site and the person (*chuang-yen tao-ch'ang*) and installation of the deities (*shao-ch'ing*) in the sanctuary. Ritual purity is maintained with great care for the duration of the rite, usually through restrictions on outside contact and diet, as well as through elaborate procedures for bathing and changing robes when entering and exiting the sanctuary. The liturgical day itself is organized according to repeated cycles of ritual worship and extended recitation or meditation. Typically these fall at six fixed intervals (*liu shih*), which are spaced evenly over the day and the night. The specific procedure for ritual worship—commonly referred to as "veneration of the Buddhas" (*li fo*) or "veneration and confession" (*li-ch'an*)—varies from rite to rite but for the most part observes the following sequence: (1) initial incense offering (*hsiang-hua kung-yang*) and generic praises to the Three Jewels (*t'an-fo*), (2) veneration (*ching-li*) of the Three Jewels (in the form of prostrations and invocation of the names of the specific deities of the given cult), (3) confession before the deities (*ch'an-hui*), (4) transference of merits (*hui-hsiang*), (5) profession of vows (*fa-yüan*), and (6) closing hymns and profession of the three refuges (*san kui-i*).[24] In certain T'ien-t'ai ritual works[25] the two additional elements of solicitation of the Buddhas to remain in the world (*ch'üan-ch'ing*) and the expression of sympathetic joy in the merits of others (*sui-hsi*) are placed between the confessional and the concluding transference and vow passages. These five members together (i.e., confession, solicitation, sympathetic joy, transference of merit, and vows) are commonly known in T'ien-t'ai circles as the "fivefold penance" (*wu-hui*).

Comparative studies of ritual materials from Chinese Buddhist movements contemporary with early T'ien-t'ai suggest that the liturgical nomenclature and structures found in Chih-i's manuals are themselves not unique but reflect a more broadly based liturgical tradition that was de-

24. At times, extended ritual circumambulation and recitation of sūtras or incantations are performed between the vow and closing refuges.

25. For later T'ien-t'ai tradition, Chih-i's *Fa-hua san-mei ch'an-i* (T 46.953a–b) became the paradigmatic source for the fivefold penance. The concept of the fivefold penance (with specific reference to the lotus samādhi) is also discussed at length in MHCK, T 46.98a12–98c17.

veloping across the board in medieval China. This lore, in turn, may be traced to conventions (and, in certain instances, to specific scriptures) of classical Indian Mahāyāna rites of *pūjā* introduced into China during the early fifth century.[26] Such evidence suggests that the basic structures informing the T'ien-t'ai rites of the four samādhis describe a relatively standardized ritual content and syntax that was adapted freely to different ritual programs, often itself supplying details of procedure not available in the sparse cultic descriptions of the original scriptural sources. This uniformity points to the existence of a transprogammatic ritual lexicon and rule of syntax which persisted beyond the context of individual cultic arrangements and paradigmatically determined the meaning and place of elements of the ritual process according to its own established logic.

Scholars of religious ritual have long noted the marked differences attending gesture and utterance performed within a ritualized context and their counterparts in ordinary existence. Although the subject has generated a diversity of models, there is general agreement on the more basic properties that characterize ritual action. Among those most often cited are: formality or stylization (implying, likewise, an especially high degree of conventionalization), prescriptive invariance (and, by association, keen attention to detail), and an implicitly hieratic sense of association with sacrality (variously understood to mean either establishing sacred presence or responding to "the sacred").[27]

These qualities describe the salient properties of the specific cults of the four samādhis. Indeed, the four samādhis are highly stylized in form; that form is essentially nonnegotiable and open to variance only within certain defined limits; and a hieratic concern for open resonance between the practitioner and the Buddhas is their express purpose. There is, however, a subsidiary aspect of these three properties that deserves further consideration—viz., the extraordinary valency that attends ritual gesture and script. By "valency" I do not simply mean the nonnegotiable or highly formalized character of ritual performance per se—that it is done a certain way simply because that *is* the way it is to be done—but a

26. See Stevenson, "The T'ien-t'ai Four Forms of Samādhi," pp. 249–464. For example, early T'ien-t'ai liturgical forms share immediate parallels with Three Stages and Shansi Pure Land ritual materials. They draw in common upon prototypes of the Indian Mahāyāna structure of the sevenfold peerless offering (*saptānuttarapūjā*) as found in such early fifth century translations as the *Shih chu p'i-p'o sha lun* (T no. 2521) and *Kuan fo san-mei hai ching* (T no. 643).

27. These characterizations have chiefly been culled from the work of Smith, "The Bare Facts of Ritual," in *Imagining Religion*, pp. 53–65; Smith, *To Take Place: Toward Theory in Ritual*, pp. 96–117; Tambiah, "A Performative Approach to Ritual"; Rappaport, "Ritual, Sanctity, and Cybernetics"; Rappaport, *Ecology, Meaning, and Religion*; Grimes, "Ritual Studies" in *The Encyclopedia of Religion*.

more fundamental sense of invocatory potency that itself generates and underscores this nonnegotiability.

J. S. Tambiah, utilizing notions developed in speech-act theory, has noted the strongly "performative" character of ritual utterance and act—"performative" in the sense that "the illocutionary speech act [itself] is 'the doing of the action' " or "performance [itself] realizes the *performative* effect."[28] Thus the primacy of invocatory power over propositional content focuses attention firmly on the content and craft of performance. This fact not only lends script and performance their inviolable formality, but it also gives them a hypervalence exceeding that attributed to ordinary action, for an extraordinary efficacy or inefficacy, benefit or even disaster, are believed to hinge on proper attention to ritual script.

We do not have to look far to find examples of such hypervalence among the ritual forms of the four samādhis. The initial incense offering and invocations—by mere profession, mere performance—make the Buddhas and bodhisattvas present in the sanctuary. Confession or the "exposing of sins" before the Buddhas and bodhisattvas properly performed removes sin and impediment. Profession of the bodhisattva vow and transference of merits actually affixes the vow as a living force in the mind-stream, generating merits on behalf of oneself and others. Thus, by implication, ritual form and syntax themselves carry the power to accomplish the Buddhist path or make the Buddha present. At the same time, however, they have an equally frightful power to accomplish the opposite, when their norms are transgressed or inattentively performed. For instance, the *Fang-teng san-mei hsing-fa*—Chih-i's most detailed manual on the vaipulya samādhi—notes at the end of its rather lengthy discussion of bathing and purificatory procedures: "If one does not maintain purity in this manner, then one will not be in accord with stipulated procedure (*ju-fa*). The practice will be without any benefit and may even invite [further] sins."[29]

The most graphic illustration of the invocatory power of the four samādhis is found in Chih-i's adaptation of a set of indigenous philosophical constructs long associated in China with discussions of divinatory, ritual, and moral efficacy—namely, the concept of *kan-ying* or "stimulus and response." *Kan-ying* was first articulated as a distinctive concept by the yin-yang/five elements correlative cosmologists and ritual theorists of the Han period. Subsequently it played a major role in *hsüan-hsüeh* discussions of the nature of the sage and the mechanisms of moral reciprocity during the third and fourth centuries. Through these auspices it became a basic component of the cultural and conceptual fabric into which Buddhist teachings were woven.

28. Tambiah, "A Performative Approach to Ritual," pp. 127–130.
29. *Fang-teng san-mei hsing-fa*, T 46.945b22–24.

The language of *kan-ying* is associated with a rather selective range of topics in fifth- and sixth-century Buddhist exegetical writings. These principally include discussions of karmic retribution,[30] the "bodies" and powers of salvific manifestation of the Buddhas,[31] and the related question—intimately bound up with the enterprise of *p'an-chiao* or "classification of the teachings"—of the mechanisms behind the historical Buddha's expedient adaptation of Buddhist doctrine to the varying circumstances and capacities of his audience.[32] Yet despite its connection to issues of such obvious urgency, *kan-ying* itself primarily remained an embedded concept. In only a handful of instances do Buddhist doctrinal works single it out as an explicit topic of discussion.[33]

A major exception, however, is to be found in Buddhist literature of a very different genre—namely, the "tales of miraculous response" (*ying-yen chi*) which appear with such profusion during the North-South Dynasties period and early T'ang. These collections principally consist of quasi-biographical and episodic testimonials of salvific power organized topically around specific Buddhas, bodhisattvas, sūtras, pilgrimage sites, relics, or images.[34] In terms of thematic focus as well as narrative design,

30. Hui-yüan authored two short treatises on this topic, which are preserved in Seng-yu, *Hung ming chi*, T 52.33b–34a (*Ta Huan Hsüan pao-ying lun*) and 34b–34c (*San pao-ying*). Discussion of karmic retribution appears in time to disassociate itself from *kan-ying* terminology, possibly due to the increasing presence of sophisticated Indian Buddhist epistemologies and models of karmic influence, maturation, and recompense.

31. It is one of the principal themes in Hui-yüan's correspondence with Kumārajīva. See Hui-yüan, *Chiu-mo-lo-shih fa-shih ta-i chang*, T 45.123b–c, 125a–c, 127a; especially 129c–130c (*Fa-shen kan-ying*); also Seng-chao, *Chao-lun*, T 45.153a–c (*Po-jo wu chih lun*) and 158a–b (Seng-chao's letter of reply to Liu I-min's queries on the nature of the Buddha's "formless" essence and powers of salvific response).

32. One of the most influential examples is Tao-sheng's *Fa-hua ching shu*, HTC 150. It is also evident in Seng-chao's *Chu wei-mo-chieh ching*, T no. 1775, Fa-yün's *Fa-hua ching i-chi*, T no. 1715 (see Fa-yün's comments to the Preface and Expedient Devices chapter [592a–610c], and in particular the Faith and Understanding [631c–645c] and Lifespan of the Tathāgata chapters [667c–672a]), and remarks of southern *Ch'eng-shih lun* and *Nirvāṇa Sūtra* exegetes preserved in Pao-liang's compendium of early medieval *Nirvāṇa Sūtra* commentaries, *Ta-pan nieh-p'an ching chi-chieh* (T no. 1763). See, for example, T 37.394b–398c, where the concept of the eternally abiding (*ch'ang-chu*) Buddha-nature is introduced.

33. Aside from an extended section on *kan-ying* in Chih-i's *Fa-hua hsüan-i*, the only other deliberate discussion in a Buddhist work (at least to my knowledge) occurs in the *Ta-ch'eng ssu-lun hsüan-i* of the seventh-century San-lun master Chün-cheng. For a survey of these materials see Ikeda Rosan, "Tendai kan'ō shisō no seiritsu igi."

34. For a basic discussion of this genre, its identity, and its features, see Gjert-

however, *kan-ying*—i.e., the responsive interaction between devotee and sacred object—functions as the linchpin. In contrast to its more implicit presence in doctrinal works, the centrality of the *kan-ying* concept to this particular genre reveals a ubiquitous and profound connection with the practical world of ritual worship and devotion.

Chih-i's applications of *kan-ying* terminology accord closely with the pattern of his contemporaries. The concept is discussed systematically in two places—the *Fa-hua hsüan-i* and the section on bodhicitta from the Synopsis of the *Mo-ho chih-kuan*[35]—and invoked with regularity throughout his longer manuals on the four samādhis. In all of these contexts, *kan* carries the familiar verbal sense of "to stimulate," "to instigate," or "to effect" as well as the nominal equivalent of "a stimulus." *Ying* represents its matching "response" or "manifestation." To these, medieval *kan-ying* discourse standardly adds a third term—the noun *chi*. Han-period thinkers postulated the existence of certain "resonantal categories" (*lei*) among the elements of heaven and earth that defined the possibilities of mutual stimulus and response between different objects or actions. *Chi* describes the pivotal element in an array of sympathetically related factors that, when acted on, will stimulate a given response. Hence it may be rendered as "switch," or more abstractly as "impetus" or "catalyst." In its Buddhist context *chi* is disassociated from such correlative categories as yin-yang and the five elemental forces. The *Mo-ho chih-kuan* and *Fa-hua hsüan-i* equate *chi* conceptually as well as in binomial compound with *yüan* ("contributory circumstances" or "conditions")—the term formally adopted by Chinese Buddhists to render the Sanskrit *hetu-pratyāya* or *pratītyasamutpāda*.[36] *Chi* thus may be said to denote the locus of causes and conditions

---

son, *Miraculous Retribution*. For a study of the three earliest texts of this genre extant today—collections associated with the figure of Kuan-yin from the Eastern Chin, Sung, and Liang, respectively—see Makita, *Rikuchō Kanzeonōgenki no kenkyū*. For an overview of the origins of Chinese *kan-ying* thought and its assimilation by Chinese Buddhists, see Sharf, "The *Treasure Store Treatise* (*Pao-tsang lun*) and the Sinification of Buddhism in Eighth Century China."

35. In both instances Chih-i pointedly takes the notion of *kan-ying* beyond its traditional unilateral sense in which the "stimulus" is initiated by the devotee and the "response" follows rather mechanistically from the deity. Through the notion of a "resonantal or symbiotic interaction of stimulus and response" (*kan-ying tao-chiao*), Chih-i makes the case for a mysterious immanence of the Buddhadharma itself working undetected within the manifest spiritual efforts or "stimuli" of the devotee. Various scholars have sought to locate in this concept a theological basis for Chih-i's emphasis on ritual veneration and confession. See Fukushima, "Tendai ni okeru kan'ō no ronri" (esp. p. 256); Ikeda "Tendai kan'ō shisō no seiritsu igi" (esp. pp. 107–108). See also Nitta Masa'aki, "Chigi ni okeru bodaishin no seiritsu konkyo ni tsuite" (esp. pp. 274–276); Nitta takes a slightly different perspective from that of Fukushima and Ikeda.

36. In certain later Chinese Buddhist works the expressions *chi* or *chi-yüan* of-

that constitutes or acts as the efficient "catalyst" behind the action of resonantal "stimulation and response" (*kan-ying*).

The language of *kan-ying* is ubiquitous throughout Chih-i's manuals on the four samādhis. Basic to the *kan-ying* infrastructure is the notion of a resonantal relationship between deity and devotee. Here we find ourselves in a universe much akin to that of the miracle tales. The deities of a given rite are represented in terms of the classic scheme of the twofold and threefold body of the Buddha or the "eternally abiding" (*ch'ang-chu*) and "historically manifest" Three Jewels—that is, the formless and universally coextensive body of dharma and the "response" body (*ying-shen*) of manifest form. The former, activated (*kan*) by the spiritual efforts of deluded beings (or in this case deliberately invoked through ritual), responds (*ying*) in appropriate measure through the expedient vehicle of the latter.

The centrality of this invocatory structure to the four samādhis is illustrated most strikingly in the instructions for mental visualization that accompany key phases of ritual performance. The opening incense offering, the invocation sequence, and the sequences for formal veneration and confession all typically require the aspirant to visualize or invoke mentally the presence of the deity, with the understanding that this act—accompanied by its appropriate physical gestures—will literally bring the deity "face to face" (*mien-ch'ien*). For instance, the *Procedure for the Lotus Samādhi Repentance* offers the following instruction for formal salutation of the deities: "In [this] procedure (*fa*) for salutation of the Buddhas, one mentally recollects with concentrated mind each Buddha that one is venerating. The dharma-body of this Buddha is all-pervading, like empty space. But in response (*ying*) to sentient beings it manifests (*hsien*) physical form and, thus, receives my salutations as though right before my very eyes."[37] In the duly-invoked presence of the deities, the practitioner confesses his sins, prays for spiritual renewal, and reaffirms his commitment to the supreme goal of Buddhahood. Through this realignment with the sacred powers the practitioner is enfolded within the grace or sustaining power of the Buddhas, and the professed goals of the practice are achieved. Hence the entire ritual sequence is not only structured to effect a resonantal "face-to-face" interaction with the deity, but the entire con-

---

ten appear to be used in the sense of "spiritual capacity" or "ability." For Chih-i, at least, the notion of spiritual capacity is more properly conveyed by the term *ken* (*mūla*), as in "wholesome and unwholesome karmic roots" or "endowment" (*shan/o ken*). Whereas the latter is substantive and personal, *chi-yüan* is complex, relational, and temporal. The primary difference between the two is apparent in their respective metaphorical associations: *chi*[-*yüan*] is represented in language of fruition—as formed or unformed, ripe or unripe. *Ken* is spoken of as dull or keen, wholesome or unwholesome.

37. *Fa-hua san-mei ch'an-i*, T 46.951b29.

cept of the rite and its contribution to spiritual progress also hinges closely on this metaphor.[38]

Much of this imagery, of course, draws on the Mahāyāna sūtras themselves, where "face to face" confession and vows before the Buddhas represent the narrative setting for most momentous events on the Mahāyāna path—such as entry into nonretrogressing bodhisattvahood (*avaivartya*) or receipt of the prediction of future Buddhahood (*vyākaraṇa*).[39] Chih-i's ritual structures themselves elaborate on this archetypal Buddhist decorum of the sacred, establishing it as a basic structure through which hierophany is symbolically organized and engaged. As a case in point, the texts of the four samādhis typically subordinate the ultimate ends of samādhi and full bodhisattvahood to the removal of sinful obstructions. The latter, in turn, is contingent on the ability, through performance of rites of veneration and repentance (*li-ch'an*), to "stimulate the Buddhas and sages to descend" (*kan* [*fo* or *sheng*] *hsiang*), or to "stimulate the Buddhas to send forth their radiant light to illumine and remove [sinful obstructions]."[40] Hence obstruction stands in relief against the sacred "presence" of the Buddha or enlightenment, and between the two works the invocatory choreography of veneration, exaltation, confession, and vows.

But, if Chih-i so persistently sets the ritual efficacy of the four samādhis within the framework of *kan-ying*, what does he see to be the essential factors that constitute or contribute to *chi*, the "causal impetus" or "locus of influences" that initiates "stimulus and response"? Here again Chih-i does not offer much in the way of systematic discussion of the subject. Nevertheless, certain patterns are discernible in his works. In the *Procedure for the Vaipulya Samādhi* he singles out two factors that interfere with ritual efficacy: "The Buddhas do not speak falsely," he says. "It is only

38. The structure of the path as presented in the chapters of the Synopsis itself displays this tendency. In lesser chapter 1, arousing the aspiration for enlightenment is conceived in terms of a "manifestation" (*ying*) of the Three Jewels initially "stimulated" (*kan*) by the maturation of the practitioner's "salvific nexus or circumstances" (*chi*). The rites of the four samādhis in lesser chapter 2 represent the practices that set the stage for lesser chapter 3, "manifestation or stimulation of the great result" (*kan ta-kuo*)—i.e., enlightenment. With entry into true bodhisattvahood—i.e., lesser chapter 4—the realized bodhisattva now takes on different appearances and freely "devises or generates teachings" (*ch'i chiao*) in spontaneous response (*ying*) to the stimulus (*kan*) he receives from other beings. With Lesser Chapter 5 the entire operation reverts to the inconceivable totality of Buddhahood.

39. Wayman, "Purification of Sin in Buddhism by Vision and Confession."

40. Equations of this sort appear regularly in Chih-i's ritual texts. See, for example, *Fa-hua san-mei ch'an-i*, T 46.949c13–15, 950b5–7; *Fang-teng san-mei hsing-fa*, T 46.948c18–20; and MHCK, T 46.92a4–15.

when a person is not wholehearted (*chih-hsin*) [in his efforts] or the conditions [of the ritual performance] are not properly met (*yüan pu-chü*) that it is impossible to predict the outcome."[41]

This particular distinction does not appear elsewhere in Chih-i's ritual writings, but its two basic provisions are echoed individually on nearly every page. The importance of proceeding "as the procedure stipulates" (*ju fa*) is often stressed by Chih-i, as is the need to guard against any casualness (*ch'ing-hsin*), incompleteness (*pu-chü, pu-ch'eng*), or impropriety (*pu ju fa*) with respect to ritual decorum. Indeed, in such statements we find the supreme testimony to the centrality and power of ritual form itself. The ritual situation is a potent one, for it places one in the presence of the Buddhas. As its highly formalized gestures are the very means by which one both constructs and defines proper relationship with the sacred truths of the Buddhadharma, to be remiss in their observance not only renders the rite ineffective (*wu li-i*) but also invites further sin and obstruction.

The idea of proper ritual observance, in turn, anticipates the importance of the second factor mentioned by Chih-i—that is, "wholeheartedness," or correct mental attitude. Throughout Chih-i's manuals "solemnity" (*yen-chung*), "utmost sincerity" (*chih-ch'eng*), and "single-minded perseverance or wholeheartedness" (*i-hsin ching-chin, chih-hsin*) are stressed as an integral aspect of "proper" ritual gesture, such that ritual gesture itself is considered incomplete if the requisite mental disposition is not fully present. In many respects this kind of sympathetic choreographing of mind and body further underscores the formalistic character of the four samādhis, especially since the mental typically moves to the rhythm of the physical. By the same token, however, when one begins to ask just what singlemindedness and sincerity actually entail, the mental dimension of performance leads seamlessly into the "inspired" domain of "contemplation of mind and religious principle." With this shift in perspective whole new vistas of interpretation begin to open on the animating power and efficacy of the four samādhis.

This last point brings us to the consideration of a second mode of discourse evident in Chih-i's works on the four samādhis. This second mode distinguishes itself by a tendency to derogate the manifest value and efficacy attached to ritual action and emphasize instead the centrality of interiorized "contemplation." In this respect it sets up a certain tension within both ritual performance and its interpretation.

The "contemplative" mode of discourse revolves around yet another indigenous Chinese philosophical construct long adapted to Buddhist usage—namely, the distinction between "principle" (*li*) and "phenomenon" or "event" (*shih*). The terms *li* and *shih* appear throughout Chih-i's writ-

41. *Fang-teng san-mei hsing-fa*, T 46.948c19–20.

ings, doctrinal as well as liturgical, and their usage there is consistent with that of most other Buddhist thinkers, certain minor points excepted. *Shih*, for Chih-i, designates the "things" and "facts" of ordinary existence, conventionally experienced and conventionally understood. Nevertheless, behind the term's manifest sense lies the uniquely Buddhist understanding of "thing" or "fact" as a composite "event"—the momentary product of "conditioned origination" (*pratītyasamutpāda*) or the complex interaction of various subaltern "causes and conditions" (*hetu-pratyāya*). Hence it is also "phenomenon" and "phenomenal," in the sense that the label *shih* applied to any datum of experience immediately implies the intrinsic presence of a more essential or noumenal perspective. That perspective is represented by *li*.

The term *li* ("principle")—or *hsing-li* ("principle of the essential nature"), as Chih-i often renders it—describes the fundamental reality that is the essence of the "phenomenal object or event" (*shih*). Expressed in terms of its analogue in Indian Buddhist tradition, *li* represents the "absolute truth" (*paramārthasatya*) of the inherent "emptiness" (*śūnyatā*) or "suchness" (*tathatā*) of all dependently originated phenomena. We must take note of the fact, however, that in Chih-i's system of classification of Buddhist doctrine (*p'an-chiao*) no fewer than four different schemes of Buddhist truth are distinguished, to which the terms *li* and *shih* are applied indiscriminately. Thus while the meaning of *shih* remains fairly constant (i.e., the domain of conventional experience), the precise meaning of *li* and its relationship to *shih* can vary considerably depending on context. This range of possibilities should be borne in mind when approaching the use of *li* in contemplative and ritual contexts as well.

Within the particular framework of ritual and meditative practice, *shih* takes on a narrower semantic focus than the generic "phenomenon," "activity," or "event" that is the subject of Chih-i's doctrinal discussions. Here *shih* refers specifically to ritual activity, as understood in full conformity with its special symbolic content, formal structures, and special order of valency. The most significant change, however, is a fundamental shift in the function of the two terms. Rather than the descriptive role that we find in doctrinal discussions, *li* and *shih* themselves become an essential part of the ritual performance. That is to say, the rite itself is undertaken according to the two modes of *li* and *shih*. Thus *li* and *shih* are prescriptive.

This structure is implicit in nearly all of Chih-i's writings on the four samādhis. The *locus classicus* for the majority of T'ien-t'ai authors, however, is Chih-i's *Procedure for the Lotus Samādhi Repentance*.[42] In the open-

42. *Fa-hua san-mei ch'an-i*, T 46.949c22–950a15. A second influential treatment of this dyad, to which we will refer shortly, occurs at the conclusion of the section on the four samādhis in the Synopsis, T 46.18c10–18.

ing sections of the text, "single-minded perseverence or application" (*i-hsin ching-chin*) to the ritual dictates and professed goal of the lotus samādhi is singled out as essential to the rite's success. A formal distinction is then introduced between cultivating single-minded perseverence on the basis of *shih* ("ritual form," "activity") and on the basis of *li* ("principle"). The former is described as, "maintaining single-minded awareness at every juncture, attending continuously to one's performance of the procedure (*fa*) at hand without allowing one's attention to wander." As such, "When one venerates the Buddhas one must single-mindedly venerate the Buddhas, with no other thought in mind; and so it goes for confession, circumambulation, reciting the sūtra, and seated meditation as well. One remains single-minded with respect to all of them."[43]

The approach of "principle" avails itself of the very same sequence of ritual acts (*shih*), but "single-minded perseverence" is construed quite differently. Focus is shifted from the explicit content and intent of "phenomenal activity" to the noetic process of cognition and action itself; and, through Madhyamaka-style critique of that process, *shih* is disabused of its specifically manifest significance and identified with the underlying noumenon of "emptiness" or the "perfect middle." As the text says:

> The practitioner reflects: "No matter what activity I undertake during this period . . . I will maintain full awareness that the mentation generated in the course of action is utterly inseparable [lit. nondual] from the essential nature of mind." How can this be so? When one venerates the Buddha, mind in its essential nature does not arise or perish. Just so, it should be known that in performance of any kind of phenomenal activity (*shih*), mind by nature does not experience the slightest arising or perishing. Contemplating (*kuan*) in this fashion, the practitioner perceives that everything is simply one [single] mind. For the nature of mind [and its objects] from the outset have always been endowed with this property of oneness.[44]

It is important to note that Chih-i is not simply advocating a symbolic or figurative "interiorization" of ritual lore here. On the contrary, the approach of "principle" is identified explicitly—via such terms as "contemplation of mind" (*kuan-hsin*) or "contemplation of principle" (*li-kuan*)—with the consummate Buddhist "deconstructive" enterprise of the contemplation (*kuan*) of emptiness and the development of liberative wisdom. Under these circumstances, the relationship between ritual activity and meditative discernment is reminiscent of the classic Buddhist use of *kasiṇa* or images of the Buddha as a basis (*ālambana*) for developing

43. *Fa-hua san-mei ch'an-i*, T 46.950a4–6.
44. Ibid., T 46.950a8–13.

"meditative calm and concentration" (*samatha*) as a prelude to "insight contemplation" (*vipaśyanā*).

The presence of *li* and *shih* as integral aspects of ritual performance introduces two elements to the four samādhis that contrast strongly with the invocatory formalism described earlier. The first of these is a reductivism reminiscent of *sui-tzu-i*: application of the designation *shih* or "phenomena" to ritual lore derogates its obligatory and hypervalent status by redescribing it in terms that equate it with a generic "phenomenal activity." The contemplative shift introduced by the presence of *li* further identifies the discursive content of ritual action with the very same processes of fictive discrimination and defilement that are responsible for the whole of deluded existence itself. Thus not only does the rite itself become an exercise in delusion of the first order (ritual language and semiological content being the most conventionalized of all conventions), but its ultimate success (enlightenment) also appears to involve nothing short of a *kuan* or insight-style exercise aimed at subversion of and liberation from the very premises of the rite itself.

The practice of recollection of the Buddha described in the pratyutpanna samādhi illustrates this point perfectly. According to the procedures set forth in the *Mo-ho chih-kuan*, the form of the Buddha Amitābha is mentally visualized while the practitioner concurrently invokes his name out loud and circumambulates his altar. Chih-i, on the basis of the *Pratyutpanna-samādhi Sūtra* itself, suggests three factors that contribute to the efficacy of this practice: the merits produced by one's observances of the disciplinary codes and stipulations of the rite, the sustaining power or grace (*adhiṣṭhāna*) of the Buddha Amitābha himself, and the power of one's own meditative concentration and insight. Together these conspire to produce "the samādhi wherein one stands face to face with all the Buddhas of the present age" (i.e., pratyutpanna samādhi itself), through which the aspirant receives the totality of Buddhadharma and enters non-retrogressing bodhisattvahood. Yet the interior contemplation of the Buddha on which the rite in good part hinges is an exercise in "consciousness only" reduction of the first order. Citing the *Pratyutpanna-samādhi Sūtra,* Chih-i instructs the practitioner to reflect: "Whence comes the Buddha [that I see before me]? [From nowhere. He does not come here, and] neither do I go off elsewhere to see him. Whatever I think of, I see. It is my mind that creates the Buddha. It is my mind itself seeing the mind that sees the mind [or thought] of the Buddha. . . . When there are thoughts in the mind it is delusion. When there are no thoughts in the mind it is nirvāṇa."[45]

This apparent denigration of religious motivation and "works" leads us to the second of our two elements: the relegation of ritual to a psycho-

45. MHCK, T 46.12c20–24.

logically therapeutic, as opposed to a formally prescriptive, role. Throughout the four samādhis section of the *Mo-ho chih-kuan*, Chih-i often suggests that "discernment of mind" (*kuan-hsin*) or "discernment of principle" (*li-kuan*) is the primary animating factor responsible for successful performance of the samādhi rites. Such an emphasis appears in his independent manuals on the four samādhis as well.[46] By way of contrast, the phenomenal dictates of ritual lore and procedure are styled "phenomenal techinques that assist awakening or the path" (*shih-hsiang chu-tao fang-fa*). Thus ritual form becomes a therapeutic expedient, whose essential role is psychological service to the interiorized contemplation of mind and principle. Dhāraṇī incantations, recitation of sūtras, and veneration and confession before the Buddhas—central ingredients of the rites of the four samādhis—are routinely prescribed in T'ien-t'ai meditative theory as "antidotes" (*tui-chih*) to impediments brought on by demons (māras) or evil karmic influences. The ritual sequence of invocation, salutation, confession, transfer of merits, and profession of vows performed "face to face" before the Buddhas is itself presented as an orchestration of great cathartic power capable of calling up and expelling (*tung-chang*) the most stubborn psychological obstructions.[47] Indeed, operating through most of Chih-i's writings on meditation we find an unwritten rule of thumb, where the heavier the impediment or the less advanced one is in practice, the heavier the use of ritual form and structure; the lighter the impediment and more skilled in practice, the less need there is for such "expedient" manipulations.[48] This distinction likewise resonates with the differentiation between "keen capacity" (*li-ken*) and "dull capacity" (*tun-ken*), which often carries polemical overtones, as when it is used to qualify the relationship between elite and vulgar religious practice or sectarian ideological stances. Putting the whole picture together, Chih-i states in one of the most celebrated passages of the Synopsis chapter:

> The four forms of samādhi differ in explicit procedure (*fang-fa*) but are the same in their contemplation of principle (*li-kuan*). Basically the procedures found in the foregoing three practices [i.e., other than *sui-tzu-i*] make liberal use of ancillary techniques designed to assist [realization of] the way (*chu-tao fa-men*). [In so doing] they also

46. On occasion the term *kuan-hui* "wisdom or insight born of discernment" is counterposed with "phenomenal activity" (*shih*) in place of "discernment of principle or mind." See, for example, *Ch'ing kuan-shih-yin ch'an-fa, Chin-kuang-ming ch'an-fa,* and *Fang-teng ch'an-fa* in *Kuo-ching pai-lu,* T 46.795b16, 796a4, and 796b22, respectively.

47. See Stevenson, "The T'ien-t'ai Four Forms of Samādhi," pp. 401–418, on the characteristics of the confessional element.

48. See ibid., pp. 130–140.

> set in motion obstructions to the way. As [the samādhi of] freely following one's thought is comparatively meager in the use of such procedures, it produces this situation to a lesser degree. Now, if one understands [a practice] solely in terms of the supportive role that its given procedures (*fang-fa*) are alleged to play, then its phenomenal [ritual] program (*shih-hsiang*) will prove ineffective [in prompting realization of the way]. But if one understands contemplation of principle (*li-kuan*), there will be no phenomenal feature (*shih-hsiang*) that will not penetrate [to realization]. Again, if one does not grasp the basic idea behind this contemplation of principle, even the assistance to the way promised by these phenomenal features will not prove successful. However, once one understands contemplation of principle, the samādhis associated with these phenomenal programs will be achieved effortlessly. Individuals who cultivate the way primarily on the basis of phenomenal content will be able to apply themselves effectively while inside the sanctuary but will not be able to maintain this when they come out. In the case of the [samādhi] of freely following one's thought (*sui-tzu-i*), however, there is no break [between the two]. It is only in the first three samādhis that explicit procedures are employed; but the contemplation of principle runs through all four.[49]

With this passage Chih-i concludes his discussion of the four samādhis. In so doing he offers a morphology of religious praxis in which discernment of "principle" represents the central animating power. By contrast, the "phenomenal" content of ritual praxis is demoted to a status no different from that of any other form of conscious discrimination—at best an expedient to entice the spiritually naive, at worst an object of misdirected belief and bondage. We are back again, it would seem, to a model of religious cultivation tailored closely to the highly rationalistic *sui-tzu-i*.

The Home-Mountain and Off-Mountain Debates of the Sung

In discussing the *Mo-ho chih-kuan* and Chih-i's ritual manuals, I have deliberately accentuated the tension between the invocatory and contemplative modes of T'ien-t'ai practice in order to clarify the lines along which they are played out as competing ideologies in later T'ien-t'ai history. Indeed, the problematic of the relative importance of cultic practice versus contemplative discernment was at the heart of the debates that animated the T'ien-t'ai tradition during the Sung dynasty (960–1279).

The tenth-century revival of T'ien-t'ai teaching in southeast China initiated a series of broad-reaching debates over doctrine and practice that repeatedly polarized the T'ien-t'ai community for the next 300 years.

49. MHCK, T 46.18c10–18.

These debates, referred to in T'ien-t'ai sectarian literature as the "home-mountain" (*shan-chia*) and "off-mountain" (*shan-wai*) controversies, are commonly distinguished into two historical phases. The earlier of these two exchanges was sparked by writings of the off-mountain master Tz'u-kuang Wu-en (912–986) and perpetuated intermittently through several generations of Wu-en's successors—notably, the masters Feng-hsien Yüan-ch'ing (d. 997), Fan-t'ien Ch'ing-chao (963–1017), Ku-shan Chih-yüan (976–1022), and their immediate disciples. The home-mountain position was defined and championed primarily by Ssu-ming Chih-li (960–1028) and a handful of close disciples. The controversy itself spanned the greater part of his career and provided the most important impetus shaping his thought and works. The second series of exchanges were internal to the emergent home-mountain line of Chih-li itself. Basically they comprise two separate (although not wholly unrelated) events: an initial controversy prompted by the "defection" of one of Chih-li's most promising disciples, Cha-ch'uan Jen-yüeh (992–1064), to a modified off-mountain position, followed several decades later by a second shift in doctrinal loyalties on the part of an eminent third-generation descendant of Chih-li, Shen-chih Ts'ung-i (1042–1091).

The terms "home-mountain" and "off-mountain" are highly polemicized labels that did not actively enter the T'ien-t'ai lexicon until the thirteenth century, when descendants of Chih-li succeeded in establishing him as the "mid-period reviver" (*chung-hsing*) of the orthodox legacy of Chan-jan.[50] Although the labels testify to the formative impact that these controversies had on later T'ien-t'ai identity, they also lend a misleading sense of partisanship and finality to a situation that was far less rigidly delineated than we might imagine. All parties involved shared a common patriarchal history, scriptural canon, institutions, and system of thought and practice. Despite their exegetical squabbles, there is no indication that any one faction ever thought to compel the other to forfeit its right to identify with the T'ien-t'ai heritage.[51] Moreover, as Andō Toshio has shown, views perilously close to those of the notorious off-mountain figures appeared frequently in the home-mountain camp without causing

50. See the construction of lineal houses in the thirteenth-century histories *Fo-tsu t'ung-chi* (T 49.194a–b, 241a) and *Shih-men cheng-t'ung* (HTC 130.826b–833b, 841a–848a). This hagiographical and historiographical feat was accomplished mainly by monks of the Kuang-chih (i.e., Chih-p'an and Tsung-hsiao) and Nan-p'ing (K'o-kuan, Tsung-yin) lines descended from Chih-li. See Shimaji, *Tendai kyōgaku-shi*, pp. 319–322; see also Andō, *Tendai shisō-shi*, pp. 137–150, 194–238.

51. This is even evident in the treatment that the off-mountain groups receive in later histories such as *Shih-men cheng-t'ung* (see HTC 130.826–833, 841–846) and *Fo-tsu t'ung-chi* (See T 49.204a–205b, 241a–242c). Although peripheral to the main line, they are nevertheless included within the sectarian fold.

any particular stir.[52] It is thus better to think of the controversies of the early Sung not so much as full-fledged internecine rivalries as the exploration of diverse interpretive possibilities at a time when the strict ideological boundaries imposed by later T'ien-t'ai historians had not yet been clearly drawn.

The early home-mountain and off-mountain exchanges began with a disagreement over which of two divergent recensions of a treatise on the *Sūtra of Golden Light* (*Suvarṇaprabhāsa Sūtra*) was the authentic version composed by Chih-i. This seemingly innocuous text-critical dispute hid in its depths substantial rifts in the interpretation of T'ien-t'ai thought and practice. In short order the original occasion for conflict reticulated into some half dozen points of intense theoretical issue, several of which generated a continuing literary exchange between the different figures involved. Over the four decades that followed, Chih-li defined the principal center of the home-mountain camp. From the start, however, the off-mountain masters were considerably more dispersed, both in personnel as well as outlook—a situation that at times makes it difficult (and even potentially misleading) to speak of a systematic off-mountain program. Nevertheless, certain common motifs and strategies of interpretation are detectable.

The off-mountain position is characterized by the tendency to read Chih-i and Chan-jan from a strongly tathāgatagarbha-oriented perspective. This interpretation was often substantiated with borrowings from such works as the apocryphal *Śūraṅgama Sūtra* (*Shou-leng-yen ching*) and the *Awakening of Faith* (*Ta-sheng ch'i-hsin lun*)[53] as well as the sophisticated syntheses of Ch'an and Hua-yen promulgated by Ch'ing-liang Ch'eng-kuan (738–839) and Kuei-feng Tsung-mi (780–841).[54] Taking Chih-i's famous metaphor of the "three-thousand realms in an instant of thought" (*i-nien san-ch'ien*), off-mountain masters equated the "single instant of thought" with the boundless and undifferentiated suchness that is the intrinsic nature of mind and phenomenal existence. Adopting an expression that originated with the Ch'an master Shen-hui and was further developed by Tsung-mi, they dubbed it "the single instant of thought as pure numinal awareness" (*i-nien ling-chih*).[55] In terms of med-

52. Andō, *Tendai shisō-shi*, pp. 37–41.

53. *Ta-fo-ting ju-lai mi-yin hsiu-cheng liao-i chu p'u-sa wan-hsing shou-leng-yen ching*, T no. 945, and *Ta-sheng ch'i-hsin lun*, T no.1666. Both are important sources for Chinese tathāgatagarbha thought, especially during the late T'ang and Sung.

54. For the definitive study of Tsung-mi's life and thought, see Gregory, *Tsung-mi and the Sinification of Buddhism*.

55. See Andō, *Tendai-gaku*, p. 338. These views of mind are set forth most clearly in the two opening sections of Yüan-ch'ing's *Shih pu-erh men shih chu chih* (on the topics of "elucidation of the nondual reality of mind only" and "elucidation of conditioned origination based on misperception and enlightenment to the

itative theory, this position translated into a subitism reminiscent of developments in the "southern" schools of Ch'an. Chih-i's perfect and sudden calming and contemplation (*yüan-tun chih-kuan*) came to be defined as "contemplation of the true mind" (*chen-hsin kuan*), where simple "awareness" (*chih*) of the true nature itself constituted the driving force of religious praxis and any additional effort at cultivation or reliance on the written word (including such canonical works as the *Mo-ho chih-kuan*) was eschewed as fruitless.

Concerning the role of the four samādhis and their ritual and cultic programs, the off-mountain master Ch'ing-chao asserts unequivocably that only the approach of what he calls "immediate practice" (*yüeh-hsing*) of discernment of principle (*li-kuan*) can "effect realization proper" (*hsiu-cheng*).[56] Without this essential animating insight, neither "phenomenal ritual form" (*shih-hsiang*) nor manipulation of "dharmas and their marks" (*fa-hsiang*)[57] can accomplish this end.[58] Since "only the contemplation of 'immediate practice' directly reveals the essential nature," Ch'ing-chao reasons, "one may dispense with the contemplation of mind on the basis of dharmas [and phenomenal distinctions]."[59]

By contrast, the ritual manuals and references to the four samādhis that abound in the writings of Chih-li, Tsun-shih, and their home-mountain compatriots are all but absent from the records of the off-mountain masters. Since the literary legacy of the off-mountain masters has not fared well at the hand of later tradition, however, it is difficult to say whether this situation reflects a complete disavowal of traditional forms of cultic practice on the part of the off-mountain lines. Nonetheless, it is

---

dharmadhātu"), HTC 100.108a–111a. For a discussion of Shen-hui's notion of "numinal knowing" and its development in the thought of Tsung-mi, see Gregory, "Tsung-mi and the Single Word 'Awareness' (*chih*)."

56. The early off-mountain demonstration of this point was achieved primarily through a tripartite expansion of the distinction between *li* and *shih* derived from Chan-jan's *Chih-kuan i-li*: (1) the approach of "immediate practice" (*yüeh-hsing*), which is "equivalent to the marvelous contemplation of principle (*li*) itself," (2) contemplation "based on dharmas and their marks" (*yüeh-fa-hsiang*), and (3) contemplation or practice that "resorts to phenomenal [ritual and cultic] distinctions" (*t'o-shih-hsiang*). The latter two categories are both *shih* or "phenomenal" approaches to practice. The first of the three categories alone is equated with the instantaneous contemplation of principle (*li*) or the "true mind"; see Chan-jan, *Chih-kuan i-li*, T 46.458a10–16. The scheme is applied at length in the off-mountain sections of the *Ssu-ming shih-i shu*, the record of Chih-li's ten-point refutation of the early off-mountain masters Yüan-ch'ing and Ch'ing-chao.

57. Contemplation of "dharmas and marks" here refers specifically to the elaborate contemplations set forth in the ten modes of discernment of the MHCK.

58. *Ssu-ming shih-i shu*, T 46.832b11–13 and 842c13–15.

59. Ibid., T 46.8329–13.

clear that the off-mountain masters placed such lore low on the ladder of spiritual capacity and praxis. Yüan-ch'ing and Ch'ing-chao, for instance, consider ritual structure and cult as little more than a didactic metaphor to inspire the novice practitioner to "orient himself to a proper understanding of the foundation of true practice" or a mnemonic tag to encourage old hands at contemplation "not to forget the fundamental [thrust] of cultivation."[60] In short, its function is little different from that of reading scripture.

Such a stance pushes the off-mountain understanding of the four samādhis in the distinct direction of *sui-tzu-i* and the view of some of the modern scholars cited earlier. Cultic lore and procedure cease to be centrally defining features of the four samādhis; and in their stead a simple physical regimen—especially constant sitting—is singled out for the support (*yüan*) it provides to an interiorized discernment of principle (*li*). The cloisters of the four samādhis themselves are considered mainly the domain of the novice, who employs them in an initial struggle to achieve the leap of faith and insight that will establish him in the "contemplation of the true mind." After this principle of "numinal awareness" (*ling-chih*) has been duly activated, the real brunt of cultivation devolves around the single practice of *sui-tzu-i*, through which one proceeds from the sequestered to the open, from the interior (*nei*) to the exterior (*wai*), and melds numinal insight with the manifold activities of daily life.[61]

Chih-li objects to the off-mountain treatment of the four samādhis on several grounds, not the least of which is their disregard for patriarchal precedent set forth in such works as the *Mo-ho chih-kuan* and Chih-i's ritual manuals.[62] Chih-li's critique does not stop here, however, but ultimately takes its stance in a fervent affirmation of the intrinsic potency of ritual cult itself. To this end he deliberately counters the off-mountain position with a forceful assertion that the ritual programs and lore of the four samādhis in and of themselves can effect full enlightenment, "without having to await [formal] pursuit of calming and contemplation [to achieve their effect]."[63] In proof of his point he frequently cites Chih-i's *Procedure for the Lotus Samādhi Repentance*, where it is claimed that the highest form of realization is accessible through "mere ritual recitation of the *Lotus Sūtra*, without entering into samādhi."[64]

60. Ibid., T 46.832b22–25, 843b19–23.

61. Ibid., T 46.838c6–839c18. This scheme of practice is, again, based on a key discussion of *sui-tzu-i* and its relationship to *li* and *shih* developed in Chan-jan's *Chih-kuan i-li*, T 46.452a20–b14.

62. *Ssu-ming shih-i shu*, T 46.845c23–27.

63. This capacity he limits to those with keen spiritual endowments; ibid., T 46.843b10–11.

64. Ibid., T 46.843b15–18. See also Chih-li, *Ch'ien shou yen ta-pei hsin chou hsing-fa*, T 46.978a21–22. The phrase comes originally from the *Kuan p'u-hsien p'u-sa*

Doubtless this enthusiasm for cultic practice finds an immediate parallel in the extraordinary attention that the practice of the four samādhis receives in the personal lives of Chih-li and his compatriot, Tsun-shih, as well as in their communities.[65] Such evidence suggests that Chih-li's impassioned defense of the four samādhis in the home-mountain/off-mountain debates echoes the voice of a seasoned devotee rather than that of a calculating patriarchal theologian. Still, Chih-li's interest in the soteriological value of ritual is not without its resonances in other aspects of his thought, which makes it difficult (and certainly unwise) to separate Chih-li the religious practitioner from Chih-li the scholar arbitrarily. One such liaison between doctrinal theory and ritual praxis may be seen in Chih-li's attempt to read the classic T'ien-t'ai formula of "three thousand realms in an instant of thought" (*i-nien san-ch'ien*) as an outright affirmation of the ontological value of form and particularity. Chih-li's predecessors and the off-mountain opponents tended toward a tathāgatagarbha-based model of perfection, where the inconceivable "encompassment" (*chü*) of the three thousand is posited in terms of an undifferentiated suchness of mind (*hsin-chü*), from which all fictions of particularity arise and within which they are ultimately resolved. By contrast, Chih-li gravitated toward a theory of "encompassment [of totality] within particulate features themselves" (*hsiang-chü*), such that in each and every mark, "all marks manifest simultaneously in perfect repleteness" (*hsiang hsiang wan-ran*).[66] Such an affirmation of the intrinsic sanctity of form would seem to hold great promise for ritual practice. But to appreciate this connection, it is best to turn to a different yet closely related area of Chih-li's thought—namely, the speculations on the immanence of the Buddha that are developed in his Pure Land writings, especially those works in which he critiques positions reminiscent of the later off-mountain figure, Cha-ch'uan Jen-yüeh.

The cult of Amitābha and the hope of rebirth in his Pure Land of Sukhāvatī were endemic to the rites of the four samādhis even in Chih-i's day.[67] However, these elements tended to hold second place to the

---

hsing-fa ching (T 9.389c22–24) and appears in *Fa-hua san-mei ch'an-i* at T 46.953c28.

65. See also the biographies of Chih-li and Tsun-shih in *Ssu-ming tsun-che chiao-hsing lu* (T 46.917b–918a, 919b–920a) and *Shih-men cheng-t'ung* (HTC 130.763b–768a, 834a–838a).

66. This development is discussed at length by Andō Toshio in his *Tendai shōgu shisō* and *Tendai shisō-shi*. See also Hibi, *Tōdai Tendai-gaku kenkyū*, pp. 315–381.

67. Amitābha is the central deity of the pratyutpanna samādhi. On the basis of the *Pratyuptpanna-samādhi Sūtra*, the MHCK alludes to the possibility of rebirth in Sukhāvatī. Similarly, Chih-i's *Procedure for the Lotus Samādhi Repentance* (*Fa-hua san-mei ch'an-i*, T 46.953b23–25) concludes with a generic prayer or vow to be welcomed into Sukhāvatī by Amitābha at the time of death. Around the time of

more immediate goal of samādhi and realization of the liberative vision of the middle truth. With the emergence of a distinctive Pure Land spirituality during the T'ang, specific interest in Amitābha and his realm of Sukhāvatī became increasingly pronounced in T'ien-t'ai circles, as it did in Ch'an and other traditions as well. By the time of the T'ien-t'ai revival at the end of the tenth century, Pure Land-oriented repentance and visualization rites were regularly included in the cultic repertoire of the four samādhis.

Three principal sources provided the basis for these new rites: the sixteen[68] contemplations of the popular *Kuan wu-liang-shou fo ching* (Sūtra on the Visualization of the Buddha Amitāyus) and two T'ang-period T'ien-t'ai Pure Land treatises falsely attributed to Chih-i—i.e., the *Ching-t'u shih-i lun* (Treatise [Elucidating] Ten Doubts About the Pure Land) and *Kuan wu-liang-shou fo ching shu* (Commentary to the Sūtra on the Visualization of the Buddha Amitāyus).[69] Through their common tendency to promote the specific soteriological end of rebirth in Sukhāvatī within the generalized framework of samādhic contemplation of the Buddha, these works heightened the inherent tension between cult ritual and meditative discernment in the four samādhis and occasioned further controversies.

The falling out between Chih-li and Jen-yüeh, which precipitated the latter's departure and his subsequent "expulsion" as an off-mountain renegade, centered around precisely such an issue.[70] As the story would have it, a dispute developed between Jen-yüeh and his brother disciple Chih-kuang Shang-hsien (d.u.) over the nature of the Amitābha meditation expounded in the *Kuan wu-liang-shou fo ching*. Ostensibly it centered around the key passage in the eighth contemplation, in which the practitioner (after having established the visualization of the Buddha's image) is instructed to reflect, "This mind creates the Buddha (*shih hsin tso fo*).

Chan-jan, Amitābha also became the central deity of the one-practice samādhi. For discussion of these points and subsequent Pure Land developments in T'ang period T'ien-t'ai, see Andō, "Tendai Chigi no jōdokyō."

68. Some traditions identify the number of contemplations as thirteen. T'ien-t'ai includes the descriptions of the three basic grades of rebirth, thereby making a total of sixteen.

69. Chih-i, *Ching-t'u shih-i lun*, T no. 1961, and Chih-i, *Kuan wu-liang-shou fo ching shu*, T no. 1750 (in one fascicle), not to be confused with Shan-tao's (613–681) famous four-fascicle commentary of the same title (T no. 1753). For details concerning these two works and the date of their composition, see Satō, *Tendai daishi no kenkyū*, pp. 567–601 and 619–643.

70. Jen-yüeh, originally one of the most promising disciples of Chih-li, contributed substantially to Chih-li's critiques of the off-mountain masters before he changed his position and parted ways with Chih-li. Later tradition especially castigates him for his betrayal of the relationship between master and disciple.

This mind is the Buddha (*shih hsin shih fo*)."[71] Chan-jan, commenting on a similar passage in the four samādhis section of the *Mo-ho chih-kuan*, waffles on the issue of whether visions of the Buddha seen in samādhi are mind-created (i.e., hallucinatory) or revelatory manifestations of the Buddhas themselves, thereby admitting both possibilities.[72] Jen-yüeh, however, maintained that the eidetic image of Sukhāvatī and the Buddha Amitābha perceived in meditation is nothing but a deluded projection of the mind—a simulacrum intended to do no more than demonstrate the "mind-only" nature of existence and the intrinsic enlightenment of the mind itself. Hence he characterized Pure Land practice as a technique to "subsume the Buddha within the mind" (*she-fo kuei-hsin*). Shang-hsien is alleged to have taken the opposite stance, stressing the primacy of the Buddha over the subjective mind with the notion that "one subsumes the mind within the Buddha" (*she-hsin kuei-fo*). Chih-li, who was asked to adjudicate, emphasized the notion of the perfect interfusion and equality of the "three dharmas"—the Buddha, the subjective mind, and sentient beings—and dismissed both positions as extreme.[73]

Although the tale is probably apocryphal, the positions attributed to the three mirror the range of interpretations characteristic of Pure Land discourse of the period. Shang-hsien's thesis, for example, is reminiscent of Shan-tao's own views on the Amitābha visualization of the *Kuan wu-liang-shou fo ching*.[74] More importantly, it is echoed among various Sung T'ien-t'ai masters—such as Tsun-shih and descendants in the line of Chih-li's disciple Shen-chao Pen-ju (982–1051)—known for their impassioned devotion to Amitābha and the goal of rebirth in the Pure Land.[75] Jen-yüeh's stance conforms not only to the basic "mind-only" view of the off-mountain monks but also to the position commonly espoused by any number of Ch'an masters of the day, including the eminent Ch'ang-lu Tsung-tse.[76]

71. *Kuan wu-liang-shou fo ching*, T 12.343a21.

72. See MHCK, T 46.12c20–24, and *Chih-kuan fu-hsing ch'uan-hung chüeh*, T 46.187b11–24.

73. The tale appears in biographies of Jen-yüeh and accounts of his controversy with Chih-li; see Andō, *Tendai-gaku*, pp. 352, 360–367; *Fo-tsu t'ung-chi*, T 49.193b; and *Ssu-ming tsun-che chiao-hsing lu*, T 46.916b.

74. Shan-tao states in his *Kuan wu-liang-shou fo ching shu* (T 37.267a4–6): "There are some practitioners who . . . make [this meditation] into a consciousness-only contemplation of the dharma body or a contemplation of the Buddha-nature that is pure in its essential self-nature. Their interpretations are truly in error."

75. See Andō, *Tendai shisō-shi*, pp. 60–80 and 127–130.

76. For a biography of Tsung-tse and discussion of his Pure Land interests, see Bielefeldt, *Dōgen's Manuals of Zen*, pp. 66–70. For additional studies of Sung

Chih-li objected to any view that would fracture the perfect interfusion of the three dharmas of Buddha, mind, and sentient being or would otherwise docetically divide the omnipresence and omniscience of Buddhahood into a formless body of enlightened dharma-esssence and a phenomenal body of manifest response. Such interpretations he dismissed as reflecting the inferior tathāgatagarbha-oriented teaching of the "separate doctrine" (*pieh-chiao*) rather than the true "perfect teaching" (*yüan-chiao*). In keeping with his multiperspectival view of the perfect middle—i.e., his notion of the mutual encompassment of totality within individual marks (*hsiang-chü*)—Chih-li advocated an equally dynamic concept of the Buddha, where "the three bodies [of dharma-essence, retribution, and manifest response] marvelously interpenetrate, such that any one is simultaneously identical with all three."[77] In the course of further controversy with Jen-yüeh and others on this same subject, Chih-li came to the radical assertion that both the dharma body (*fa-shen*) and the highest domain of the Buddha (i.e., the "realm of eternal quiescence and radiance," *ch'ang-chi-kuang-t'u*) are not an undifferentiated suchness but an inconceivable totality in which the marks of phenomenal existence are preserved replete within them (*fa-shen yu-hsiang, chi-kuang yu-hsiang*).

This emphasis on the immanence of Buddhahood within phenomenal existence held significant implications for the efficacy of ritual and cultic form as well, implications that Chih-li exploited in his discussions of the sixteen contemplations of Amitābha and the other rites of the four samādhis. On the basis of his peculiar reading of the T'ien-t'ai notion of the inseparability of Buddha, mind, and sentient being, Chih-li advocated a unique "resonance of stimulus and response" (*kan-ying tao-chiao*) that operated between contemplation of the mind and contemplation of the Buddha, such that mental contemplation of the "phenomenal" features (*shih*) of Amitābha Buddha's form (known as *cheng* or "primary [form]") and the Pure Land (known as *i* or "environmental setting") has the power to "stimulate" (*kan*) the "nature of Buddha *qua* mind" to "manifest" (*ying*) as the "vision of wondrous principle" (*miao-li-kuan*).[78] As Chih-i explains in his subcommentary to the *Kuan wu-liang-shou fo ching shu*:

---

period Ch'an figures with Pure Land interests see Andō, *Tendai shisō-shi*, pp. 127–130, 335–336.

77. Chih-li, *Kuan wu-liang-shou fo ching shu miao-tsung ch'ao*, T 37.221c16. (Hereafter cited as *Miao-tsung ch'ao*.) The text is a subcommentary to the *Commentary on the Sūtra of the Visualization of Buddha Amitāyus* attributed to Chih-i. According to the *Ssu-ming tsun-che chiao-hsing lu* (T 46.858a), it was composed in 1021, some years after Jen-yüeh had departed.

78. See Chih-li, *Kuan-ching jung-hsin chieh* (in *Ssu-ming tsun-che chiao-hsing lu*), T 46.866b.

> The Mahāyāna practitioner knows that one's own mind contains within it the nature of all the Buddhas. Taking [mind] as the ground or sphere [of discernment] and cultivating [mindful recollection of] the Buddha [on its basis], the features of the Buddha thereupon appear. Here [in the sixteen discernments] we contemplate the primary [form] and environmental [setting] of Amitābha as the object of discernment. [This practice] perfumes the essential nature of mind, and the primary [form of the Buddha] and environmental [realm] of Sukhāvatī inherently replete within the mind manifest due to this perfuming.[79]

Then again, anticipating the objections of persons who would exclude the phenomenal features of cult (*shih*) altogether from the domain of the inconceivable three truths (*li*), Chih-li remarks in his *Kuan-ching jung-hsin chieh* (Explanation of the Interfusion of Mind [and Buddha-visualization] in the Sūtra on the Visualization [of the Buddha Amitāyus]):

> People suspect that the [principle of the] three views would be impeded by the visualization of the [phenomenal] primary form and environmental setting [of Amitāyus and Sukhāvatī]. Here I will say outright that the three views [themselves] are able to manifest this form and setting. As the three contemplations gradually increase in strength, the primary form and environmental setting become progressively clearer. Because they share a common substance within the one mind, they mutually issue forth [with it].[80]

For Chih-li the entire cultic program of the sixteen contemplations of the *Sūtra on the Visualization of the Buddha Amitāyus*—from the contemplation of the setting sun and *vaiḍurya* terrain, to the phenomenal details of the nine grades of rebirth—becomes a vehicle for discernment of principle (*li-kuan*). This differs from Jen-yüeh and various other Sung figures of the "mind-only" persuasion, who advocated that either all sixteen contemplations or all but the ninth contemplation of Amitābha's inconceivable form and radiance were "phenomenal."[81]

The possibilities that this line of thinking held for affirming the invocatory side of ritual practice are demonstrated in various ways in Chih-li's writings. Essential to understanding Chih-li's views on this subject is a qualitative distinction that he makes between cultic phenomenal content

79. Chih-li, *Miao-tsung ch'ao*, T 37.197c.

80. In *Ssu-ming tsun-che chiao-hsing lu*, T 46.867b. The treatise was composed in 1014, apparently prior to Jen-yüeh's departure. See ibid., T 46.857c.

81. See Shioiri Ryōdō, "Chō-Sō Tendai ni okeru jissen-men no kōsatsu," p. 79. Off-mountain figures such as Yüan-ch'ing, Ch'ing-chao, and Chih-yüan dismissed all sixteen discernments as "phenomenal." See Nakayama Shōkō, "Chō-Sō Tendai to jōdokyō," p. 207.

that is conducive to principle (*shun-li shih-hsiang*) and profane phenomenal content that contravenes principle (*ni-li shih-hsiang*). The former—exemplified by the sacred iconography of Amitābha and the Pure Land—resonates with the principle of the perfect middle and hence has the power to invoke principle when engaged. But the latter, because it involves "defiled and obstructed features" (*jan-ai chih hsiang*) that are solely the product of the saṃsāric mind, is not only powerless to manifest principle but must also ultimately be refuted and transformed. "When one engages phenomena in a way that contravenes principle," Chih-li tells us, "then illumination causes those phenomena to be effaced. But if contemplation proceeds in conformity with principle, it actually causes [phenomena] to become fully replete."[82]

Chih-li attributes the same invocatory potential to the cultic lore of the other rites of the four samādhis. Thus the *Lotus Sūtra* in the lotus repentance and the dhāraṇī incantations and visualizations in the Avalokiteśvara and vaipulya repentances are all classed as phenomena conducive to principle. The one notable exception is the practice of *sui-tzu-i*, which is excluded from the fold by the fact that it possesses no such cultic content or invocatory potential, being grounded in the discernment of "defiled" activities.[83]

Chih-li's position contrasts strongly with that of his compatriots in the off-mountain camp. He reevaluates the simplistic distinction between *li* as an interiorized principle of enlightenment and *shih* as deluded discrimination or "outer" activity, thereby giving special status to the semiotic content of cult and affirming the invocatory function of "stimulus and response" (*kan-ying*). This emphasis carries over into the liturgical forms and syntax that provide the structure for ritual performance as well. Much in keeping with his passion for the practices of the four samādhis, Chih-li's writings repeatedly stress the necessity for what he calls "the conjoined cultivation of primary and ancillary [techniques]" (*cheng-chu ho-hsing* or *cheng-chu shuang-hsing*)—that is, the coordinated use of "phenomenal" ritual forms of veneration and confession with "discernment of principle."[84] Speaking of the Amitābha rites, for example, Chih-li explains: "Contemplation of the marvelous is primary; purificatory acts [of confession, and the like] are ancillary. When primary and ancillary are cultivated in unison, one can manifest (*kan*) the four levels of Pure Land and perceive the threefold body of Amitābha."[85] The frequency of

82. *Kuan-ching jung-hsin chieh* (in *Ssu-min tsun-che chiao-hsing lu*), T 46.867b.

83. See ibid., T 46.866b and 867b; see also *Miao-tsung ch'ao*, T 37.195b, 202b.

84. See, for example, his preface to the *Miao-tsung ch'ao*, T 37.195c2–4; and *Hsiu-ch'an yao-chih* (*Ssu-ming tsun-che chiao-hsing lu*), T 46.868b21–23 and 869b12–18.

85. Chih-li, *Miao tsung ch'ao*, T 37.196c.

such statements, combined with Chih-li's promotion of the ritual manuals of the four samādhis, has prompted Shioiri Ryōdō and others to single out this emphasis on ritual penance as one of the distinguishing features of Chih-li's thought on religious practice.[86]

The positions on the four samādhis and ritual cult that we have outlined here are historically specific to the series of home-mountain and off-mountain controversies that split the T'ien-t'ai tradition during the Sung period. As two discontinuous moments in T'ien-t'ai history, when differing interpretive stances were carved out of a single collective discourse, they illustrate the way in which ambiguities within the *Mo-ho chih-kuan* continued to play themselves out as fundamental paradigms that shaped T'ien-t'ai discourse. Even identifying these positions too narrowly with a given historical event—such as the home-mountain and off-mountain debates—runs the risk of historicizing a process that is essentially paradigmatic in nature. As Andō Toshio has noted in his monumental studies of Sung-period T'ien-t'ai, the off-mountain and home-mountain ideologies were not nearly so demarcated from one another as their labels imply. For, indeed, there are numerous instances in which views typical of the off-mountain figures or the alleged Pure Land essentialist Chih-kuang Shang-hsien appear among Chih-li's descendants without touching off any cry of heterodoxy.

The two modes of discourse that we have emphasized in our discussion of T'ien-t'ai religious practice also resonate closely with other well-known dichotomies in Chinese Buddhism, including that between Ch'an and Pure Land and the attendant distinction between "elite" and "popular" Buddhism. Such categories rest as much on the normative conventions of East Asian Buddhist historiography as they do on the "projections" of modern Western scholars. A growing recognition of both facts—but especially an appreciation of the rhetorical nature of sectarian ideology and historiography—has led to a rethinking of the basic criteria by which we describe "tradition" in Chinese Buddhist history. The result has been a shift toward an appreciation of sectarian tradition as an integral part of a larger cultural discourse. Placed properly within its extended cultural context, the seemingly self-contained world of a particular religious "school" (such as T'ien-t'ai, Ch'an, or Pure Land) reveals itself to be involved in a ceaseless dialogue with the Buddhist tradition at large. As Bernard Faure has noted in regard to Ch'an, the familiar fault line so rigidly dividing Ch'an and the "mediate" traditions of popular Buddhism and Pure Land "did pass not only between them but also through them."[87] Hence, the properties by which we typically differentiate Ch'an and Pure Land, for example, as two utterly distinct entities are not so

86. Shioiri, "Chō-Sō Tendai ni okeru jissen men no kōsatsu," p. 81.
87. See Faure, *The Rhetoric of Immediacy*, p. 79.

much the exclusive feature of one tradition or the other as they are a part of a larger discourse that includes them both.

The *Mo-ho chih-kuan* and the T'ien-t'ai legacy of ritual and contemplative discourse offer a significant contribution to this newly emerging understanding of Chinese Buddhism and the paradigmatic structures that shaped it. To begin with, Chih-i's works anticipate, within a singular field of discourse, the Ch'an and Pure Land rift well before this polarity ever took form as discrete sectarian ideologies. Hence it represents one important instance where the fault line, so to speak, clearly runs within rather than between traditions. Even more compelling, however, is the rich body of material that has grown up around the *Mo-ho chih-kuan* and Chih-i's ritual treatises, material that illustrates the process by which the polarity between cultic and contemplative modes of praxis has continuously reinscribed itself onto various ideological positions over the course of T'ien-t'ai history.

Although the tension between contemplative and ritual discourse at times generated open conflict within the tradition, it nevertheless constituted a unitary discursive field for both Chih-i and later T'ien-t'ai thinkers. Both modes were integral to Chih-i's understanding of religious practice. Just as ritual performance was deemed ineffective if it remained bound to a naïve piety that did not lead to a more sophisticated understanding was ineffective, so Chih-i also cautioned against using the more theoretical perspective of principle to reject ritual form. If either pole were missing, T'ien-t'ai practice would lose its efficacy.

Part II

An Annotated Translation of the First Chapter of the *Mo-ho chih-kuan*

Introduction by Kuan-ting

The Lineage of the Teaching

[1a7] Calming and contemplation as luminosity and tranquility:[1] [this teaching] had not yet been heard of in former generations when Chih-i,[2] beginning on the twenty-sixth day of the fourth month of the fourteenth year of K'ai-huang (594), at the Jade Spring Monastery (Yü-ch'üan ssu) in Ching-chou,[3] expounded this work twice a day[4] over the course of the summer, compassionately raining down [his wisdom]. Although his desire to preach knew no bounds,[5] once he completed the section on the

1. Chan-jan (T 46.142b6–9) says: "The two words 'calming and contemplation' express directly the essence (*t'i*) of [the teaching] heard [in Chih-i's lectures on the *Mo-ho chih-kuan*]. The two words 'tranquility and luminosity' extol the meritorious properties of this essence. That is to say, the essence of calming is tranquility, and the essence of contemplation is luminosity. Whether one is speaking of the ten modes of discernment or the ten greater chapters [as a whole], from beginning to end there is not any [aspect of the MHCK] that does not involve this essence of calming and contemplation, [which is] tranquility and luminosity."

2. Kuan-ting refers to Chih-i by the honorific title of Chih-che (the "Wise One"), which was bestowed on Chih-i by the Sui prince Yang Kuang in 591 (see Satō, *Tendai daishi no kenkyū*, p. 54). For the sake of convenience, his dharma name "Chih-i" is used throughout.

3. Located in Tang-yang county, Ching-chou prefecture, Hupei province, Jade Spring Monastery (Yü-ch'üan ssu) was founded by Chih-i (as I-yin ssu) in 593. The following year Emperor Wen of the Sui bestowed on the monastery an imperial plaque and the new name, Yü-ch'üan ssu, or Jade Spring Monastery. Along with becoming a focal point for Northern Ch'an, Vinaya, and esoteric Buddhist traditions, the monastery continued to function as a major center of T'ien-t'ai learning and practice up to the time of the Buddhist persecutions of the ninth century.

4. Chan-jan (T 46.142c24) identifies these two periods as morning and late afternoon.

5. Chan-jan (T 46.143a7–13) identifies "desire or joy in preaching" as the

sphere of views,[6] he brought to a halt the turning of the wheel of the dharma[7] and did not discourse on the final sections of the work.[8]

[1a10] Yet drawing water from a stream, one seeks its source, and scenting an aroma, one traces its origin. The *Great Treatise* says, "In my practice I have not had a teacher."[9] Yet a sūtra says, " 'I (Śākyamuni) received the prophecy of Buddhahood from the Buddha Dīpaṃkara."[10] A [secular] writing says, "Those who are born with knowledge are the highest. Next come those who attain knowledge through study."[11] The Buddhist teachings are a vast and subtle truth. Do they shine of themselves with the heavenly light of truth or is their blue derived from the indigo plant?[12]

[1a13] If a practitioner hears the lineage of the transmission of the treasury of the dharma, he will recognize the origins of [our ancestral] line (*tsung*).[13] Through aeons [of former lives] the Greatly Enlightened

---

greatest of four forms of eloquence, notably, the power to expound, limitlessly and freely, the entirety of the Buddhadharma from a single term or passage.

6. "Discernment of the sphere of views" is the seventh among the "ten spheres of discernment" (*kuan-ching*) discussed in greater chapter 7 on Cultivation of Calming and Contemplation Proper.

7. Stopped preaching.

8. Thus Chih-i never completed the last three spheres of discernment in greater chapter 7 or the proposed greater chapters 8, 9, and 10.

9. From the *Ta-chih-tu lun*, or *Treatise on the Great Perfection of Wisdom [Sūtra]*, T 25.65a (hereafter referred to as the *Great Treatise* in the text and TCTL in the notes). TCTL is a commentary to the *Pañcaviṃśati-sāhasrika-prajñā-pāramitā Sūtra* (The Perfection of Wisdom in Twenty-Five Thousand Lines; hereafter, *Pañcaviṃśati*), translated into Chinese by Kumārajīva during the early fifth century.

10. From the *T'ai-tzu jui-ying pen-ch'i ching*, T 3.473a.

11. From the *Lun-yü* of Confucius, 16:9; see D. C. Lau, trans., *Confucius: The Analects*, p. 140.

12. In other words, is their wisdom derived secondarily from texts and/or a teacher, or is it transhistorical? The simile of the indigo plant is derived from the opening lines of the *Hsün Tzu*, which compares the knowledge that a pupil receives from his teacher with the blue derived from the indigo plant (see Watson, trans., *Basic Writings of Hsün Tzu*, p. 15).

13. For discussion of the use of this rather complex term *tsung* ("lineage," "trunkline ancestry," "doctrinal theme," "school") in medieval Chinese Buddhism, see Stanley Weinstein, "The Schools of Chinese Buddhism" in Kitagawa and Cummings, eds., *Buddhism and Asian History*, pp. 257–265.

The lineage of the transmission of dharma that Kuan-ting now proceeds to set forth consists of two parts. The first is a line of twenty-three (or twenty-four) eminent Indian and Central Asian masters known as the "patriarchal transmission from the golden-mouthed one" (*chin-k'ou tsu-ch'eng*). Its list is derived from the *Fu fa-tsang yin-yüan chuan* (History of the Transmission of the Dharma Treasury), T 50.297a-322b. The second—the "patriarchal transmission of current masters" (*chin-shih tsu-ch'eng*)—is the line of Chinese masters who are more immediately

World-Honored One fulfilled every sort of religious discipline. For a period of six years he suppressed false views in himself and [finally] subdued Māra[14] by raising a single finger. He first preached at the Deer Park,[15] after that, at Vulture Peak,[16] and finally at the Śāla grove.[17] He transmitted the dharma to his disciple Mahākāśyapa (1), who, after the Buddha's death and cremation, divided the Buddha's relics[18] into eight portions [to distribute among his followers] and [convened the first council] in order to compile the tripiṭika.[19] He, in turn, transmitted the dharma to Ānanda (2). Ānanda entered the wind-producing samādhi amid the river Ganges and magically divided his body into four parts.[20] He had previously entrusted the dharma to Śāṇavāsa (3). Śāṇavāsa, the nectar of the dharma raining from his hands, manifested 500 accesses to

---

responsible for establishing the T'ien-t'ai teachings—Hui-wen (n.d.), Nan-yüeh Hui-ssu (515–577), and T'ien-t'ai Chih-i (538–597) (see Chan-jan, T 46.145a20–24 and 147b19). Unlike the Ch'an tradition, no direct succession is established between the Indian and Chinese "patriarchs." The connection remains primarily a "literary" one—through the works of the thirteenth Indian patriarch, Nāgārjuna.

The *Fu fa-tsang yin-yüan chuan* first appeared at the end of the fifth century. Although it purported to be a translation from a Sanskrit original, modern scholars suspect that it was composed in China (see Mochizuki, *Bukkyō daijiten* 5.4493–4494). Sanskrit equivalents for proper names have been taken from Yampolsky, *The Platform Sutra of the Sixth Patriarch*, p. 8. With the addition of Vasumitra between Miccaka (6) and Buddhanandi (7), the genealogy given in the *Fu fa-tsang yin-yüan chuan* became incorporated into the standard lineage of Ch'an/Zen patriarchs (see Yampolsky's chart in *The Platform Sutra of the Sixth Patriarch*, pp. 8–9). There are a few minor discrepancies between the names given in the *Fu fa-tsang yin-yüan chuan* and the MHCK; for a comparative listing see the foldout chart at the back of Yanagida, *Shoki zenshū no kenkyū*.

14. While in meditation beneath the bodhi tree, at the time of his great enlightenment.

15. In Benares.

16. Near Rājagṛha.

17. Where he died, near Śrāvastī.

18. The Chinese word is a transcription of the Sanskrit *śarīra*.

19. At Rājagṛha.

20. *Fu fa-tsang yin-yüan chuan*, T 50.303b. Knowing he was about to die, Ānanda left Magadha for Vaiśālī, north across the Ganges. Ajātaśatru, still the king of Magadha, sent soldiers out to stop him, while the king of Vaiśālī, hearing of Ānanda's impending arrival, sent soldiers out to greet him. Ānanda was halfway across the river when he saw these two hosts on the opposite banks of the river, so in order to be equitable, he rose into the air and cremated himself, causing his ashes and unburnt "relics" to fall half on the northern bank and half on the southern bank, so that there were some for each king. A third portion was sent up to the Trayastriṃśa heaven atop Mount Sumeru, and another portion down to the nāga-king in the ocean, making four parts in all.

dharma and transmitted the dharma to Upagupta (4). The latter obtained the third of the four fruits while still a layman and, after having accepted the monastic code, obtained the fourth fruit.[21] He transmitted the dharma to Dhṛtaka (5).[22] Dhṛtaka, when he first mounted the ordination platform to become a monk, had [already] obtained the first fruit, but, by the time he had thrice repeated the ordination confessional, he realized the fourth and highest fruit. He transmitted the dharma to Miccaka (6), who in turn transmitted it to Buddhanandi (7). The latter transmitted it to Buddhamitra (8), who administered the three refuges[23] to a king and defeated a numerologist in debate. He transmitted the dharma to the bhikṣu Pārśva (9). When Pārśva emerged from the womb, his hair was already white.[24] His hands emitting light, he took in them a Buddhist sūtra.[25] He transmitted the dharma to Puṇyayaśas (10), who himself defeated Aśvaghoṣa (11) in debate, shaved the latter's head, and made him his disciple. Aśvaghoṣa wrote the *Rāṣṭrapāla*, a drama that dealt with transience, suffering, and emptiness. Those who witnessed it became enlightened to the path. He transmitted the dharma to Kapimala (12), who wrote a treatise on no-self (*anātman*); false views were annihilated wherever this treatise was current. He transmitted the dharma to Nāgārjuna (13). Nāgārjuna was born into his physical body beneath a tree (*arjuna*) and achieved the dharma-body through the instrumentality of a serpent deity (*nāga*).[26] He transmitted the dharma to Kāṇadeva[27] (14). Kāṇadeva gouged out the eye of a golden statue of a god, then miraculously provided him with a myriad fleshly eyes. He transmitted the dharma to Rāhulata (15). The latter recited from memory a book containing the names of demons and thereby overwhelmed an unbeliever with his marvelous ability and converted him. He transmitted the dharma to

21. The four stages of sainthood (*ārya*) in the Hīnayāna: stream-winner, once-returner, never-returner, and full arhatship.

22. The original reading of the name in the *Fu fa-tsang yin-yüan chuan* is followed here (as the MHCK has reversed the last two characters).

23. Profession of refuge in the Buddha, dharma, and saṅgha.

24. According to Chan-jan (T 46.146a26–27), he had been in the womb for sixty years.

25. As *Shiki* (1.46) points out, the phrase "his hands emitting light, he took in them a sūtra" in the *Fu fa-tsang yin-yüan chuan* (T 50.315a) actually belongs to the account of the next patriarch, Puṇyayaśas. The latter caused Aśvaghoṣa to accept the Buddhist sūtras through this act.

26. The *Fu fa-tsang yin-yüan chuan* (T 50.317b) says: "His birth occurred beneath a tree (*arjuna*), and he realized enlightenment through a nāga. Thus he is known by the name 'Nāgārjuna.' "

27. MHCK only has *t'i-p'o* (deva). The reading in *Fu fa-tsang yin-yüan chuan* (T 50.318c) has been followed here.

Saṅghānandi[28] (16), who, speaking in verses (*gāthās*),[29] tested the understanding of an arhat and transmitted the dharma to Saṅghayaśas (17).[30] Saṅghayaśas saw a city while wandering along the seashore and there preached in verses. He transmitted the dharma to Kumārata (18), whose powers were such that once, on seeing a myriad horsemen, he was able to remember the color of each horse and know the name and distinguish the clothing of each horseman. He transmitted the dharma to Jayata (19). For the benefit of certain monks who had committed grave offenses against the monastic code, Jayata magically created a fiery pit and made them enter and do penance there. The pit was transformed into a pond and their sins were extinguished. He transmitted the dharma to Vasubandhu (20), who in turn transmitted it to Manorhita (21).[31] Manorhita used the Ganges to divide the populace into two parts and converted the group [south of the river].[32] He transmitted the dharma to Haklenayaśas (22), who in turn transmitted it to Siṃha (23). Siṃha was mortally wounded by order of the king of Damiḷa.[33] When he was put to the sword, milk flowed from his wounds.

[1b6] There were twenty-three persons who transmitted the treasury of the dharma, beginning with Mahākāśyapa and ending with Siṃha. But [counting both] Madhyāntika[34] and Śāṇavāsa, who received the dharma at the same time, there were altogether twenty-four.[35] These teachers all received prediction [of future Buddhahood] from the Golden-Mouthed Ones. They were all saints who were able to benefit great numbers of people.

28. MHCK gives his name as *Seng-fa-nan-t'i*; *Fu fa-tsang yin-yüan chuan* (T 50.320a) gives it as *Seng-ch'ieh nan-t'i.*

29. According to the *Fu fa-tsang yin-yüan chuan* (T 50.320a), the gāthās formed a riddle: "What is it that is born from the seed of a wheel-turning king (*cakravartin*) and enters nirvāṇa, but is neither a Buddha, an arhat, nor a pratyekabuddha?" Unable to answer, the arhat consulted Maitreya in the Tuṣita heaven about it. The answer that Maitreya gave him was "a clay vessel," for this object is made by applying mud to a potter's wheel (thus the potter becomes the "wheel-turning king") and eventually breaks (i.e., enters nirvāṇa), but is not a Buddha, arhat, or pratyekabuddha.

30. *Fu fa-tsang yin-yüan chuan* (T 50.320a) gives *Seng-ch'ieh-yeh-she*, whereas the MHCK gives *Seng-fa-ye-she.*

31. Or Manura.

32. Following Chan-jan (T 46.147a5–7).

33. Skt. Draviḍa. According to Hsüan-tsang this was in South India, 1,500–1,600 *li* south of Coḷa.

34. Said to be contemporaneous with Śāṇavāsa.

35. Counting Madhyāntika and the Buddha himself, the lineage contains twenty-five people.

[1b9] In former times there was a king who decided not to establish a stable [for his elephants] in the vicinity of a hermitage but placed it instead near a slaughterhouse.[36] How much more likely [than beasts in a stable] are humans, when in the proximity of saints, to benefit from their teachings. Again, a brahmin was selling skulls, of which a rod could be passed clean through some, half through others, and not at all through the remainder. Buddhist laymen built a stūpa for those which the rod passed completely through, performed veneration and made offerings to them, and were consequently reborn in the heavens.[37] The essential feature about hearing the dharma is that it has such merit. It is in order to confer this benefit that the Buddha has transmitted the treasury[38] of the dharma.

[1b13] In this treatise on calming and contemplation, the master T'ien-t'ai Chih-i has explained the approach to dharma that he practiced within his own mind.[39] When Chih-i was born, light filled the room, and in his

36. From the *Fu fa-tsang yin-yüan chuan*, T 50.322a. It seems that a certain king used a fierce elephant to trample criminals to death. A time came when the elephant refused to carry out his task, merely smelling and licking his supposed victims without harming them. On inquiring among his ministers, the king found that the elephant's stable had recently been moved to the neighborhood of a Buddhist hermitage, and the animal was being influenced by the teachings he heard emanating from the monastery. The king therefore ordered the stable moved to the vicinity of a slaughterhouse, whereupon the elephant soon regained his blood lust.

37. Ibid., T 50.322b. The brāhmin had at first no success in selling the skulls and so became angry, cursing and vilifying those who refused to buy them. The Buddhist laymen of the city were frightened at this and agreed to buy. First, however, they tested the skulls by slipping a rod through the ear holes, saying that they attached the greatest value to those which could be penetrated completely so that the rod came out the other side. They explained that such skulls had belonged to persons who in life had heard the Buddha's wondrous preaching and had thereby attained great wisdom (literal vacuity of mind). Their veneration of these sacred relics earned them rebirth as devas.

38. Or "storehouse." This word is used for the Pāli or Skt. *piṭaka*, "basket," meaning the "three baskets" (tripiṭika) that comprise the Buddhist scriptures in their traditional division: sūtra, vinaya, and abhidharma. Here it may be taken to refer broadly to the Mahāyāna scriptures as well.

39. Chan-jan (T 46.147b19–29) says: "[Now comes] the patriarchal transmission through current masters. [The statement] here offers a preliminary summation of the dharma that is the transmission and the person [through whom it is transmitted]. The line that reads, '[this text] expounds the practice that [Chih-i] used within his own mind,' represents Chang-an [Kuan-ting's] hint that he obtained from the grand master the practice that [Chih-i] himself used. Thus he mentions the practice in order to clarify the transmission. If there is transmission

eyes there were double pupils. Later he performed the repentance [based on] the *Lotus Sūtra*, [as a result of which] he manifested dhāraṇīs.[40] Then, taking the place of the teacher from whom he had received the dharma,[41] he lectured on the golden-lettered *Prajñāpāramitā Sūtra*.[42] The Ch'en and Sui states esteemed him and gave him the title of "imperial teacher." He died in the meditation posture, having attained the stage of the five classes of disciplehood.[43]

[1b16] Therefore it says in the *Lotus Sūtra*, "[The accumulated merit of] one who gives the seven precious jewels[44] to each being in 400 billion *nayutas* of countries, who converts and endows them all with the six superhuman powers, is not equal to even the one-thousand-millionth part of the merit of one who experiences the first glimmer of joy [at hearing

---

but no practice, or words but no practice, how would one prove that what has been transmitted is not useless? Thus [by this passage] one knows that what has been transmitted is what [Chih-i] 'himself personally practiced.'

"This [statement] is also intended to prevent later generations from practicing in ways that go against [what has been] taught, for this one text is thereby established as [containing] the basic features of practice. Some people say that there is a special transmission of the essentials of mind (*hsin-yao*) apart from the three [basic texts on calming and contemplation of MHCK, *Tz'u-ti ch'an-men*, and *Liu-miao fa-men*] and, therefore, that these three works are useless. But even if there were an oral transmission given face to face, it could only amount to a verification of one's personal realizations before a master. The technique for contemplating and settling the mind presented in this text would still stand as sufficient unto itself. How much the more so if later practitioners do not have a personal transmission to rely on. Apart from this [text] what else is there to speak of? Thus one should have faith in the fact that this [teaching] represents the transmission."

40. The practice in question is the twenty-one-day lotus samādhi repentance described in the section on part walking/part sitting samādhi in the second chapter of the Synopsis, Engaging in the Great Practice or the Four Samādhis. Chih-i experienced his first major spiritual awakening on the fourteenth day of this practice, as a result of which he "manifested dhāraṇī" (i.e., incantations for the securing of religious power or truth) in the form of profound insight. For a translation of this account from his biography, see Hurvitz, "Chih-i," pp. 108–109.

41. Hui-ssu.

42. Hui-ssu is said to have copied the *Pañcaviṃśati* in gold characters.

43. The five classes of disciplehood (*wu p'in ti-tzu wei*) were systematized by Chih-i on the basis of references in the Discrimination of Merits chapter of the *Lotus Sūtra* (T 9.44c–46b; Hurvitz, pp. 249–257). They rank just below the standard fifty-two stages of the perfect path and correspond to the stage of identity in meditative practice—the third in a system of six identities also used in T'ien-t'ai to mark progress on the perfect path. Chan-jan (T 46.148c11–12) claims that Chih-i attained the fifth of the five classes.

44. Listed in the *Lotus Sūtra* (T 9.46c) as gold, silver, *vaiḍūrya*, mother of pearl, agate, coral, and amber.

the dharma]."[45] How much less is it comparable to the merit achieved by the fifth [and highest] class of disciplehood! [The *Lotus*] also says, "[Those who expound the *Lotus Sūtra* are] the emissaries of the Tathāgata, deputed by the Tathāgata to perform the work of the Tathāgata."[46] The *Nirvāṇa Sūtra* says, "This is a bodhisattva at the first stage [of the four grades of bodhisattva on whom the world relies]."[47]

[1b20] Chih-i served Nan-yüeh [Hui-ssu] (515–577) as his master. The latter's religious practice was inconceivably profound; for ten years he did nothing but recite scripture. For seven years he practiced the vaipulya [repentance].[48] For three months he sat constantly in meditation, and in a single instant he attained perfect realization. The dharma-gates of both the Mahāyāna and Hīnayāna luminously opened forth for him.[49] Hui-ssu studied under the dhyāna-master Hui-wen. During the reign of Kao-tsu (550–560) of the Northern Ch'i dynasty, the latter wandered alone[50] through the region between the Yellow and Huai rivers,[51] his approach to dharma unknown to his age.[52] Indeed, people [daily] tread the

45. Paraphrased from the *Lotus Sūtra* (T 9.46c; Hurvitz, pp. 258–259). Joy occurs specifically from hearing the *Lotus Sūtra*. Joy in hearing the dharma (i.e., the *Lotus*) represents the first of the five classes of disciplehood—i.e., a stage of spiritual development that Chih-i is said to have achieved.

46. Ibid., T 9.30c; Hurvitz, p. 175.

47. From the *Nirvāṇa Sūtra*, T 12.637a. The "four dependables" (*ssu-i*) describes four kinds of humans on which people in the world may rely or depend: those who are not yet rid of their *kleśas* but who nevertheless are able to benefit the world; stream-winners and once-returners; nonreturners; and arhats. While these distinctions draw explicitly on Hīnayānist categories, in T'ien-t'ai works they are identified with stages of the perfect teaching—the five classes of disciplehood and the stage of the purity of the six senses; the ten abodes; the ten stages of action and the ten stages of diversion; and the ten stages (*bhūmi*) proper, together with the stage of penultimate Buddhahood, respectively.

48. The vaipulya repentance is one of the practices of the part walking/part sitting samādhi described in the second chapter of the MHCK Synopsis, Engaging in the Great Practice or the Four Samādhis.

49. Chan-jan (T 46.149a15–16) says: "From this point on his eloquence and enlightenment were so substantial that he could understand on his own without the slightest doubt scriptures he had never heard expounded. Thus the text says, 'dharma-gates of the Hīnayāna and Mahāyāna luminously opened forth.' "

50. Chan-jan (T 46.149a22) says: "Because he did not vie with others for converts the text says 'wandered alone.' " Muranaka (p. 16), following later Japanese and Chinese T'ien-t'ai glosses, reads the line differently, interpreting it to mean that Hui-wen was "especially peerless or renowned."

51. Chan-jan (T 46.149a22–23) says: "Yellow (Ho) [River] and Huai [River mean [the regions of] Ho-pei and Huai-nan."

52. Chan-jan (T 46.149a23–24) comments: " 'He traveled and taught in the world, yet [the text] says '[his approach to dharma] was not known to his age.'

earth and gaze at the heavens,[53] yet have no idea of the earth's thickness nor heaven's loftiness. Hui-wen's mental discipline was exclusively based on the *Great Treatise*, which was expounded by Nāgārjuna, the thirteenth patriarch in the line of those who transmitted the treasure of the dharma. It says in Chih-i's *Treatise on Contemplating the Mind*, "I entrust myself to the master Nāgārjuna."[54] By this we can verify that Nāgārjuna is the founding ancestor (*kao-tsu*) [of our line].

[1b27] Q: Skeptics say, "The *Middle Treatise*[55] [of Nāgārjuna] clears away, while calming and contemplation builds up. How could they be the same?"

[1b28] A: There are seventy Indian commentaries to Nāgārjuna's verses in all; one should not accept only that of Piṅgala,[56] while rejecting those by other teachers.[57] Furthermore, it says in the *Middle Treatise*, "Whatever dharma arises through causes and conditions, that I declare to be identical to emptiness. It is also a provisional designation. This, furthermore, is the meaning of the middle way."[58]

This means that, since his realization was profound, it was not something others knew about."

53. From *Tso-chuan*, fifteenth year of Duke Hsi; see also *Shuo yüan*, 18:24.

54. *Kuan-hsin lun*, T 46.585c, paraphrased. The *Kuan-hsin lun* was delivered orally by Chih-i as a final testament or behest to his disciples shortly before his death in 597. See Satō, *Tendai daishi no kenkyū*, pp. 62–63.

55. The *Chung-lun* (T no. 1568), Kumārajīva's Chinese translation of Nāgārjuna's *Madhyamaka-kārikās* together with the prose commentary of Piṅgala (*Ch'ing-mu*).

56. This is Richard Robinson's hypothetical and not altogether satisfactory Sanskritization of the Chinese name Ch'ing-mu, "blue-eyes," the author of the prose commentary in the *Chung-lun* (see his *Early Mādhyamika in India and China*, p. 29).

57. Chan-jan (T 46.149c2–9) mentions in particular three other commentaries that were known in China: the *Shun-chung-lun* (T 30.39c–50b) by Asaṅga; a no-longer extant work by Rāhula, also called the *Chung-lun*; and the *Prajñā-pradīpa* (*Pan-jo teng lun-she*, T 30.50c–135c) by Bhāvaviveka. Chan-jan cites Chinese Buddhist opinion that the commentary by Piṅgala is inferior to the others and hence not to be taken as the only standard.

58. *Chung-lun*, T 30.33b (chapt. 24, verse 18 of the *Madhyamaka-kārikās*). This verse became an important scriptural locus for the T'ien-t'ai three truths (i.e., emptiness, provisionality, and the middle). In this capacity it is cited repeatedly throughout the first chapter of the Synopsis, Arousing the Great Thought [of Enlightenment].

Chan-jan responds (T 46.149c10–13) to the skeptic in the text as follows: "The first line of the [verse from] the [*Middle*] *Treatise* reads, 'whatever dharma arises on the basis of causes and conditions.' It implies 'building up.' [The line], 'I declare to be empty' represents 'clearing away.' 'Provisional designation' and 'middle way' again are 'building up.' "

The Three Kinds of Calming-and-Contemplation

[1c1] Chih-i transmitted Hui-ssu's three kinds of calming and contemplation: (1) the gradual and sequential, (2) the variable, and (3) the perfect and sudden. These all belong to the Mahāyāna. They all take ultimate reality (*shih-hsiang*) as their object [of contemplation] and are alike called calming and contemplation. The gradual [calming and contemplation] is shallow at the beginning but later becomes deep, like [climbing] a ladder or stairs. In the variable [calming and contemplation],[59] the earlier and later [stages] mutually shift around, just as the color of a diamond thrust into the sunlight varies depending on its position.[60] In the perfect and sudden [calming and contemplation], beginning and end are not two [different things], so that the practice is comparable to someone with supernatural powers mounting into space.[61] It is for the sake of three basic types of [spiritual] capacity that we teach these three approaches to dharma and cite these three similes.[62] Having finished the abbreviated explanation of the three kinds of calming and contemplation, we continue now with the expanded explanation.

Gradual and Sequential Calming-and-Contemplation

[1c6] Even at the beginning of gradual [calming and contemplation] one is aware [of the nature] of ultimate reality. This reality is difficult to understand, but the gradual and sequential method is easy to practice.[63]

59. Literally, "unfixed" or "unspecified" (*pu-ting*).

60. From the *Nirvāṇa Sūtra*, T 12.754a. Here it is stated that the "color" or outward appearance of one in the state of *vajra-samādhi* is like the color of a diamond thrust into the sunlight. When among the populace, such a bodhisattva is seen differently by each person who looks at him. *Vajra-(upama-)samādhi* is here equated with calming and contemplation. For a discussion of the *vajra-samādhi*, see Buswell, *The Formation of Ch'an Ideology in China and Korea*, pp. 104–115.

61. Chan-jan (T 46.150a28–b3) says: " 'Perfect' means perfectly interfusing or perfectly full. 'Sudden' means reaching its furthest limit 'all-at-once,' or 'instantaneously' becoming fulfilled. Furthermore, 'perfect' means complete. . . . Because its essence (*t'i*) is not established gradually, it is 'sudden or instantaneous.' But although in essence it [is already] fulfilled or at its limit, one still must use the twenty-five techniques as preliminary expedients and rely on the ten modes of discernment for cultivation [of contemplation] proper."

62. Chan-jan (T 46.150b6–8) says: "These three approaches to calming and contemplation apply to spiritual capacity differently. Although from the phenomenal perspective (*shih*) there are differences [among them], they take the same sudden principle (*li*) as their object. Beyond [this principle of] the perfect teaching there is really no other capacity to speak of. Thus one should be aware that the three [approaches to calming and contemplation] all orient themselves to the perfect principle and that their distinguishing of three courses of practice [on this basis] is referred to as 'three types of spiritual capacity.' "

63. Chan-jan (T 46.150b19–23) says: "Five stages are enumerated here, but in

One begins by taking refuge in the monastic code (*kuei-chieh*), thereby turning away from depravity and approaching the good. [The paths of] fire, blood, and the knife[64] are brought to a halt, and one reaches the three wholesome destinies.[65] At the next stage one takes up the practice of meditative concentration,[66] through which one restrains the far-ranging net of desire and achieves the concentrations of the realms of form and formlessness.[67] Next one cultivates [insight that brings] freedom from outflows (*wu-lou*),[68] thereby terminating one's imprisonment in the three realms and reaching the path to nirvāṇa. After that one cultivates loving kindness and compassion, disregarding one's own progress toward enlightenment and reaching the bodhisattva path.[69] Finally one cultivates [the vision] of reality [itself], thereby arresting in oneself the biases of the two extreme views and achieving the eternally abiding way.[70] These are

---

concept they actually include thirteen distinctions. The five are: (1) submitting to the precepts, (2) meditative concentration, (3) [cultivating insight or wisdom] devoid of outflows, (4) kindness and compassion, and (5) ultimate reality. As for the thirteen subsidiary points, the first stage contains six, which are the three evil [destinies] and three good [destinies]. The third stage contains four, which are the two [tripiṭaka and shared] teachings and the two vehicles. Together with the previous six they make ten. Add in the remaining three, without any changes to their number, and the total comes to thirteen. Throughout the thirteen, ultimate reality remains the object of focus. But taking into consideration the fact that [this reality] is the same as for the sudden, it should not be counted as a point of difference [among the three calmings and contemplations]. It is for this reason that later in the questions and answers [the text] speaks of 'twelve points of dissimilarity or difference.' "

64. Standing for the three painful destinies of hell, animals, and hungry ghosts.

65. Asuras, humans, and devas.

66. Cultivation of mundane states of dhyāna and samādhi.

67. This refers to the three realms of (in ascending order) desire, form, and formlessness: *kāmadhātu*, *rūpadhātu*, and *arūpadhātu*. States of mundane meditative concentration are charted according to them.

68. "Outflows" (*āsrava*) are equivalent to *kleśas*, the passions or afflictions that bind an individual to cyclic birth and death within the three realms. Cultivation of techniques for eradicating the defiling "outflows" (i.e., the techniques of insight or *vipaśyanā* peculiar to Buddhism) lead to deliverance from the mundane condition of the three realms of saṃsāra. In T'ien-t'ai parlance, this represents "entering emptiness from the provisional" (*ts'ung-chia ju-k'ung*). Hence Chan-jan associates this stage with the two vehicles of śrāvaka and pratyekabuddha or the tripiṭaka and shared teachings.

69. Here the practitioner vows to return to saṃsāra and work toward the enlightenment of other beings. In T'ien-t'ai parlance, it is equivalent to realization of the provisional truth or "reemerging into the provisional from emptiness" (*ts'ung-k'ung ch'u-chia*).

70. Traditionally the most common representation of the two extreme views is

the features of the gradual and sequential calming and contemplation, which is shallow at the start but profound at the end.

Variable Calming-and-Contemplation

[1c12] There is no particular sequence of stages in the variable calming and contemplation.[71] At times it may employ the gradual method, which we have outlined above, and at times it may employ the sudden method, which we discuss below,[72] alternating between these two, now shallow and now deep. Sometimes [it focuses on] phenomenal distinctions (*shih*), at other times on principle (*li*).[73] In some cases it points to the worldly [siddhānta] as the [siddhānta of] ultimate truth, or treats the [siddhānta of] ultimate truth as the individualized and therapeutic [siddhāntas].[74] It

---

eternalism (*śāśvatavāda*) and annihilationism (*ucchedavāda*) of the self and/or dharmas. In T'ien-t'ai discussions, however, they are usually presented in terms of the "three truths"—emptiness, provisionality, and the middle. Thus the two extremes are "emptiness" and "provisionality," which are "simultaneously eradicated and simultaneously illumined" (*shuang-fei shuang-chao*) in the realization of the perfect "middle" truth that is ultimate reality.

71. Chan-jan (T 46.150b29–c1) says: "The term 'variable' is devised in reference to the two previous [approaches of] the gradual and sudden. Sometimes it is gradual; sometimes it is sudden; it does not focus exclusively on any one approach. Thus it is 'variable.' "

72. Following Chan-jan, T 46.150b26–28.

73. Originally an indigenous philosophical concept developed by early medieval Confucian and Hsüan-hsüeh thinkers, the distinction between "principle" (*li*) and "phenomena" (*shih*) was adapted to classic Indian Buddhist polarities of emptiness (*śūnyatā*) and existence, or "ultimate truth" (*paramārtha-satya*) and "conventional truth" (*saṃvṛti-satya*). In Hua-yen and later T'ien-t'ai the nuances surrounding these terms become quite complex. Chih-i himself frequently uses *shih* to refer to concrete features of religious practice, ritual activity, and cultic lore. *Li*, on the other hand, represents an interior insight whereby one sees these very distinctions as devoid of any absolute status in and of themselves (i.e., empty) and experiences them as intrinsically identical to the transcendent "middle truth." Hence *li* (as "principle") may be taken loosely to mean "essential principle of truth or reality"; and *shih*, "phenomenal appearance."

Chan-jan (T 46.150c4–6) says: "As for 'principle' and 'phenomena,' sometimes the mundane realms [of saṃsāra] are considered 'the phenomenal'; and the supramundane, 'principle.' Or [the pairs of] conventional truth (*saṃvṛti-satya*) and ultimate truth (*paramārtha-satya*), the three siddhāntas and the one siddhānta [are identified with the phenomenal and principle, respectively]. [Here in the variable calming and contemplation] they also mutually shift around."

74. This sentence refers to the second and third of the four siddhāntas (*hsi-t'an*)—four strategies for expounding the teachings and guiding beings to perfection. They derive from the TCTL, T 25.59b–61b. Chih-i, following his teacher Hui-ssu, understood the term *hsi-t'an* as a mixture of Chinese and Sanskrit, meaning "universally giving" (i.e., interpreting *hsi* in its ordinary Chinese meaning of "universal" and *t'an* as the Sanskrit *dāna*, "giving"). In fact the whole word, and

may involve the pacification (*hsi*) of contemplation (*kuan*) in order to achieve calming (*chih*); or it may involve the illumination (*chao*) of calming (*chih*) to achieve contemplation (*kuan*).[75] That is why it is called the "variable" calming and contemplation.

[1c16] Q: A skeptic might say, "[These three types of calming and contemplation] belong to the same [Mahāyāna] teaching, have the same [reality] as their object, and have the same name.[76] But in terms of the features [of their practice] they are still utterly different."

[1c16] A: Though they are the same, they are not the same; and though they are not the same, they are the same.[77] There are six [distinctions within the first stage of] the gradual calming and contemplation: three each of good and bad destinies.[78] There are three general aspects to [the cultivation of] freedom from outflows, so that we have in all twelve points of difference.[79] The reason we adopt the name "variable" [for this calming and contemplation] is that we are speaking from the perspective of its manifoldness.

[1c19] Q: The types of calming and contemplation discussed in this section are in the same Mahāyāna, they aim at the same ultimate reality, and are the same in being called "calming and contemplation." Why then is this section called "elucidating differences?"[80]

---

not merely half of it, is a transcription of the Sanskrit word *siddhānta*. The four siddhāntas are: (1) the "worldly siddhānta," where one instructs beings in accordance with their existing (conventional) desires and motives; (2) the "individualized siddhānta," which devises instruction in accordance with the capacities of beings to receive the teaching; (3) the "therapeutic siddhānta," which takes the approach of preaching dharma in accordance with specific evil mental states and behavior that need to be counteracted; and (4) the "ultimate siddhānta," or preaching in direct accordance with the true nature of reality.

75. Chan-jan (T 46.150c13–14) says: "In some cases, by applying illumination to calming, calming [itself] becomes contemplation. By applying pacification to contemplation, contemplation becomes calming."

76. Calming and contemplation.

77. *Kōgi* (1.86–87): they are the same in teaching, object, and name but different in details of practice (*hsing-hsiang*).

78. Hell, hungry ghosts, and animals; asuras, humans, and devas.

79. These distinctions are made only with respect to the gradual calming and contemplation. Cultivation of freedom from outflows is, as above, the third stage of the five. Each of the other three stages remains undivided, thus giving a total of twelve. The three aspects of freedom from outflows are not clearly explained by commentators, although Chan-jan (T 46.150c26–151a1) suggests that the three are a condensation of four, possibly the four fruits of stream-winner, etc. The fact that this list differs from Chan-jan's previous analysis of the gradual path into twelve points (not including "reality," the thirteenth) (T 46.150b) makes the passage even more confusing.

80. Chan-jan (T 46.151a19–20) explains that the title for this section was used in earlier editions of the MHCK (i.e., the *Yüan-tun chih-kuan*). Although the title

[1c20] A: Though they are the same, they are not the same; and though they are not the same, they are the same. Within the [stages of the] gradual and sequential [calming and contemplation] there are nine[81] points of difference, while within the variable [calming and contemplation] there are four points of difference,[82] making in all thirteen points of difference. The reason we use the expression "not the same" is that we are stressing multiplicity in our choice of words. It is the same idea as saints treating unconditioned dharmas[83] as having differences.

Perfect and Sudden Calming-and-Contemplation[84]

[1c23] The perfect and sudden calming and contemplation from the very beginning takes ultimate reality (*shih-hsiang*) as its object.[85] No matter what the object of contemplation might be, it is seen to be identical to the middle.[86] There is here nothing that is not true reality (*chen-shih*). When one fixes [the mind] on the dharmadhātu [as object] and unifies one's mindfulness with the dharmadhātu [as it is],[87] then there is not a single

has been dropped here, its name is retained in the text of the question and answer.

81. *Sic. Kōgi* (1.93) informs us that this figure is arrived at by counting the first of the five stages as six, and each of the next three stages as one (the fifth stage is here omitted from the computation). Again the meaning of the computation is unclear.

82. Again the precise meaning of this enumeration is unclear (see Chan-jan, T 46.151a22–15b19). *Kōgi* (1.90) suggests that the four represent the two pairs of the worldly siddhānta/ultimate siddhānta and calming/contemplation, in which each member of a pair can be considered from the point of view of the other, making four permutations.

83. *Asaṃskṛta-dharmas*. The Buddhist schools posited various numbers of unconditioned dharmas—three in the case of the Sarvāstivādins and Sthaviravādins, and six in the case of the Yogācārins—although they were all in agreement that ultimately there was only the one reality.

84. This paragraph is known as the "core" statement of the MHCK, its distilled essence. For centuries it has been chanted by T'ien-t'ai and Tendai monks as a part of their daily religious offices.

85. Chan-jan (T 46.151c16–17) says: "[The passage from] 'from the [very] beginning takes [ultimate] reality as its object' to 'true reality' [in the line that follows] represents the object that calming and contemplation focuses on."

86. That is, whatever phenomenal event or experiential condition (*ching*) one may encounter or produce (*tsai*) in the course of contemplation. The term "object" should be understood in light of the ten experiential spheres of discernment.

87. The line originates from the *Wen-shu shuo-ching* (T 8.731a–b). Chan-jan (T 46.151c18–20) says: " 'Mindfulness' itself is the constant illumination that attends [the mind] in quiescence. 'Affixing' is the constant quiescence that attends the illumination of [unified] mindfulness. Since subjective and objective [aspects] are one, how much the more so calming and contemplation."

sight nor smell that is not the middle way.[88] The same goes for the realm of self, the realm of Buddha, and the realm of living beings.[89] Since all aggregates (*skandha*) and sense-accesses (*āyatana*) [of body and mind] are thusness, there is no suffering to be cast away.[90] Since nescience and the afflictions are themselves identical with enlightenment (bodhi), there is no origin of suffering to be eradicated. Since the two extreme views are the middle way and false views are the right view, there is no path to be cultivated. Since saṃsāra is identical with nirvāṇa, there is no cessation to be achieved. Because of the [intrinsic] inexistence of suffering and its origin, the mundane does not exist; because of the inexistence of the path and cessation, the supramundane does not exist. A single, unalloyed reality (*shih-hsiang*) is all there is—no entities whatever exist outside of it. That all entities are by nature quiescent (*chi*) is called "calming" (*chih*);[91] that, though quiescent, this nature is ever luminous (*chao*), is called "contemplation" (*kuan*).[92] Though a verbal distinction is made between earlier and later stages of practice, there is ultimately no duality, no distinction

88. Chan-jan (T 46.151c20–23) says: "The middle way is itself the dharmadhātu. The dharmadhātu is itself calming and contemplation. Calming and contemplation are not two separate things; wisdom and the object it perceives are a mysterious unity. Subjective [contemplator] and object [contemplated] are spoken of together in order to clarify [the quality of] quiescent illumination."

Chan-jan subsequently remarks (T 46.151c): "There are two meanings to the term 'middle way.' The first, which simply means to depart from [the two extreme views of] annihilationism and eternalism, belongs to the two vehicles. The second, which is [the middle way of the] Buddha-nature, belongs to the two subsequent teachings [of the separate and perfect doctrines]. The latter together present two approaches to Buddha-nature: one provisionally expedient, the other real. Thus there is the [concept of Buddha-nature as something] 'apart' [from phenomena and the afflictions] and the [concept of Buddha-nature as] 'identical' [to phenomena and the afflictions]. Here the text takes the perspective of the 'identical.' Therefore it says 'every sight, every smell is the middle way.' People today unanimously take these words 'sight' and 'smell,' etc. to signify the insentient. But while they admit that 'every sight, every smell can be the middle way,' they disclaim the notion of the intrinsic Buddha-nature of the insentient as deluded and excessive."

Chan-jan, of course, is renowned for elaborating the theory that the Buddha-nature is also intrinsic to the insentient. In the lines that follow in the commentary he offers ten points in support of his position (T 46.151c28–152a21). For a discussion of Chan-jan, his works and ideas, see Hibī, *Tōdai tendai-gaku kenkyū.*

89. The "three dharmas" of the Avataṃsaka Sūtra (T 9.465c)—personal mind, sentient beings, and the Buddha—which according to that sūtra are utterly identical.

90. Beginning here, the four noble truths are discussed from the standpoint of the sudden calming and contemplation.

91. *Śamatha*: calming, concentration, stopping, cessation, serenity.

92. *Vipaśyanā*: contemplation, insight.

between them. This is what is called the "perfect and sudden calming and contemplation."

Scriptural Verification of the Three Kinds of Calming-and-Contemplation[93]

[2a2] Now omitting the gradual and the variable calming and contemplation from the discussion, we shall further explain the perfect and sudden calming and contemplation by reference to the sūtras.

[2a3] The bodhisattva Bhadraśiras of the subtle qualities, who had penetrated to the extremely profound, said, "When a bodhisattva dwelling in saṃsāra first gives rise to the thought of enlightenment (*bodhicitta*) and when he seeks enlightenment single-mindedly, firmly, and without vacillating, then the merit contained in that single thought is profound, vast, and limitless, and even the Tathāgata, when describing in detail that merit, cannot exhaust it, though he expound on it to the end of time."[94] This bodhisattva hears the perfect dharma, gives rise to perfect faith, establishes perfect practice, dwells in the perfect stages, adorns himself with perfect merit, and by means of his perfect energy establishes living beings in the dharma.

[2a8] What does it mean to hear the perfect dharma? One hears that saṃsāra is identical to the dharma-body, that the afflictions are identical to prajñā, that bondage[95] is identical to liberation. Though there are three names [for reality], there are not three substances (*t'i*).[96] Though this is only one substance, three names are given it. These three are but a single mark (*hsiang*); in reality there is no distinction between them. Since the dharma-body is ultimate, prajñā and liberation are also the ultimate; since prajñā is pure, the other two are also pure; since liberation is unimpeded, so are the other two. For hearing any dharma it is the same—each contains fully the totality of the Buddha-dharma, without any diminution. This is what "hearing the perfect dharma" means.

[2a14] What is perfect faith? It is the conviction that all dharmas are empty, that they are nevertheless provisionally existent, and that they are

93. Kuan-ting now gives scriptural proof for all three varieties of calming and contemplation from four sūtras, for the gradual alone from one sūtra, and for the sudden alone from six sūtras. Finally he ties them up with another quotation from the *Avataṃsaka*.

94. Paraphrased from the *Avataṃsaka Sūtra*, T 9.433a–441b.

95. Literally, karma due to defilement.

96. According to Chan-jan (T 46.152c1–2), the three circuits of saṃsāra (*san-tao*) here correspond to three meritorious qualities of Buddhahood (*san-te*) into which they are transmuted—the dharma-body, prajñā or wisdom, and liberation, respectively (see the introduction, as well as chapter 5, Returning to the Great Abode, of the Synopsis).

the middle between these extremes.[97] Though ultimately there are not one, two, or three [separate views], yet there are one, two, and three [separate views]. To say that these three do not exist [separately] forestalls the notion that they are one, two, and three, while to say that the three do exist [separately] illumines this [multiplicity of] one, two, and three. When there is neither forestalling nor illuminating, all are alike ultimate, pure, and unimpeded. When hearing of the profundity not to fear, and the vastness, not to doubt, and to be bold in hearing that they are neither profound nor vast—this is what is called having "perfect faith."[98]

[2a18] What is perfect practice? Intently and single-mindedly to seek unsurpassed enlightenment;[99] to know that the extremes themselves are identical to the middle and not to entertain any further biases; perfectly to cultivate the three truths without finding extinction and quiescence in the absence of extremes, or suffering agitation by the presence of extremes; and to enter directly into the middle way without agitation or extinction—this is what is meant by "perfect practice."

[2a21] What is it to enter the perfect stages? It is, on entering the stage of the first abode, to realize that any one stage is all stages, that they are all ultimate, pure, and unimpeded.[100] This is what is meant by the "perfect stages."

[2a23] What is the adornment of perfect mastery?[101] The *Avataṃsaka* extensively explains the features of perfect mastery.[102] As it says, one may [freely] enter samādhi through one sense-faculty and arise from samādhi to expound the dharma with another sense-faculty, or one may simultaneously both enter and arise from samādhi with the same sense-faculty, or one may neither enter nor leave it with any particular sense-faculty.

97. The well-known "three views" or "three truths" of T'ien-t'ai.

98. Chan-jan (T 46.153a3) adds that faith arises in dependence on reality and is in turn the foundation of practice.

99. *Anutttura-samyak-saṃbodhi.*

100. Entry into the first abode represents entry into the forty-two ranks of full non-retrogressing bodhisattvahood of the perfect teaching. Each stage eliminates one measure of nescience and strengthens the wisdom of the middle truth by one measure. Thus, qualitatively speaking, there are no stages, and one is already identical to a Buddha; but, quantitatively, wisdom still must be progressively matured and deepened before full Buddhahood is actually reached. This is the path of the T'ien-t'ai perfect teaching.

101. This paragraph should explain "adorns himself with perfect merit," as above, but the "himself" (*tzu*) has become "perfect mastery" (*tzu-tsai*) in Kuan-ting's commentary on the passage at this point. Actually, chapter 8 of the *Avataṃsaka* (T 9.438b–c) speaks of both these subjects consecutively, whereas Kuan-ting appears to treat them as the same thing. The explanation of "perfect mastery" below is abbreviated from the sūtra.

102. T 9.438b.

The same holds for each of the six senses. One may enter samādhi with respect to one sense-object, or leave it and expound the dharma with respect to another, or both enter and leave with respect to a single sense-object or neither enter nor leave thus. The same holds for each of the six sense-objects. One may enter samādhi in this direction or leave it and expound in that direction, or in the same direction both enter and leave, or neither enter nor leave. Or one may enter samādhi with respect to one object, or rise and expound with respect to one object, or both enter and leave, or neither enter nor leave from samādhi with respect to one object. To be exact, when even with respect to one sense or sense-object one enters and emerges from samādhi, or both, or neither, then one is self-sovereign with respect to every form of primary and environmental [karmic] retribution.[103] This is what is meant by "the adornment of perfect mastery." It is comparable to how the sun, in revolving about the four great continents,[104] causes it to be noon in one place, morning in another, evening in another, and midnight in another. It is because its position varies as it revolves that, though there is but a single sun, it is seen differently from these four places.[105] The freedom of a bodhisattva is like this.

[2b8] What is it to establish animate beings perfectly in the dharma? By emitting a single beam of light, a bodhisattva can bring animate beings the benefit [of the realization that all things are] identical to emptiness, identical to provisionality, and identical to the middle way. And he can confer the benefit of being able to enter samādhi, depart from it, do both [at the same time], or do neither [in any and all circumstances]. This holds for walking, standing, sitting, lying down, speaking, being silent, or any activity whatever. Whoever is so destined by previous karmic affinity will see [this reality], just as a person with eyes sees light. One without such karmic predilection [for the perfect teaching] will not perceive it, just as it is always dark for the blind.[106]

103. These two types of karmic retribution refer, respectively, to the psychophysical being of the entity itself and the features of external environment or circumstance.

104. In Buddhist cosmology these surround Mount Sumeru, the center of the world. Starting in the south and moving counterclockwise, they are Jambudvipa (our world, or alternatively, India), Pūrvavideha, Uttarakuru, and Aparagodānīya.

105. Chan-jan (T 46.153a20–23) clarifies the analogy by identifying noon with both entering and leaving samādhi, morning with rising and expounding, evening with entering samādhi, and midnight with neither entering nor leaving samādhi.

106. In Chih-i's writings, the perfect teaching and perfect and sudden calming and contemplation are exclusively intended for beings of keen karmic capacity or endowments.

[2b12] Hence we cite the dragon-king as an illustration.[107] In height he encompasses the six heavens of the realm of desire and in breadth reaches across the four continents. He raises all manner of clouds, wields all manner of thunder, flashes all manner of lightning, and causes all manner of rain to fall, all without budging from his own palace. His activity appears different to everyone who sees him. This is what a bodhisattva is like. Having attained internally for himself full realization of the simultaneous identity of emptiness, provisionality, and the middle, he is able, without disturbing the dharma-nature, externally to cause animate beings to gain a variety of benefits and engage in a variety of activities [to effect their salvation]. This is what is called "establishing animate beings in the dharma by means of his perfect energy."

[2b17] At the [stage of] first arousing the thought [of enlightenment][108] it is already like this—how much more so is this true for the intermediate and later stages. The Tathāgata untiringly extols this dharma; those who hear it rejoice.[109] Sadāprarudita sought wisdom in the east.[110] Sudhana sought the dharma in the south.[111] The bodhisattva Bhaiṣajyarāja burnt his own arm as a sacrifice to the Buddha.[112] Samantaprabhāsa risked having his own head cut off.[113] Even if one should

107. From the same section of the *Avataṃsaka*, T 9.440b.

108. That is, the first of the ten abodes of the perfect path, which is known as the "abode of first putting forth the thought [of enlightenment]."

109. An allusion to the *Lotus Sūtra*, T 9.6b (the Chapter on Expedient Devices) and T 9.49c (the chapter on Merits of the Dharma-Preacher).

110. The story of Sadāprarudita "the ever-weeping one" is found in the *Pañcaviṃśati* and its accompanying commentary, the TCTL (T 25.731a). He was tireless in his pursuit of prajñā-pāramitā, until one day he heard the Buddha's voice speaking from the air and telling him to go eastward, to be absolutely indefatigable, not to spare life or limb lest concern for them bind him to saṃsāra. After having begun his journey eastward, he realized he had forgotten to ask the voice how far he should go and whom he should seek out. In sorrow, therefore, he wept for seven days and seven nights as bitterly as if he were mourning a son, whence his name, "the ever-weeping one." Eventually the voice spoke again from the air and gave him proper directions.

111. From the *Gaṇḍavyūha*, the last chapter of the *Avataṃsaka*, T 9.676a, where the story is told of how this bodhisattva sought the dharma from a series of fifty-three acquaintances, achieving realization finally on encountering Mañjuśrī.

112. This story is found in the chapter of the *Lotus Sūtra* titled "Former Deeds of Bodhisattva Medicine King" (T 9.53c; Hurvitz, pp. 293–302). Ultimately Bhaiṣajyarāja immolated his whole body in offering to the dharma, thereby achieving profound realization.

113. From the *Jen-wang pan-jo p'o-lo-mi ching*, T 8.830a. Although the translation of this sūtra is attributed to Kumārajīva, most scholars today regard it as an apocryphal text of Chinese origin. The Sanskrit name here is a "reconstruction" from the Chinese, P'u-ming. The TCTL has a version of the same story but calls

thrice a day give up his own life as often as there are grains of sand in the Ganges, this would still not compare to the power of the merit attained by one who writes down, preaches, and so forth a single verse of the dharma.[114] How then could the feat of carrying a burden on one's shoulders for a billion kalpas ever repay the blessing of the Buddha's dharma. This represents one particular citation from one sūtra;[115] but in other sūtras we find [examples of this teaching] as well.

[2b22] Q: A skeptic might say that he would like to hear firm scriptural proof for the other [two] types of samādhi.[116]

[2b22] A: [It is true that this would be desirable,] but the sūtras and treatises are vast and cannot be cited in detail. Nevertheless we shall briefly mention one or two.

[2b23] The *Vimalakīrti Sūtra* says, "When the Buddha first sat beneath the bodhi-tree and by his power overcame Māra, he attained nectar-like nirvāṇa and won enlightenment. He thrice turned the wheel of the dharma[117] for the billion worlds. The wheel was fundamentally and forever pure, which is attested to by the fact that gods and men have been enlightened thereby. It was then that the three jewels[118] appeared in the

---

the protagonist by his more usual name of Sutasoma. See Lamotte, *Traité* 1.261, for additional Pāli, Sanskrit, and Chinese sources for this tale. According to the story, this king was seized by a prince Kalmāṣapāda, who had vowed to kill 1,000 kings in order to become a king himself. Sutasoma begged for time to fulfill a promise he had made to a mendicant to give him alms and was given a temporary reprieve. He promised to return, however, and risked his life to fulfill that promise, whereupon Kalmāṣapāda finally spared his life and released his other captives as well.

114. From the *Diamond Sūtra*, T 8.750c.

115. The citation referred to here is the one from the *Avataṃsaka*, according to *Shiki* (1.132). Chan-jan disagrees (T 46.154c3–5), saying that the phrase refers to the entire section—the citing of one example from each sūtra.

116. In other words, samādhi here refers to cultivation of samādhi through the gradual and variable forms of calming and contemplation.

117. Chan-jan (T 46.154c23–25) explains that the wheel can signify the crushing of the afflictions (*kleśa*), while the three turns of the wheel signify indicating (*chih*), exhorting (*ch'üan*), and proving (*cheng*), respectively. This refers to the way in which the Buddha expounded the four noble truths to his first five disciples in the Deer Park. In the "first turn of the wheel" he "indicated" the meaning of each of the four truths. In the second turning of the wheel he "exhorted" his disciples to realize these truths fully, and in the third turning he offered himself as "proof" that full realization was possible. These three turnings of the wheel of the dharma should not be confused with the better-known schema found in the *Saṃdhinirmocana Sūtra* and elaborated by Bu-ston, namely the Hīnayāna, Madhyamaka, and Yogācāra traditions.

118. Buddha, dharma, and saṅgha.

world."[119] This was the beginning of the gradual teaching.[120] The *Vimalakīrti* also says, "The Buddha expounds the dharma with a single sound, but each type of animate being understands it in its own way. Some fear and some rejoice, some develop aversion, and some are freed from doubt. This is an example of his superhuman and unique power."[121] This is the scriptural proof for the variable teaching. The *Vimalakīrti* also says, "The Buddha teaches that dharmas neither exist nor inexist, for it is by reason of causes and conditions that they arise. Yet though there is no self, no doer, and no recipient [of karmic retribution],[122] still this does not mean that good and evil karma are also done away with."[123] This is the scriptural proof for the sudden teaching.

[2c2] It says in the *Pañcaviṃśati*, "There is a sequential approach to practice, a sequential approach to study, and a sequential approach to [realization of the] way."[124] This is scriptural proof of the gradual calming and contemplation.[125] The *Pañcaviṃśati* also says, "When a jewel is wrapped in cloth of various colors and placed in water, the color of the water varies according to the color of the substance used to wrap the jewel."[126] This is scriptural proof of the variable calming and contemplation or teaching. It also says, "From the moment of first arousing the thought [of enlightenment] they sit in the place of enlightenment,[127] turn the wheel of the dharma, and save animate beings."[128] This is scriptural proof of the sudden calming and contemplation.

[2c6] It says in the *Lotus*, "Such persons will by this dharma enter gradually into the wisdom of the Buddhas."[129] This verifies the gradual calming and contemplation. The *Lotus* also says, "If they should not believe

119. T 14.537c.

120. According to later T'ien-t'ai doctrine, the gradual teaching describes the basic pedagogical strategy that informed the Buddha's historical career. It is identified with the five periods of (1) the *Avataṃsaka*, (2) the Deer Park, (3) the vaipulya [scriptures], (4) the prajñā (scriptures), and (5) the *Lotus* and *Nirvāṇa* sūtras. This is the second of the five.

121. T 14.538a.

122. That is, dharmas do not exist.

123. T 14.537c.

124. T 8.384b; see also TCTL, T 25.666b.

125. Chan-jan (T 46.155b5–9) understands "practice, study, and the way" to represent the six perfections: "practice" corresponds to giving (*dāna*) and exertion (*vīrya*), "study" to discipline (*śīla*) and meditation (dhyāna), and "the way" to forbearance (*kṣānti*) and wisdom (prajñā).

126. T 8.291c; see also TCTL, T 25.477b.

127. *Bodhimaṇḍa*.

128. Ibid., T 8.226a; see also TCTL, T 25.342b.

129. T 9.25c.

this dharma, then let other profound dharmas show, teach, benefit, and delight them."[130] This verifies the variable calming and contemplation. The *Lotus* also says, "I [the Buddha] have openly cast away the expedient [teaching][131] and expound now only the supreme way."[132] This verifies the sudden calming and contemplation.

[2c10] The *Nirvāṇa Sūtra* says, "From the cow there comes milk, [from milk comes cream, from cream come butter curds, from butter curds comes butter, and from butter] there ultimately comes ghee."[133] This verifies the gradual calming and contemplation. It also says in the *Nirvāṇa Sūtra,* "When poison is put in milk, then the milk can kill people. This is true as well [for all the progressive refinements of milk] up to ghee, which also can kill people if poison is put in it."[134] This proves the variable calming and contemplation. The *Nirvāṇa Sūtra* also says, "In the Himalayas there is a grass called *kṣānti.* If a cow eats it then one instantly obtains ghee from the cow's milk."[135] This proves the sudden calming and contemplation.

130. T 9.52c.

131. *Upāya.* This refers to the provisonal teachings of the three vehicles used previously in the Buddha's teaching career. In their place the "real" teaching of the one vehicle [i.e., perfect teaching] is revealed.

132. T 9.10a. From the famous verses concluding the chapter on Expedient Devices. See Hurvitz, pp. 42–47 for the context.

133. T 12.690c–691a. This is the *locus classicus* of the well-known simile of the five flavors (*wu-wei*), adopted by Chih-i and developed by subsequent T'ien-t'ai masters as a scheme to classify the respective phases of development or unfolding of the Buddha's historical teaching (i.e., the "five periods"). The sūtra continues, "By using the ghee one eradicates all sickness, for all medicines are contained within it. Oh sons of good family, it is also thus with the Buddha and his teaching. From the Buddha come the twelve divisions of scripture, from the twelve divisions of scripture come the sūtras, from the sūtras come the vaipulya [i.e., Mahāyāna] sūtras, from the vaipulya sūtras come the prajñāpāramitā, and from the prajñāpāramitā comes the *mahāparinirvāṇa,* which is to be compared with ghee (the ultimate essence). Ghee is analogous to the Buddha-nature."

For discussion of the historical development of this scheme in T'ien-t'ai, see Chappell, *T'ien-t'ai Buddhism,* pp. 21–42, and Hurvitz, "Chih-i," pp. 230–244.

134. T 12.784c. The quotation may be continued to clarify the point: "All the five progressive essences contain poison, yet milk is not called 'cream,' nor is cream called 'milk,' and this is so for the different stages right up to ghee. Although the names change, the poisonous essence is not lost. If the ghee is taken, even it can still kill people, though in fact that poison has not been put directly into the ghee. It is the same with the Buddha-nature of animate beings: though they dwell in five different destinies [of saṃsāra] and are incarnated in different bodies, still their Buddha-nature is always one and unchanging."

135. T 12.770b. To continue the quote from the sūtra: "There are also other grasses, but if the cow eats them, then no ghee is produced. Yet despite the ab-

[2c13] It says in the *Sūtra of Illimitable Meaning*, "When the Buddha turned the wheel of the dharma, he first rained down little drops to wash away the dust of all desires, thus opening the gate to nirvāṇa, fanning the wind of liberation, eradicating the keen sufferings in the world, and bringing into existence the purity and coolness of the dharma. Next he rained down the doctrine of the twelve causes and conditions of dependent origination, by which he washed the land of nescience and blotted out the glare of false views. Finally he poured forth the unexcelled Mahāyāna, arousing the thought of enlightenment in all beings."[136] This verifies the gradual calming and contemplation.

[2c18] It says in the *Avataṃsaka Sūtra*, "When the sea-dragons rain into the ocean drops the size of carriage axles, the ocean alone is capacious enough, other places cannot endure it. The perfect sūtras were preached for beings of superior capacity; adherents to the two vehicles were as if deaf and dumb."[137]

[2c19] It says in the *Vimalakīrti*, "When entering a *campaka* grove, only the strong perfume of the *campaka* tree's flowers, but no other scent, can be smelled. In the same way, one who enters this room perceives nothing but the fragrance of the merit of Buddhas."[138]

[2c21] It says in the *Śūraṅgama-samādhi Sūtra*, "If one grinds a myriad kinds of incense together into a ball, and a single particle of this ball is burnt, the smoke is endowed with all the component vapors."[139]

[2c22] It says in the *Pañcaviṃśati*, "If a bodhisattva desires through om-

---

sence of ghee in this case, one cannot say that there is no *kṣānti* grass in the Himalayas. It is the same with the Buddha-nature. The Himalayas represent the Tathāgata, the *kṣānti* grass represents the great nirvāṇa, and the other grasses represent the twelve divisions of scripture. If living beings are able to listen to, receive, and be enlightened by this great nirvāṇa, then they will perceive the Buddha-nature. Though one does not hear from the twelve divisions of scripture, it cannot on that account be said that there is no Buddha-nature."

136. *Wu-liang-i ching*, T 9.384b. This sūtra presents itself (and has been traditionally accepted) as a prelude to the *Lotus Sūtra*. It is an apocryphal work produced in China during the mid-fifth century.

137. T 9.573a. The original text of the sūtra reads: "For example, it resembles the great rain that the sea-dragon kings rain down, in that only the great ocean, and no other place, can receive it. Bodhisattva-mahāsattvas are like this ocean, but none of the ordinary animate beings, nor śrāvakas, nor pratyekabuddhas, nor bodhisattvas even up to the ninth stage of the ten stages of bodhisattvahood can fully receive the . . . Tathāgata's great rain of the dharma. Only those bodhisattvas dwelling in the realm of the dharma-cloud of the tenth stage, all of them, can receive and keep it."

138. T 14.548a. The text in the sūtra goes on, "and does not delight in smelling the perfume of the inferior merit of śrāvakas and pratyekabuddhas."

139. *Shou-leng-yen san-mei ching*, T 15.633b.

niscient knowledge of all modes to know all dharmas, Śāriputra, he should train in the perfection of wisdom."[140]

[2c23] It says in the *Lotus*, "[The bodhisattvas and wheel-turning kings, gods, and dragons come,] each with his hands joined reverently, wishing to hear of the perfect way."[141]

[2c24] It says in the *Nirvāṇa Sūtra*, "For example, it is as if there were someone swimming in the great ocean; know that in so doing he makes use of the water of all rivers."[142]

[2c25] It says in the *Avataṃsaka Sūtra*, "For example, it resembles the rising of the sun: first at sunrise the peaks of the high mountains alone are illuminated, then their valleyed [slopes], and then plains."[143] The plains correspond to the variable, the valleys to the gradual, and the high mountains to the sudden calming and contemplation.

[2c27] Everything quoted above is the authentic word from the golden mouth of the Buddha. It is the dharma as revered by the Tathāgatas of past, present, and future. It has no beginning, no matter how far back in

140. T 8.218c; TCTL, T 25.137c. "Omniscient wisdom of all modes" is the highest of three wisdoms presented in TCTL, T 25.259a, where it is described as the Buddha's wisdom, as opposed to bodhisattva's wisdom (wisdom of the modes of destinies, *tao-chung-chih*) and the wisdom of adherents to the two vehicles (omniscient wisdom, *i-ch'ieh-chih*).

141. T 9.6c.

142. T 12.753b. The sūtra adds, "A bodhisattva-mahāsattva is like this. Know that when he practices the diamond (*vajra*) samādhi, he thereby practices all samādhis."

143. T 9.616b. This concludes Kuan-ting's series of twelve scriptural proofs. The passage in the sūtra reads in full: "For example, it resembles the shining of the sun: first at sunrise the kings of all great mountains are illuminated; next the sun illuminates all the rest of the great mountains; next it illuminates the diamond (*vajra*) mountains; only then does it completely illuminate all the great earth. The rays of the sun do not think, 'we shall first illuminate the kings, and so on until we completely illuminate the great earth.' It is because the mountainous territory has higher and lower elevations that there is an earlier and a later in regard to illumination. The Tathāgata, the one deserving offerings, the perfectly enlightened one, is like this. . . . The 'sun,' that is, the wisdom of the boundless dharmadhātu, emits the infinite, unimpeded light of wisdom; it first illuminates all the kings of mountains—the bodhisattva-mahāsattvas, then the pratyekabuddhas, then the śrāvakas, then the beings who have been determined to have a favorable capacity for enlightenment, for beings are converted in accordance with their capacity for response to the teaching. Only then does the light of wisdom illuminate the rest of living beings, including even those determined to be of evil nature, and create the causes and conditions for their future benefit. The sunlight of the Tathāgata's wisdom does not think, 'I will first illuminate bodhisattvas, and so on up until those determined to be of evil nature.' He simply emits the light of great wisdom, and thus illuminates all sons of the Buddha everywhere."

the past; it is unlimited and boundless in the present; and it will roll ceaselessly on into the future. Its nature is inconceivable in any of the three times. Know that calming and contemplation is the teacher of all these Buddhas. Since the dharma is eternal, the Buddhas are also eternal. So, too, is it blissful, personal, and pure.[144] How could anyone fail to believe such scriptural proof?

[3a4] Once one has faith in this dharma of the three kinds of calming and contemplation, one needs to know the three texts in which it is set forth. The first of these is the *Graduated Approach to Dhyāna*,[145] which altogether would equal thirty fascicles. The extant ten-fascicle version was personally taken down in writing by the monk Fa-shen[146] of the Ta-chuang-yen monastery. The second of these is the text on variable calming and contemplation, the *Six Wondrous Dharma-gates*.[147] In accordance with the meaning of "variable," it touches on the practices of the twelve dhyānas,[148] the nine meditations on death,[149] the eight liberations,[150] [the four approaches to dhyāna of] discernment, refinement, perfuming, and cultivation,[151] [the twelve] causes and conditions, and the six perfections.

144. The *Nirvāṇa Sūtra* (T 12.652b) teaches the revolutionary doctrine that reality (rather than being altogether impermanent, painful, devoid of self, and impure), when properly understood according to the Mahāyāna, is ultimately permanent, blissful, personally endowed with selfhood, and pure in its essential nature.

145. *Tz'u-ti ch'an-men* is an abbreviated form of the fuller title, *Shih ch'an p'o-lo-mi tz'u-ti fa-men* (Elucidation of the Graduated Approach of the Perfection of Dhyāna), T no. 1916. The treatise represents one of Chih-i's earliest works, taken down from a series of lectures delivered at Wa-kuan ssu in Chin-ling between 568 and 575. See Satō, *Tendai daishi no kenkyū*, pp. 103–126, for details.

146. In 571. It was later edited by Kuan-ting. See Hurvitz, "Chih-i," pp. 174–175.

147. *Liu-miao fa-men*, T no. 1917. The work expounds the six phases of mindfulness of the breathing (*ānāpāna-smṛti*) according to sudden, gradual, and variable perspectives.

148. These are the four basic concentrations or dhyānas from the Hīnayāna tradition, the four emptinesses (of marks, inexistence, own-being, and other-being), and the four infinite states of mind (*brahmavihāra*) (of loving-kindness, compassion, sympathetic joy, and equanimity).

149. In these originally Hīnayāna meditations one contemplates nine progressive stages of putrefaction and disintegration of a human corpse in order to counteract fleshly attachments.

150. *Vimokṣas*. See TCTL, T 25.215a–216a. These are dealt with in the *Dīgha-nikāya* no. 15 (English translation in Rhys Davids, *Dialogues of the Buddha*, pt. 2, pp. 68–70, "The Eight Stages of Deliverance").

151. Four levels of approach to or mastery of the techniques of dhyāna: discernment applies methods and produces dhyāna individually, refinement and perfuming link and master them in sequence, and cultivation develops total sov-

[This text] makes the rounds of the aforementioned techniques freely and without constraints, both vertically and horizontally. The president of the department of affairs of state, Mao Hsi, requested Chih-i to produce this work.[152] The third text is the *Perfect and Sudden* [*Calming and Contemplation*],[153] taken down in ten fascicles by the monk Kuan-ting in the Jade Spring Monastery in Ching-chou. Though there are three texts, do not warp or harm your own understanding by adhering biasedly [to mere provisional distinctions among them]. The *Great Treatise* says, "Whether they perceive the perfection of wisdom or not, everyone is in bondage and everyone is liberated."[154] The way in which such texts ought to be regarded is analogous to this.

[3a11] Q: A skeptic would say that since all dharmas ultimately have the mark of nirvāṇa, [this mark] is impossible to put into words.[155] The *Nirvāṇa Sūtra* says, "The origination of something existent cannot be explained, and the failure of something inexistent to originate cannot be explained."[156] Whether one attempts to discourse in summary or in detail, the path of language is cut off, and there is neither anyone to explain nor anything to be explained. Moreover, Śāriputra said, "I have heard that in regard to liberation there is nothing to be said; therefore I do not know what to say about it."[157] Furthermore, the *Vimalakīrti* says, "What is expounded lacks the capacity to be expounded or indicated. Those who listen to the dharma being expounded can neither hear it nor attain to an understanding of it."[158] Thus neither does a person have the ability to expound it, nor is the dharma expoundable, yet you speak of teaching people.

[3a18] A:[159] But you mention only one of the two extremes,[160] without taking the other into consideration. The *Nirvāṇa Sūtra* says, "Because of

---

ereignity over different techniques and levels of dhyāna, where any one of them can freely produce or be transmuted into the others.

152. For details, see Satō, *Tendai daishi no kenkyū*, pp. 151–171.

153. That is, the *Mo-ho chih-kuan* known by the title used for its two earlier editions. See Satō, *Tendai daishi no kenkyū*, pp. 364–399.

154. TCTL, T 25.190c. The passage reads: "One who does not perceive the perfection of wisdom is in bondage; but one who does perceive the perfection of wisdom is also in bondage. One who perceives the perfection of wisdom gains liberation; but one who does not perceive the perfection of wisdom also gains liberation."

155. From the *Lotus Sūtra*, T 9.10a.

156. T 12.733c.

157. *Vimalakīrti Sūtra*, T 14.548a.

158. T 14.540a.

159. Here follow eleven sūtra quotes supporting the utility of expounding the dharma.

160. That is, the extreme of inexistence, corresponding to emptiness.

causes and conditions, it is nevertheless possible to expound the dharma."[161] The *Lotus Sūtra* says, "The Buddhas expound the dharma for animate beings by recourse to numberless expedients and a variety of causes and conditions."[162] It also says, "It was by the power of expedients that Śākyamuni expounded the dharma to the five monks."[163] In fact the dharma can be expounded, both in summary and in detail. It says in the *Nirvāṇa Sūtra*, "A person with normal eyes describes the color of milk to one who is blind."[164] This shows that ultimate truth can be explained. The *Pravara-devarāja-paripṛcchā Sūtra* says, "Though a dhāraṇī ultimately lacks words and letters, yet words and letters express an incantation."[165] This shows that the conventional truth can be explained. Besides, the Tathāgata always relies on these two truths to preach the dharma.[166] The *Vimalakīrti* says, "Being separate from the essence of words and letters—this is identical with liberation."[167] Thus expounding is ultimately identi-

161. T 12.733c, following almost immediately after the passage quoted by the skeptic above (see note 156).

162. T 9.7b.

163. T 9.10a. This *Lotus* quote follows immediately on the quote in which the skeptic framed his objection above (see note 155). This refers to the time of the first turning of the wheel of the dharma, directly after Śākyamuni's enlightenment under the bodhi tree.

164. T 12.688c. Kuan-ting has here summarized a long passage from the sūtra: "Oh son of good family, all these unbelievers (*tīrthikas*) are foolish and childish, without either wisdom or expedients; they are unable to fully comprehend [impermanence] or permanence, suffering or bliss, purity or impurity, self or nonself, life or nonlife, beings or nonbeings, reality or unreality, existence or inexistence. They grasp only a small part of the Buddha's dharma. Falsely imagining that there is permanence, bliss, selfhood, and purity, they in fact do not understand the real permanence, bliss, selfhood, and purity. It is just as with a person blind from birth, who, not knowing the color of milk, asks another, saying, 'What is the color of milk like?' The other answers, 'The color is white like a seashell.' The blind one asks again, 'Is this color of milk then like the sound of a seashell?' 'No.' 'What is the color of a seashell like?' 'It is like the tip of an ear of rice.' The blind one asks again, 'Is then the color of milk soft like the tip of a rice-ear? What again is the color of the tip of a rice-ear like?' The other answers, 'It is like snow.' The blind one asks again, 'Is then the tip of a rice-ear cold like snow? What again is the color of snow like?' 'It is like a white crane.' Thus, although this person, blind since birth, hears four similes, he is ultimately unable to arrive at the real color of milk. It is the same with unbelievers, who are ultimately unable to realize the permanent, blissful, personal, and pure nature of reality."

165. *Sheng-t'ien-wang pan-jo p'o-lo-mi ching*, T 8.720c.

166. Possibly an allusion to the *Middle Treatise* (*Chung-lun*), T 30.32c, although Chih-i and Kuan-ting seem to cite consistently from sūtras here rather than from treatises.

167. T 14.548a. This follows soon after the first of the two *Vimalakīrti* passages quoted by the skeptic (see note 157). The MHCK text, however, is apparently

cal to not-expounding. The *Nirvāṇa Sūtra* says, "If a bodhisattva should understand that the Tathāgata never expounds the dharma at all, then he is one who has heard much of it."[168] This shows that non-expounding is itself expounding. The *Viśeṣacintabrahma-paripṛcchā* says, "The Buddha and his disciples constantly engage in two forms of practice, now expounding and now being silent."[169] The *Lotus Sūtra* says, "Whether he is going or coming, standing or sitting, the Buddha constantly expounds the wondrous dharma like a downpour of rain."[170] It also says, "If you wish to seek the Buddhist dharma, follow constantly those who have heard much of it,"[171] and "A worthy friend[172] is an important cause and condition for enlightenment, for he converts and leads you and enables you to see the Buddha."[173] The *Nirvāṇa Sūtra* says, "Clouds and thunder in the air produce flowers on ivory."[174] How could there ever fail to be preaching of the dharma?

[3b2] If one sets expounding and silence in opposition to each other, then one fails to understand the meaning of the teaching and departs further and further from principle (*li*). There is, however, no principle

---

corrupt here, omitting a crucial negation that stands in the *Taishō* text of the *Vimalakīrti*, so that the MHCK text should read here, "Not being separate. . . ." The sūtra passage itself may be rendered, "Speech, words, and letters—these all have the mark of liberation. Why is this? Because liberation is not within nor without, nor is it between the two; and words and letters too are not within nor without, nor between the two. For this reason, Śāriputra, liberation cannot be expounded without words and letters. Why is this? Because all dharmas have the mark of liberation."

168. T 12.764c.

169. T 15.50c.

170. T 9.208.

171. T 9.60c, paraphrased. The match is a dubious one.

172. *Kalyāṇamitra* or "good spiritual friend."

173. T 9.60c.

174. T 12.652b. The sūtra says: "For example, when in the sky thunderbolts flash and clouds arise, flowers [seem to] appear on all ivory. Without thunderbolts no flowers would appear, nor would there even be names for them. The Buddha-nature of animate beings is like this, for being constantly obscured by the defilements, it cannot be seen. This is why I teach that animate beings are without self. If one can hear this marvelous scripture called *Mahāparinirvāṇa*, then he perceives [his own] Buddha-nature, like flowers on ivory. Even if he has heard all the samādhis of the [Hīnayāna] sūtras, he will not understand the subtle marks of the Tathāgata if he has not heard this sūtra, just as no flowers can be seen on ivory without a thunderbolt. But having heard this sūtra, he will understand the secret treasury of the Buddha-nature preached by all the Tathāgatas, just as flowers may be seen on ivory by the light of a thunderbolt. Having heard this scripture, he will immediately understand that all the numberless animate beings have a Buddha-nature."

apart from the expounding of it, and no expounding apart from principle, for expounding and non-expounding are identical to each other. There is no duality, no difference between them; the phenomenal (*shih*), as it stands, is the real. The compassionate one preaches because he takes pity on all those who have not heard the dharma. It is as though the moon were hidden behind a mountain range, and one raised a round fan to create a semblance of it; or as though the blowing of the wind had ceased, and one shook a tree to indicate the effect the wind would have. These days people's minds are dull, and to attain profound vision is accordingly difficult. But by the eye's relying on visible form one is able to see; and through recourse to the written word [understanding] is made easier for them. But if one were then to damage his understanding by imprisoning himself in the written text, then it would be essential for him to realize that a text is not an absolute text. And having penetrated to the realization that all written words are ultimately neither absolute valid writings nor non-valid writings, then he can achieve complete understanding through a single text. It is in light of this principle that these three texts have been used to create a gate through which the one [ultimate reality] is achieved.

[3b10] This completes the brief explanation of the origination of the *Mo-ho chih-kuan*.[175]

175. Here ends Kuan-ting's introduction to the MHCK. The next section, still preceding the MHCK proper and its greater chapter 1, the Synopsis, is usually thought to be Chih-i's own words, taken down and edited later by Kuan-ting.

Introduction by Chih-i

[3b10] We shall now list the ten chapters [of the text]. Chapter 1 is the Synopsis (*ta-i*). Chapter 2 concerns the explanation of terms.[1] Chapter 3 elucidates the features of that essence [which the terms "calming" and "contemplation" describe].[2] Chapter 4 demonstrates how all dharmas are encompassed [by the practice of calming and contemplation].[3] Chapter 5 [distinguishes between] one-sided (*p'ien*) and perfect (*yüan*) [calming and contemplation].[4] Chapter 6 sets forth [preparatory] expedients [for calming and contemplation].[5] Chapter 7 discusses contemplation proper

1. The terms "calming" (*chih*) and "contemplation" (*kuan*) are discussed in this chapter according to the four perspectives of relative, absolute, conflation, and differentiation, and their shared inherence in the three meritorious qualities of enlightenment (see T 46.21b–23c). A similar thematic focus on calming and contemplation pertains for the other eight chapters of the MHCK as well. Chan-jan (T 46.157c1–2) notes: "From the general synopsis of calming and contemplation to the tenth chapter on the returning of the purport in calming and contemplation, anyone expounding [this text] should always gloss it with reference to calming and contemplation."

2. MHCK, T 46.23c–29c. Four perspectives are used to elicit the essential substance (*t'i*) of the perfect calming and discerning: its relative place among the classifications of the four teachings, the various wisdoms or eyes, the spheres or objects [of wisdom], and final contribution or loss.

3. See T 46.29c–32a. Calming and contemplation encompass all dharmas in six ways—by comprehensively encompassing all principles (*li*), all delusions, all forms of wisdom, all practices, all stages, and all teachings.

4. See T 46.32a–35c. Biased or one-sided (*p'ien*) and perfect or rounded (*yüan*) calming and contemplation are distinguished according to (1) greater and lesser vehicles, (2) partially (*pan*) and completely (*man*) stated meaning, and the doctrinal perspectives of the (3) one-sided and perfect, (4) gradual and sudden, and (5) the provisional and real.

5. "Expedients" here refers to the well-known T'ien-t'ai formula of the twenty-

(*cheng-kuan*).[6] Chapter 8 concerns the results and recompenses [of calming and contemplation]. Chapter 9 is on the generation of teachings [from calming and contemplation]. Chapter 10 treats the returning of the purport [to the ultimate abode]. This division into ten is simply a convention of enumeration, the number ten being neither too many nor too few.[7] The opening chapter shows that the final goal [of the practice] lies in *ḍha*, while the concluding chapter conveys this basic theme of the text to its ultimate end.[8] Thus [the text] begins in excellence and ends in excellence, proceeding as a unified whole through these ten chapters.

---

five preliminary expedients: the (1) fulfilling of the five conditions, (2) reproval of the five desires (of sense), (3) removing of the five hindrances or coverings (*nivaraṇa*), (4) adjusting and harmonizing (of body, breath, and mind), and (5) the five expedient practices. These define the optimum environment for calming and contemplation as well as establish the mental and physical tenor necessary for effective application of calming and discerning—meditative discernment proper. For this reason, the twenty-five expedients are often referred to as "preliminary expedients" (*ch'ien fang-pien*) or "remote expedients" (*yüan fang-pien*) in contrast to the techniques of "cultivation proper" (*cheng hsiu*) or "near expedients" (*chin fang-pien*) represented by calming and contemplation proper. The twenty-five preliminary expedients are explained at length in Chih-i's *Tz'u-ti ch'an-men* (T 46.483c–491c), *Hsiao chih-kuan* (T 46.462c–466c), and MHCK chapter 6 (T 46.35c–48c), as well as Kuan-ting's *Kuan-hsin lun shu* (T 46.603c–607c). English translations of the *Hsiao-chih-kuan* are available in Luk, *Secrets of Chinese Meditation*, and Goddard and Wai-tao, *A Buddhist Bible*.

6. An abbreviation of the full title of the chapter, "Cultivation of Calming and Contemplation Proper" or, as the case may be, "Right Cultivation of Calming and Contemplation" (*cheng hsiu chih-kuan*). This is the most central and extensive of the ten chapters of the MHCK, occupying well over half of the entire work (T 46.48c–140c). It is divided into ten subsections, corresponding to what are known as the ten objects or spheres of contemplation (*kuan-ching*). To each of these ten spheres the famous ten modes of discernment (*kuan-fa*) are in turn applied as the principal method of contemplation. The text of the MHCK itself ends with the seventh of the ten spheres (contemplation of the sphere of views), leaving undiscussed the last three spheres of greater chapter 7 as well as the last three chapters of the work as a whole—greater chapters 8 through 10.

7. Although both Chih-i and Chan-jan refrain from drawing any formal connection with the *Avataṃsaka*, Chan-jan (T 46.157c3) notes that "In the *Avataṃsaka Sūtra* the various series of dharma gates are enumerated in sets of ten." See, for example, chapters 12 through 14 (in the sixty-fascicle text) describing the practices and merits associated with manifesting the thought of enlightenment and entry into the ten abodes (T 9.449a–462c).

8. The syllable *ḍha* represents the last in a series of forty-two syllables of the Siddham Sanskrit alphabet that are equated in the *Pañcaviṃśati* and TCTL with various thematic permutations of the liberative wisdom of the nonarising of dharmas. Regarding this final syllable, TCTL says (T 25.409a): "One who hears it realizes that all dharmas are incapable of being attained. There are no letters

[3b14] As for the production and origination of this text, we consider simply the sequential progression of the ten chapters. The ultimate principle (*li*) is quiescent and extinct, lacking both production and producer, origination and originator. However, by dint of cause and condition, the ten chapters as a whole are produced and originated.[9] Should we distinguish [the text] according to the particular [content of its chapters], preceding chapters produce [subsequent ones], while subsequent chapters originate [from preceding ones].[10] The same [sort of analysis] can be

---

beyond *ḍha*." Chih-i, following a precedent first established in Hui-ssu's *Ssu-shih-erh tzu-men* (Gates of the Forty-two Syllables), matched the forty-two syllables from *a* to *ḍha* with the forty-two ranks of the *Ying-lo ching* and *Avataṃsaka Sūtra* to describe a set of bodhisattva stages for the path of the perfect teaching. Just as all syllables are permutations of the primal syllable *a*, so each of the forty-two stages from arousing the thought of enlightenment to full Buddhahood is simply a further intensification of the original insight of nonarising on which the path is founded. Thus progress toward Buddhahood is marked not by qualitative changes in insight or stage but by a seamless maturation or intensification of the insight that brought forth the first arousing of the thought of enlightenment. Although in quality it is no different from the first letter, *a*, the last letter, *ḍha*, represents the final culmination of the path in the achievement of Buddhahood.

Chan-jan (T 46.157c10–12) comments: "The five lesser chapters of the Synopsis commence with the arousing of the great thought [of enlightenment] and aspire to the final goal [of returning the mind] to the great abode. The 'great abode' is none other than the three meritorious qualities [of Buddhahood] to which 'the purport returns.' The three meritorious qualities are themselves the ultimate meaning that is the syllable *ḍha*. 'Concluding [chapter]' refers to the returning of the purport. The three meritorious qualities that mark the returning of the purport represent [the end] to which the myriad practices [for cultivation of] self and other lead. Thus [the text] says, 'conveys to its ultimate end.' "

9. This passage, according to Chan-jan, offers a "universalistic" (*t'ung*) explanation of the "production and origination" of the MHCK as a whole. Chan-jan states (T 46.157c16–18): "[From the perspective of] principle (*li*) there is no arising or production to speak of, nor is there any subject [who initiates such an arising], due to the matter of the cause and effect [relationship that pertains between] self and other. For this reason the text says, 'cause and condition.' [Chih-i's] explanation contains both universal (*t'ung*) and particular (*pieh*) [perspectives]. According to that of the universal, each chapter [as it is] contains the two senses of producing and originating."

10. For his specific or particular (*pieh*) analysis of the production and origination of the text, Chih-i introduces a distinction between *sheng* as "producing" and *ch'i* as "originating." Chan-jan states (T 46.157c19–20): "According to the specific perspective, [to say that] 'production occurs with the preceding chapters' means that they act to produce the subsequent [chapters]. [To say that] 'origination occurs with the subsequent chapters' means that the subsequent originate from the preceding." Chan-jan's reading of the passage has been followed here.

made [using the expressions] "conditional basis" and "thematic progression."[11]

[3b18] Having been veiled in stupidity and delusion for numberless aeons, unaware that nescience is itself enlightenment, one becomes alerted to one's condition for the first time [on encountering this treatise]. Thus [chapter 1] is called "the synopsis or overview." Once having understood the identity of nescience and enlightenment, one is no longer subject to the flux [of saṃsāra]. This we refer to as "calm" (*chih*). The lustrousness and great purity [of this realization] we call "contemplation" (*kuan*).[12] Upon hearing these terms [explained] one apprehends the essence (*t'i*) to which they refer.[13] This essence itself encompasses all dharmas,[14] including both the one-sided and the perfect.[15] Through an understanding of [the difference between] the one-sided and perfect, expedients are devised.[16] Once expedients are instituted, right

11. Chan-jan states (T 46.157c20–22): "Production and origination are alternately referred to as 'conditional basis' and 'thematic progression' [respectively]. That is to say, the preceding chapters act as the conditional basis for the subsequent chapters. And the subsequent chapters represent thematic progressions from the preceding ones. This is [the analysis] according to the particular (*pieh*) perspective. From the universal (*t'ung*) perspective, every chapter contains both conditional basis and thematic derivation."

12. The preceding two sentences correspond to chapter 2, Explanation of Terms. Explaining the use of the two terms "calming" and "contemplation," Chan-jan (T 46.158a1–3) says: "Having awakened [to one's condition] one no longer seeks after the one-sided or lesser nirvāṇa—this is what is meant by 'not being subject to flux.' The fact that one is no longer defiled by the three delusions is what is meant by 'great purity.' "

13. Corresponding to chapter 3. Chan-jan (T 46.158a4–6) says: "Names are able to perform the function of elucidating. The 'essence' is [the object] that is elucidated. Because of the name one knows that there is [an object] to be elucidated. It is in this sense that [the text] uses the term 'apprehend.' It is not stating that [this 'essence'] is apprehended in the form of an actual realization (*cheng-te*)."

14. Corresponding to chapter 4. Chan-jan (T 46.158a6–7) says: " 'Essence itself encompasses all dharmas' is to say that that essence refers to reality, and reality is able to include the provisional. Thus the provisional and real [together] encompass all dharmas."

15. Corresponding to chapter 5. Chan-jan (T 46.158a7–8) says: "The provisional and real that are encompassed do not go beyond the one-sided and perfect. Thus reality and the provisional are distinguished on the basis of the one-sided and perfect."

16. Corresponding to chapter 6. Chan-jan (T 46.158a8–10) says: "The rest of the passage can be understood accordingly. Although the ten chapters produce and originate [in the fashion described above], the text is above all concerned with generating practice on the basis of understanding. For this reason the last three chapters are listed only in brief and not explained."

contemplation[17] is established; and having established right contemplation, one gains the wondrous result or recompense.[18] On the basis of one's personal attainment of the dharma, one generates teachings and trains others.[19] Self and other both achieve peace and, together, revert to eternal quiescence.[20] It is only because we have not attained to nonproduction and nonorigination that the production and origination [of these ten chapters] takes place. For, once one comprehends nonproduction and nonorigination, mental impulses are extinguished. The path of language is cut off, and there is perfect quiescence and purity.

[3b26] [The text] is divided [into discrete sections] because the meritorious virtues offered in these ten chapters are like a jewel in a bag: if it were not groped after and brought out for display, no one would be able to see it.[21] Of these ten chapters, which deal with the true, which with the conventional, and which with neither the true nor the conventional? Which deal with the preaching of saints, which with their silence, and which with neither their preaching nor their silence? Which deal with meditative concentration (samādhi), which with wisdom (prajñā), and which with neither concentration nor wisdom?[22] Which deal with the eyes, which with the legs, and which with neither the eyes nor the legs?[23] Which deal with cause, which with effect, and which with neither cause nor effect? Which deal with self, which with other, and which with neither self nor other? Which deal with shared dharmas, which with unshared dharmas, and which with neither shared nor unshared dharmas?[24] Which deal with universals (*t'ung*), which with particulars

17. Or "contemplation proper is established." It corresponds to greater chapter 7, "Cultivation of Calming and Contemplation Proper."

18. Chapter 8.

19. Chapter 9.

20. Chapter 10.

21. According to Chan-jan, the likening of explanations of the perfection of wisdom to the bringing forth of a jewel from a sack comes from TCTL, T 25.518a. Chan-jan comments (T 46.158a19–22): "[This] explains the reasons for distinguishing [the text into ten chapters]. Without the organization of the ten chapters according to these ten topics, it is likely that people would never know of the wealth contained in them. . . . The richness of meaning of the ten chapters is like a jewel in a sack. Their differentiation according to the [ten] topics is equivalent to groping after [the jewel] and bringing it out for display."

22. That is, samādhi and prajñā. They correspond, respectively, to the practices of calming and contemplation.

23. From a metaphor in the TCTL, T 25.640c: "It is as if, in hot weather, there were a cool and pure pond. Anyone with eyes and legs can enter it." Eyes, according to Chan-jan (T 46.148b20–22), correspond to insight and understanding of the teachings, legs to practice.

24. Although there is a traditional list of eighteen "unshared" dharmas or qualities that are unique to a Buddha (i.e., the *āveṇikā buddhadharmāḥ*), the expression

(*pieh*), and which with neither universals nor particulars? Which offer extended explanations, which abbreviated, and which neither extended nor abbreviated? Which are horizontal, which vertical, and which neither horizontal nor vertical?[25] Let questions be put forward freely regarding such diverse distinctions.[26]

[3c3] The first eight chapters deal with the true, although under the auspices of the conventional.[27] The single chapter 8, Result and Recompense, deals with the conventional, although on the basis of the true. Chapter 10 on the Returning of the Purport deals with neither the true nor the conventional. Chapter 7 on Contemplation Proper corresponds to the silence of the sages, while the other eight chapters excluding the last correspond to the preaching of the sages. Chapter 10 on the Returning of the Purport corresponds neither to preaching nor silence. Part of chapter 7 on Contemplation Proper concerns meditative concentration, while the remaining parts of chapter 7 together with the other eight chapters[28] are on wisdom. Chapter 10 on the Returning of the Purport concerns neither meditation nor wisdom.[29] The chapters from the Syn-

---

as it is used here is understood by Chan-jan (T 46.158b26–29) to refer to qualities that are unique to saints (*ārya*) and "not shared" with ordinary unenlightened beings (*pṛthagjana*).

25. A "vertical" explanation is defined by Chan-jan (T 46.158c1–17) as one in which a point is presented by a sequential progression through different levels of profundity. A "horizontal" explanation presents the entire picture in a lateral synthesis.

26. The answers to the preceding questions are not given in exactly the same order as the questions. The answer to the fourth question, on eyes and legs, is inserted after the answer to the sixth, on self and other.

27. Chan-jan points out (T 46.158b7) that this should be the first seven chapters plus the ninth, not the first eight. Chan-jan (T 46.158b8–11) says: "Because the eight do not involve actual realization of the true, they are represented as conventional. But, by the fact that this conventionality in its very essence is fundamentally true, we say 'the true under the auspices of the conventional.' The result and recompense that is realized [as a consequence of practice] represents the conventional as [it operates] beyond the [three] realms [of cyclic birth and death]. The conventional [in this sense] derives from realization of the true; actual realization of the essence (*t'i*) gives rise to function (*yung*), and this function is itself the conventional. Thus the text says, 'the conventional under the auspices of the true.' "

28. Excluding the last chapter, chapter 10.

29. Chan-jan explains (T 46.158b16–17): "The previous listing of chapters [refers to chapter 7 as] 'Cultivation of Calming and Contemplation Proper.' Here the 'cultivation and calming' have been abridged and the text just says 'contemplation proper.' But cultivation proper does not exceed the two procedures of calming and contemplation. Whatever concerns calming belongs to [the aspect of] meditative concentration. Anything that concerns contemplation belongs to wisdom.

opsis up through Contemplation Proper are the cause. Chapter 8 on Result and Recompense is the effect.[30] Returning of the Purport is neither cause nor effect. The first eight chapters are on self-practice, chapter 9 on Generation of the Teachings concerns conversion of others, and Returning of the Purport is on neither self nor other. The Synopsis chapter up through Generation of the Teachings corresponds to the eyes, chapter 6 on Expedients through chapter 8—Result and Recompense—corresponds to the legs, and Returning of the Purport to neither the eyes nor the legs.[31] The Synopsis through Contemplation Proper are on shared dharmas, Result and Recompense as well as Generation of the Teachings are on unshared dharmas, while Returning of the Purport is on neither shared nor unshared dharmas.[32] Only the Synopsis is universal, while the next eight chapters are particular, and Returning of the Purport is neither universal nor particular.[33] The Synopsis is abbreviated, the next eight chapters are expanded, and Returning of the Purport is neither abbreviated nor expanded.[34] Chapter 3 on the Characteristics of

---

In the other chapters, the fact that they tend primarily to the side of understanding does not mean that they are contrary to the notion of calming. But, as a whole, they belong mainly to the aspect of understanding, and understanding is included in [the aspect of] contemplation."

30. The order of the text is skewed here. Chan-jan adds (T 46.158b18) that chapter 9, on Generating Teachings, should be included under effect as well.

31. Chan-jan (T 46.158b19–23) notes: "In keeping with principle, [the text] should say that the first five chapters together with the Generating Teachings chapter are the eyes. Eyes represent understanding. The first five chapters are the eyes of self-oriented practice. The one chapter of Generating Teachings causes others to develop the eye [of understanding]. [The chapters on] Expedients through Result and Recompense are the feet. Feet signify practice. Expedients and Contemplation Proper represent practice that is marked by effort (*ābhoga*); the stages [described in] Result and Recompense from the first abiding on are characterized by effortless practice (*anābhoga*)."

Later, at the beginning of chapter 7 (T 46.48c–49a), Chih-i remarks that the first six chapters deal with "eyes" or wisdom, so that chapter 6 changes categories.

32. According to Chan-jan (T 46.158b26–29), the first seven chapters are "shared" because they present teachings or practices that apply in common to both the ordinary being (*pṛthagjana*) and the enlightened saint (*ārya*). The qualities described in the chapters on Generating Teachings and Result and Recompense are the special domain of the saint. Thus they are "unshared."

33. Chan-jan (T 46.158c1–2) says: " 'Universal' means to be universal [in the Synopsis' inclusion of] cause and effect, self and other. Particular means to be particular in terms of the mutual distinctions that pertain among the eight chapters."

34. Chan-jan does not comment on the "abbreviated/expanded" distinction here, although later in his commentary to MHCK (T 46.159a3–4) as well as in his *Chih-kuan ta-i* (T 46.459b17–18) he refers to the Synopsis chapter as "abbreviated" and the remaining nine chapters as "expanded."

the Essence is vertical, the next eight chapters are horizontal, and Returning of the Purport is neither horizontal nor vertical.[35]

[3c13] Q: What is the difference between the abbreviated description and the Synopsis?[36]

[3c14] A: From the perspective of general [content] (*t'ung*) only the terms are different, the meanings being the same. But from that of particular [content] (*pieh*), the abbreviated description deals with all three kinds of calming and contemplation, while the Synopsis deals only with the sudden calming and contemplation.

[3c15] Q: If you discuss an openly revealed contemplation in relation to the openly revealed teaching, then you should also discuss a secret contemplation in relation to the secret teaching.

[3c16] A: We have already distinguished between the openly revealed and the secret. Now I elucidate only the openly revealed without expounding the secret teaching.[37]

35. According to Chan-jan's rather lengthy discussion of this dyad (T 46.158c2–18), because chapter 3 (Characteristics of the Essence) explicitly organizes itself according to the shallow and the profound, it alone may properly be called vertical. The other chapters, except chapter 10, are provisionally declared horizontal; but on closer inspection all but chapter 2 (Explanation of Terms) may be found to have variations in profundity and hence may be thought of as both horizontal and vertical.

36. Chan-jan (T 46.158c25–159a1) insists that this first question and answer were inserted by Kuan-ting, for they reflect a textual arrangement that was first introduced in Kuan-ting's second edition of the MHCK. (The remaining questions and answers he considers to be the work of Chih-i himself.) Thus the "abbreviated description" refers to a discussion of the three calming and contemplations that was originally included as part of Chih-i's introduction to the Synopsis but was subsequently emended by Kuan-ting and, in the third edition, removed from the text and placed by Kuan-ting in his own separate preface. "Synopsis" refers to the chapter of that name, where the focus is primarily on the sudden and perfect calming and contemplation. Also see Chan-jan, *Chih-kuan fu-hsing sou-yao chi*, HTC 99.234b.

Chan-jan (T 46.159a4–18) argues vociferously against the idea that the sudden and perfect calming and contemplation treated in the Synopsis (and main text of MHCK) is anything other than the sudden and perfect practice that is included as "one among the three" forms of calming and contemplation outlined in the "abbreviated description" of Kuan-ting's preface. The attention he gives this point suggests that there were individuals who thought there was an "absolute" perfect and sudden calming and contemplation that stood as a "one outside the three."

37. Chan-jan (T 46.159a19–28) points out that the question, to begin with, is based on a confusion of the three kinds of calming and contemplation—gradual, sudden, and variable—with the four pedagogical approaches to teaching known as the four methods of conversion (*ssu hua-i*). The first three of the four methods of conversion, taken together, are the "openly revealed teaching" as opposed to the "secret teaching." In the latter case the Buddha preaches "with a single voice"

[3c17] Q: While I can conceive of making such a distinction [between the openly revealed and secret] in terms of doctrine or teaching, can [a secret contemplation] actually be discussed or not?

[3c17] A: In some cases it can; in some it cannot.[38] The teachings are words with which the exalted sage regales lower beings. The sage is able to expound both openly and in secret, while the preachments of ordinary people can convey only the openly revealed and not the secret explanation. What then could listeners rely on to fashion or perform a secret contemplation? As for those who are capable [of conveying a secret contemplation], they are the ones who have reached the stage of purity of the six sense faculties.[39] Since they can fill the billion worlds with a single subtle sound of dharma[40] and can make this reach anywhere and everywhere at will, they are capable of transmitting a secret teaching. If one trains in contemplation, one manifests dharmas of the openly revealed teaching in which one has explicitly trained. One does not develop dharmas in which one has not trained. One may, however, speak of a secret contemplation when it comes to those people who [in the course of contemplation] manifest karmic influences from past lives.

[3c23] Q: Being first shallow and afterwards profound is called gradual contemplation. Which kind of contemplation is first profound and afterwards shallow?

[3c24] A: That would be the variable contemplation.

[3c24] Q: Which kind of contemplation is shallow from start to finish?

---

but each listener, fancying himself the only one spoken to, hears only what he is capable of understanding. He is, as it were, closeted with the Buddha, receiving private instruction, the content of which is "indeterminate" because it is determined not by the spokesperson but by the listener. Hence it is the "secret indeterminate teaching." See Hurvitz, "Chih-i," pp. 244–247; Chappell, *An Outline of the Fourfold Teaching*, pp. 55–61.

The names of three of the four modes of teaching being identical to the names of the three kinds of calming and contemplation, one might expect there also to be a fourth "secret" calming-contemplation corresponding to the secret teaching. In fact, the two sets of categories are quite different and the analogy is an inappropriate one.

38. Chan-jan (T 46.159a29–b13) analyzes Chih-i's response from two perspectives: those who might teach a "secret" calming and contemplation and those who might receive or be trained by it.

39. According to the scheme of the perfect teaching, this is equivalent to the ten stages of faith among the fifty-two stages, and the fourth—identity of resemblance—among the six identities. It represents a stage of "proximate" enlightenment that is on the cusp of full sainthood (*ārya; sheng*) and formal entry into nonretrogressing bodhisattvahood.

40. From chapter 19 (Merits of the Dharma-Preacher) of the *Lotus Sūtra*, T 9.49c; Hurvitz, pp. 273–274. This chapter, as a whole, is the *locus classicus* for the notion of "purification of the six sense faculties."

[3c25] A: That would be the Hīnayāna sense of contemplation. It is not a characteristic of the three kinds of calming and contemplation.

[3c25] Q: The Hīnayāna is also the teaching of the Buddha; why then do you exclude it [from the three forms of calming and contemplation]? If you insist on excluding it, you should not even speak of the "gradual" [calming and contemplation].

[3c3c26] A: We have already distinguished between the Mahāyāna and the Hīnayāna, and the Hīnayāna is not my topic of discussion here. The "gradual" that we speak of here is simply the gradual transition from obscured to fully manifest [realization].[41] The Hīnayāna knows reality neither at the start nor the finish [of the path of religious discipline], so it is not the "gradual" [calming and contemplation] that concerns us here.

[3c28] Q: You have referred to three texts [on calming and contemplation], and texts belong to the category of visible form.[42] Does this "visible form" function as a gate [to reality] or does it not? If you assert that visible form does serve as such a gate, form itself is ultimate reality. What penetration could there be to speak of? On the other hand, if visible form is not such an access, then how could you still say that every shape and smell is the middle way?

[4a2] A: Texts and gates are both reality. Animate beings for the most part [are afflicted by] inverted views and have little sense of the noninverted. This fact is revealed through texts, whereupon they realize that text itself is [at one and the same time] text, no text, and neither text nor nontext.[43] Texts are that aforesaid gate, for one reaches reality through them. Texts are that very gate, and in that gate all dharmas are contained. [They are], at once, a gate, no gate, and neither gate nor nongate.

[4a6] The "Explanatory Discourse" [that now follows] refers to the discourse of the ten chapters.[44] We begin with the Synopsis. It is the bag that contains [the teaching of the ten greater chapters in its entirety]

41. In other words, in the gradual calming and contemplation one is aware of the nature of reality from the start but approaches it through a graduated sequence of steps. Chan-jan explains (T 46-159b22–24): "The lesser is dismissed as wrong in order to sever attachment to it. This is based on the premise that [the lesser vehicle] has yet to reveal [itself as] provisional, and, so, [adherents to the lesser vehicle] are not actually aware of the real. As such, in the gradual [calming and discerning of the greater vehicle] even the most minuscule [cultivation of the] good belongs to the great [vehicle]."

42. Ostensibly, the *Tz'u-ti ch'an-men*, the present MHCK, and the *Liu-miao fa-men* mentioned by Kuan-ting in the preface.

43. Chan-jan explains (T 46.159c6–7): "Text represents the truth of the conventional; nontext, that of the true; and the negation of both, the ultimate truth."

44. Actually only greater chapter 1 and its five parts—the five "lesser chapters" of the MHCK—are now discussed.

from beginning to end. It is the cap that crowns all from first to last.[45] Because the overall thrust of the work is diffuse and difficult to perceive, here [its chief points] are abstracted in the form of the five lesser chapters [of the Synopsis]. They are: Arousing the Great Thought [of Enlightenment]; Engaging in the Great Practice; Manifesting the Great Result; Rending the Great Net; and Returning to the Great Abode.[46]

[4a8] What does "Arousing the Great Thought" mean? Since animate beings are benighted, have an inverted view of reality, and fail to awaken to the truth by themselves, this text stimulates them, causing their awakening—both their upward quest for their own enlightenment and their downward transforming of other beings.[47]

[4a10] What does "Engaging in the Great Practice" mean? Even though the thought of enlightenment has already been aroused, beings may simply gaze down the road without ever taking a step. So doing, they will never see the day when they reach their objective. This text stimulates their resolute endeavor and urges them to apply themselves to the practice of the four forms of samādhi.[48]

[4a12] What does "Manifesting the Great Result" mean? Even though one does not seek birth in the Brahma-heaven, rebirth there comes as an automatic response [to one's efforts].[49] [The text] by extolling this wondrous recompense gladdens the heart [of the aspirant].[50]

[4a13] What does "Rending the Great Net" mean? The various sūtras

45. Following Chan-jan's gloss of the passage, T 46.159c11–20.

46. Chan-jan explains (T 46.159c23–25): "[The Synopsis] is titled *Ta-i,* and the five lesser chapters have 'great' (*ta*) in their titles because the general purport of the nine chapters—which are all 'great'—is outlined here."

47. The bodhisattva is devoted to both his own enlightenment and that of other lesser beings, so he goes "up" and "down" at the same time, "upwardly seeking" and "downwardly transforming."

48. "Samādhi" here refers to programs of religious discipline designed to effect the experience of samādhi or meditative concentration. The four, which are discussed at length in lesser chapter 2, include: cultivation of samādhi through (1) constant sitting, (2) constant walking, (3) part walking and part sitting, and (4) neither walking nor sitting.

49. From the *Nirvāṇa Sūtra,* T 12.613c. The Brahma-heaven is the lowest of the heavens in the realm of form, only one step above our realm of desire. A story is told in the sūtra about an impoverished woman who, by her compassion, was rewarded by rebirth in the Brahma-heaven. The sūtra states at this point, "Even though such a person does not seek liberation, it comes of itself to such a one."

50. Chan-jan (T 46.160a23–24) says of "wondrous recompense": "It characterizes the entire course, from the first [of the ten] abodes through wondrous enlightenment [of Buddhahood]. The present text especially singles out the first abode. But there are also many beings who have never heard of the wondrous merits of the first abode. As such, they [either] boast or grieve over their accomplishments. We expound the wondrous recompense to uplift and gladden them."

and treatises [are intended to] open people's eyes, but people adhere to some of these and doubt others, affirm one and deny the rest.[51] [The blind man in trying to gain an understanding of the color of milk] hears the word "snow" and says "cold," hears "crane" and says "it moves."[52] This chapter shows how the sūtras and treatises all interpenetrate. It loosens bonds [of subjective adherence to one particular interpretation] and releases us from the cage of [misconstruing the provisional and the real].[53]

[4a16] What does "Returning to the Great Abode" mean? In the dharma there is no opposition of beginning and end. In the dharma there is no opposition of passage (*t'ung*) and blockage (*she*).[54] If one realizes the dharmadhātu, one knows it to be without beginning or end, passage or blockage. It is void, radiant, unhindered, and free.

We have produced the five lesser chapters in order to express the meaning of the ten greater chapters.

51. Chan-jan (T 46.160a29–b3) explains: "For example, prior to the preaching of the *Lotus* beings were utterly confused about the provisional and the real, emptiness and existence, principle and phenomenal affairs [as they appeared in the Buddhist] teachings. But once properly classified so that the provisional [teachings] were opened up and the real was disclosed, the provisional and real were prevented from exceeding [their bounds] and [beings] were brought to understanding of the fundamental intent of the teachings. The net of doubt that comes from clinging to teachings was destroyed, and [beings] realized the one principle beyond which there is nothing else. They achieved the great essence of [all] approaches to dharma and realized that the myriad teachings all have a [common] end."

52. From the *Nirvāṇa Sūtra*, T 12.688c.

53. Following Chan-jan, T 46.160b19–20.

54. Chan-jan explains (T 46.160b22–26): "When transforming of beings becomes complete [all] revert to the secret treasury (*mi-tsang*). As for the notion that the essence of the secret treasury is 'without beginning or end,' and so on, [it is to be understood as follows]: there is no beginning, and yet it begins, for one begins [the path] with cultivation of the three discernments. It is without end, yet it does end, for ultimately one arrives at the three meritorious qualities [of Buddhahood]. It is without blockage, yet blockage is present, which we provisionally refer to as 'the three obstacles.' It is without passage, yet passage occurs, which we provisionally call 'the three meritorious qualities.' "

LESSER CHAPTER 1

Arousing the Great Thought [of Enlightenment]

[4a18] There are three sections to this chapter on Arousing the Great Thought: first, [the meaning of] the term [*bodhicitta*] in different languages; next, excluding the wrong; and last, revealing the right [arousing of the thought of enlightenment].

"Bodhicitta" in Sanskrit and Chinese

[4a19] *Bodhi* is an Indian term for what is in China called "the way" (*tao*).[1] *Citta* is an Indian term for what is in China called "mind" (*hsin*), that is, the mind of cognitive reflection. But our word *hsin* has another sense[2]—the pure essence of an aggregate or the heart of a plant—which is akin in meaning to the Indian *hṛdaya*.[3]

Excluding the Wrong

[4a23] Now, in excluding wrong interpretations we dismiss the understanding of *hsin* as the essence of an aggregate or heart of a plant and settle solely on the interpretation of *hsin* as the mind of cognitive reflection. [The term] *tao* or "way" also has universal and particular usages, which we will now go on to exclude on the basis of ten [general topics].[4]

1. P'u-t'i is a transliteration of the Indian term *bodhi*, while the Chinese translation for the same Indian term is *tao*. The latter is the older Buddho-Taoist translation of bodhi, which by Chih-i's time was generally rendered by the newer and more accurate translation of *chüeh*, "awakening."

2. Although their meanings in Sanskrit and English are entirely different, *citta* or "mind" and *hṛdaya* "heart" are both translated as *hsin* in Chinese.

3. Chih-i gives us two transliterations of *hṛdaya*, differing only in the first of the three characters that comprise the word.

4. As careful as he has been to focus on the correct meaning of *citta*, Chih-i in

DISCUSSION OF PARTICULAR USAGES OF [THE TERM] "THOUGHT OF ENLIGHTENMENT"

[4a25] (1) Suppose that in every moment of thought one's mind is preoccupied with craving, anger, and delusion.[5] Though one tries to bring [these afflictions] under control, they will not be restrained; and though one attempts to uproot them, they will not come out.[6] Instead, they increase overwhelmingly with the passing of days and months so that one commits the ten evil acts to an extreme degree,[7] like the five eunuchs.[8] This is tantamount to arousing the mentality of a hell-being and proceeding along the path (*tao*) of fire.[9]

[4a27] (2) If one's mind desires at every moment the increase of one's retinue, like the sea drinking in all rivers or fire consuming kindling, and

---

his discussion of the arousing of *bodhicitta* or the *tao-hsin*—the "thought or mind of the way"—chooses to play on the original polyvalence of the Chinese term *tao*. The ten "ways" or "paths" (*tao*) that he discusses in the passages that follow do not refer to *tao* as an ultimate "sacred order or reality" (i.e., bodhi) but to *tao* as unfavorable "paths" or "destinies of rebirth," hence *gati* in Sanskrit rather than *bodhi*. Thus Chih-i excludes the lesser and wrongful "ways" (*tao*) of false paths and wayward quests in order to illumine the right "way" wherein one seeks the *tao* as bodhi—the enlightenment of a Buddha. The first six of these ten wrong "ways" are the same as the traditional six destinies of saṃsāra that range from the hells to the deva realms.

5. The well-known three poisons—*rāga*, *dveṣa*, and *moha* in Sanskrit—except that in the process of transition to China, *dveṣa* (aversion or hate) became "anger."

6. Chan-jan (T 46.160c25–26) notes: "[The line] 'tries to bring them under control but they will not be restrained' means that one applies calming but is unable to settle or stop them. 'Attempts to uproot them but they will not come out' means that one uses contemplation but is unable to refute or eradicate them."

7. The ten evil acts are killing, stealing, adultery, lying, slander, harsh speech, frivolous speech, covetousness, anger (or hatred in the Sanskrit tradition), and wrong views. According to TCTL (T 25.663a), they may be committed in three degrees: great, which corresponds to hell; middling, the animal realms; and lesser, the realm of hungry ghosts or pretas.

8. The story of the five eunuchs is contained in the **Mahā-māyā Sūtra*, T 17.583c. These were originally five lazy monks, who in a time of famine posed as sages, pretending to be deeply immersed in meditation, but were actually harboring all sorts of evil thoughts. Though they succeeded in gaining a handsome livelihood for themselves, the ultimate result of their deception was to plunge them for aeons into hell. After that they were reborn in various lowly destinies until they finally ended up in the human realm—four born as castrated palanquin-bearers in a royal palace, and one as a cleaner of latrines. All still resisted the dharma, even when confronted by the Buddha.

9. The path or destiny (*gati*) of fire, the path of blood, and the path of knives correspond to the three lowest of the six realms of rebirth—namely, the hells, the realms of animals, and hungry ghosts.

if one thus commits the ten evil acts to a middling degree, like Devadatta, who enticed a multitude of 500 monks to follow his schismatic views,[10] then this amounts to arousing the mentality of an animal and proceeding along the path of blood.

[4b1] (3) Suppose that one's mind desires at every moment to have one's name heard throughout the four remote lands[11] and the eight directions, there to be praised and exalted. Even though one is without true inner virtue of one's own, one compares oneself vainly to saints and sages and gives rise to the ten evil acts to the lesser degree, much like Mākaṇḍika.[12] This, then, represents the arousing of the mentality of a hungry ghost and proceeding along the path of the knife.

[4b3] (4) Suppose that one's mind desires at every moment to be superior to others and is unable to bear being looked down upon. One ridicules others and esteems oneself, like a kite bird, who flies high and looks down [on all below]. Putting on an outward display of the five virtues of humanity, righteousness, decorum, moral discernment, and faithfulness,[13] one thereby arouses the good mind of the lesser degree[14] and follows the path of asuras.

[4b6] (5) If one's mind delights at every moment in worldly pleasures, gratifying the stinking body and pleasing the foolish mind, then this is the arousing of the good mind of the middling degree and following the path of human beings.

[4b8] (6) If one's mind understands at every moment the extent of tor-

10. From the *Nirvāṇa Sūtra*, T 12.812a. Devadatta tried to persuade the Buddha to let him take charge of the saṅgha, then failing to gain consent, tried to do so without the Buddha's permission, thus committing the grave sin of "fomenting discord in the saṅgha," one of the five heinous sins, all of which he ultimately committed.

11. According to Chan-jan (T 46.161c22–26), a general term for barbarian countries in the north, south, east, and west.

12. From the TCTL, T 25.63c–64a, 82b. Mākaṇḍika is cited as the founder of the eponymous religious order whose adherents believed that the mere sight of the corpse of their founder would guarantee their attainment of the way of purity. The Buddha refutes this position by asserting that the way is not something that can be attained by mere views (*dṛṣṭi*), tradition (*śruti*), knowledge (*jñāna*), or moral conduct, nor by the absence of these, but is rather to be attained by the abandoning of all attachment. Mākaṇḍika argued in reply that it should be attainable by simply saying nothing at all. The TCTL quotes the stanzas containing Mākaṇḍika's heretical view and the Buddha's refutation of it from the *Atharvargīya* (T 4.180), the Pāli version of which is to be found in the *Māgandiya-sutta of the Suttanipāta*.

13. The five cardinal virtues of Confucianism, although Chan-jan (T 46.162a23) discusses their "outward display" with particular reference to chapter 38 of the *Lao Tzu*.

14. In which the ten good acts are practiced to the lesser degree.

ment to which beings of the three evil paths[15] are subject, how pain and pleasure are intermingled for humans, and how among the gods there is only pleasure, so that to achieve the bliss of the deva heavens one stops up the six senses, neither allowing them to issue forth or the six corresponding sense-objects to enter[16]—then this represents the arousing of the good mind of the higher degree and proceeding along the path of the devas.

[4b10] (7) If one's mind desires great power and authority at every moment, so that people comply with one's every whim of body, speech, or mind, then one gives rise to the mentality of the lord of the sixth and highest heaven of the realm of desire, and one follows the path of Māra.

[4b12] (8) If one's mind desires at every moment to acquire keen intelligence, perspicacity, superior talent, and courageous wisdom that extends throughout all directions with utmost clarity, then one gives rise to the mind of mundane wisdom and follows the path of the Nirgranthas.[17]

[4b14] (9) If in one's mind there is at every moment little obscuring by external pleasures arising from the five sense-objects and the six desires,[18] but one's mind is heavily imbued with the internal bliss of the first three dhyānas, which are like a stone spring,[19] then one gives rise to the Brahma-mind[20] and follows the path of the realm of form and the formless realm.[21]

15. That is, the three lower realms of the hells, animals, and hungry ghosts.

16. Chan-jan (T 46.162b12–13) says of this path: "One must [at least] be endowed with the power of the preliminary grade of samādhi before one can be born in this realm." That is to say, blocking sense distraction is the basis for meditative concentration, which is necessary for rebirth in heavens of the form and formless realms as well as in certain heavens of the desire realm.

17. Originally this referred to one of the six non-Buddhist ascetic schools at the time of Śākyamuni, namely the Jains. According to Chan-jan (T 46.162b14–15), here it is used in a wider sense to mean any non-Buddhist pursuing religious emancipation.

18. This part of the text is possibly corrupt. The "six desires" are a list of miscellaneous lustful attachments to the human form—color, physical form, enticing gesture, artful speech, soft and smooth skin, and attractive faces of men and women. They are to be overcome by the nine meditations on death and decomposition. See TCTL, T 25.217a–218c; see also *Tz'u-ti ch'an-men*, T 46.535c–537b.

19. TCTL (T 25.120c) distinguishes between externally and internally derived bliss or pleasure. The latter is represented by the bliss of nirvāṇa, which, like the water that spontaneously wells up from the recesses of a stone spring, is not produced by outside objects. The latter analogy is extended to the bliss of dhyāna concentration as well. As for the reference to the three dhyāna, the factor of bliss characterizes the first three of the four dhyāna, but with the fourth it disappears and is replaced by perfect equanimity.

20. That is, the mind that practices the four *brahma-vihāras* or abodes of Brahma: kindness or goodwill, compassion, sympathetic joy, and equanimity.

21. These, along with the realm of desire, make up the three realms. Tradi-

[4b16] (10) Suppose that one's mind is aware at every moment of the matter of cyclic transmigration through the three good and three evil destinies. One knows that the common person is mired in it, while it is denounced by the sages and saints; and one understands how the destruction of evil is based on purified wisdom, purified wisdom is based on purified meditative concentration, and purified meditative concentration is based on purified morality.[22] If one thus esteems these three dharmas like a person who is starving and parched [craves for food and drink], then one gives rise to a mind [that seeks] freedom from defiling outflows and follows the path of the two vehicles.[23]

General Discussion of the Thought of Enlightenment

[4b19] Whether it is the thought (*citta*) or the way (*bodhi*) that is being discussed, the erroneous meanings [to be excluded] are extremely numerous. It is for the sake of brevity alone that we mention only ten. One could elaborate on the higher degrees and condense the lower, or elaborate on the lower degrees and condense the higher—the number ten is used only to establish a conveniently round number.[24]

[4b21] Discussion [of these ten classses] proceeds according to one class at a time, with the rationale that it is the dominant tendency [in the mind of an animate being] that acts as the primary influence [for determining retribution in the destinies].[25] It is in this sense that the *Great Treatise* says,

tionally, the Brahma-heaven (*brahma-loka*) represents the first of the four dhyāna heavens in the realm of form. It, in turn, is subdivided into three grades or Brahma-heavens. However, the term is often used loosely to apply to all the heavens of the realm of form. Here Chih-i seems to extend the meaning of the term even further to include the formless realm.

22. This refers to the aforementioned triad of the three disciplines: moral purity (śīla), meditative concentration (samādhi), and wisdom (prajñā).

23. The two vehicles of the śrāvaka and pratyekabuddha are characterized by the personal quest for release through removal of the defiling outflows (*āsrava*) that keep one bound to saṃsāra. Chan-jan (T 46.162c5–29) notes that this is still inferior (and incorrect) because it does not take into account the salvation of others.

24. Chan-jan (T 46.162c2–5) explains: " 'Higher' refers to the two vehicles; 'lower,' to the asuras. Since the text condenses the two vehicles, it mainly elaborates on the lower. That is to say, it elaborates on the asuras as distinct from [the other destinies of the] hungry ghosts and animals. The *Lotus* speaks of six destinies; the *Vimalakīrti*, five paths, depending on whether the asuras are distinguished separately or combined [with other destinies]."

25. Chan-jan (T 46.162c9–11) says: "To follow the 'dominant tendency' does not mean that the other mentalities are not present. At the moment of death, the retribution [that will occur in the next life] is especially influenced by the dominant [mental] tendency [at that instant]. Thus [we speak of] producing one par-

"An immoral mind falls to hell, an avaricious mind falls to the destiny of hungry ghosts, and a shameless mind falls to the destiny of animals."[26]

[4b23] It may be a wrong thought that is first aroused, or it may be a right thought that is first aroused, or both right and wrong may be simultaneously aroused. For example, elephants, fish, and the wind can all muddy the water of a pond. The elephants symbolize external [influences], the fish symbolize internal [influences], and the wind symbolizes both of these arising together. Again, the elephants symbolize wrong states of mind that originate from without; the fish symbolize how inner contemplation, when feeble, is agitated by the two extremes [of annihilationism and eternalism]; the wind symbolizes how the inner and the outer merge and intermingle in their defiling [of the mind's original purity].[27]

[4b27] Again, the nine [lower paths] affirm [involvement in] cyclic birth and death and may be compared to silkworms entwining themselves in their own cocoons.[28] The last [or tenth] path affirms [pursuit of] nirvāṇa and is analagous to the solitary prancing of a fawn; though beings in this class achieve their own liberation, they are not yet in full possession of the dharma of the Buddhas. Because both [the first nine and the tenth path] are wrong, they are excluded [from the true meaning of arousing the thought of enlightenment]. The first nine are mundane [paths]. Unable to shake [the causes of suffering],[29] they fail altogether to lead one out of [saṃsāra]. The tenth path does emerge from saṃsāra but is lacking in great compassion.[30] Both [the former and the latter] are wrong; hence both are excluded.

[4c2] The same [sort of distinctions] may be made with regard to a variety of doctrinal categories, such as conditioned and unconditioned, with outflows and without outflows, good and evil, defiled and pure, fettered and liberated, ultimate truth and conventional truth.[31] For exam-

---

ticular mentality; it is not to say that the other nine are wholly absent. Because among the ten we [tend to] follow one [as dominant], the text says 'one class.' "

26. TCTL, T 25.219a. The third of these phrases is not in the TCTL and was apparently added by Chih-i to match his comments on the three lowest destinies. The passage occurs in the TCTL within an extended discussion on mental state at the moment of death and its impact on future rebirth.

27. This simile might well be from a sūtra, but neither the commentators nor secondary sources locate a source for it (see "*Makashikan* inyō tenkyo sōran (1)," p. 75).

28. From the *Nirvāṇa Sūtra*, T 12.660b. In the sūtra it is, specifically, the *icchāntika* who is compared to the silkworm.

29. Following Chan-jan, T 46.163a1.

30. For the Hīnayānists pay no heed to the suffering of others, being devoted solely to their own liberation.

31. The first nine paths correspond to the first member of each of these pairs,

ple, the nine lower paths remain involved in the truth of the suffering of the world,[32] while the tenth path rejects it as wrong. Though the latter dismisses [the condition of] suffering as wrong, beings in this class have warped [understanding], are inept [in their efforts at salvation], hold [that nirvāṇa necessarily involves the reduction of the body to] ashes and the extinction [of consciousness], and tarry near [the conjured city].[33] Hence both the first nine and the tenth path are wrong, and both are excluded [from the correct meaning of arousing the thought of enlightenment].

[4c5] [The first nine paths are] "conditioned" and "possessed of outflows" and, therefore, wholly involved in the truth of the origin of suffering. The latter or tenth path rejects [this condition] as wrong.[34] Even though it rejects [involvement in] the origin of suffering as wrong, [followers of this path] are warped, tarry near, affirm the doctrine of ashes, and are inept. Thus once again both the first nine paths and the tenth path are wrong and are excluded.

[4c6] Next, with respect to the noble truth of the path, [one may distinguish] "good" and "evil," "defiled" and "pure."[35] [As opposed to the previous nine], the latter path affirms the truth of the path as correct. But though this is the case, it is excluded along with the other nine above.

---

the tenth (Hīnayāna) path, to the second. Though the Hīnayāna bears on the unconditioned, the absence of outflows, the good, the pure, liberation, and the truth, it still remains incomplete and biased, and hence "incorrect," when compared to the "correct" path of the Mahāyāna.

32. *Duḥkha*, the first of the four noble truths. Chan-jan points out that, because the above items are listed in contrasting pairs, MHCK presents a one-sided explanation of them. Their explanation in terms of the four noble truths could also be presented in a contrasting fashion. Chan-jan (T 46.5a2–4) says of the first two pairs: "[The truths of] suffering and origin both involve being 'conditioned' and 'possessed of outflows.' Even though suffering is explained first, if one were to explicate them in contrast to one another, [the text] should read, 'conditioned and with outflows represent the truth of suffering; unconditioned and without outflows represent the truth of cessation.' "

33. Following Chan-jan's reading of the passage (T 46.163a5–6). The "conjured city" refers to the famous parable from the *Lotus Sūtra* (T 9.26a; Hurvitz, pp. 148–155), in which the expedient (Hīnayāna) teaching of the Buddha is compared to an illusory city magically conjured up for exhausted treasure-seekers by the leader of the expedition to give them a rest on the way to their goal (the true treasure lode). Once they recover their strength he causes it to disappear.

34. That is, Hīnayānists advocate the conquering of craving. Chan-jan (T 46.163a6–8) notes: "If explained in contrast, [the text] should also say that 'conditioned' and 'devoid of outflows' are the truth of the path."

35. The eightfold path, fourth of the four noble truths. Chan-jan (T 46.163a8–9) says: "If one were to take them up singly [according to the noble truths], it should simply read, 'good' and 'pure.' But because [the truth of cessation] is contrasted with [the truth of the] origin [of suffering] they are presented as pairs."

[4c8] Then again, [one may distinguish] "fettered" and "liberated," "ultimate truth" and "conventional truth," with respect to the noble truth of cessation.[36] Although the tenth path also affirms the truth of cessation as correct [while the other nine do not], it is excluded as above.

[4c9] If you have understood the meaning of the above discourse, then at all times you must strive to discern carefully and not allow turbid states of mind to arise, regardless of the thoughts or fluctuations in mental state that occur when immersed in the senses and their objects, the three deeds, and the four modes of physical activity.[37] Should [unwholesome mental states] arise, quickly eliminate them. An intelligent person in the world can distance himself from the myriad evils just as [effectively as] a clear-sighted person is able to avoid a poor and hazardous road. Even a beginning practitioner is fit to act as a refuge for the world if he has understood the meaning of the above discourse.

[4c13] Q: Does the practitioner himself arouse the thought of enlightenment, or does someone else arouse it in him through the act of teaching?[38]

[4c13] A: [Such distinctions of] self and other, together or separately really do not apply here. We are discussing the arousing of the thought of enlightenment only in the sense of the mutual resonance between stimulus [on the part of the practitioner] and [the Buddhadharma's] response (*kan-ying tao-chiao*).[39] It is comparable to a child falling into water or fire and his parents frantically rescuing him. The *Vimalakīrti Sūtra* says, "When their only child falls ill, the father and mother also fall ill."[40] And the *Nirvāṇa Sūtra* states, "A father and mother especially favor a sick

36. Chan-jan (T 46.163a10–11) says: "[The contrasting pairs] 'fettered' and 'liberated' and so forth can be understood according to the same procedure."

37. The three deeds include those of body, speech, and mind. The four bodily postures are walking, standing, sitting, and reclining.

38. Chan-jan (T 46.163a15–18) says: "First, as regards the question, although it is free of the previous ten erroneous [views of the thought of enlightenment], since the potential for fault is still present it is grouped together with the erroneous. As for the answer, when one has truly departed from the potential for fault and, as such, understands stimulus and response from the perspective of the inconceivable [realm], then [arousing of the thought] may truly be called correct. The saintly ones respond with nonresponding and, so doing, reach the four capacities (*chi*). The recipient stimulates by nonstimulation and, so, gains the four benefits."

39. Chan-jan (T 46.5a21–22) refers the reader to the extensive discussion of stimulus and response in Chih-i's *Fa-hua hsüan-i*, T 33.646c–649c.

40. T 14.544b. The passage in the sūtra continues: "If the child recovers, the father and mother also recover. In the same way, bodhisattvas love all animate beings as their own children. When the beings are ill the bodhisattvas are also ill, and when the beings recover, the bodhisattvas also recover."

child."[41] [A Buddha or bodhisattva] moves [the immovable] mountain of dharma-nature and enters the sea of saṃsāra [to save beings].[42] Hence they engage in the illness-practice and the child-practice.[43] This is what is meant by arousing the thought of enlightenment through stimulus and response.

[4c18] It says in a dhyāna sūtra, "The Buddha expounds the dharma by according [with the listeners' capacities] in four ways: according with what they find pleasurable, according with what is appropriate, according with the impurities in them which are to be suppressed, and according with truth itself."[44] Respecting their basic intentions, he expounds those things that will delight their minds. Taking cognizance of karmic propensities accumulated from past lives, he [instructs in a way that] makes it easy for them to accept the practice. Discerning the relative gravity of their illness, he provides them with the appropriate amount of medicine. When, in the course of time, their particular circumstances for achieving the way (*tao-chi*)[45] have ripened, upon hearing [the highest truth] they

41. T 12.724a. The passage in the sūtra reads: "It is like a man with seven children, one of whom falls ill. Though the father's and mother's feelings toward the children are not unequal, they are nevertheless especially partial to their sick child. Great king, the Tathāgata is like this. Though his feelings toward living beings are not unequal, he is nevertheless especially partial toward sinners."

42. Chan-jan (T 46.163a22–24) states: "Dharma-nature is immovable like a mountain. Beings' evils are deep like the ocean. If one does not have great vows and consummate skill in the use of expedients, how could one possibly move this mountain so difficult to move or enter this ocean so difficult to enter?"

43. These correspond to the fifth and fourth items in the famous set of five practices listed in the *Nirvāṇa Sūtra* at T 12.673b and discussed over subsequent chapters. The child-practice (4) involves expounding the lesser Hīnayānistic teachings out of a sense of compassion for immature capacities, as when the Buddha treats beings like his own children. Illness-practice (5) means treating the specific illnesses that cause beings' suffering.

44. Source uncertain; possibly an early dhyāna sūtra no longer extant. As Chan-jan (T 46.163b1) notes, the "four types of accordance" (*ssu-sui*) and four siddhāntas are evidently identical.

45. Although often translated as "salvific capacity," the Chinese term *chi* has a distinct meaning in Chinese philosophical discourse that is not properly conveyed by this English equivalent. In neo-Taoist as well as in Chinese Buddhist usage, *chi* stands together with two other important indigenous terms—*kan* ("stimulus") and *ying* ("response")—as an integral system for describing the mechanisms by which the Tao (or the transcendent Buddhadharma) responds to the phenomenal human condition. Thus *chi* represents a "locus of influences" that, when properly formed, acts to instigate a connection with the Tao or the Buddhadharma and, hence, "stimulate" (*kan*) it to "manifest" or "respond" (*ying*). According to the usage of the term *chi* in the works of Chih-i, it is the extended circumstances and Buddhist teachings acting on the individual capacity that serve to fashion a *chi* ("a

awaken fully to the way. How could this be anything but the benefit that comes from stimulus (*kan*) and response (*ying*) [functioning] in accord with salvific circumstance (*chi*)? In the *Great Treatise* the four siddhāntas are expounded.[46] The "worldly" [siddhānta] is so named, [because it takes into account] the boundaries and differences consistent with worldly dharmas. The "individualized" [siddhānta] takes its name from the fact that [religious discourses are devised] in accordance with what a being can manage. These two siddhāntas are the same as those [set forth in] the four forms of accordance [described above].[47] They also are informed by the concept of stimulus and response.

[4c24] We cite in addition the five "moreovers" from the *Great Treatise*: the Buddha "moreover" preached the prajñāpāramitā sūtras (1) in order to elucidate the various practices of bodhisattvas, (2) in order to cause bodhisattvas to grow stronger in the samādhi of recollection of the Buddha (*nien-fo san-mei*), (3) in order to demonstrate the qualities [of one who has attained] *avaivartya*,[48] (4) in order to eliminate the evils and depravities of the disciples [of the Hīnayāna], and (5) in order to teach the ultimate truth.[49]

[4c27] These five "moreovers" are not different from the four forms of accordance and four siddhāntas. They are also the same as the five causes and conditions.[50] If in preaching one fails to accord with the listener's salvific circumstances (*chi*), then one merely torments him instead

---

network of proper salvific circumstances"). Thus *chi*, metaphorically, is almost always described as "ripe" or "unripe," "formed" or "unformed." The notion of "spiritual capacity," by contrast, is more properly expressed by the Chinese term *ken*, "karmic roots" or "karmically determined faculties." It is *ken* that is regularly described as "keen" (*li*) or "dull" (*tun*), "good" (*shan*) or "bad" (*e*).

46. T 25.59b.

47. The third and fourth siddhāntas of the TCTL are not only identical in meaning to the third and fourth types of accordance (as given in the unidentified dhyāna sūtra) but identical in name as well. The first and second of each group differ in name only; thus there is a one-to-one correspondence between the members of the siddhāntas and accordances. See also Chan-jan, T 46.163a29–b1.

48. *Avaivartya* or "nonretrogression" refers to the stage on the path where a bodhisattva can no longer backslide but is assured of future attainment of Buddhahood.

49. These are from a list of some twenty reasons for preaching the prajñāpāramitā sūtras that are discussed in the first chapter of the TCTL (T 25.57c–62c). The five correspond respectively to the first, second, fourteenth, fifteenth, and sixteenth in the sequence.

50. The "five causes and conditions" is simply another name for the five lesser chapters that make up the Synopsis chapter of the MHCK: (1) Arousing the Great Thought, (2) Engaging in the Great Practice (i.e., four samādhis), (3) Manifesting the Great Result, (4) Rending the Great Net, and (5) Returning to the Great Abode.

of helping him, and no benefit accrues from one's teaching. But if one acts with the thunder-rain of great compassion, then [the listener's vision] can proceed from dim to clear.[51]

[5a1] It says in the [*Middle*] *Treatise*, "The true dharma, those who expound it, and those who hear it are hard to find. As such, saṃsāra neither has an end nor is it endless."[52] Reality is neither difficult nor easy to attain, neither existent nor inexistent—that is what is meant by "the true dharma."[53] Those who expound and those who listen in accordance with it are the "true expounders and listeners."[54] That there is benefit to be gained through the first three siddhāntas is what is meant by "having an end," while the benefit obtained from the ultimate siddhānta is what is meant in the statement "neither having an end nor endless."[55] Thus it is

51. Chan-jan (T 46.163b18–19) says: "As these five moreovers (*wu fu-tz'u*), four accordances, four siddhāntas, and five causes and conditions represent techniques for stimulus and response and adaptation to salvific circumstances (*chi*), there is not any [element of them] that is not informed by great compassion and [desire to] benefit living beings."

52. The *Treatise* here is the *Chung-lun*, T 30.39a—Kumārajīva's translation of Nāgārjuna's *Madhyamaka-kārikās* with commentary. In the Sanskrit of the *Kārikās* there are thirty stanzas in chapter 27 as against thirty-one in the Chinese of Kumārajīva, and this stanza (25) is the one missing from the Sanskrit originals and its commentaries.

Chan-jan (T 46.163b20–22) states: "[The references to] 'true dharma' and 'expounder' illustrate that the wondrous response (*ying*) is difficult to stimulate (*kan*). That 'those who hear it are hard to find' shows how it is difficult to produce the wondrous circumstances of salvation (*chi*). The three words [in Chinese], 'because [it is] difficult to obtain,' are intended summarily to refer to the three items: wondrous dharma, wondrous response, wondrous [nexus of] salvific circumstance (*chi*)."

53. Chan-jan (T 46.163b22–25) states: "[The text] from 'as such' explains the aforementioned 'true dharma.' Whatever is preached through wondrous response or stimulated by wondrous salvific circumstance (*chi*) is fully identical to the middle way. For this reason the pairs [of opposites] are [simultaneously] negated. Neither 'having' nor 'not having' [an end] simultaneously negates conventional and ultimate [truths]. Although the words speak of simultaneous negation, their [actual] point is the mutual identity [of these opposites]."

54. Chih-i obviously understands "true" (*chen*), the first character in the quote, to apply to expounders and listeners as well as to the dharma, whereas the original context of the quote as well as *Piṅgala's commentary on it (T 30.39a16–20) suggest that the word is applied only to the dharma.

55. Chan-jan (T 46.163b26–29) states: "Reiteration of the four siddhānta brings [discussion of] the true dharma to its conclusion. Its point lies in showing that the four siddhāntas are analogous in concept to the two truths as well as to stimulus and response. The middle way is thereby revealed and established as the ultimate truth. This is different from the monolithic [concept of the] true [as conceived in opposition to the conventional truth]. It is for this reason that [such pairs

precisely through understanding [the truth of] conditioned origination that the great event[56] of [a Buddha appearing in the world] can be accomplished. And this, itself, is the basic import of stimulus and response. Thus, although the names of the four forms of accordance, four siddhāntas, and five causes and conditions are different, in meaning they are the same.

[5a7] Now to explain further: the four forms of accordance emphasize the benefit that accrues [to the listener] as a result of the resonantal response of the greatly compassionate ones. The four siddhāntas emphasize the universal imparting of the dharma [by the compassionate ones] out of their empathy and concern. [These two] are no more than the difference between left and right.[57] As for the expression "causes and conditions," in some cases we attribute cause to the sage [who instructs] and condition to the ordinary being [who receives it]. In other cases the cause is located in the ordinary person and condition lies with the sage.[58] This simply expresses the resonantal interaction of stimulus and re-

---

of opposites] are simultaneously negated. As such, one should realize that stimulus and response do not exceed the two truths."

56. The *Lotus Sūtra*, in the chapter on Expedient Devices (T 9.7a), says: "The Buddhas, the World Honored Ones, for one great cause alone appear in the world . . . because they wish to cause beings to hear of the Buddha's knowledge and insight and thus enable them to gain purity, . . . to demonstrate the Buddha's knowledge and insight to beings, . . . to cause beings to understand, . . . to cause beings to enter into the path of the Buddha's knowledge and insight. Śāriputra, this is the one great cause for which the Buddhas appear in the world." See Hurvitz, p. 30.

57. Chan-jan (T 46.163c2–6) says: "The four accordances gain their name from the fact that [the saints], out of great compassion, accord with the salvific circumstances of living beings. The four siddhāntas gain their name from the fact that [the saints], out of empathy [for the plight of beings], universally dispense the medicine of dharma. Great compassion and empathy are different names for a single substance. It is analogous to there being a single object with no inherent differences; but when one stands to the left of it, one says the object is on the right. When one stands to the right of it, one says the object is on the left. The [five] causes and conditions are none other than the five lesser chapters [of the MHCK Synopsis]."

58. Chan-jan (T 46.163c6–10) states: "The alternate applications of the two terms 'cause' and 'condition' [may be explained as follows]: If an animate being arouses the thought of enlightenment with particular boldness, that being is considered to be the [efficient] cause and the saint to be the [contributory] condition, even though he may avail himself of the response of a saint. If a being's wholesome roots (*ken*) are meager and a saintly person spurs him [to arouse the thought of enlightenment], then the response of the saint is the [efficient] cause and the animate being is the [contributory] condition. The immediate [impetus for] production is the 'cause'; remote ancillary contribution is 'condition.' "

sponse (*kan-ying tao-chiao*). Know, then, that when there is proper correspondence between word and meaning within each of these three categories their point is the same.[59]

[5a10] [The term] "in accordance with their desires" stresses what people value in the way of the causal influences that they cultivate [through mental habit] (*hsiu-yin*), whereas [the term] "worldly siddhānta" stresses partition and difference with respect to the retributions (*pao*) that people receive. This is merely the difference between [karmic] cause and effect. [The term] "in accordance with what is appropriate" means selecting the teaching and determining the [appropriate] person accordingly. [The term] "individualized siddhānta" means observing the person and devising the teaching (*tou-fa*) [to fit him]. This is merely the difference between the [subjective] enjoying of something and the [object that is] enjoyed.[60]

[5a13] As for the five causes and conditions,[61] on the basis of the beliefs and desires of animate beings the Buddhas preach that one dharma is all dharmas. This corresponds to the great thought of enlightenment. In the sūtra[62] it is [equivalent to] "acting in accordance with their desires," while in the *Great Treatise*[63] it is known as the "worldly siddhānta." With ener-

59. According to Chan-jan (T 46.163c10–11), these three are the four types of accordance, the four siddhāntas, and the five causes and conditions. The five moreovers have been omitted from the summation.

60. Chih-i here compares the first and second types of accordance to the first and second siddhānta respectively but leaves the third and fourth of each group uncontrasted, since both their meanings and names are identical. Chan-jan (T 46.163c16–18) states: " 'Desires' simply means fondnesses and joys. Therefore we say it conforms with [the idea of] cause. 'World' is simply the aggregates (*skandha*) and sense-accesses (*āyatana*). Therefore we say it conforms with [the idea of] effect. 'World' takes 'partition and difference' as its main concept; 'desires' simply indicates that preferences are not the same. Although there is the distinct difference of cause and effect, their meaning is one and the same. 'Appropriate' involves determining which person is appropriate for a given dharma [that has already been established]. 'Individualized' determines what dharma the person might delight in by taking into account the [nature of the] individual who is to be treated. When focusing on the person, one must select what is appropriate; when selecting [first] a [given] dharma, one must determine whether [the person] can manage it. The [subjective] delight and the [object that] is attended to [for delight] together constitute a single concept."

61. Chan-jan (T 46.163c22–23) states: "Here the [five] causes and conditions are matched up with the accordances and siddhāntas and their meanings shown to be the same." The five causes and conditions, as stated earlier, refer to the five lesser chapters of the Synopsis.

62. The unidentified dhyāna sūtra mentioned above, from which the four types of accordances are derived.

63. TCTL, T 25.59b.

getic zeal and boldness on the part of beings as the cause, the Buddhas preach that one practice is all practices; this corresponds to the four samādhis. In the sūtra it is called "acting in accordance with what is appropriate," while in the *Great Treatise* it is the "individualized siddhānta." Beings in possession of the great wisdom of sameness represents the cause, [and this] stimulates the Buddhas to preach that the eradication [of one affliction] is the eradication of all [afflictions]. They thereby gain the supreme result and recompense and fully penetrate the sūtras and treatises. In both the sūtra and the *Great Treatise* this is called the "therapeutic."[64] Beings possessing the wisdom-eye of the Buddha serve as the cause, and [through this] they stimulate the Buddhas to preach that one ultimate is all ultimates. This is expounded as the returning of the purport to quiescent extinction. In both the sūtra and the *Great Treatise* it is referred to as the siddhānta and accordance of "ultimate truth."[65]

[5a21] Now [to match] the five causes and conditions with the five moreovers: (1) The "thought of enlightenment" is the basis of all practice. In the [*Great*] *Treatise*[66] a variety of practices are mentioned, but the difference between [the thought of enlightenment] and these practices is merely that between root and branch.[67] (2) The "four samādhis" [describe] practice in universal terms, while "recollection of the Buddha" (*nien-fo*) is a particular form of practice. Thus their difference is merely that of universal and particular.[68] (3) The "supreme recompense," more

64. Here the third (Manifesting the Great Result) and fourth (Rending the Great Net [of Doubt]) lesser chapters together correspond to the third siddhānta and third accordance (i.e., the "therapeutic").

65. Chan-jan (T 46.164a4–7) states: "Once beings acquire the three wisdoms and the three eyes within a single instant of thought, they will penetrate the secret treasury (*pi-tsang*). With this functioning as cause, they will stimulate the Buddhas to reveal to them how [all] purport ultimately reverts to the three meritorious qualities [of Buddhahood]. Their own practice will then be wondrously fulfilled and their training of others wondrously accomplished. Both are called 'ultimate.' "

66. Reference uncertain, but the TCTL presents a vast array of practices connected with the bodhisattva path. These are, in turn, set forth in detail (according to their original sequence) in Chih-i's treatise on the gradual and sequential calming and contemplation, the *Tz'u-ti ch'an-men*, T 46.508a–548c.

67. Chan-jan (T 46.164a9–11) says: "The thought of enlightenment guides practice, as the branch must proceed from the root. And practice gives fulfillment to the vow, as the root must avail itself of the branch [to be a root]. Though root and branch differ, together they make up the tree of enlightenment."

68. *Buddhānusmṛti* is the practice of maintaining recollection of the Buddha's form and spiritual qualities, at times accompanied by recitation of the Buddha's name. The great emphasis placed on exclusive recitation of the name is actually a product of later Pure Land developments in Japan. Chan-jan (T 46.164a11–13) states: "The four samādhis are referred to as 'universal' because they include all

precisely stated, covers the habitual (*hsi-kuo*) and the retributory (*pao-kuo*) fruition, in both environmental and primary [spheres].[69] The term *avaivartya* concerns itself predominantly with the characteristics of the habitual fruition (*hsi-kuo*) of [formal] entry into the stages [of bodhisattvahood].[70] Their difference is merely one of mentioning a single or both members of a pair. (4) "Removing impediment and doubt with respect to the scriptures and treatises" places emphasis on the sūtras and treatises as the places where doubt and attachment are generated. "Eliminating the evils and depravities of the disciples" places emphasis on the persons who give rise to error. Their difference is merely one of place and person. (5) It is easy to see that "absolute identity of root and branch"[71] as well as "ultimate truth" are essentially the same in name but different in perspective. The reason that they are not different lies in the fact that their meaning is the same.

[5a28] Now the preaching of the saints can take many different ap-

---

practices completely. The samādhi of recollecting the Buddha is just one practice among the many; thus it is described as 'particular.' "

69. Chan-jan (T 46.164a20–21) says: " 'Result and recompense' signifies [recompense] pertaining to [both] primary and environmental [spheres]. The 'environmental' must have [its counterpart of] the 'primary' [recompense]. 'Retributory' [karmic influence and effect] must have [its counterpart of] 'habitual' [karmic influence and effect]. Thus 'result and recompense' includes both pairs."

The "habitual" (*hsi*) and "retributive" (*pao*) represent two of six types of karmic cause distinguished in Abhidharmic systems. Technically, the "habitual" (*niṣyanda*) influence is defined as an influence that produces an effect of the same valency or nature; the "retributory," as an influence that produces an effect that is different in valency or nature from its cause. These two categories receive extensive discussion in Chih-i's *Tz'u-ti ch'an-men* (T 46.494a–c) and MHCK (T 46.112a–b), as well as in *Fang-teng san-mei hsing-fa* (T 46.946b–947a). The English rendering given them in this translation accords with Chih-i's particular understanding and usage: karmic causal influences (*yin*) and fruition (*kuo*) of the "habitual" (*hsi*) sort represent subjective mental or emotive qualities that perpetuate themselves uninterruptedly as a part of the mental continuum itself. They are "primary or subjective" (*cheng*) because their sphere of operation is the mental and physical makeup of the individual being. Karmic influences and fruits of the "retributory" (*pao*) sort involve the formation or maturation of seeds occasioned by specific events or actions. Because they pertain primarily to interaction with other beings and the general surroundings, they are "environmental" (*i*).

70. *Bodhisattvaniyāma.*

71. From the *Lotus Sūtra*, T 9.5c (Hurvitz, p. 23). This is the last of the ten "such-likes" (*ju-shih*) by which Chih-i adumbrates the nature of dharmas in his theory of "the three thousand realms in a single moment of thought" (*i-nien san-ch'ien*). Here it is used to refer to the final chapter of the Synopsis—the fifth of the five causes and conditions. Chan-jan (T 46.164a26–27) says: "Arousing the thought is the root; reverting together [to the great abode] is the branch."

proaches.[72] In some instances they preach by graduated sequence; in others they do not. In some instances they preach comprehensively, in others they do not. In some instances they preach in mixed fashion, in others, not.[73] Moreover, living beings gain benefit [from the teachings] in dissimilar ways. In some instances benefit is realized in a graduated sequence. In others it is not. In some instances it comes comprehensively; in others it does not. In some instances it comes in mixed fashion; in others, not. Sometimes the four siddhāntas are made to correspond [perfectly] to the five causes and conditions, or the five causes and conditions made to correspond to the four siddhāntas.[74] Then again, at times the four siddhāntas [are condensed] to correspond to a single cause and condition, or a single cause and condition made to correspond to a single

72. Chan-jan embarks here upon an interesting discussion of the significance of calming and contemplation to the textual structure of the Synopsis as a whole. He ends with a critique—much like that found in the commentary to the beginning of this chapter (T 46.158c29–159a)—of individuals who would posit a separate "single form of calming and contemplation beyond the [usual] three." Again this underscores the fact that Chan-jan's interpretation of the T'ien-t'ai three forms of calming and contemplation is but one among a diversity of interpretations current during his day.

Chan-jan (T 46.164b2–11) says of this passage: "It concludes with the three forms of calming and contemplation. The passages on stimulus and response for the most part must conclude with all three. But if the point of the passage is narrowly focused, [sometimes the text] uses only one [calming and contemplation], as in the [sections on] the four vows and six identities that follow. . . . Or, sometimes three and one are both used, as in the present passage. When one [calming and contemplation] is used, it is a universal [explanation]. When three are used, it is a particulate [explanation]. If [a reader] does not perceive this point, he will give rise to a lot of wayward ideas. Question: Why is it necessary to conclude with calming and contemplation? [Answer:] These three dharmas, as a whole, crown all [teachings and practices]. Since the text of the five lesser chapters [of the Synopsis] is universalistic in its focus, passages from place to place use the three or one to conclude. Moreover, this text [of the MHCK] carries the overall title of 'calming and contemplation.' There is not a point in it that is not [presented in terms of] calming and contemplation. [Since it deals with the path in its entirety,] one must not think that it is always referring to a method of religious practice whenever it concludes [a section] with calming and contemplation. For example, in the [sections on] 'principle' and 'name'—[the first two] of the 'six identities'—both conclude with calming and contemplation, as does the present passage concerning simply stimulus and response. How can one possibly construe [from the text that] there is a separate single [form of calming and contemplation] beyond the [usual] three?"

73. Chan-jan (T 46.164b17–18) says: " 'Sequential' refers to the gradual; 'comprehensive,' the sudden; 'mixed,' the variable [calming and contemplation]."

74. Chan-jan (T 46.164b22) says: "Because each of the four siddhāntas and five causes and conditions are set in mutual opposition to one another, it is the gradual [calming and contemplation]."

siddhānta.[75] Or, each and every cause and condition may be made to contain all four siddhāntas, and each of the four siddhāntas made to contain all of the five causes and conditions.[76] Thus [these] different categories may be made to correspond mutually and reveal one another in a variety of ways. If we return to sum them up according to three forms of calming and contemplation, the idea can be understood along similar lines. Then again, they may also be summed up on the basis of the single expression "calming and contemplation." To arouse the thought of bodhi is "contemplation," and to put an end to depraved mentalities is "calming."[77]

[5b7] Moreover, the five lesser chapters [of the Synopsis chapter] are nothing but the ten greater chapters [in abbreviated form]. The first five greater chapters are concerned with the single point of arousing the thought of enlightenment.[78] [Greater chapter 6 on] Expedients and [greater chapter 7 on] Contemplation Proper are nothing but the four samādhis.[79] The one [greater] chapter on Result and Recompense[80] is concerned mainly with explaining contrary and proper [forms of recompense]. The contrary represents results [that fall] within the two extremes, while the proper represents [results that promote] the supreme and wondrous recompense.[81] The [greater] chapter [9] on Generating Teachings[82] turns from individual practice to the issue of benefiting others. In some instances, the provisional and the real may be conferred

75. Chan-jan (T 46.164b22–23) says: "Because the one and the four are variously combined, this is the variable [calming and contemplation]."

76. Chan-jan (T 46.164b23) says: "Because in singling out any one dharma all dharmas are included, it is the sudden [calming and contemplation]."

77. Chan-jan (T 46.164b27–c1) says: "Since this passage equates arousing the thought [of enlightenment] with contemplation and the halting of depravity with calming, one should know that the five causes and conditions [of the Synopsis], the moreovers, the four types of accordance, and the four siddhāntas do not have any meaning that is not included within arousing the thought [of enlightenment] and halting depravity. Likewise, the three forms of calming and contemplation do not go beyond arousing the thought and halting depravity. Thus one would know that the [references to] one and three [calmings and contemplations] simply represent the [difference between] universal and particular [perspectives, and not substantial differences in religious praxis]."

78. That is, lesser chapter 1, Arousing the Great Thought.

79. That is, lesser chapter 2, Engaging in the Great Practice.

80. Greater chapter 8.

81. Chan-jan (T 46.164c10–12) says: " 'Contrary' means one-sided bias toward emptiness or one-sided bias toward the provisional. It says 'two extremes' because [these extremes] are 'contrary' to the perfect roundedness of the middle. 'Proper' means [that one is] perfectly oriented with respect to the middle or perfectly oriented with respect to principle. Because one 'properly accords' with reality it is called 'supreme and wondrous.' "

82. Greater chapter 9.

through taking the physical form of a Buddha.[83] Or, by taking on the likenesses [of beings] of the nine lower realms[84] one dispenses the gradual and sudden [teachings] appropriately (*tui-yang*), evolves (*chuan*) gradual into sudden, or pervasively disseminates (*hung-t'ung*) gradual and sudden.[85] [Greater] chapter 10 on the Returning of the Purport, likewise, is the same as [the lesser chapter] of Returning to the Great Abode, [which involves returning to] the midst of the secret treasury (*pi-mi chih tsang*).[86] Know then that the basic point of the greater and lesser chapters is the same.

Revealing the Right [Arousing of the Thought of Enlightenment]

[5b13] The Revealing of the Right [Arousing of the Thought of Enlightenment] contains three sections: first, the fourfold four noble truths; next, the four extensive vows; and last, the six identities.

The Fourfold Four Noble Truths

[5b14] The names and the features of the doctrine of the fourfold four noble truths derive from the chapter on Saintly Conduct in the *Nirvāṇa Sūtra*.[87] The four levels [of interpretation] include: arising-and-perishing, nonarising-and-perishing, the innumerable, and the unconstructed.[88]

83. Highest of the realms or destinies of the tenfold dharmadhātu.

84. The six realms or destinies of saṃsāra together with those of arhat, pratyekabuddha, and bodhisattva.

85. Chan-jan (T 46.164c27–165a2) explains: " 'Dispensing sudden and gradual appropriately' refers to the Buddha preaching the *Avataṃsaka*, the [four] *Āgamas*, and the *Prajñāpāramitā* [appropriately, according to the degree of maturation of the assembly]. 'Transforming [gradual into sudden]' refers to the Avataṃsaka [where gradual ranks are used to describe the perfect path]. 'Transforming [sudden into gradual]' refers to the [sūtras of the] vaipulya [period]. The injunctions to 'widely disseminate' that appear at the end of all sūtras are what is meant by [the expression] 'pervasively disseminate.' "

86. From the *Nirvāṇa Sūtra*, T 12.616a–b. The expression also appears throughout the *Lotus Sūtra*, T 9.31b, 39a, 52a. The *Lotus Sūtra* itself is referred to as the "treasure-store of the secret essentials of the Buddhas" because it preaches the marvelous dharma of the one Buddha vehicle, which is the "secret essence" of the Buddhas (T 9.10b).

87. T 12.676b–683a. The formulation of the fourfold four noble truths is a contribution of Chih-i that is based principally on terms and ideas expounded in this chapter of the *Nirvāṇa Sūtra*. However, Chih-i's terminology also parallels a discussion of the four noble truths contained in the *Śrīmālā Sūtra*, T 12.221a20–b7. The four levels of interpretation of the four noble truths are identified with the T'ien-t'ai four teachings—the tripiṭaka, shared, separate, and perfect teaching, respectively.

88. The term "unconstructed" has been chosen to render this fourth item

[5b15] **Arising-and-Perishing.** [At this level of understanding] suffering and the origin of suffering[89] are the mundane cause and effect, while the path and cessation [of suffering][90] are the supramundane cause and effect. Suffering represents the shift [of dharmas] through the three phases [of arising, transformation, and perishing].[91] The origin of suffering is [understood as] the flux of the four mental states.[92] The path counteracts and eliminates [the afflictions], while cessation annihilates existence and causes it to revert to inexistence. Whether [we consider them in their] mundane or supramundane aspects, they always involve change and difference.[93] That is why they are called the four noble truths of arising-and-perishing.[94]

[5b19] **Nonarising-and-Perishing.**[95] [At this level of understanding] suffering no longer inflicts itself on the practitioner, for all things are understood to be empty. How indeed could something that is empty drive away something else that is also empty? This very form is identical with emptiness, and the same is true for sensation, cognition, impulses, and consciousness.[96] Hence [suffering] lacks all mark of infliction.

[5b21] By the same token, the origin of suffering lacks any mark of

---

on the basis of discussions of the fourfold four noble truths in Chih-i's *Fa-hua hsüan-i* (T 33.701b7–8): "Phenomena precisely as they are are the middle [way]. Because there is no deliberate pondering [of this reality], no recollecting [of this reality], no one who constructs or fashions [this reality], it is called [the] 'unconstructed' [four noble truths]." For a complete English translation of this section of the *Fa-hua hsüan-i*, see Swanson, *Foundations of T'ien-t'ai Philosophy*, pp. 226–234.

89. The first two noble truths.

90. The fourth and third noble truths, as they are traditionally listed. Chih-i always reverses their order, placing "the path" before "cessation."

91. According to Chan-jan (T 46.165a27–b1), these are the "four marks" that describe the momentary arising, persistence, transformation, and perishing of all dharmas, minus the second item—"persistence or abiding." Chan-jan explains this lacuna by saying that "abiding" has been collapsed into "transformation" in order to avoid giving people the notion that dharmas have constancy.

92. Chan-jan (T 46.165b1–3): "The 'four mental states' are the four basic afflictions. Because they are inevitably activated by the three marks, the [text] says 'flux.' This 'flux' is none other than cyclic birth and death." *Kōgi* (1.226) identifies them as craving, anger, pride, and stupidity.

93. That is, the Hīnayāna teaching centers on establishing explicit distinctions between dharmas and demonstrating the fact that these dharmas are in constant flux and change.

94. The four noble truths interpreted at the level of arising-and-perishing correspond to the tripiṭaka teaching of the Hīnayāna.

95. This corresponds to the shared teaching (see Chan-jan, T 46.165b13).

96. Possibly from the *Heart Sūtra* as translated by Kumārajīva (T no. 251), although this passage happens to be closer to the better-known translation of Hsüan-tsang (T no. 252), which postdates Chih-i.

coordinate correspondence [between cause and effect], for both cause and effect are empty. How, then, could a cause that is empty join in correspondence with an effect that is empty? The same holds for all the variations of craving, anger, and stupidity.[97]

[5b22] The path is marked by nonduality; there is ultimately no agent that acts to counteract [the afflictions] nor are there [any afflictions] to counteract. In emptiness there is not even [a mark of] oneness to be found; how then could there be two? Since dharmas have originally never blazed up into existence, there is no need to extinguish them now. Because they neither blaze up nor are extinguished the four noble truths at this level are called the four noble truths of nonarising-and-perishing.[98]

[5b25] **The Innumerable.** Analytical investigation [of existence] discloses countless aspects to suffering. The suffering in a single realm [of the tenfold dharmadhātu] comes in a vast plurality of forms.[99] How much more incalculable must be its variety in all ten realms. [This variety] can never be known by the two vehicles, whether by their wisdom or their eyes, but it can be comprehended by bodhisattvas. Thus there are numerous differences in [the suffering endured by those in] hell—being scourged with swords, chopped up, roasted, minced, and many more, so many they cannot all be named nor their number estimated. How much the more is this so for the [aggregate of] material form in the other nine realms, as well as [the aggregates of] sensation, cognition, impulses, and consciousness. Like grains of sand or drops in the sea, how could they ever be exhausted? Hence the four noble truths at this level are beyond the understanding of the two vehicles, but the wisdom-eye of bodhisattvas can penetrate them.

[5c2] The origin of suffering as well has innumerable features. That is to say, the variety of deeds that arise through body, speech, and mind [due to the influence of] craving, anger, and stupidity cannot be reckoned. It is just as when the body bends, its shadow becomes skewed, or when the voice calls out loudly, its echo indistinctly resounds.[100] Bodhisattvas illumine all of this without erring.

[5c5] There are also innumerable aspects to [the noble truth of] the path, such as analytical (*hsi*) and immediate (*t'i*) [forms of wisdom],[101]

97. *Rāga, dveṣa,* and *moha*—the three root poisons that are the foundation of suffering.

98. For a more detailed explanation of this shared teaching, Chan-jan (T 46.165b13) refers the reader to the *Viśeṣacintabrahma-paripṛcchā,* T no. 586.

99. Following Chan-jan here (T 46.165b19).

100. According to Chan-jan (T 46.165b26–27), body and voice correspond to the origin or cause of suffering, whereas shadow and echo correspond to the effect or suffering itself.

101. The former achieves emptiness by reductively analyzing the phenomenal

clumsy and skillful expedients, or winding and straight, long and short [paths],[102] and provisional and real [teachings]. Bodhisattvas elucidate this faultlessly and with precision.

[5c6] There are also innumerable aspects to [the noble truth of] cessation. Certain expedients are able to remove [the afflictions that pertain to] intellectual view; other expedients extinguish [afflictions pertaining to] cultivation.[103] Each of these expedients has innumerable primary and ancillary supportive aspects. Bodhisattvas perceive them all perfectly without being off the mark even by a hair. Then again, while the expedients that [establish existence as] inherently empty have multiple primary and ancillary aspects of this sort, ultimately there is no such plurality whatsoever. Yet even though there is no such plurality, bodhisattvas do not err or suffer confusion when they distinguish their numerous varieties. Moreover, certain expedients are able to annihilate by analysis the four grounds of delusion pertaining to intellectual view and cultivation.[104] Then again, other expedients have the power to annihilate the four grounds through immediate [insight]. Certain expedients are able to annihilate the delusion that obscures multiplicity.[105] Other expedients have the power to annihilate fundamental nescience.[106] Though

---

world into concomitant parts. The latter realizes emptiness directly, as an inherent absence of self-existence or self-nature.

102. An allusion to the parable of the conjured city in the *Lotus Sūtra*, T 9.26a; see Hurvitz, pp. 148–149.

103. Literally, these are the "afflictions that are removed in the path of vision" (*darśana-mārga prahātavya-kleśa*) and "afflictions that are removed in the path of cultivation" (*bhāvanā-mārga prahātavya-kleśa*). The former represent delusions of view or intellect; the latter delusions pertain more to emotional or volitional habit.

104. The *Śrīmālā Sūtra* (T 12.219c–220a) classifies the afflictions of view and afflictions of cultivation into four major "grounds of delusion": intellectual delusions (i.e., erring in the four noble truths) and three varieties of emotional delusions (i.e., attachment in the realms of desire, form, and formlessness). A fifth and more fundamental ground of delusion is added as the source of the other four: that of *avidyā* or timeless nescience. All but *avidyā* are eradicated by the two vehicles. *Avidyā* in its entirety is eradicated only by Buddhas. Chih-i, relying in part upon the *Śrīmālā Sūtra*, developed a system of three grounds or bases of delusion: the delusions of view and cultivation, the delusion that obscures multiplicity, and fundamental nescience. Each obscures, respectively, one of the three views or truths—emptiness, the provisional, the middle.

105. The second in the T'ien-t'ai system of three grounds of delusion. Chan-jan (T 46.165c7–8) states: " 'Dust and sand' here [underscores] the inability to know multiplicity." Because of their attachment to emptiness and extinction, followers of the two vehicles are incapable of expediently viewing the multiple aspects of deluded existence as numerous as the sands [of the Ganges]. The bodhisattva removes this obstruction of emptiness, realizes the truth of provisionality, and thus is able to function expediently amidst birth and death.

106. The third of the three delusions. By eliminating this delusion the bodhi-

they are innumerable in their variety, [the bodhisattva sees] each for what it is and does not mix them up.

[5c13] Furthermore, there are numerous [variations] because of the distinctions [that the bodhisattva makes when applying] the three siddhāntas. However, there is no such plurality where the ultimate siddhānta is concerned. Yet even though there is no such plurality, because our discussion at this level is from [the perspective of] the many, the word "plurality" is used. This we call "the innumerable four noble truths."

[5c15] **The Unconstructed.**[107] [At this level of understanding the four noble truths in all their aspects] are ultimate reality, utterly inconceivable. This is not to say that [the siddhānta of] absolute truth alone is devoid of all plurality. In fact, the three lower siddhāntas and all other dharmas also lack plurality. Since this idea can be inferred [from the previous discussion], no further details about it need be noted here.

[5c18] If the fourfold four noble truths are brought into correspondence vertically with the four types [of Buddha] land,[108] some lands have more and others have less [of the fourfold four noble truths].[109] All four are present in the Co-dwelling Land, while there are three in the Land of Expedients,[110] there are two in the Land of Recompense of the Real,[111]

---

sattva eliminates the nescience that conceals the middle truth and acquires the wisdom of Buddhahood.

107. Associated with the perfect teaching.

108. Four types of land or realm corresponding to the three bodies of Buddha and four levels of spiritual development: the Co-dwelling Land, where ordinary people and sages may both be found; the Land of Expedients, where imperfectly realized Hīnayānistic śrāvakas and pratyekabuddhas dwell; the Land of Real Recompense, where the bodhisattvas are; and the Land of Eternal Quiescence and Illumination, the domain of the Buddhas as they are in and of themselves. Of the three bodies of the Buddha, the body of enjoyment or recompense (*pao-shen*) and dharma-body (*fa-shen*) correspond respectively to the third and fourth of these lands, while two bodies of manifestation or response (*ying-shen*)—one superior, the other inferior—are distinguished in accordance with the first and second of the Four Lands (see Muranaka, p. 350). For the origins of this system see Andō, *Tendai-gaku*, pp. 160–164.

109. Chan-jan (T 46.165c17–19) explains: "Teachings are established in response to salvific circumstance (*chi*); and because there are differences in degree with respect to circumstance, there will be differences in the teachings. Because the lands are matched to the teachings on the basis of superiority and inferiority and the number [of teachings present], it is called 'vertical.' "

110. They are the "nonarising-and-perishing," "innumerable," and "unconstructed" interpretations of the four noble truths, which correspond to the shared, separate, and perfect teachings, respectively.

111. The "innumerable" and "unconstructed" interpretations of the four noble truths or the separate and perfect teachings.

and there is only one in the Land of Eternal Quiescence and Illumination.[112] If the fourfold four noble truths and the four lands are matched horizontally, then the Co-dwelling Land corresponds to arising-and-perishing; the Land of Expedients, to nonarising-and-perishing; the Land of Recompense of the Real, to the innumerable; and the Land of Eternal Quiescence and Illumination, to the unconstructed.[113]

[5c21] Furthermore, when [this teaching] is expounded in comprehensive form, it is called the four noble truths. When it is expounded in specific form, it is known as the twelve causes and conditions.[114] Suffering corresponds to the seven items of consciousness, name-and-form, the six sense faculties, contact, sensation, birth, and old age and death.[115] The origin [of suffering] is represented in the five items of nescience, impulses, craving, attachment, and existence.[116] The path corresponds to the expedients employed to counteract the twelve causes and conditions. Cessation is equivalent to the annihilation of nescience on through to annihilation of [the twelfth link of] old age and death. Hence the *Nirvāṇa Sūtra* distinguishes the fourfold four noble truths as well as four levels [of interpretation of] the twelve causes and conditions.[117] By contemplating the causes and conditions with the lower wisdom, one attains the enlightenment of a śrāvaka. By contemplating with the middling degree of wisdom, one attains the enlightenment of a pratyekabuddha. By contemplating with the superior wisdom, one attains the enlightenment of a bodhisattva; and by contemplating with supreme wisdom, one attains the enlightenment of a Buddha.

[5c27] Then again, in the gāthā of the *Middle Treatise*,[118] "whatever dharma arises on the basis of causes and conditions" corresponds to the

112. The "unconstructed" four noble truths, or the perfect teaching.

113. This means that the lands should also correspond to the four teachings. However, the fit is not a good one, for the lowest land is for ordinary people, and the second for Hīnayānists, whereas in the four teachings it is the lowest teaching that corresponds to the Hīnayāna.

114. *Pratītyasamutpāda.*

115. These are numbers 3–7 and 11–12 of the twelve. In Abhidharma theory the first group is regarded as the effect (suffering) in the present life; and the second group, as the effect in the future life.

116. Numbers 1–2 and 8–10 of the twelve. The first group is the cause in the past life; the second group the cause in the present life.

117. The latter occurs at T 12.768c. Actually the sūtra distinguishes four kinds or levels of wisdom that discern causes and conditions. Chih-i's adaptation of these wisdoms is presented in the lines that follow.

118. Chap. 24, verse 14, from the *Chung-lun*, T 30.33b: "Whatever dharma arises through causes and conditions, that I declare to be identical to inexistence [Chih-i uses the word "emptiness"]. It is also a provisional designation. This, again, is the meaning of the middle way."

level of arising-and-perishing. "That I declare to be empty" corresponds to the level of nonarising-and-perishing. "It is also called 'provisional designation' " represents the level of the innumerable; and "it is also called the meaning of the middle way" corresponds to the level of the unconstructed.[119] Moreover, one may interpret [the gāthā] in such a way that "causes and conditions" represent the origin of suffering, "what is produced by them" is suffering, the "expedients" that eradicate suffering are the path, and the disappearance of suffering and the cause of suffering is cessation. Or else, when the gāthā speaks of "causes and conditions," causes and conditons may be regarded as identical to nescience,[120] whereas "what is produced" through them are impulses,[121] name-and-form, the six sense organs, and so forth.

[6a3] Hence it says in a passage [from the *Middle Treatise*], "The Buddha taught his disciples of keen capacity (*li-ken*) the nonarising and nonperishing aspect of the twelve causes and conditions." This refers to the first twenty-five chapters [of the *Middle Treatise*]. [And the *Treatise* says,] "He taught his disciples of dull capacity (*tun-ken*) the arising-and-perishing aspect of the twelve causes and conditions." This refers to the last two chapters [of the *Middle Treatise*].[122]

[6a6] Know, then, that when the gāthā[123] of the [*Middle*] *Treatise* is interpreted in comprehensive fashion, [its four lines] correspond to the fourfold four noble truths. When it is interpreted in specific fashion, its four lines correspond to the four kinds of wisdom that view cause and condition.[124] This completes the analysis of the fourfold four noble truths.[125]

119. Here Chih-i has matched up the four lines of the famous gāthā with the four levels of interpretation of the four noble truths. Chan-jan (T 46.166a17–18) says: "Moreover, cause and condition are fundamental to all dharmas; but, due to differences in the way they are contemplated, there are the [three views or truths of] emptiness, provisionality, and the middle. Thus, while there are differences in terms of the teaching that one realizes, they are the same in their [common] contemplation of cause and condition."

120. *Kōgi* (1.241) thinks that "impulses" (*saṃskāra*, second in the chain) should be added to "nescience" here.

121. *Kōgi* (1.241) cites *Kōroku* to the effect that "consciousness" should be substituted here for "impulses."

122. From the prose commentary to chap. 1, verses 1 and 2 of the *Chung-lun* (T 30.1b), somewhat paraphrased. The last two chapters of the treatise concern the twelve causes and conditions (*pratītyasamutpāda*) and false views (*dṛṣṭi*), respectively.

123. That is, chap. 24, verse 14; T 30.33b.

124. Kōgi (1.242) regards this difference as essentially temporal in nature—the twelve causes and conditions introduce the distinction of past, present, and future, which is not explicit to the four noble truths.

125. Chan-jan (T 46.166b6–9) states: "The four noble truths are principle (*li*).

Ten Occasions for Arousing the Thought of Enlightenment [on the Basis of the Fourfold Four Noble Truths]

[6a7] The sūtras elucidate a variety of circumstances for arousing the thought of enlightenment: (1) the thought of enlightenment may be aroused by inference from various [doctrinal] principles (*li*); (2) the thought of enlightenment may be aroused by seeing the various marks of the Buddha; (3) by seeing the various [manifestations] of the Buddha's supernormal powers; (4) by hearing various dharmas; (5) by traveling to various lands; (6) by observing different types of animate beings; (7) by seeing the performance of various religious practices; (8) by witnessing the destruction of various dharmas;[126] (9) by seeing various transgressions [committed by beings]; or (10) by seeing the different sufferings experienced by others. Having begun by briefly mentioning ten [basic circumstances for arousing thought of enlightenment], we will now explain in detail.[127]

[6a13] **(1) Arousing the Thought of Enlightenment by Inference from Principle (*li*).**[128] The dharma-nature is utterly perfect in itself. The arising of suffering cannot defile it, suffering itself cannot afflict it, the path cannot penetrate to it, and cessation cannot purify it. Like the moon, which may be hidden but is never harmed by clouds, the dharma-nature is perceived the instant the afflictions are cleared away.[129] It says

---

There is no instance of arousing the thought of enlightenment where principle is not the basis. For this reason, when it cites the ten ways [of arousing the thought of enlightenment, the text] places principle at the beginning."

126. That is, the persecution and destruction of the Buddhist teachings.

127. In the passages that follow, Chih-i only discusses the first four of the ten. Chih-i's list of ten, according to Chan-jan (T 46.166b10–27), represents a selective condensation of several similar lists found in various Buddhist sūtras, including: **Daśabhūmika-vibhāṣa Śāstra* (TT 26.35a–b), **Upāsaka-śīla Sūtra* (T 24.1035b), *Avataṃsaka Sūtra* (T 9.450b), and *Ta-fang-pien fo pao-en ching* (T 3.136a–b).

128. "Principle" primarily means insight into the doctrine of the four noble truths here. In the section that follows, Chih-i devotes a paragraph to each of the four levels of interpretation of the four noble truths.

129. Chan-jan points out that this description seems similar to the separate teaching of the Mahāyāna but is really still at the level of the tripiṭaka teaching of the Hīnayāna—i.e., the teaching of the "arising-and-perishing four noble truths." He says (T 46.166c20–25): "Here the tripiṭaka teaching also asserts that dharma-nature is self-so, and [in this respect] does not appear to be much different from the separate [teaching]. For this reason we should distinguish between a provisional [sense of the] dharma-nature and the real dharma-nature. Since the tripiṭaka teaching considers that 'arising [of suffering] cannot defile it and cessation cannot purify it,' there must be a dharma-nature that it regards as standing utterly apart from the four noble truths."

in a sūtra, "Cessation is not itself the truth; it is through cessation that one realizes the true."[130] If even cessation is not the truth, how could the other three noble truths ever be? That there is no enlightenment in the afflictions, and no affliction in enlightenment—this is called arousing the thought of enlightenment through inference from the four noble truths at the level of arising-and-perishing. So doing one [resolves] upwardly to seek for the enlightenment of a Buddha and downwardly strives to train and transform living beings.

[6a19] Arousing the thought of enlightenment by inferring from the four noble truths at the level of nonarising-and-perishing: The dharma-nature is not different from suffering or the origin of suffering. It is simply that, by erroneously straying into suffering and the origin of suffering, one loses sight of the dharma-nature. It is like water when it freezes to form ice—there is no ice apart from the water.[131] The instant one realizes that suffering and the origin of suffering are [inherently] devoid of suffering and any arising of suffering, one comes to merge with the dharma-nature. If this is true even for suffering and its origin, how much more so it must be for the path and cessation. It says in a sūtra, "The afflictions are identical with enlightenment; enlightenment is identical with the afflictions."[132] This is called arousing the thought of enlightenment, upwardly seeking and downwardly transforming, by inferring from the four noble truths at the level of nonarising.

[6a24] Arousing the thought of enlightenment by inference from the four noble truths at the level of the innumerable: Now the dharma-nature is known as ultimate reality. This does not even fall within the realm of the two vehicles—much less that of ordinary unenlightened beings.[133] Beyond the two extremes[134] there separately exist pure dharmas. It is like the ten similes of the **Buddhagarbha* [*Sūtra*].[135] This is called arousing the

130. *Kōgi* (1.247) and "*Makashikan* inyō tenkyo sōran," p. 76, give the *Nirvāṇa Sūtra*, T 12.682c, as the source for this citation. Although the sense is similar, MHCK is quite far from the sūtra passage.

131. Chan-jan (T 46.166c27–a1) comments: "The analogy of ice and water resembles the perfect teaching. But here ice merely symbolizes cause and effect within the six destinies [of the three realms]. The dharma-nature as truth is represented by water, which it establishes as distinct [from the ice]. Although in name they are equated, [the use of the analogy here] still does not demonstrate the three truths and three thousand world-realms as themselves the nature of mind."

132. *Viśeṣacintabrahma-paripṛcchā Sūtra*, T 15.39b29. Earlier in his commentary (T 165b13) Chan-jan identifies this sūtra closely with the shared teaching—the teaching with which the four noble truths of nonarising-and perishing is affiliated.

133. That is, *pṛthagjana*.

134. The two extremes of existence and inexistence, arising and nonarising.

135. Or, the *Tathāgatagarbha Sūtra*, T 16.457c. This sūtra expounds ten famous

thought of enlightenment, upwardly seeking and downwardly transforming, by inferring from the four noble truths at the level of the innumerable.[136]

[6a27] Arousing the thought of enlightenment by inferring from the four noble truths at the level of the unconstructed: Here the dharma-nature and totality of dharmas are not two, not separate. If this is true even for dharmas of the ordinary [person], how much more so for the dharmas of the two vehicles. To seek reality apart from dharmas of the ordinary is like leaving empty space in one place to look for it in another. The dharmas of the ordinary are themselves the dharma of ultimate reality. There is no need to renounce the ordinary or turn toward the saintly. A sūtra says, "Saṃsāra is identical with nirvāṇa."[137] Every shape and every smell is the middle way. This is called arousing the thought of enlightenment, upwardly seeking and downwardly transforming, by inferring from the four noble truths at the level of the unconstructed.

[6b3] By inferring from any given dharma, one fathoms the entire dharmadhātu, reaching to its outermost limits and plumbing its deepest depths. Both horizontal and vertical are realized to the full, and one comprehends simultaneously phenomena (*shih*) as well as principle (*li*).[138] Upward seeking and downward transforming are [encompassed] completely within [this realization]. Only when this is the case can it [properly] be called arousing the thought of enlightenment. Enlightenment (bodhi) is

---

similes (among others) to show how the tathāgatagarbha or the "embryo of the Tathāgata" is present in all beings.

136. Chan-jan (T 46.167a2–4) says: "[In the separate teaching] the principle (*li*) of the dharma-nature 'transcends the two extremes.' The two previous teachings (i.e., the tripiṭaka and shared) are still caught up in existence and inexistence. The concealing and revealing [illustrated in] the ten similes of the *Tathāgatagarbha Sūtra* appear to resemble the [similes used for the] previous tripiṭaka teaching. But [their views regarding] the essence of principle are utterly different."

137. "*Makashikan* inyō tenkyo sōran," p. 76 (probably based on *Kōgi*), identifies this source as the *Viśeṣacintabrahma-paripṛcchā Sūtra*, T 15.41a.

138. Chan-jan (T 46.167a11–13) states: "Question: In what way is the inference on the basis of principle [discussed here] any different from the four truths [given previously]? Answer: The previous reference to the four truths was intended to provide a comprehensive term that could serve as a common basis for discussion. In the inference from principle [that is discussed] here, particular distinctions are being made with respect to dharma-nature. [That is to say,] the four types of practitioner [arouse the thought of enlightenment] through inference from two types of dharma-nature. Because of this difference between comprehensive and particular [approaches], the discussion is repeated here [with respect to dharma-nature]." According to *Kōgi* (1.252), "horizontal" means all the dharmas of the ten destinies, "vertical" means the three truths. "Phenomena" and "principle" are equated with the multiplicity of dharmas, on the one hand, and with the three truths, on the other.

also known as "the way" (*tao*). The way can lead directly to the other shore of both the horizontal and vertical. This is what is meant by the expression "the perfection of arousing the thought of enlightenment."[139] Hence, even though we make fine distinctions between shallow and profound ways of inferring from principle, phenomena and principle are themselves universally coextensive. From here on, each and every dharma is to be viewed in this way.

[6b15] **(2) Arousing the Thought of Enlightenment by Seeing the Marks and Excellences of the Buddha.**[140] Suppose that one sees the Tathāgata in the body born of his father and mother, the marks on his body vivid and prominent, each clearly occupying its proper place, resplendent and radiant. It is a body such as even the divine craftsman Viśvakarman could not have made,[141] with marks and excellent qualities superior to those adorning even wheel-turning kings, so rare in the world. There is nothing like the Buddha anywhere in the heavens above or the world below, he has no peer in any of the world-realms of the ten directions. Then one vows: "May I attain Buddhahood and be the equal of this king of the holy dharma! I vow to deliver incalculable and inexhaustible numbers of animate beings."[142] This is arousing the thought of enlightenment, upwardly seeking and downwardly transforming, by seeing the marks of the [inferior] body of manifest response (*ying-shen*) of the Buddha.[143]

139. Actually, this is not found among the classic set of six perfections (*pāramitās*), nor even among the ten perfections. Although modern scholarship accepts that *pāramitā* means "perfection" or "great virtue," the traditional etymology used in China is "arriving at or reaching the other shore."

140. This refers to the thirty-two major marks and eight minor excellences that characterize the body of a Buddha. Chih-i's list appears to derive from TCTL, T 25.90a–91a. For lists of these marks in English, see Hurvitz, "Chih-i," pp. 353–361; Dayal, *The Bodhisattva Doctrine in Buddhist Sanskrit Literature*, pp. 300–305.

141. TCTL, T 25.90b. This statement is made of the second mark, the thousand-spoked wheel on the soles of the Buddha's feet. Viśvakarman, whose name means "maker of everything," "the omnipotent one," is a creator god of the late Vedas.

142. Chan-jan treats these two statements as condensations of the famous "four extensive vows," which are discussed at length in the section that follows the four noble truths. He states (T 46.167b5–8): "[To say] 'I myself vow to become a Buddha' is equivalent to the [fourth] vow, 'The unexcelled enlightenment of a Buddha I vow to attain.' [To say] 'I vow to save beings' is the same as the [first] vow, 'Animate beings without limit I vow to deliver.' In order to deliver animate beings one must 'cultivate the accesses to dharma.' In order to obtain the enlightenment of a Buddha one must 'sever afflictions.' Thus the text only mentions two of the [four] extensive vows and incorporates the other two into them."

143. This corresponds to the tripiṭaka teaching, the lowest of the T'ien-t'ai four teachings.

[6b20] Suppose that, on seeing the Tathāgata, one realizes that there is no Tathāgata in the Tathāgata; and seeing his marks, one realizes that the marks are no-mark.[144] The Tathāgata and his marks are both like empty space. In emptiness there is no Buddha, much less any mark or excellence. To see that the Tathāgata is no-Tathāgata is to see the Tathāgata. To see that the marks are no-mark is to see the marks. Then one vows: "May I attain Buddhahood and be the equal of the king of the holy dharma! I vow to save beings incalculable and inexhaustible in number." This is arousing the thought of enlightenment, upwardly seeking and downwardly transforming, by seeing the marks of the [superior] body of response (*ying-shen*) of the Buddha.[145]

[6b26] Suppose that when one sees the Tathāgata, his marks are such that there is no form not manifested [in them], like a clear mirror, in which one sees a myriad images reflected. Neither ordinary person nor saint can fathom their limit.[146] For example, even the god Brahma cannot see the mound of flesh (*uṣṇīṣa*) on the crown of the Buddha's head;[147] and even Maudgalyāyana cannot fathom his voice.[148] A treatise says,

144. Chan-jan (T 46.167b11–14) says: "When one sees the marks of the Buddha according to the shared [teaching], it is simply a matter of seeing the emptiness of the marks and excellences of the previous tripiṭaka teaching. The Tathāgata is that which is adorned, the marks do the adorning. Since the object that is adorned is empty, how can there be an adorning. Adorning mark and object represent cognition and its object as construed from the perspective of the practitioner. As for the use of the term 'emptiness' here, the marks are themselves 'no-mark.' But this is not to be understood as [true] 'marklessness.' People use this [concept] far too loosely. One must be very judicious about it."

145. This arousing of the thought of enlightenment corresponds to the shared teaching.

146. Chan-jan (T 46.167b19–20) explains: "As for the 'marks of the Buddha's body of recompense,' because it is a body like a clear mirror [acquired] through realization of the dharma-nature, there is no image that does not appear manifested within it. To say that 'the limit of every mark and excellence is beyond the reach of ordinary person and saint' means that the ordinary person and saint within the two previous teachings, as well as beings who have not yet reached the [ten] stages (*bhūmi*) in the present [separate] teaching, are incapable of fathoming the limit of the marks of the body of recompense."

147. From the **Guhyaka-vajrapāṇi Sūtra* in the *Ratnakūṭa* collection of sūtras (*Ta pao chi ching*, T 11.54a). Above the mound of flesh on the crown of the Buddha's head there is an "invisible" *uṣṇīṣa*, which even Brahma—the most peerless among the devas of the heavens of form—cannot perceive.

148. From the the **Guhyaka-vajrapāṇi Sūtra*, T 11.56c–57a. This wonder-working disciple of Śākyamuni wanted to find how far the Buddha's voice reached, but no matter how far he magically transported himself, the voice was still as clear and distinct as if the Buddha were standing right before him. The story also appears in the TCTL, T 25.127c.

"The peerless essence that itself is formless is [what is meant by] 'the adornment that does not adorn.' "[149] Then one vows: "May I attain Buddhahood and be the equal of the king of the holy dharma!" This is arousing the thought of enlightenment, upwardly seeking and downwardly transforming, by seeing the marks of the body of recompense (*pao-shen*) of the Buddha.[150]

[6c2] Suppose that on seeing the Tathāgata one becomes aware that the Tathāgata's wisdom deeply fathoms the marks of beings' sins and meritorious blessings, illuminating everything throughout the ten directions. The thirty-two marks that endow his subtle and pure dharma-body are each in themselves identical to ultimate reality; and one perceives that the dharmadhātu and reality are contained entirely replete and undiminished [within them].[151] Then one vows: "May I attain Buddhahood and be the equal of the king of the holy dharma!" This is arousing the thought of enlightenment, upwardly seeking and downwardly transforming, by seeing the marks of the dharma-body (*fa-shen*) of the Buddha.[152]

[6c6] **(3) How Is the Thought of Enlightenment Aroused by Seeing the Various Spiritual Transformations [Produced by the Buddha]?** Suppose that one sees the Tathāgata relying on the power of the foundational dhyānas[153] to concentrate his mind [on a single phenomenon]

149. From the **Vajracchedika-prajñā-pāramitā-sūtra Śāstra,* T 25.786a. The work is a commentary on the *Diamond Sūtra* consisting of summary verses by Maitreya, with prose expositions by Asaṅga. Chan-jan (T 46.168a7–10) comments: " 'Formless' refers to the dharma-nature. 'Adornment' refers to the [two accumulations of] wisdom and merit. Wisdom and its object are mutually established and function in universal response with the dharmadhātu. Only those of the same level [of attainment] can see this nonadorning [adornment]. . . . It is perceived by bodhisattvas who have ascended to the [ten] stages (*bhūmi*) [of the separate teaching]."

150. This corresponds to the separate teaching.

151. This corresponds to the perfect teaching. Chan-jan (T 46.168a10–13) says: "Because [the Tathāgata's] 'wisdom' resorts to the dharma-body, it is characterized as 'deeply penetrating.' To indicate that the dharma-body itself is the foundation or source of all the marks [the text] says, 'the thirty-two marks that endow the dharma-body.' Furthermore, as [described] in the *Avataṃsaka* [*Sūtra*], each mark and excellence is fully conterminal with empty space."

152. Chan-jan (T 46.168a19–20) sums up the section on arousing the thought of enlightenment through seeing the marks of the Buddha: "Each of the passages [in this section] begins with the words, 'When one sees the Tathāgata.' All, therefore, take the Tathāgata of the tripiṭaka teaching as their fundamental object [of discussion and contemplation]. However, the four perspectives differ in their perception of these material marks."

153. *Maula-dhyāna.* The four basic dhyānas and four formless *samāpattis* are each distinguished into "foundational" or "fully apprehended" (*maulya*) and "partially apprehended" conditions, depending on whether the afflictions associated

and produce that single [phenomenon], not many.[154] Perhaps one sees him emit a single beam of light, which fills every place from the Avīci hell to the Bhavāgra heaven[155] with the resplendency of fiery light, so that everything in heaven and earth is clearly illuminated, and sun and moon seem to cease their double shining, their natural light dimmed and hidden [by its brilliance]. Then one vows: "May I attain Buddhahood and be the equal of the king of the holy dharma!"

[6c10] Suppose that one sees the Tathāgata responding to animate beings by relying on the Tathāgata's essential principle (*li*) of nonarising.[156] Without depending on dualistic features he is able to cause each being to see the Buddha as if he were standing in front of that being alone. Then one vows: "May I attain Buddhahood and be the equal of the king of the holy dharma!"

[6c12] Suppose that one sees the Tathāgata immersed in the perfect equipoise of samādhi, relying on the tathāgatagarbha to produce incarnations that engage in the four physical activities throughout the reaches of the ten directions.[157] Yet all the while in his essential dharma-nature [the Tathāgata] remains ever unperturbed. Then one vows: "May I attain Buddhahood and be the equal of the king of the holy dharma!"

[6c15] [Then again] one may see the Tathāgata as not different from his magical transformations, [the two being] utterly nondual. The Tathāgata produces spiritual transformations and the spiritual tranformations

---

with the level of meditative concentration preceding it have been merely suppressed or entirely eradicated.

154. Chan-jan (T 46.168a26–29) explains: "It is the same as when a magician speaks, his apparition speaks; when the magician is silent, his apparition is silent. As with speaking and silence, so it is with other activities. Thus it is not a true manifestation, in the sense that it does not have its own [self-soveriegn powers of] activity."

155. Respectively, the lowest hell and the highest heaven in the formless realm.

156. Chan-jan (T 46.168b15–16) says: "Because here one resorts to principle, it is different from [the previous] tripiṭaka [teaching] where one resorts to the fundamental dhyānas. Also, because there is no mark of duality, it is different from the tripiṭaka teaching where one 'concentrates the mind on a single phenomenon and produces that single phenomenon.' "

157. Chan-jan (T 46.168b21–24) states: " '*Garbha*' here means the essential nature that is principle itself (*li-hsing*). [This tathāgatagarbha] is unable to manifest transformations [as it is]. One must ascend to the level of the [ten] stages (*bhūmis*), fulfill the conditional practices, and manifest true cultivation before one can effect these sorts of transformations. It is quite distinct from the foundational [meditations of the tripiṭaka teaching] and principle of nonarising [that is the basis of the shared teaching]. The 'perfect equipoise of samādhi' signifies the level of the first [of the ten] stages, where one performs the work of the Buddhas throughout one hundred realms of the ten directions."

themselves create the Tathāgata.[158] Thus, in an inexhaustible process of transmutation beyond all reckoning, apparitions produce yet other apparitions, with each being utterly inconceivable and each identical to ultimate reality. In this fashion they accomplish the work of the Buddhas. Then one vows: "May I attain Buddhahood and be the equal of the king of the holy dharma!"

[6c18] **(4) How is the Thought of Enlightenment Aroused Through Hearing Various Dharmas?**[159] One may hear the dharma from Buddhas and from worthy spiritual friends, or one may hear it from the rolls of the sūtras. Hearing a single phrase on the [four noble truths] of arising-and-perishing, one may come to understand that all mundane and supramundane dharmas are ever newly arising and perishing and changing from moment to moment. Thereupon one realizes that the quiescence that comes from moral precepts, wisdom, and liberation is the truth.[160] Then one vows: "May I attain Buddhahood and come to be able to preach the path of purity."

[6c22] Or, on hearing the teaching of arising-and-perishing, one may realize that the four noble truths are utterly devoid of arising and perishing. Since in emptiness there is no thorn [of suffering whatsoever to be found], what is there to extract?[161] Who suffers? Who experiences the arising of suffering? Who engages in religious practice? Who becomes enlightened? [The four truths] are ultimately pure; subject and object are both quiescent.[162] Then one vows: "May I attain Buddhahood and be able to preach the path of purity."

158. Chan-jan (T 46.168c4–5) says: "[The term] 'spiritual transformations' does not only refer to bodily [manifestations]. All mental artifices of speech and mind are also 'spiritual tranformations.' "

159. Chan-jan (T 46.168c23–24) says: "Beginning with this [first section on] hearing [the teaching of] the arising-and-perishing [four noble truths], the dharmas of the four teachings [are presented in sequence]. Each, in turn, is interpreted from four different perspectives." Thus each of the four teachings (presented in the form of the fourfold four noble truths) is interpreted again according to the four teachings, thereby producing sixteen possibilities.

160. This corresponds to the perspective of the tripiṭaka teaching (i.e., the arising-and-perishing four noble truths). Chan-jan (T 46.168c25–28) says: "Arising takes place ceaselessly. Therefore [the text] says, 'ever newly.' Because [this process] is marked by the four marks [of arising, persisting, changing, and perishing], the text says it 'changes.' This signifies the truths of suffering and the origin of suffering. 'Precepts and wisdom' summarily refer to the truth of the path; and 'liberation,' to the truth of cessation, both conditioned as well as unconditioned. Quiescence is the principle of extinction that is realized."

161. From the *Nirvāṇa Sūtra*, T 12.78la.

162. This corresponds to the perspective of the shared teaching (i.e., the non-arising four noble truths). Chan-jan (T 46.169a3–4) says: "Because there is no subject [to effect realization], therefore [subject and object] are 'empty.' [Because

[6c25] Then again, on hearing the teaching of arising-and-perishing, one may understand that arising-and-perishing and nonarising-and-perishing represent paired opposites. Neither arising-and-perishing nor nonarising-and-perishing, then, is the middle. This middle way is pure and preeminent, transcending all predication in terms of saṃsāra and nirvāṇa. Thereupon one vows: "May I attain Buddhahood and be able to expound to animate beings the supreme way, preeminent and transcendent like the lotus flower that rises above the muddy water, like the moon in the sky."[163]

[6c29] Or else, on hearing the teaching of arising-and-perishing, one may understand at once both arising-and-perishing and nonarising-and-perishing as well as neither arising-and-perishing nor nonarising-and-perishing. Illumining simultaneously arising-and-perishing as well as nonarising-and-perishing, one finds any one [alternative] to be identical to the other three, and the three identical to the one. Thus [one comes to know] the secret treasury of the dharmadhātu, which is perfectly replete in its permanence and bliss.[164] Thereupon one vows: "May I attain Buddhahood and be able to expound the secret treasury to living beings, transforming them just as a person of great merit can take a stone and make it a jewel, or take poison and make it medicine.[165]

[7a4] [Moreover,] on hearing the nonarising-or-perishing [four noble truths], one may realize that the two vehicles attain nonarising [as deliv-

---

they are] empty, [the text] says they are 'pure.' 'Subjective agent' refers to cessation and the path; 'object,' to suffering and its origin. Because subjective agent and object are nondual, [the text says they are] 'quiescent.' "

163. This corresponds to the perspective of the separate teaching (i.e., the innumerable four noble truths). Chan-jan (T 46.169a5–7) states: "Here the extremes themselves are not actually identified with the middle. Rather, the middle is postulated on the basis of the [two] extremes [of emptiness and the provisional]. Thus, in the similes that follow, the flower of the middle way rises above the water of the two extremes, and the moon of wisdom comes forth from the darkness [of the clouds] and abides in the sky of dharma-nature."

164. This corresponds to the perspective of the perfect teaching (i.e., the unconstructed four noble truths). Chan-jan (T 46.169a7–9) says: "Although the three [truths] are mutually identified [with one another], the nature of this middle [truth] is such that [all extremes] are simultaneously eradicated [and simultaneously illuminated]. This mutual identity of the three and the one is [likewise] perfectly equal with the dharmadhātu. In name [the truths and the dharmadhātu] differ but in meaning they are the same."

165. Chan-jan (T 46.169a13–15) states: "Stones and jewels, poisons and medicines are originally not two separate things. Depending on what the circumstances of the subject necessitate (i.e., stimulate), each is regarded and treated differently. It is the same for the teachings of the dharma. Originally they are all [one and the same] dharmadhātu."

erence from rebirth] in the three realms,[166] while bodhisattvas do not [experience this sort of] nonarising.[167] Then again, on hearing the teaching of nonarising, one may come to understand that all three vehicles attain the state of nonarising in the three realms.[168] Or, on hearing the teaching of nonarising, one may realize that the two vehicles do not partake of even a portion [of the true nonarising], and that [nonarising in its genuine sense] pertains only to bodhisattvas.[169] [The reason lies in the fact that] bodhisattvas first achieve deliverance from rebirth[170] in the common [saṃsāra] of fixed divisions and allotments and then achieve deliverance from arising in the supernally transformed [saṃsāra].[171] Finally, on hearing the teaching of nonarising, [one may realize that] one nonarising is all nonarisings.[172]

[7a8] Should one hear a line of teaching concerning the innumerable

166. Desire, form, and formlessness.

167. The perspective or interpretation of the tripiṭaka teaching. Chan-jan remarks (T 46.169a17): "Here the four interpretations are generated upon hearing the nonarising-or-perishing (four noble truths)." The bodhisattvas do not attain this sort of nonarising because the "biased" form of extinction espoused by the tripiṭaka teaching is anathema to them.

168. The perspective of the shared teaching. Chan-jan (T 46.169a19) says: "[From the perspective of the shared teaching], the three vehicles engage in a common practice and all eradicate [the afflictions of view and cultivation that keep beings bound to the three realms]. Thus they all realize nonarising."

169. The perspective of the separate teaching. Chan-jan (T 46.169a19–21) explains: "If nonarising is construed solely in terms of the severing of the afflictions of view and cultivation, then the two vehicles 'share in a portion' of it. But here [according to the perspective of the separate teaching] nonarising is understood to mean the severing of fundamental nescience [that conceals the middle truth]. Thus [the two vehicles] 'share in no portion' of it."

170. The term used here (i.e., *sheng*) can mean birth as well as arising or production.

171. These are two kinds of saṃsāra that are distinguished in the *Śrīmālā Sūtra*, T 12.219c. The first, "the common saṃsāra of fixed divisions and allotments," represents the mundane experience of saṃsāra as cyclic rebirth among the six fixed destinies in accordance with one's karma. The second, "the supernally transformed saṃsāra," represents a saṃsāra of expedience that is spontaneously produced and experienced by enlightened bodhisattvas who freely take birth in saṃsāra in order to deliver other beings.

172. The perspective of the perfect teaching. Chan-jan (T 46.169a22–23) explains: "Hearing the teaching of the [Sanskrit] syllable *a*, one thereupon realizes all [of the forty-one syllables and their teachings] in totality. This is the perspective of the perfect [teaching]." The letter *a*, according to the perfect teaching, represents true nonarising and the realization of the middle truth. The remaining forty-one syllables, which are equated with the forty-one stages of the perfect path subsequent to the first abiding, are simply modes of this fundamental insight.

[four noble truths] it works much the same way.[173] On hearing the teaching of the innumerable [four noble truths], one may understand it to mean that such features of the two vehicles as the path of expedients, the four noble truths, and the sixteen truths[174] are "innumerable." Or, on hearing the teaching of the innumerable, one may realize that although the two vehicles employ it to suppress their own delusions, they are unable to use it to transform others; only bodhisattvas use this teaching of the innumerable to eliminate their own delusions and transform others as well.[175]

[7a11] Or, on hearing the teaching of the innumerable, one may [understand it to] mean that the two vehicles have absolutely no part in it, that it is exclusive to bodhisattvas alone.[176] Bodhisattvas employ it to eradicate their mundane delusion that obscures multiplicity and also suppress their supramundane delusion that obscures multiplicity.[177] Or, on hearing the teaching of the innumerable, one may [understand it to] say that the two vehicles have no part in it, that it is exclusive to bodhisattvas, and the bodhisattvas employ it to eradicate both their mundane and supramundane [delusion that obscures] multiplicity and also to suppress nescience.[178] Then again, on hearing the teaching of the innumerable, one may [understand it to be] exclusive to bodhisattvas, who employ it to both suppress and eradicate nescience.[179]

173. Chan-jan (T 46.169a23) states: "Now comes the generation of the four interpretations due to hearing the innumerable [four noble truths]."

174. The perspective of the tripiṭaka teaching. The sixteen truths represent sixteen stages of eradicating intellectual delusions with respect to the Hīnayāna four noble truths. They are the partial and complete realization of the four noble truths in the realm of desire (eight items), and the partial and complete realization of the four noble truths in the form and formless realms (eight items). For details, see Mochizuki, *Bukkyō daijiten*, 3.2288c.

175. The perspective of the shared teaching.

176. The perspective of the separate teaching.

177. The dustlike delusions—the second ground in the T'ien-t'ai system of three grounds of delusion—represent an obsession with emptiness that impedes the bodhisattva's perception of the provisional truth and, hence, his expedient salvific function.

178. Third of the three delusions. Nescience conceals the truth of the middle.

179. *Kōgi* (1.278–279) is perplexed that this section ends with the suppression and eradication of nescience, for it seems to represent nothing more than the culmination of the sequence of the gradual path of the separate teaching described previously. Thus the perfect teaching appears to have been omitted by Chih-i. To resolve this ambiguity *Kōgi* suggests that the statement "both suppress and eradicate nescience" must describe the perfect path, wherein suppression and eradication are understood, simultaneously, to mean no-suppression/no-eradication and all suppressions and eradications. Chan-jan himself makes no reference to the perspective of the perfect teaching here whatsoever.

[7a16] Finally, hearing the unconstructed [four noble truths] may work in similar fashion [to arouse the thought of enlightenment].[180] On hearing the teaching of the unconstructed [four noble truths], one may [understand it to] mean that [the reality] is not something that Buddhas, devas, men, or asuras have acted to produce. The two vehicles both realize the unconstructed.[181] As the *Viśeṣacintabrahma-paripṛcchā* [*Sūtra*] says, "We have cultivated the unconstructed and so have achieved its realization, but bodhisattvas cannot attain this realization."[182]

[7a19] Or, on hearing the teaching of the unconstructed, one may [understand it to] say that the three vehicles are all able to attain it.[183] Then again, on hearing the teaching of the unconstructed, one may [take it to] mean that it is not within the [experiential] domain of the two vehicles, much less that of the ordinary person. By this [realization], bodhisattvas refute the provisional sense of the unconstructed [peculiar to the two vehicles] and attain the real unconstructed.[184] Finally, on hearing the teaching of the unconstructed, one may understand it to mean that right in the provisional [view of] the unconstructed one attains the real unconstructedness.[185] Once this point is grasped, on hearing any single phrase

180. Chan-jan (T 46.169b7) says: "[Here begins] the generation of the four interpretations [from hearing the teaching of] the unconstructed [four noble truths]."

181. That is, the two vehicles realize the "unconstructed" according to their particular understanding of it. *Kōgi* (1.280) cites the *Saṃyuktāgama* (T 2.85b) as the source for this statement. The attribution seems questionable.

182. T 15.37a. According to the *Viśeṣacintabrahma-paripṛcchā Sūtra*, 500 bhikṣus listening to the Buddha's discourse on nirvāṇa as unconstructed claim: "We have now realized [the true nature and, hence, extinction] of all the defilements and act though unable to act. . . . Nirvāṇa has the nature of unconstructedness. Because we have attained it we say that we act [and construct] though unable to act." The phrase "bodhisattvas cannot attain it" is not part of this sūtra passage, although the commentators treat it as if it were. Chan-jan (T 46.169b8–9) says: "[From the perspective of the tripiṭaka understanding of the unconstructed, bodhisattvas do not eradicate their defilements and, hence, do not attain the unconstructed."

183. The perspective of the shared teaching.

184. The perspective of the separate teaching. Chan-jan (T 46.169b10) states: "The [thirty ranks of the bodhisattva path] that lie prior to the ten stages represent the provisional. Entry into the [ten] stages is the real."

185. The perspective of the perfect teaching. Chan-jan (T 46.169b11–12) says: "[According to the separate teaching] the two truths [of emptiness and the provisional] characterize [practice at all] levels [of the bodhisattva path] prior to the [ten] stages (*bhūmi*). But here, [all such stages and perspectives on emptiness and the provisional] are understood to be identical to the middle truth that is realized upon entry to the ten stages. Thus it says that 'provisional and real are mutually identified with one another.'"

[of the teaching], all phrases [of the dharma] are comprehended, to the point where all phrases and all dharmas are mutually unimpeding.

[7a22] Now, because there are multiple interpretations for each level of discourse [of the fourfold four noble truths], their meaning is difficult to clarify. Therefore, we will provide another explanation, this time in reference to the gāthā of the *Middle Treatise*.[186]

[7a23] [The gāthā] says, "Whatever arises through causes and conditions, that I declare to be identical with emptiness." But having mentioned "that which arises through causes and conditions," how does one arrive at its "identity with emptiness?" One must first analyze (*hsi*) these causes and conditions exhaustively; only then will one understand their emptiness. Thereupon one declares this emptiness that is anticipated [through analysis] to be "identical with emptiness."[187] [The line from the gāthā that reads] "It is also called 'provisional designation' " means at this level that existence is too insubstantial and weak to stand alone and is established only through provisional reliance on a multitude of conditions. It is provisional because it is dependent on conditions, not because it is conferred as a provisional expedient.[188] [The line] "It is also called the meaning of the middle way" at this level is understood to mean the middle way that departs from the two extreme views of annihilationism and eternalism.[189] This is not the middle way of [the intrinsic] Buddha-nature. When the gāthā is interpreted in this manner, although the three

186. *Chung-lun*, T 30.33b. The verse in question reads: "Whatever dharma arises on the basis of causes and conditions, that I declare to be identical with emptiness (or inexistence). It is also provisional designation. This, furthermore, is the meaning of the middle way." Chan-jan (T 46.169b15–16) says of this section: "[Here the text] employs the [*Middle*] *Treatise*'s [discussion of the] mutual identity [of the three truths] in order to sum up the four interpretations."

187. Chan-jan (T 46.169b17–20) says: "This may be likened to declaring a man falling from a cliff dead before he reaches the ground. The [analytic] 'only then' means something like 'must be.' When one cultivates [contemplation of] impermanence, even though one has yet to know it to be [truly] 'identical with emptiness,' the sense that it 'must be' empty is already imputed to the object."

188. Chan-jan (T 46.169b20–23) explains: "There are two sorts of provisionality established on the basis of conditions, each distinct unto itself. The same may be said for [the views of] emptiness and the middle. The false and illusory provisionality that is discussed here is produced through dependence on the myriad [causes and] conditions. It is not the same as the [deliberate] bringing forth on the basis of emptiness various provisional expedients designed to benefit living beings."

189. *Ucchedavāda* and *śāśvatavāda*. Chan-jan (T 46.169b23–24) says: "A middle [truth] in the form of departing from eternalism and annihilationism is also attained by the two vehicles. But because the fruit of Buddhahood is far superior to that of the disciples of the three vehicles, it [alone] receives the distinction of being called the 'middle [truth].' "

phrases quoted from the gāthā are all empty, the meaning of "identical with emptiness" remains incomplete, to say nothing of "identical with provisionality" or "identical with the middle." This, then, is the meaning of the four noble truths at the level of arising-and-perishing.[190]

[7b2] Suppose that dharmas "that arise through causes and conditions" are perceived in their very essence (*t'i*) as being identical with emptiness, so that one does not resort to reduction or destruction in order to achieve emptiness, but they are not yet completely identified with provisionality or the middle as well. In such a case, even though one may posit provisionality and the middle, they will both have a tendency to be subsumed into emptiness. Why is this? Dharmas are identical with emptiness due to their lack of own-being; their provisionality is identical with emptiness, because they are established as entities only in a provisional sense; and their middleness is also identical with emptiness, because it is a middle that [merely] departs from the two extremes of annihilationism and eternalism. Although the above three statements differ verbally, they all tend toward dissolution in emptiness. Thus, although they do not fall back into the inferior analytical dharma of the two vehicles, neither do they advance to the [dharma of] the separate or perfect [teachings]. They are nothing more than the notion of a commonly shared emptiness, as in the simile of the three animals crossing the river.[191]

[7b8] Suppose that one understands [the three statements of] "identical to emptiness," "identical to provisionality," and "identical to the middle way" in a mutually permuting manner but with each [interpretation] standing distinctly apart from the others.[192] That is to say, the three statements of the gāthā are all empty because [dharmas that arise from conditions] are without own-being, are insubstantial postulates,[193] and

190. This is the perspective of the tripiṭaka teaching.

191. From the *Nirvāṇa Sūtra* (T 12.746b); also cited in the **Upāsaka-śīla Sūtra* (T 24.1034). When a rabbit, a horse, and an elephant cross a river, the rabbit swims only on the surface, the horse is more deeply submerged, and the elephant plants its feet firmly on the bottom. These represent differences in the realization of dharma-nature on the part of the three vehicles: śrāvakas, pratyekabuddhas, and bodhisattvas, respectively.

192. Chan-jan (T 46.169c15–16) says: "Because the three truths are actually present, [this perspective] is not the same as those of the tripiṭaka and shared [teachings]. Thus it is not to be deprecated. But it must be faulted for the fact that it takes a sequential approach [to the three truths] and cannot yet be called 'perfect.' . . . Although the three truths are all empty, all provisional, and all [identical with] the middle, together they still retain a sequential arrangement."

193. Chan-jan (T 46.169c18) says: "From the mind of emptiness one brings forth provisionality. Thus, in response to the provisional illnesses of others, one provisionally establishes the medicine of dharma. Hence, both the illness and medicine are identical to emptiness."

belong to neither extreme.[194] The three statements are all provisional, because they all involve the use of names.[195] The three statements are all the middle, because the first is the middle with respect to truth, the second is the middle in terms of salvific circumstance (*chi*), and the third is the middle with respect to reality [itself].[196] This [understanding] achieves the separate [teaching] but still falls short of the perfect [teaching].

[7b12] Suppose that one understands [the three statements of] "identical with emptiness," "identical with the provisional," and "identical with the middle" in such a way that though they are three, they are all one. And though they are one, they are still three. [That is to say,] they do not impede each other in any way whatsoever. All three [statements] are empty because the path of speech and discursive thought is cut off. All three are provisional because they are name only. All three are the middle because they are identical with ultimate reality. [The term] "emptiness" is merely used as a name; thus it implicitly includes the provisional and the middle. If one awakens to emptiness, then one [simultaneously] awakens to the provisional and the middle. It is the same for the other two as well.

[7b16] Know, then, that when a single dharma is heard, a whole variety of interpretations may arise, and a variety of vows may be put forth. These, in turn, suggest a variety of different ways in which the thought of enlightenment may be aroused.[197]

194. Chan-jan (T 46.169c20) says: "[This is] the principle of the middle devoid of all [notions of opposite] extremes. It is none other than ultimate emptiness."

195. Chan-jan (T 46.169c23–24) says: "Although the three truths are name only, there is nevertheless a sequential arrangement of prior and after. Thus [the three statements] remain distinct."

196. Chan-jan (T 46.169c24–28) says: "That the 'three are all the middle' also resembles the [perfect teaching], where one middle is all middles. However, a sequential arrangement is still retained overall, and the designation 'middle' is contrived mainly in a provisional and expedient sense. Thus the three truths still describe an explicit sequence [where each is distinguished in contrast to the others]. Because [emptiness] departs from [the extremes of] annihilationism and eternalism, it is called the 'middle with respect to the truth.' This level corresponds to the stages of the ten abodes. Because [the provisional] is not off the mark when it comes to [responding to] salvific circumstance, it is called 'middle in terms of salvific circumstance.' This level corresponds to the stages of the [ten] actions and [ten] transferences. Because [the middle abides in] the reality limit of the dharma-nature itself, it is called 'the middle with respect to reality.' This level corresponds to the ten stages."

197. Chan-jan (T 46.170a6–9) says: "Dharma is the object [to be realized]. This object we define in terms of the four noble truths. On the basis of [perceiving] this object, understanding arises. Through understanding, vows arise. Therefore, the vow is called 'arousing the thought of enlightenment.' People of the world

[7b18] **(5–10) The Remaining Ways of Arousing the Thought of Enlightenment.** The various other ways of arousing the thought of enlightenment that have been listed above—i.e., through (5) [traveling to various] Pure Lands, (6) [seeing] assemblies of followers, (7) [witnessing] the performance of various religious practices, (8) [experiencing] the destruction of the dharma, (10) [observing] the sufferings [of others], and (9) [seeing] various transgressions[198]—may be understood in a similar fashion. No further details about them shall be recorded here.[199]

[7b19] We have already discussed at length many ways of arousing the thought of enlightenment. Now we shall sum them up according to the [three forms] of calming and contemplation.

[7b20] Q: Now, the dharma-nature does not even admit a dharma of oneness. How [can its meaning] be inferred from three [kinds of calming and contemplation] or four [levels of interpretation of the four noble truths]?[200]

[7b21] A: Here, when we speak of one, two, three, or four it is to explain that the dharma-nature is the object with regard to which we err; suffering and the origin of suffering represent the subjective erring. The subjective erring may be slight or severe, and the object of error may be considered identical to or separate [from the practitioner]. Then, when we distinguish the mundane and supramundane,[201] there are altogether four kinds of suffering and origin of suffering. Moreover, when we consider the capacities of animate beings to grasp principle (*li*), there are one, two, three, four, or more differences. If someone of dull capacity within the [three] realms errs severely with respect to the truth, his suf-

---

today for the most part look upon sitting in meditation and settling the mind (*an-hsin*) [through contemplation] as arousing the thought [of enlightenment]. Such persons utterly fail to identify just what the object of their efforts is. They have absolutely no anticipated goal in mind and are wholly without the aspect of 'upward seeking.' Nor do they have a clear idea of what great compassion is and so are completely without the 'downward transforming.' Thus [one should be aware that] the arousing of the thought of enlightenment takes place on the basis of great compassion."

198. The sequence of the last two items is reversed from that given at the beginning of this section on arousing the thought of enlightenment.

199. Although Chih-i and Kuan-ting have nothing further to say about them, Chan-jan in his commentary (T 46.170a10–c9) discusses each of these remaining items with considerable detail. Witnessing the destruction of dharma, for example, may arouse the thought of enlightenment by stimulating one to defend and protect the dharma. Seeing others commit faults may do so because one thereby perceives the cause of suffering in action.

200. Following Chan-jan (T 46.170c16–17).

201. Literally, "distinguish between what is subject to the three realms of desire, form, and formlessness and what is beyond them."

fering and origin of suffering will also be severe. If someone of keen capacity errs only slightly with regard to the truth, his suffering and cause of suffering will also be slight. The same differences obtain in the supramundane realm for the slight and severe [erring of persons of] keen or dull capacities.

[7b26] The dharma-nature is the object to be understood, while the path and cessation refer to the subjective understanding. The object of understanding may be considered either identical or separate [with the practitioner], while the subjective understanding may be either skilled or inept.[202] For the dull person subject to the mundane realm, the object of understanding is considered to be separate, and the subjective understanding itself is inept. But the object of understanding is considered to be identical for those of keen capacity, and subjective understanding itself is skilled. The same distinctions obtain in the supramundane realm for the views of identity and separateness and the skilled or inept [understanding] of [persons with] keen or dull [capacity].[203] Why is this? Because when the phenomenal order (*shih*) and principle (*li*) are construed as separate, benighted delusion is already severe.

[7c1] It is, for example, like a father and son who think of each other as strangers, so that both their anger and the subsequent blows they inflict on each other are severe. Anger represents the origin of suffering, and the blows represent suffering. If one understands that the afflictions are themselves identical to the dharma-nature, and that phenomena and principle are identical to each other, then suffering and the origins of suffering are slight. Even though the two persons may not actually be of the same flesh and bone, if they should think of each other as father and son their anger and blows will be slight.[204]

202. Chan-jan (T 46.170c20–23) says: "Truth and dharma-nature are different in name but the same in meaning. The keen and dull individuals of the mundane realms err with respect to truth. Keen and dull of the supramundane realms err with respect to the middle way. Whether one errs with respect to truth or errs with respect to the middle, although the object of one's erring and the object of one's understanding are one and the same dharma-nature, subjective understanding and error differ in their skill and ineptness. Thus they altogether come to four."

203. Chan-jan (T 46.170c24–27) says: " 'Keen' implies 'identical.' 'Dull' implies 'separate.' 'Skilled' and 'inept' work the same way. 'Separate' means that suffering and its origin are considered to be 'separate from' dharma-nature. 'Identical' means that dharma-nature itself is identical to suffering and its origin. That the object of understanding is construed as separate is because the subjective understanding is inept. That the object is construed as identical is because the subjective understanding is skilled."

204. Chan-jan (T 46.171a5–6) says: "Thus the notion that suffering and its origin are ever different from the dharma-nature exemplifies persons of the tri-

[7c4] The same considerations apply for pairs of opposites like the coarse and the subtle, branch and root, the shared and the separate, the all-encompassing and the restricted, the difficult and the easy. One might say that suffering and the origin of suffering are "severe" and "slight," because in the mundane realm they lurk in the depths, while in the supramundane realm they have arisen and departed. Or one might speak of "shallow," because the delusions of the mundane realms are skin-deep, and "deep," because the delusions of the supramundane realm are flesh-deep. Or one might say "inept," because in the mundane realms one follows others' ideas, and "skilled," because in the supramundane realm one follows one's own. Or one might say "skilled," because in the mundane realms one accords with the specific salvific circumstances (*chi*) of beings, and "inept," because in the supramundane realm one does not. Or one might say "coarse," because in the mundane realms there exist both subject and object, and "subtle," because in the supramundane realm there is no distinction between subject and object. Or one might say "subtle," because in the mundane realms the ultimate end of the Hīnayāna lies in the conjured city, and "coarse," because in the supramundane realm the ultimate of the Mahāyāna lies in the treasure lode.[205] Or one might say "branch," because in the mundane realms there is adventitious defilement, and "root," because in the supramundane realms [defilement and truth] are ultimately the same substance. Or one might say "root," because the mundane realms are at the beginning, and "branch," because the supramundane comes later. Or one might say "shared," because the mundane realms are common to both the Hīnayāna and the Mahāyāna, and "separate," because the supramundane is peculiar to the Mahāyāna. Or one might say "small," because the mundane realms are one-sided, and "separate," because they are shallow, or "great," because the supramundane realm is perfect, and "shared," because it has no barriers in it. Or one might say "restricted," because [the scope of] the mundane realms is truncated, or "universal," because the supramundane encompasses the entire dharmadhātu. Or one might say "universal," because the mundane is common to all saints and worthies, and "restricted," because the supramundane is the exclusive provenance of those affiliated with the great [vehicle].[206] Or one might say "difficult to eradicate," because in the mundane realms only the expedients of the two vehicles are

piṭaka and separate teachings. . . . The notion that suffering and its cause are identical to the dharma-nature, therefore, typifies persons of the shared and perfect teachings."

205. From the parable of the conjured city in the *Lotus Sūtra*, T 9.26a. The conjured city is a mere way station on the path to perfect enlightenment, which is the treasure lode in the parable.

206. Following Muranaka, p. 78.

employed, or "easy to eradicate," because in the supramundane realm one relies solely on unimpeded wisdom. Thus one may expound by using various pairs of opposites interchangeably like this.

[7c20] Now if we sum this up it can be easily understood. If we take the first two pairs, "shallow/deep" and "slight/severe," this is the sense of the gradual and sequential contemplation. If we establish the idea that there is no difference between the one reality and the four noble truths, then this is the sense of the perfect and sudden contemplation. If we take all the pairs like "slight/serious" and so forth and reciprocally interchange them, this is the sense of the variable contemplation.

[7c23] All [three present] Mahāyāna dharmas and their features. Therefore, one should be familiar with them. Whoever sees the meaning of this understands [the three kinds of calming and contemplation]—the gradual and sequential revealing of the right [arousing of the thought of enlightenment], the variable revealing of the right [arousing of the thought of enlightenment], and the perfect and sudden revealing of the right [arousing of the thought of enlightenment].

[7c25] Q: If there are four ways of viewing the origin of suffering, why are there only two ways of seeing the effect of suffering?

[7c26] A: If the delusions follow from [defects in] the understanding, then there are four kinds of sufferings, [corresponding to the four levels of the four noble truths]. If the defects in the understanding follow from the delusions, then one only experiences the two kinds of saṃsāra. For example, when in the Hīnayāna delusions follow from defects in the understanding, the latter are divided into two, namely delusions pertaining to intellect or view and those pertaining to cultivation. If the defects in the understanding follow from the delusions, then there is only the common saṃsāra of fixed division and allotment.

[7c29] Q: [It is feasible that] suffering and the origin of suffering might be equated with the line from the gāthā that speaks of "dharmas that arise through causes and conditions." But why are the path and cessation also included [at the level of the arising-and-perishing four noble truths]?[207]

207. This question refers to the one-to-one correspondence made by Chih-i between the four teachings and the four lines of the gāthā (7a24ff), beginning with "dharmas that arise on the basis of causes and conditions." The questioner understands how the first saṃsāric pair of noble truths could be considered statements on conditioned dharmas, but he has difficulty grasping how the second pair of noble truths could be statements on the conditioned.

Chan-jan (T 46.171b18–21) says: "Suffering and its origin have delusion and error as their basis and can certainly be regarded as subjective causes and conditions. But the path and cessation eradicate error. How can one claim that they arise on the basis of causes and conditions? The reply that follows explains that the suffering and origin of suffering to be eradicated are in essence conditionally produced. [Furthermore] if there were no suffering and its origin, there would

[8a1] A: Suffering and the origin of suffering are what is to be eradicated, while the path and cessation are what do the eradicating. At the level of the four noble truths of arising-and-perishing, the eradicating pair are denoted according to what they eradicate. Both pairs then belong to the category of "dharmas that arise through causes and conditions." Hence it says in the *Nirvāṇa Sūtra*, "With the annihilation of nescience as the cause one attains the shining lamp of perfect enlightenment."[208] This is also causation.

[8a3] Q: The dharma-nature is that in which one errs. [Since it is unitary and beyond all distinguishing marks,] how can it be two, and how can it be four?

[8a4] A: Because the dharma-nature is considered from the standpoint of both the provisional and the real, we speak of two. Because differences in individual capacity and circumstance are taken into account, we speak of four.[209] If this point has been understood, then the other nine ways of arousing the thought of enlightenment—from seeing the marks [of the Buddha] and hearing the dharma to seeing the commission of transgressions—as well as the four ways of arousing the thought of enlightenment within each of these, can be elaborated and discussed along similar lines.

The Four Extensive Vows[210]

[8a7] Here we reveal the right [arousing of the thought of enlightenment] with reference to the four extensive vows. [The correct arousing of the thought of enlightenment] has already been elucidated in the preceding sections on inference from [the principle of] dharma-nature,

---

be no path and cessation. These designations derive from the others; thus they also are based on conditionality."

208. T 12.732a.

209. Chan-jan (T 46.171b28–29) explains: "Provisional expedients are initially elaborated in order [ultimately] to reveal the reality of the one single dharma-nature. Because provisional expedients are instituted on behalf of the real, a distinction is made between the provisional and the real. With respect to [these] provisional and real [teachings], capacities for understanding will be different. Thus for each of the two—the provisional and real—keen and dull [capacities are distinguished]."

210. Chan-jan (T 46.171c2–4) explains: "As for the term 'four extensive vows,' 'extensive' means 'vast.' 'Vow' means to 'restrain or make a pledge.' Thus the term can be interpreted to mean 'swearing to a certain restraint.' Here one restrains or disciplines the elementary thought [of enlightenment] by means of the four stipulations."

The four extensive vows originate from the *P'u-sa ying-lo pen-yeh ching* (T no. 1485), an apocryphal Buddhist scripture probably composed in late fifth century China. These four vows, which have been recited widely by Buddhists throughout East Asia since the seventh century, include: "Animate beings without limit I vow to deliver. Afflictions without end I vow to eradicate. Dharma-gates without measure I vow to practice. Unexcelled Buddhahood I vow to attain."

hearing the dharma, and so forth. For the benefit of those who have not clearly understood we once again treat it here, but this time with respect to the four extensive vows.

[8a8] Moreover, the four noble truths mainly explain upward seeking and downward transforming in terms of intellectual understanding. The four extensive vows explain upward seeking and downward transforming with an emphasis on resolve.[211] Then again, while the illustration of upward seeking and downward transforming in terms of the four noble truths extends universally to Buddhas of all three times, the four extensive vows concern only future Buddhas.[212] Also, the four truths, in explaining upward seeking and downward transforming, apply to [the activities of] all the sense faculties, while the four vows deal exclusively with the faculty of the mind or cognitive sense.[213] Analyses of this sort make [the arousing of the thought of enlightenment] easier to comprehend; but those who have already understood need not await [this additional explanation].

[8a14] **The Four Vows and the Arising-and-Perishing Four Noble Truths.**[214] Thoughts in the mind do not come into being wholly on their

211. Chan-jan (T 46.171c7–11) says: "Although the arousing of the thought [of enlightenment] has already been discussed extensively on the basis of the [four noble] truths, students without much understanding may not realize how the four noble truths themselves serve as the object for the four extensive [vows]. Thus [the text] once again expounds [the four truths] in relation to the extensive vows. . . . The four truths are the object [of wisdom]. From this object, understanding arises. Thus [the text] says, 'in terms of understanding.' As for 'the four extensive vows,' resolution is developed on the basis of understanding. Thus [the text] says, 'with an emphasis on resolve.' Moreover, because the four truths include both cause and effect, they extend across the three times. But vows are concerned exclusively with what is to come, thus they belong to the future."

212. Chan-jan (T 46.171c12–13) says: "The four [noble] truths are concerned with principle. Principle extends throughout the three times. The four vows are pledges, and a pledge is realized in the future."

213. *Mana-indrīya*, the sixth of the six sense faculties—the seat of cognitive awareness and thought. In Chinese the term has the additional meaning of "intent" or "will," which possibly explains Chih-i's particular identification of the *mana-indrīya* with the making of vows.

Chan-jan (T 46.171c18–21) notes: "The four truths pervade the three activities [of body, speech, and mind], and the three activities extend in common to the six sense faculties. Since the making of vows does not really require [the presence of] body and mouth, it may [be said to] involve mind alone. However, this represents a very general perspective. If one were to discuss [the matter] in detail, [the making of vows] should also involve all three [activities]. Mind focuses on the object or referent of the vow; the mouth professes the vow out loud; and the body displays signs of reverence [for it]."

214. Chan-jan (T 46.171c28–172a2) says: "Q: Previously you explained [the

own but must depend on [other dharmas as] conditions in order to arise. The faculty of the mind sense acts as the efficient cause, mental and physical objects are the contributing conditions, and the thought that is aroused is the dharma that is produced by [this interaction of] cause and condition. The sense organs and what they perceive, the subject and its objects, shift through the three phases,[215] stealthily arising and stealthily departing. Ever newly do they arise and perish, without enduring for even a moment of thought. Like lightning they flicker and [pass by] as quickly as a rushing stream.

[8a17] Material form is like a bubble; sensations, like foam; cognition, like a flame; volitional impulses, like mirages;[216] consciousness, like an illusion of magic.[217] One's country, fields, house, wife, children, and material wealth—all such things that pertain to the retribution of environment[218]—are lost in an instant. They are here one moment and gone the next. The three realms are impermanent, while [the body itself] is like a basket [of vipers], promising nothing but suffering.[219] Should the four mountains close in on you from the four directions, there would be no place to escape to. [Just so], the only thing left [for one caught up in saṃsāra] is to focus the mind wholly on morality, meditation, and wisdom.[220]

---

arousal of the right thought of enlightenment in terms of] a series of ten categories. Why do you now single out the [four] truths? A: The four truths represent the universal [perspective]; the ten categories, the perspective of the particular. For this reason, when explaining the ten items, the [four] truths are placed at the very beginning. Should any of these ten items be lacking [in the perspectives of] principle (*li*) and phenomena (*shih*) then they will be the same as the preachings of Māra. For this reason generalizations are made for the rest of the ten by exclusive reference to the meaning of the [four noble] truths."

215. Arising, changing, and perishing. As before, persistence, the fourth dharmic state, is omitted.

216. According to Chan-jan's (T 46.172a21) treatment of this passage, the original at T468a17 should probably be emended to read "city of the Gandharvas." They represent mirages that, when seen from afar, resemble cities with towering spires.

217. A well-known set of similes for insubstantiality found in the *Saṃykuktāgama* (T 2.48b) as well as in the *Pañcaviṃśati*, T 8.217a.

218. That is, *i-pao*, the aspect of karmic retribution that determines particulars of external circumstance or environs (*niśraya*) as opposed to the aspect that determines the subjective or primary form of the being itself.

219. From the *Nirvāṇa Sūtra* (T 12.742c–743a), where the four elements that compose the body and the sense organs are compared to four poisonous snakes imprisoned in a basket.

220. Paraphrased from the *Nirvāṇa Sūtra*, T 12.781c, with emendations. Chanjan (T 46.172b7–8) states: "The four mountains represent the four elements. The four directions represent birth, old age, sickness, and death."

[8a20] Vertically one eradicates the inverted views.[221] Horizontally one parts the ocean of saṃsāra.[222] Thereby one crosses the stream of conditioned existence. A sūtra says, "I [the Buddha] was once like all of you, oblivious to the four noble truths. For this reason I revolved in saṃsāra for ages."[223] If the "burning house" is like this, why, then, remain "immersed in self-indulgent play" [instead of trying to escape the flames]?[224]

[8a23] In this manner, out of loving kindness and compassion one gives rise to the four great vows and strives to uproot the sufferings of others and confer joy on them. It is the same idea as when Śākyamuni saw the plowing of the field[225] or when Maitreya saw the destroyed watchtower.[226] Because of one's clear understanding of the four truths, one is not in any of the nine states of bondage; and because of having made the four extensive vows, one is not in the single state of solitary liberation.[227] This is the arousing of the true and proper thought of enlightenment [that knows] neither bondage nor solitary liberation. Thus the idea of revealing the right [arousing of the thought of enlightenment] is here clarified.

[8a26] **The Four Vows and the Nonarising Four Noble Truths.** Then again, simply by contemplating how a single moment of thought

221. The inverted views include: seeing permanence, pleasure, selfhood, and purity where there is none.

222. Chan-jan (T 46.172b9–11) says: " 'Vertically eradicating the inverted views' refers to the cause [or arising] of suffering. 'Horizontally parting the ocean of saṃsāra' refers to the elimination of suffering [itself]. In extinguishing the delusions one must begin with the coarse and proceed to the subtle. Thus it is described as 'eradicating vertically.' Because the cessation of suffering involves no relative progression, it is 'horizontally severing.' "

223. The *Nirvāṇa Sūtra,* T 12.693b. The sūtra goes on to state that it was seeing the four noble truths that put an end to the Buddha's entrapment in saṃsāra.

224. From the famous parable of the burning house in the Parable chapter of the *Lotus Sūtra,* T 9.14a–b; Hurvitz, pp. 68–69. A father, seeing his children "immersed in self-indulgent play" while the house is being consumed by flames, contrives to lead the children to safety with promises of a sheep-drawn cart, a deer-drawn cart, and an ox-drawn cart waiting outside the wall.

225. According to Chan-jan (T 46.172c2), this example is from the *T'ai-tzu jui-ying pen-ch'i ching* (T 3.475c). The young Siddhārtha experiences deep compassion for the insects turned up by a plowshare, whom birds came to harass and devour.

226. From the *Mi-lo hsia-sheng ch'eng-fo ching,* T 14.424b. A jewelled tower was presented to Maitreya as a gift, which he in turn presented to a brāhmin. On seeing it torn down by the brāhmin, he became aware of how all things are subject to dissolution and consequently resolved to seek Buddhahood.

227. In other words, one is not subject to any of the ten negative conditions that were excluded in the first section of this chapter as "wrong" forms of the thought of enlightenment. The first nine falsely affirm the value of mundane existence and, hence, remain bound to cyclic birth and death. The liberation of the Hīnayāna remains mired in an annihilationist nirvāṇa.

arises through the mutual interaction of sense faculty and sense object, one may understand that there is no aspect of producer or produced[228] that is not empty. Although we commonly speak of the arising of thoughts, there is in this arising neither own-being, other-being, nor both together, nor causelessness.[229] When [a thought] arises, it comes about neither through itself, nor through another, nor through both, nor through neither. When it perishes, it goes neither east, west, south, nor north. This thought does not reside within, nor without, nor between the two. Nor has it a permanent self-existence all its own. All there is is a name, and that name is "the thought." This label ["thought"] neither persists nor fails to persist. Since it is inapprehensible, the arising [of thought] is itself devoid of arising and even devoid of nonarising. Existence and inexistence are both quiescent. Worldly simpletons speak of what "exists," but the wise know inexistence. It may be likened to [a child who] reaches out to touch the moon in the water, rejoices at the thought that it is really there, and then grieves over the thought that he has lost it. For adults [who know that this is all imagined], the disappearance [of the moon's image] holds no grief, its appearance holds no joy.[230] Reflections in a mirror and tricks of magic work the same way.

[8b6] It says in the *Viśeṣacintabrahma-paripṛcchā* [*Sūtra*], "Suffering is without arising, the origin [of suffering] is without coordinate aggregation, the path is nondual, and cessation does not arise."[231] It says in the *Nirvāṇa Sūtra*, "[Bodhisattvas] understand that there is no suffering in suffering and are thus in possession of the truth, and they understand that there is no cessation in cessation and are thus in possession of the truth."[232]

[8b8] Since the origin of suffering is itself identical with emptiness, one should not be like the thirsty deer that chases after the shimmering heat of the spring sun [thinking it to be water].[233] Since suffering is identical

228. Sense organs and sense objects (or the subjective self) are what produces; the thought is what is produced.

229. A paraphrase of one of the opening verses of Nāgārjuna's *Madhyamaka-kārikās* (*Chung-lun*, T 30.2b): "Dharmas do not arise by themselves, nor through the auspices of another, nor through both together, nor without cause. Thus one should know them to be unarisen."

230. From TCTL, T 25.102b.

231. T 15.39a.

232. From T 12.682c. According to the sūtra, ordinary people are subject to the four noble truths but have no understanding of them. Followers of the Hīnayāna understand the noble truths in part but do not grasp their ultimate meaning. The bodhisattvas fully apprehend the ultimate truth in the four noble truths.

233. Possibly an allusion to the *Laṅkāvatāra Sūtra*, T 16.491a, which describes a herd of deer tormented by thirst, which mistakes the shimmering of the air under the spring sun for water.

with emptiness, one should not grasp at the moon in the water like the foolish monkey.[234] As the path [likewise] is identical with emptiness, one should not say, "I am engaging in practice that recognizes things as they are to be empty and am avoiding the practice that does not recognize things as intrinsically empty."[235] It is as in the simile of the raft:[236] if the dharma is to be discarded, how much more should anything that is not the dharma be discarded. [Finally,] since cessation is itself identical with emptiness, one should not speak of it [in relative contrast to] the fixed life span of animate beings. For who could possibly intuit [the true character of] cessation through such a [mundane concept of] annihilation? Since cyclic birth and death itself is identical with emptiness, how could it ever be discarded? Since nirvāṇa itself is identical with emptiness, how could it ever be attained?

[8b14] It says in a sūtra, "I do not admit any cultivation of the path in [this] dharma of nonarising, whether from the four stations of mindfulness to the eightfold noble path;[237] I do not admit the attainment of any result in [this] dharma of nonarising, whether it be from the level of stream-winner to that of arhat."[238] It follows from this example that one should also say, "I do not admit within this dharma of nonarising either form, sensation, cognition, impulses, or consciousness; nor do I admit in this dharma of nonarising craving, anger, or stupidity."[239]

234. From the *Mahāsaṃghika Vinaya* (*Mo-ho-seng-chi-lü*), T 22.284a. Here Devadatta in his misleading of the community of monks is compared to a monkey chieftain who saw the moon in a well under a tree. Thinking to take it for himself, he held a branch of the tree while having his retainers hang from his tail to get it. Unfortunately, the branch broke and they all fell.

235. Chan-jan (T 46.173b3–5) says: "If everything is empty, how could one possibly [affirm] the practice of 'identity' [with emptiness as right] and exclude [what is] 'not identical' [with emptiness as wrong], for there is no 'non-identical' that lies outside of emptiness. Should anything be excluded, it would be like shunning space in one place to seek it in another."

236. An allusion to the famous analogy between the dharma and a raft, both of which are constructed solely to ferry one to the "opposite shore." See the *Madhyamāgama*, T 1.764b–c; see also the *Diamond Sūtra*, T 8.748b.

237. The four stations of mindfulness and eightfold noble path represent the first and last of the seven categories of practice ("seven branches") that make up the thirty-seven factors of enlightenment. Here they imply the presence of all thirty-seven.

238. Paraphrased from the *Pañcaviṃśati*, T 8.271b, or TCTL, T 25.437b. The stream-winner and the arhat are the first and fourth of the Hīnayāna "four fruits" (the other two being the once-returner and the never-returner).

239. Chan-jan (T 46.173b28–c2) says: "The *Pañcaviṃśati*, in its explanation of the dharma of non-arising (*anutpattika*), asserts that the truth of the path—which is none other than the thirty-seven factors of enlightenment—is from the outset unarisen. The fact that there are 'no four fruits' indicates that the truth of cessa-

[8b18] One's empathy for animate beings is alone sufficient[240] to inspire the vow to relieve them of the two kinds of suffering[241] and bestow on them the two kinds of joy. But because of realizing the emptiness of suffering and its origin, one is not subject to the nine [states of] bondage; and, because of realizing the emptiness of the path and cessation, one is not in the one [state of] solitary liberation. This represents the arousing of the true and proper thought of enlightenment [which knows] neither bondage nor liberation. The meaning of revealing the right [arousing of the thought of enlightenment] is thus clear.

[8b21] **The Four Vows and the Innumerable Four Noble Truths.**[242] Simply by contemplating the [interaction] between sense faculty and sense object and the arising of a single moment of thought, one may see that this arising of thought is itself just a provisional [designation], and that such provisionally designated thoughts are [themselves] the basis of both delusion and understanding. Thus one comes to recognize the four noble truths as having innumerable aspects.[243]

[8b23] There are no distinct dharmas in the three realms; all are but the product of one single mind.[244] Mind is like a skilled painter, producing all sorts of forms.[245] It constructs the six destinies, introducing innu-

---

tion is originally unarisen. The line [that begins], 'it follows from this example,' represents the great master [Chih-i's] own extension of this example: since the [truths of the] path and cessation do not exist, how can there be suffering and its origin?"

240. Chan-jan (T 46.173c6–8) states: "[The passage] should say, 'Empathy for living beings without any knowledge of the principle that they are non-arisen apparitions.' "

241. Suffering that is internal in origin (i.e., bodily illness, emotional disturbance, etc.), and external in origin (i.e., caused by external factors such as bandits, wild animals, natural disasters, etc.).

242. Chan-jan (T 46.173c13) says: "Now comes the [four vows, as understood from the perspective of] the innumerable [four noble truths] of the separate teaching."

243. Chan-jan (T 46.173c20–21) says: "This being the case, the four noble truths of the separate [teaching] encompass all four [levels of interpretation] of the four noble truths, for [the two aspects of] self and other [and progression from] beginning to end entail a comprehensive [approach to] practice. Because what one must learn is so multifarious, it is called 'innumerable.' "

244. From the *Daśabhūmika* portion of the *Avataṃsaka Sūtra*, T 9.558c. *Kōgi* (1.316) also cites the TCTL, T 25.276b.

245. This is a reference to a very celebrated passage from the *Avataṃsaka Sūtra* (Chapter on the Verses of the Bodhisattvas of the Suyama Heaven), T 9.465c: "The mind is like a master painter, who paints [with] all manner [of combinations of] the five aggregates. Throughout all the world-realms [of the universe] there is no dharma not created by it. Whether the mind or the Buddha, it is so for both. Whether the Buddha or animate beings, it is the same as well. Mind, Buddha, and

merable distinctions in appearance and value [among them]. It is these false views and attachments[246] that are the distinguishing features of the origin of suffering [in its various degrees of] lightness and gravity, both within and beyond the three realms. Moreover, it is saṃsāra experienced under such conditions that represents the mark of suffering [itself], in its various degrees of lightness and gravity both within the common saṃsāra [of fixed divisions and allotment] as well as within the supernal saṃsāra. By going back and overturning this [deluded] mind, one produces understanding—just as the painter first washes away the previous forms, applies white plaster, [and is then able to] paint anew.[247]

[8b28] When one contemplates the body as impure [and proceeds in sequence through the four stations of mindfulness] to contemplation of the mind as impermanent,[248] such an approach to the [thirty-seven] limbs of enlightenment leads in roundabout fashion to the conjured city.[249] [Then again,] contemplating the body, one may find the body to be empty, or contemplating the mind, realize that the mind is empty. In this emptiness one finds no impermanence nor any impurity. The [thirty-seven] factors of enlightenment approached in this fashion lead directly to the conjured city.[250] [Then again,] on contemplating the imperma-

---

animate beings—these three are without distinction. The Buddhas know that everything is evolved from the mind."

246. The afflictions of view (*chien*) and emotive attachment (*ai*) are the equivalent of the afflictions of intellectual view (*chien*, or *darśana-prahātavya-kleśa*) and afflictions of cultivation (*ssu*, or *bhāvanā-prahātavya-kleśa*).

247. Chan-jan (T 46.174a3–6) says: "The master painter represents the bodhisattva himself. The hand [of the artist] is analogous to the essential nature of the bodhisattva's mind. The brush is analogous to the [deluded] mind or mental states that are [the object of] contemplation. The forms are the cause and effect of the six destinies [of saṃsāra]. To 'wash away the previous forms' is to eradicate cause and effect [of the six destinies]. To 'apply white plaster and paint anew' represents [the truths of] the path and cessation. Then again, to cultivate emptiness is analogous to 'wiping away the previous forms.' The provisional discernment is analogous to 'painting anew.' "

248. The first and third, respectively, of the four stations of mindfulness. The remaining two (which are implied here) include mindfulness of sensation (as painful) and mindfulness of dharmas (as devoid of self). Chan-jan (T 46.174a12–13) says: "If one were to speak of the truth of the path in full, one should explain all seven sections [of the thirty-seven factors of enlightenment]. But here the mindfulnesses alone are explained and the other six abridged."

249. Once again, the conjured city parable from the *Lotus Sūtra*, T 9.26a. The conjured city, which is equated with the liberation from saṃsāra of the two vehicles, is achieved according to Chan-jan (T 46.174a13–14) when "[the delusions of] intellectual view and cultivation are eradicated."

250. Chan-jan (T 46.174a15) says: "In this case contemplation is skilled and,

nence of the body, one may realize that impermanence is itself identical with emptiness, or, contemplating the dharma-nature of the body, realize that it is neither permanent nor impermanent, neither empty nor nonempty. It is the same [for all aspects of the four stations of mindfulness], down to contemplating the mind. Such an approach to the [thirty-seven] factors of enlightenment leads in roundabout fashion to the treasure lode.[251] [Finally,] on contemplating the dharma-nature of the body, one may realize that it is neither pure nor impure, while simultaneously realizing that it is both pure and impure. Or, contemplating the dharma-nature of the mind, one realizes that it is neither permanent nor impermanent, while simultaneously realizing that it is both permanent and impermanent. Such an understanding of the [thirty-seven] factors of enlightenment leads directly to the treasure lode.

[8c7] [According to the perspective of the arising-and-perishing four noble truths],[252] if a person's [delusions of intellectual view] have been annihilated [through the vision of truth], he is known as a stream-winner;[253] and if the delusions of cultivation have also been annihilated, he is called an attainer of one of the three fruits [that follow].[254] [From the perspective of the nonarising four noble truths],[255] when a person's intellectual delusions have been annihilated, he is said to be at the stage of vision.[256] When his delusions of cultivation are annihilated, he is said to be at the level of sparse [desire], the level of separation [from desire], the level of the task accomplished, or the level of [final] onslaught against residual karmic influences. Then he is called a pratyekabuddha.[257]

---

hence, does not proceed in the same [roundabout fashion] as the previous inept or clumsy [contemplation of the tripiṭaka teaching]."

251. In the parable of the conjured city from the *Lotus Sūtra*, the "treasure lode" represents the supreme goal of Buddhahood—the goal of the bodhisattvas of the Mahāyāna.

252. That is, the tripiṭaka teaching.

253. Literally, the "[afflictions that are] removed [in the path of vision] through the vision of truth" (*darśana-[mārga] prahātavya-kleśa*). With the eradication of false views and the first substantial vision of the four noble truths, one gains the stage of the *darśana-mārga* and verges on the first of the four saintly fruits of the Hīnayāna—that of the stream-winner.

254. Once-returner, never-returner, and arhat.

255. That is, the shared teaching.

256. The stage of the *darśana-mārga*, equivalent to the stream-winner. The "stage of vision" represents the fourth stage in the system of ten stages of the shared teaching. For an English explanation, see Chappell, *T'ien-t'ai Buddhism*, pp. 119–129; see also Hurvitz, "Chih-i," pp. 260–262. This system, which was developed by Chih-i into the system of the "shared teaching," is based on the *Pañcaviṃśati*, T 8.346b, 259c, and the TCTL, T 25.417a.

257. Stages five through eight, respectively, of the ten stages of the shared

[8c10] [From the perspective of the innumerable four noble truths],[258] the cessation of the person's delusions of intellect and cultivation is called the ten abodes.[259] The cessation of the delusion that obscures multiplicity is known as the ten stages of action and the ten stages of transference.[260] The cessation of nescience is called the ten stages (*bhūmi*) proper, as well as near-enlightenment and wondrous enlightenment.[261] [From the perspective of the unconstructed four noble truths,][262] the cessation of both the person's delusions of intellect and cultivation, as well as his delusion that obscures multiplicity, is called the ten stages of faith.[263] The cessation of nescience is called the ten abodes, ten stages of action, the ten stages of transference, the ten stages proper, penultimate enlightenment, and wondrously perfect enlightenment.[264]

[8c13] Thus at this level [of the four vows seen from the innumerable four noble truths], we differentiate the path, cessation, [suffering, and the origin of suffering] into a total of sixteen different teachings,[265] until

---

teaching. At stage seven ("the task accomplished") both the delusions of view and cultivation in their primary manifest form are eradicated. This is equivalent to the arhat of the Hīnayāna. However, residual karmic influences (*vāsanā*) remain, which must be fully eradicated in order to reach the eighth stage of pratyekabuddha. Stages nine and ten correspond to those of bodhisattvahood and Buddhahood, respectively. Thus the ten stages of the shared teaching draw all three vehicles together into a "common" path.

258. That is, the separate teaching.

259. Here the bodhisattva first eradicates the delusions of view and cultivation, realizes the truth of emptiness, and achieves liberation from saṃsāra of the three realms.

260. Here the bodhisattva, out of his vow of compassion, gives rise to provisional expediency from emptiness and returns to saṃsāra to save others. It corresponds to suppression and eradication of the delusion that obscures multiplicity, realization of the provisional truth, and the effort to view both emptiness and provisionality simultaneously.

261. In these remaining twelve stages, the bodhisattva progressively eradicates basic nescience and reveals the unalloyed middle truth.

262. That is, the perfect teaching.

263. Lowest ten of the fifty-two stages of the perfect path, equivalent to the identity in resemblance. This involves eradication of the delusions of view and cultivation and the delusion that obscures multiplicity, as well as suppression of nescience, through which a proximate vision of the perfect middle truth is achieved.

264. The remaining forty-two, corresponding to the identity of increments of truth and ultimate identity. Here nescience is progressively eradicated and the wisdom of the middle progressively clarified.

265. Chan-jan (T 46.174b9) explains: "The four approaches of the four teachings, with each approach multiplied by the four noble truths."

we ultimately arrive at Buddhist teachings as numerous as the sands of the Ganges. [Thus] there are so many distinctions and evaluations as to be beyond all expression and estimation. Yet the mind [of the bodhisattva knows them all] without error, just as lucidly as seeing a fruit in the palm of one's hand, for all of them are born of the mind and come from nowhere else. By contemplating [the arising of] a single thought in this way, one is able to know indescribable [numbers of] mental states. And through these indescribable numbers of mental states, one is able to penetrate inexpressible [varieties] of dharmas.[266] And through these inexpressible [varieties of] dharmas one is able to penetrate inexpressible [forms of] nondharma and nonmental state.[267] For the contemplating of any and all thoughts, it is the same.

[8c18] The ordinary person subject to the nine states of bondage fails to perceive or to understand [this vast richness]. He is like the blind heir of a wealthy merchant, who sits in his treasure chamber utterly unaware of the [riches around him]. When he moves about, he is impeded and hurt by the jewels instead. [Then again,] the two vehicles in their feverish delirium take the jewels for demons, tigers, dragons, and snakes, so that they abandon them and hasten away, reeling and in pain for some fifty years.[268] Although solitary liberation and the nine states of bondage differ from each other, they are alike in that they are both bereft of the incomparably precious treasure of the Tathāgata. But [realizing this fact, the bodhisattvas of the Mahāyāna] generate great vows of loving kindness and compassion, in which they vow to eliminate suffering and confer joy [on others]. This is neither bondage nor solitary liberation but the arousing of the true and proper thought of enlightenment. The meaning of "revealing the right [arousing of the thought of enlightenment]" is then clear.

266. *Kōgi* (1.322) cites Chan-jan's *Mo-ho chih-kuan fu-hsing sou-yao-chi* (HTC 99.247) to support the interpretation that *hsin* in this instance means "thoughts or cognitive states" and that *fa* means "dharmas."

267. Chan-jan (T 46.174b13–14) says: "Here, 'dharmas and mental states' designate provisionally produced discriminations. Penetrating the dharma-nature is what is known as 'non-dharmas and non-thoughts.' "

268. An allusion to the parable of the prodigal son from the *Lotus Sūtra*, T 9.17b; Hurvitz, p. 88. The heir of a wealthy merchant runs away, becomes lost, and forgets his home. Only after some fifty years of bitter wandering and suffering is his true heritage revealed. Chan-jan (T 46.174b19–21) says: "As for [the expression] 'fifty odd years,' it simply means that due to turning their backs on the treasure trove, affliction gets the advantage of them. After falling away from the Mahāyāna they revolve amid the five destinies. Because the abode of the asuras is placed between the hungry ghost and animal [realms], it says 'some' [fifty years]."

[8c23] **The Four Vows and the Unconstructed Four Noble Truths.**[269] Next, on contemplating the arising of a single moment of thought through the interaction of sense faculty and sense object, one may find that it is, at once, identical with emptiness, identical with provisionality, and identical with the middle. Whether we speak of sense faculty or sense object, both are the dharmadhātu, both ultimate emptiness, both the tathāgatagarbha, and both the middle way.

[8c26] In what way is [this thought] identical with emptiness? Because [all factors of its arising][270] come into being through conditions: whatever originates conditionally lacks subjective own-being, and to lack own-being is to be empty. How is it identical to provisionality? Because despite their lack of own-being, [the factors involved in the production of this thought] still arise. Consequently, they are to be considered provisional. How is it identical to the middle? Because at no time do [its concomitant factors] depart from the dharma-nature. They are all identical to the middle. Know, therefore, that [each and every] moment of thought is identical with emptiness, identical with provisionality, and identical with the middle.[271] What is more, it is ultimate emptiness, it is the tathāgatagarbha, and it is ultimate reality. Though [these truths] are not three, they are three; though they are three, they are not three.[272] [The three

269. Chan-jan (T 46.174c5) says: "Here the [four] extensive vows are clarified [from the perspective of] the unconstructed [four noble truths] of the perfect teaching. The essential substance (*t'i*) of the four noble truths is none other than the three truths. Thus the three truths are used as a general means to illustrate the object [on which] the vows [are formulated]. The 'single instant of the arising of thought' is here no different from the manner in which it was discussed before. But the contemplative wisdom that subjectively discerns [this moment of thought] is completely different from [the wisdom employed in the three] previous [teachings]. Here the 'one instant of thought' is itself identical to the three truths, and there is no further consideration of [this moment of thought] as a 'basis for delusion and understanding.' Whether [one is speaking of] the sense object or sense faculty, all aspects [of the arising of thought] are the dharmadhātu. 'Dharmadhātu' is just an alternate name for the three truths."

270. Chan-jan (T 46.174b8–10) and *Kōgi* (1.325) both note that all dharmas and factors acting as conditions for the arising of thought are indicated here.

271. Chan-jan (T 46.174c11–14) says: " 'All aspects of conditioned arising' refers to both the single moment of thought as well as the hundred realms and thousand such-like [dharmas] implicit in it. This sort of conditioned arising is utterly without subjective own-being. Being without subjective own-being, it is 'empty.' But as it is simultaneously identical to the thousand such-like [dharmas], it is called 'wondrous provisionality.' Moreover, because it is identical to dharma-nature, it is called 'the wondrous middle.' "

272. Chan-jan (T 46.174c14–16) says: " 'Though they are not three, they are yet three' represents the provisional. 'Though three, they are yet not three' rep-

truths] are not merged [into a single principle] nor dispersed [into three]. Yet [at the same time] they are both merged and dispersed, as well as neither unmerged nor undispersed.[273] One cannot say that they are one and the same; nor can one say that they are different. Yet, in a sense they are the same, and in a sense they are different.

[9a2] They are analogous to the relationship between a mirror and its luminosity.[274] The [intrinsic] luminosity [of the mirror] represents "identity with emptiness." The reflected image represents "identity with provisionality"; and the surface of the mirror [where all interact without impediment] represents "identity with the middle." These three are neither merged [into one and the same entity] nor dispersed [as utterly separate], and yet they are as though merged and dispersed. They are not [in a sequential order of] one-two-three, yet two and three [may be present] without hindrance.[275] This one moment of thought is not to be understood through vertical or horizontal [representation of the three truths]. [Its real nature] is inconceivable.

[9a5] [The interfusion of three truths within one moment of thought] applies not only for oneself personally but for all other animate beings and the Buddhas as well. It says in the *Avataṃsaka Sūtra*, "One's own mind, the Buddha, and other animate beings—there is no difference between these three."[276] Know, therefore, that your own mind here and now contains replete within it the whole of the Buddha's dharma. The *Viśeṣacintabrahma-paripṛcchā* [*Sūtra*] says, "It is only when a person is deluded with respect to the aggregates (*skandha*), sense factors (*dhātu*), and sense accesses (*āyatana*) [of his mental and physical being] that he seeks

---

resents emptiness. It should also go on to say, 'neither three nor not three,' which would be the middle. Since the text does not have this, it is abbreviated."

273. Chan-jan (T 46.174c17–19) says: " 'Neither merged nor dispersed' is the simultaneous negation [that reveals] the middle way. 'Merged' represents emptiness. 'Dispersed' represents the provisional. 'Neither unmerged nor undispersed' utterly negates the first set of negations. It is tantamount to the simultaneous illumination [of both extremes that reveals the middle way]. The first is equivalent to the simultaneous eradication of both [extremes], and the last, to the illumination of both [extremes]."

274. That is, the power of the mirror to reflect clearly.

275. Chan-jan interpolates the word "one" into the second line here (T 46.175a8).

276. From the chapter on the Verses of the Bodhisattvas of the Suyama Heaven contained in the *Avataṃsaka Sūtra*, T 9.465c29. See note 89 to Kuan-ting's Introduction. These became the famous "three dharmas of Master Nan-yüeh [Hui-ssu]," which (according to the T'ien-t'ai system of the perfect teaching) are utterly interpenetrating and mutually identified. For a translation of Chih-i's discussion of these in the *Fa-hua hsüan-i*, see Swanson, *Foundations of T'ien-t'ai Philosophy*, pp. 177–199.

enlightenment. For these are identical to [enlightenment]. There is no enlightenment apart from them."[277] The *Vimalakīrti* says, "The Tathāgata's liberation is to be sought in the mental processes of animate beings themselves."[278]

[9a10] If beings are already identical with enlightenment, then there is nothing further to obtain. If beings are already identical with nirvāṇa, then there is nothing further to annihilate. This being the case for a single thought, it is the case for all thoughts and for all dharmas as well. The *Sūtra on the Visualization of the Bodhisattva Samantabhadra* is making the same point when it says, "The Buddha Vairocana is omnipresent."[279] Know, therefore, that all dharmas are the Buddha's dharma, for they are all the dharmadhātu of the Tathāgatas.[280]

[9a13] Q: If this is so, then why is it also said, "Disport your mind in the dharmadhātu as though it were empty space,"[281] and "Nescience and illumination are themselves identical to ultimate emptiness"?[282]

[9a15] A: [Both of the quotations] that you mention take the word "emptiness" as their point of departure for discussion. But emptiness is identical to the nonempty, as well as the neither-empty-nor-nonempty.[283] Moreover, it also says [in the scriptures], "Each single mote of dust contains a billion rolls of sūtras."[284] Thus the whole of the dharma of the

277. T 15.52b.

278. T 14.544c6.

279. *Kuan p'u-hsien p'u-sa hsing fa ching*, T 9.392c. The *Sūtra on the Visualization of the Bodhisattva Samantabhadra* was translated by Dharmamitra during the early fifth century. Because of its connection with the Encouragements of Samantabhadra Chapter of the *Lotus Sūtra*, it came to be recognized by many as an extension of the *Lotus* itself.

Chan-jan (T 46.175a22–24) says: "[The name] 'Vairocana' translates as 'omnipresent.' The essence (*t'i*) of the afflictions is pure. The myriad virtues [of Buddhahood] are already possessed in full. Bodily form and realm are mutually interdependent and pervade all places universally. This elucidates [the idea from] the two previously cited sūtras that the principle [intrinsic to] living beings is universal."

280. Following Muranaka, p. 91 and Nitta, p. 238.

281. From the *Avataṃsaka Sūtra*, T 9.409c.

282. *Kōgi* (1.330) and "*Makashikan* inyō tenkyo sōran," p. 78, identify the source of this quote as the *Nirvāṇa Sūtra*, T 12.651c, but the match is not a clear one. Chan-jan (T 46.175a26) identifies the reference to "ultimate emptiness" with the *Pañcaviṃśati* and TCTL but provides no indication of the chapter.

283. Chan-jan (T 46.175b1–2) says: "Because emptiness itself contains all three [truths], it says, 'the empty is identical to the non-empty.' Why should emptiness alone be thus. It is the same for provisionality and the middle as well. As such, [the text] cites [the passages on] the 'infinitessimal mote of dust' and the 'middle way' [in order to show] that each [truth] contains all three [truths] within it."

284. From the Nature Origination chapter of the *Avataṃsaka Sūtra*, T 9.624a and 625a. It also appears in the *Ratnagotravibhāga*, T 31.827b.

Buddhas is contained in a thought,[285] as seeds [are contained] in the earth,[286] or [fragrances are contained in] a ball of different kinds of incense.[287] These similes take the idea of existence as their point of departure. But existence is identical to inexistence and to neither-existence-nor-inexistence. It is also said that "There is no sight nor smell that is not the middle way."[288] This takes the word "middle way" as the point of departure. But the middle is identical to the extremes [of existence and inexistence] and, at the same time, is neither identical nor not identical to these extremes. [All perspectives are contained within it,] utterly replete and undiminished. Hence do not damage the perfect [truth] by conforming too narrowly to words, thereby misrepresenting their holy purpose.

[9a21] If you are able to understand this, then [you will know] that when a single moment of thought arises [through the interaction of] sense faculty and object, the sense faculty contains within it [all the] 84,000[289] treasuries[290] of the dharma. The same goes for the sense object. And within the arising of the single moment of thought, [all the] 84,000 treasuries of the dharma are contained as well. [The very arising of thought on the basis of sense faculty and object] is nothing more than the dharmadhātu of the Buddhas coming into contact with the dharmadhātu itself and thereby giving rise to the dharmadhātu.[291] There is nothing that is not the Buddha dharma.

[9a24] Saṃsāra is itself identical to nirvāṇa. This is called the truth of suffering. In one sense object there are three sense objects,[292] and in one

285. Or, "in the mind" (*hsin*).

286. *Kōgi* (1.331) and "*Makashikan* inyō tenkyo sōran," p. 78, identify the **Suṣṭhita-mati-devaputra-paripṛcchā* from the *Ratnakūṭa* collection of Mahāyāna sūtras (*Pao-chi ching*, T 12.128a) as the source for this simile. However, the connection is not a clear one.

287. From the *Śūraṅgama-samādhi Sūtra*, T 15.633b. Here it is stated that bodhisattvas are permeated through and through by the six perfections, each perfection interfusing with the others just as different kinds of aromatic would interfuse if ground up and mixed into a ball.

288. From the preface to the MHCK itself, T 46.1c–2a.

289. In other words, an unlimited number. Chan-jan states (T 46.17524–25): "The afflictions number 84,000, and [the Buddha] preached 84,000 dharma medicines [to alleviate them]. Simply to indicate a countless number, one says, '84,000.' "

290. "Collections of discourses" or *piṭakas* of the Buddha's preaching of dharma.

291. Chan-jan (T 46.175c16) says: "The 'dharmadhātu of the Buddha' is the sense faculty. The 'dharmadhātu that is contacted' is the sense object. 'Giving rise to the dharmadhātu' is consciousness."

292. *Kōgi* (1.336): According to whether it is liked, disliked or regarded with indifference.

thought there are three thoughts.[293] Each of these sense objects is accompanied by the 84,000 gates to affliction, and the same goes for each thought. Craving, anger, and stupidity are identical to enlightenment, and all the afflictions [as a whole] are identical to enlightenment. This is called the truth of the origin of suffering.

[9a27] When it is turned over, each gate to affliction itself becomes a gate to the 84,000 samādhis. It also becomes a gate to the 84,000 *dhāraṇī*;[294] it [produces] 84,000 methods of counteracting [the afflictions];[295] and it brings about the attainment of 84,000 pāramitās.[296] Nescience when turned around itself transforms into illumination,[297] just as ice becomes water when it melts. [Enlightenment] is not something distantly removed, nor does it come from some other place. It is completely present in each and every moment of thought. It is like [the precious jewels and objects] produced by the wish-fulfilling gem: they are neither contained fully within it, nor are they absent from it. If you say that they are not there, you speak falsely. But if you say they are there, you broach a depraved view. [The reality of it] cannot be cognized with the mind nor truthfully expressed in words.

[9b5] Animate beings who dwell amid this unthinkable and unfettered dharma nevertheless create fetters for themselves through their own mentation (*ssu-hsiang*).[298] In dharmas that are devoid of liberation, they seek liberation. [Contemplating in this fashion, bodhisattvas] generate great loving kindness and compassion, and these in turn arouse the four extensive vows—that is, the vows to eliminate the two kinds of suffering and confer the two kinds of joy. This is known as arousing the true and proper thought of enlightenment [within the condition] that knows neither bondage nor liberation. In the previous three sections [concerning the arising, nonarising, and innumerable perspectives], discussion centered around the four noble truths. Here, [from the perspective of the unconstructed four noble truths], discussion is focused on [the 84,000] treasuries of the dharma, gates to affliction, samādhis, and pāramitās. Nevertheless, the basic idea is the same.[299]

293. *Kōgi* (1.336): Pleasure, pain, and equanimity.

294. Chan-jan (T 46.175c13–14), citing the TCTL (T 25.269a), says: "Dhāraṇī has the nature of wisdom. Samādhi has the nature of meditative concentration."

295. Chan-jan (T 46.175b15) identifies this with the truth of the path.

296. Chan-jan (T 46.175c16) identifies this with the truth of cessation.

297. From the *Nirvāṇa Sūtra*, T 12.652a.

298. Chan-jan (T 46.175c24–25) says: " 'Mentation' means making discriminations within this interpenetrating and wondrously singular dharmadhātu, such as ordinary and saintly, ultimate truth and conventional truth, animate and inanimate."

299. Chan-jan (T 46.175c29–176a4) says: "In these four [levels of interpretation] of the four extensive vows, each speaks of discerning 'one moment of [the

[9b10] Q: In the previous [section on] excluding the wrong [forms of the thought of enlightenment], the [teachings of the two vehicles][300] were both dismissed as "wrong." Now in this section on revealing the right [thought of enlightenment], why are they again included among the "right"?

[9b11] A: The reasons for which they are included here as "right" are as follows: Both are "right" in this instance because [bodhisattvas, even in the teachings of the two lower vehicles,] are neither subject to bondage nor [immersed in] solitary liberation. This is because [bodhisattvas in general] are all in the process of upward striving. Also, they are deemed "right" because [bodhisattvas of the two lower vehicles] arrive at reality gradually by successive stages. Moreover, they are "right" because, even though reality is difficult for them to know, they [are able ultimately to] reveal the real through following [teachings that are] provisional expedients. These three explanations make their claim [that bodhisattvas of the lower vehicles] are within the "right" on the basis of the worldly siddhānta.

[9b14] Then again, while provisional expedients do not include the real, the real does encompass provisional expedients. [Bodhisattvas of the lower vehicles] are treated as "right" in order to make this [principle of] inclusiveness clearly and easily understood. This particular [argument for] including [the lower vehicles] as "right" is based on [the principle of] the individualized siddhānta. Then again, one arousing of the thought of enlightenment is all thoughts of enlightenment. If we did not expound [on one], then all of them would be unknown to us. Hence they are affirmed as "right." This particular argument for establishing them as "right" is patterned on the therapeutic siddhānta. Finally, if one speaks at the ultimate level, the first three [explanations or siddhāntas] belong to the [teaching of] provisional expediency, and the fourth and final one to the real.[301] It is analogous to a skilled physician with a secret method

---

arising of] thought,' which is simply the thought that arises as a result of the contact between sense faculty and object. As for its differentiation according to the four [teachings], the first two teachings both advocate the cessation of thought as the highest fruit, even though they have their respective differences regarding the clumsiness and skillfulness [of their approach]. The follower of the separate [teaching takes the one moment of thought] to be the basis of [both] delusion and understanding. The follower of the perfect [teaching] knows that the thought itself is the dharmadhātu."

300. That is, the two vehicles of the śrāvaka and pratyekabuddha, whose doctrines are represented in the tripiṭaka and shared teachings, respectively. Following Chan-jan, T 46.176a6–7, as well as Chan-jan, *Mo-ho chih-kuan fu-hsing sou-yao-chi*, HTC 99.248b. Muranaka (p. 93) offers a slightly different interpretation.

301. Following Chan-jan (T 46.176a19–20) and Muranaka (p. 94) here, who both take the numbers three and four to refer to the siddhāntas themselves. Nitta

of treatment that includes within it all other methods. Or it is like the panacea *agada*, which incorporates the virtues of all other medicines.[302] Or it is like eating a mixture of milk and gruel, where nothing more is needed. Or it is like the wish-fulfilling gem, which contains everything within itself.[303] [Having heard this explanation] of the revealing of the right [thought of enlightenment] made on the basis of provisional expediency and the real, the idea should be clearly evident.[304]

[9b22] Then again, we may speak of one [form of the thought of enlightenment] as right, and that is because [arousing the thought] is itself the cause and condition that brings about the one great event [of a Buddha appearing in the world].[305] Why is it "one"? Because it is a single reality that is not false; because it is the one way that is [ultimately] pure; and because it is the one way by which all those who have freed themselves from impediments depart from saṃsāra.[306] Why is it "great"? [It is great] because, being by nature broad and vast, it subsumes many things: it is the great wisdom, it is the great eradication [of afflictions], it is the vehicle ridden by the great, it is the roar of the great lion, and it greatly benefits both the ordinary person and the saint.[307] The reason the word

---

(p. 244) differs in taking them to refer to the three and four teachings or levels of explanation of the vows (excluding the perfect).

302. From the *Avataṃsaka Sūtra*, T 9.461c. The curative powers of *agada* (the "panacea medicine") are compared to the wondrous powers of wisdom, which remove all afflictions.

303. Properties of the wish-fulfilling gem are discussed in the *Avataṃsaka Sūtra*, T 9.575b. Chan-jan (T 46.176a18–21) says: "Various similes are introduced here in order to illustrate the real. The 'secret method [of healing]' represents the teaching; *agada*, wisdom; milk and gruel, practice; and the wish-fulfilling gem, principle. They also express the concept of the four siddhāntas."

304. Following Nitta, p. 243.

305. The notion of defining the thought of enlightenment and Buddhist practice as the "cause and condition that brings about the one great event [of the Buddhas appearing in the world]" (*i-ta-shih yin-yüan*) originates primarily with the Expedient Devices chapter of the *Lotus Sūtra*, T 9.7a; Hurvitz, p. 30.

306. Chan-jan (T 46.176b4–6) says: " 'One reality that is not false' represents wondrous principle (*li*). 'One way that is ultimately pure' represents wondrous wisdom and practice. 'One way of those who have freed themselves from impediment,' etc. means that people by resorting to this path come into tally with principle. It signifies the wondrous stages [of the perfect path] but in intent implies the other three dharmas as well."

307. Chan-jan (T 46.176b10–12) says: "As for [the term] 'lion,' [it refers to] one who has entered the stages [of true bodhisattvahood] and [begun] to expound the teaching for the benefit of others. As such, the 'lion's roar' means expounding this wondrous dharma [of the perfect teaching]. It is expounded by one who has realized the fruit [of practice]."

"event" is used is because this is the prescribed manner in which all the Buddhas of the ten directions and the three times conduct themselves.[308] By this [very conduct] one can attain the enlightenment of the Buddhas for oneself, and by this [conduct] one can accomplish the deliverance of other living beings. It is called the "cause and condition [for enlightenment]" because it is through this as a cause that animate beings effect (*kan*) [the manifestation of] the Buddhas, and through this as a condition that the Buddhas manifest in response (*ying*).

[9b29] Again, the right [thought of enlightenment] cannot be said to be threefold [according to the three truths], nor can it be said to be one [according to a single reality]. Nor is it both three and one nor neither-three-nor-one. This is why it is called the inconceivable right [thought of enlightenment].[309]

[9c2] Again, the right [thought of enlightenment] is not something that is constructed;[310] it is not produced by Buddhas, gods, men, or asuras. The eternal object-realm [of reality] is without distinguishing features. The eternal wisdom [that realizes it] takes hold of nothing as a referent. By this referentless wisdom one takes as object the featureless object-realm [of reality]. The featureless object-realm conversely functions as the feature that referentless wisdom [perceives].[311] Wisdom and object are a mysterious unity, yet provisionally speaking [we distinguish between] "object-realm" and "wisdom." This is why it is called "unconstructed."

[9c5] Again, with regard to the right [thought of enlightenment] the *Sūtra of Mañjuśrī's Questions on Bodhi* says: "The eradication of any and all notion of 'arousing' is what is called 'arousing the thought of enlightenment.' [Yet] the thought of enlightenment must be aroused by always conforming with the characteristics of enlightenment."[312] Then again, although [the thought of enlightenment] is devoid of all arousing, it is still

308. Chan-jan (T 46.176b13–14) says: "Elaborating provisional expedients in order to [ultimately] reveal the real, seeking to increase the way and diminish [the realms of deluded] sentiency, these are all the [prescribed] 'conduct' of the great beings who are the Buddhas."

309. Following Chan-jan, T 46.176b16–18.

310. Chan-jan (T 46.176b21–22) says: "The essence (*t'i*) of [this] unconstructed[ness] is the reality [that is the true mark or characteristic of things]. This reality is, itself, markless; and this marklessness is also void."

311. Following Chan-jan, T 46.176b23–26.

312. *Wen-shu-shih-li wen p'u-t'i ching* (or **Gayāśirsa Sūtra*) translated by Kumārajīva, T 14.482a, to be distinguished from the entirely different *Wen-shu-shih-li wen ching* (T no. 468), translated by Saṅghaphala, which serves as a scriptural basis for the T'ien-t'ai one practice samādhi described in the section on the four samādhis that follows.

aroused; and although it is devoid of all accordance [with features], it is nevertheless in accord with [the features of enlightenment].[313] Furthermore, it transcends all eradication [of features] and transcends all accordance [with features]; yet it simultaneously illumines both [extremes] of eradication [of features] and accordance [with features]. This is what we call "arousing the thought of enlightenment." These three ways [of describing the thought of enlightenment] are neither one and the same nor different. They are equivalent to [the perspectives of] principle (*li*), phenomena (*shih*), and neither-principle-nor-phenomena, [respectively]. That is why it is called the "right" [arousing of the thought of enlightenment]. On the basis of this idea, doctrinal formulae such as "unconstructedness," "inconceivability," the "cause and condition of the one great event," and so forth all speak of eradication [of features], all speak of accordance [with features], all speak of neither eradication nor accordance [with features], and all [assert] the simultaneous illumination of both eradication and accordance.

[9c12] Then again, the first three interpretations [of the right thought of enlightenment] are what the lower, middling, and higher [forms of] wisdom perceive, whereas the final teaching is what the supreme wisdom perceives.[314] The first three [have stages] in common, whereas the final one is unique.[315] The first three are shallow, near, and roundabout, whereas the final one is profound, far, and direct.[316] The first three represent the "great" among the "lesser" [vehicles], whereas the final one is the greatest among the great, highest of the high, most perfect of the perfect, most complete of the complete, most real of the real, truest of the true, most fully disclosed of the fully disclosed, the mystery of mysteries, most wonderful of the wonderful, and most inconceivable of the

313. According to Chan-jan (T 46.176c15–17), "accordance" with characteristics means to "establish" characteristics.

314. The four forms or levels of wisdom that perceive conditioned origination from the *Nirvāṇa Sūtra*, T 12.768c. Chan-jan (T 46.177a1) says: "Classifying [these four interpretations] according to provisional expediency and the real, the perfect [teaching is the real and] corresponds to the 'supreme' [wisdom]."

315. Chan-jan (T 46.177a1–3) says: " 'Common' and 'unique' are distinguished on the basis of stages [of the path]. The stages of the [ten] abodes and [ten] activities of the separate [teaching] are held in common with the previous two tripiṭaka and shared teachings. The perfect [teaching] alone is unique."

316. Chan-jan (T 46.177a3–5) says: " 'Shallow' and 'near' are classifications based on [form of] practice. The practices of the first two [teachings] are 'near' [because they only lead to the conjured city]. The practice of the separate [teaching is distant because it arrives at the treasure lode but] is still 'roundabout' [because it does not lead directly to the goal as does the perfect teaching].' "

inconceivable. Those who are thus able to exclude the wrong and reveal the right as they arouse the thought of enlightenment, [who are able to] grasp the essence of provisional expediency yet know the real,[317] such beings are the seed of the Buddhas.[318]

[9c18] [Arousing the right thought of enlightenment] is like adamant (*vajra*). [Just as adamant] originates from the essence of the metal [element], the thought of [achieving] the enlightenment of a Buddha originates in great compassion, which precedes all other religious practices.[319] [Arousing the thought of enlightenment] is like taking the *asaru* herb:[320] one first swallows the pure water of compassion, chief among religious practices. Just as the life-faculty[321] is the most important of all the faculties, this thought [of enlightenment] is the most important of all the Buddha's right dharma and right practice. It is like a prince who, from birth, bears the physical markings and manner of a king, so that government ministers revere him and he wins great renown.[322] It is like the *kalaviṅka*, whose song excels those of other birds even when it is still in the egg.[323] Thus this thought of enlightenment has tremendous power. It is like a lute string made of lion sinew,[324] like a lion's milk,[325] like a hammer made

317. Chan-jan (T 46.177a23–25) says: "To 'grasp the essence of provisional expediency' means to avoid clinging to the expedient [teaching] thinking it wrongly to be the real. To know the expedient to be an expedient device and that beyond the expedient there is no real—this is to know the real."

Kōgi (1.350) explains that "to realize the provisional" means to use expedients skillfully so as to accord with the ordinary world of secular emotions, while "to know the real" means to realize that the mundane world is itself nothing but the subtle activity of the dharma-nature.

318. Chan-jan (T 46.177a26–27) says: "By putting forth the thought of enlightenment on the basis of the real, all the Buddhas are born. Thus it is called 'seed of the Buddhas.' "

319. See TCTL, T 25.298b. Chan-jan (T 46.177b14–15) says: "The enlightenment of the Buddhas has great compassion as its essential nature and is, thus, produced from great compassion."

320. *Bhumea lacena*. Mentioned in the *Avataṃsaka Sūtra*, T 9.779b.

321. According to the Hīnayānist Sarvāstivādin school this *jīva* is the substance created by karma that supports the continuation of warmth and consciousness in the body while it is alive.

322. See TCTL, 25.609c. The reference is to the traditional thirty-two marks of a "wheel-turning king," *cakravartin* or universal monarch.

323. From the TCTL, T 25.267a.

324. From the *Avataṃsaka Sūtra*, T 9.778c. Such a string is so prominent that it drowns out the sounds of the other lute strings, as this perfect thought of enlightenment overpowers all others.

325. Ibid., T 9.778c. Lion's milk, when added to a vessel containing cow's, horse's, and sheep's milk, will supposedly make the other kinds of milk disappear.

of adamant,[326] like Nārāyaṇa's arrow,[327] and like the wish-fulfilling gem, which contains within it [the promise of] a multitude of treasures and can wipe out the misery of poverty. Even if one tends to be indolent or loses touch with the proper majesty [of the practice], [by the thought of enlightenment alone] one still surpasses the accomplishments of the two vehicles. In a word, this thought [of enlightenment] itself contains the merit of all bodhisattvas and is able to bring about unsurpassed and perfect enlightenment throughout the three times.

[9c28] If this thought of enlightenment is [truly] understood, then one effortlessly carries out calming and contemplation. Contemplation is the unaroused yet unimpeded [vision of this thought of enlightenment]. Calming is the quiescent extinction that is its essential nature. Calming and contemplation are themselves identical to enlightenment (bodhi), and enlightenment is identical to calming-and-contemplation. It says in the *Ratna-rāśi Sūtra*, "If a bhikṣu does not cultivate the dharma of a bhikṣu, then in the chiliocosm[328] there will be no place for him even to spit, much less to receive the offerings of laymen.[329] Sixty bhikṣus wept bitterly and said to the Buddha, 'We are soon going to die[330] and cannot receive the offerings of laymen.' The Buddha said, 'You harbor thoughts of shame; very good, very good.' One bhikṣu asked the Buddha, 'Which bhikṣus may receive offerings?' The Buddha answered, 'Those who practice the proper conduct of a bhikṣu in the assembly of bhikṣus and thus earn the benefits of being a bhikṣu may receive offerings.' " The four incipient and four fully realized fruits are the assembly of bhiksus.[331] The thirty-seven factors of enlightenment are the proper conduct of a bhikṣu, and the four fruits represent the benefits of being a bhikṣu. "The bhikṣu again asked the Buddha, 'What about bhikṣus who have given rise to the Mahāyāna thought of enlightenment?' The Buddha answered, 'If one gives rise to the Mahāyāna thought of enlightenment and seeks omni-

326. Chan-jan (T 46.177c4) says: "Wielding the hammer of omniscient wisdom one smashes the mountain peak of biased views."

327. From the *Ta-chuang-yen ch'ang-che wen fo na-luo-yen li ching*, T 14.853a. The cosmic man in Indian tradition, often identified with Brahmā. Chan-jan (T 46.177c4–5) says: "Nārāyaṇa's arrow can pierce a disk of iron, as a bodhisattva's unconditioned compassion can destroy anything."

328. This expression means 1000^3, i.e., one billion. The sūtra has *ta-ti*, whereas the MHCK has *ta-ch'ien*; so following the sūtra we should read "on the great earth" instead of "in the chiliocosm (cosmos)."

329. Including food, clothing, incense, and everything necessary to sustain a monk's life and practice.

330. The sūtra adds, "without gaining the fruit of arhatship."

331. The stream-winner, once-returner, never-returner, and arhat are each subdivided into incipient and perfect levels.

science, then even though he may not conform to[332] the rules of the assembly of bhikṣus, practice the proper conduct of a bhikṣu, or have earned the benefit of being a bhikṣu, he still may receive offerings.'[333] The monk was astonished and asked, 'How can such persons receive offerings?' The Buddha said, 'Should such persons receive clothes sufficient to cover the whole earth and food equal in volume to Mount Sumeru, they will still be able to requite in full the almsgivers' kindness.' "[334] Know, therefore, that even the highest fruit of the Hīnayāna is still inferior to the very first thought of enlightenment in the Mahāyāna.

[10a13] Furthermore, as it says in the **Tathāgata-guhya-garbha Sūtra*, "If a person harms his father, who has become a pratyekabuddha; or steals property belonging to the three jewels; or defiles his mother, who has become an arhat; or slanders the Buddha with untrue allegations; or [seeks to ingratiate himself] with saints and worthies through double talk; or vilifies saints with hateful speech; ruins or confuses seekers of dharma with lascivious talk; or has anger sufficient to commit the first of the five depravities;[335] or is avaricious enough to appropriate things belonging to those who observe the monastic code; or foolish enough to adhere to the extreme views [of eternalism and annihilationism]—then, oh Kāśyapa, such a person is evil even within the ten evil acts.[336] But if this evil person understands the Tathāgata's teaching that there is in conditioned dharmas no self, person, animate being, or life substance, no arising nor perishing, no defilement nor attachment, and that their essential nature is pure—and if he understands, holds in faith, and penetrates [this fact that] all dharmas in their essential nature are pure—then I do not teach, oh Kāśyapa, that such a one is destined for retribution in the hells or the other evil destinies. Why is this? Because, [oh Kāśyapa,] there is in dharmas no accumulation [or aggregation], no arising [of suffering] nor [subsequent] affliction. Dharmas all fail to either arise or persist; their arising takes place due to a confluence of causes and conditions, and they perish as soon as they arise. [Kāśyapa,] if thoughts perish as

332. Following the emendation suggested by Donner in his dissertation and by Muranaka, p. 98.

333. This section in the MHCK quote relating to the virtue of a Mahāyānistic monk who does not keep the monastic code does not appear either in the original sūtra or in Chan-jan's citation of the sūtra (T 46.177c14).

334. Paraphrased from the *Ratna-rāśi Sūtra* in the *Ratnakūṭa* collection of Mahāyāna sūtras (*Pao-chi ching*), T 11.640a–b.

335. The five depravities are: killing one's father, killing one's mother, killing an arhat, shedding the blood of a Buddha, and destroying the harmony of the saṅgha.

336. The first three of the ten evils are physical, the next four are verbal (essentially variations on the prohibition against lying), and the last three are mental (the well-known three poisons of craving, anger, stupidity).

soon as they arise, then all the fetters also perish as soon as they arise. Understood in this way, there is no commission [of sin]. For sin to exist or endure is utterly impossible. We may compare this to a room, dark for a hundred years, wherein a lamp is lit. The darkness could not then say, 'Having dwelt here so long, I am the master of this room. I do not consent to leave.' For, in fact, once the lamp is lit, the darkness immediately vanishes."[337]

[10a26] The meaning of what I am saying is the same [as what is expounded in this sūtra]. This sūtra indicates precisely the nature of the four types of thought of enlightenment [discussed] previously.[338] "If one understands the Tathāgata's exposition of conditioned dharmas" corresponds to the first thought of enlightenment. "If one understands that there is no arising nor perishing" represents the second thought of enlightenment. "If one understands that [they are] pure in their essential nature" is the third thought of enlightenment; and "if one understands that all dharmas in their essential nature are pure" corresponds to the fourth thought of enlightenment. If even the first of these [four types of] thought of enlightenment is already capable of eradicating the karma produced by the gravest of the grave transgressions of the ten evil acts, then how much more efficacious must the second, third, and fourth thoughts of enlightenment be! The practitioner who hears of this supreme and wondrous merit of the thought of enlightenment must spontaneously rejoice at his good fortune, for [its arising] is like the dark becoming light, or the stinking castor-oil seed becoming a fragrant sandalwood tree.[339]

[10b4] Q: The term "causes and conditions" has been used as a universal designation applicable to all four levels of explanation [of the four vows and four thoughts of enlightenment]. Why is it now applied to only the first view?

[10b5] A: This term is applied [to the thought of enlightenment of the first level] because it occurs in the first [line of the gāthā from the *Middle Treatise*]. Furthermore, the explicit phenomenal features of cause and condition are especially suitable for contemplation at the elementary level. However, if one speaks of [cause and condition in relation to] arising and perishing, then it takes on a particular meaning. The three examples that follow it [i.e., nonarising, innumerable, and unconstructed] have both a universal and particular [usage of the term "cause and con-

337. Paraphrased from the **Tathāgata-guhya-garbha Sūtra* (*Ju-lai mi tsang ching*), T 17.844c–845a.

338. That is, the four interpretations of the four extensive vows based on the levels of the fourfold noble truths or four teachings.

339. From the *Nirvāṇa Sūtra*, T 12.727c–128a. The castor-oil plant and the sandalwood tree are often paired to represent the *kleśa* and bodhi, respectively.

dition"]; but it is from the particular that they derive their individual names.

The Six Identities[340]

[10b7] Q: As for revealing the right thought of enlightenment with respect to the six identities, is this 'rightness' present when one first arouses the thought [of enlightenment], or is this 'rightness' something that only comes with later [stages of cultivation]?[341]

[10b8] A: As with the simile of the burning wick in the *Great Treatise*, "It is neither at the beginning nor apart from the beginning, neither at the end nor apart from the end."[342] If wisdom and faith are both present,

340. The term "identity" alludes specifically to such stock aphorisms from the sūtras as "afflictions themselves are 'identical to' enlightenment" or "all beings are themselves 'identical to' great nirvāṇa" (*Viśeṣacintabrahma-paripṛcchā Sūtra*, T 15.52b; *Vimalakīrti Sūtra*, T 14.549a, 550c–551c), both of which are used regularly by Chih-i to illustrate the principle of the six identities in the perfect teaching (see Chih-i's *San-kuan i*, HTC99.98b). In T'ien-t'ai of the late T'ang and Sung periods, where considerable discussion is generated around the precise meaning of the terms 'identical to' (*chi*) and 'implicitly contained' (*chü*), the notion of 'identity' is frequently expressed in terms of the T'ien-t'ai formulae "a single instant of thought itself 'contains' [*chü*] the 3,000 world-realms" or "a single instant of thought is itself 'identical to' (*chi*) emptiness, identical to provisionality, identical to the middle."

Hsing-man says in his *Meaning of the Six Identities* (*Liu-chi i*) (HTC 100.805a): "Within a single instant of thought one is able to contemplate the three truths, perfectly and completely. Wisdom and its object are a mysterious unity. These three themselves are yet one; the one, yet three. Cause and effect are [inherently] complete. In this manner should the term 'identity' be understood." Also see Chih-li's famous discussions of the terms 'identity' and 'implicitly contained' in the *Shih-pu-erh men chih-yao ch'ao* (T 46.707a21–b4, 710a16–b8), as well as various other materials associated with the T'ien-t'ai "home mountain and heterodox line" debates.

Chan-jan (T 46.178c13–15) says: "There are lecture [masters] in the world today who all regard the [stage of the] first abode as the fruit of Buddhahood [itself]. This also comes from their lack of grasp of the six identities. If it is this way for lecturees, how much more so for ignorant dhyāna practitioners."

For discussion of the six identities in T'ien-t'ai thought and especially their relevance to this issue of doctrinal or meditative excess, see Donner, "Sudden and Gradual Intimately Conjoined," pp. 201–226.

341. Chan-jan (T 46.178c16–18) says: " 'First' means [identity] in principle. 'Later' means ultimate [identity]. The question is asking whether the present arousing of the thought [of enlightenment] derives its description of 'revealing the correct' in reference to principle, or whether it is only called 'revealing the correct' when it reaches the ultimate [stage of enlightenment]."

342. From the *Pañcaviṃśati* or the TCTL, T 25.584c–585c. The flame of enlightenment cannot be identified exclusively with either the first glimmer when

then when one hears that any single instant of thought is itself the right [thought of enlightenment], one's faith will prevent one from disparaging [this teaching], while one's wisdom will prevent one from fearing it. In this case the beginning and the end will both be "right." But if one lacks faith, one will think of the saintly realms as so lofty and far-removed that one has no stake in their wisdom, while if one lacks wisdom, one will become exceedingly arrogant, declaring oneself to be the equal of the Buddha. Under such circumstances, beginning and end will both be in error. Because of these [sorts of] problems one needs to understand the [concept of] the six identities.[343] They are: identity in principle, verbal identity, identity in meditative practice, identity in resemblance, identity in increments of truth,[344] and ultimate identity. These six identities range from the [level of] the ordinary person to [that of] the saint. Because they begin with the ordinary [unenlightened] condition, they eliminate doubt and fear; and because they end with the saintly, they eliminate arrogance.[345]

[10b15] **Identity in Principle.** Identity in principle means that each single moment of thought is itself identical to the [ultimate] principle (*li*)

---

the wick is lit or the final fire blazing from the torch; it is both and neither at the same time.

Chan-jan (T 46.179a4–7) says: "In terms of the fundamental underlying principle, there is no division between beginning and end. But on the basis of phenomenal differences, distinctions are made in the progressive ascent of the six stages. Combined use of the term 'six' and the term 'identity' expresses the idea that, throughout the practice of the perfect teaching, from the moment of first arousing the thought one is neither wholly identified with [principle] nor apart from it."

343. Chan-jan (T 46.179a13–17) says: "He has faith that [enlightenment] is replete within the first thought and so does not disparage [the principle of the perfect] teaching, saying that it is not the case. [He knows that when this intrinsic] wisdom is developed to the highest, [the path is] fulfilled. Thus he does not fear that he has no stake in [the achievements of the saints]. In this respect, 'beginning and end are both correct.' To say that the ultimate achievement belongs only to the Buddhas and that ordinary beings have no stake in it is to be in error about the end. To say that ordinary beings are already endowed with principle and, thus, are themselves identical to the Buddhas is to be in error about the beginning. To avoid such errors with respect to beginning and end [of the perfect path] one must be familiar with the six identities."

344. Also at times referred to as "identity in incremental realizations [of the real]" (*fen-cheng [chen] chi*).

345. Chan-jan (T 46.179a19–21) says: "Benighted dhyāna practitioners are for the most part [afflicted with] overweening arrogance. Text-bound [exegetes] tend to relegate [the fruit of the path] to only the most accomplished [saints]. Both [errors] arise from interpreting [the notion of] 'identity' without knowing the six identities."

of the tathāgatagarbha. It is identical to emptiness because of its [intrinsic] suchness *(tathā)*, identical to provisionality because of its treasure-store or embryonic (*garbha*) nature,[346] and identical to the middle because it is [the ultimate] principle (*li*). [These] three wisdoms are fully present in any single thought, utterly inconceivable. As we have explained above, [they are at one and the same time] three truths and one truth but also neither three nor one. Every sight and every smell contains all dharmas, and so it is for each and every thought as well.[347] This is what is called the right thought of enlightenment [at the level of] identity in principle. It is also calming and contemplation [at the level of] identity in principle. [That each moment of thought] is intrinsically quiescent is calming. [That each instant of thought] is intrinsically luminous is contemplation.

[10b20] **Verbal Identity.** Even though in principle [thought] is perfectly correct just as it is, one may be unaware of this in one's daily activities.[348] Without hearing the doctrine of the three truths one will remain completely incognizant of the dharma of the Buddhas.[349] It is like having the eyesight of cattle or goats, who have no sense whatsoever of the [four] cardinal or [four] intermediate directions.[350] But if one should hear—

346. *Tsang*, which renders the Sanskrit *garbha* (embryo or womb), can also have the meaning of "storehouse" or "treasury." In important medieval Chinese Buddhist works such as the *Awakening of Faith* (T no. 1666), the "womb or treasure-store of the Tathāgatas" (tathāgatagarbha) signifies the omnipresent reality of suchness "stored" in a condition of concealment beneath the adventitious delusions of ordinary existence.

347. Chan-jan (T 46.179b1–4) says: "As for explaining the principle of tathāgatagarbha in terms of the three truths, [it is to say that] all living beings are endowed to the full with the tathāgatagarbha as well as with the three truths. As expounded previously in the [explanation of the] four vows and four truths from the perspective of the perfect teaching, this principle has been present from beginningless time, but beings have never heard its name [i.e., its existence]. By virtue of this principle there is not a hair's breadth of difference between [sentient beings and] the Buddhas."

348. Chan-jan makes a play on words here. Taking the line "in daily life (or regular activity) they remain unaware of it" and, reading it in reverse, he interprets it to mean "make use of the sun [regularly] but remain unaware of it." Chan-jan (T 46.179b7–9) says: "Because there is principle there is cyclic birth and death. Cyclic birth and death relies on principle. But because one is not aware that birth and death is itself identical to principle, [the text] says 'one [regularly] makes use of the sun but is never aware of the fact.' It is like people of the world making use of the sun without having any sense of their indebtedness to its light."

349. Chan-jan (T 46.179b9–10) says: "Because one has never heard of its name [or existence], one remains unaware that one's essential nature of principle contains the three truths in full. Thus one does not recognize the fact that the dharma of the Buddhas is present in the ordinary."

350. Chan-jan (T 46.12–14) says: "Although cattle and goats see [the cardinal

either through personal acquaintances or from the rolls of the sūtras—of the singular reality of enlightenment described above, one will acquire a verbal comprehension of the fact that all dharmas are the Buddha-dharma.[351] This represents [the right thought of] enlightenment[352] [at the level of] verbal identity. It is also calming and contemplation [at the level of] verbal identity. For the restlessly seeking mind to come to rest, having finally heard what it has chased about everywhere to hear—this is called calming. To place one's faith solely in the dharma-nature and not in the manifold [forms in which it manifests]—this is called contemplation.

[10b26] **Identity in Meditative Practice.** One who does no more than hear the terms and [blindly] repeat them in discourses to others is like an insect that accidentally produces a meaningful sign by its random gnawing on wood, all the while unaware of whether it is a word or not.[353] Unless one truly penetrates [the meaning of the words] how can it be considered enlightenment? It is essential that one's contemplation of the

---

directions], they have no sense of their [directional significance]. Thus one should know that the ordinary [person] and [followers of] the lesser [vehicles] have no comprehension of the cardinal and intermediate directions [with respect to] reality. The real within reality corresponds to the cardinal directions. Provisionally expedient [representation] of the real corresponds to the 'intermediate directions.' "

351. Chan-jan (T 46.179b14–16) says: "By hearing [the teaching] one gains knowledge. That is, one comes to know about the principle of reality described above. If one does not hear its name, how will one ever gain understanding? People in the world today who spurn doctrinal teachings and esteem [only] the contemplation of principle (*li-kuan*) are so mistaken, so mistaken!"

352. From the second identity on, Chih-i (or Kuan-ting) drops the word *hsin* or "thought" from the compound, "thought of enlightenment." Although the difference may seem significant, neither Chan-jan nor any other commentators remark on it. This would suggest that the passage is to be read in a manner similar to the first identity—"the right thought of enlightenment at the level of identity in principle."

353. From the *Nirvāṇa Sūtra,* T 12.618b. In the sūtra this simile is used to illustrate the point of another simile—that of an unskilled doctor who indiscriminately applies a powerful medicine to treat all illnesses. Some it cures, many others it harms; but he clings ignorantly to his accidental successes as proof of the efficacy of his approach. Both similes are invoked at the end of the chapter on the four samādhis (Engaging in the Great Practice) as illustrations of unskilled dhyāna masters who denounce effortful religious practice due to a wrongful understanding of the doctrine that afflictions are themselves enlightenment.

Chan-jan (T 46.179b17–18) says: "[Here] at the beginning, in order to establish the superior and dismiss the inferior, [the text emphasizes that] practice is superior to [merely] hearing [the teaching]. The point of hearing [the teaching] lies in practice, not in simply repeating [it] verbally in discourses [to followers]."

mind be clear and comprehending, and principle and wisdom be in perfect mutual accord (*hsiang-ying*).[354] One's actions must match one's words, and one's words match one's actions. It says in the *Kuśala-mūla-saṃparigraha*, "For the most part, people fail to practice what they preach. It is not with words, but with the mind that I strive for enlightenment."[355] When mind and mouth are in correspondence with each other (*hsiang-ying*), then it is the [thought of] enlightenment [at the level of] identity in meditative practice.

[10c2] The four lines of verse in the *Great Treatise* [may be used to] evaluate whether one's wisdom achieved by hearing [the dharma] (*wen-hui*) is sufficient.[356] When the eye obtains sunlight, it illumines things clearly and without distortion. So it is with meditative practice as well.[357] Even though one has yet to achieve [full] tally with principle, one's contemplation of the mind does not fade. It is like the simile in the *Śūraṅgama-samādhi Sūtra* of shooting arrows at a target.[358] This is called the

354. Chan-jan (T 46.179b24–27) says: "[The passage] from 'it is essential' reiterates [the previous] exhortation. 'Contemplation of the mind must be clear and comprehending' emphasizes that understanding must first be established with respect to principle, and [this, in turn,] gives rise to practice. 'Principle and wisdom in mutual congruence' advocates that practice must first be established with respect to principle, and [this, in turn,] gives rise to understanding. As such, discerning of mind and principle function in mutual response. In one's practice one establishes contemplation on the basis of principle. In speaking, one's preachings are based on practice."

355. *Hua-shou ching*, T 16.140b.

356. TCTL, T 25.101b. Actually these come to six pairs of five character lines. The text reads: "(1) One who has inherent wisdom but has not heard much of the dharma does not know reality: it is like being in utter darkness with healthy eyes but nothing to see. (2) Nor can one know reality if one has heard a great deal of the dharma but lacks wisdom: it is like being in a brightly lit area with a lamp but no eyes. (3) One who has heard much and whose wisdom is keen is fit to receive the dharma. (4) But one who has neither heard the teachings nor possesses wisdom we call an ox in human form."

Chan-jan (T 46.179c11–12) says: "When 'wisdom produced from hearing is sufficient' one perceives the principle of the three truths."

357. From the *Diamond Sūtra*, T 8.750c. The sūtra passage says, "Subhūti, when a bodhisattva practices in his mind the perfection of giving while dwelling in dharmas, it is like a person entering the darkness and seeing nothing. If, on the contrary, a bodhisattva practices in his mind the perfection of giving without dwelling in dharmas, it is like a person having eyes and in the brightness of sunlight seeing a variety of forms."

358. T 15.633c–634a. The Buddha here compares the course of practice leading to the *śūraṅgama samādhi* with learning archery. Just as in the latter discipline one begins by aiming at large targets, then gradually reduces the size of the target until one is able finally to hit the hundredth part of a hair, so too in religious

[thought of] enlightenment [at the level] of identity in meditative practice. It is also known as calming and contemplation [at the level of identity in] meditative practice. To bear this thought in mind constantly is contemplation, and to halt all other thoughts is calming.

[10c6] **Identity in Resemblance.** As contemplation becomes ever clearer and calming ever more serene, [the practitioner nears his objective] as the archer with diligent practice comes ever closer to his mark. This is called the wisdom born of contemplation (*kuan-hui*) that bears a resemblance [to the true wisdom of enlightenment]. [At this level] one experiences no conflict with any of the mundane occupations for sustaining existence, and all one's speculations and assessments [regarding Buddhist teachings] turn out to be [in perfect accord with] what has been previously expounded in the sūtras of the Buddhas.[359] It is as explained [in discussions of] the purification of the six sense faculties.[360] At this stage the perfect suppression of nescience is referred to as calming, and the wisdom that bears a resemblance to the middle way, contemplation.[361]

---

practice one begins with the foundational practices and gradually proceeds to the abstruse. One's early practice may not "match" the ultimate truth, but eventually one does achieve this through a gradual deepening.

Chan-jan (T 46.179c27) says: "[Chih-i] adopts the simile but not the method from the sūtra, [which belongs to the separate teaching]. Thus the person in the perfect teaching contemplates the sudden [approach to] principle. The archer from the very start shoots for the bull's eye. His skill improves and he gets closer [to the mark], but the target itself doesn't change. This passage illustrates the perfect teaching."

359. Paraphrased from the Merits of the Dharma-Preacher chapter of the *Lotus Sūtra* (T 9.50a; Hurvitz, p. 276)—the chapter where the merits of purification of the six sense faculties (i.e., the stage of identity of resemblance) are described in detail.

Chan-jan (T 46.180a12–16) says: "[One's wisdom] simply accords with and bears a resemblance to [the full wisdom of] reality and so 'experiences no opposition.' [The text] merely says that 'all one's thoughts turn out to be in accord with what is expounded in the sūtras of the previous Buddhas,' so one cannot [yet] say that what one expounds is itself a sūtra. If it were the case of someone at the stage of [identity in] increments of the real displaying himself as a Buddha [and undergoing] the eight characteristic phases [leading to Buddhahood], then it would be analogous to the example of Vimalakīrti, where even though one turns the wheel of dharma it is still known as the practice of a bodhisattva. The latter is the practice that characterizes a bodhisattva from the stage of the first abode on."

360. Purification of the six sense faculties is expounded in the Merits of the Dharma-Preacher chapter of the *Lotus Sūtra*, T 9.47c–50b. Purification of the six senses and the identity in resemblance are equivalent to the stages of the ten faiths in the fifty-two-stage scheme of the perfect teaching.

361. Practitioners at this level sever the delusions of intellectual view and cul-

[10c11] **Identity in Increments of Truth.**[362] Through the power of contemplation [achieved at the level of] resemblance, the practitioner now enters the stage of the copper wheel.[363] For the first time he begins to eradicate nescience and perceive the Buddha-nature, open up the treasure lode [of true dharma], and reveal true thusness. [According to the scheme of fifty-two stages,] this corresponds to [the forty-one stages] from the abode of the arousing of the thought[364] through [the stage of] penultimate enlightenment.[365] Nescience grows increasingly negligible and wisdom becomes increasingly prominent, just as between the first and fourteenth days of the lunar month the radiant disk of the moon becomes ever more round and the darkened area vanishes.[366] If a person is to achieve deliverance through [perceiving] the form of a Buddha, then [a bodhisattva at this stage] will [display] the eight stations [of a Buddha's life] and his attainment of bodhi.[367] If [a being] is to achieve enlightenment [through perceiving] a form from one of the other nine

---

tivation, as well as the delusion that obscures multiplicity, but merely suppress root nescience. Thus they achieve a semblance of the realization of the middle truth, but the unalloyed middle truth is not yet firmly in their grasp.

362. This identity coincides with the next forty-one of the fifty-two stages of the perfect teaching. Only Buddhahood itself ("wondrous enlightenment") is excluded, for it corresponds to the sixth identity—the "ultimate identity." At each of these forty-one stages one measure of nescience is eliminated and one measure of wisdom of the middle way obtained. Thus the perfect wisdom that perceives the middle or "the real" is intensified in "increments."

Chan-jan (T 46.180a21–23) says: "At the first [abode] one eradicates one measure [of nescience] and perceives the threefold Buddha-nature. One opens up the treasure-store of the three meritorious qualities [of Buddhahood] and reveals one increment of principle. As one progresses toward penultimate enlightenment, [these qualities are] gradually deepened and gradually made more prominent. Thus is the gradual [development] of the aspirant [on the] perfect [path]."

363. From the *Ying-lo ching*, T 24.1012c. Six wheel-turning kings are described, each with a wheel of a different composition. They are identified, respectively, with the ten stages of faith, the ten abodes, the ten stages of action, ten stages (*bhūmi*) proper, and the stage of equivalent enlightenment. The "copper wheel [-turning king]" corresponds to the stages of the ten abodes.

364. The first stage in the ten abodes, where nescience is first severed and the middle way first grasped.

365. *Teng-chüeh*, the fifty-first stage just prior to perfect Buddhahood.

366. The simile is from the *Nirvāṇa Sūtra*, T 12.724b.

367. These are the traditional eight stages of a Buddha's life: (1) descending from the Tuṣita heaven, (2) entering the womb, (3) dwelling in the womb, (4) issuing from the womb, (5) leaving his home, (6) achieving the way (becoming enlightened under the bodhi tree), (7) turning the wheel of the dharma, and (8) entering *mahāparinirvāṇa*. In the T'ien-t'ai tradition, the third stage is omitted and "overcoming Māra" is inserted between 5 and 6 of the above list.

realms [of the dharmadhātu], then [the bodhisattva] will display "universal manifestations" of the sort that are expounded at length in [the *Lotus*] *Sūtra*.[368] This is known as [the thought of] enlightenment [at the level of] identity in increments of truth. It is also called the calming and contemplation [at the level of] increments of truth, as well as wisdom and eradication at the level of increments of truth.

[10c17] **Ultimate Identity.** A single step beyond [the stage of] penultimate enlightenment and [the practitioner] enters into the marvelous enlightenment [of Buddhahood]. When the light of his wisdom is so perfectly full that no further increase is possible, this is called the final fruit of enlightenment (bodhi). When in the great nirvāṇa [afflictions] have been eradicated to the point where there remains nothing further to eradicate, this is called the fruit of fruits. [Those at the stage of] penultimate enlightenment cannot fathom [this attainment]; it is known to Buddhas alone. Beyond the [syllable] *ḍha*[369] there is no further way[370] to be expounded. Thus it is called [the thought of] enlightenment [at the level of] the ultimate identity, as well as calming and contemplation [at the level of the] ultimate.[371]

[10c21] We will now sum up by illustrating [the six identities] with a parable. Suppose there is a pauper with a cache of treasure around her house of which she is totally unaware. A friend shows her where it is buried, whereupon she comes to know of its existence. She clears away the weeds and trash and begins to dig it out. Gradually she gets closer and closer, until, on reaching it, she opens the cache of treasure, takes it all out, and puts it to use. By applying this sixfold illustration, [the six identities] can be understood.[372]

368. The Universal Gateway or *Samantamukha* chapter (*p'u-men p'in*) of the *Lotus Sūtra* describes the power of Avalokiteśvara to respond universally to the salvific needs of beings by manifesting in any of thirty-three different forms.

369. *Ḍha* is the last syllable in an arrangement of forty-two syllables of the Siddham alphabet. On the basis of theories in the Four Mindfulnesses Chapter of the TCTL (T 25.407c), Hui-ssu matched these forty-two syllables with the forty-two stages of the complete path ranging from the ten abodes through wondrous enlightenment. Thus the first syllable, *a*, represents the first realization of the wisdom of the middle, or the unarisen nature of dharmas. The final syllable, *ḍha*, represents the maturation of this wisdom into full Buddhahood.

370. That is, *tao*, "way" or "enlightenment."

371. Chan-jan (T 46.180b12–14) says: "For each of the six [identities the word] 'bodhi' [or 'enlightenment'] is used. The name 'calming and contemplation' is also applied. They are just alternate terms for 'identity.' In each of the identities, [the section] concludes with 'calming and contemplation' at the very end. Thus one should know that all [of these stages] are called 'calming and contemplation,' whether it is that of principle, the verbal, or the final fruit."

372. The simile is from the *Nirvāṇa Sūtra*, T 12.407b. Chih-i introduces the distinctions that match it to the progress of the six identities.

[10c25] Q: What is the meaning of the five kinds of bodhi or "enlightenment" [expounded] in the *Great Treatise*?[373]

[10c25] A: The *Great Treatise* vertically classifies the stages of the separate teaching,[374] whereas here the stages of the perfect teaching are classified vertically.[375] If we match up the two sets,[376] the "first arousing of the thought [of enlightenment]" corresponds to [the level of] verbal identity;[377] "suppressing [the afflictions of] the mind"[378] corresponds to identity in meditative practice; "illumining or clarifying the mind"[379] corresponds to identity in resemblance; "emerging toward[380] [enlightenment]" corresponds to identity in increments of truth; and the

373. TCTL T 25.438a. These five, in ascending order, are: the first arousing of the thought, suppressing the mind [of affliction], illumining the mind, emerging toward [Buddhahood], and the supreme mind.

374. The T'ien-t'ai separate teaching presents the system of the fifty-two stages of the *Ying-lo ching* as a process of vertical ascent through the three truths of emptiness, the provisional, both in consort, and the middle.

375. The same system of fifty-two stages of the *Ying-lo ching* is reinterpreted according to the perfect teaching. Thus, although a vertical ascent is described, it represents the clarification and intensification of a single vision of practice—the three truths fully replete within each instant of thought.

376. According to Chan-jan (T 46.180c15–16), identity in principle is omitted because practice has not yet begun and the thought of enlightenment is still completely unmanifested at this stage.

377. The TCTL (T 25.438a3–5) says: "Still in the infinite sea of birth and death, one has the thought of supreme perfect enlightenment. In this sense it is called 'enlightenment' or 'bodhi.' It is equivalent to speaking of the effect or result that lies implicit in the cause." Chan-jan (T 46.180c15) says: "At this [stage of] arousing the thought [of enlightenment] one has not yet begun actually to practice. Thus it is equivalent to verbal identity."

378. TCTL (T 25.438a5–6) says: "Here one severs the afflictions and suppresses the [defiled] mind through the practice of the [six] perfections." Chan-jan says (T 46.180c16): "In this suppressing [of the afflicted] mind the actual eradication of [afflictions] has not yet been accomplished. Thus it is equivalent to the identity in meditative practice."

379. TCTL (T 25.438a6–9) says: "One perceives clearly the features, both distinctive and shared, of dharmas in past, present, and future. And one realizes that the real character of all dharmas is absolute purity." Chan-jan (T 46.180c16) says: "With this illumining of the mind one expels the darkness. It is equivalent to [the identity in] resemblance."

380. TCTL (T 25.438a9–12) says: "Within the perfection of wisdom one obtains the power of expediency, and thus one is also not attached to the perfection of wisdom. One extinguishes all afflictions, perceives all the Buddhas of the ten directions, attains the forbearance of the non-arising of dharmas (*anutpāttikadharmakṣānti*), departs from the three realms, and reaches the [ocean of] *sarvajñā*." Chan-jan (T 46.180c16–17) says: "Reaching *sarvajñā* [or 'omniscient wisdom'] is equivalent to increments of truth."

"unexcelled [mind]"[381] corresponds to the ultimate identity. Moreover, these [five] names [from the *Great Treatise*] may also be used to describe the [fifty-two] stages of the perfect [teaching]. The "first arousing of the thought [of enlightenment]" represents the ten abodes; "suppressing [the afflictions of] the mind" represents the ten stages of action.[382]

[10c28] Q: [According to the perfect teaching,] the afflictions are already eradicated in the ten abodes. Why does "suppressing" occur again in the subsequent [ten stages] of action?[383]

[10c29] A: Here it is by means of the true way[384] that suppression [is accomplished]. One may take a parallel example from the Hīnayāna, where destroying delusions of intellect or view is [at times] called "eradicating," while [destruction of] the delusions of cultivation is called "suppressing."[385] [To continue our pairing of the five terms from the *Great Treatise* with the fifty-two stages,] "illumining or clarifying the mind"[386] represents the ten stages of transference; "emerging toward [enlightenment]" represents the ten stages (*bhūmi*) proper; and the "unexcelled mind" is the wondrous enlightenment [of Buddhahood itself]. Then again, beginning with the ten abodes, these five kinds of enlightenment or bodhi [from the *Great Treatise*] are [already] completely present; but the five reach their ultimate fulfillment with the wondrous enlightenment [of Buddhahood]. Hence it says in the *Daśabhūmika-vyākyāna*[387] that every level from the first stage on contains replete within it the merits of all ten stages.[388] That is the meaning of the present discussion.

381. TCTL (T 25.438a13) says: "Achieving supreme, perfect enlightenment." Chan-jan (T 46.180c17) says: "Being supreme and unsurpassed, it is equivalent to the ultimate [identity]."

382. The third, fourth, and fifth kind of bodhi from the TCTL should be mentioned at this point, but another question-and-answer pair is first interposed.

383. Chan-jan (T 46.180c22) notes: "In all the teachings suppression precedes eradication."

384. That is *tao*, which may also be read as "bodhi" or "enlightenment."

385. *Shiki* (1.388) remarks here that eradicating and suppressing apply to both the delusions of intellect and cultivation. According to this scheme the eradication of the delusions of intellect or view actually precedes the suppression of the delusions of cultivation. They are two different sets of affliction that are dealt with at different stages on the path.

386. Here we return to the alignment of the five kinds of bodhi or "enlightenment" from the TCTL with the fifty-two stages of the perfect path.

387. *Shih-ti ching lun*, T 26.175c–176b. The work was composed by Vasubandhu and translated by Bodhiruci during the first half of the sixth century. It spawned an important tradition of doctrinal exegesis known as the *Ti-lun* line, after the Chinese title of the treatise.

388. The *Daśabhūmika-vyākyāna* (T 26.176b) says: "One mounts the vehicle of all the perfections from the very first stage." Elsewhere (T 26.175c) it says: "In

[11a4] Q: Why is [the doctrine of] the six identities expounded [exclusively] in reference to the perfect teaching?

[11a5] A: When one contemplates dharmas on the basis of the perfect [teaching], one always speaks of it in terms of the six identities. Hence one uses the concept of the perfect [teaching for distinguishing] all the dharmas and always employs six identities to assess the stage of one's [spiritual] progress. This is not the case for the other [teachings], which is why we do not apply [the doctrine of the six identities to the other teachings]. Why would it be inappropriate to apply [these six identities] to those teachings? Because they are "shallow and near"[389] and do not expound the proper meaning [of the perfect teaching].

[11a8] Thus in the [section] above where we excluded the wrong [forms of the thought of enlightenment], we first did so with respect to the truth of suffering and [the notion of] ascending or sinking within the mundane world.[390] In the next section we excluded those kinds of wisdom whose view of the four noble truths is round about, clumsy, shallow, and near. Then we took up the four extensive vows[391] and, finally, the stages of the six identities. The [text] thus develops by degrees of profundity and subtlety, until the "right" [thought of enlightenment] stands [perfectly] revealed.[392] Know, therefore, that "the wondrous pearl

---

each of the ten stages, bodhisattvas are completely endowed with all the partial dharmas that facilitate enlightenment."

389. From the parable of the conjured city in the *Lotus Sūtra*, T 9.26a; Hurvitz, p. 148. According to Chan-jan (T 46.181a7–12), they are shallow because they do not penetrate (at least directly) to the principle of the perfect teaching and are near because they tarry in the vicinity of the conjured city and do not proceed to the treasure lode.

390. Chan-jan (T 46.181a13–14) says: " 'Sinking' refers to the nine forms of bondage [within the mundane world] of suffering. Solitary liberation from suffering is 'ascending.' Both [are excluded as] wrong in order to reveal the right."

391. Chih-i (or Kuan-ting) skips over the section on the other ten ways of correctly arousing the thought of enlightenment here, although the doctrine of the four noble truths may be regarded as implicit to them as well.

392. Chan-jan (T 46.181a16–20) says: "Previously in the [section on the fourfold] four noble truths, understanding is generated by taking [the principle of the four noble truths] as object. Since there are [differences between] superior and inferior [forms of wisdom], the inferior are then excluded and the superior are used to reveal the right [thought of enlightenment]. Here, in the [section on the four extensive vows], the vow to practice is generated from understanding, for knowledge must find its fulfillment in practice. Furthermore, since there are differences according to [the form of truth that is] the object [of understanding], exclusions are also made with respect to the four extensive vows [themselves]. [Thus] even though there is the vow to practice [in all four teachings], [the vows formulated according to] the first three teachings are wrong, and [only that of] the wondrously [perfect teaching] is right. For this reason [the text] again makes

that is as clear as the moon lies at the bottom of a chasm nine levels deep, beneath the jaws of a black dragon,"[393] but those with sufficient determination and merit will surely reach it. Otherwise, one will be like the ordinary people of the world, coarse, shallow, and aimlessly drifting, who vie for tiles, rocks, grass, and sticks, which they deludedly think to be objects of great value.[394] Practitioners of the latter age [of dharma] receive such a precious [teaching] yet end up having no knowledge of it whatsoever.[395]

---

exclusions by means of the six identities. Thus [the text] says, 'it develops and unfolds by degrees of profundity and subtlety.' "

393. From *Chuang-tzu*, cf. Watson, *The Complete Works of Chuang Tzu* (p. 360): "A pearl worth a thousand in gold could only have come from under the chin of the Black Dragon who lives at the bottom of the ninefold deeps."

394. A simile from the *Nirvāṇa Sūtra*, T 12.617c. Those who take [the Hīnayāna teaching of] impermanence, suffering, egolessness, and impurity to be the ultimate truth are compared to "people who, swimming and playing in a great pond in springtime, drop a lapis lazuli into deep water. They all jump into the water to hunt for the jewel and fight over the different tiles, rocks, grass, sticks, sand, and pebbles they find. Each person tells himself he has found it, and rejoices, but then emerges from the water to realize he is mistaken and does not have the real jewel."

395. Chan-jan (T 46.182a2–5) says: "Shallow students of the latter age [of decline] have no idea that the revealing of the correct [thought of enlightenment] resides solely with the perfect and wondrous [teaching], or that [the entire process of] initially creating [expedient teachings] in order to reveal [the real] lies in one [moment of] thought. [Under such circumstances] what will they use as a goal for arousing the thought [of enlightenment]? Without a goal, where will their arousing lead? The [chapter on] arousing the great thought is here completed."

LESSER CHAPTER 2

Engaging in the Great Practice or the Four Samādhis

[11a21] In this second [chapter] we encourage undertaking the practice of the four forms of samādhi (*ssu-chung san-mei*)[1] in order to enter the ranks of full bodhisattvahood.[2] One who wishes to ascend to such marvelous levels [of bodhisattvahood] will make no progress without engaging in religious practice. But if one understands well how to agitate and

1. Along with the more traditional sense of a state of meditative concentration, Chih-i often uses the word "samādhi" to include the program of religious practice that is designed to induce such experiences. Thus the expression "*ssu chung san-mei*" may be more profitably understood to mean "the four programs or rubrics for cultivating samādhi."

A second description of the four forms of samādhi, which is textually close to that of the MHCK, appears in the *Kuan-hsin lun shu* (T no. 1921), a work by Kuan-ting, Chih-i's disciple and the editor of MHCK. Recent scholarship suggests that much *Kuan-hsin lun shu* material is taken from a version of MHCK that is earlier in date and more pristine in form than the highly emended text that we have today. Thus, in certain instances, it illumines the MHCK text significantly (see Satō, *Tendai daishi no kenkyū*, pp. 364–400). For a general overview of the practices of the four forms of samādhi, their cult, literature, and significance in the early T'ien-t'ai religious community, see Stevenson, "The Four Kinds of Samādhi in Early T'ien-t'ai Buddhism," pp. 45–97. For a detailed analysis of the ritual content of the four forms of samādhi and its origins, see Stevenson, "The T'ien-t'ai Four Forms of Samādhi and Late North-South Dynasties, Sui, and Early T'ang Buddhist Devotionalism."

2. Chan-jan (T 46.182a12–13) says: "Though one may have aroused the thought of enlightenment already, one can hardly speak of 'stages' without engaging in practice." Entry into or assurance of full bodhisattvahood (*ju p'u-sa wei; bodhisattvaniyāma*) is a technical distinction designating the point on the bodhisattva mārga where the bodhisattva achieves the insight of a Buddha, receives prediction of future buddhahood, becomes truly irreversible (*avaivartya*), and is assured of future Buddhahood. Depending on whether classical Indian or Chi-

skim [the raw milk], he will be able to produce the ghee (*t'i-hu*) [of true enlightenment].[3] In the *Lotus Sūtra* it says, "I furthermore see sons of the Buddha performing all manner of religious practices in order to seek the path to Buddhahood."[4] Methods of practice are numerous, but we summarize them according to four sorts: [cultivation of samādhi] through (1) constant sitting; (2) constant walking; (3) part walking and part sitting; and (4) neither walking nor sitting.[5]

[11A25] What is generally denoted by the term "samādhi" is "taming," "rectifying," and "stabilizing" the mind.[6] It says in the *Great Treatise*, "When one is adept at fixing the mind on a single point so that it settles

---

nese Mahāyāna schemes are operating, in the more traditional gradualistic models of the path it is associated either with entry into the ten bhūmi or, more specifically, with achievement of the eighth bhūmi. In the T'ien-t'ai system of the "perfect" teaching (or mārga), the path is radically collapsed, and *bodhisattvaniyāma* is equated with entry into the ten abodes or the identity of incremental or partial realization of the real.

3. The fifth of the "five flavors" or stages in the manufacture of ghee from milk. The simile is used in the *Nirvāṇa Sūtra* (T 12.530b–532a) to illustrate the distillation of progressively finer essences of the dharma. Among Chinese exegetes the analogy is usually understood to describe the different doctrinal strategies evolved by the Buddha over the course of his historical career. Here, however, "essence of ghee" refers more specifically to the wisdom of a Buddha or the insight of the middle way associated with the perfect teaching. Chan-jan (T 46.182a17–20), in a rather unconventional approach to this metaphor, matches the remaining four flavors to the stages of the perfect teaching: "The condition of the ordinary being (*pṛthagjana*) and the five grades of disciplehood are analogous to plain milk. [Purification of] the six senses is analogous to cream, butter, and melted butter. From the first abode on it is called 'finest essence of ghee.' Anyone skilled in training himself in the four forms of samādhi should know that [purification of] the six senses and the first abode can be realized thereby." The MHCK text has been emended here on the basis of Chan-jan and alternative readings given in the *Nirvāṇa Sūtra*.

4. T 9.3a3–4.

5. The methods are thus classified broadly according to the dominant form of physical activity. The categories of sitting and walking were most likely selected in order to accommodate the ritual stipulations of the specific cults of the pratyutpanna, one practice, and lotus samādhis, and the vaipulya and Avalokiteśvara repentances, all of which were already prominent in the communities of Hui-ssu and Chih-i. See Stevenson, "The Four Kinds of Samādhi in Early T'ien-t'ai Buddhism," pp. 49–50.

6. The same definition appears in an earlier work of Chih-i, *Shih mo-ho pan-jo p'o-lo-mi ching chüeh-i san-mei*, T 46.622b19. Chan-jan (T 182a3–5) says: "Mind from beginningless time has been crooked and convoluted. Entering [samādhi] . . . mind is straightened, just as a snake, which habitually moves in meandering coils, becomes rigidly straight when it crawls into a bamboo tube."

there without stirring, this is called 'samādhi.' "[7] The dharmadhātu is such a single spot. With right contemplation one can abide in it without wavering. The four activities [of walking, sitting, etc.] serve as the objective basis (*ālambana*) [for meditative concentration]. In discerning the mind one resorts to this basis in order to tame [deluded thoughts] and rectify [the wayward mind]. Hence all four methods are called "samādhi."[8]

Constantly Sitting Samādhi

[11a28] First [among the four forms for cultivating samādhi] is [the practice of] constant sitting. This derives from the two prajñā sūtras of *Mañjuśrī's Discourse [on Prajñā]*[9] and *Mañjuśrī's Queries.*[10] It is also referred to

7. TCTL, T 25.110b.

8. Chan-jan (T 46.182a28–b3) says: "The four practices uniformly resort to the single spot of the dharmadhātu [and, thus, the term 'samādhi' serves as a generic designation]. However, in giving them distinct titles such as 'constant sitting,' or 'neither walking nor sitting,' names have been devised on the basis of physical deportment. [Then again,] when one distinguishes them according to [specific] dharma or method, constant sitting is called 'one practice'; constant walking, 'Buddha standing'; part walking/part sitting, 'vaipulya and lotus [repentances]'; and neither walking nor sitting, 'following one's thought.' "

9. The two-fascicle *Wen-shu-shih-li so-shuo pan-jo p'o-lo-mi ching* (**Mañjuśrī-nirdeśa-prajñā-pāramitā Sūtra,* T no. 232; hereafter cited as *Wen-shu shuo ching*) cited by Chih-i and Kuan-ting as the scriptural basis for this practice was translated into Chinese by Mandrasena during the Southern Liang in 503. The sūtra is more commonly known by the Sanskrit title *Saptaśatikā-prajñā-pāramitā.* An English translation of the two-fascicle text of Mandrasena is available in Chang, ed., *A Treasury of Mahāyāna Sūtras,* pp. 100–114.

10. The second scripture, *Wen-shu-shih-li wen ching* (**Mañjuśrī-paripṛcchā Sūtra,* T no. 468; hereafter cited as *Wen-shu wen ching*), is not titled as a prajñāpāramitā sūtra nor generally included among that class of scripture. Kuan-ting in the *Kuan-hsin lun shu* (T 46.600b22–23) does not specifically cite this text as a second source for the "constantly seated" or "one practice" samādhi but instead invokes "various sūtras of the Buddha."

The main passage from the *Wen-shu wen ching* (T 14.507a) upon which the MHCK account of the constantly sitting samādhi draws reads as follows: "Mañjuśrī asked the Buddha, 'By what further means can one bring about this samādhi?' The Buddha said, 'By shame, repentance, reverence, and giving alms, you can serve and speak to the people of the dharma as if making offerings to the Buddha. You can bring about samādhi by these four methods. Then for ninety days have no thoughts of self. Simply sit, concentrating your thought, without mixing in other mental activity. Except for eating, walking, and attending to your natural functions, you may not rise at all."

as the one practice samādhi.[11] We shall first clarify the procedure for the practice (*fang-fa*), then give exhortations to engage in it (*ch'üan-hsiu*). Procedure is discussed according to what should and should not be done with the body, what should be spoken and when to be silent with the mouth, and the application of calming-and-contemplation to the mind.[12]

Procedure for Practice

[11b2] **Body.** As for bodily posture, one should remain constantly seated and refrain from walking about, standing, or reclining. Practice in a group is permissible,[13] but it is better to be alone. Sit in a special chamber for quietude (*ching-shih*)[14] or out of doors in a peaceful place apart from all clamor. Set up a single rope chair [for meditation],[15] and provide no other seats of any kind. Over a fixed period of ninety days sit in proper meditation posture—legs intertwined, the neck and backbone perfectly

11. One practice samādhi (*i-hsing san-mei*) is listed as the eighty-first member in the list of 108 samādhis of the Mahāyāna found in the *Pañcaviṃśati* and TCTL (T 25.401b20–25). However, the *locus classicus* for most Chinese discussions of the samādhi (including that of Chih-i) is the brief account in *Wen-shu shuo ching*, T 8.731a26–b8. For a discussion of the significance of the one practice samādhi in medieval Chinese Buddhist discourse as well as information concerning relevant Japanese scholarship on the subject, see Faure, "The Concept of One Practice Samādhi in Early Ch'an," pp. 99–128.

Chih-i is ambivalent about the precise meaning of the binome "one practice" (*i-hsing*), but Chan-jan (T 46.182b3–6) says: "The expression 'one practice' abstracts the dominant mode of physical activity and dismisses concern for attendant phenomenal activities. Thus [this practice] is called 'one practice.' It does not derive the name 'one practice' from the fact that principle (*li*) serves as the object of meditation. Among the four practices or activities, there isn't one that doesn't take reality as the basis or object of contemplation."

12. The *Kuan-hsin lun shu* (see T 46.600b23–24) uses a tripartite structure for presenting the contents of the four samādhis: features of phenomenal activity [of the ritual cult] (*shih-hsiang*), procedure of contemplation (*kuan-fa*), and exhortation to practice (*ch'üan-hsiu*). The section on phenomenal activity corresponds to the MHCK subsections on the activities of speech and body; and the section on the method of contemplation, to the calming and contemplation of the mind.

13. Chan-jan (T 46.182b8) says: " 'practicing together in a group' means in a meditation hall (*ch'an-t'ang*)."

14. The term *ching-shih* or "room of quietude" has a formal usage in early medieval Taoist sources, where it refers to rooms or buildings specially sanctified for use in Taoist rites or meditation.

15. *Pītha*, a chair strung with rope constructed and used specifically for meditation. Its dimensions are prescribed in various Vinayas (see Mochizuki, *Bukkyō daijiten*, 3.2545d).

erect.[16] Do not fidget or waver;[17] do not allow yourself to droop or lean on anything. Vow to yourself that, while sitting, you will not even let your ribs touch the sides of the chair,[18] much less sprawl out like a corpse,[19] stand up, or dally about. [Periods for] walking meditation (*ching-hsing*),[20] taking meals, and relieving oneself are to be the only exceptions [to this rule].[21] Sit facing squarely in the direction of [one's chosen Buddha][22] and maintain this practice continuously without a moment's lapse. The activity prescribed is sitting and sitting only. What is prohibited must not be violated. Do not cheat the Buddha. Do not betray your own heart. Do not deceive animate beings.

16. Constant sitting in meditation for a fixed period of ninety days is stipulated in the *Wen-shu wen ching*, T 14.507a. No such statement appears in the *Wen-shu shuo ching*.

17. Following Chan-jan (T 46.182b16).

18. The reference to ribs in this sentence makes it clear that Chih-i is speaking of sitting in a chair with a back (or side), not merely a mat or a platform.

19. Chan-jan (T 46.182b18–19) says: "One should not allow oneself to recline even if one lies properly on the right side, how much more so like a corpse. 'Lying like a corpse' means to recline looking upward. It is also called, 'the reclining posture of the wanton woman.' "

20. *Caṅkrama* is a slow-paced walking exercise (generally to and fro, along a straight path) used between periods of sitting meditation. In addition to its power to counteract drowsiness, *caṅkrama* is said by Chan-jan (citing the *Ssu-fen-lu* or Dharmagupta Vinaya) to have five benefits (T 46.182b22–27): it (1) develops the ability to walk great distances, (2) develops contemplation, (3) reduces illness, (4) helps the digestion, and (5) enables one to abide in meditative concentration for long periods of time. *Shiki* (1.404) distinguishes it from ritual circumambulation proper (*hsing-tao* or *hsüan-jao*).

21. Chan-jan (T 46.182b28–29) says: "[Along with walking meditation], taking meals and relieving oneself are also acceptable activities. But one may not use them as occasions to dawdle or indulge oneself. Once the activity is completed [i.e., drowsiness is eliminated or the meal is over], it is not to be engaged in."

22. Neither the MHCK, *Kuan-hsin lun shu*, nor any other early reference to one practice/constantly seated samādhi suggests a specific identity for this Buddha. Chan-jan's commentary to the passage, however, shows evidence of a growing interest in Amitābha among T'ien-t'ai circles (T 46.182b29–c4): "The direction one faces should be due west, for, whenever impediments arise, it is expediently helpful to recollect the Buddha according to the direction [in which that particular] Buddha (*nien-fo*) is located. The sūtras do not specify facing in the westernly direction and [merely state] that when impediments arise one should concentratedly invoke one Buddha. But in the various teachings, it is Amitābha who is extolled more than any other [Buddha]. Thus we make the western direction the standard one." For a classic discussion of possible Pure Land tendencies in Chih-i's works and their perceived tension with more "interiorized" samādhi practices, see Ando, "Tendai Chigi no jōdokyō," in his *Tendai shisō-shi*.

[11b9] **Speech.** When to speak and when to be silent:[23] If exhaustion becomes extreme due to sitting, one is troubled by illness or overcome by sleepiness, and internal or external obstacles[24] impinge upon right mindfulness to the point where one is unable to expel them, then one should recite intently the name of a Buddha and, with a keen sense of shame, repent and entrust one's life to him.[25] The merit obtained from such a practice is fully equal to that gained by reciting the names of all the Buddhas of the ten directions.

[11b13] How does this work? When people become choked up with joy or grief,[26] should they raise their voices in song or wailing, their sadness and delight will find release. It is the same with the practitioner. When the vital breath (*ch'i*) strikes seven places in the body, the physical act [of speech] takes shape; and when the echo of the voice emerges from the lips, the vocal act is completed.[27] The two together can assist the mind, forming a causal nexus (*chi*) that stimulates (*kan*) the Buddhas [and causes them] to descend (*hsiang*) [to the practitioner's aid].[28] It is analo-

23. Chan-jan (T 46.182c20) says: "One remains silent in order to be in proper keeping with the practice; one speaks in order to remove impediments."

24. Chan-jan (T 46.182c24–26) says: "The afflictions—such as false views, overweening pride, etc.—are known as internal obstacles. The māras and evil acquaintances are the external obstacles."

25. From the *Wen-shu wen ching*, T 14.507a. Chan-jan (T 46.182c25–26) says: "Having no alternative but concentratedly to invoke the Buddha, this is known as confession. To put one's entire being into it without reluctance is to 'entrust one's life to him.' "

26. Chan-jan (T 46.183a1–2) says: " 'Choked up' means that the mental intention does not express itself. Heavy grief and great joy remain in the mind and do not come forth [and disperse]. Thus one uses the wailing and song of body and speech to assist it."

27. This morphology of the act of speech is drawn from the TCTL, T 25.103a. Here it is said that *udāna*, one of the five vital airs of the human body, rebounds (echoes) from the navel and impinges on seven bodily parts (the top of the head, the gums, teeth, lips, tongue, throat, and chest) before issuing from the mouth as speech. The TCTL, unlike Chih-i, makes no special distinction between the bodily and vocal act. For the TCTL, the emphasis is on the idea that the sound of speech is brought into existence through a variety of causes, but there is no real speaker; the voice is a simile for the unreality of dharmas.

28. Chan-jan (T 46.183a12–16) says: "Although the [*Fa-hua*] *hsüan-wen* makes the case that the activity of mind alone comprises the causal nexus (*chi*) [for stimulus and response], this is not the sense that 'mind' carries in the passage here. In this case one is urged to cultivate the auxiliary support [of body and speech] because one cannot accomplish [the task] on the basis of mind or mental-intent alone. The scripture itself incorporates all three vehicles, but the present reference to 'mind' carries the exclusive sense of the perfect teaching and does not extend to the shared or separate [teachings]. Even though, in order to remove

gous to a person who tries to pick up a heavy load, but whose strength is insufficient to move it. Should he enlist the help of a bystander, the object can be lifted with ease. For religious practitioners it is much the same. If their minds are weak and incapable of expelling obstacles [on their own], by reciting the name of a Buddha and beseeching the latter's protection and support they can prevent unfavorable conditions from ruining them.

[11b18] If you are not completely clear about this practice (*fa-men*), you should approach someone who understands prajñā and practice as instructed by them. You will thereby be able to enter the one practice samādhi, see all the Buddhas face to face, and mount to the stage of true bodhisattvahood.

Compared to perfect quietude, even reciting sūtras or incantations is noisy; how much noisier yet is worldly talk![29]

[11b21] **Mind.** To practice calming-and-contemplation of the mind,[30]

---

impediments, one is now instructed to recollect [the body of] the Buddha of manifest response, later in the section on calming and contemplation of the mind one is instructed to recollect the dharma-body. Thus it is exclusively [based on the] perfect [teaching]."

29. Chan-jan (T 46.183a21–25) says: "The activity [of reciting sūtras] is excluded from this practice of constant sitting, but one should not think that these stipulations apply equally for the other three forms of samādhi. Therefore, although in constant sitting 'recitation of sūtras is avoided; much less, worldly talk,' the prohibition against reciting sūtras applies only in this instance. Prohibition against vulgar talk, however, applies for all four [forms of samādhi]. As such, in all four samādhis one must sever all connection with persons from outside. Neither walking nor sitting samādhi also has certain stipulations based on the sūtras. Even though it extends [practice unrestrictedly to] all sense perceptions and forms of physical activity, vulgar talk and deeds are not advocated."

30. Chan-jan (T 46.183a25–b5) says of this section on "calming and contemplation of the mind" as well as its counterpart in the samādhis that follow: "In each [of the sections on the four samādhis] from here through neither walking nor sitting, the statements regarding contemplation are organized crudely around material from the original sūtras. Although [their form] may resemble the ten modes of discernment [i.e., the formal system of meditation set forth at length in greater chapter 7 of MHCK], the passages in all cases are highly abbreviated. One cannot rely [on these descriptions] to distinguish the practice of contemplation in all its aspects. The same holds true for all [of the five sections of the Synopsis], from the first [lesser] chapter on the arousal of the thought of enlightenment, through the three [concluding] chapters that follow [this section on the four samādhis]. It is for this reason, in fact, that the five [lesser] chapters are called the 'Synopsis.'

"The text here resorts to very general examples from the two [Mañjuśrī] sūtras. The passages themselves are disjointed and their import abstruse. They must not be analyzed speciously. If you want to elucidate them fully, you must master the chapters on the ten modes of discernment that follow. Only then will you be free of error. However, if you resort to the latter [part of the] text, [the discussion of

just sit in proper posture and maintain right mindfulness (*cheng nien*). Dispel evil thoughts and discard confused fantasies. Allow no other mental reflections to intrude and refrain from grasping after distinguishing features.[31] Fix your mind on the dharmadhātu as the object [of meditation] and that alone.[32] Unify your mindfulness (*nien*) completely with the dharmadhātu. "Fixing the mind on the dharmadhātu as the object" is calming, and "unifying mindfulness with the dharmadhātu" is contemplation.[33]

[11b23] Have faith that every one among the myriad dharmas is itself the Buddha dharma.[34] There is no prior and no after, no temporal or spatial boundary whatsoever between them. [What is more] there is no knower and no expounder [of the dharma]. If there is neither knower nor expounder, then [truth and its realization] neither exist nor do not exist. If there is no knower, then neither is there a nonknower. Departing from these two extremes, one dwells where there is nothing in which to

---

the ten modes] lacks details concerning the four activities or practices [of the four forms of samādhi]. In this respect, the section of the text [on the ten modes of discernment] itself may be considered abbreviated. Then again, because the text here is not complete with respect to the ten modes of discernment, it also is abbreviated. Thus the five lesser chapters [of the Synopsis] are called 'abbreviated' because, from the perspective of meditative discernment, they are abridged and one-sided. But they are not so with respect to phenomenal activities (*shih*)."

31. Chan-jan (T 46.183b10–12) identifies the first half of the sentence with "calming" and the latter half with "contemplation."

32. From the central passage on one practice samādhi in *Wen-shu shuo ching*, T 8.731a–b. The four characters of this line and the four of the one that follows also appear in the core statement on the "perfect and sudden calming and contemplation" in the preface of MHCK (see T 46.1c24). There is a persistent tendency among Japanese scholars to render the four characters of *chi yüan fa-chieh* as "fix (or identify) (*chi*) all mental objects/conditions (*yüan*) in (or with) the dharmadhātu (*fa-chieh*)" (see Muranaka, p. 112 and Ōno, "Shishu-zammai no tenkyo to sono kōsatsu—jō: jōza-zammai to jōgyō-zammai," p. 286). In the *Wen-shu shuo ching*, as well as throughout Chih-i's writings, *chi-yüan* functions regularly as a verbal binome (transitive) with the technical meaning "to fix the mind on a specified *x* [as the object of meditation]"—see Chih-i, *Hsiao chih-kuan* (T 46.467a6–8) and *Tz'u-ti ch'an-men* (T 46.492a6–10.) The conventional Japanese reading is not supported by the original text or by Chan-jan's commentary (T 46.183b6 and 151c).

33. Chan-jan (T 46.183b14–15) comments on the passage: "This explains quiescence and illumination, calming and contemplation on the part of the one who discerns. Even though one 'fixes one's mind [on the object]' or 'practices mindfulness,' one never departs from the dharmadhātu. Whether one cultivates calming or practices contemplation, quiescence and illumination are perfectly simultaneous."

34. From the *Wen-shu shuo ching*, T 8.731c.

dwell.[35] One settles in the perfectly quiescent dharmadhātu, wherein all the Buddhas dwell.

[11b27] Do not be alarmed upon hearing this profound dharma! For this dharmadhātu is also known as "bodhi," "the realm of the inconceivable," "prajñā," or "the nonarising and nonperishing." Thus, there is no duality, no separation between the myriad dharmas and the dharmadhātu. When you hear that there is no duality or separation, you must harbor no doubts about this in your mind. One who is able to contemplate in such fashion contemplates the ten epithets of the Tathāgata.[36]

[11c2] When contemplating the Tathāgata[37] one does not think of the Tathāgata as the Tathāgata. There is here no Tathāgata that is a Tathā-

35. Ibid., T 8.728b. Chan-jan (T 46.183b15–22) says: " 'Having faith that all dharmas, etc.,' exhorts one to have faith. One must have faith that 'there is no prior or after,' because the dharmadhātu is not encompassed by the three times. Things or entities represent 'spatial delimitation'; being first, etc., represents 'temporal delimitation.' Because the substance of the dharmadhātu is all pervading, there is 'no temporal or spatial boundary.' Inner realization is 'knowing'; training others is 'expounding.' Knower and expounder are not separate from the dharmadhātu; thus it says, 'no knower, no expounder.' Being beyond dualistic extremes, the dharmadhātu is neither existent nor nonexistent. Because it is not worldly (i.e., supramundane), there is 'no knower.' But because it is also not empty, neither is there a 'nonknower.' In keeping with its sublimity we say that [the dharmadhātu] 'departs from all extremes.' But because the middle and the [dualistic] extremes are themselves identical, 'one dwells where there is nothing in which to dwell.' All the Buddhas take the dharmadhātu as the place in which they settle (*an*). We shall dwell in the dharmadhātu as the Buddhas dwell in it. Thus it says, 'the place where one settles.' "

36. The ten epithets are listed in the *Wen-shu wen ching*, T 14.506c18–19: (1) Tathāgata or "thus-come-one," (2) arhat, (3) the one who has awakened to full perfect enlightenment, (4) fully practiced in (and endowed with) the illuminations, (5) well-gone, (6) knower of the world, (7) the supreme one, (8) teacher of men and gods, (9) the Buddha, and (10) the World-Honored One. Sometimes the tenth is divided into two separate items; in other instances the epithet *jina*, "the victorious," is added.

Chan-jan (T 46.183b28–c12) says: "Simply by contemplating the dharmadhātu, the ten epithets of the Tathāgata that describe the body of manifest response are found to be equivalent to the dharmadhātu itself. One thereby comes to know the ten epithets of the Tathāgata as they pertain to the dharma body as well. How so? [The Buddha] is called 'Tathāgata' because he comes into tally with the true object-realm through his resorting to the wisdom of nonduality. . . . The ten epithets of the body of manifest response and the dharma body are a single substance, devoid of duality."

37. 'Tathāgata' or 'thus-come-one' is the first of the ten epithets. Chan-jan (T 46.183c19) says: "The previously mentioned dharma body described in the first passage functions as the object here."

gata, nor is there any Tathāgata's wisdom by which [the condition of] Tathāgata could be known. For Tathāgatahood and the wisdom by which Tathāgatahood is known both lack all mark of duality.[38] They lack all marks of motion and all marks of production. They are neither situated in any direction nor apart from all direction. They are not subject to the three times nor removed from the three times. They are not characterized by dualistic extremes, nor yet do they stand apart from dualistic extremes. They are distinguished neither by defilement nor by purity. This contemplation of the Tathāgata is extraordinarily rarefied.[39] Like space, it is without defect. [Contemplating in this manner,] right mindfulness is increased.

38. The entire passage here is based on *Wen-shu shuo ching*, T 8.728a. Chan-jan comments (T 46.183c17–21): "[The passage] from 'contemplate the Tathāgata' on explains that the object [of wisdom] and the wisdom [that discerns it] are not two separate things. The previously mentioned dharma body set forth in the opening passage functions as the object here. How are we to know that the object [of wisdom] itself derives from the wisdom that does the discerning? Because at the beginning it is established that 'one is not to think of the Tathāgata [as the Tathāgata].' 'Not to think' is itself the wisdom that knows [things as] inapprehensible. The line 'there is no [Tathāgata]' illustrates that the object of contemplation is featureless. The line 'nor is there any wisdom by which Tathāgatahood is known' establishes that wisdom is featureless. The line from 'the Tathāgata and wisdom' demonstrates that wisdom and its object are not two." *Kōgi* (1.415) says: "For if the object-realm is eradicated, the subject-realm must likewise vanish. . . . Their identity results from their inexistence."

39. *Wen-shu shuo ching*, T 8.726b. Chan-jan (T 46.183c22–184a1) comments: "That wisdom and its object are a mysterious unity is the meaning of the phrase 'lack the mark of duality.' That wisdom and its object completely pervade one another in substance is the meaning of 'no mark of movement.' That wisdom and its object are originally present as such is what is meant by 'no mark of production.' That they pervade one another universally without any sign of pervasion is what is meant by 'not situated in any direction.' Because, although markless, they actually do pervade universally, they are described as 'nor apart from directions.' Because they are not mundane or conventional, they are 'not of the three times.' But because they also do not lie outside the conventional world, they are described as 'nor apart from the three times.' The middle [truth] wherein [the two extremes are] simultaneously eradicated is indicated by 'not marked by duality.' The middle [truth] wherein [the two extremes are] simultaneously illumined is indicated in the line 'nor yet apart from dualism.' 'Not defiled' means that they are not admixed with delusion. 'Not pure' means that they are not admixed with wisdom. The line [beginning with] 'this contemplation' concludes with the praising of this contemplative wisdom. 'Extraordinarily rarefied' means that it is utterly self-sustaining and unique. It is 'like empty space' because it is universally pervading yet also extinct. It is 'without blemish' because it does not rely upon sequential stages. Because it advances the tally [of wisdom and object], it 'augments right mindfulness.' "

[11c8] [One should think of] the vision of the Buddha's major and minor marks to be like viewing one's own reflection shining from the mirrorlike surface of water. At first one sees a single Buddha, then [innumerable] Buddhas throughout the ten directions. It is not that one uses superhuman powers to travel elsewhere to see the Buddha. But, remaining right where one is, one sees the Buddhas, hears them expound the dharma, and comprehends the meaning of thusness (*tathatā*).[40]

[11c11] View the Tathāgata [in his form aspect] so as to benefit other animate beings, but do not seize upon any mark of a Tathāgata.[41] Transform all animate beings with the teaching and turn them toward nirvāṇa, but do not seize upon any explicit feature of nirvāṇa. Display [the two] great adornments[42] so as to benefit all living beings, but do not perceive any sign of these adornments.[43] For [reality] is devoid of both form and feature; it cannot be seen, heard, or known as an object.[44] As for a Buddha, he does not attain or realize anything whatsoever.[45] This, indeed, is

40. The entire passage is based on the *Wen-shu wen ching*, T 14.506c–507a. Chan-jan (T 46.184a2–5) says: "When the contemplation is successfully completed one will see the Buddha [in a vision]. Through this contemplation one sees the Buddha of the body of [manifest] form. Even though it was not the original expectation or design of the practice, the power of contemplation brings it about as such. For this reason the vision that one perceives is likened to a reflection in a mirror. Without employing superhuman powers of penetration, one sees throughout the ten directions. Dwelling in the abode of the dharmadhātu one is able to see all the Buddhas."

41. Chan-jan (T 46.184a6–7) says: "Through the power of great compassion one sees the marks, while through the power of great wisdom one avoids seizing upon them. Nirvāṇa and the two adornments are to be treated in the same way."

42. The two adornments that the bodhisattva perfects in order to be established in Buddhahood—the adornment or accumulation of merits (*puṇya-saṃbhāra*) and the adornment or accumulation of wisdom (*jñāna-saṃbhāra*).

43. From the *Wen-shu shuo ching*, T 8.726b.

44. Chan-jan (T 46.184a11–13) says: "Form is the substance (*t'i*), features are the external presentation (*wai-piao*) of the dharma. Though one sees the Tathāgata and hears his preaching, one knows that the real meaning of the dharma is devoid of seeing and hearing, etc."

45. Following Chan-jan's reading (T 46.184a12–16): "The Buddha himself knows no realization or attainment of the dharma. How could the practitioner possibly speak of any such attainment? The lines that follow explain the example introduced above: what the Buddha realizes is just the one single dharmadhātu. The dharmadhātu knows no realization nor any attainment. For realization involves taking hold of a fruit or result; acquisition involves clinging to or abiding in a dharma, and both are done away with here. This is why the text says, 'nothing.' "

extraordinarily rarefied and sublime. Why? Because the Buddha himself is identical to the dharmadhātu.[46] To suppose that the dharmadhātu realizes the dharmadhātu would indeed be meaningless prattle. There is no realization and no attainment.

[11c16] Contemplate the mark of sentient existence as if it were the mark of Buddhahood, and the domain of animate beings as identical in scope to the domain of the Buddhas. The domain of the Buddhas is inconceivable in its scope, and the domain of animate existence is likewise inconceivable.[47] Dwelling in the domain of animate existence is the same as dwelling in open space. By dint of [this] dharma of nondwelling and dharma of marklessness, one dwells in the very midst of prajñā.[48] If one does not find any dharma of worldliness, how can it be renounced? If one does not find any dharma of saintliness, how can it be acquired?[49] The same goes for saṃsāra and nirvāṇa, defilement and purity.[50] Neither renouncing nor appropriating anything, one simply dwells in the limit of reality (*bhūtakoṭi*). In this manner one contemplates animate beings as the true dharmadhātu of the Buddhas.

[11c22] When contemplating the various afflictions, such as craving, anger, and stupidity, always think, "These are impulses (*saṃskāra*) of perfect quiescence—impulses devoid of activity. They are not dharmas of birth and death; yet neither are they dharmas of nirvāṇa."[51] Cultivate the

46. *Wen-shu shuo ching*, T 8.728b.

47. Chan-jan (T 46.184a19–21) says: "There is no separation or distinction between the domain of animate beings and [that of] Buddhas; nor is there any difference in their scope. Because they are perfectly equal in terms of principle (*li*), they are also perfectly equal in number and type. One must not cause them to impede one another by seizing upon phenomenal distinctions."

48. *Wen-shu shuo ching*, T 8.726c. Chan-jan (T 46.184a25–28) says: "In the explanation of the mutual 'sameness' of Buddhas and animate beings, the point is that one should contemplate animate beings to be 'the same as or like' the Buddha. Because the basic substance (*t'i*) of this 'sameness' is without distinguishing marks, it is likened to open space. Although likened to open space, wisdom—which is itself like empty space—discerns the object-realm that is like empty space. Therefore it says that 'one dwells in prajñā by virtue of the dharma of nondwelling.' "

49. Chan-jan (T 46.184a28–29) says: "Since animate beings are identical to Buddhas, there is no worldliness to reject. Since Buddhas are identical to animate beings, there is no saintliness to acquire."

50. *Wen-shu shuo ching*, T 8.727a. According to Chan-jan, this describes the "unconstructed four noble truths" (T 46.184a29–b2): "In the unconstructed four noble truths, there is nothing acquired, nothing renounced. 'Neither acquiring nor renouncing' comes with abiding in the reality limit."

51. Chan-jan (T 46.184b4–8) seeks, with difficulty, to align the clause in quotation marks with the three truths: "Impulses of perfect quiescence are impulses [as understood from the perspective of] the truth of the real. Impulses devoid of activity are impulses of the provisional truth. 'Not [dharmas of] birth and death,

path to Buddhahood without either abandoning false views or abandoning inaction (*wu-wei*).[52] Neither practice the way nor do not practice the way.[53] This is what is known as properly dwelling in the dharmadhātu of the afflictions.

[11c25] When contemplating the gravity of different deeds (karma), there is no deed as serious as the five depravities.[54] And yet, the five depravities are themselves identical to bodhi. Bodhi and the five depravities are without any mark of duality.[55] There is no perceiver, no knower, no maker of discriminations.[56] The mark of sinfulness of the depravities and the mark of ultimate reality are both inconceivable, indestructible, and utterly devoid of own-being. All karmic causation takes place within the limit of reality. It does not come, does not go, and constitutes neither cause nor effect.[57] This is what is meant by contemplating karma as itself the seal of the dharmadhātu.

[12a1] The seal of the dharmadhātu cannot be destroyed even by the four māras;[58] the māras cannot affect it.[59] Why not? Because the māras

---

etc.' refers to impulses of the middle way." *Kōgi* (1.423) endeavors to make "motionless impulses" fit provisionality better by saying that these "impulses" conform infallibly to things—for since "things" fall in the category of the "provisional," this can be fitted to the truth of provisionality.

52. Chan-jan (T 184b5–7) says: "Not abandoning false views represents provisionality; not abandoning inaction represents emptiness; cultivating the path to Buddhahood under these circumstances represents the middle."

53. *Wen-shu shuo ching*, T 8.730a.

54. The five cardinal sins in Buddhism, also known as the *pañca ānantaryāṇi karmāṇi* or five deeds resulting in rebirth in the hells of uninterrupted torment. The five include matricide, killing an arhat, patricide, destroying the harmony of the saṅgha, and shedding the blood of a Buddha.

55. Chan-jan (T 46.184b23–24) says: "They are nondual because the depravities and bodhi do not depart from the essential nature of mind."

56. The *Wen-shu shuo ching*, T 8.728c. "The word 'perceiver' is used because one identifies or recognizes the nature of mind. Since there is no 'perceiver or perceiving' [of this truth], we say 'no perceiver.' It is called 'perceive' in the sense that it stands in contrast to [an opposing] object. 'Knowing' designates inner understanding. Knowing and perceiving are identical in their essential substance and do not differ in meaning. 'No maker of discriminations' means the absence of a subject who differentiates inner and outer [realizations]. Then again, recognizing the nature of the five depravities is 'perceiving'; illumining bodhi is 'knowing'; and knowing these two dharmas [in turn] is 'discriminating.' "

57. Ibid., T 8.728b.

58. They include: (1) Maheśvara Māra, or the divine Māra who is lord of the realm of desire, (2) the māras of the defilements, (3) the māras of the five psychophysical aggregates or skandhas, and (4) the māra of death (see TCTL, T 25.99b). Together the four māras describe all those factors that seek the destruction of good in the world.

59. *Wen-shu shuo ching*, T 8.732c.

themselves are the seal of the dharmadhātu. How could the seal of the dharmadhātu destroy the seal of the dharmadhātu? If you extend this idea to all dharmas, then you will understand [their true nature]. Everything said here is based on the text of the [Mañjuśrī] sūtras.[60]

Exhortation to Practice

[12a4] In the exhortation to practice we extol the true merits to be derived from the practice in order to encourage practitioners. The dharma of the dharmadhātu is itself the true dharma of the Buddha, and it is the seal of the bodhisattva. If you can hear this dharma without being alarmed or taking fright, then you are one who, for aeons, has planted roots of merit throughout a hundred thousand million million Buddha-fields.[61] It is analogous to a rich man who, having lost a precious jewel, later recovers it, and his heart becomes filled with joy. In the same way, before the four assemblies[62] have heard this dharma, they are in a state of suffering and affliction. But once they hear it and come to develop faith and understanding in it, they become joyful.[63] Know therefore that such people have seen the Buddha. In the past they have already heard this dharma from Mañjuśrī.[64]

[12a9] Śāriputra says [in the *Sūtra of Mañjuśrī's Discourse*], "One who understands thoroughly the meaning of this teaching we call a bodhisattva-mahāsattva." Maitreya replies, "Such a person comes near the seat of the Buddha, for the Buddhas are ones who have awakened to this dharma."[65] Hence Mañjuśrī says, "To hear this dharma without being

60. Chan-jan uses this reference to the "seal of the dharmadhātu" as an occasion to make several interesting observations about the place of the *Wen-shu shuo ching* in the emergence of Chinese Ch'an, in particular the transition from East Mountain Ch'an to the development of southern (Yangtze valley) and northern (imperial capital and Yellow River basin) lines. He (T 46.184c11–13) comments: "Because it is the 'seal of the dharmadhātu,' the dhyāna/*ch'an* master [Tao-]hsin originally used this sūtra for his 'essentials of mind' (*hsin-yao*). People of later generations followed his precedent but came to differ in their personal interpretations. This brought about the discrepancies between the lines (*tsung*) of Ch'an beyond the Yangtze and in the vicinity of the capital and the Ḥo."

61. *Wen-shu shuo ching*, T 8.727b.

62. Monks, nuns, Buddhist laymen, and laywomen.

63. This passage possibly resonates with the first of the five grades of discipleship in the path of the perfect teaching, which is known as the "grade of joy [in the dharma]."

64. Mixed paraphrase and quote from *Wen-shu shuo ching*, T 8.730a–b.

65. Chan-jan (T 46.184c21–24) comments: " 'Seat' describes that on which [the Buddha] relies. He relies on the principle of reality. The text says 'comes near the seat,' because one who hears this dharma approaches the principle of reality. The Buddha is the one who awakens; the dharma is that to which he awakens. To

alarmed is to see the Buddha."[66] And the Buddha says, "Such a person dwells in the stage of no back-sliding (*avaivartya*), fulfills the six perfections, and becomes endowed with all the dharma of the Buddhas."[67]

[12a13] Those who wish to acquire the dharma of the Buddhas in its entirety, their marks, excellent qualities, and noble demeanor, the Buddha voice that expounds the dharma,[68] as well as the ten powers[69] and the fearlessnesses,[70] should engage in this one practice samādhi. By practicing diligently without remiss, one will be able to enter it.[71] It is like caring for a jewel: the more it is polished, the more it shines.[72] By this practice one acquires unthinkable merit. If a bodhisattva is able to learn it, he or she will quickly win enlightenment. If monks and nuns hear this practice expounded without becoming alarmed, they will truly be following the example of the Buddha in their abandonment of the household

---

come near what the Buddha has awakened to is to 'come near the seat of the Buddha.' "

66. Chan-jan (T 46.184c26–27) says: "To hear this dharma and not become alarmed is to perceive the dharma body of the Buddha."

67. *Wen-shu shuo ching*, T 8.727c–728a and 730c. Chan-jan (T 46.184c27–29) says: "If one attains the first [of the ten] abodes and sees the dharma body of the Buddha, then this marks nonretrogression of mindfulness. If one realizes purification of the six sense faculties and achieves a proximate vision [of the dharma body] of the Buddha, it marks nonretrogression with respect to stage and practice. When these three types of nonretrogression [have been achieved], all of the perfections are fulfilled. Then they are known as 'pāramitā.' "

68. The Buddha's lion-roar (*siṃha-nāda*).

69. Two different versions of the "ten powers" (*daśa-bala*) may be found in Buddhist works—an older list common to both the *Āgamas* and various Mahāyāna scriptures and a later formulation peculiar to certain Mahāyāna works. As evidenced in other writings of Chih-i where such listings appear (see *Fa-chieh tz'u-ti ch'u-men*, T 46.665a; *Tz'u-ti ch'an-men*, T 46.481b), Chih-i generally resorts to the TCTL for his Mahāyāna technicalia. Thus *Fa-chieh tz'u-ti ch'u-men* (T 46.694a–c), drawing on TCTL (T 25.235c–236a), gives the more ancient formulation of the ten powers: knowledge of (1) whether a location is suited to the path or not, (2) deeds and their respective retributions, (3) meditative states and techniques, (4) differences in the strength of beings' faculties, (5) the range of beings, hopes, or desires, (6) dharmas and their natures, (7) the different destinies or abodes of existence, (8) one's own past existences, (9) karmic destinies of other beings, and (10) exhaustion of outflows.

70. The four fearlessnesses (*vaiśāradya*) of a Buddha. According to Chih-i's *Fa-chieh-tz'u-ti ch'u-men* (T 46.694c) and TCTL (T 25.235c–236a) they include: the fearlessness (1) that comes with omniscient wisdom, (2) that comes with knowledge of exhaustion of outflows, (3) in pointing out obstructions to the dharma and the path, and (4) in preaching the path that leads to the extinction of suffering.

71. *Wen-shu shuo ching*, T 8.730c and 731b.

72. Ibid., T 8.731b.

life. If laymen and laywomen hear it without being dismayed, then this is truly taking refuge in the Buddha.[73] The encomium [of merits] offered here is drawn from the two [Mañjuśrī] sūtras.

Constantly Walking Samādhi

[12a19] Second is the constantly walking samādhi.[74] We begin with the procedure for practice (*fang-fa*) and, following it, give the exhortation to practice (*ch'üan-hsiu*). Under procedure for practice we distinguish what should and should not be done with the body, what to utter and when to be silent with the mouth, and the calming and contemplation of the mind.

[12a20] This teaching originates from the *Pratyutpanna-samādhi Sūtra*, which, translated, means "[the Sūtra Wherein] the Buddhas Stand [Before One]."[75] There are three essential points in [this] "Buddha-Standing" [practice]:[76] first is the awesome sustaining power (*adhiṣṭhāna*) of the

73. Ibid., T 8.731c.

74. Early catalogues credit Chih-i with a separate manual on the pratyutpanna samādhi titled *Pan-chou cheng-hsiang hsing-fa* (Procedure for Performing Pratyutpanna [Samādhi] and Signs for Verification of Successful Realization), no longer extant; see Tao-hsüan, *Ta T'ang nei-tien lu*, T 55.284b, and Satō, *Tendai daishi no kenkyū*, pp. 78–81.

75. The common Sanskrit title of the sūtra is *Pratyutpanna-buddha-saṃmukhāvasthita-samādhi Sūtra* or "The Sūtra of the Samādhi in Which All the Buddhas of the Present Age Stand Face to Face Before One." The Chinese version of the sūtra used by Chih-i transliterates the title as *Pan-chou san-mei ching*. The name of the samādhi itself (*pratyutpanna-buddha-saṃmukhāvasthita samādhi*) is often rendered in Chinese works as *[chien] chu-fo hsien-ch'ien san-mei* or "the samādhi wherein [one sees] all the Buddhas manifesting or appearing before one" (see, for example, *Shih-chu p'i-p'o-sha lun*, T 26.68c17–18). For an extensive discussion of the samādhi and its great significance to early Mahāyāna Buddhism, consult Lamotte, *Traité*, 5.2263–2272.

The *Pratyutpanna-samādhi Sūtra* is also known by the title *Bhadrapāla-bodhisattva Sūtra*, after the scripture's chief interlocutor. The four Chinese translations of the text (dating from the second through the sixth centuries) extant today represent various redactions that range in length from one to five fascicles. Chih-i relies on the three-fascicle *Pan-chou san-mei ching* (T no. 418), said to have been translated by Lokakṣema in 179. For an excellent discussion of these different Chinese translations and their attributions, as well as an English translation of the Tibetan version of the sūtra, see Harrison, *The Samādhi of Direct Encounter with the Buddhas of the Present*.

76. According to the *Pan-chou san-mei ching*, T 13.905c, these three factors are responsible for bringing about the phenomenon of the Buddha, or Buddhas, manifesting before the practitioner. Chan-jan (T 46.185a28–29) says: "With the coming together of [the proper] causes and conditions there occurs the interactive

Buddha; second is the power of samādhi; and third is the power of the practitioner's own basic merits. By these it is possible, while absorbed in meditative concentration, to see all the present Buddhas of the ten directions standing before one.[77] One will see the Buddhas of the ten directions as vividly and in as much profusion as a person with keen sight sees stars on a clear night. This is why it is called the samādhi where the Buddhas stand [before one].

[12a25] The **Dasabhūmika-vibhāṣa Śāstra* says in the gathās, "The abodes of this samādhi may be distinguished into lesser, middling, and greater. Their respective features must be discussed."[78] "Abodes" refers to the fact that, by arousing these powers,[79] this samādhi can be produced in either the first, second, third, or fourth dhyāna. That is why the term "abodes" is used. [Samādhi produced in] the first dhyāna is the lesser abode, the second is the middling, and that of the third and fourth [dhyānas] is the greater. Then again, "lesser" may refer to the fact that one abides in samādhi for a short time. Or it may be called "lesser" because one sees a small number of realms or sees only a few Buddhas. The same applies for "middling" and "greater."[80]

---

resonance of stimulus and response (*kan-ying tao-chiao*). For this reason one must have the three powers."

77. *Pan-chou san-mei ching*, T 13.905a.

78. *Shih-chu p'i-p'o-sha lun*, T 26.88b13–14 (hereafter referred to by its reconstructed Sanskrit title, **Daśabhūmika-vibhāṣa Śāstra*). The text itself is attributed to Nāgārjuna and was translated by Kumārajīva at the beginning of the fifth century. It consists of root verses and prose commentary on the first two of the ten bodhisattva stages of the *Daśabhūmika Sūtra*. (Although circulated as an independent scripture, the latter is also incorporated as part of the *Avataṃsaka Sūtra*, a fact that ensured the great popularity of the *Daśabhūmika Sūtra*, its system of stages, and its Indian commentaries in China).

Extensive citations and discussion of features from the *Pratyutpanna-samādhi Sūtra* appear in the twenty-fifth chapter of the **Daśabhūmika-vibhāṣa Śāstra*, on Practices that Assist Buddha Mindfulness Samādhi (T 26.86a–88c). This chapter, together with two preceding sections on Buddha Mindfulness (T 26.68c–71c) and the Forty Dharmas Unique to a Buddha (T 26.71c–83c), is consulted by Chih-i as a second locus for the practice of pratyutpanna samādhi.

79. The powers discussed here are not the same as the three powers mentioned in the *Pratyutpanna-samādhi Sūtra* above. They represent three degrees of meditative prowess associated, respectively, with (1) initial contemplation of the thirty-two marks and eighty excellences of the Buddha's body of form, (2) contemplation of his dharma-body in the form of the Buddha's forty unique spiritual powers and merits, and, finally, (3) contemplation of the Buddha as unconditioned reality itself; see **Daśabhūmika-vibhāṣa Śāstra*, T 26.86a7–19.

80. This paragraph is taken virtually verbatim from the prose commentary to the root verses of the **Daśabhūmika-vibhāṣa Śāstra* cited in note 78; see ibid., T 26.88b16–20.

Procedure for Practice

[12b1] **Body.** Regarding the body, constant walking is what is prescribed. When practicing this dharma, avoid unworthy acquaintances as well as foolish people, relatives, and people hailing from your native place.[81] Dwell alone in a fixed place and harbor no expectations nor seek for any assistance from others.[82] Always beg for the food that you eat but do not accept special invitations for repasts.[83] Decorate resplendently a sanctuary for practice (*tao-ch'ang*), providing it with all necessary ritual implements, incense, ritual food,[84] and sweet fruits [for offering]. Wash your body,[85] and whenever exiting the hall from the left and entering from the right, change clothes accordingly.[86] Concentrate solely upon circumambulating [the altar to Amitābha Buddha] for a fixed period of ninety days.[87] One should have a knowledgeable and experienced teacher who

81. From the *Pratyutpanna-samādhi Sūtra*, T 13.904b–c, much abbreviated. Chan-jan (T 46.185b22–23) explains: "Because relatives and persons hailing from one's native place entail many entangling responsibilities, one must keep them at a distance."

82. *Pratyutpanna-samādhi Sūtra*, T 13.909c.

83. Ibid., T 13.909c and 916c. Chan-jan, citing various scriptures, offers a lengthy discourse on the advantages of begging for food over accepting invitations or taking regular meals with the saṅgha of monks. "Because the mind [under the latter circumstances] becomes scattered and confused and departs from the way," he cautions, "one should beg for meals" (T 46.185c17–18). Elsewhere in MHCK (T 46.42a–b), however, Chih-i distinguishes three means of sustenance suitable for meditative cultivation (each adapted to one of three environments): (1) gathering fruits, etc., if one is practicing alone deep in the mountains or forests, (2) begging for alms if one is practicing *dhūta* within walking distance of a village, and (3) regular support from donors and "external protectors" (*wai-hu*) if one is practicing in a cloistered room within the precincts of a monastery. As will become clear shortly, the support of "external protectors" is an implicit feature of Chih-i's pratyutpanna samādhi.

84. Following Kuan-ting's reading in *Kuan-hsin lun shu* (T 46.601b15–16), where he distinguishes "ritually prepared delicacies, sweet fruits, incense, and flowers." The term *hsiao*, rendered here as "ritually prepared delicacies," traditionally refers to cooked meats and fish used for ritual offerings and banquets. Chan-jan (T 46.185c20–21) takes *hsiang-hsiao* as a binome meaning "fragrant ritual delicacies." He equates the expression with *hsiao-ts'ai*, which he describes as "ritually cooked vegetables . . . that do not involve coarse grains." Obviously meat was not offered.

85. Specifically, washing of the hands and face, according to Chan-jan (T 46.185c21–22).

86. Kuan-ting notes in *Kuan-hsin lun shu* (T 46.601b16–17): "When exiting from the left and entering from the right, change clothes according to the usual procedure."

87. Kuan-ting explains in *Kuan-hsin lun shu* (T 46.601b17): "One should only

is well versed in both the internal and external disciplinary codes and is able to remove impediments to the practice.[88] Look upon the teacher from whom you hear this samādhi as if he were the World-Honored One himself. Do not despise or be angered at him and do not critically dwell on his shortcomings and strengths.[89] You should be willing to rend your very skin and flesh in offering to your teacher—how much the more [sacrifice] any other object. Serve the teacher as a servant would an eminent family, for if you should develop loathing of him, it will be all the more difficult to achieve this samādhi that you seek.[90] You should have external protectors who [treat you] as a mother would care for her child and fellow practitioners [who tend to one another] as though they were together traversing a precipitous path.[91] Set your goals and vow as follows:

---

circumambulate and not engage in the other three postures [of standing still, sitting, or reclining]."

88. Chan-jan (T 46.185c23–25) says: "Codes for body and speech are external; codes for mind are internal. Both the Hīnayāna and Mahāyāna have [this latter aspect of] mental disciplinary codes. They encompass violations of the [twenty-five] preliminary expedients [of meditative practice] as well as the latter three items of the ten wholesome and evil deeds. . . . Also, [the disciplinary codes of] the Hīnayāna can be considered 'external,' and those of the Mahāyāna, 'internal.' If a person is only versed in the codes of behavior and is not acquainted with [signs of] obstruction or impediment [in the practice], one is still not fit to occupy the position of teacher." For further reference to the distinction between internal and external codes, see Chih-i, *Fang-teng san-mei hsing-fa*, T 46.947b7.

89. *Pratyutpanna-samādhi Sūtra*, T 13.909c.

90. Chan-jan quotes both the **Daśabhūmika-vibhāṣa Śāstra* (T 26.115c–116a) and the TCTL (T 25.414b–c) at length on the interesting problem of the proper attitude a disciple should have toward a teacher of less than supreme merit. Both texts agree strongly that a teacher is to be respected whatever his or her faults, for the sake of extinguishing the disciple's arrogance if for no other reason. Chan-jan (T 46.186a12–16), citing the latter source, says: "Don't seize upon good qualities and reject evils simply on the basis of worldly convention. If [a teacher] is able to elucidate prajñā, then venerate him to the full and don't think of his other faults. Don't throw out the gold because the sack in which it is kept happens to stink. If an evil man is walking a perilous road at night with candle in hand, you won't reject its light because the one who holds it happens to be bad. The bodhisattva is also like this. He goes for the light of wisdom and doesn't consider other flaws."

91. "External protectors" (*wai-hu*) refer to laypersons or members of the monastic saṅgha who attend to the needs of the retreatants. "Fellow practitioners" (*t'ung-hsing*) are fellow participants in the practice. For further discussion of these terms, see MHCK (T 46.43a–b) and *Kuan-hsin lun shu* (T 46.605c22–29). Here we have followed the sense that Kuan-ting gives in a parallel passage from the Kuan-hsin lun shu (T 46.601b20–22): "One must have external protectors who, day and night, regulate one's meals and are diligent and patient, like a mother caring for her children. Also one must have excellent fellow practitioners of serious

"Though my flesh and bone may waste away, I will train in this samādhi without rest until I have achieved it."

[12b11] Arouse in yourselves such great faith that nothing can despoil it; pour forth such great effort that nothing can equal it; let the wisdom that you attain be so great that no one can challenge [or lead it astray]; and always attend your good teacher faithfully.[92] Until the three months are over do not entertain worldly thoughts or desires for even as long as it takes to snap your fingers. Until the three months are over do not go off to lie down[93] for even as long as it takes to snap your fingers. Until the three months are over walk up and down (*ching-hsing*) without pausing, except when sitting down to take meals or when [exiting] from the left and [entering] from the right [in order to relieve oneself, etc.].[94] Expound the scriptures to others without any expectation of clothing or

---

demeanor and firm discipline, who act like persons traveling together on a perilous road."

Chan-jan (T 46.186b2–3) says: " 'External protectors like mothers,' etc., means that they should not starve you nor overfeed you but treat you in a way that is both loving, yet strict. [The idea that] 'fellow practitioners should be like individuals together traversing a precipitous path' means that if one is lost, all are destroyed. Fellow practitioners should [approach the practice in] this way."

92. The four items in this sentence are the first of four such sets of four listed in the third chapter of the *Pan-chou san-mei ching*, titled, "the four activities or items." Together they are presented as essential conditions that hasten a bodhisattva's attainment of this samādhi (T 13.906a). They are also listed in the **Daśabhūmika-vibhāṣa Śāstra*, T 26.86b–c. For translation from the Tibetan, see Harrison, *The Samādhi of Direct Encounter with the Buddhas of the Present Age*, pp. 45–46.

93. The three-fascicle *Pratyutpanna-samādhi Sūtra* (T 13.906a) has the same expression as the MHCK here—"lie down or leave." However, the one-fascicle version (T 13.899c) as well as the **Daśabhūmika-vibhāṣa Śāstra* (T 26.86c) have "sleep" or "become drowsy." The Tibetan agrees closely with the latter two versions: "not give in to sloth and torpor" (*styāna-middhi*). We have followed Chan-jan (T 46.186b11–12) here in rendering the line "go off to lie down."

94. As noted previously, the binome *ching-hsing*, which renders the Sanskrit term "*caṅkrama*," technically refers to the meditative exercise of slowly pacing to and fro along a straight line. In China (notably in T'ien-t'ai and Pure Land works) it comes to be used interchangeably with such terms as *hsüan-jao* and *hsing-tao* to designate the ritual action of *pradakṣiṇā* or "clockwise circumambulation of an altar or holy site." Although the Sanskrit original here (according to the Tibetan) indicates *caṅkrama*, Chih-i and other medieval Chinese advocates of pratyutpanna samādhi clearly define the practice as ritual circumambulation or *pradakṣiṇā* around an altar to Amitābha (see MHCK, T 46.12b5; *Kuan-hsin lun shu*, T 46.601b17). We have followed Chan-jan here (T 46.186b19–20), who, noting discrepancies between the **Daśabhūmika-vibhāṣa Śāstra* and the sūtra, insists that the line from the śāstra that reads "except for relieving oneself, eating, sitting down and rising" belongs with the third in this set of four items.

food from them in return.[95] It says in the gāthās of the **Daśabhūmika-vibhāṣa Śāstra* "[In order to bring about this samādhi,] become intimate with worthy spiritual friends. Persevere diligently without slacking off. Let your wisdom be extremely firm, and the power of your faith incapable of being shaken or led astray."[96]

[12b18] **Speech.** When to speak and when to keep silent with the mouth: while the body walks for ninety days without pausing, for ninety days the mouth ceaselessly chants (*ch'ang*) the name of Amitābha Buddha without pausing, and for ninety days the mind recollects (*nien*) [the form and meritorious qualities of] Amitābha Buddha without pausing. One may chant and recollect simultaneously, or first recollect and then chant, or first chant and then recollect. But reciting and recollecting are, nevertheless, to be carried out continually without a moment's pause.[97] The merit that accrues from chanting [the name of] Amitābha is equal to that of chanting [the names of all] the Buddhas in the ten directions. However, Amitābha alone is to be regarded as the focus of this practice. Every step, every utterance, and every thought should be centered solely upon the Buddha Amitābha.

[12b24] **Mind.** With respect to mind we discuss calming and contemplation. One should mentally recollect the Buddha Amitābha ten trillion Buddha lands to the west, in a jewelled pavilion, under a jewelled tree, on an island in a jewelled pond in a jewelled land, expounding sūtras while sitting amid a congregation of bodhisattvas.[98] Recollect the Buddha

95. This is the second set of four conditions listed in chapter 3 of the three-fascicle *Pratyutpanna-samādhi Sūtra* (T 13.906a17–20) and the **Daśabhūmika-vibhāṣa Śāstra* (T 26.86c). Chih-i omits the third and fourth sets, perhaps for the reason that they appear to be far more peripheral to the actual ninety-day rite than the two sets listed here.

96. T 26.86b17–25. We have followed Chan-jan (T 46.186b20–23) here, who treats the four as separate conditions. Muranaka (pp. 120–121), apparently following the prose commentary of the **Daśabhūmika-vibhāṣa Śāstra* (T 26.86b), takes the verses conditionally: "If you become intimate with a worthy spiritual friend and persevere unremittingly, your wisdom will become keen and your power of faith unshakeable." Chan-jan (T 46.186b10–11) says of the good teacher: " 'Good' in this case means skill in identification of the signs of impasse and progress in the [cultivation of] samādhi."

97. Chan-jan (T 46.186b24–26) explains: "[The passage] that begins with 'ninety days' and runs through 'mentally recollects Amitābha Buddha without pause' instructs [the practitioner] in the application of the three activities [of body, speech, and mind]. . . . Although it speaks of 'prior to,' 'after,' or performing them 'simultaneously' with the mind, from one instant to the next one must allow no lapse in [at least] one of these elements [of recitation and recollection]."

98. *Pratyutpanna-samādhi Sūtra*, T 13.905a. In the sūtra the number of Buddha lands is one quintillion. No mention is made of the jewelled scenery.

(*nien-fo*) continually like this for three months.[99] How should you think of him? Mentally recollect his thirty-two marks, one by one in reverse order, from the thousand-spoked wheel on the sole of each foot to the invisible mark at the top of his head.[100] Then you should review all the marks in the proper order, from the mark at the top of his head to the thousand-spoked wheels on his soles and think to yourself, "Let me come to have these marks as well."

[12b29] Ponder in this way: "Do I apprehend the Buddha via the mind? Do I apprehend the Buddha via the body? No, the Buddha is not to be apprehended through the mind, nor is the Buddha apprehended through the body; nor is the form of the Buddha to be apprehended via the mind, nor is the mind of the Buddha to be apprehended via form."[101]

99. T 13.905a–8. The sūtra here specifies a period of seven days for the practice, but a fixed period of three months is also specified in the four sets of ancillary disciplines from chapter 3 of the *Pratyutpanna-samādhi Sūtra*.

100. An aspect of the *uṣṇīṣa* or fleshy lump on the Buddha's cranium. It is "invisible" to beings of the three realms of delusion but can be perceived by saints. Technically it is one of the eighty minor excellences. The reference to the invisible mark (as well as the vow that concludes this paragraph) is from the *Pratyutpanna-samādhi Sūtra*, T 13.905b. The procedure for recollecting the Buddha's marks in proper (*shun-yüan*) and reverse (*ni-yüan*) sequence does not originate from the *Pratyutpanna-samādhi Sūtra* but from the highly influential *Kuan-fo san-mei hai ching* (T 15.648c13–16) introduced by Buddhabhadra in the early fifth century. Likewise, the *Pratyutpanna-samādhi Sūtra* does not offer a description of the thirty-two marks and eighty minor excellences; but a detailed account of these is provided in both the *Kuan-fo san-mei hai ching* (T 15.648c–668b) and the **Daśabhūmika-vibhāṣa Śāstra* (*Shih-chu pi-p'o-sha lun*), T 26.68c–70c.

101. A rather free paraphrase of the *Pratyutpanna-samādhi Sūtra*, T 13.908b. The Tibetan text has the concept of the "achieving of *sambodhi*" or "the full awakening of Buddhahood" itself as the object of reflection here (see Harrison, *The Samādhi of Direct Encounter with the Buddhas of the Present Age*, pp. 68–69). But the Chinese text, by using the character for "Buddha" (*fo*) rather than for bodhi, creates a certain amount of ambiguity in the passage. It is not clear as to whether the verb-object "*te-fo*" is to be read as "the visual apprehending of the Buddha or qualities of Buddhahood in contemplation and samādhi" or the concept of "attaining or achieving Buddhahood (*saṃbodhi*) itself." We have followed Chan-jan, who reads the passage predominantly as a dialectic analysis of the eidetically conceived image of the Buddha and Buddhahood.

Chan-jan (T 46.186c19–21) explains: "The first part of the passage briefly analyzes (*t'ui*) [the relationship between] one's own body and mind and the [qualities of] the Buddha [as envisioned in] samādhi. Through whose auspices is this body and mind of Buddha apprehended? The first two lines represent the main analysis. In the lines beginning with 'the Buddha is not apprehended through,' etc., having analyzed one realizes that [one's own] mind and the Buddha are both inapprehensible. How can I perceive the body and mind of the Buddha through my own body and mind? This sets out the four alternatives of the tetralemma:

[12c3] Why? As concerns "mind," the Buddha is without mind; as concerns "physical form" the Buddha is without form. Hence perfect enlightenment (*sambodhi*) is not to be apprehended or achieved via "physical form" or "mind." The material form of the Buddha is already extinct, [and so it is for the other aggregates] up to consciousness, which is also extinguished.[102] The foolish do not understand this extinction as it is expounded by the Buddha, but the wise comprehend it well. Buddhahood is not to be apprehended via body or speech, nor is Buddhahood to be apprehended even via wisdom.[103] Why? Because no matter how deeply one seeks for wisdom, wisdom is inapprehensible, [just as] when the self seeks to know self, it is ultimately unable to apprehend it. Nor is there anything to be seen. All dharmas are fundamentally lacking in content. One must destroy any notion of a fundament and eradicate the very idea of a foundation![104]

[12c8] It is like dreaming that one has obtained the seven precious jewels and all one's relatives are filled with joy: upon waking and remembering the dream, one will not be able to find where they have disappeared to, no matter how one tries. Recollect the Buddha (*nien-fo*) in this way.[105] Again, it is like the story of the wanton woman named Sumanā of Śrāvastī.[106] Hearing of her, a certain man [living in Rājagṛha] rejoiced. At night he dreamt that he had intercourse with her, but upon awakening

---

that 'Buddhahood is not achieved or apprehended through the mind' means that I do not apprehend this mind of Buddha through my mind; 'not achieved or apprehended through the body' means that I do not apprehend the body of Buddha through my body. [The lines] 'not apprehend the form of the Buddha through the mind,' etc., reverse the arrangement. The word 'my' has simply been abridged here."

Kōgi (1.444) notes: "This visualization of the Buddha is elucidated on the basis of consciousness only. That is to say, the object is itself simply mind."

102. That is, sensation, conception, and volitional responses.

103. From the *Pratyutpanna-samādhi Sūtra*, T 13.908c.

104. Paraphrased from the *Pratyutpanna-samādhi Sūtra*, T 13.908c. Chan-jan (T 46.186c21–25) explains: "A Buddha's body [of material form] and mind are devoid of mark, utterly inapprehensible. My own body and mind are also like this. Body and speech represent corporal form. Wisdom represents mind. The very existence of material form and mind derives from the [false notion of] self. Because self ultimately does not exist, [the text] says, 'dharmas are originally inexistent.' Yet, in order to eradicate [any notion of] such a fundamental inexistence, [the text] says, 'destroy the fundament.' In order also to sever any notion of 'destroying' it says, 'eradicate the very idea of a foundation.' "

105. Here begins a series of six similes, all from the *Pratyutpanna-samādhi Sūtra*, T 13.905a–c.

106. This story also occurs in the TCTL, T 25.110b. In both this source and the *Pratyutpanna-samādhi Sūtra* there are three wanton women and three sex-starved men dreaming of them from afar.

and recalling his dream to mind he realized, "She did not really come to me, nor did I really go to her. Yet I did enjoy her in just the way I dreamed of." This is the way in which you should recollect the Buddha. Again, it is like a parched and starving man walking through a great swamp. Falling asleep, he dreams of delicious food, but when he awakens he finds that his belly is still empty. Thinking to yourself that all dharmas are as dreams, you should practice recollection of the Buddha (*nien-fo*) in the same way, pondering this over and over again without pause. Applying recollection in this manner you will be reborn in the land of the Buddha Amitābha.[107] This is called "maintaining recollection [of the Buddha] in accordance with his distinguishing marks."[108] Again, it is as when a

107. The western Pure Land of Sukhāvatī or "Highest Bliss." In the three-fascicle *Pratyutpanna-samādhi Sūtra* (T 13.905b) the Buddha Amitābha is made to say: "Recollect (*nien*) me continually if you wish to be reborn in my Pure Land." However, the single-fascicle version (T 13.899a29–b1) has: "Recollect or recite my name (*nien-ming*) continually." The single-fascicle text came to be favored by the Shansi Pure Land masters Tao-ch'o and Shan-tao, who began to emphasize the soteriological end of rebirth in the Pure Land through devoted recitation of the Buddha's name and the invocation of the power of Amitābha's original vow (see Shan-tao, *Kuan-nien fa-men*, T 47.24a19–20).

For such T'ien-t'ai masters as Chih-i and Chan-jan, it was the self-reliant act of mental concentration, the development of samādhi, and insight into the nature of mind itself that held primacy. With the steady growth of interest in Pure Land devotionalism among T'ien-t'ai circles of the late T'ang and Sung, however, there erupted a controversy over the status of the Buddha and his relation to the intrinsic nature of mind, especially as it pertains to contemplation. Is the Buddha invoked through contemplation and the mechanisms of salvation reducible simply to "mind" or "mind only," or does the Buddha maintain a distinctive "otherness," such that mind is subordinated to the power and reality of the Buddha? For an introductory discussion of this issue see Andō, *Tendai gakuron: shikan to jōdo*; and the same author's *Tendai shisō-shi*.

108. Chan-jan (T 46.186c25–187a2) explains the similes of the three dreams as follows: "As for this dreaming, the essential nature of mind is the perceptual ground or field (*ching*); the discerning or visualizing (*kuan*) is analogous to conjuring up the thought [of the object] (*yüan-hsiang*); and the full development of this discernment is analogous to the dream. This conforms perfectly with the perspective of the individual engaged in practice. Then again, the dharma-body is analogous to the perceptual ground or field; the body of retribution to the conjuring of the thought; and the body of response or manifestation to the dream. This conforms to the perspective of the [functioning that characterizes] the sphere of Buddhahood. Furthermore, the Buddha [that is visualized] is analogous to the perceptual ground; the practitioner [who visualizes] corresponds to the conjuring of the thought; and the vision of the Buddha, to the dream. This conforms to the perspective of stimulus and response. The [arrangement] works the same way for all three dreams. Therefore, whenever one generates meditative visualization, and that visualization emerges as an actual perception of features,

person holds another jewel over a piece of crystalline *vaiḍūrya*, so that the image of the one appears in the other. Or, it is as when a monk performs the white bone contemplation, and various rays of light seem to emanate from them: there is neither anyone who brings the light to his eyes, nor is the light within the bones themselves. What he sees is nothing but the work of his own mind. Again, it is like an image in a mirror, which neither enters the mirror from outside nor manifests [by itself] internally. One sees the image only because the mirror is clean.[109]

[12c19] If the material form (*rūpa*) of the practitioner is pure, then whatever he has[110] is pure. If he wants to see the Buddha, he will see the Buddha. Having seen him, he will beseech the Buddha to expound the dharma. Having beseeched, he will be answered, hear sūtras, and greatly rejoice.[111]

[12c20] Think to yourself,[112] "Whence comes the Buddha [that I see

---

in all cases it is endowed with these three aspects. Should one seek for the Buddha within this ultimate emptiness, [the Buddha] is unobtainable. Thus one should know that the first and third of the three dreams illustrate how [the image of the dream] is inapprehensible even though it is visible. The second dream illustrates how, although unobtainable, the dream is still seen."

109. Chan-jan (T 46.187a16–20) says: "The three similes of the jewel, etc., are essentially the same as those of the dream. The second jewel represents the subjective mind that focuses on the object; the crystalline *vaiḍūrya* represents the perceptual field [or ground of mind] itself; and the manifesting of the reflected image is analogous to the dreamlike vision. The contemplation of the bones and the image in the mirror likewise include these three aspects. From a slightly different perspective, [we may consider] the so-called manifestation of the provisional on the basis of emptiness: The crystalline *vaiḍūrya* is analogous to emptiness; and the manifesting of the reflected image is analogous to the [appearance] of provisional reality. There originally being no bones is analogous to emptiness, while the manifestation of their radiant light is analogous to [manifestation of] provisionality. The clear mirror is analogous to emptiness, the manifestation of the image to provisionality. The previous three [similes of the dream] also encompass the two perspectives of emptiness and provisionality, for on the basis of the mind of emptiness they bring forth the provisional."

110. The translation of this passage from the Tibetan by Harrison reads: "Because the forms are good and clear the reflections appear" (*The Samādhi of Direct Encounter with the Buddhas of the Present Age*, p. 37). Chan-jan (T 46.187a22–23) says: "The practitioner here is referred to as 'the material form (*rūpa*) of the practitioner.' Material form means the body. By 'whatever he has' we mean that whatever mark or feature he mentally conjures up, it appears."

111. Also from the *Pratyutpanna-samādhi Sūtra*, T 13.905c.

112. Although extremely influential, this whole paragraph is quite corrupt, greatly at variance in different recensions, and notoriously difficult to read. Alternate Chinese versions of it may be found in the following: the single-fascicle *Pan-chou san-mei ching* (T 13.899b–c), three-fascicle *Pan-chou san-mei ching* (T 13.905c–906a), *Pa-p'o p'u-sa ching* (T 13.923a1–6), *Ta-fang-teng ta-chi ching hsien-*

before me]? [From nowhere. He does not come here, and] neither do I go off elsewhere to see him. Whatever I think of, I see. It is my mind that creates the Buddha. It is my mind itself seeing the mind that sees the mind[113] of the Buddha. This mind or thought of the Buddha is my own mind seeing the Buddha. Mind does not itself know mind; mind does not itself see mind. When there are thoughts in the mind it is the deluded mind, while having no thoughts is nirvāṇa. This dharma cannot ultimately be indicated in words,[114] for [such efforts] are all products of

---

hu fen (T 13.877b–c), and TCTL (T 25.276b). The paragraph is absent from the Tibetan, but for Harrison's translation of the Chinese, see *The Samādhi of Direct Encounter with the Buddhas of the Present Age*, p. 43. The MHCK version of the passage agrees perfectly with that offered by Kuan-ting in the *Kuan-hsin lun shu* discussion of the constantly walking samādhi (T 46.601c24–27).

In our translation we follow Chan-jan's gloss of the passage (also see Muranaka, pp. 124–125), which we include in full here. Chan-jan (T 46.187b10–21) comments: "Now we explain the passage at hand in its entirety: The first line can be understood from the context of the sūtra. Next, the word 'Buddha' that appears in the various lines beginning with 'that I recollect,' etc., in every case encompasses two meanings. The first is the [eidetic] vision of the Buddha that is produced in samādhi through [the power of] one's own mind. The second is the [actual] Buddha of the western direction [whose presence] is invoked through causal stimulation (*yin-kan*). Here both senses are included, and together they constitute a single object or referent. [However], in order to accord with principle (*li*) the passage is explained on the basis of the first perspective [i.e., the eidetic image of the Buddha produced in samādhi]. Once samādhi has been achieved, whatever one thinks of will thereupon appear. The fact that this visionary experience is itself the essential nature of mind is what is meant by [the phrase] 'mind creates or produces the Buddha.' Because this Buddha is produced by the mind, when one sees a vision of the Buddha it is called '[mind] seeing one's own mind.' If one sees one's own mind, it is tantamount to 'seeing the Buddha's mind,' for that mind or thought of the Buddha is in fact one's own mind. [The line from] 'this mind or thought of the Buddha' to 'seeing the Buddha' explains that the Buddha perceived [in the vision] is not different from one's own mind. [The line from] 'mind does not itself known mind' to 'see the mind' explains that even though one sees the Buddha, when one seeks for the perceiver, the mind-sense, object, and act of cognition, they are all found to be unobtainable. The thrust [of the contemplation], then, is that one simply discerns one's own mind as well as the vision of the Buddha to be inseparable from the dharma-nature. As such, seeing the mind of the Buddha is the same as seeing one's own mind. One's own mind and the Buddha's mind are themselves none other than the middle way. It is not necessary to go on to establish further predications, such as the mutual eradication of the pair, etc."

113. The Chinese term used here, *hsin*, can also be understood to mean "thought," in the sense that the Buddha that is seen is the "thought of the Buddha" created by the meditator's mind.

114. The different Chinese recensions of the *Pratyutpanna-samādhi Sūtra* are at

thought. [Thus] even when there are thoughts present, they are to be understood as empty and inexistent.

[12c25] It says in the gāthās, "Mind does not know mind: what has mind cannot see mind. When thoughts arise in the mind, this is delusion; when thoughts are absent this is nirvāṇa."[115] The sūtra also says, "The Buddhas attain liberation via the mind.[116] When the mind is without stain it is called, 'pure.'[117] Even in the lower five destinies it is fresh, pure, and not subject to material form.[118] Whoever understands this attains the great way."[119] This is called the "seal of the Buddha" [in the sūtra].[120] There is [in this seal of the Buddha] nothing to be coveted, nothing to be attached to, nothing to be sought after, and nothing that could be an object of thought. All existence [of an object] is exhausted, and all desire exhausted.[121] Hence there is nowhere whence the seal of the Buddha

---

variance here, some offering *lo* "take delight or pleasure in" or *chien* "firmness, substantiality" in place of the MHCK *shih* "indicate in words." The Tibetan apparently reads more in conformity with the sense of "*chien*"—i.e., "these dharmas are insubstantial"—rather than the MHCK reading of "this dharma cannot be indicated in words," or the other scriptures that read "these dharmas offer no delight or pleasure." We have followed MHCK and Chan-jan.

115. From the *Pratyutpanna-samādhi Sūtra*, T 13.906c.

116. Chan-jan (T 46.187b6–7) says: "All the Buddhas attain Buddhahood through discerning that their own minds are not different from the Buddha-mind."

117. MHCK is at variance with the sūtra here (T 13.908c–909a). Chan-jan (T 46.187b28–29) says: "This explains [the nature of] the mind that is the object of discernment mentioned in the previous line. Mind is like the Buddha-mind. The Buddha-mind is free of all stain, and so is one's own mind."

118. Chan-jan (T 46.187b29–c3) says: "The five destinies [of rebirth] arise from the mind. The essential substance of mind is fundamentally pure. Although it pervades the five destinies, it is unaffected by their forms. It is analogous to a person with eye disease, who sees flowers all over the sky. Even though the flowers pervade the sky, the sky is unaffected by them. It is the same with [the different states] of ice, waves, flowing water, and steam [which do not impinge upon the essential nature of water]."

119. *Pratyutpanna-samādhi Sūtra*, T 13.909a.

120. Ibid., T 13.919b. "The Seal of the Buddha" is the title of the last chapter of the three-fascicle *Pratyutpanna-samādhi Sūtra*. Chan-jan (T 46.187c4) says: " 'Buddha seal' demonstrates [the nature of] the foregoing object of contemplation: since it is none other than reality itself, we call it 'the Buddha seal.' "

121. Chan-jan (T 46.187c5–8) says: "This elucidates the features of the contemplation itself: one 'does not crave' for existence, 'does not become attached' to emptiness, and 'does not seek after' the middle. Because one is free of these three thoughts, we say that 'all existence or presence [of an object] and all desire are exhausted.' 'Existence [of an object]' refers to the objective field of contemplation; 'desire' refers to the wisdom that contemplates. Subject and object both vanish;

could arise, and nowhere whither it could vanish. There is nothing that could be annihilated. This is the essence of the way, the foundation of the way. Adherents of the two vehicles[122] cannot despoil this seal.[123] How much less could it be destroyed by the depravities of the māras!

[13a3] The **Daśabhūmika-vibhāṣa Śāstra* explains that a bodhisattva who has newly put forth the resolution to seek perfect enlightenment first recollects the thirty-two physical marks of the Buddha.[124] Each mark is contemplated, respectively, in terms of its substance, action, effect, and function.[125] Contemplating in this manner he attains the lesser degree of power. Next he recollects the forty unique or unshared dharmas of a Buddha and thereby attains the middling degree of power. Then he recollects the Buddha as ultimate reality and so attains the superior degree of power [in the practice]. Yet [in all three of these levels of Buddha recollection] he must become attached neither to the form body nor to the dharma body of the Buddha.[126]

[13a6] It says in the gāthās [of the **Daśabhūmika-vibhāṣa Śāstra*], "Be attached to neither the form-body nor the dharma-body, but be fully aware that all dharmas are eternally quiescent, like space."[127]

---

because they vanish, there is 'no arising' [of any Buddha seal] 'nor any means for [such a seal] to arise.' Not arising, there is also 'no perishing.' "

122. Chan-jan (T 46.187c13–14) says: "Even the annihilationism of the two vehicles cannot despoil it."

123. The entire paragraph is a paraphrase of the *Pratyutpanna-samādhi Sūtra*, T 13.919b.

124. T 26.86a. This is from a four-line gāthā that reads, "If a bodhisattva who has just put forth the thought of enlightenment recollects the Buddha in terms of the marvelous features denoted by the ten epithets of the Buddha, then he will not lose the image of the Buddha, just as if he were looking at his own image in a mirror."

125. Ibid., T 26.64c27–29. The śāstra distinguishes only three perspectives for contemplating the marks: the substance of the mark, the action or karmic cause [that produces] the mark, and the effect or result of the mark. MHCK and Chan-jan elicit a fourth perspective not mentioned in the śāstra: the function of the mark. Chan-jan (T 46.188a4) explains the latter as follows: "Each [mark] has its unique function of benefitting others."

126. Ibid., T 26.86a. These three degrees of power in the practice of "Buddha recollection or mindfulness samādhi" (*nien-fo san-mei*) are matched with three levels of contemplation of the Buddha: (1) the ten epithets (*shih-hao*) and thirty-two marks of the body of form (*rūpa-kāya*), (2) the forty unshared or unique dharmas (i.e., spiritual powers and merits), which are referred to in the śāstra as the dharma body (*dharmakāya*), and (3) the Buddha as ultimate reality or *sarvadharmabhūtatā*. A list of eighteen unique or unshared dharmas (*aveṇikāḥ dharmāṇ*) is more commonly encountered in Mahāyāna works.

127. Ibid., T 26.86a.

Exhortation to Practice

[13a7] The exhortation to practice: if one should wish to acquire wisdom as vast as the ocean, so that no one could be considered one's teacher,[128] and if one should wish, while sitting here and without resorting to superhuman powers, to be able to see all the Buddhas, hear everything they expound, and take in all that one hears from them,[129] then the constantly walking samādhi is the best of all meritorious practices. This samādhi is the mother of the Buddhas, the eye of the Buddhas, the father of the Buddhas. It is the unproduced, greatly compassionate mother. All Tathāgatas are produced from these two dharmas [of father and mother].[130]

[13a12] If a billion worlds with all their grasses and trees were to be pulverized, and each mote of dust were to become a Buddha-world, and if one were to fill all these Buddha-worlds with treasure to use as alms, then the merit derived from this would be exceedingly great. Yet it would not compare to the merit obtained from hearing this samādhi without astonishment or fear, much less to the merit obtained from receiving [this teaching] in faith, keeping it, reading, reciting, and expounding it for others. Or, even more so, the merit obtained from practicing it with concentrated mind. It is like the field that indirectly produces the cow's milk. How much greater again will be the benefit if one is able to perfect this samādhi! Hence the merit obtained from this samādhi is incalculable, immeasurable.[131]

[13a16] The **Daśabhūmika-vibhāṣa Śāstra* says, "If the fires at the end of the kalpa, officials, bandits, malice, poison, nāgas, noxious pneuma, wild beasts, and a host of diseases should assail this person, it would not make the slightest bit of difference.[132] The person [who performs this samādhi]

128. From the *Pratyutpanna-samādhi Sūtra*, T 13.903b.

129. The **Daśabhūmika-vibhāṣa Śāstra*, T 26.68c.

130. The *Pratyutpanna-samādhi Sūtra* states (T 13.913c): "This samādhi is the eye of bodhisattvas, the mother of all bodhisattvas, the refuge of all bodhisattvas, that from which all bodhisattvas are born." The **Daśabhūmika-vibhāṣa Śāstra* (T 26.25c) says: "Pratyutpanna samādhi is the father, great compassion and the patience of the nonarising [of dharmas] is the mother; all tathāgatas are born from these two dharmas." See also TCTL, T 25.314a, where similar claims are made.

Chan-jan (T 46.188b13–16) explains: "The wisdom that knows reality is the mother of the Buddhas. To see the middle [truth] is the eye of the Buddhas. Skillful use of expedient devices (upāya) is the father. Unconditioned compassion is [again] the mother. Question: Why are there two items for the mother? Reply: The wisdom that knows reality is the generative [mother]; compassion is the nurturing [mother]. If compassion and wisdom are not both present, the true son will not reach full [adulthood]."

131. All from the **Daśabhūmika-vibhāṣa Śāstra*, T 26.87c–88a. The same simile is found, however, in the *Pratyutpanna-samādhi Sūtra*, T 13.907c–908a.

132. The śāstra also mentions his being assailed by malicious bandits (in

will be constantly protected, thought of, and praised by all the devas, nāgas, and other members of the eight divisions of superhuman beings as well as by all the Buddhas. They will all want to see him and come to wherever he is. Those who hear of this samādhi and sympathetically rejoice in the above four kinds of merit cause all the Buddhas and bodhisattvas in the three times to rejoice sympathetically as well. [But the merit of actually performing this samādhi] exceeds even the above four kinds of merit."[133] Not to practice such a dharma means to lose an incalculably precious treasure, and both men and gods will grieve over this. [One who, upon hearing it, does not practice this samādhi,] resembles a person with a benumbed sense of smell who has his hands full of sandalwood yet is unable to smell it,[134] or the farm lad who wagered a precious jewel against a mere ox.[135]

Part Walking/Part Sitting Samādhi[136]

[13a24] Third is the explanation of the samādhi that involves part walking and part sitting. Again the procedure for practice (*fang-fa*) is treated first, followed by the exhortation to practice (*ch'üan-hsiu*). The procedure

---

MHCK the characters for "malicious" and "bandits" have been inverted), lions, tigers, wolves, vicious beasts, nāgas ("dragons"), poisonous snakes, *yakṣas*, *rākṣasas*, *kumbhāṇḍas*, *piśācās*, humans, nonhumans, as well as by diseases of the eye, ear, nose, tongue, mouth, and teeth, among others.

133. **Daśabhūmika-vibhāṣa Śāstra*, T 26.88a–b (see also *Pratyutpanna-samādhi Sūtra*, T 13.912c–913a). The MHCK paraphrase of the **Daśabhūmika-vibhāṣa Śāstra* is quite garbled here. The śāstra (T 26.88b2–12) says: "If there were a person who had merely heard of this samādhi, he would still be joyful in four ways that would turn him toward supreme enlightenment: (1) when constantly seeking to hear much of how the Buddhas of the past practiced the bodhisattva path, he rejoices in their samādhis, while thinking, 'I too will be like that'; (2) when hearing of the Buddhas of the present he rejoices in their samādhis, thinking 'I too will be like that'; (3) when hearing of how the Buddhas of the future will practice the bodhisattva path, he rejoices in their samādhis, thinking 'I too will be like that'; (4) when hearing of the samādhis that the bodhisattvas of the past, future, and present practice . . . thinking, 'I also rejoice.'. . . Such sympathetic joy is not a hundredth part, not a hundred quadrillionth part of the supreme merit of actually performing the samādhi. The merit derived is beyond expression by numbers. The actual practice of this samādhi confers incalculable, unlimited recompense."

134. From the *Pratyupanna-samādhi Sūtra*, T 13.907a, in which the man not only cannot smell its actual fragrance but also claims that it stinks.

135. Ibid., T 13.907a–b. In the sūtra a merchant offers to sell a jewel, so bright it can be used at night to light the way, to a farm youth. The youth does not recognize the true value of the jewel and is willing to pay only one ox for it.

136. The translation of the title is literal; it actually means "the practice of samādhi while alternately walking and sitting."

for practice, in turn, is divided into: what should and should not be done with the body, what to utter and when to keep silent with the mouth, and the calming and contemplation of the mind. This rubric of part walking and part sitting derives from two sūtras. The first of these, the **Mahā-vaipulya-dhāraṇī Sūtra*[137] says, "Circumambulate for 120 rounds. Then retire to sit and ponder [the sūtra]."[138] The *Lotus Sūtra* says, "If the person recites this sūtra while either walking or standing, or ponders it while sitting, I, Samantabhadra, will appear to him mounted on a white elephant with six tusks."[139] By these citations one may know that both sūtras espouse part walking and part sitting as their basic procedure.

Vaipulya Repentance[140]

[13a29] The vaipulya [repentance] is most exalted and must not be treated casually. If one wishes to practice it, the [guardian] spirits must

137. *Ta fang-teng t'o-lo-ni ching* (T no. 1339), a quasi-esoteric sūtra said to have been translated by Fa-chung during the Northern Liang (early fifth century). Its practice was widespread in China by the time of Hui-ssu and Chih-i. See Stevenson, "The T'ien-t'ai Four Forms of Samādhi," pp. 175–188; and Ōno, "*Hōtōdara-nikyō* ni motozuku sembō."

138. T 21.645b. The sūtra says: "Recite this text 120 times while circumambulating 120 times, then retire, sit, and ponder. Having finished pondering, recite this text again. Continue like this for seven days."

139. T 9.61a–b. The passage is from chapter 28, "The Encouragements of Universal Worthy," the *locus classicus* of the twenty-one-day lotus repentance (see Hurvitz, pp. 333–337).

140. In the **Mahāvaipulya-dhāraṇī Sūtra*, liturgical specifications for the vaipulya repentance are sparse and appear scattered over its four fascicles. The main seven-day rite (together with the receiving of the twenty-four precepts) is described in the first fascicle (T 21.645b2–c9); the ten dharma princes and various forms of offering, in the second fascicle (T 21.650b); and clothing (T 21.651a) and preparations for the rite and the preliminary beseeching of the twelve dream-kings, in the third fascicle (T 21.652a–b). In addition to this brief account in the MHCK, Chih-i also compiled two independent manuals for the vaipulya repentance, both of which treat the aspect of ritual performance in far more depth. They are *Fang-teng ch'an-fa* ("Procedure for the Vaipulya Repentance"), contained as document 6 in the KCPL (T 46.796a–798c), and the *Fang-teng san-mei hsing-fa* (T 46.943a–949a). The latter text—by style and content clearly a work of Chih-i—seems to have disappeared in China during the early T'ang period, only to be reintroduced from Japan in the eleventh century. Of Chih-i's three descriptions of the vaipulya rite, the *Fang-teng san-mei hsing-fa* is the earliest; the KCPL *Fang-teng ch'an-fa* from the middle of Chih-i's career; and the MHCK, the latest. See Satō, *Tendai daishi no kenkyū*, pp. 190–220.

Chan-jan (T 46.46.189a14–15) notes: "The details of ritual procedure (*shih-i*) given here are too insufficient to use [as a guide] for actual practice, so the text [of the MHCK] itself directs one to the [*Fang-teng ch'an-fa*] in the *Kuo-ch'ing pai-lu*."

grant confirmation.[141] Thus first you must seek a vision of the dream-kings. If you succeed in obtaining one, [it is a sign] that you are permitted to undertake the repentance.[142]

Procedure for Practice

[13b1] **Body.** Adorn a sanctuary for practice (*tao-ch'ang*) in a quiet and untrammeled place.[143] Daub the floor with scented plaster, as well as the inner and outer walls of the chamber. Fashion a round altar and paint it brightly.[144] Hang rainbow-colored pennants [about the room], burn in-

141. According to the **Mahāvaipulya-dhāraṇī Sūtra* (T 21.641c17–642c27), the dhāraṇī for this rite was revealed (by the Buddha King of Jewels) to the Bodhisattva Bouquet of Flowers so that the latter might subdue māras that were afflicting the Bhikṣu Sound of Thunder. When Sound of Thunder invoked the spell, his demonic tormenters submitted and pledged forever more to act as guardians of the vaipulya-dhāraṇī and the vaipulya rite. Thus they became the twelve dream-kings, whose permission must be sought (in the form of a divine sign) in order to perform the practice.

142. The Buddha says in the third fascicle of the sūtra (ibid., T 21.652a5–b10): "Whether I am still alive or whether I have already departed this world, if a son or daughter of good family comes to where you live and seeks (to be taught this) dhāraṇī sūtra, then have him seek for the twelve dream-kings. If he sees one, then you should teach him the seven-day practice." The names of the twelve dream-kings, as well as descriptions of auspicious dreams that confirm their sanction, follow (see also the first fascicle, T 21.642a).

Details concerning this preparatory phase of the rite are also provided by Chih-i in *Fang-teng san-mei hsing-fa* (T 46.b16–20): "For seven days [prior to the actual rite] one should practice circumambulation and recitation of the incantation until they are smooth. Confess [one's sins] with utmost sincerity, summon and pray to the dream-kings to reveal their forms to you. If you succeed in conjuring one of them, you have permission to undertake the repentance." See also KCPL, *Fang-teng ch'an-fa* (T 46.797a8–17).

Fang-teng san-mei hsing-fa (T 46.943a–944a), drawing on the fourth fascicle of the sūtra (T 21.656a–657b), also includes a list of ancillary penance rites that may be used by members of the sevenfold saṅgha to absolve grave sins that obstruct permission to perform the main seven-day rite.

143. Chan-jan (T 46.189b23–25) says: "One should set up the sanctuary in a *saṅghāraṇya* or *saṅghārāma* (i.e., hermitage or monastery maintained by the monastic saṅgha). If one has worldly involvements, an ordinary household is permissible. This refers to two assemblies of laypersons [i.e., male and female]."

144. Chan-jan (T 46.c10–11) says of fashioning the round altar (*t'an*): "In the [*Record of*] *Rites* it says to make it by piling up earth. The Buddhist dharma follows this practice but fashions [the altar] in the shape of a lotus flower. Thus the text says to make a round altar and color it brightly." He says of the banners or pennants (T 46.189c14–16): "In the making of any banner or pennant it is not permissible to put the image of a Buddha or bodhisattva on it. Pennants are implements of offering to be offered to the object of offering."

cense from the seaside,[145] and light lamps. Set out thrones (*kao-tso*) [on the altar]; then invite [and install] in the sanctuary the images of the twenty-four deities.[146] If you wish to add more, it will make no difference. Set out foods of ritual offering [for the deities],[147] expending the utmost effort [in their preparation]. One's robes and sandals should be clean and new;[148] but if you do not have a new set, wash what you have that is old. When changing clothing as one enters or exits the sanctuary, take care not to allow this [purified set] to become mixed with [impure clothing].[149] Over the course of the seven days observe the postnoon fast[150] and bathe the body three times daily.[151]

145. See the **Mahāvaipulya-dhāraṇī Sūtra*, T 21.657a. The sūtra also instructs (T 21.650a): "Daub plaster throughout the inside wall of the chamber, and draw on it with colored strokes." Apparently it is here referring to the making of frescoes. See *Fang-teng san-mei hsing-fa* (T 46.945a7–18) and KCPL, *Fang-teng ch'an-fa* (T 46797a17–29), for additional details concerning preparation and purification of the ritual site. Details concerning incense and aromatics are discussed in the sūtra, T 21.646b, 650b, 652b, passim. Chan-jan (T 46.189c16–17) identifies "incense from the seaside" as a form of sandalwood.

146. The sūtra (T 21.646b15–16) specifies that twenty-four deities are to be enshrined as the objects of veneration and offering but does not give a clear listing of who they might be. Chih-i in the *Fang-teng ch'an-fa* (T 46.797b4–20) sequence for summoning the deities (*chao-ch'ing*) lists the following: the ten Buddhas of the sūtra (venerated individually), the father and mother of the dhāraṇī (inclusive as a single item), ten dharma princes (individually), the Bhikṣu Sound of Thunder and Bodhisattva Bouquet of Flowers, the twelve dream-kings (venerated as a single inclusive item), and the śrāvakas (Śāriputra, etc., inclusive)—a total of twenty-five items. For the names of the ten dharma princes, see T 21.650b; for the ten Buddhas, see T 21.650c.

147. Following Chan-jan, T 46.189c25–26; see also T 46.185c20–21.

148. For specifications regarding clothing, see **Mahāvaipulya-dhāraṇī Sūtra*, T 21.651a. No mention of sandals appears in the sūtra. Details for clothing and footwear are given in both *Fang-teng ch'an-fa* (T 46.797a) and *Fang-teng san-mei hsing-fa* (T 46.944c–945a). Chan-jan (T 46.189c27) notes that, as with the robes, different sets of footwear are to be used inside and outside of the sanctuary.

149. According to *Fang-teng san-mei hsing-fa* (T 46.944c, 945a, 945b), the purified set of robes is retained solely for use within the inner sanctum of the hall, and clothing is changed upon exiting and entering. The following cautions are made against happenstance pollution of the sanctuary (T 46.945b23–24): "If one does not safeguard purity in this way, one will not be acting in accordance with the prescribed procedure. [The performance of] the rite will be of no benefit and may even result in further sins. Thus the participants must exert themselves to maintain purity carefully."

150. This is the regular practice for monks and one of eight special *uposatha* observances for laypersons. Chan-jan (T 46.190a2) says: "Throughout this [practice] they observe the rule of not eating after noon."

151. See the **Mahāvaipulya-dhāraṇī Sūtra*, T 21.645b26–27. Details for the bath

[13b6] On the first day make offerings to all the monks present, as much or as little as you feel is appropriate.[152] Then ask one who understands both the internal and external disciplinary codes to be your teacher.[153] Accept from him the twenty-four precepts of conduct[154] and the dhāraṇī incantation[155] and confess to the teacher any sins that you have committed.[156] [The rite must commence] on the eighth or the fifteenth day of the lunar month[157] and last for a fixed period of seven days.[158] By no means should this number of days be reduced, but one

---

house and the procedure for bathing are given in *Fang-teng san-mei hsing-fa*, T 46.945b.

152. See the **Mahāvaipulya-dhāraṇī Sūtra*, T 21.646b. The *Fang-teng san-mei hsing-fa* says (T 46.945a20–22): "One must perform one offering [to the monks] on the first day of the practice and another offering upon completion of the seven days. On the day when the [participants are] released from the sanctuary, they invite a congregation of monks. There is no prescribed number."

153. See the **Mahāvaipulya-dhāraṇī Sūtra* (T 21.645b), as well as *Fang-teng san-mei hsing-fa* (T 46.946a–b) and KCPL, *Fang-teng ch'an-fa* (T 46.797a), for details.

154. The twenty-four precepts are given in the **Mahāvaipulya-dhāraṇī Sūtra* at T 21.645c–646b, where they are described specifically as "twenty-four precepts of bodhisattva mahāsattvas" (T 21.646b7). Outside of its specific place among the T'ien-t'ai four forms of samādhi, the vaipulya repentance and its twenty-four precepts played a significant role as a tradition of bodhisattva precept ordination in China. See Stevenson, "The T'ien-t'ai Four Forms of Samādhi," pp. 176–188.

155. The incantation for the seven-day rite is given in the **Mahāvaipulya-dhāraṇī Sūtra* (T 21.645b) and in the *Fang-teng san-mei hsing-fa* (T 46.944a). Additional incantations are provided for aspirants who, due to having committed grave sins, must perform remedial purifications of a preliminary sort in order to receive permission to practice the seven-day rite. See the sūtra (T 21.656b–658b) and the *Fang-teng san-mei hsing-fa* (T 46.943b–944a) for details.

156. Chan-jan (T 46.190a25–27) comments regarding the qualifications of the master/confessor: "[This person] must be pure [in his practice], thoroughly versed in the features and details of doctrinal classification, and familiar with the [signs] of impediment. If he himself is guilty of grave offenses and knows nothing about [the nature of] impediments [to the path], how can he possibly be fit to function as a basis for the eradication of sins?"

157. See the **Mahāvaipulya-dhāraṇī Sūtra*, T 21.645c2. We have followed *Fang-teng san-mei hsing-fa* (T 46.945a7) and KCPL, *Fang-teng ch'an-fa* (T 46.797b2–3), here. Chan-jan (T 46.190a27–28) states: "As for the eighth and the fifteenth days of the lunar month, the two lunar fortnights of the dark [or waning] moon and light [waxing] moon are each marked by two days [i.e., first and eighth days for the waxing moon, fifteenth and twenty-third for waning]. Most resort to the waxing moon [i.e., the eighth day]. The lotus repentance (*fa-hua ch'an-i*) specifies any [of the six] *uposatha* days."

158. The **Mahāvaipulya-dhāraṇī Sūtra* suggests that the practice may be extended beyond seven days, "for as long as one deems suitable" (T 21.649b, 651a). Both *Fang-teng san-mei hsing-fa* (T 46.944a, 945a21, 946a9) and KCPL, *Fang-teng*

may extend the practice for as long as one is able to endure it. Up to ten persons are permitted to take part in the rite, but no more than this.[159] It is also open to laypersons.[160] All participants must prepare the requisite set of three garments sewn with single seams and have mastered beforehand Buddhist ceremonial procedures (*fo fa-shih*).[161]

[13b12] **Speech.** [Next we deal with] what to vocalize and when to be silent. One should memorize beforehand the dhāraṇī spell [from the sūtra], to the point where it can be recited smoothly. At the first interval of worship [on the first day], chanting in unison,[162] summon three times the three jewels [in the specific form of] the ten Buddhas [of the sūtra],[163] the father and mother of the *Vaipulya Sūtra* [dhāraṇī], and the ten princes of dharma.[164] This procedure for invitation (*chao-ch'ing fa*) appears in the

---

ch'an-fa (T 46.797c2) specify a fixed length of seven days. Chan-jan (T 46.190a29–b1) states: "Seven days represents the minimum length. One may not reduce it. But if one wishes to [continue to] pursue this practice he may do so for as long or as short as he desires. Thus Nan-yüeh [Hui-ssu] did it for over seven years."

159. See the **Mahāvaipulya-dhāraṇī Sūtra*, T 21.650b27. Also *Fang-teng san-mei hsing-fa* (T 46.945a) and *Fang-teng ch'an-fa* (T 46.797b). All specify a maximum of ten persons. Chan-jan (T 46.190b2), commenting on the use of this rite during the early T'ang, says: "Nan-shan [Tao-hsüan] relates, 'I have seen performances of the vaipulya [rite] in the capital where there are sometimes as many as one hundred people, at other times, half that number.' "

160. See the **Mahāvaipulya-dhāraṇī Sūtra*, T 21.650c–651a; also *Fang-teng san-mei hsing-fa*, T 46.944c.

161. For specifications in the sūtra regarding the robes, see the **Mahāvaipulya-dhāraṇī Sūtra*, T 21.651a. *Fang-teng san-mei hsing-fa* (T 46.944c–945a) stipulates that three sets of robes (of varying purity) are to be prepared. The purified robe worn in the sanctuary by laypersons is essentially the same as that of the mendicant, except for the fact that it must be of a single seam (T 46.944c29–945a2): "This robe is taken up and put on when entering the sanctuary to perform the rites for the Buddhas of the three times. Although one wears the robe of a mendicant, [the layperson] does not shave his or her head." Chan-jan (T 46.190b15–16) explains that the layperson is permitted the robe of a single seam but not the "patched" robe of the mendicant.

162. Following Chan-jan (T 46.190b19–21): "The 'first interval of the day' refers to the interval for early morning [worship]. A person with a bright and clear voice should be selected from the assembly to function as lead cantor (*hsien-tao*). As his voice trails off, the others join in in harmony."

163. The ten Buddhas are identified in KCPL, *Fang-teng ch'an-fa* (T 46.797b), as "Ratnarāja Buddha and the rest of the ten Buddhas, all derived from the [*Vaipulya*] sūtra." A somewhat different list is given in the sūtra itself (**Mahāvaipulya-dhāraṇī Sūtra*, T 21.650c3–5), which includes Amitāyus and the seven Buddhas of the past. Chan-jan (T 46.190b22) suggests that it is something of a selective combination of the two: "Ratnarāja, etc., together with the seven Buddhas."

164. Chan-jan (T 46.190b28) says: "The Buddha is the dharma king; the bodhisattvas are his sons (i.e., princes)." The ten dharma princes refer to ten great

Kuo-ch'ing pai-lu.[165] After the summoning, burn incense and mentally visualize the offering of the three deeds (*san-yeh kung-yang*).[166] When the offering is finished, venerate [with prostrations] the three jewels, which you have just summoned.[167] Following veneration, with a heart of utmost sincerity and tears of lament, proceed to confess your sins. When you are done, arise and perform 120 circuits of circumambulation. One round of circumambulation should correspond to one full recitation [of the spell]. You should neither dawdle nor move too hurriedly, and the recitation

---

bodhisattvas, including Mañjuśrī, Ākāśagarbha, and Avalokiteśvara, listed in the **Mahāvaipulya-dhāraṇī Sūtra* (T.21.650b).

165. See the "procedure for invitation" (*chao-ch'ing fa*) in KCPL, *Fang-teng ch'an-fa,* T 46.797b. The three jewels are invoked in the specific cult form of: (1) the ten Buddhas of the sūtra (each summoned individually), (2) the mother and father of the dhāraṇī (one item), (3) the ten dharma princes of the sūtra including Kusumaketu Bodhisattva (each individually), (4) all the śrāvakas and pratyekabuddhas including Śāriputra (inclusively), (5) Brahmā, Indra, and the twelve dream-kings (inclusively). Each is summoned with the formula, "With singleness of heart I humbly invite you! Homage to. . . ." The entire sequence is repeated three times.

This sentence was clearly inserted into the MHCK by Kuan-ting after Chih-i's death, for the KCPL was compiled in 605, twelve years after Chih-i passed away.

166. Chan-jan (T 46.190c5–7) says: "In offering of the three deeds, the body kneels with torso raised erect. With the mouth one chants aloud, and with the mind one visualizes. Nan-shan [Tao-hsüan] says that [this procedure] has been handed down from the ancients without ever having been standardized. The rite (*shih-i*) used for visualization [and offering] here is entirely as expounded in the *Samantabhadra Repentance* of Master T'ien-t'ai [Chih-i]."

The incense hymn and visualization used in KCPL, *Fang-teng ch'an-fa* (T 46.797b6–10) for the "offering of the three deeds" (and described at length in Chih-i's *Fa-hua san-mei ch'an-i,* T 46.950b–c) comes directly from Buddhabhadra's *Kuan-fo san-mei hai ching* (T 15.695a); see Stevenson, "The T'ien-t'ai Four Forms of Samādhi," pp. 362–372.

167. Chan-jan (T 46.190c7–11) says of this ritual veneration or salutation (*li*): "In all cases one's intentions must be absolutely sincere. With the body one performs the gesture of prostration (*li*). The general idea behind the method of prostration is as follows: the two knees should reach [the floor] first, then the two elbows [or forearms] follow, and finally the forehead touches the ground, so that the whole body bows down flush with the ground. One visualizes that one is at the feet of the Buddha, then extends one's hands and receives his feet, as though he were right before one's very eyes. In the posture of kneeling with knees flush, the three limbs [i.e., head and two forearms] are erect. One bends the torso slightly [i.e., in humility] and, with palms joined, fixes one's gaze on the true demeanor [of the Buddha]. People of recent times are quite remiss in this and completely neglect the proper form of kneeling. So long as the banner of arrogance is not cut down, the sea of karma will be difficult to overturn."

should be neither too loud nor too soft. Upon completing the circumambulation and recitation of the spell, venerate once more the ten Buddhas, the *[*Mahā*]*vaipulya-dhāraṇī Sūtra*, and the ten princes of dharma. When all this is done, withdraw [from the inner sanctum] to sit and ponder.[168] After meditating, arise once more to circumambulate and recite the spell. Then retire to sit and ponder again. When this cycle has been completed, begin the whole process over again. Continue in this way to the end of the seven days. Beginning with the second period (i.e., ritual cycle), one should omit the invitation sequence but continue to perform all the other procedures as usual.[169]

[13b21] **Mind.** Next we discuss calming-and-contemplation of the mind.[170] When the sūtra recommends "pondering," it means to ponder the "great incantation that burns away [evil] and secures [the good]" (*mahāḍahanadhāraṇī*).[171] Translated, this means "the great secret essence that

168. Chan-jan (T 46.190c15–16) says: "Pondering is as discussed in the section on calming and contemplation of the mind."

169. The **Mahāvaipulya-dhāraṇī Sūtra* (T 21.645b27–29) gives only the most minimal description of the rite: the three periods of bathing, change of clothing, 120 rounds of circumambulation and recitation of the spell, sitting and pondering, followed by another cycle of recitation and circumambulation. KCPL, *Fang-teng ch'an-fa* (T 46.797b), and MHCK, which are in close agreement with one another, expand on this format considerably. Regrettably, *Fang-teng san-mei hsing-fa* (T 46.943b) is missing its fifth chapter, which is alleged to describe in detail the ritual cycle.

The only important difference between the MHCK and the KCPL text here is that in the last of the seven sentences ("Starting on the second day . . .") the former (T 46.13b21) says "from the second period or interval drop the invitation sequence," where the latter has, "from the second day drop the invitation sequence." Chan-jan (T 46.190c16–17) asserts: "This refers to the mid-morning [interval of worship]. The first ritual cycle has been completed, and the second cycle is beginning. There is no need to invite the deities [again], so one proceeds directly to veneration of the Buddhas." *Kōgi* (1.469) disagrees and defends the KCPL, *Fang-teng ch'an-fa*, reading by invoking the norms of esoteric Buddhist ritual practice. Based on parallel evidence in *Fa-hua san-mei ch'an-i* (T 46.950a21–23, 954b14–17), there is a clear precedent for Chan-jan's interpretation.

170. Chan-jan (T 46.190c17–20) says: "Here [the text] first elucidates the method for discernment of reality (*shih-hsiang kuan-fa*). Then it explains the method for contemplation as it is applied to phenomenal activities (*li-shih kuan-fa*). For any sūtra or treatise it should be like this, not just the passage here."

171. *Mo-ho-t'an-ch'ih t'o-lo-ni*, the central incantation of the seven day rite. *Mo-ho* transliterates the Sanskrit *mahā*, meaning "great"; in Chinese *t'an* means to "strip away" or "block"; and *ch'ih*, "to secure." The character *t'an* may also be taken as a transliteration of the Sanskrit letter *ḍa*, possibly giving, as Mochizuki (*Bukkyō daijiten*, 4.3183d–3184a) suggests, the Sanskrit reading *mahāḍahana*, "greatly burning," as in "burning away the defilements."

checks evil and secures the good."[172] "Secret essence" (*pi-yao*) means nothing other than ultimate reality, the middle way, true emptiness.[173]

[13b24] In the **Mahāvaipulya-dhāraṇī Sūtra* it says, "I come from the midst of true reality. True reality has the mark of quiescent extinction (i.e., nirvāṇa). There is nothing to be sought in the mark of quiescent extinction. The seeker too is empty, as is the one who attains, the one who is attached,[174] the one who treats things as real,[175] the one who comes and goes during the samādhi practice, the one who speaks, and the one who questions. All these are empty too. Quiescent extinction is also utterly empty, as is the entire expanse of space, with its myriad realms and divisions. It is therefore in the midst of having nothing to seek that I seek [true reality]. This emptiness, which is itself empty, is the dharma of true reality. How should one seek it? Seek it through the six perfections."[176]

[13b29] This resembles the eighteen kinds of emptiness in the *Pañcaviṃśati*.[177] Furthermore, the *Nirvāṇa Sūtra*'s emptiness of the city of Kapilavastu, emptiness of the Tathāgata, and emptiness of *mahāparinirvāṇa* are not different from this emptiness.[178] If you employ the wisdom of

172. This translation offered by Chih-i appears to have no basis in the sūtra or the title of the incantation itself.

173. Chan-jan (T 46.190c28–29), possibly alluding to similar expressions in the *Lotus* and *Nirvāṇa* sūtras (e.g., *pi-mi chih tsang* or *pi-mi chih yao*), says: " 'Great' refers to the fact that it reveals and removes biased [clinging to] the lesser [teachings]. 'Secret' means that all the dharmas are in themselves but one dharma; 'essence' means that this one dharma encompasses all dharmas."

174. Chan-jan (T 46.191a22–23) says: "That is to say, the person who becomes attached to samādhi."

175. Following Chan-jan (T 46.191a23–24).

176. Condensed from the **Mahāvaipulya-dhāraṇī Sūtra*, T 21.645a11–22.

177. Discussed at length in the chapter on the eighteen emptinesses in the TCTL, T 25.285b–296b, they represent eighteen progressive refutations or realizations of emptiness, beginning with the emptiness of interior, exterior, and interior-exterior, and ending with the emptiness of both the existence and inexistence of the dharmas. For an English listing of them (expanded to twenty items), see the appendix of Murti, *The Central Philosophy of Buddhism*, pp. 351–356.

178. T 12.765c. The *Nirvāṇa Sūtra* explains here how the teaching that dharmas have an own-being is only for worldlings. That dharmas are without own-being (*svabhāva*) is a teaching reserved for the wise, for there is actually nothing that is really seen. Prajñā cannot be practiced; nirvāṇa cannot be entered. The six perfections, the five skandhas, the Tathāgata, are all empty. "That is why," says the Buddha, "I told Ānanda at Kapilavastu not to grieve" (for the destruction of the city and its inhabitants). Ānanda said then, "But Tathāgata, World-honored One, all my relatives have been exterminated. Why should I not mourn? Both the Tathāgata and I were born in this city, are of the Śākya clan, and have the same relatives. Why should the Tathāgata be the only one who does not mourn?" The Buddha replied, "Ānanda, you see Kapilavastu as something really existing, but I

this realization of emptiness to everything that you encounter, there will be nothing that will not function as a basis for contemplation.

[13c2] The word "vaipulya" (*fang-teng*) can mean "broad and level." But in this case *fang* means "method." There are four methods by which one may approach prajñā. That is to say, the four gates that lead to the pure and cool pond [of wisdom] represent "method" (*fang*).[179] *Teng* ("equal") means that the principle (*li*) with which one comes into tally is none other than the great wisdom of perfect equality and sameness.

[13c5] Requiring the practitioner to seek [a sign from] the dream-kings signifies the preliminary expediency of the first two views.[180] The sanctuary for practice represents the realm of cleanliness and purity: here one [threshes the grain], winnows the "chaff" of the five grounds [of delusion], and reveals the "rice kernels" of reality.[181] Also this signifies

---

see it as empty, quiescent, and inexistent. You see the Śākya clan all as relatives of yours, but because I practice the view of emptiness, I do not see any of them as really existing. For this reason, you become grief-stricken, while my body and visage shine more brightly than ever."

179. The remainder of the MHCK text on the vaipulya repentance is quite close to (and likely based upon) the section of KCPL, *Fang-teng ch'an-fa*, titled "[Symbolic] Representation of the Rite" (T 46.798a20–b18). Here *fang* could also mean "direction," with the four gates representing gates of the cardinal directions. The simile of the pure and cool pond is from the *Pañcaviṃśati* and its accompanying commentary, the TCTL (T 25.640c). Here Subhūti is presented as believing that only the clever can "enter the gate" to the pool of prajñāpāramitā, but the Buddha corrects him, explaining that one's potential for this feat depends not on the sharpness or dullness of one's faculties but simply on one's diligence, right thinking, and mental concentration. He distinguishes the "four gates" or teachings as perspectives devised to fit the differing capacities of beings. Chih-i later in MHCK (T 46.73c–75b) glosses the four gates as the four alternative perspectives of the existence tetralemma: the gate of existence, the gate of inexistence, the gate of both, and the gate of neither.

180. Chan-jan (T 46.191b13–14) says: "In the practice of contemplation one must first cultivate emptiness and provisionality. [The words] 'first cultivate' can also refer to the fact that one resorts to phenomenal [ritual activities] as the basis for performing contemplation."

181. None of the four commentators gives a scriptural source for this metaphor. We follow Chan-jan (T 46.191b17–23), who provides an ancient interpretation of the word *ch'ang* (from the compound *tao-ch'ang*, "sanctuary") as that portion of a field where, after the grain is harvested, the earth is leveled and packed down so that it may be used as a threshing floor. The five abodes or grounds probably refer to the five grounds of delusion or defilement (*vāsabhūmi*), although they are not explicitly identified as such by Chan-jan here. The *Śrīmālā Sūtra* (T 12.230a–c) lists them as: (1) delusions pertaining to view in the three realms, delusions pertaining to cultivation in the (2) desire realm, (3) form realm, and (4) formless realm, and (5) fundamental nescience. Chih-i generally uses a modified form of this arrangement, which includes (1) delusions pertaining to

the dharma body being adorned with meditation and wisdom. Daubing with scented plaster represents supreme moral purity (śīla). The five-colored canopy signifies how the contemplation of the five aggregates (skandha) and liberation from the fetters arouse great kindness and compassion that cover the dharmadhātu. The round altar represents the unshakable ground of reality. The silken pennants[182] signify the [flag of] dynamic and liberative understanding that is produced when [the flag of] the delusions [that flies] over the dharmadhātu is toppled. That the pennants and the altar are not separated from each other illustrates that there is no distinction between the dynamic and nondynamic [aspects of enlightenment].[183] The incense and lamp signify morality and wisdom.[184] The thrones show that all dharmas are empty and the Buddhas dwell amidst this emptiness.[185] The twenty-four images signify the enlightened wisdom that contemplates the twelve causes and conditions in both their proper and reverse sequences. The foods for ritual offering represent the vinegar of impermanence and painfulness, which serve as contemplations that assist the way (*chu-tao kuan*). The clean new clothes symbolize forbearance of quiescent extinction.[186] The accumulation of anger and the other delusions is called "old," while the overturning of anger and the other delusions and realization of this forbearance is called "new." The seven days of the practice signify the seven limbs of enlightenment.[187] The one-day [cycle] represents the one truth of reality. And the

view and (2) delusions pertaining to cultivation (both grouped together as delusions that involve the apprehending of marks), (3) the delusions that obscure multiplicity and inhibit the bodhisattva's expedient function or grasp of the provisional truth), and (4) fundamental nescience. See Nitta, *Tendai jissō-ron no kenkyū*, pp. 448–454.

182. The fact that they should be silk does not appear in the foregoing MHCK passage to which this line refers (T 46.13b3), but such a specification is present in the sūtra as well as in KCPL, *Fang-teng ch'an-fa* (T 46.797b4–5).

183. Chan-jan (T 46.191b22–23) says: "Delusion is identical to the dharmadhātu; therefore we say they are 'not separate.' "

184. Chan-jan (T 46.191b23) says: "The incense or fragrance of the precepts suffuses everywhere; the light of the lamp of wisdom illumines fully and completely."

185. Chan-jan (T 46.191b24): "The Buddhas, endowed with the wisdom of perfect enlightenment, dwell in the emptiness which is the realm of principle (*li*)."

186. This is the fifth in a sequence of five kinds of forbearance or patience (*kṣānti*) described in the *Jen-wang pan-jo p'o-lo-mi ching* (Sūtra of Benevolent Kings, T 8.826b–827b), where progress toward Buddhahood is correlated with the patience or acquiescence achieved with (1) suppression of the defilements, (2) faith, (3) being in accord with the way, (4) nonorigination or nonarising of the dharmas, and (5) quiescent extinction (nirvāṇa) of Buddhahood itself.

187. The seven *bodhyaṅga*: (1) mindfulness, (2) right understanding or discern-

three periods of bathing illustrate how contemplation of this one reality and cultivation of the three discernments may wash away the three obstacles and purify the three wisdoms.[188] The one teacher signifies the one truth of reality. The twenty-four precepts signify contemplation of the twelve causes and conditions in both proper and reverse order, which produces the precepts that arise with [realization of] the way.[189] To incant is to secure a matching response.[190] The *Ying-luo ching* explains that there are ten modes to the twelve causes and conditions, making a total of 120 items.[191] Each incantation of the spell corresponds to one item of the 120. These 120 items can be summed up simply as the three circuits of suffering, karma, and the afflictions.[192] To incant [the dhāraṇīs] with

---

ment of dharma, (3) zealous application, (4) joyousness, (5) ease, (6) samādhi or concentration, and (7) equanimity.

188. The three obstacles (corollaries of the three circuits) include the afflictions, karma, and retribution (i.e., circumstances of endowment and environment). The three wisdoms (based on TCTL, T 25.257c–260c) are omniscient wisdom (i.e., emptiness, *sarvajña[tā]*), wisdom of modalities of the destinies (*mārgākarajña[tā]*), which in T'ien-t'ai parlance corresponds to the view of provisionality, and omniscient wisdom of all modes (*sarvākarajña[tā]*) or the middle. Chan-jan (T 46.191c6–7) comments: "That which is washed away is the delusion; that which does the washing is contemplation. Since the body is without impurity, actor and object are both simultaneously pure."

189. The fifth among ten levels of moral purification or observance of the disciplinary codes listed in the *Tz'u-ti ch'an-men* (T 46.484c22–23) and MHCK (T 46.36c27–28); sixth in another anomalistic listing given at MHCK (T 46.17a). Also referred to as "precepts that accord with the way," this level of precept observance is said to "arise with the path or way" because it comes with the first substantial realization of the way in the *darśana-mārga* and the cusp of entry into sainthood (*ārya*). According to the *Abhidharmakośa* (T 29.72b), this is the highest of three levels of observance of Hīnayāna monastic discipline, which pertains to the practice of saints. It is a consequence of their undefiled (*anāsrava*) meditation in the form and formless realms.

190. Following Muranaka, p. 133. Chan-jan (T 46.191c9–10) says: "It is called 'securing a matching response' because the dharma is established with flawless match. That the incantation destroys the three circuits without error means that it 'matches or tallies.' "

191. *Pu-sa ying-luo pen-yeh ching*, T 24.1015a. The ten are given as (1) seeing the twelve in terms of self-hood, (2) mind being the twelve, (3) the twelve as nescience, (4) the twelve dependently arising from each other, (5) the twelve aiding each other's completion, (6) the twelve in the three acts (body, speech, mind), (7) the twelve in the three times, (8) the twelve in the three kinds of suffering (physical torment, loss or destruction of the pleasant, and impermanence), (9) the twelve as devoid of own-being, and (10) the dependently originating twelve. The sūtra offers no further explanation of their significance.

192. They are known as the three circuits (*san-tao*) because the (1) root afflictions (*kleśa*) cause (2) karma, which in turn brings (3) suffering (*duḥkha*) in the

respect to these [120] causes and conditions is equivalent to incanting [the dhāraṇīs] with respect to the three circuits. This may be construed as "repentance."

[13c22] Repentance performed on the basis of phenomenal activities (*shih ch'an-hui*) repents the circuits of suffering and karma, while repentance that accords with principle (*li ch'an-hui*) repents the circuit of the afflictions.[193] The text of the sūtra says, "Should a person break any of the rules of conduct, from those for novices to those for full mendicants, then by this [rite of] repentance he or she cannot fail to be restored to life [as a due member of the saṅgha]."[194] This is the passage in the sūtra that signifies repentance of the circuit of karma.[195] "The purification of the eye, ear, and the other six sense faculties" is the passage that represents repentance of the circuit of suffering.[196] "On the seventh day one will see the Buddhas of the ten directions, hear them expound the dharma, and attain the stage of no backsliding" is the passage in the sūtra that indicates repentance of the circuit of the afflictions.[197] When the three obstacles are eliminated, the tree of the twelve causes and conditions is toppled.[198] It also means that the hut of the five aggregates is

---

form of reciprocity. Suffering completes the cycle by generating renewed afflictions. As noted above, they are corollary to the three obstacles (*san-chang*). They may be said to represent a condensation of the cyclic action of the twelvefold chain of causation.

193. Repentance that accords with principle removes the root of nescience through the wisdom of emptiness, whereas repentance of phenomenal activity affects only the phenomenal elements of deeds and their potential reciprocity (see MHCK, T 46.39c3–41c6). For what is perhaps Chih-i's most lucid and thorough discussion of the different forms of repentance, see *Tz'u-ti ch'an-men*, T 46.485b6–487a16.

194. **Mahāvaipulya-dhāraṇī Sūtra*, T 21.656b1–4, 26. Chan-jan (T 46.191c6–7) says: "One who has committed serious infractions is a dead man as far as the dharma is concerned. But [this repentance] can restore one to purity and restore to life the essence of the precept [body]. If the repentance practice is performed successfully, there is no sin that will not be eliminated."

195. KCPL, *Fang-teng ch'an-fa* (T 46.796b), first matches the three circuits to specific items of the twelvefold chain of causation. Thus the circuit of the afflictions is assigned to members 8 and 9 (craving and attachment), the circuit of karma is assigned to members 2 and 10 (volitional impulses and existence), and the circuit of suffering is assigned to members 3 and 4 (consciousness and name-and-form), etc. Subsequently, the passages from the sūtra that follow here are assigned to the three obstacles rather than to the three circuits.

196. Location of this passage in the sūtra is unclear. KCPL, *Fang-teng ch'an-fa* (T 46.796c), cites an entirely different passage from the **Mahāvaipulya-dhāraṇī Sūtra* (T 21.645c2–7): "Anyone afflicted with leprosy, should he repent wholeheartedly, will without fail be cured."

197. Ibid., T 21.653b–c.

198. Chan-jan (T 46.192a9–11), citing the *Mahāvibhāṣa*, says that of the twelve

empty. By pondering reality one truly eradicates [the three obstacles]. That is why this [rite] is referred to as the repentance of "the real dharma of the Buddhas."[199]

Exhortation to Practice

[13c29] Next is the exhortation to practice. When the Buddhas attain the way, they all do so by means of this dharma. This is the father and the mother of Buddhas, the supremely great treasure of the world.[200] Whoever is able to practice it gains this treasure in its entirety. One who is able to read and recite it gains a middling portion of the treasure, and one who performs offerings to it with flowers and incense gains an inferior portion of the treasure. In the sūtra the Buddha and Mañjuśrī explain that even the inferior portion of the treasure is inexhaustible. Vaster yet are the middling and the superior parts. If one were to pile treasure from the earth up to the Brahma heaven as an offering to the Buddha, the merit from such an act would still be less than the merit gained by providing one who keeps this sūtra with a single meal, thereby satiating his body.[201] The merit to be gained is expounded at length in the sūtra.

Lotus Samādhi[202]

[14a5] For the lotus samādhi as well, the explanation is divided into procedure (*fang-fa*) and exhortation to practice (*ch'üan-hsiu*).

---

links of *pratītya-samutpāda*, the first two (from the past) may be considered the root of the "tree" of saṃsāra; the next five (of the present), its trunk and branches; the next three (of the present) its flowers; and the last two (future) links, its fruit.

199. From the **Mahāvaipulya-dhāraṇī Sūtra*, T 21.645b11–12.

200. The text of MHCK from the second half of this sentence down to the next to last line of the paragraph is condensed from ibid., T 21.647c22–648a16.

201. Ibid., T 21.649a16–20.

202. The lotus samādhi draws its name and basic inspiration from the *Lotus Sūtra*, the main scriptural source around which its cultus is organized and to which it is directed as an object of ritual veneration (for background see Shioiri, "Hokke sembō to shikan," pp. 307–336). In early T'ien-t'ai, two basic programs are described for the lotus samādhi: the first, which is often referred to as the lotus or Samantabhadra repentance (*fa-hua ch'an-fa or p'u-hsien ch'an-fa*), is a highly structured ritual repentance of twenty-one days' length that is based on procedures outlined in chapter 28 of the *Lotus* ("Encouragements of Samantabhadra") and the *Sūtra on the Procedure for Visualization of the Bodhisattva Samantabhadra* (*Kuan p'u-hsien p'u-sa hsing-fa ching*, T no. 277). The latter scripture (viewed as an extension of the last chapter of the *Lotus*) was translated by Dharmamitra during the first part of the fifth century and (along with another work claiming affiliation with the *Lotus*, the *Wu-liang-i ching*) was in time incorporated loosely into the extended cycle of the *Lotus Sūtra*.

The second program for the lotus samādhi, known as the "easeful and pleasurable course" (*an-le hsing*), is based on the eponymous chapter 14 of the *Lotus*. Unlike the twenty-one-day repentance, the easeful course is unstructured—

The Procedure for Practice

[14a6] The procedure once again covers what should and should not be done with the body, what to utter and when to be silent with the mouth, and the calming and contemplation of the mind.

[14a6] **Body.** Physical action involves ten aspects:[203] (1) adornment and purification of the sanctuary (*tao-ch'ang*), (2) purification of the person;[204] (3) offering of the three deeds (*san-yeh kung-yang*),[205] (4) invitation of the

---

completely fluid in form and open-ended in terms of length—and is presented as a course for more advanced practitioners who wish to dispense with ritual constraints and concentrate upon long-term cultivation of samādhi.

Scholarship has shown that the lotus/Samantabhadra repentance was practiced well before and beyond the confines of the T'ien-t'ai community; but this particular distinction between the twenty-one-day repentance rite and the easeful course appears to be peculiar to Hui-ssu and Chih-i. It is set forth for the first time in Hui-ssu's *Fa-hua ching an-le hsing-i* (T 46.700a9–b8) as well as in Chih-i's *Fa-hua san-mei ch'an-i* (T 46.949c12 and 955b18–c4)—the two early T'ien-t'ai treatises that stand as the *locus classicus* for the T'ien-t'ai lotus samādhi. Much of the discussion in the MHCK centers around these two sources and their twofold program of the lotus samādhi. For a brief description of the lotus samādhi based on early T'ien-t'ai sources, see Stevenson, "The Four Kinds of Samādhi in Early T'ien-t'ai Buddhism," pp. 67–72.

203. These ten ritual phases or procedures are based directly on Chih-i's *Fa-hua san-mei ch'an-i* (hereafter referred to in citations as *Ch'an-i*). The *Ch'an-i* is divided into five main chapters: exhortation to practice, preliminary expedients, method for developing single-minded perseverance upon entering the sanctuary, procedure for actual performance of the rite, and clarifying the signs that verify successful realization. The fourth chapter, "the actual performance," is in turn divided into ten sections, which set forth in detail the basic phases, gestures, and litanies of the ritual. The ten aspects or procedures listed here in the MHCK correspond to the ten ritual phases (*fang-fa*) of chapter 4, "the actual performance," with the exception that item 5 of the original list in *Ch'an-i* (praising the three jewels) has been dropped and the larger chapter 5, "signs that verify success," has been tacked on as the tenth item. See T 46.950a17–23; for an annotated translation of Chih-i's *Fa-hua san-mei ch'an-i,* see Stevenson, "The T'ien-t'ai Four Forms of Samādhi," pp. 468–537.

204. As with the vaipulya repentance, the ritual site is first purified with the scouring of fragrant plasters and the sprinkling of perfumed waters, and an altar is installed. However, in this rite no images of deities are enshrined; a copy of the *Lotus Sūtra* alone is enthroned upon the altar as the object of worship (see *Ch'an-i,* T 46.950a27–29). New and/or purified robes are provided for use in the sanctuary. For a full week prior to the rite the participants purify their bodies and minds, focus their thoughts, practice the ceremonies, and memorize the litanies (see *Ch'an-i,* T 46.949c13–21 and 950b9–13).

205. Offerings through the media of body, speech, and mind are made to the eternally abiding three jewels throughout the dharmadhātu by means of the same incense offering and visualization described previously in the vaipulya repentance (see note 166). Referred to regularly in T'ien-t'ai literature as the "offering of the

Buddhas (*ch'ing-fo*),[206] (5) veneration of the Buddhas (*li-fo*),[207] (6) confession of the six sense faculties (*liu ken ch'an-hui*),[208] (7) circumambulation [of the altar] (*hsüan-jao*),[209] (8) recitation of the sūtra (*sung-ching*),[210] (9) seated meditation (*tso-ch'an*),[211] and (10) [distinguishing the] signs of success in the practice (*cheng-hsiang*).[212] There exists a separate work of one

---

three deeds" (*san-yeh kung-yang*), this procedure is described in detail in the *Ch'an-i* (T 46.950b14–c3): It begins with the igniting of incense in a hand-held censer and verbal salutations and prostrations to the eternally abiding three jewels throughout the ten directions. As the *Kuan-fo san-mei hai ching* incense hymn (T 15.695a) is intoned, the offering is visualized (along with the cloud of incense) as suffusing throughout the Buddha lands of the ten directions. There it rains down offerings and stimulates the Buddhas' salvific work. It concludes with prostrations and verbal salutation to all beings. Also see KCPL, *Fang-teng ch'an-fa* (T 46.797b6–12); KCPL, *Ching-li fa* (T 46.794a3–6); KCPL, *Ch'ing kuan-shih-yin ch'an-fa* (T 46.795c7–12); MHCK (T 46.13b15, 14c28–29).

206. As in the vaipulya repentance (KCPL, *Fang-teng ch'an-fa*, T 46.797b) and repentance for invoking Avalokiteśvara (KCPL, *Ch'ing kuan-shih-yin ch'an-fa*, T 46.795b–c), the three jewels are invited or summoned into the sanctuary in specific form—in this instance, the Buddhas, the scripture, and saintly assemblies of the *Lotus Sūtra* (see *Ch'an-i*, T 46.950c–951b).

207. The specific deities of the rite (representing the three jewels) are venerated in sequence through the three activities of verbal salutation, five-limbed prostration, and simultaneous visualization of their presence (see *Ch'an-i*, T 46.951b–952b). The *Ch'an-i* (and, indeed, most T'ien-t'ai rites) precede this part of the rite with a brief phase known as "invocatory hymns and praises of the Buddha" (*t'an-fo chou-yüan*). See *Ch'an-i* (T 46.951b); KCPL, *Ching-li fa* (T 46.794a26); KCPL, *P'u-li fa* (T 46.795a22); KCPL, *Fang-teng ch'an-fa* (T 46.797b18–20).

208. Recitation of six passages offering generic confession of sins committed through the six senses (they are drawn from the *Sūtra on the Visualization of Samantabhadra*, T 9.391c–392c). According to the sūtra (T 9.391a1–5) this repentance or confession leads to "purification of the six senses" (*liu-ken ch'ing-ching*), which in T'ien-t'ai parlance is equivalent to the stage of the ten faiths or the identity of semblance (i.e., the cusp of sainthood and irreversibility) on the path of the perfect teaching. The *Ch'an-i* (T 46.952b–953b) incorporates confession, together with four other items, into a single ritual sequence known in T'ien-t'ai as the "five-fold penance" (*wu-hui*): confession, solicitation or exhortation (*ch'üan-ch'ing*), sympathetic rejoicing (*sui-hsi*) or celebration, dedication or transfer of merits (*hui-hsiang*), and making of vows (*fa-yüan*).

209. See *Ch'an-i*, T 46.953b29–c16. Recitation of the *Lotus Sūtra* is performed while circumambulating.

210. According to the *Ch'an-i* (T 46.953c–954a), the single chapter of the Easeful and Pleasurable Course may be recited if the practitioner has not learned to recite the *Lotus Sūtra* in its entirety. Recitation of the sūtra may also be extended into the period of seated meditation that follows circumambulation.

211. Ibid., T 46.954a–b. The *Ch'an-i* stipulates that the periods of circumambulation and seated meditation, as well as the activities of silent contemplation and recitation of the sūtra, may be adjusted to the practitioner's ability and state of mind.

212. Rather than being an actual part of the ritual performance, "clarification

fascicle [on this rite] titled, the *Lotus Samādhi Repentance*, written by master T'ien-t'ai [Chih-i]. It is extant today and is esteemed as authoritative by practitioners [of the way].[213]

[14a10] **Speech.** Since the above list includes the category of raising the voice as well as being silent, we shall not discuss this under a separate heading.

[14a11] **Mind.** The calming and contemplation of the mind:[214] The *Sūtra on the Visualization of the Bodhisattva Samantabhadra* says, "Just recite the Mahāyāna sūtras without entering into samādhi."[215] At the six designated intervals of day and night [one is instructed to] repent sins committed with the six sense faculties.[216] The chapter on the Easeful and Pleasurable Course (*an-le hsing p'in*) [from the *Lotus Sūtra*] says, "Among all the dharmas there are none in which the bodhisattva courses. . . . He neither practices nor makes discriminations [with regard to them]."[217]

---

of signs verifying success in the practice" refers to the fifth and final chapter of the *Ch'an-i* (T 46.954b–955c), in which different forms of religious experience provoked by the rite are classified according to three basic grades.

213. Understood to be a reference to the *Fa-hua san-mei ch'an-i*, T no. 1941. That Chih-i is the author of this work is indisputable; however, the current *Taishō* (and Chinese canonical) version of the text (titled *Fa-hua san-mei ch'an-i*) represents a critical edition prepared and published by the T'ien-t'ai master Tsun-shih (964–1032) during the Northern Sung. The best text-critical discussion of this work remains Satō, *Tendai daishi no kenkyū*, pp. 127–151.

214. Regarding this section on calming and contemplation of the mind, Chan-jan (T 46.192b21–22) remarks: "One could also say that calming and contemplation of the mind extends throughout [the other activities of body and speech] as well. The independently circulated text [of the *Ch'an-i*] [discusses contemplation] solely in terms of investigation on the basis of the tetralemma. Therefore, [Chih-i] here elaborates on the contemplation of [the iconography of] the elephant in order to supplement this other work."

215. *Kuan p'u-hsien p'u-sa hsing-fa ching*, T 9.389c. The context in which the passage appears in the sūtra is as follows: "Ānanda, if there should be monks or nuns, laymen or laywomen, devas or nāgas or any other of the eight divisions of superhuman beings, or any animate beings, who recite Mahāyāna sūtras, engage in Mahāyāna practice, and aspire to the Mahāyāna, who wish to see the physical form of the bodhisattva Samantabhadra, the stūpa of the Buddha Prabhūtaratna, the Buddha Śākyamuni and his magical incarnations, who wish to purify their six sense organs—then they should learn this contemplation, which by its merit will eliminate every obstacle and allow them to see the marvelous form of Samantabhadra. Even without entering into samādhi, but just because they recite and remember Mahāyāna sūtras, and concentrate their minds on them continuously with every thought, never separating themselves from the Mahāyāna, for from one day to three-times-seven days, they will be able to see Samantabhadra."

216. See *Kuan p'u-hsien p'u-sa hsing-fa ching*, T 9.390c27–391a5. The six confessions appear in the pages that follow.

217. T 9.37a. The missing line here reads, "But views the dharmas in keeping with their true mark." See Hurvitz, p. 208.

[14a13] These two sūtras were originally devised together [as a single teaching].[218] How could anyone think to set them in oppostion, cling to one text and reject the other?[219] The order in which they are presented here is merely a matter of circumstance [and is not to be taken as significant], for there is no substantial difference between them. In the Chapter on the Peaceful and Easeful Course are not "protecting, keeping, reading, reciting, and expounding the sūtra"[220] and "offering veneration [to all the bodhisattvas of the ten directions] reverently from the bottom of one's heart"[221] practices that involve phenomenal activity (*shih*)? Then again, the *Sūtra on the Visualization* [*of Samantabhadra*] also explains the repentance that is devoid of mark: "Since one's mind is of itself void, there is no subject in which sin or merit could inhere,"[222] and "The sun of wisdom can clear away the frost and dew of sins." [223] How is this not [practice based on] principle (*li*)?[224]

[14a18] Master Nan-yüeh [Hui-ssu] spoke of the "easeful course en-

218. Muranaka (p. 135) takes this line to mean, "The two sūtras supplement or complete one another." Chih-i regarded the *Kuan p'u-hsien p'u-sa hsing-fa ching* as an integral part of the cycle of *Lotus* discourses; thus a more literal reading of this passage is feasible.

219. The previous two passages are cited by Hui-ssu as the basis for his distinction between the "easeful and pleasurable course devoid of features" (i.e., the easeful and pleasurable course proper) and the "easeful and pleasurable course endowed with features" (i.e., the highly ritualized twenty-one day lotus repentance). See *Fa-hua ching an-le hsing i*, T 46.700a18–b7. Apparently there were divergent views in the T'ien-t'ai community regarding the role of these two approaches, for Kuan-ting and Chih-i go to great lengths to reconcile them in the lines that follow.

220. The *Lotus Sūtra*, T 9.37a; Hurvitz, p. 208.

221. The *Lotus Sūtra*, T 9.38a; Hurvitz, p. 216.

222. *Kuan p'u-hsien p'u-sa hsing fa ching*, T 9.392c. This is from the famous passage: "What is sin, what is merit? Since one's own mind is itself void, sin and merit are without a subject. So it is with all other dharmas as well: they are devoid of abiding, devoid of destruction. Such a repentance—in which one contemplates the mind as lacking the nature of mind, and the other dharmas as not abiding in themselves, but sees them all as liberated, as the noble truth of annihilation, and as quiescent—this is called the great repentance, the majestically adorned repentance, the repentance free of all mark of sin, the repentance that destroys mind and consciousness."

223. Ibid., T 9.393b.

224. In *Ch'an-i* (T 46.949c5–946a15, also 955b–c) Chih-i introduces the distinction between "developing single-minded perseverance on the basis of phenomenal ritual activity (*shih*)" and "single-minded perseverance on the basis of principle (*li*)," to which this section appears to allude. The *Ch'an-i* is careful to point out that both approaches may be applied to the twenty-one-day lotus repentance, depending upon the capability of the practitioner. However, the more fluid easeful and pleasurable course (*an-le hsing*) is geared more directly to the discernment of principle.

dowed with distinguishing features" (*yu-hsiang an-le hsing*) and the "easeful course devoid of distinguishing features" (*wu-hsiang an-le hsing*).[225] Don't these expressions, "with features" and "featureless," basically mean phenomenal activity (*shih*) and principle (*li*)? The reason [Hui-ssu] calls it "endowed with features" is because the pracititioner works through the medium of phenomenal activity (*shih*) and performs repentance of the six senses as an expedient to induce[226] enlightenment. What he calls the "featureless" approach represents the expedient of contemplating directly the emptiness of all dharmas. At the moment of marvelous realization both of these approaches are abandoned. Once this point is understood, one will no longer be perplexed by the apparent differences between the two sūtras.

[14a22] Now we shall describe how the practice of contemplation may be applied to the written text.[227] Where the sūtra says, "A white elephant

225. Hui-ssu, *Fa-hua ching an-le hsing i* (T 46.700al8–b7), states: "Practice devoid of features (*wu-hsiang hsing*) is none other than the easeful and pleasurable course [of the *Lotus Sūtra*]. While in the very midst of the dharmas, [the practitioner discerns that] the features of mind are quiescent and extinguished and ultimately do not arise at all. For this reason it is called 'practice devoid of features.' He is ever immersed in all manner of profound and wonderful dhyāna absorptions, because in all activities—walking, standing, sitting, reclining, eating, or speaking—his mind is always settled in samādhi. . . . Because there is no mental fluctuation whatsoever, it is called practice devoid of distinguishing features. . . . Then again, there is the practice endowed with features, which is the practice of reciting the *Lotus Sūtra* and striving diligently with the ordinary scattered mind as taught in the chapter on the Encouragements of Samantabhadra. A person undertaking this approach neither cultivates dhyāna nor strives to enter samādhi. Whether sitting, standing, or walking, he concentrates his whole attention on the words of the *Lotus Sūtra* and perseveres earnestly without lying down to rest, as though he were trying to extinguish a fire blazing on his head. This is known as the practice endowed with features [that resorts to] the written text."

226. Following Chan-jan (T 46.192c14–17).

227. The iconography of Samantabhadra presented below derives from the following passage in the *Kuan p'u-hsien p'u-sa hsing-fa ching* (T 9.389c–390a): "By the power of his wisdom the bodhisattva Samantabhadra appears magically before the practitioner mounted on a while elephant with six tusks and seven legs. Beneath the seven legs grow seven lotuses. The elephant is a brilliant white, whiter than crystal or even the [snow-capped] Himālayas, and his body is 450 leagues (*yojanas*) long and 400 leagues high. At the tip of the six tusks are six bathing pools, and in each of these grow fourteen lotuses equal in size to the pools, blooming as luxuriantly as the most excellent of celestial trees (*pārijāta*). There is a bejeweled maiden upon each blossom, scarlet of countenance and more radiant than a nymph, with five harps appearing magically in her hands, and 500 other musical instruments accompanying each harp. . . . On the head of the elephant are three magically produced men: one holds a golden wheel, one a jewel, and the third a vajra-prod with which he guides the elephant. The elephant does

with six tusks," this signifies the six undefiled superhuman powers of the bodhisattva Samantabhadra, for the keen action of the tusks is as quick as the superhuman powers of penetration.[228] The great strength of the elephant signifies the [enormous capacity of] the dharma body to bear and uphold. It is because there is no defilement or stain that the elephant is white. The three men on his head—one holding a diamond prod, one holding a diamond wheel, and one holding a wish-fulfilling gem—signify that the three wisdoms abide at the summit of freedom from the outflows (*anāsrava*). The guiding of the elephant by the prod signifies how wisdom guides religious practice. The turning of the diamond wheel signifies issuing forth into the provisional [from the empty]. The wish-fulfilling gem signifies the middle. That there are pools on the tusks signifies that the eight degrees of liberation are the substance of the meditative concentrations (dhyāna),[229] and the six superhuman powers are the functional activity produced by the power of samādhi: for substance (*t'i*) and function (*yung*) are not separate from each other. At the tips of the tusks are pools, and in the pools are lotus flowers. The flowers signify the wondrous cause.[230] The [wondrous] cause is the purifying of Buddha lands and the benefiting of animate beings by the activity of the superhuman powers of the bodhisattva. This cause arises from the superhuman powers just as the flowers emerge from the pools. In each flower there is a maiden signifying goodwill. If she lacked unconditional goodwill, how could she even with the aid of superhuman power shrink herself until small enough to enter this sahā world of ours? The superhuman powers

---

not tread on the ground but seven feet up in the air; yet he leaves footprints, each with the mark of a perfect thousand-spoked wheel. From between each spoke of each wheel grows a great lotus, and from each lotus appears magically another elephant with seven legs, following the first, so that every stride of the great elephant produces 7,000 elephants to follow him as his retinue. . . . On a pedestal on the elephant's back sits a bodhisattva, cross-legged in the lotus posture, named Samantabhadra, his body pure as a white jewel . . . with rays of golden light streaming from every pore of his body."

228. The six superpowers free of *āsravas* or "defiling outflows."

229. *Shiki* (1.493) cites the *Vimalakīrti Sūtra* (T 14.549c) as the source for this equation: "The water of samādhi brims full in the bathing pools of the eight (degrees of) liberation." The eight degrees of liberation represent a sequence of eight techniques for the refinement of meditative concentration that correspond to the four dhyāna and four formless samāpatti.

230. The wondrous cause is the great religious practice of a bodhisattva of the perfect teaching. As described by Hui-ssu in his *An-le hsing i* (T 46.698b–c) and Chih-i in *Fa-hua hsüan-i* (T 33.682b, 771c–774c), the flower blossom represents cause, and seed or fruit, the result. In the case of the lotus blossom (symbolic of the perfect teaching), flower and fruit are formed at the same time, not sequentially. The causal ground of practice is, simultaneously, the salvific function of the result.

are set in motion by goodwill in the same way as the maidens are held aloft by the flowers. The maidens hold musical instruments, signifying the four inducements.[231] When goodwill is practiced both physically and verbally, various kinds of equalizing actions and beneficial actions are manifested. That the two kinds of giving—that of possessions and the dharma—may take many diverse forms depending on the person is analogous to the infinite variety of tones produced from the 500 musical instruments. [Samantabhadra's] displaying himself in a form that beings find joyous to behold represents the samādhi wherein physical form is manifested universally [throughout the dharmadhātu].[232] Whatever [form] will benefit and delight a being is manifested for him. It does not necessarily have to come as the pure white jadelike image [of Samantabhadra]. Verbal dhāraṇī[233] signifies that speech is suffused with goodwill and a variety of dharmas are thereby expounded. All of this is simply an alternate name for the lotus samādhi. Whoever fully grasps its import will be able to assume the seat atop the elephant and freely create his or her own teachings.

Exhortation to Practice

[14b11] Now we give the exhortation to practice: It says in the *Sūtra on the Visualization of Samantabhadra* that if anyone in the seven assemblies[234]

231. The four modes of inducement (*saṃgraha-vastu*) are methods for winning over beings and leading them toward enlightenment. They include *dāna*, giving beings what they ask for, whether wealth or teachings; *priya-vāditā*, beguiling their minds with skillful parables; *artha-caryā*, arousing their good physical, verbal, and mental activity, and *samānārthatā*, causing them to act the same as oneself, the teacher.

232. The "samādhi whereby one manifests forms universally [throughout the dharmadhātu]" (*p'u-hsien se-shen san-mei*) figures regularly as a *summum bonum* in the tales of various bodhisattvas from the *Lotus Sūtra* (see Hurvitz, pp. 294, 307–309), as well as in the *Kuan p'u-hsien ching*. Tsuda Sōkichi, in his classic discussion of the lotus samādhi, sees it as graphically descriptive of the interpenetrating three truths and the wondrous salvific powers that are the fruit of the T'ien-t'ai perfect teaching and the lotus samādhi (see his "Chigi no hokkezammai").

233. *Kuan p'u-hsien p'u-sa hsing fa ching*, T 9.390c says, "After practicing in this way day and night for three times seven days, the practitioner will gain the dhāraṇī of turning or revolving. By this dhāraṇī he will remember and not forget the subtle dharma expounded to him by the Buddhas and bodhisattvas." A similar claim appears in the Samantabhadra chapter of the *Lotus Sūtra* (T 9.61b7–8): "[Having seen me] he shall straightaway attain samādhis and dhāraṇīs , the latter named the turning dhāraṇī" (Hurvitz, p. 333).

Chih-i, in an explanation of this passage from the *Lotus Sūtra* in his *Ch'an-i* (T 46.955b5–8), remarks: " 'Dhāraṇī' is great wisdom, for, upon obtaining this great wisdom, one is able to retain without ever forgetting and comprehend without impediment anything that the Buddha expounds."

234. All the male and female members of the Buddhist community: monks,

breaks the disciplinary code and wishes to "expunge in the time it takes to snap one's fingers the sins committed over a hundred quadrillion incalculable eons of saṃsāra";[235] if one wishes to arouse the thought of enlightenment, and enter nirvāṇa "without eradicating the defilements, purify his sense organs without separating himself from the five kinds of desire associated with them, and see what is beyond the obstructions";[236] if one "wishes to see the corporal manifestations [of the Buddha Śākyamuni] as well as the two Buddhas Prabhūtaratna and Śākyamuni";[237] if one wishes to acquire the lotus samādhi and the sum total of all verbal dhāraṇī, enter the chambers of the Tathāgata, put on the robes of the Tathāgata,[238] sit on the throne of the Tathāgata, and there expound the dharma to devas, nāgas, and the rest of the eight kinds of superhuman beings; if one wishes to have the vision of "the great bodhisattvas Mañjuśrī and Bhaiṣajyarāja, and stand in attendance upon them while holding incense and flowers";[239] then one should "practice this *Lotus Sūtra*, read and recite the Mahāyāna sūtras, and be mindful of the activities of the Mahāyāna."[240] Bringing one's mind into mutual resonance with this wisdom of emptinesss, one should maintain mindfulness of the mother of all bodhisattvas. It is from the pondering of ultimate reality that such supreme [powers of] expediency are born. "The myriad sins are like frost and dew: they are cleared away by the sun of wisdom."[241] If one can manage this, there is no task that one will not be adequate to meet. "Whoever is able to keep this sūtra will be able to see me, [Samantabhadra,] will be able to see you, [the Buddha Śākyamuni,] and will also [be able to] make offerings to Prabhūtaratna and the other corporal projections [of Śākyamuni], thereby causing all the Buddhas to rejoice."

[14b24] It is all as the sūtra describes at great length. Who could hear such a dharma and fail to give rise to the thought of enlightenment? Only the base, the stupid, the benighted, and the ignorant.

Neither Walking nor Sitting Samādhi

[14b26] Fourth is [the cultivation of] samādhi [through] neither walking nor sitting. The preceding methods resort exclusively to either walking or sitting, but this approach differs from the above. The name "neither walking nor sitting" is adopted simply to complete the four alternatives

---

nuns, novices of both sexes, laypeople of both sexes, and the *śikṣamāṇās* (a special class of female novice).

235. *Kuan p'u-hsien p'u-sa hsing-fa ching*, T 9.393c6–7.

236. Ibid., T 9.389c7–9.

237. Ibid., T 9.389c19–20.

238. Ibid., T 9.391a12.

239. Ibid., both of these phrases are at T 9.393b20–21.

240. Ibid., T 9.389c.

241. Ibid., T 9.393b12.

[of the tetralemma].[242] In actuality this practice encompasses walking and sitting, as well as all forms of activity (*shih*). As such, master Nan-yüeh [Hui-ssu] styled it "[the samādhi of] freely following one's thought" (*sui-tzu-i*).[243] That is to say, whenever any thought or cognitive involvement arises, one uses it to cultivate samādhi right then and there. The *Pañcaviṃśati* calls this "the samādhi of maintaining wakeful awareness of thought" (*chüeh-i san-mei*).[244] Whatever turn thought or cognition (*i*) may take, one strives to maintain clear and wakeful awareness (*chüeh*) of it. Although there are three different names, it is really one and the same method of practice.

242. This fourth category of "neither walking nor sitting" is not intended as a repudiation of the activities of walking and sitting per se but is devised in order to complete the set of four alternative propositions that may be formulated on the basis of the two original designations of "walking" and "sitting."

243. Hui-ssu composed a single-fascicle work by this title that is still extant today: *Sui-tzu-i san-mei* (HTC 98). The date of composition and impact of this work are discussed in Satō, *Zoku Tendai daishi no kenkyū*, pp. 241–268. For a brief description of its contents and their relation to the "neither walking nor sitting samādhi," see Stevenson, "The Four Kinds of Samādhi in Early T'ien-t'ai Buddhism," p. 75.

244. *Chüeh-i san-mei* (*bodhyaṅga samādhi*) appears as the seventy-second member in the list of 108 samādhis of the Mahāyāna found in Kumārajīva's translation of the *Pañcaviṃśati-sāhasrikā-prajñāpāramitā Sūtra* (*Mo-ho pan-jo p'o-lo-mi ching*, T 8.251b). The term *chüeh-i* is a binome commonly used (prior to Hsüan-tsang) to refer to the technical Buddhist formula of the seven *bodhyaṅga* or "limbs of enlightenment"—i.e., discrimination of dharmas, energetic zeal, joy, tranquility, mindfulness, concentration,. and equanimity. The various Chinese and Sanskrit redactions of the *Pañcaviṃśati* explain this *bodhyaṅga samādhi* or *chüeh-i san-mei* to be a samādhi "wherein all samādhis are furnished with the seven limbs of enlightenment (*bodhyaṅga*) and one rapidly achieves perfection" (see *Ta pan-jo p'o-lo-mi-to ching*, T 7.76b18–20; *Kuang-tsan pan-jo ching*, T 8.192a). The sūtra's Chinese commentary, the TCTL (T 25.401a25–27), fully affirms this interpretation: "By dwelling in this samādhi one is able to render all samādhis devoid of outflows and bring them into response with the seven limbs of enlightenment, just as one *chin* of the mineral *shih-han* can transform 1,000 *chin* of copper into gold."

Chih-i composed a separate manual for the *chüeh-i san-mei*—the *Shih mo-ho pan-jo p'o-lo-mi ching chüeh-i san-mei* (T no. 1922; hereafter abbreviated as *Chüeh-i san-mei*)—sometime during the early to middle part of his career. It draws on conventions established in Hui-ssu's *Sui-tzu-i san-mei*, which, in turn, it develops and passes on to such seminal works as the *Hsiao chih-kuan* and MHCK. The organizational concept as well as large segments of the MHCK section on the "neither walking nor sitting samādhi" are lifted practically verbatim from the *Chüeh-i san-mei*. These emendations are thought to have been made not by Chih-i himself but by Kuan-ting in the course of his editing of the MHCK. For discussion of the dating, authorship, and influence of the *Chüeh-i san-mei*, see Satō, *Tendai daishi no kenkyū*, pp. 173–189. The meditative procedure set forth in the work is described in Stevenson, "The Four Kinds of Samādhi in Early T'ien-t'ai Buddhism," pp. 75–84.

[14c1] Now we shall explain the name ["samādhi of wakeful awareness of thought"] on the basis of the sūtra.[245] "Wakeful awareness" (*chüeh*) means illumined understanding, and "thought" or "cognitive activity" (*i*) refers to the factors of mentation. "Samādhi" is as explained previously.[246] When the factors of mentation arise, one should turn back to reflect upon and discern them thoroughly (*fan chao kuan-ch'a*). So doing, one finds neither origin or terminus, whence or whither, to this evolving flow of thought.[247] In this sense it is called "maintaining wakeful awareness of thought."

245. Despite its well-established technical meaning of *bodhyaṅga*—with which Chih-i is fully familiar (see his *Chüeh-i san-mei,* T 46.621c23–622a9)—here Chih-i assigns a reading to the binome *chüeh-i* that departs radically from the original sense signaled in the sūtra and its commentary (i.e., TCTL). *Chüeh* and *i* he takes as verb-object, thereby interpreting the formula *chüeh-i san-mei* in a way that conforms closely with Hui-ssu's *sui-tzu-i san-mei,* "samādhi of following one's thought." Why Chih-i chose to drop Hui-ssu's designation (*sui-tzu-i*) and adopt the name *chüeh-i san-mei* in its stead remains something of a mystery. However, it is possible that he saw in *chüeh-i san-mei* and the *Pañcavimsati* a more substantial scriptural basis for the practice than Hui-ssu's rather tenuous identification of *sui-tzu-i* with the *Śūraṅgama-samādhi sūtra.*

246. "Taming, rectifying, and stabilizing or affixing"; see MHCK, T 46.11a25–26.

247. The four character expression *fan-chao kuan-ch'a,* which we render "turn back to reflect upon and discern," is an extremely significant formula that appears frequently throughout Chih-i's and Hui-ssu's works on meditation. *Fan-chao,* which literally means "to turn back and illumine" or "to turn back one's illumining," carries an almost cosmogonic sense of returning to the source or reversing the stream of deluded thought from which the entirety of deluded existence evolves.

Chih-i states in the opening lines of his *Chüeh-i san-mei* (T 46.621a10–12): "Any practitioner who desires to cross the sea of birth and death and ascend to the other shore of nirvāṇa must comprehend thoroughly the root-source of delusion and be well-versed in the essentials for attaining the way. The root of delusion is itself the very reality limit of mind. The essentials for realizing the way are what we call 'turning back to illumine (*fan-chao*) the well-spring of mind.' "

Again, in his discussion of "skillful settling of the mind through practice of calming and contemplation"—the third of the ten modes of discernment found in the main body of the MHCK—Chih-i (T 46.56b24–28) says: "Upon reverting to the source and returning to the root, the dharmadhātu [is found to be] utterly quiescent. This is what we mean by 'calming.' When one performs 'calming' in this fashion, all derivative mental flow and production comes to a halt. When 'contemplating' one discerns that, at its source, the mind of nescience is wholly equanimous with dharma-nature and, fundamentally, empty. Likewise, all subsequent deluded thoughts and good and evil [actions] are as empty space—nondual and indivisible from it."

The point that Chih-i and Hui-ssu make explicitly in this practice of *chüeh-i san-mei* and *sui-tzu-i san-mei* (and implicitly in the other practices of the four samādhis)

[14c4] Q: Mental factors are incalculable in number. Why do you discuss wakeful awareness solely on the basis of [the faculty of] cognitive activity or thought (*i*)?[248]

[14c5] A: If one seeks out the source of the myriad dharmas, one will find that they are all the product of cognition or thought (*i*). Therefore, we take the word "thought" or "cognitive activity" (*i*) as our verbal point of departure.

[14c5] The sentient awareness of objects that distinguishes us from trees and stones is called "mind" (*hsin*; *citta*). Next, the power of mind to make discursive evaluations [with respect to these objects] is called "thought" or "cognitive activity" (*i*; *manas*). And full discriminative identification is called "consciousness" (*vijñāna*; *shih*). Whoever [clings to] such distinctions as absolute falls into perverted mind, perverted thoughts,

---

is that "turning back to illumine and discern the well-spring of mind" should be cultivated with each moment of thought amidst any and all circumstances.

248. The triune compound that Chih-i invokes here—*cittamanovijñāna*—is a formulation with a long yet complicated usage in Buddhist tradition. Due to the fact that, from earliest times, Buddhist models of mind and consciousness were problematic and, hence, ever-evolving, it is difficult to locate a suitable fixed interpretation from Indic Buddhist tradition. However, generally speaking, *manas* (*i*) represents the "mind sense" or "faculty of cognitive activity" that coordinates the other five sense faculties and takes as its object various "mental" dharmas that arise from their activity. *Vijñāna* or "consciousness" is sense specific, being produced when a given sense faculty contacts its respective object.

The meaning of these terms is rendered even more complex by the ambiguities introduced by the Chinese equivalents of *hsin* "mind," *i* "mental design or intent," and *shih* "conscious identification, recognition." Chih-i no doubt adopts the formula because of its widespread usage in early medieval China but clearly turns it to his own particular purposes. Chan-jan, in his commentary to this passage, underscores the ambiguity of its meaning by citing some four different interpretations. Chan-jan (T 46.193a26–b3) states: "Some say that past [reflection] represents 'cognitive activity' or 'thought' (*i*), that the future [generation of thoughts] represents 'mind' (*hsin*), and that the present represents 'consciousness' (*shih*). Others say that 'mind' is construed in reference to the sense fields (*dhātu*), that 'thought' or 'cognitive 'activity' is construed in reference to the accesses (*āyatana*), and that 'consciousness' is construed in reference to the aggregates (*skandha*). Still others assert that the miscellaneous forms of materiality represent 'mind,' as the six destinies of birth derive from the mind. Affixing or inherence represents 'thought' or 'cognitive activity,' just as the other five sense faculties inhere in the 'mind sense' (*manas*). Speech and thought represent 'consciousness,' as discrimination is the property of consciousness. The *Kośa* says, 'Dependent origination is called mind. Discursive evaluation is thought or cognitive activity, and full discursive discrimination is consciousness' (T 29.21c). However, all of these [interpretations] derive from the traditions of the lesser [vehicle]. These three designations are really but different names for one and the same thing. For this reason the text here explains that one must not adhere [to any such designation] as definitive, whether it be the notion that they are three, one, merged or dispersed."

and perverted views.[249] How could this be called "wakeful awareness"? Wakeful awareness is understanding fully that in "mind" (*hsin*), [the faculty of] "thought" or "cognitive activity" (*i*) is neither included nor not included, and "consciousness" (*shih*) is neither included nor not included; that "thought" neither includes nor does not include "mind" and neither includes nor does not include "consciousness"; and that "consciousness" neither includes nor does not include "thought" and neither includes nor does not include "mind." Since mind, thought, and consciousness are not one and the same, three names are established; and since they are not three, we teach that there is only a single nature. If one understands that "name" is "no-name," then "nature" likewise is "no-nature." Since "name" is refuted, [these aspects of mind] are not three; and since "nature" is refuted, they are not one. Not being three, they are not dispersed; not being one, neither are they merged or conjoined.[250] Since they are not merged, [these three aspects] are not absolutely empty; and since they are not dispersed, they are not absolutely existent. Since they do not absolutely exist, they are not eternal; and since they are not empty, they are not inherently annihilated. If one holds to neither the view of eternality nor the view of annihilation, then in the end one perceives neither uniformity nor difference.[251]

249. *Chüeh-i san-mei* (T 46.621c8–9) reads: "This constitutes the distinction between mind, thought or cognitive activity, and consciousness. If one seizes on these disctinctions as such, one will fall into perversion of mind, perversion of thought, and perversion of views."

250. The *Chüeh-i san-mei* and MHCK have the characters for "merged" and "dispersed" reversed here. The same problem occurs with "empty" and "existent" in the line following. Given the context of the passage, in both cases MHCK seems the more logical reading (see T 46.621c15–16).

251. Most of the critical categories that Chih-i uses in his dialectics can be traced to Nāgārjuna's *Madhyamaka-kārikās* (*Chung-lun*)—for "sameness/uniformity" (*i*) and "difference" (*i*) see chapters 1 (Cause and Condition) and 6 (Defilement and Defiled) (T 30.8a–c); for "merged" (*ho*) and "dispersed" (*san*), also see chapters 6 and 7 (the Three Marks) (T 30.9a–12b).

Chan-jan (T 46.193b15–24) states: "Having refuted the three names and their discriminations as erroneous, one should contemplate their essential nature as beyond designation. For this reason, whenever [the text] says 'not present or existent' in any of these six lines, it means that they are identical in substance. When it says 'not absent or inexistent,' it means different in name. Furthermore, one must not reckon in terms of name, substance, sameness, or difference. Thus it also concludes, 'not being one we say it is three; not being three we say it is one.' The rest, including 'merged' and 'dispersed,' can be explained accordingly. [The text] from 'if one knows name to be no-name' contains altogether six statements that, in convoluted fashion, reiterate this point. These six statements together effect the simultaneous refutation and simultaneous illumination (*shuang-fei shuang-chao*) [of the two extremes]. Provisional designation and essential nature are both inapprehensible. If one uses this passage to establish the three discernments, re-

[14c17] If one contemplates "thought" or "cognitive activity" (*i*), it necessarily includes both "mind" (*hsin*) and "consciousness" (*shih*), as well as all other dharmas. If one repudiates [the faculty of] "thought," then nescience is also destroyed, and the other afflictions likewise all vanish.[252] This is why, although there are many dharmas, we select "thought" or "cognitive activity" (*i*)[253] alone to explain this samādhi. Through contemplation one tames and rectifies[254] the mind. That is why we call it "the samādhi of maintaining wakeful awareness of thought."[255] [The other names,] "freely following one's thought" and "neither walking nor sitting," may be understood along the same lines.

[14c20] We divide this discussion into four parts: the first is [the cultivation of samādhi] on the basis of [practices outlined in] the sūtras; the second, [cultivation of samādhi] by resorting to wholesome dharmas; the third, [cultivation of samādhi] on the basis of evil dharmas, and the fourth, cultivation with respect to neutral dharmas.

Cultivation on the Basis of the Sūtras

[14c21] Any method of practice from the sūtras that does not fit into the rubric of the previous three forms [of samādhi][256] belongs to the [sam-

---

futing their oneness and establishing them as three, then it represents the provisional. Refuting the three and expounding the one is emptiness. And to establish name as no-name and nature as no-nature is the middle. The other five statements may be treated accordingly. If, through this rather involved process, one succeeds in penetrating the essential nature of mind, then this constitutes the wondrous realm of the inconceivable three truths [that is the object of the perfect course of contemplation]."

252. Chan-jan (T 46.193b25–8) states: "The contemplation of the perfect [teaching] not only discerns thought or cognitive activity (*i*) as the basis of all dharmas but also destroys the well-spring of nescience and the defilements. Thus one should know that not only does thought and cognitive activity include [all dharmas], but cognitive activity is itself identical to nescience. When nescience is eliminated, all the defilements are retained freely as they are (*an-tsai*)." As *Kōgi* goes on to point out, mind may be viewed as identical both to the dharmakāya—i.e., ultimate reality—and to the defilements that obscure it; to understand this double identity is simultaneously to realize truth and to destroy nescience. Thus truth and nescience are but two names for the same "thing," "fact," or "condition."

253. *Chüeh-i san-mei* (T 46.621c21) reads: "Thus we use wakeful awareness of thought or cognitive activity to elucidate this samādhi."

254. Ibid., T 46.622b19.

255. Chih-i's *Chüeh-i san-mei* at this point follows with a second explanation of the title of this samādhi, which is based closely on the original interpretation found in the *Pañcaviṃśati* and the TCTL. That is to say, he demonstrates how *chüeh-i san-mei* as *bodhyaṅga samādhi* enables one to endow all other samādhis with the *bodhyaṅga* or "seven limbs of enlightenment" (see T 46.621a23–622b23).

256. In other words, if a given practice does not fit the physical description of constant sitting, constant walking, or part walking/part sitting.

ādhi of] following one's thought. However, here we shall explain the features of this samādhi with specific reference to the [rite from] the *Invocation of Avalokiteśvara* [*Sūtra*].[257]

[14c23] Adorn a sanctuary for practice (*tao-ch'ang*) in a quiet place, using banners, canopies, incense, and lamps.[258] Invite the Buddha

257. *Ch'ing kuan-shih-yin p'u-sa hsiao-fu tu-hai t'o-lo-ni ching* (T no. 1043; Sūtra of the Dhāraṇī that Invokes the Bodhisattva Avalokiteśvara for Eliminating Poison and Suppressing Harmful Influences; hereafter abbreviated as *Ch'ing kuan-yin ching*). The *Ch'ing kuan-yin ching* is a quasi-esoteric sūtra that was introduced to China by the Indian layman Nandin during the last years of the Eastern Chin (317–420). The rite described here is known in T'ien-t'ai circles as the Repentance for the Invocation of Avalokiteśvara (*Ch'ing kuan-yin ch'an-fa*), its name being derived from the title of the scripture. Two independent manuals for this practice are known to have circulated in the early T'ien-t'ai community. The first of these—*Ch'ing kuan-shih-yin ch'an-fa*—is preserved as item 4 in the KCPL (T 46.795b16–796a3; hereafter referred to as KCPL, *Ch'ing kuan-yin ch'an-fa*). It offers a brief account of the liturgy of offering, veneration, repentance, and recitation that comprises the heart of the ritual cycle of the Repentance for the Invocation of Avalokiteśvara. Contemplative practice is mentioned but not described. The second manual is no longer extant, but a listing of its chapters is provided in the *Ch'ing kuan-yin ching shu* (T 39.973a19–23), an early T'ien-t'ai commentary to the *Ch'ing kuan-yin ching*. Along with the previous liturgical details, this second manual apparently contained a major section on seated meditation. Both manuals are thought to be by Chih-i (see Satō, *Tendai daishi no kenkyū*, pp. 504–508).

Chan-jan (T 46.193c20–24) mentions both the KCPL, *Ch'ing kuan-yin ch'an-fa*, as well as the second "older" manual, but as he appears to know of the latter only through the *Ch'ing kuan-yin ching shu*, the text must already have been lost by his day. A third manual on the repentance for the invocation of Avalokiteśvara, much later in date, was composed by the Sung T'ien-t'ai master Tsun-shih when he revived the rite during the eleventh century. His text supplements the ritual structure of the KCPL, *Ch'ing kuan-yin ch'an-fa*, with procedural details from Chih-i's comprehensive *Fa-hua san-mei ch'an-i* (see *Ch'ing kuan-shih-yin hsiao-fu tu-hai t'o-lo-ni san-mei i*, T no. 1040).

An additional work relevant to the study of the Repentance for the Invocation of Avalokiteśvara and its place in T'ien-t'ai is the above-mentioned commentary to the sūtra, the *Ch'ing kuan-yin ching shu*. This commentary (in particular its discussion of the operative power of the three dhāraṇī of the sūtra) became an important source for the theory of the inherent inclusion of evil within Buddha-nature (*hsing-e*) that was advanced by the T'ien-t'ai master Ssu-ming Chih-li (960–1028) in the Sung. Although later catalogues ascribe the *Ch'ing kuan-yin ching shu* to Chih-i, recent scholarship has challenged this view by marshaling evidence that it is more likely the work of his disciple Kuan-ting (for views of the two main proponents of this controversy see Andō, *Tendai-gaku*, pp. 330–356 and Satō, *Tendai daishi no kenkyū*, pp. 475–516; Satō, "Shō'o shisō no sōshōsha wa Chigi ka Kanjō ka?"; and Satō, *Zoku Tendai daishi no kenkyū*, pp. 411–428).

258. The KCPL, *Ch'ing kuan-yin ch'an-fa*, adds that the rite should be performed for a fixed period of either twenty-one or forty-nine days (T 46.795b16).

Amitābha and the two [attendant] bodhisattvas Avalokiteśvara and Mahāsthāmaprāpta by installing images of them on the western side of the chamber.[259] Set out tooth-cleaning sticks[260] and purified water for them. [When entering and exiting the hall] from the left and right or [going in and out] to relieve oneself, you must smear your body with aromatics,[261] wash youself thoroughly, and put on new and clean robes.

259. The KCPL, *Ch'ing kuan-yin ch'an-fa*, offers a different arrangement: "Install an image of the Buddha facing south and, apart from it, an image of Avalokiteśvara (Kuan-shih-yin) facing to the east" (T 46.795b18–19). It is unclear which Buddha should be installed on the north wall. The liturgy offers special veneration to both Śākyamuni Buddha and Amitāyus. Tsun-shih's *Ch'ing kuan-yin san-mei i* (T 46.968c24) places Avalokiteśvara and Mahāsthamaprāpta facing east and (apart from them) Amitābha to the left of Avalokiteśvara facing south. Śākyamuni may be installed with them wherever room is available.

260. The "tooth-cleaning stick" or *dantakāṣṭha* (which, as rendered in Chinese, literally means "willow sprig") is not the familiar leafy branch of willow later associated with the bodhisattva Avalokiteśvara in China but a common tool of oral hygiene used traditionally in India. It is a short, soft segment of twig that is chewed and worked against the teeth and gums. As one of the items of offering prescribed for this rite by the *Ch'ing kuan-yin ching* (T 20.34c), the tooth-cleaning stick represents the power and desire to cleanse. Thus Kuan-ting, commenting on its significance in the *Ch'ing kuan-yin ching shu* (T 39.973a), says: "This is to promote the acquiring of the two causes that act as the primary instigation [for enlightenment]: the tooth-cleaning stick sweeps away, thereby symbolizing insight. Purified water is clear and cool, thereby symbolizing [the stability of] meditative absorption."

Chan-jan (T 46.193c24–25) states: "As for setting out the tooth-cleaning stick ("willow-sprig") and so forth, because Avalokiteśvara holds a willow sprig in his left hand and vase for bathing in his right, the supplicant must prepare these two items." *Kōgi* (1.506) correctly points out that this description is not present in the *Ch'ing kuan-yin ching*. Nor do we find it in Kuan-ting's commentary. The iconographical form of Avalokiteśvara given by Chan-jan anticipates the familiar configuration of Avalokiteśvara holding a flowing willow branch and a vase of ambrosia, which began to appear in Chinese paintings of the bodhisattva from the latter part of the T'ang.

261. KCPL, *Kuan-yin ch'an-fa* (T 46.795b20–21), reads: "Up to ten persons may participate in the practice. They should face in the westerly direction and be seated on mats. However, if the ground is rough or damp, they may set up a low dais. They must remove their purified robes when [leaving the chamber] and enter from the right and exit from the left. After they have bathed they again don the purified robes [to enter the chamber]."

The *Ch'ing kuan-yin ching* says to smear oneself with "ashes" rather than "aromatics" here (T 20.35c). *Kōgi* and *Shiki* support the MHCK reading with the claim that there has been a copyist's error in the sūtra. However, in the preceding vaipulya repentance the ritual bathing (prior to donning purified robes) is performed with a solution of ash and perfumed water (*Fang-teng san-mei hsing-fa*, T

One of [the six monthly days of] the *uposatha* should be chosen as the time to commence the rite.[262]

[14c27] Facing squarely toward the west, drop to the ground in five-limbed prostration[263] and venerate the three jewels [in the form of] the seven Buddhas,[264] Śākyamuni Buddha, Amitābha Buddha, the three dhāraṇīs,[265] the two bodhisattvas [Avalokiteśvara and Mahāsthāmaprāpta], and the assembly of saints.[266] Having finished doing obeisance, assume the foreign kneeling posture to burn incense and scatter flowers.[267] With utmost attentiveness carry out the mental visualization [for

46.945b2), and Tsun-shih chooses to retain the original reading of "ash" (see *Ch'ing kuan-yin san-mei i,* T 46.968c5).

262. The six days of *uposatha* include the eighth, fourteenth, fifteenth, twenty-third, twenty-ninth, and thirtieth days of the lunar month. The KCPL, *Ch'ing kuan-yin ch'an-fa* (T 46.795b21–3), adds: "Everyday [the practitioners] should make an exhaustive effort to provide offerings. But if they are unable to make the necessary arrangements, they must by all means provide a full array on the first day. Then each person takes up an incense censer and facing to the west, with single heart and single purpose, drops to the ground in five-limbed prostration."

263. Chan-jan (T 46.193c27–9) states: "Dropping to the ground in five-limbed prostration is as it is commonly performed by monks: . . . where the two elbows, two knees, and crown of the head all touch the floor. It is also known as the 'five-fold wheel,' because the five spots [where the limbs touch] form a circle." The *Ch'ing kuan-yin ching shu* (T 39.972a–b) identifies these bodily members symbolically with the five skandhas: the left hand and leg are *yin* and associated with *saṃskāra* and *rūpa* (impulses and form), respectively; the right hand and leg are yang and associated with *saṃjñā* and *vedanā* (perception and sensation), and the head is naturally associated with *vijñāna* (consciousness).

264. See *Ch'ing kuan-yin ching,* T 20.35c. The Seven Buddhas of Antiquity include Vipaśyin, Śikhin, Viśabhū, Krakucchanda, Kanakamuni, Kaśyapa, and Śākyamuni.

265. The three dhāraṇī or incantations that represent the core of the rite: the dhāraṇī for eradicating poison and harm, the dhāraṇī for destroying evil karma, and the dhāraṇī of six-syllable phrases (they are given in the *Ch'ing kuan-yin ching,* T 20.35–36). There is actually a fourth dhāraṇī given in the sūtra—the *abhiṣeka dhāraṇī;* however, it does not figure significantly into either the rite or the commentary.

266. As is clear from the litany of venerations provided in the KCPL, *Ch'ing kuan-yin ch'an-fa* (T 46.795b25–c6), the three jewels are saluted in the particular form of the individual Buddhas, dhāraṇī , and bodhisattvas that are central to the *Ch'ing kuan-yin ching.* Each "veneration" begins with the profession, "Wholeheartedly I salute with the crown of my head [name X] . . ." and concludes with five-limbed prostration. Along with Avalokiteśvara and Mahāsthamaprāpta, veneration of the ṣangha includes the general multitude of bodhisattva mahāsattvas, śrāvakas, pratyekabuddhas, and assembly of saints and worthies.

267. Described in Chih-i's *Fa-hua san-mei ch'an-i* (T 46.950b24) as "right knee

this offering of the three deeds] according to the usual procedure.[268] When the offering is completed, assume the lotus posture with legs intertwined and properly compose body and mind.[269] Fix your attention on the counting of the breaths, making each [cycle of mindfulness] correspond to ten cycles [of inhalation and exhalation].[270] When ten [cycles of] mindfulness have been completed, arise, burn incense, and, on behalf of

---

placed to the ground, body poised erect," the "foreign kneel" receives its name from the fact that it is a formal posture of veneration derived from Indic and Central Asian Buddhist traditions. According to Tao-hsüan (*Shih-men kuei-ching i*, T 45.863c), the right knee rests firmly on the ground and the left knee is raised. The buttocks should be suspended ever so slightly above the two heels. The torso should be erect and inclined slightly forward, and the two palms are joined in reverence.

268. The "burning of incense and scattering of flowers"—often referred to in Chih-i's manuals as "offering of the three deeds" (*san-yeh kung-yang*)—is accompanied by the intoning of the incense hymn and visualization of offerings typical of the preceding lotus and vaipulya repentances. The KCPL, *Ch'ing kuan-yin ch'an-fa* (T 46.795c8–12), instructs: "Taking up incense and flowers, [the participants] should make offering according to [the usual] procedure. When visualization of the offering to the three jewels of the tenfold dharmadhātu is complete, in all sincerity they profess the following outloud: 'May this cloud of incense and flowers suffuse universally throughout the realms of the ten directions and provide offerings for all the Buddhas, the dharma, the bodhisattvas, and the assembly of countless śrāvakas. May they use it to erect a terrace of light that spans realms without limit. And throughout infinite Buddha lands may it be received and used to perform the work of the Buddhas, thereby perfuming all living beings and causing them to generate the aspiration for enlightenment.' "

269. The *Ch'ing kuan-yin ching* prescribes that the left hand should be placed over the right (T 20.36c), which is contrary to the usual Indian practice but in accordance with Chih-i's writings on meditation as well as later Chinese Buddhist tradition. This prescription would seem to be quite an anomaly for an Indian text.

270. *Ch'ing kuan-yin ching*, T 20.34c. The KCPL, *Ch'ing kuan-yin ch'an-fa* (T 46.795c13–14) adds: "One should keep the mind from becoming scattered. Do not count the breath if breathing is winded, constricted, or coarse." According to Chih-i's discussion of the twenty-five preliminary expedients for meditation in *Tz'u-ti ch'an-men* (T 46.490a3–17) and *Hsiao chih-kuan* (T 46.466a1–10), these three conditions will impede meditative development. Contemplation can only be carried out effectively under a fourth condition—where breathing is "fine" or "at rest" (*hsi*)—which he likens to "a continuous thread of fine silk that sometimes seems to be present and sometimes seems to have vanished."

Chan-jan (T 46.194a6–18) expands at length on the meaning of breath counting according to the perspectives of mundane religious praxis as well as according to the four dharmas of the tripiṭaka, shared, separate, and perfect teachings. In the perfect teaching the breath is contemplated in conformity with "the three truths in a single instant of thought." His discussion is mostly based on the *Ch'ing kuan-yin ching shu* (T 36.972c).

all living beings, invite three times [the specific deities of] the three jewels listed above.[271] Once invoked, chant the names of [these deities of] the three jewels three times through.[272] Also chant the name of Avalokiteś-vara. Then, with the palms and ten fingers joined [in reverence], recite the four-line gāthās.[273] After that, recite the three incantations. You may do this one time through, or seven times, depending on the lateness of the hour.[274] When you have finshed reciting the spells, confess and re-pent your sins. Recollect to yourself the rules that you have transgressed. When you have exposed them fully, imagine that you are washed clean of them. Then venerate [the deities] whom you summoned previously. When the veneration is finished, let one person mount the high seat to chant or recite the text of this *Sūtra* [*of the Invocation of Avalokiteśvara*], while the others in the group listen attentively. This procedure should be

271. Both the KCPL, *Ch'ing kuan-yin ch'an-fa* (T 46.795c19–21), and the outline of the lost manual in *Ch'ing kuan-yin ching shu* include offering of the water and tooth-cleaning stick as part of this invitation of the three jewels. The former states: "Each kneels with knees flush and invites: 'With single heart I invite you! Salutations to our Original Master Buddha Śākyamuni! [Three times he invites each of the deities in the preceding list of the three jewels.] Having invited you, I have also prepared tooth-cleaning stick and purified water. May you show great compassion and pity and accept it from me!' "

272. The KCPL, *Ch'ing kuan-yin ch'an-fa* (T 46.795c22), in close agreement with MHCK, appears to distinguish this recitation as another cycle of veneration or salutation (*li*) to the specific list of deities of the three jewels, but the outline of the manual in *Ch'ing kuan-yin ching shu* fails to distinguish it from the invitation and offering sequence. Chan-jan (T.46.194a19) states: "[Reciting three times through] symbolizes removal of the three obstacles [of retribution, karma, and the afflictions]. Details of the procedure are provided in the main ritual manual from the [*Kuo-ch'ing*] *pai-lu* as well as the in *Cheng hsing i* [of Nan-shan Tao-hsüan]. Thus the text says that one may consult the sūtra to supplement the prac-tice."

273. The gāthās, provided in the *Ch'ing kuan-yin ching* (T 20.34c) as well as by Chan-jan (T 46.194a), read: "I beseech you to save me from suffering and disas-ters, to include everything as the object of your great compassion, to shine beams of pure light everywhere, and to annihilate the darkness of nescience. That I may be released from suffering, afflictions, and all manner of disease, may you come unfailingly to where I am and confer great peace upon me. I now bow my head in salutation to you, the one who, upon hearing his name, saves those who speak it from disasters; now I entrust myself to the father, who has good will and com-passion toward the world. I ask only that you come unfailingly, to release me from the sufferings created by the three poisons and to confer upon me happiness in this life and great nirvāṇa thereafter."

274. Following the first and second dhāraṇī , the KCPL, *Ch'ing kuan-yin ch'an-fa* (T 46.795c23–26), inserts recitation of select prose passages from the sūtra as well as the names of the deities of the three jewels.

used at morning and early evening [intervals of worship].[275] For the other four periods use the standard liturgy.[276] Anyone who dislikes omissions and abbreviations may consult the sūtra to supplement the practice.

[15a9] The [*Invocation of Avalokiteśvara*] *Sūtra* says, "The eye responds to form; how then can it be concentrated and made to abide? The faculty of mental cognition (*i*; *manas*) responds to the objects of mind; how can it be concentrated and made to abide [in one place]?"[277] The *Mahāsaṃnipāta Sūtra* says, "[It is called] abiding in the mind just as it is."[278] This "just as it is" is none other than emptiness. The passage in this text that reads "each and every one [of the six senses] enters into the limit of the real" is just another way of saying emptiness and suchness.

[15a12] [Śāriputra says in the *Invocation of Avalokiteśvara Sūtra*,] "The element earth lacks solidity."[279] If we say that earth exists, then by "exists"

275. Chan-jan (T 46.194b12–13) states: "The two times of day and night each has its beginning interval. Therefore [the text] says morning and early night."

276. KCPL, *Ch'ing kuan-yin ch'an-fa* (T 46.796a2), says here, "During the other [four worship] intervals [of the day and night], sitting in meditation and veneration of the Buddhas should proceed according to the usual practice." This "usual procedure" is described in Chih-i's *Li chih-fa* (Establishing of Regulations) as "four periods of sitting in meditation and six periods or intervals of venerating the Buddhas" (KCPL, T 46.793c8–9). The two rites commonly used at the Kuo-ch'ing Monastery on Mount T'ien-t'ai for this daily cycle of worship (the *Ching-li fa* and *P'u-li fa*) are included as items 2 and 3 of the KCPL (T 46.794a–795b); for further discussion, see Stevenson, "The Four Kinds of Samādhi in Early T'ien-t'ai Buddhism," pp. 45–48.

277. *Ch'ing kuan-yin ching*, T 20.37a. In the sūtra, an earnest and devout monk named Upasena asks Śāriputra, "How, while I am counting breaths and petitioning the Honored One to expound liberation to me, can I maintain concentration? For my eye and visual consciousness respond to form; how then can I maintain my concentration? . . . My mind and mind consciousness (*manovijñāna*) respond to objects of mind (dharmas); how then can I maintain my concentration? . . . Thus these consciousnesses are thieves of the attention, prancing about like monkeys. How then can I maintain my concentration in the face of these gamboling six sense organs and the ubiquitous dharmas that are their objects?" Śāriputra's answer to this question follows immediately in the sūtra, but in the MHCK a quote from the *Mahāsaṃnipāta* (*Ta-chi ching*) and another passage from the *Ch'ing kuan-yin ching* are first interposed.

278. *Ta-chi ching* (*Mahāsaṃnipāta Sūtra*), T 13.168c, is identified by *Kōgi* (1.508) as the source of the quote; the correspondence, however, is not exact.

279. *Ch'ing kuan-yin ching*, T 20.37a. The passage from the sūtra cited here refutes in succession the essential properties of the four material elements: "Then Śāriputra told Upasena, 'You should now contemplate the element earth as lacking the nature of solidity, the nature of the element water as not to abide, the nature of the element wind as unimpedability, . . . and the nature of the element fire as unreal; . . . form, sensation, perception, impulses, and consciousness are each in their nature and features the same in this respect as (earth), water, fire,

we mean "substantiality" or "reality," and "substantiality" is what "solid" means. But if we say that earth inexists, or that it both exists and inexists, these descriptions still imply phenomenal substantiality; hence they too are included in the meaning of the term "solid." Here [the sūtra] repudiates the supposed nature of solidity by demonstrating that it is utterly inapprehensible.

[15a15] "The nature of water is not to abide anywhere." If we say that water exists, then by "exists" we mean "abides." Similarly, to go on to say that water neither exists nor inexists is still to consider that it "abides." Now water does not abide in the existence tetralemma, nor in the inexistence tetralemma, nor even in the indescribable. That is why [the sūtra] says, "The nature of water is not to abide."

[15a18] "The nature of wind is unimpedability." If we contemplate wind as existing, then "existing" means in this case "impeded." To go on to say that "wind neither exists nor inexists" is also inapplicable. Even the inexistence tetralemma fails [to characterize wind]. That is why it is said, "The nature of wind is unimpedability."

[15a20] "The element fire is insubstantial." Fire does not arise from itself, nor from something else, nor from both, nor without a cause. It fundamentally lacks an own-being and exists only in dependence upon causes and conditions. That is why the sūtra says it is insubstantial. As it is this way for the contemplation of material form, so "sensation, perception, impulses, and consciousness likewise each enter into the limit of the real."

[15a23] The contemplation of the five aggregates being like this, the twelve links of cause and condition are [similarly shown] each to be like an echo in a canyon, as solid as the core of a banana tree, as evanescent as dew or lightning, etc.[280] Thus at each moment of mental activity one may bring to completion the discernment of emptiness. One should strive to develop this contemplation assiduously so as to bring one's own mind into resonance [with the principle of reality]. This foundation of contemplative insight (*kuan-hui*) must not be lacking.[281]

---

and wind. All enter into the limit of the real.' When Upasena had heard these words, his body became like water and fire. He achieved the samādhi of the four elements, comprehended perfectly the emptiness and featurelessness of the five aggregates, killed the bandits of his mind, the defilements, attained vast clarity of mind, became an arhat, and, spewing fire from out of his body, burnt himself to ashes and entered nirvāṇa."

280. Examples from the ten *upamāna* or 'semblances' (i.e., ball of foam, bubble, mirage, trunk of a banana tree, magical illusion, dream, reflection, echo, cloud, and flash of lightning) used frequently in Buddhist scriptures to illustrate the insubstantiality and evanescence of dharmas (for references, see Lamotte, *L'Enseignement de Vimalakīrti*, pp. 132–133, n. 23).

281. Chan-jan (T 46.194c25–195a1) states: "If there is no [foundation of] con-

[15a25] The dhāraṇī for eliminating poison and suppressing harmful influences has the ability to destroy the obstacle of retribution.[282] [Upon hearing the Buddha teach them to intone verses, recite the names of the three jewels and the incantations of Avalokiteśvara,] the people of Vaiśālī were returned to their original state of health.[283]

[15a27] The dhāraṇī for eradicating evil karma has the ability to destroy the obstacle of karma, for, by reciting it, even a person who violates the rule of chaste conduct can clear away the filth and restore himself or herself to purity.[284]

---

templative insight (*kuan-hui*), then the practice becomes profitless asceticism. For this reason one must use the meditative discernment [that perceives objects to be] like a mirage, etc., in order to realize the emptiness of essential nature and distinguishing mark and enter the limit of reality. There are two [understandings] of the limit of reality: the two vehicles resort [to the sense found in] the shared [teaching], which [interprets the limit of reality as] the true or real. The separate and perfect [teachings] rely on the [vision of] the middle and do not hold anything in common with the lesser [vehicles]. Here [the MHCK] still carries the [sense of] the shared [teaching]. But when it comes to the dhāraṇī of six-syllable phrases below, it accords with the [view of] the middle way. This is all the more the case for the section on the contemplation of evil [dharmas] that follows later, which relies wholly upon the perfect contemplation. Thus you should know that the fundamental import of the present section is that of the perfect [teaching]."

282. The first of the three dhāraṇī from the *Ch'ing kuan-yin ching* (T 20.35a6–15) used in this rite. The sūtra itself gives this dhāraṇī the title "incantation for summoning the Buddhas of the ten directions to save and protect animate beings," which is different from the title adopted by Chih-i. Chih-i's name for the dhāraṇī ("the dhāraṇī that eliminates poison and suppresses harmful influences") is actually the title that the sūtra gives to the second dhāraṇī (i.e., the "incantation that destroys the obstruction of evil karma, eliminates poison, and suppresses harmful influence") (see T 20.35a23–24).

The "obstacle of retribution" is one of the "three obstacles" (*san chang*)—i.e., those of the afflictions, karma, and retribution. The obstacle of retribution refers to limitations of physical or mental endowment as well as environment that arise from karmic influences of the past. The pairing of the obstacles of retribution and affliction with the first and third dhāraṇīs is reversed in the MHCK and *Ch'ing kuan-yin ching shu* (see T 39.973a24–29).

283. *Ch'ing kuan-yin ching*, T 20.35a20. This dhāraṇī heals the terrible illnesses with which the population of Vaiśālī had become afflicted.

284. Ibid., T 20.35a22–b11. The second of the three dhāraṇī, it is matched with the obstacle of karma or deed precisely because the sūtra gives its title as "the dhāraṇī incantation that destroys the obstruction of evil deeds, eliminates poison, and suppresses harm." The *Ch'ing kuan-yin ching* says of its efficacy (T 20.35b8–13): "All fears, poisons, and harmful influences will disappear. All evil spirits, tigers, wolves, and lions will, upon hearing this dhāraṇī, have their mouths closed and stopped up and be unable to cause harm. Even a person who violates the rule of chaste conduct and commits the ten evil acts will, upon hearing this dhāraṇī,

[15a28] The dhāraṇī of six-syllable phrases has the power to destroy the obstacle of the afflictions.[285] There can be no doubt that it purifies the sense organs of the three poisons and brings about the achievement of Buddhahood. The "six syllables" [of its name] signify the six [incarnations] of Avalokiteśvara, which together are capable of destroying the three obstacles in each of the six destinies.[286] The Avalokiteśvara of Great Compassion destroys the three obstacles in the destiny of hell; it is because the suffering in this destiny is so intense that it is appropriate for him to employ his great compassion. The Avalokiteśvara of Great Kind-

---

have the filth washed away and be restored to the state of purity. Even if your karmic obstacles are filthy and bad, call on the bodhisattva Avalokiteśvara and recite and remember this dhāraṇī. Your obstacle of karma will then be destroyed and you will see the Buddhas before you."

285. Ibid., T 20.36a6–12. The third of the three dhāraṇīs. The name of this dhāraṇī—"six-syllable phrases"—is problematic, for it does not appear to have any immediate connection with the fifty odd characters that make up the incantation in Chinese, aside from the fact that the dhāraṇī does contain a succession of some twelve words, each containing three characters or syllables.

Chan-jan (T 46.195b18–29), resorting to the *Ch'ing kuan-yin ching shu*, states: "Some people say that it refers to the names of the three jewels, with each jewel containing two syllables: as in 'Buddha,' 'dharma,' and 'saṅgha.' Others say that the three jewels represent three syllables or characters, and the name 'Kuan-shih-yin,' three characters. But there is really no evidence for these in the text [of the sūtra itself]. Therefore, we dismiss them. In its analysis of the passages from the sūtra, the [*Ch'ing kuan-yin ching*] commentary suggests three interpretations of the [term] 'six syllables.' The first treats the six syllables from the perspective of recompense or fruit. After the verses [the sūtra] explains in detail how, upon being heard by the fourfold assembly, the six syllables have the power to uproot the suffering of the six destinies [of rebirth]. Next, it treats the six syllables from the perspective of cause: where Upasena, upon hearing the six syllable phrase, is made to contemplate the psychic channels, the six marvelous accesses [of meditation upon the breath] are explained in detail. Third, the six sense faculties are equated with the six syllables. Where Śāriputra answers Upasena in the forest saying, 'When eye responds to form,' [the sūtra] elucidates in depth the six sense faculties. Each of these three passages [in the sūtra] is summed up with the statement, 'Because they heard the six-syllable phrase. . . .' Thus the meaning of the six syllables does not lie outside of these three sections. The present text [of MHCK] adopts two of these interpretations—the first and the last." See also *Ch'ing kuan-yin ching shu*, T 39.975b13–c11.

Oda's *Bukkyō daijiten* (1827c) cites Hōtan's (1654–1738) unpublished commentary on the *Ch'ing kuan-yin ching*, the *Kannon sangenki*, claiming that the six syllables refer specifically to the six characters *an-t'o-li pan-t'u-li* (**aṃdali-paṃdali*) contained in the dhāraṇī. This phrase also occurs within the preceding two dhāraṇī. Hōtan takes it to mean *ānāpānasmṛti* or "contemplation of the breath."

286. Neither Chan-jan nor the *Ch'ing kuan-yin ching shu* offers a clear explanation of the origin of these six incarnations of Avalokiteśvara.

ness destroys the three obstacles in the destiny of hungry ghosts; it is because there is starvation and thirst in this destiny that it is appropriate for him to employ his great beneficence. The Avalokiteśvara of Leonine Fearlessness destroys the three obstacles in the destiny of animals; it is because the king of beasts is majestic and fierce that it is appropriate for him to employ his fearlessness in this destiny. The Avalokiteśvara of the Universal Shining Radiance destroys the three obstacles in the destiny of the asuras; it is because of the preponderance of envy and distrust in that destiny that it is appropriate for him to employ his attribute of universal radiance. The Divine Hero Avalokiteśvara destroys the three obstacles in the destiny of human beings; in the human realm there are to be found both the principle [of reality] (*li*) and phenomenal affairs (*shih*); he is called "divine" because he uses phenomenal means to subdue people's arrogance and "hero" because he uses principle to enable people to see their own Buddha nature. The Avalokiteśvara as Mahābrahmā the Profound destroys the three obstacles in the destiny of the gods; Brahmā is the lord of the gods, so that by indicating their lord, one includes the vassals as well.

[15b10] Enlarging upon this, we may consider the six Avalokiteśvaras to signify the twenty-five samādhis.[287] The Avalokiteśvara of Great Compassion represents the undefiled samādhi; the Avalokiteśvara of Great Kindness signifies the samādhi of mental delight; the Leonine Avalokiteśvara signifies the samādhi of nonretrogression; the Avalokiteśvara of Great Shining Light signifies the blissful samādhi; the Heroic Avalokiteśvara signifies the four samādhis beginning with the apparitional samādhi; the Mahābrahmā Avalokiteśvara signifies the seventeen samādhis beginning with the unshakable samādhi. Think on this yourself and you will see what is meant.

[15b14] This sūtra may be used for repentance by persons from any of the three vehicles. Thus if one disciplines and delivers oneself, killing the bandits that are the fetters, one will achieve the status of an arhat. If one's

287. From the *Nirvāṇa Sūtra*, T 12.690b. These samādhis are correlated in the sūtra to the so-called twenty-five "states of existence," with one samādhi matched to annihilate each "existence." The twenty-five existences are simply a vertical breakdown of the three realms. Thus the realm of desire contains fourteen levels of existence broadly grouped according to the six destinies—one state of existence for each of the hell, animal, hungry ghost, and asura realms; four states of existence (corresponding to the four continents) for the human destiny; and six levels of existence for the heavenly destiny. The realm of form contains seven states of existence, grouped according to the four dhyānas. The formless realm contains four states of existence, namely the four formless meditations (*samāpatti*). A detailed discussion of the relationship of these twenty-five samādhis to the twenty-five states of existence (and their place on the bodhisattva course) appears in Chih-i's *Ssu chiao i*, T 46.755c29–758b28.

merit is abundant and capacity keen, then upon contemplating nescience, impulses, and the rest [of the twelve causes and conditions], one will achieve the status of a pratyekabuddha. If one gives rise to great compassion, one's body will come to shine like crystalline *vaiḍūrya* and Buddhas will appear as though in every pore. One will attain the *śūraṅgama samādhi* and dwell in the stage of no backsliding.[288]

[15b17] Throughout the Mahāyāna sūtras there are practices of this type, such as the repentances of the seven buddhas and the eight bodhisattvas,[289] or the repentance involving 800 days of cleaning privies that is described in the *Sūtra on the Visualization of Bodhisattva Ākāśagarbha.*[290] All such practices as these are encompassed by [the samādhi of] freely following one's thought (*sui-tzu-i*).

Contemplation amidst Good Dharmas

[15b20] Second is the section on [contemplation] as applied to good [dharmas]. This falls into two parts: first, we distinguish the four phases of thought and, next, deal with their application to the myriad wholesome [activities].

The Four Phases of Thought

[15b21] We begin with an explanation of the four phases of thought. Mind and consciousness, being formless, are impossible to preceive in and of themselves; but their [temporal operation][291] may be distin-

288. *Ch'ing kuan-yin ching*, T 20.35c, 38a6–7. Chan-jan (T 46.196c1–2) states: "Through generating great compassion and taking the reality limit as one's object one realizes nonretrogression. This stage is equivalent to either the first abode or first stage (*bhūmi*) [depending upon whether one is using the scheme of the separate or perfect path], where mindfulness no longer backslides."

289. From the *Ch'i fo pa p'u-sa shuo t'o-lo-ni shen-chou ching* (T no. 1332; The Dhāraṇī Sūtra Spoken by the Seven Buddhas and the Eight Bodhisattvas). Chan-jan (T 46.196c9–14) states: "[This sūtra] first reveals that each of the seven Buddhas has a dhāraṇī and goes on to explain that dhāraṇī's effectiveness as a means of repentance. Next the text discusses the eight bodhisattvas, . . . for each of whom there is an incantation and effective procedure for repentance."

290. The *Kuan hsü-k'ung-tsang p'u-sa ching*, T 13.677a–677c. According to Chan-jan (T 46.196c8–197a19), who cites the scripture, this practice entails a daily routine of secretly cleaning latrines, meditating on the bodhisattva Ākāśagarbha, and repenting before the thirty-five Buddhas of confession. The practice is to be carried out for a continuous period of 800 days.

291. This entire introductory section on the four phases of thought (from T 46.15b21 to 15c16) is taken, with some abridgment and rearrangement, from chapter 4 of Chih-i's *Chüeh-i san-mei* (T 46.623a8–b23). This chapter (Clarification of the Marks of the Four Phases) begins with the question, "If a practitioner wishes to enter this samādhi, which particular mental marks should he take as the basis for contemplation?" Chih-i then explains that the four temporal phases of

guished in terms of the four successive phases of not-yet-thinking, about-to-think, thought-proper, and thinking-completed. "Not-yet-thinking" denotes the condition where mind has yet to generate [any involvement with a given object]. "About-to-think" refers to the condition where mind is on the verge of generating [involvement with the object]. "Thinking-proper" is the condition where mind dwells in full involvement with the object. "Thinking-completed" denotes the condition where, having reached its culmination, mental involvement with the given object fades and vanishes.[292] Anyone who can comprehend these four [phases] fully will penetrate the one mark that is no-mark.[293]

---

mental activation are used as the basis for contemplation (rather than any fixed external or material referent), precisely because they appear, consistently and repeatedly, through each moment of thought and activity. Asked to explain how these are to be construed as marks for contemplation, Chih-i responds (T 46.623a19–23): "That which allows something to be apprehended and, as such, distinguished is known as a 'mark.' The dharmas of mind and consciousness are without form. If not distinguished by means of the four marks of the activation of thought, they are difficult to know. If one is unable to know [mind as object] clearly, contemplation will be impossible to perform. Therefore, one must first distinguish [mind and its temporal operation] by means of the marks of the four [phases]. If one discerns and distinguishes to the point where one clearly realizes that these marks are no-mark, then one will enter the perfect equality of the one mark."

Chan-jan (T 46.197a26–b4) states: "'*Yün*' (phase, cycle) means movement. From 'not-yet' one arrives at 'about-to'; from 'about-to,' at 'actual or proper'; from 'actual,' at 'completed.' Thus [the phases] are generically construed as movement. . . . In [the contemplation of] the [six] activities and [six] sense perceptions that follows, if one does not first distinguish the [four phases] clearly, contemplation of mind will have no basis."

292. This particular reading has been reconstructed on the basis of the passage in *Chüeh-i san-mei* from which the lines in MHCK have been abstracted (see T 46.623a10–11).

293. Chan-jan here embarks on a critique of certain misinterpretations of the "samādhi of following one's thought," as well as on a lengthy statement of what he considers to be the correct approach to its practice. The passage in question figures prominently in the debates over meditation carried on between the "home mountain" and "off mountain" circles of Sung period T'ien-t'ai. We translate it in full (with a minor abridgment).

Chan-jan (T 46.197b4–28) states: "Furthermore, people in the world today for the most part assert that the mind in which thought has arisen (*sheng-hsin*) is false, and one should contemplate the mind [wherein thought is] annihilated. [The latter, they claim,] is real. So saying, these people end up avoiding [the practice of] meditative discernment completely, thinking that [such an approach] represents the nonarising or nonproduction [of thought]. Their error is grave indeed. These commonplace practitioners of dhyāna all [claim to] contemplate nonarising but have no clue as to where this 'nonarising' is to to be found. Is [this condition of

[15b25] Q: The [phase of] not-yet-thinking [means that thought] has not arisen, and thinking-completed [means that it has] already gone. There is no mind or mentation (*hsin*) present in either of these. And since there is no mind, there is likewise no mark. How then can these [phases] be contemplated?[294]

[15b26] A: Although in not-yet-thinking no arising has taken place, it

---

nonarising] previously existent or present? Is it previously nonexistent or not present? If you say it is already present, then you must have already realized non-arising. If you say it is not already present, then how can you call it a contemplation? . . .

"[Contemplation] is like putting out a fire: [its coals] must be extinguished completely. If one just extinguishes the visible [flames and smoke] and fails to extinguish its potential [to flare up again], one will eventually be scorched by flames that have yet to appear. To contemplate mind [in the phases of] 'not-yet-arisen' or 'already-completed' is truly to extinguish [mind that is] 'about-to-arise' and 'arisen-proper.' People who [occupy themselves with this misconceived] contemplation of nonarising [of thoughts] only know how to discern mind in its full state of generation and force it not to generate thoughts. They do not know how to discern mind before it has generated thought. The essential substance of mind is originally inexistent. Its inexistence being something that is fundamental, its generation or activation is, likewise, no-generation. . . .

"Furthermore, contemplation of the four phases [of thought] is a method of meditative discernment that is designed to pursue the branch tips and follow along with phenomenal activities (*shih*), wherever thought happens to lead (*sui-tzu-i*). On the other hand, approaches such as the constantly seated samādhi are concerned exclusively with the discernment of principle (*li*) or [the fact that] there is no dharma that is not identical to dharma-nature. Thus one should know that neither of these two approaches can be dispensed with in the cultivation of samādhi. It is with such an idea in mind that the *Chan-ch'a ching* (T 17.908a–b) says: 'There are two modes to meditative discernment. One is [the approach of] consciousness-only, where all is [realized to be] mind only. The second is contemplation of reality [itself] or the discerning of true suchness.' 'Consciousness-only' corresponds to [contemplation] carried out amidst phenomenal activities (*shih*). 'Suchness' is the contemplation of principle (*li*). The contemplation of the four phases as applied to [the manifold phenomena of] the tenfold dharmadhātu that is described in the text here is the equivalent of the discernment of all [dharmas] as mind-only set forth in the *Chan-ch'a ching*. It is with this sense in mind that the passage here states: 'If one can comprehend fully the four [phases], one will penetrate marklessness.' "

For a discussion of the *Chan-ch'a shan-e yeh pao ching* (T no. 839), with reference to recent Japanese scholarship, see Lai, "The *Chan-ch'a ching*: Religion and Magic in Medieval China."

294. This question and response are taken from *Chüeh-i san-mei*, T 46.623a24–b8: "It is feasible that one might discern the two mental phases of about-to-think and thinking-proper. But as not-yet-thinking has not arisen, there is no mentation or mind present. With no mentation there is no mark to distinguish."

does not mean that [mind] is ultimately inexistent.[295] It is analogous to a person who has not yet performed an action deciding suddenly to do it. You cannot say that there is no person simply because he has not yet undertaken to act. If you assert absolutely that there is no person present at that point, then who performs the action afterwards? It is precisely because there is a person who has "not-yet-performed" the action that there can be a performance of the action to begin with. It is the same with mind or mentation (*hsin*): it is on account of there being a not-yet-thinking that there can be an about-to-think. How could an about-to-think exist if there had been no not-yet-thinking? Hence, although it is true that [mentation in] its phase of not-yet-thinking is not yet fully present, it does not follow from this fact that thinking as a whole is completely inexistent.[296] As for the thinking-completed, it can still be contemplated even though [thinking per se] has perished, just as when a person has finished an action one cannot say that the person himself no longer exists. If there is really no person present at that point, then who has just performed the action? The same applies for the notion that mind perishes when thinking is completed: one cannot say that the perishing is eternal, for to do so is to commit the fallacy of annihilationism—the utter denial of cause and effect.[297] Hence, although it is true that [the thought]

295. The word "mind" (*hsin*) here is supplied from the *Chüeh-i san-mei* passage, T 46.623a27. Chan-jan (T 46.197c9–10) states: "Because [thought at this point] has not yet arisen one can refer to it as inexistent. But since [mind] is not forever or wholly inexistent [at this moment], one still must contemplate [it]." *Kōgi* (1.534) says that though there are vicissitudes in the mind's activity, its substance does not vanish.

296. Chan-jan (T 46.197c12–14) states: "Thinking and not-yet-thinking each resorts to its prior conditional basis. Although these conditions may come and go, the mind itself is indestructible. Being indestructible, the mind as such is able to produce the entire range of thoughts. Therefore, in contemplating the mind one prevents it from taking the delusions or defilements—the nine realms of the dharmadhātu—as its conditional basis. So doing one enters into the Buddha mind."

297. If mind utterly perished with the perishing of each thought, continuity of karmic cause and effect (and, hence, religious practice as well) would be impossible. This, of course, was one of the basic grounds for positing the Yogācāra thesis of an *ālaya-vijñāna* (the repository for karmic seeds) and *kliṣṭa-manovijñāna* (the deluded grasping or positing of the *ālaya* as self) as a continuing substratum of mental activity that undergirds the arising and perishing of momentary consciousness (*manas* and *vijñāna*). Although the contemplation of the four phases of thought is quite reminiscent of classic early Buddhist meditations upon the momentary arising and perishing of the cognitive/mental consciousness (*manovijñāna*) and its concomitant factors (i.e., the operation of the *skandhas*, *āyatanas*, and *dhātus*), Hui-ssu, Chih-i, and Chan-jan all tend to work implicitly within certain proto-Yogācāra-tathāgatagarbha models of mind that were current in medieval China.

in its phase of thinking-completed has perished, contemplation can still be performed.

[15c6] Q: What is past is gone; what is future has yet to arrive; and what is present does not persist. Yet it is unthinkable that there should be some other mind apart from the three times.[298] What sort of mind would you have us contemplate?

[15c8] A: Your question is erroneous. For if the past were permanently extinguished, one could ultimately not have knowledge of it; if the future were entirely yet to come, one could not have knowledge of it; and if the present did not persist at all, one could not have knowledge of it. How then could the saints know the minds [of beings throughout] the three times? Even demons and gods know [the affairs] of themselves and others in the three times.[299] How then could practitioners of the Buddha's dharma hold such annihilationist, tortoise-hare, and rabbit-horn views [as you suggest by your question]?[300] Know then that, although mind in the three times lacks any concrete reality, it is nevertheless possible to have knowledge of it.

[15c12] Hence it is said in gāthās, "What the Buddhas have expounded is that, although [the mind] is empty, it is not utterly inexistent, and that, although it continues successively, it is not eternally unchanging. Thus neither sin nor merit is lost."[301] One who upholds the view of the inherent extinction of mind resembles a blind person encountering color: for such an individual there will be no eye of right contemplation with respect to the Buddha's teaching, and religious practice will be futile, bring-

298. This question and answer sequence is taken virtually verbatim from *Chüeh-i san-mei*, T 46.623b8–23. Chan-jan (T 46.197c16) identifies this statement with the *Diamond Sūtra*, although the match is not exact—see *Chin-kang pan-jo p'o-lo-mi ching* (T 8.751b27–28): "Subhūti! The past mind is impossible to apprehend, the present mind is impossible to apprehend, and the future mind is impossible to apprehend."

299. Knowledge of the destiny of others by means of the divine eye, knowledge of one's own and others' karmic legacy from past lives, and the power to know other beings' present thoughts represent the first, third, and fourth of the five *abhijñā* or "superpowers." These five are classed as mundane powers that may be realized by gods and certain spiritually powerful individuals. In addition to the five, saints of the Buddhist tradition realize a sixth, "supramundane," power that is peculiar to the Buddhist tradition—the exhaustion of outflows.

300. Chan-jan (T 46.198a5–8) states: "Chih-i uses these two similes to illustrate the view of annihilationism. The opponent cites the passage where 'the three times are inapprehensible' to make the point that there is ultimately no mind. This is equivalent to the two [similes], which themselves are wholly inexistent. It is known as 'annihilationist views.' "

301. TCTL, T 25.64c. The preceding lines to the verse read: "If there is a deed, there is also its fruition. The inexistence of the agent of the act as well as the fruit is the ultimate and profound law that was discovered by the Buddha."

ing no attainments. Once the practitioner knows that there are four temporal phases to thought, then, in accordance with whatever good and evil thoughts his mind produces, he uses wisdom that is free of attachment to reflect back upon and discern it.[302]

Application of the Four Phases to Wholesome Activities

[15c17] Next we deal with the application [of this contemplation] to wholesome activities. [The variety of such activities] is vast, but here we shall discuss them on the basis of the six perfections.[303] When confronted with the six objects of sense one should be even-minded and detached toward the six perceptions. When one lacks material provisions one

302. *Chüeh-i san-mei*, T 46.623c2. Kuan-ting in this passage alludes to a specific process of meditative development set forth at length in Chih-i's *Chüeh-i san-mei*. According to the latter (T 46.623b25–624c19), the practitioner of the "samādhi of maintaining wakeful awareness of thought" must first tame the mind through application of the six perfections and foster the keen conviction that mind and all dharmas are empty. Then, with "a mind that is free of all clinging," he "turns back to reflect upon and discern" the four mental phases in each moment of thought. When the four phases are fully established as an object of contemplation, they are then shown to be inapprehensible through investigation of the four alternatives of the tetralemma. The *Chüeh-i san-mei* (T 46.624b23–27) says: "Contemplating the [phases of] not-yet-thinking and about-to-think in this manner, if one does not apprehend any dualistic extremes, one will not grasp after dualistic extremes. Not grasping after dualistic extremes, one will no longer cling to dualistic extremes, [nor go on to] generate all manner of afflictive deeds (karma). Once one is free of dualism, free of the deeds that induce bondage, free of obstructions, then the mind of right contemplation [will appear], lucid and pure like empty space. As a result of this, the genuine insight of the middle way will brilliantly open forth, and [the practitioner] will come to illumine the two truths simultaneously."

According to *Chüeh-i san-mei* the "right contemplation" described here represents the foundation of the "samādhi of maintaining wakeful awareness of thought." What is more, there is a deliberate procedure to its cultivation. Correct contemplation must be developed first through seated meditation—a practice that Chih-i calls the "general or universal discernment" (*tsung-kuan*). Only when contemplation of the four phases and their inapprehensibility is stable enough to be maintained effectively through other activities is seated meditation dispensed with as a regular practice. The fluid application of this contemplation to all activities—i.e., the six sense perceptions and six modes of physical action under both good and evil circumstances—is known as "discernment in specific applications" (*pieh-kuan*). This basic model for development of "right contemplation" functions as a central structure of Chih-i's *Hsiao chih-kuan* (T 46.466c28–467a3), as well as the formal discussion of "contemplation proper" in greater chapter 7 of MHCK (T 46.100b16).

303. Giving (*dāna*), morality (*śīla*), patience or forbearance (*kṣānti*), exertion (*vīrya*), meditation (*dhyāna*), and wisdom (*prajñā*).

should engage in the six acts [in order to provide for oneself].[304] Taken together, this even-mindedness [of the senses] and performance [of the six actions] comes to twelve forms of activity (*shih*) in total.

[15c19] **The Six Sense Perceptions and the Perfection of Giving (*dāna*).** First we will consider the moment when the eye perceives form.[305] Not-yet-seeing, about-to-see, seeing-proper, and seeing-completed—in neither of these four phases can seeing take place—yet it is not valid to say that one does not see. Turning the focus of contemplation back to the mind that is aware of form,[306] we find that it does not come from outside, for if it did, the image would not be present within oneself. Nor does it emerge from inside, for if it did, it would not be dependent upon causes and conditions. As it originates from neither within nor without, neither is it from somewhere in between. Nor is it eternally self-existent. One should know, then, that the act of perceiving form is ultimately empty and quiescent. The form that is being contemplated is the same as space, and the one who contemplates form is as good as blind.[307]

304. Walking, standing, sitting, reclining, speaking, being silent, and miscellaneous actions. These derive from Hui-ssu's *Sui-tzu-i san-mei* (HTC 98.344a) and the *Chüeh-i san-mei* (T 46.624c21–24), with the exception that for "reclining" Hui-ssu has "sleeping," and instead of "miscellaneous actions" he has "eating."

305. The first of the six sense perceptions; see *Chüeh-i san-mei*, T 46.625b3–12.

306. Ibid., T.46.625b6–10. *Chüeh-i san-mei* states: "[The factors of] sense faculty, object, [intervening] space, and light are incapable of seeing and discriminating on their own. Through their coming together as causes and conditions, they produce visual consciousness. With visual consciousness as cause and condition, mental consciousness is produced. When mental consciousness emerges, one is able to discriminate the various types of form. Also, visual consciousness, in turn, comes into existence through dependence on mental consciousness. By visual consciousness one is able to perceive form, as a result of which one gives rise to attachment. For this reason one must turn back to reflect upon and contemplate the mind that is aware of form."

307. Chih-i's twofold approach to discernment described here—refutation of the categories of temporal process and refutation of lateral factors of cause and condition—is paradigmatic for all of the remaining five sense perceptions and six activities. These two approaches to contemplation, along with a third, are discussed at length in the fourth of the ten modes of discernment (i.e., "Eradication of Dharmas Completely") in MHCK, greater chapter 7 (T 46.63a7–65a2), as well as in Chih-i's San kuan i (HTC 99.79a–80b). They are discernments used to counter three respective conventional assumptions about mind: production on the basis of lateral causal factors (*yin-ch'eng*), successive temporal continuity [of mental consciousness] (*hsiang-hsü*), and mutual relativity [of mind to the concept of no-mind] (*hsiang-tai*). The basic method for all three is to "demonstrate the inapprehensibility of each position by systematic refutation of the alternatives of the tetralemma " (*ssu-chü t'ui-chien pu-te*).

Chih-i claims to derive the entire system from Nāgārjuna's *Mūlamadhyamakakā-*

[15c24] [The same analysis applies to the other five kinds of sense perception], up to the sixth, the awareness of dharmas on the part of the cognitive faculty or mind sense (*i*; *manas*). In each of its four phases—not-yet-aware, about-to-be-aware, aware-proper, and awareness-completed—the thought is incapable of being apprehended. Turning the focus of contemplation back to the mind that is aware (*chüeh*) of dharmas,[308] we find that it too neither comes from outside nor emerges from inside. There are no dharmic objects nor is there anyone who could regard them as dharmas; both are the same as emptiness. Such is the contemplation of the six kinds of perception.

[15c27] The eye, form, space, and light are all necessary for seeing to take place,[309] but none of these can see or discriminate on its own. Causes and conditions combine to produce the visual consciousness, while the visual consciousness as cause and condition produces cognitive or mind consciousness. When mind consciousness arises one is able to discriminate. Also, visual consciousness in turn comes into existence on the basis of mind consciousness.[310]

---

rikā (see MHCK, T 46.63c16–21). While there is an unmistakable similarity between these discernments and the third ("Discernment of the Six Senses"), second ("Discernment of Coming and Going") or seventh ("Discernment of the Three Marks"), and first ("Discernment of Cause and Condition") chapters of Nāgārjuna's treatise, the match is not a perfect one (see *Chung-lun*, T 30.1b–6b).

308. *Chüeh-i san-mei* (T 46.625c29–626a2) states in the section on contemplation of mental perception: "One turns the focus of contemplation back to discern the well-spring of mind, cognitive activity or thought, and consciousness. Upon carefully discerning this mind, one does not find any mind that abides persistently; nor [any mind from which] the various dharmas and their marks arise and perish. If there is no place where mind abides, nor production and destruction of dharmas and marks, then one should know that this mind is inapprehensible."

309. Chan-jan (T 46.198b16–18) asserts that consciousness itself should be added to this list to make five factors that combine to produce the visual event in the mind: "When the eye sees form, five factors must come into coordination before one is able to see: space, light, sense faculty, object, and consciousness. The [perceptions of] ear, nose, tongue, and body, do not require the factor of light."

310. This entire paragraph (as well as the first several lines of the one that follows it) is taken from *Chüeh-i san-mei* (T 46.625b6–10; see note 68 above). Chan-jan (T 46.198b24–27) explains the passage as follows: "As for the 'visual consciousness serving as cause and condition for production of mind consciousness,' the visual consciousness acts as the primary cause (*hetu*), but it also has sense faculty, object, space, and light as contributory conditions (*pratyaya*). In instantaneous and interrupted succession it [in turn] produces mind consciousness. The [notion that] 'visual consciousness comes into existence on the basis of mind consciousness,' is simply based on the fact that the cause for the [subsequent] instantaneous perishing of the cognitive or mind consciousness is established by the cognitive or mind sense: when the [mind sense shifts to] confront other [mental]

[16a1] By visual consciousness one is able to see. Having seen, one gives rise to craving, and, defiled by the longing for visual form, one breaks the rules of conduct that one has accepted—these are the four phases of thought that lead to the destiny of hell.[311] When in reality one's mind thirsts for form, but one conceals and denies it, this is the operation of the four phases of thought [leading to] the destiny of hungry ghosts. If one develops an attachment to form, such that one calculates everything in terms of me and mine, these are the the four phases of thought [that produce] the destiny of animals. When one discriminates between one's own form and that of others, thinking, "I am superior, he is inferior," this is the operation of the four phases of thought [that produces] the destiny of asuras. When one does not take objects from others that are not freely given,[312] and so develops human-heartedness, deference, righteousness, faith, and intelligence with respect to these forms—in short, the five rules of discipline and the ten good acts—this is the operation of the four phases of thought [that produces] the destinies of humans and gods. When in contemplating thought in its four phases one directs attention to the arising-and-perishing of the features of the thought, the impermanence of each thought, the three kinds of sensation[313] in each thought, the lack of autonomy of each thought, and the fact that each thought arises in response to causes and conditions,[314] then this is the operation of the four phases of thought [that produces] the destinies of the two vehicles.

[16a8] Upon contemplating the four phases of thought in oneself, one

---

objects visual consciousness is once again generated. Thus the two consciousnesses alternately function as cause for one another."

Kōroku (quoted by *Kōgi* [1.542]) believes the phrase "the other objects" refers solely to dharmic objects of the cognitive or mind sense, but *Kōgi* criticizes this interpretation, saying instead that it means the objects of awareness of the other senses as well.

311. Chan-jan (T 46.198b28–c1) states: "Next the text distinguishes individually the ten realms [of the dharmadhātu]. The statement for the first four destinies—where it says 'by visual consciousness one is able to see,' etc.—is based on the sūtras and quite close in sense to the lesser vehicle. As such it states that 'consciousness sees.' [Mental] evolution takes place on the basis of this, with [visual and mind consciousnesses] acting alternately as cause and condition for one another. In this manner, the ten realms of the dhramadhātu are gradually produced."

312. Following Chan-jan (T 46.198c6–13).

313. Pain, pleasure, and neutral sensations.

314. Chan-jan (T 46.198c17–20) identifies the first four of these as the meditation of the four stations of mindfulnesses (*smṛtyupasthāna*)—impermanence, impurity, painfulness, no-self—which together represent the practice of the śrāvakas. The fifth element, identified as meditation upon conditioned origination (*pratītyasamutpāda*), is the practice of pratyekabuddhas.

will find ample evidence of the errors and disasters described here. Contemplating the four phases evident in others, it will be just the same. So doing, one arouses good will and compassion, which inspires the practice of the six perfections.[315]

[16a10] What is the reason [for the practice of the six perfections]? From countless ages past we have witlessly and stubbornly clung to these [naive notions] of the nature and features of the six objects of perception. So doing, we find it impossible to renounce them. And when we have managed to renounce them, we have found it impossible to dispel them.

[16a12] If one now contemplates sense objects as nonobjects, then there will be no perception of an object; if one contemplates one's own sense faculties as nonfaculties, then there will be no attachment to the self; and if one contemplates the other person as inapprehensible, then there will be no [notion of] any recipient [of the gift]. The realization that these three factors[316] are all empty is what is meant by "perfection of giving" (*dāna-pāramitā*).

[16a14] The *Diamond Sūtra* says, "For a person to give while dwelling in forms, sounds, odors, tastes, tangible sensations, and dharmas is called practicing giving while dwelling in features. It is comparable to a man entering a dark room and seeing nothing. But not to dwell in sounds, tastes, etc., is the featureless giving. It may be likened to a man with eyes seeing the whole array of forms displayed in the light of the sun."[317]

[16a17] Simply to say that [the bodhisattva] sees no features is elliptical and difficult to understand. Actually he does not see form as either endowed with features, devoid of features, both, or neither. Wherever there are features to which he has been attached, he withdraws from them and dispels them from his mind. He does not develop any of the sixty-two false views[318]—this is what is called "featureless giving." When,

315. Identified by Chan-jan (T 46.198c20) as the realm of bodhisattvas.

316. The gift (sense object), giver (sense faculty), and recipient.

317. This citation is pieced together and paraphrased from two different passages of the *Diamond Sūtra*, T 8.749a12–15 and 750b29–c3.

318. The sixty-two false views represent, in effect, the totality of false views. Chan-jan offers a detailed breakdown of several definitions of the sixty-two, based primarily on Kuan-ting's commentary to the *Nirvāṇa Sūtra* (*Ta-pan nieh-p'an ching shu*, T 38.169a–b). The former offers the following explanation: the five skandhas in the desire realm are multiplied by the four phrases of the existence tetralemma, making twenty views. They are again multiplied by the four phrases of the tetralemma for the form realm, producing an additional twenty. Since there is no form in the formless realm, four skandhas are multiplied by the four phrases, making sixteen. The two extreme views of eternalism and annihilationism are added for each of the three realms, producing another six views and a total of sixty two. Chih-i in *Fa-hua wen-chü* (T 34.56b5–8) offers the following explanation: the five skandhas can be viewed as the self, or as separate from the

from here to the other shore, the practitioner enlists all dharmas in his practice of giving and thus perfects the Mahāyāna, this is the operation of the four phases of thought for bodhisattvas.

[16a21] Again, if one contemplates the four phases of thought as being equivalent to empty space, this is [to contemplate their intrinsic] permanence; not to perceive them is [to experience their intrinsic] pleasantness; not to generate karma because of them is [to know their essential] selfhood; and to be incapable of being defiled by them [is to know their intrinsic] purity. This is the operation of the four phases of thought for Buddhas.[319]

[16a23] Although the four phases of thought are in this way empty, one may actually see in emptiness various manifestations[320] of the four phases of thought and other dharmas until one sees everywhere the dharmas of the Buddha as numberless as the sands of the Ganges. Thus the view of the Mahāyāna is perfected. These are the four phases of thought of provisional designation.

[16a25] If it is empty, it should not contain the ten realms of the dharmadhātu.[321] Since these realms [of the dharmadhātu] arise through causes and conditions, in essence they should be nonexistent. Not having any substantial existence, they are empty. But not being empty, they yet exist. Without apprehending either emptiness or existence, one simultaneously illumines their emptiness and existence. Contemplating the three truths in just this way is to be in possession of the Buddha's insightful vision and fully to understand the four phases of thought. The three truths are naturally replete, and one acquires the wise vision of the Buddhas. Thus through the four phases of thought one comes to perfect and complete understanding.

[16a28] In the same way, when one contemplates the four phases of thought in the remaining five perceptions of sound, smell, taste, touch, and dharmas, one likewise achieves perfect realization of the inconceivability of the three truths. This may be understood by reference to the

---

self, or as greater than the self, or as smaller than the self, making twenty possibilities. This is multiplied by the three times to yield sixty, and the two fundamental false views of permanence and annihilation are added to make sixty-two.

319. The four inverted views used in the lesser vehicle to describe the mechanisms of deluded existence are redefined in the *Nirvāṇa Sūtra* as the four meritorious qualities of the Buddha-nature or intrinsic enlightenment (T 9.648a–653c).

320. Chan-jan (T 46.26–27) states: "Because in emptiness one finds contained in full the four phrases of the ten realms [of the dharmadhātu] the text says, 'various.' "

321. In this context *fa-chieh* has to be interpreted as *gati*, "destiny" or "realm," rather than as dharmadhātu.

preceding discussion, and I shall not trouble to give further details here.[322]

[16b9] **The Six Acts and the Perfection of Giving.** Next we discuss the [perfection of] giving while contemplating the six acts. In contemplating not-yet-thinking of walking, about-to-walk, walking-proper, and walking-completed, one realizes that the four phases of walking, whether they occur slowly or rapidly, are incapable of being apprehended, and that even this inapprehensibility cannot be perceived. Directing one's contemplation back to the mind that is aware of [the nature of] walking, one realizes that it neither comes from outside, arises from within, occurs between the two, nor is permanently self-existent. Neither walking nor the walker exists; both are ultimately empty and quiescent.

[16b12] Even so, because of the activity of the mind there is going and coming. This going and coming may be for the purpose of breaking the disciplinary code,[323] or it may be for the purpose of deceiving others, or it may be for the purpose of congregating together in a group, or it may be for the purpose of establishing superiority over others, or it may be for the purpose of righteousness and deference, or it may be to engage in good acts and meditative concentration,[324] or it may be to gain nirvāṇa, or it may be for the purpose of practicing good will and compassion. When one engages in the six acts having developed detachment with respect to the six sense objects, then the expedient activities of going and coming, raising the foot and lowering it, will all be like magical apparitions. Entranced and abstracted,[325] the practitioner forgets both self and other. A journey of a thousand miles he would not consider far; nor a spot a few steps away, near. Whenever he undertakes anything, he neither calculates its merit nor anticipates its [karmic] reward. Abiding thus in giving, he gathers in the entirety of the Buddhas' dharma, as vast as the sands of the Ganges. He becomes fully endowed with the Mahāyāna and is able to reach the other shore.

[16b19] Then again, in contemplating a single moment [of walking], one realizes that all of the ten realms [of the dharmadhātu] are contained

322. Use of the term "record" or "note" (*chi*) suggests that this is an insertion by Kuan-ting.

323. Chan-jan (T 46.200a8) states: "[This] activation of the mind is the origin of the ten realms [of the dharmadhātu]." He matches each of the ten activities that follow with one of the ten realms: breaking the precepts with hell, and the remainder with the destinies of hungry ghosts, animals, asuras, humans, gods, śrāvakas and pratyekabuddhas, and bodhisattvas, respectively.

324. Chan-jan (T 46.200a11–12) identifies these "good acts" with the ten wholesome deeds leading to and practiced by gods of the desire realm; and the four states of meditative concentration (dhyāna), with the heavens of the realm of form.

325. Following Muranaka, p. 154.

fully within it. This one moment of thought is not unconditionally one, hence it can be the ten realms. The ten are not unconditionally ten, hence they can be one. It is neither one nor ten, yet also both one and ten. Thus the three truths are fully replete in each single moment of thought.

[16b22] For standing, sitting, lying down, speaking, being silent, and other miscellaneous actions, it is the same [as with walking]. They all may be understood by reference to the preceding discussion. The *Lotus Sūtra* therefore says, "Again, I see sons of the Buddha giving beautiful robes and excellent garments as alms in order to seek the Way of the Buddha through the virtue of giving."[326] This is the same idea that I am expounding.

[16b24] **The Other Five Perfections in the Six Senses and Six Acts.** In the preceding we have discussed the twelve items[327] collectively under the rubric of the perfection of giving. We shall now discuss, in sequence, the [fulfillment of all the] six perfections with respect to each of the twelve items.[328]

[16b26] When the practitioner walks,[329] he regards animate beings with the eye of great compassion, not apprehending their worldly features. In so doing beings are able to approach the bodhisattva free of fear. This is to practice [the perfection of] giving while walking. There are no beings whom he injures or causes loss, nor does he apprehend their evils or their meritorious qualities. This is called [the perfection of] morality. When he walks, thoughts do not arise in his mind; nor does he suffer any perturbation or settle into any particular abode. The aggregates, sense accesses, and sense fields display no fluctuation whatsoever.[330] This is called [the perfection of] forbearance. When he walks, he

326. Paraphrased from *Miao-fa lien-hua ching*, T 9.3b; Hurvitz, pp. 9–10.

327. That is, the six internal sense perceptions and six external activities.

328. Chih-i (or Kuan-ting) is not always consistent in the sections that follow, but his basic point is clear. Chan-jan (T 46.200a28–b2) explains: "For each [of the twelve items] the text explains the ten realms [of the dharmadhātu] and the six perfections. But because the passages are often abbreviated, sometimes they discuss nine realms, sometimes only the Buddha realm. [In any case], whether expanded or condensed, their form is in mutual agreement; and together they all take the perspective of the perfect teaching. Then again, why should each of the twelve items merely fulfill the six perfections? Each of the six should also contain the other six. Thus each perfection is adorned by the other five."

329. This entire paragraph on the practice of the six perfections is lifted nearly verbatim from the opening lines of Hui-ssu's *Sui-tzu-i san-mei*, HTC 98.344d.

330. Chan-jan (T 46.200b27–28) states: "Because thoughts do not arise it is called 'not suffering any perturbation.' Being everywhere is what is meant by 'having no abode.' Because the aggregates, etc., are themselves identical to the dharmadhātu, they 'do not fluctuate.' "

does not apprehend the raising or the lowering of his feet. In his mind there is no sequence of first pondering something and afterwards understanding it.[331] There is for him no arising, persistence, or perishing of the dharmas.[332] This is called [the perfection of] exertion. He does not apprehend his body or mind, saṃsāra or nirvāṇa.[333] Among all the dharmas there are none that he senses, thinks of, or develops an attachment to. He neither savors [nirvāṇa] nor falls prey to the confusion [of saṃsāra].[334] This is called [the perfection of] meditative concentration. When he walks, his head and the other six parts of his body are like clouds to him, like shadows, dreams, apparitions, echoes or phantoms, without arising or perishing, extinction or permanence.[335] He realizes the aggregates, sense accesses, and sense fields to be empty and quiescent, and he [conceives himself to be] neither bound nor liberated. This is called [the perfection of] wisdom. The details are as stated at length in the *Śūraṅgama-samādhi Sūtra.*[336]

[16c7] The bodhisattva is quiescent and endowed with the characteristics of samādhi even while walking.[337] But if the practitioner does not investigate this carefully, he may give rise to tainted craving for samādhi and cling to the flavor of meditation. Should he now contemplate this mind of samādhi, he will realize that there is not even any mind to this mind. Where, then, is this concentration [of samādhi] to be located?[338] Know, therefore, that this [entire notion of] samādhi arises from in-

331. Chan-jan (T 46.200b29–c1) states: "In each moment of thought he resorts directly to principle and is completely free of the process wherein understanding comes only after discursive reckoning."

332. Chan-jan (T 46.200c3–4) states: "Because thought after instant of thought is identical to the dharmadhātu, there occurs no division between arising and perishing."

333. Chan-jan (T 46.200c5) states: "He does not apprehend the two extremes because the extremes are themselves identical with the middle."

334. Following Chan-jan (T 46.200c6–7).

335. Chan-jan identifies the six limbs as the head, torso, two arms, and two legs.

336. *Shou-leng-yen saṇ-mei ching*, T 15.633b–c. The citation is included in the original passage from Hui-ssu's *Sui-tzu-i san-mei*. For a brief discussion of the relevance of this sūtra for Hui-ssu's text, see Stevenson, "The Four Kinds of Samādhi in Early T'ien-t'ai Buddhism," pp. 95–96. For a translation of the scriptural passage see Lamotte, *Concentration de la marche heroique*, p. 152.

337. This entire section (extending from the three paragraphs that follow down to the end of the discussion of the three samādhis and four māras) is taken, virtually verbatim, from Chih-i's *Chüeh-i san-mei*, T 46.626a14–b9.

338. Chan-jan (T 46.201a2–3) states: "One contemplates the mind that has just developed an attachment, realizing thereby that it is no mind. [Without any mind to be in samādhi] how could one further imagine a place where *śūraṅgama samādhi* occurs?"

verted views. When one contemplates in this fashion, one sees neither emptiness nor nonemptiness. All sign of samādhi is thereby eradicated, and attachment does not arise. To arise or produce for the purpose of expediency,[339] this is the bodhisattva's [proper] understanding [of samādhi].

[16c11] If the practitioner is not yet sufficiently awakened, he may take note of his own powers of contemplation, thinking to himself, "This mind of mine is marvelously wise." Clinging to the idea of his own wisdom, he thinks himself exalted. This is called the wisdom obstacle.[340] In the same way as those adhering to the non-Buddhist paths, one fails to achieve liberation. But if one reflects back upon this mind that is the agent of contemplation, one will find that it abides nowhere and is completely devoid of arising and perishing. Ultimately there exists neither a contemplator nor a noncontemplator. The contemplator being inexistent, who then contemplates the dharmas? Not apprehending any mind that contemplates, one thereupon leaves behind all thought of contemplation.

[16c15] The *Great Treatise* says, "Once thoughts and opinions have been eliminated, minds that have given rise to nonsensical prattle all enter into extinction. Thereupon, the countless multitudes of sins slough away and the pure mind is revealed in its eternal oneness. The individual of such noble and marvelous attainment we regard as one who is able to see prajñā."[341]

[16c17] The *Mahāsaṃnipāta Sūtra* means the same thing when it says, "Contemplate the mind [that is contemplated] and the mind [that contemplates]."[342] Within such practices as these are contained the three

339. Following the sense suggested by Chan-jan (T 46.201a6–7): "To know oneself as identical in substance with the dharmadhātu and universally respond to all things—this is what is meant by 'arising or production for the sake of expediency.' "

340. *Jñeyāvaraṇa*. For a discussion of Chih-i's multivalent use and understanding of this term, see Swanson, "Chih-i's Interpretation of *Jñeyāvaraṇa*: An Application of the Threefold Truth Concept." In essence Chih-i regards the "wisdom obstacle" as an obstruction of the unalloyed insight of the middle truth. Chan-jan, commenting on this passage, states (T 36.201a9–12): "For there is to be 'one who reckons' at all, the sense of self must already be quite coarse. How much more so if one 'exalts oneself.' Since when is this to be considered 'wisdom'? The clinging mind obstructs wisdom; therefore it is called 'wisdom obstacle.' Followers of the non-Buddhist paths all make this claim [to self-exaltation]. Since the self-exaltation here is no different from that of the nonBuddhist paths, how can it be construed strictly as a lapse with regard to the wisdom of the middle way?"

341. TCTL, T 25.190b; the citation is not exact.

342. *Ta-chi ching*, T 13.177b–c. This passage occurs in the *Pao-chi p'u-sa p'in* (*Ratnacūḍa-paripṛcchā*) section of this sūtra collection: Here the discussion centers

samādhis.[343] In the first of these contemplations, one does away with all the various mundane features of existence, perceiving neither an inner nor an outer—this is called the samādhi of emptiness. In the next contemplation one is able to destroy the mark of emptiness—this is called the samādhi of marklessness. In the final contemplation, one does not perceive even the doer—this is the samādhi of actionlessness. Furthermore, by destroying the three inversions[344] and the three poisons, transcending the stream of the three realms of existence, and overcoming the malice of the four māras, one then attains the six perfections.[345] Yet how could the encompassing of the entire dharmadhātu, as well as the progressive augmentation [of the path] to the point of full mastery of all approaches to dharma, possibly end with the six perfections and the three samādhis? Just as one can perfect all the dharmas in the activity of walking, so it is for the other eleven items as well.

[16c24] **The Perfection of Morality (*śīla*).** Next, when the bodhisattva is again passing among the six sense objects, he combats their attraction and holds his mind steady, [restrained and as oblivious to distracting thoughts] as if he were trying to carry a jar brimful of oil without spilling a single drop.[346] Also when engaged in any of the six acts, he displays similar dignity of deportment, acting and retiring with perfect orderliness. This is called observing the rules of conduct. The karmic reward of observing the rules of conduct is to rise in one's next life to a higher destiny, there to experience joy. Yet without the element of sam-

around the question of whether the mind one is trying to contemplate in meditation is the same as or different from the mind that is doing the contemplating. The Buddha then discourses on the contemplation of mind, stating that the nature of mind cannot be perceived in either internal or external *āyatanas* (i.e., the sense organs and sense objects), or both, in the *skandhas*, or in the *dhātus* (T 13177b11–13).

343. A list unrelated to Chih-i's four forms of samādhi, these are also known as the three gates to liberation (*vimokṣa-dvāra*). The third of these, given as "actionless" here, is generally rendered by Kumārajīva and later translators as "wishlessness" (*wu-yüan*).

344. Inversion of mind, or the inability to awaken to the true nature of mind; inversion of view, or the false imputing of existence to sense objects and failure to realize their true nature; inversion of thought, or the generation of deluded thinking and attachment (mentioned in *Nirvāṇa Sūtra*, T 12.498b).

345. The māras of the afflictions, the aggregates (*skandha*), sense accesses (*āyatana*), and sense fields (*dhātu*), death, and Maheśvara, lord of the realm of desire. They represent all factors that destroy good. See Chih-i's *Tz'u-ti ch'an-men*, T 46.506c–507a for details.

346. This simile, taken from the *Nirvāṇa Sūtra* (T 12.740a), is used to illustrate the attentiveness of the bodhisattva: a man is ordered by his king to pass among a crowd of people carrying a jar brimful of oil, but not to spill a single drop, or else he will be instantly slain by a second man following him with a drawn sword.

ādhi it is not to be termed a "perfection." However, if he attains to the wisdom born of contemplation (*kuan-hui*), morality will be perfected automatically in the twelve activities.

[16c28] It has been said that as one contemplates the four phases of form not-yet-seen, form about-to-be-seen, form being-seen, and form having-been-seen and investigates them from various perspectives [of the tetralemma], neither the thought that arises nor the mind that contemplates can be apprehended.[347] The mind is not inside, not outside, does not come, does not go.[348] It is quiescent and lacks both arising and perishing.

[17a2] If, in this fashion, one is able to contemplate[349] the seven evil acts of body and speech[350] as pure like space, then this is to observe the three kinds of discipline: the faultless, the unbroken, and the unpierced.[351] To destroy all evil thought and view in the four phases of thought is to observe the unmixed rule of conduct. Not to be confused by the four phases of thought is to observe the rule of conduct that accords with samādhi. For the four phases of thought not to arise at all is to observe the rule of conduct that accompanies study of the path. To be able to discriminate among the various manifestations of the four phases of thought without becoming mired in these distinctions is to observe the nonattached rule of conduct. To discriminate the four phases of thought unerringly is to observe the rule of conduct that is praised by the wise. To understand how the four phases of thought encompass all dharmas is to observe the self-sustaining rule of conduct of the Mahāyāna. To be aware of the four meritorious qualities [of enlightenment] in the four phases of thought is to observe the ultimate rule of conduct.

347. Following Chan-jan (T 46.201c7–8). The "thought that arises" he glosses as the "realms of the six destinies of rebirth." Chan-jan identifies this sequence with the discernment of the first of the three truths—emptiness.

348. Chan-jan (T 46.201c10) says: " 'Neither inside nor outside' refers to the emptiness of the six sense perceptions; 'neither comes nor goes,' to the emptiness of the six acts."

349. Chan-jan identifies this paragraph with contemplation at the level of the provisional truth.

350. That is, the ten evil acts minus those of mind. These are killing, stealing, and adultery (for the body), and lying, slander, harsh speech, and frivolous speech (for speech).

351. Here and below Chih-i presents a list of ten degrees or levels of observance of the rules of conduct (although these are not, strictly speaking, rules of discipline). The contents are not derived from any one particular source but assembled from several, particularly the TCTL (T 25.225c–226a) and the *Nirvāṇa Sūtra* (T 12.675a). The list given here differs slightly from another listing of the ten that appears in MHCK (T 46.36b–c), as well as from Chih-i's earliest work, the *Tz'u-ti ch'an-men* (T 46.484c18–485a5). The discrepancy mainly centers around the identity of the sixth and tenth items.

[17a9] Once the mind has become clear and unsullied, it simultaneously eradicates the two extremes [of emptiness and the provisional] and enters truly into the middle way.[352] One then simultaneously illumines both extremes. The inconceivable realm of Buddhahood is perfected to the full and, thereafter, knows no diminution.

[17a11] The perceiver of form, the form as dharma [or object], and the act of perceiving are alike incapable of being apprehended. That these three all vanish [upon being contemplated] is [the perfection of] giving. To allow one's mind to repose unwaveringly in the form and the perceiver of the form is called [the perfection of] forbearance. To remain free of defilement by form and the perceiver of form is called [the perfection of] exertion. Not to be thrown into confusion by form and the perceiver of form is called [the perfection of] meditation. And to view form and the perceiver of form as a mirage or a magical apparition is called [the perfection of] wisdom.

[17a16] To regard form and the perceiver of form[353] as resembling space is called the samādhi of emptiness, [the first of the three samādhis]. Not to apprehend this emptiness is called the samādhi of marklessness. The absence of both subject and object is called the samādhi of actionlessness. Not only the three truths, the six perfections, and the three emptinesses,[354] but all the dharmas of the Buddha as numerous as the sands of the Ganges may be understood analogously. Having contemplated in this manner the sense object of form, [contemplation of] the other five sense objects may be understood to proceed in the same way, as should the six kinds of sense perception and the six acts. The *Lotus Sūtra* accordingly says, "I further see the sons of the Buddha, scrupulous in their observance of the rules of discipline, thereby seeking the way of the Buddha."[355]

[17a20] **The Perfection of Forbearance (*kṣānti*).** Next we deal with [contemplation] as applied to the wholesome dharma of forbearance. Reflecting upon the six acts and the six kinds of perception, it is clear that for any of them there are times when events are contrary, and times when events are compliant. Being in compliance means that events proceed as we would like, while being contrary means events proceed in a way counter to our wishes. A bodhisattva is neither angered when events are contrary nor attached when events are compliant. There is for him

352. According to Chan-jan (T 46.201c15), this begins the discourse on contemplation at the level of the middle, the third of the three truths.

353. Chan-jan (T 46.201a19–21) adds the act of perceiving, so as to maintain the parallelism with the three items of the previous paragraph.

354. The three samādhis mentioned above.

355. A condensation of *Miao-fa lien-hua ching*, T 9.3b; Hurvitz, p. 17.

neither seeing nor seer, neither act nor actor. Everything else which could be said about forbearance is as explained above.

[17a23] **The Perfection of Exertion (*vīrya*).** Next we deal with [contemplation] as applied to the wholesome dharma of exertion. It has been said of old that "exertion has no peculiar form to it; it simply means the diligent performance of everything one does."[356] However, when one broadly ponders its significance with respect to other practices, one would expect it to have a special or separate identity.[357] It is analogous to nescience, which permeates all the lesser afflictions, yet stands as a separate affliction called "nescience."

[17a25] Now if one were to rely solely on the recitation of sūtras to discipline and inspire one's mind, this would be considered an example of exertion. Yet even though one were to do this unremittingly both day and night, becoming fluent and skillful in recitation, still this would not be considered equivalent to either samādhi or wisdom. But if one were to contemplate the breath [during this recitation], one would realize as it touches the seven places in the body and converges to produce the voice that it resembles an echo. It has neither inside nor outside, neither reciter nor recited present in it. If all this is investigated fully in terms of the four phases of thought, one will not posit a perceiver of the sound, nor an agent who produces the sound, among these various contributing conditions. Should one recite the scripture with a mind uninterrupted by the afflictions, every thought will flow into the great sea of nirvāṇa. This is what is called "exertion."

[17b1] **The Perfection of Meditation (*dhyāna*).** Next we deal with the application [of contemplation] to different forms of meditative concentration. The basic [dhyānas], the nine meditations on death, the eight degrees of liberation, and so on, are all merely [mundane] meditative concentrations.[358] They are not the perfection of meditation. However,

356. Source uncertain, but probably TCTL (T 25.629b5–7): "If a bodhisattva begins by putting to use the dharma-gate which is exertion, he will enter into all the other perfections. 'Exertion' means that he diligently practices the other five perfections, vigorous in both body and mind, neither pausing nor stopping. 'Exertion' has no peculiar or separate form to it."

357. According to Chan-jan (T.46.202a4–9) the "other practices" are the other five perfections. He insists that exertion should have special status because it "directs or leads the other five perfections."

358. According to Chih-i's *Tz'u-ti ch'an-men* (T 46.480a–b) these "basic meditative concentrations" refer to the four dhyāna and four *samāpatti*. The nine meditations on death are a technique for visualizing the successive stages of decomposition of a corpse. The ninth contemplation involves cremation or utter disappearance of the corpse and, hence, can result in elimination of both contemplator and object. The eight renunciations are a sequence of methods for producing and refining the basic dhyāna and *samāpatti*.

if a person were to contemplate the four phases of thought upon entering into samādhi, he or she would find the mind unobtainable. What, then, could be considered the locus of this samādhi? It is at this point that the true character of meditative concentration is realized, and meditation comes to subsume all the other dharmas.[359] This is why, in the fifth fascicle of the *Great Treatise*, after elucidating eight meditations on death, the author explains all the dharmas, including the ten powers and the four kinds of fearlessness.[360] Nowadays treatise masters do not grasp the profound meaning of this passage. They all say that the *Treatise* is in error, but they should not say this.[361] The reason that the author of the *Treatise* explains all these other dharmas in such detail is to show how the eight meditations on death produce the features of the Mahāyāna.

[17b7] **The Perfection of Wisdom (*prajñā*).** Next we deal with the application [of contemplation] to wisdom. In the *Great Treatise* prajñā is understood in eight ways.[362] Now mundane wisdom can be used to contemplate the six kinds of perception and the six acts. Then when one analyzes this mundane wisdom[363] by means of the four phases of

359. Chan-jan (T 46.202b9–11) states: "As the distracted mind is inexistent, how could one yet locate a concentrated mind? Concentration here refers to the nine meditations, eight renunciations, etc. Not seizing on either the concentrated or scattered [mind], one realizes the true character of meditative concentration. And [this] reality universally encompasses all the dharmas."

360. TCTL, T 25.402c–406b. In this passage the sūtra and the śāstra both omit mention of the traditional ninth meditation on the cremation of the body. In the MHCK (T 46.121c) section on dhyāna (the sixth of the ten objects for contemplation), it says that a person should practice all but the last of the nine. This is evidently because cremation and its contemplation imply complete annihilation (in nirvāṇa), which is anathema to the Mahāyāna. The ten powers represent ten different powers of wisdom possessed by the Buddhas. The four fearlessnesses include a Buddha's fearlessness in announcing his omniscience, his complete eradication of the defilements, his exposition of all the obstacles to enlightenment, and his exposition of the path to overcome them (see TCTL T 25.241b–c).

361. The identity of these treatise masters is unknown.

362. The TCTL passage in question is at T 25.139a–140a. The Buddha here explains six definitions of wisdom current in the world: as the root of undefiled wisdom; as defiled wisdom; as every level of wisdom from the first arising of *bodhicitta* to final realization; as both defiled wisdom and undefiled wisdom; as undefiled, unconditioned, invisible nonduality; and as inexpressible and utterly beyond the bounds of all proposition on the basis of the existence tetralemma. The "seventh definition" is actually the statement that all of these six are correct, a position that the Buddha rejects. The "eighth definition" is the statement that the sixth alone is correct, which is the position that the Buddha adopts.

363. The first and lowest of three kinds of wisdom described in the *Laṅkāvatāra Sūtra* (T 16.16.500c), the other two being supramundane wisdom and supreme supramundane wisdom. Chih-i introduces similar distinctions for dhyāna—mun-

thought, one finds it to be inapprehensible. It is all just as explained above; and so it goes for all other wholesome dharmas or activities.[364]

[17b10] Q: If, as you say, one dharma includes all dharmas, contemplation alone should be sufficient. What need is there to employ calming as well? One perfection should be sufficient; why employ the other five?

[17b11] A: The six perfections perfectly supplement and complete one another. It is just like soldiers who must remain close together when they don armor and advance into the ranks of the enemy. Contemplation is like a lamp, and calming like a closed room; they are like washing and rinsing clothes; or grasping and cutting grass.[365] Yet it is also true that the perfection of wisdom is itself the dharmadhātu and includes everything within itself. From this standpoint there is no need for other dharmas. But the other dharmas are also the dharmadhātu. Each of them includes everything in itself as well and has no need of wisdom, for, ultimately, the perfection of wisdom is identical to all other dharmas, and each of these is identical to the perfection of wisdom. There is no duality, no difference between them.

Contemplation amidst Evil Dharmas

[17b16] Third, we discuss application of freely following one's thought to the array of evil activities.

[17b17] Now good and evil have no fixed nature. For example, the obscurations[366] are considered evil, and the perfections, as performed at the phenomenal level, are thought of as good. But when the karmic rec-

dane, supramundane, supreme supramundane—on the basis of the three wisdoms on the *Laṅkāvatāra Sūtra*; see his *Chüeh-i san-mei*, T 46.621c5–622a4.

364. Chan-jan (T 46.202c18–19) says: "[The line] should read: 'In the application of each and every one of all the wholesome dharmas to the twelve items [it is just the same].' However, the passage is abbreviated."

365. These are two of nine similes from the *Nirvāṇa Sūtra* (T 12.793c24–794a10) used to illustrate the joint action of samādhi and prajñā. First one impregnates with soap, then rinses with clean water; first one grasps the grass firmly, then cuts with the scythe.

366. Chih-i in *Chüeh-i san-mei* (T 46.622b5–623a4) matches the six perfections to six obscurations that stand as their opposites: lust or craving, immorality (violation of precepts), anger or malice, indolence, distractedness, and dull-mindedness or stupidity. The formulation originates from the TCTL (T 25.303c–304b). Unlike Kuan-ting's arrangement here, the *Chüeh-i san-mei* (T 46.623a1–4) treats attendance to the six perfections as "preliminary expedients" necessary to tame the mind of the six obscurations and elicit correct meditative discernment: "The six perfections encompass all expedients. Once you become skilled in applying them to subdue the coarse mental states of the six obscurations and are able to make the mind supple and harmonious, only then will you be able to discern with a subtle mind and, so, enter the gate of right contemplation. They are known as the expedients for cultivating truly deep samādhi."

ompense [from good deeds such as these] is exhausted in the destinies of humans and gods, one falls back once more to the three turbid destinies. So, again, [one could say] they are evil.[367] Why? Because neither [indulgence in] the obscurations nor [phenomenal performance] of the perfections can extricate one [from the cycle of birth and death]. As such, both of these are in essence "evil."

[17b19] Now the two vehicles do deliver one from suffering, for which reason they may be called "good." Yet though the two vehicles are "good," they are only capable of effecting one's own personal deliverance. Therefore they do not set forth the features of the truly "good" person.[368]

[17b20] The *Great Treatise* says, "I would sooner think of becoming an evil and leprous fox than set out to become a śrāvaka or pratyekabuddha."[369] One should know, then, that saṃsāra and nirvāṇa are both "evil." What we call "good" is the bodhisattvas endowed with the six perfections who, out of loving kindness and compassion, work toward the salvation of both [themselves and other living beings]. Yet even though they are able to work to save both [themselves and others], what they do is comparable to storing food in a poisoned vessel, which then indiscriminately kills whomever eats it.[370] This again is evil.

[17b24] The three vehicles are alike in that they eradicate [the afflictions], and this can be considered "good." But they fail to perceive the distinctive principle[371] [of the unalloyed middle way] and regress to one or the other of the two extremes [of emptiness and provisionality]. Having failed to spit out [this basic] nescience, they are still "evil."

[17b25] The separate teaching is "good." However, even though practitioners at this level are aware of the distinctive principle [of the middle], they continue to resort to expedients and are unable to conform [di-

367. Either the phenomenal performance of the perfections or retribution in the turbid realms of the hells, animals, and hungry ghosts could be the subject here.

368. For example, the bodhisattva or Buddha, who seeks to effect the salvation of all beings.

369. Source unidentified.

370. A simile from TCTL (T 25.262a). This passage makes the point that unless a bodhisattva rids himself of the three poisons, he is like a poisoned jug that vitiates any nectar (merit) that is poured into it. Chan-jan (T 46.203b14–16) states: "The Bodhisattva's person is like the poisoned vessel. To be possessed of the afflictions is what is meant by 'poison.' Cultivating Buddhadharma [under these conditions] is like putting ambrosia in [the poisoned] vessel. By teaching this approach to others, [the bodhisattva] causes them to lose the 'life' that is the eternally abiding [Buddha-nature]."

371. According to which the middle is recognized as a single unalloyed reality that both transcends and includes the two perspectives of emptiness and provisionality.

rectly] to principle. The *Nirvāṇa Sūtra* says, "Up to now, we could all be described as holders of depraved views."[372] Are not "depraved views" evil?

[17b28] The dharma of the perfect [teaching] alone is properly called "good." Whatever accords well with reality (*shih-hsiang*) is called "the way," while whatever runs counter to reality is called "the nonway."[373] But if one achieves the realization that evil things are not evil, that everything is reality, then one achieves the way of the Buddha through practicing the nonway.[374] On the other hand, if one develops an attachment to the way of the Buddha and fails to efface (literally, digest) its ambrosial taste, then the way turns into the nonway.

[17c2] When good and evil are discussed in such a [generic] fashion, they can ultimately mean the same thing. We shall now discuss them insofar as they are distinct [from one another].[375] That is to say, the perfections at the level of phenomenal activity we will consider to be "good," and the obscurations, "evil." However, having already dealt with the contemplation of good dharmas above, we now go on to elucidate the contemplation of evil.

[17c4] **On the Mind that Contemplates Evil.** Despite one's prior efforts at contemplation of the good, the obscurations may not have ceased [their activity]. Rather, growing all the more vigorous, [it may seem that] there is hardly a moment when the afflictions are not arising in the mind. If one goes on to observe the minds of others, evils will surely appear to be beyond all measure. For example, when one performs the meditation that views the world as utterly without cause for joy,[376] one

372. T 12.648a28. The Buddha has just expounded to Kāśyapa the four meritorious virtues of ultimate reality (i.e., permanence, pleasure, selfhood, and purity), and Kāśyapa responds that from this day forth he is enlightened.

373. Chan-jan (T 46.203b20–23) says: "To regard the act of according [with reality] as the 'good' and going counter [to reality] as 'evil' represents a relative position. In the next [line where it says] 'if one achieves realization,' etc., attachment is regarded as evil and realization is good. One must depart from evil in both its relative and absolute senses. To cling to [the notion of] a perfect [teaching] is still evil. How much more so any other [teaching]."

374. An expression derived from the *Vimalakīrti Sūtra*, T 14.549a.

375. Chan-jan (T 46.203b24–25) says: "Here evil in its most crude sense is distinguished in detail. This is intended to function as the basis for contemplation. First the essential substance (*t'i*) of evil is elicited, namely the six obscurations." *Kōgi* (2.3) says: "This applies to the beginner's contemplation alone."

376. The fifth item in a list of ten reflections from TCTL (T 25.229a–232c). They include a series of thematic reflections on: impermanence, suffering, absence of self, and impurity of the body (which rectify the four inverted views), death, impurity of one's food, the fact that the world is utterly without cause for joy, and the three features of nirvāṇa (i.e., severence, separation from, and exhaustion of the afflictions). The ten reflections are also discussed at length in Chih-i's *Tz'u-ti ch'an-men*, T 46.538c–540b.

perceives no good people nor any good country anywhere.[377] All one sees is the evil of the obscurations and sees oneself as completely enmeshed in it.

[17c8] Even though people may not be subject to all the obscurations, they will certainly commit evils as a result of particular influences. Some persons may show a preponderance of craving and lust, while others may be mainly given to infringement of the moral codes, maliciousness, indolence, or indulgence in alcoholic spirits. Easily deprived of their native faculties,[378] inevitably they suffer mishap. Who among us is without such failings?

[17c10] There are persons who abandon the household life and part from the world, but who are incomplete in their practice and, like the laity, continue to enjoy the objects of desire; they are not true practitioners of the way. Evil is their lot, and, even if they become arhats, they will continue [to suffer the influence of] residual defilements. How much more is this true for ordinary folk! Should ordinary persons (*pṛthag jana*) wantonly indulge in evil, they will be crushed [in their next lives] and plummet [into one of the lower destinies], there to remain with no hope of escape for a long, long time. This is why one must learn to cultivate contemplative insight (*kuan-hui*) in the midst of evil.

[17c13] Take, for example, householders who lived when Śākyamuni was still in the world: some were burdened with responsibility for wives and children; others were involved in governmental duties or worldly enterprises; but all were still able to achieve the way. In the case of Aṅgulimālīya, the more people he slew, the greater grew his goodwill.[379] Jeta

377. TCTL (T 25.232a9–12) reflects upon the evils that occasion joylessness from these two basic perspectives: beings and lands.

378. The match between these items and the six obscurations is not an exact one. Chan-jan (T 46.203c14–17) tries to explain the passage as follows: "The six obscurations are mentioned briefly here in order to illustrate 'generation through a particular preponderance [of obscuration].' The first four are as they usually appear. Alcoholic spirits, being a cause of confusion, represent the obscuration of distraction of mind. 'Easily deprived of native faculties' is equivalent to the obscuration of stupidity." Muranaka (p. 164) offers a more feasible reading, which we have followed here.

379. From the Mahāyāna **Aṅgulimālika Sūtra* (*Yang-chüeh-mo-li ching*, T 2.512b). The story runs as follows: a young brāhmin student, lusted after by his teacher's wife, refused to satisfy her. She became enraged and falsely reported to her husband that the young man raped her; in consequence the teacher ordered that he could only expiate his crime and receive proper initiation if he killed a thousand people. He followed the teacher's orders and terrorized the populace as a result, taking a finger (*aṅguli*) from each of his victims to fashion a necklace (*mālā*), whence his name. He was on the verge of killing his last victim, who happened to be his own mother, but was stopped in the nick of time by the Buddha's

drank and Mālikā gave people wine, yet they were moral in their behavior.[380] Vasumitra remained chaste though she engaged in sexual intercourse,[381] and Devadatta's false views were actually right ones.[382]

[17c16] If amidst the evils everything were wholly evil, such that the practice of the way were impossible, then people would forever remain unenlightened. But because the way is present even within evil, it is possible to attain saintliness even though one may engage in the obscurations. Know therefore that evil does not obstruct the way.[383] Nor does the

---

arrival on the scene. The Buddha first lured him away from his mother, then expounded the dharma to him, whereupon he attained arhatship and acquired the six superhuman powers.

380. From the **Mahā-māyā Sūtra* (T 17.585a–b). As one of the sons of King Prasenajit of Śrāvastī, Jeta (or Jetṛ) was often compelled to drink alcoholic sprits on social occasions. Although he was careful to control himself, he felt that drinking with people was important and promoted good relations overall. Thus he asked the Buddha to be released from his vow to keep the five prohibitions for laymen and receive instead the rule for avoidance of the ten evil acts, which includes no prohibition against alcohol. The Buddha congratulated him on his insight and approved of his motives.

The same sūtra (T 17.585b–586a) recounts the tale of Mālikā, the wife of King Prasenajit, who lies, seductively adorns her body, entertains, and serves wine to the king. These unlawful things she does in order to mollify the king's anger and keep him from taking the life of a cook who has angered him. Because her motives were wholesome and pure, the Buddha praises her actions.

Chan-jan (T 46.205a4–7) notes: "This [story] tells of breaking the precepts to save beings because of the bodhisattva's basic desire to benefit others. As such it is known as 'good in the midst of evil.' . . . Anyone wishing to follow this example must assess his or her motives judiciously. If one is just indulging desire it is not on the order of observance [of the precepts]."

381. From the *Gaṇḍavyūha* section of the *Avataṃsaka Sūtra,* T 9.716c–717b. Vasumitrā—one of fifty-three spiritual teachers whom the pilgrim Sudhana visits on his famous journey toward perfect realization—was a beautiful and wise woman who made a practice of inviting men to enjoy her in order that she might have an opportunity to teach them the dharma.

382. From the Devadatta chapter of the *Lotus Sūtra,* T 9.34b–35a; Hurvitz, pp. 195–197. Although he is conventionally seen as an evil rival of the Buddha who propounded false views and instigated schism in the sangha, the *Lotus* presents Devadatta as a great bodhisattva destined for Buddhahood.

383. Chan-jan (T 46.205c22–24) states: "The words 'does not obstruct' mean that evil can be transformed. They encourage one to apply oneself to calming and contemplation even while in the midst of evil. However, one must not [take this as a license to] indulge in evil without restraint, otherwise one will forever remain an ordinary being. It does not mean that deliberately promoting evil offers no impediment [to the way]. [The text] also says 'the way does not obstruct evil' in order to show that even though one may have attained the way, evils can still remain."

way obstruct evil. For example, the stream-winner's carnal desires grew and grew;[384] Pilindavatsa was still arrogant, despite being a monk;[385] and Śāriputra became angry.[386] Yet with respect to their freedom from [defiling] outflows, what possible impact—detrimental or otherwise—could [such lapses] have? It is like the play of light and dark through empty

384. Chan-jan identifies this as the story of Nanda, alluded to but not recounted in detail in TCTL (T 25.70c), the same source from which the next two illustrations are taken. All three of these stories are given as illustrations of how arhats and pratyekabuddhas differ from Buddhas. The story of Śāriputra shows that traces of aversion may remain; the story of Nanda, traces of craving; and Pilindavatsa, traces of pride. The story of Nanda is a famous one, and appears in many places in Buddhist literature and iconography (see Lamotte, *Traité*, 1.118). Nanda, half-brother of the Buddha, left his wife to join the saṅgha but continued to be plagued by memories of her. In order to extinguish his longings, the Buddha took him to the Trāyastriṃśa heaven and showed him nymphs incomparably more beautiful than his wife, telling him he could have any one of them after he died if only during this life he stayed with the saṅgha as a monk. When the Buddha told the other disciples what had happened, they all laughed at Nanda. Ashamed, Nanda renounced his concupiscence and quickly attained to the state of an arhat.

As the story appears in the *Udāna-varga* (T 4.699b–c), there was once a woman who was hounded by the excessive sexual demands of her husband. In despair she consulted a monk for advice, who suggested asking her husband rhetorically if such conduct befitted a stream-winner (first of the four fruits leading to arhatship). She followed the monk's advice, whereupon her husband was ashamed and as a result attained the stage of nonreturning (third of the four fruits). Chan-jan's explanation of this passage in MHCK appears to be a conflation of the two.

385. TCTL, T 25.71a. The monk Pilindavatsa wanted to cross the Ganges to beg for food. Coming to the river's edge, he snapped his fingers and said to the river: "Lowly slave, stop flowing!" The river parted for him and let him pass, but its god went to the Buddha and complained about being addressed with such contempt. The Buddha then told Pilindavatsa to apologize to the river god. He obediently went and, joining his palms, said to the god: "Lowly slave, do not be angry. I apologize to you." All those within earshot laughed to hear what appeared to be a renewed insult. The Buddha, however, reassured the river god that the apology had been sincerely meant. It was just that Pilindavatsa, as a result of having been a brāhmin throughout his last 500 lives, was used to being arrogant and vilifying others. Though he was not truly arrogant any more, he could not help using his old forms of expression. Thus, concludes the TCTL, even though arhats have eliminated their afflictions, the latter may still persist in a residual form (*vāsana*).

386. TCTL, T 25.70c–71a. Śāriputra, told by the Buddha that he had eaten impure food, vomited it all up and angrily vowed not to accept any more invitations to eat or associate with lay donors. King Prasenajit was quite nonplussed at this and complained to the Buddha that he could hardly acquire great faith under such conditions, used as he was to listening to Śāriputra's fine expositions of the

space, where the one does not exclude the other. This is the idea behind the emergence of a Buddha's enlightenment.[387]

[17c22] If a person has, by nature, a great number of desires and is seething with defilements—so that despite his efforts to counter and suppress them, they continue to increase by leaps and bounds—then he should simply direct his attention wherever he wishes. Why? Because without the arising of the obscurations, he would have no chance to practice contemplation.[388]

[17c24] It is like going fishing. If the fish is strong and the fishing line weak, the fish cannot forcibly be pulled in.[389] Instead, one simply lets the baited hook enter the fish's mouth and, depending on how close the crea-

---

dharma. The Buddha explained to the king that Śāriputra's mind could not be changed, for as a result of karmic influence from his previous lives he was exceedingly stubborn. Once he had been a poisonous serpent who had bitten a king. Summoned magically by the king's doctor to swallow down his own poison or else be forced into a blazing fire, he chose the latter.

387. The source of this illustration is a lengthy passage in the introductory section to Chih-i's *Chüeh-i san-mei*, T 46.621a14–b5. Chan-jan (T 46.206b5–8) explains: "In empty space there is no light or dark, for light and dark are dependent on form to obstruct each other. In the same way, the 'space' of the dharma-nature fundamentally contains neither good nor evil. It is only on the basis of the opinions of the ordinary person that we say good and evil impede each other. Thus the fact that good and evil—as they are understood according to the lesser vehicle and the ordinary person—do not impede one another is because in their essential nature and substance (*t'i-hsing*) they are not two. One who comes to such a realization will assuredly manifest bodhi. This is the reason for encouraging people to cultivate calming and contemplation in the midst of evil. To realize that evil is not evil and perceive the essential nature of evil is to know that, in its essential nature, there is fundamentally neither good nor evil." *Kōgi* (2.19) takes Chan-jan's words as a springboard to argue for the inherent inclusion of evil in the Buddha-nature.

388. Chan-jan (T 46.206b11–15) explains: "Even though one employs the nine meditations, etc., to cut off and suppress [the afflictions], [these afflictions may, on the contrary,] grow increasingly troublesome. Therefore one should use the four phases mentioned here in order to analyze them. One relaxes restraint of the mind but continues to control body and speech. Investigating [the desirous mind] exhaustively through meditative discernment, one thereby destroys desire. It is with this thought in mind that [the text] says, 'Without the arising of the obscurations he would have no chance to practice contemplation.' "

389. Chan-jan (T 46.19–26), explaining this paragraph, says: "Heavy desires are like the strength of the fish. The feebleness of contemplation is like the weakness of the line. One fears that, one's powers of meditation being minuscule, they will be bested by desire. Since [desire] cannot be severed in one swoop, one yields to it and employs contemplation. It is for this reason that the text cautions, '[the fish] cannot be hauled in all at once.' The method of contemplation is the hook; allowing [desires] to arise is the bait."

ture approaches, allows it to dive and surface freely. Then before long it can be laid hold of and landed.[390] The practice of contemplation on the basis of the obscurations is much the same. The obscurations are represented by the evil fish; and contemplation, by the baited hook. If there were no fish, there would be no need for hook or bait. The more numerous and large the fish are, the better.[391] They will all follow after the baited hook without rejecting it. Similarly, the obscurations will soon give way and be ready to be brought under control.

[17c29] **Application of the Four Phases to the Obscuration of Desire.** How then should this contemplation be practiced?[392] If a desire arises, then contemplate it minutely in its four phases: not-yet-desiring, about-to-desire, the act of desiring-proper, and desiring-completed.[393] In order for the about-to-desire to arise, must the not-yet-desiring first perish? In order for the about-to-desire to arise, does the not-yet-desiring not perish? Does it both perish and not perish, or neither perish nor not perish? [394]

390. This simile appears to originate from the TCTL (T 25.526b): "It is like a fish who nibbles at a hook: though he may still disport himself in the water of the pond, one knows that it will not be long before he leaves it. A practitioner of the way is like this too, for if he deeply believes and delights in the perfection of wisdom, he will not continue to live for long in saṃsāra."

Chan-jan (T 46.206b27–28), explaining the expression "getting hold of and landing," says: "When desire is severed and the contemplation is successfully completed, it is known as 'getting hold of and landing.' Initial success in contemplation is what is meant by 'getting hold of.' Full entrance into the ranks of [bodhisattvahood] is what is meant by 'landing.' "

391. The meaning of the text is unclear here.

392. The procedure for applying the tetralemma described in the passage that follows (down to realization of ultimate emptiness and simultaneous illumination of the two truths) is a condensation of an extended section of the *Chüeh-i san-mei*, T 46.623c4–624b28.

393. Chan-jan (T 46.206c8–9) says: "Desire or craving is treated first, for it is placed first in the list of six obscurations."

394. A typical application of the tetralemma or "four alternatives" (*catuṣkoti*), referred to in T'ien-t'ai works as "the investigation [of inapprehensibility] on the basis of the four phrases or propositions" (*ssu-chü t'ui-chien [pu-te]*)." Here naïve notions about the successive arising and perishing of each of the four phases of mental activation are analyzed rigorously according to these alternatives: (1) *x*, (2) not *x*, (3) both *x* and not *x*, (4) neither *x* nor not *x*. That is to say, inquiring into the actual mechanisms of the origin of a thought (in this case, desire) to determine precisely what sort of process takes place as it transpires from not being present to being present. Does its prior inexistence (the first of the four phases) cease in order that its impending existence might take place? Or does its impending existence come into being without the previous inexistence ceasing? Or both? Or neither? The particular structure that Chih-i uses in the four dialectical analyses that

[18a4] If the not-yet-desiring perishes in order for the about-to-desire to arise, then do the perishing and the arising coincide[395] or are they separate? If they coincide, then we have the contradiction of arising and perishing being simultaneous. If separate, then the arising lacks a cause.[396]

[18a6] If the not-yet-desiring does not perish in order for the about-to-desire to arise, then do these two coincide or are they separate? If they coincide, then both would be in existence together, and there would be no limit to the origination of new entities.[397] If separate, then the arising would again lack a cause.

[18a7] As for the notion that not-yet-desiring may both perish and not perish when the about-to-desire arises, if the arising [of the about-to-desire] can take place with the perishing [of the not-yet-desiring], then inclusion of [the second element of] not-perishing is pointless. Similarly, if arising can occur through not-perishing, then to speak of perishing is pointless.[398] How could such an indeterminate cause produce a deter-

---

follow appears to be based closely on chapter 7 (Discernment of the Three Marks) of Nāgārjuna's *Madhyamaka-kārikā* (*Chung-lun*, T 30.9a).

395. Do they occur as one event at the same point in time?

396. Chan-jan (T 46.206c13–15) says: "Perishing and arising are opposites. If arising occurs coincident to or in identity with perishing, then this constitutes a contradiction. It is analogous to saying that the state of the lamp perishing is called light shining. There is simply no basis for it. On the other hand, to say that arising takes place in separation [from perishing] is to imply that arising occurs apart from perishing—in isolation and wholly on its own. Thus it is tantamount to 'causelessness.' It is like light flaring up entirely on its own without the 'perishing' of the [prior condition of the unlighted] lamp. Moreover, if one allows that arising may occur without a cause, arising should be found to occur in all manner of instances where there is no cause, such as curds appearing when there is no milk or thought arising in wood and stone."

397. *Chüeh-i san-mei* (T 46.623c23–624a4) states: "If arising [of the phase of about-to-think] occurs coincident to the not-perishing [of the phase of not-yet-thinking], not-perishing already implies the presence of arising. How can this arising then take place? If this [previously] arisen [condition] can [secondarily] produce this [new] arising, then there should occur yet additional arisings. Arising would be limitless. If there is one identity of substance to this arising, its oneness should not admit multiple arisings, just as there are not multiple fingers included in one finger. If arising is something different from its substance, it can't be called 'arising.'. . . If one posits that the arising of about-to-think takes place in separation from the not-perishing of the phase of not-yet-thinking, then on what basis does about-to-think arise? If arising has no basis for arising it is arising without cause."

398. Chan-jan (206c25–29) says: "If both [the perishing and not perishing of the phase of not-yet-desiring] are simultaneously present [when the phase of about-to-desire arises], then we have contradictory causes producing [a single]

minate effect? Even if the perishing and the nonperishing of not-yet-desiring were the same in substance, they would differ in their fundamental nature, while if they were different in substance, there could be no relationship between them.

[18a11] Assuming that the not-yet-desiring must neither perish nor not perish when the about-to-desire arises, is the locus of this double negation existent or inexistent? If existent, then how can we say it is doubly negated? If inexistent, how could inexistence be capable of producing anything?

[18a13] Applying in this manner the four alternatives of the tetralemma, one cannot account for the arising of the phase of about-to-desire.[399] When, in turn, one [analyzes the second half of the statement] according to the four alternatives, the phase of about-to-desire cannot be found to either arise, not-arise, both-arise-and-not-arise, or neither-arise-nor-not-arise when the phase of not-yet-desiring perishes.[400] It is just as has been expounded above. Contemplating in this way, the obscuration of craving is found to be ultimately empty and quiescent. Yet simultaneous illumination [of the two truths] is also lucid and clear.[401] Again, it

---

fruit. Thus they both cancel each other out as unnecessary. Because it [purports to] involve both perishing and not-perishing [at the same time] we say [the cause is] 'indeterminate.' How could [such an indeterminate cause] produce a determinate result—namely, the definitive arising [of the phase of about-to-desire]?"

399. Chan-jan (T 46.207a9–11) states: "This marvelous contemplation provisionally establishes guest and host [i.e., the artificial rubric of both the object of contemplation and the method of analysis]. Then, thought after instant of thought, it examines with them relentlessly, so that there is not a moment when [the mind] escapes [their scrutiny]. When [all notion of] essential nature and attribute dissolves, it is called 'emptiness.' Because [the mental phases and their evolution] are empty, one does not perceive any arising of the phase of about-to-desire."

400. Chih-i and Kuan-ting in this passage are concerned not so much with the four phases of thought in and of themselves as with the transitions among the four phases. Each transition implies the interaction of two phases. If, on the basis of the tetralemma, one works out all the possible permutations for the mutual perishing and arising of the two phases, there are sixteen possible alternative formulations for each juncture. There being four gaps between phases (including the gap from the last back to the first), this comes altogether to sixty-four formulations. Chih-i has explicitly discussed only four and (in the last paragraph) suggested another four. Chan-jan in his commentary (T 46.207a11–207c23) works their permutations out to the full.

401. Chan-jan (T 46.207c23–208a2), pressed to account for the hyperbolic convolutions of this meditation, states: "Altogether there are sixteen possible propositions for each of four [junctures]. Of course, if one can achieve enlightenment the instant one engages in contemplation, one of the propositions alone is sufficient. What need is there to labor through all of the sixty-four? It is because

is as explained above. This is what we call the baited hook. When and wherever the obscurations arise, this contemplation will always illuminate them.[402] Though you will perceive neither their arising nor the illumination [of their arising], nevertheless they will both arise and be illuminated.

[18a18] Again, in contemplating this obscuration of desire, consider from which sense object it has arisen. Was it from form? Was it from another of the six? Consider, too, from which act it has arisen. From walking? From another of the six? If it arose in response to the seeing of form, was it in response to the not-yet-seeing of the form, the about-to-see, the seeing-proper, or the seeing-completed? If it arose in response to walking, was it in response to the not-yet-walking, the about-to-walk, the walking-proper, or the walking-completed?

[18a20] What was the phenomenal objective for which the desire arose? Was it for the breaking of the moral code? For conformity with the group? Was it out of jealousy? Out of kindness and deference? Was it a desire for the good or meditative concentration? For solitary nirvāṇa? For the four meritorious qualities?[403] For the six perfections? For the three samādhis?[404] For the Buddha's dharma, vast as the sands of the Ganges?[405]

---

persons of dull capacity tend to give rise to [false] suppositions with the unfolding of each step that we are compelled to refute the sixty-four propositions in their entirety. The discussion of the tetralemma with respect to the three provisionalities that appears in fascicle 5 [of the *Mo-ho chih-kuan*] expounds this to the full. But if one considers the basic point of that chapter, immediate investigation of any one [proposition] should reveal the realm of the inconceivable. The present passage resorts to a sequential and particulate approach to explaining [the practice]. Thus the sixty-four propositions are simply said to effect 'entry into emptiness.' Now, for one who has prior knowledge of the inconceivable principle, the instant that the thought of desire is refuted the wondrous realm stands perfectly replete. But even for this individual, phenomenal [techniques] for assisting [the path] are still necessary. The primary (*cheng*) and the ancillary (*chu*) must be used together."

402. According to Chan-jan (T 46.208a12–20), the presence of arising and illumination, even though there is no perception of arising and illumining, illustrates that emptiness does not occlude provisionality, but that both are illumined simultaneously.

403. Although, ordinarily, this refers to the four virtues of Buddha-nature described in the *Nirvāṇa Sūtra*, here it means the four stages of sainthood that culminate in arhatship.

404. Emptiness, featurelessness, wishlessness.

405. Various phenomenal objectives are matched roughly to the ten realms or destinies of the dharmadhātu. The fifth realm, that of the asuras, is skipped; the six perfections and the three saṃādhis belong together at the ninth level, that of the bodhisattva.

[18a24] When one contemplates in this way, one realizes that there is no perceiver of the sense object and no subject that acts upon the circumstances [of mental cognition]. Yet, even so, the simultaneous illumination[406] of the sense object and the perceiver, the mind sense and its supporting conditions is keen and bright. [The three perspectives that see desire as] a magical apparition, as emptiness, and as true dharma-nature, do not impede each other.[407] Why? Because, if obscurations impeded the dharma-nature, it would involve the destruction of the dharma-nature, while if the dharma-nature impeded the obscurations, the latter would not be able to arise at all. Know, therefore, that the obscurations are themselves identical with the dharma-nature. When an obscuration arises, it is the dharma-nature itself arising; and when the obscuration ceases to be, it is the dharma-nature itself ceasing.[408]

[18a29] The *Sarva-dharma-pravṛtti-nirdeśa* [*Sūtra*] says, "Desire is identical to the way, and the same is true for anger and stupidity. The whole of the Buddha's dharma is contained in these three dharmas. If one should seek enlightenment apart from desire, one would be as far from it as earth is from heaven."[409] Desire is identical to enlightenment.

[18b2] The *Vimalakīrti* says, "By following the nonway, a bodhisattva achieves the Buddha's way."[410] "All animate beings are already identical to the mark of enlightenment, so they cannot further attain it; they are already identical to the mark of nirvāṇa, so they cannot further extinguish anything."[411] "To those of overweening pride the Buddha preaches that separation from craving, anger, and stupidity is what is called liberation. But to those without arrogance he preaches that the nature of craving, anger, and stupidity is itself identical to liberation."[412] "The defilements are the seeds of the Tathāgata."[413]

[18b7] The color of mountains and the taste of the sea are always the same. Just so, one should contemplate all evils as the principle of the

406. Simultaneous illumination of both emptiness and provisionality.

407. The three truths of provisionality, emptiness, and the middle.

408. Chan-jan (T 36.208b14–16) states: "This mutual unimpededness of the dharma-nature and obscuration is expounded on the basis of principle. It is like waves and water not obstructing one another. All of this, up to the [passage concerning] the mutual identity of dharma-nature and the obscurations in their arising and perishing, is intended expressly to illustrate that dharma-nature is to be discerned right in the obscurations."

409. A paraphrase of the *Chu-fa wu-hsing ching*, T 15.759c.

410. T 14.549a. Chan-jan (T 46.208b29) says: "The nonway is the obscurations. The way of the Buddha is the essential nature [of things]."

411. Ibid., T 14.542b.

412. Ibid., T 14.548a.

413. Ibid., T 14.549b. Mañjuśrī explains here that, just as lotus seeds must be planted in the mud and will never germinate in empty space, so the seeds of Buddhahood will flourish only when planted in the mire of worldly afflictions.

inconceivable.[414] If one constantly attends to the development of contemplative insight (*kuan-hui*), the obscurations and principle will be in mutual resonance with one another, like shape and shadow. This is called the stage of identity in meditative practice.[415] One who is able to view all evil dharmas and mundane means of livelihood as not in contradiction with reality is at the stage of the identity in resemblance.[416] Advancing further, one enters the stage of the copper wheel[417] and begins to destroy the root of the obscurations. That root is nescience. Through the bending of the root and the snapping of the twigs Buddha-nature comes to be revealed. This is the stage of the identity of incremental realization of the truth.[418] Finally, as a Buddha, to extirpate completely the fountainhead of the obscurations—this is called the stage of ultimate identity. Within the obscuration of craving there is contained, vertically, all of the six identities and, horizontally, the six perfections. This holds true for all other dharmas as well.[419]

[18b14] Next we deal with contemplation of the obscuration of anger.[420] There are persons who tend toward a preponderance of anger, who ceaselessly surge with emotion and are prone to such frequent out-

414. The simile of the taste of the ocean possibly comes from the *Nirvāṇa Sūtra*, T 12.805a–b. Here *mahāparinirvāṇa* is said to be unthinkable in eight ways like the sea. The third way is that it is all the same salty taste. TCTL (T 25.752a5) also contains such a simile. The simile of the color of the mountains occurs in TCTL (T 25.752b–c), according to which non-Buddhist books speak of Mount Sumeru, the center of the world, as being of only a single color.

415. The third of the six identities. The first two (identity in principle and verbal identity) have been omitted as not pertaining to practice.

416. Fourth of the six identities, equivalent to the ten stages of faith or the first set of ten in the fifty-two stages. Here the practitioner achieves a proximate or semblance of realization of the truth of the middle way.

417. The second of six "universal monarchs" or "wheel-turning kings" (*cakravartin*) described in the apocryphal *Jen-wang p'o-lo-mi ching* (Sūtra of Benevolent Kings) (T 8.826b–829a). In the T'ien-t'ai perfect teaching it is interpreted as a metaphor for the stages of the bodhisattva path and is matched to entry into the ten abodes or the identity of increments of truth.

418. Also known as "identity in increments of truth," it is the fifth of the six identities. It is only here that the basic nescience obscuring the unalloyed reality of the middle truth begins to be eliminated. This identity contains forty-one of the fifty-two stages, ranging from the ten abodes to the stage of "penultimate enlightenment" that lies just shy of the supreme fruit of full Buddhahood. Over these forty-one stages, nescience is progressively eliminated and the wisdom of the middle way progressively strengthened.

419. Chan-jan (T 46.208c28–29) says: "The six identities illustrate differences in shallowness and depth; thus they are described as vertical. But the six perfections all inhere upon one another without any particular one taking precedence; thus they are described as horizontal."

420. This is the third, not the second, in the list of the six obscurations.

breaks of temper that they are utterly unable to arrest or control themselves even for a moment. Such an individual should allow his anger to arise freely so that he can illuminate it with the practice of calming and contemplation. In contemplating the four phases of the anger, he should inquire from whence they arise. If their arising cannot be apprehended, then neither can their perishing.[421] He should then consider each of the twelve items,[422] asking from whom the anger arises, who is the angry one, and who is the object of that anger. Contemplating in this manner, he realizes that the anger is utterly inapprehensible. Its coming and going, the traces it leaves behind, as well as its manifest features, are all both empty and quiescent.[423] He contemplates anger as the ten realms [of the dharmadhātu][424] and contemplates anger as the four meritorious qualities,[425] just as has been explained above. Thus one attains the way of the Buddha through the nonway of anger.

[18b20] One should contemplate in this fashion the remaining obscurations—immorality, laziness, mental distractedness, and the stupidity of adherence to false views—as well as all other evil forms of phenomenal activity.

Contemplation amidst Neutral Dharmas

[18b22] Fourth is the contemplation of [activity and perception] that is neither good nor evil—that is to say, those dharmas whose nature is morally neutral or nonvalent.[426] The reason it is necessary to contemplate such dharmas is that there are some people who by nature do neither good nor evil. If only good or evil dharmas were used for contemplation, there would be no way for such persons to achieve deliverance from the

421. Chan-jan (T 46.209a5–6) asserts that application of the first set of sixteen among the sixty-four alternative propositions is implied in the terms "arising" and "perishing" here.

422. The six acts and six perceptions.

423. Chan-jan (T 46.209a9) says: "Quiescence and extinction of manifest features represents the view of emptiness."

424. Chan-jan (T 46.209a9–10) says: "The ten realms represent the view of provisionality."

425. Chan-jan (T 46.209a10) says: "The four meritorious qualities [i.e., permanence, pleasure, purity, and selfhood] represent the view of the middle."

426. Chan-jan (T 46.209a28) states: "If one were to discuss them in detail, all other dharmas outside of the perfections and obscurations could be called nonvalent or neutral. For this reason contemplation of the neutral must be included." *Kōgi* (2.42), citing the *Abhidharmakośa*, takes issue with Chan-jan, insisting that the designation is more specific. Among the forty-six mental dharmas in the system of seventy-five dharmas elaborated by the *Abhidharmakośa*, there are six classes: three kinds of evil dharma (totaling eighteen), ten good dharmas, ten ubiquitous dharmas, and eighteen indeterminate dharmas (T 29.84a–b).

world through [the practice of] freely following one's thought (*sui-tzu-i*). Then what could these people do?

[18b25] The *Great Treatise* says, "The perfection of wisdom is also present in the morally neutral."[427] By this we know that the contemplation of neutral thoughts is admissible.

[18b26] In contemplating these neutral thoughts, one should examine whether they are different from or the same as good or evil thoughts.[428] If the same, then they are not neutral after all. If different, then does this neutrality arise with the perishing of the prior mark of valency? Does it arise with the nonperishing of the mark of valency, or both, or neither?[429] In seeking the valency [of good and evil thoughts], one realizes it cannot be apprehended; how much the less could one apprehend neutrality! Is the nonvalent one and the same with or different from the valent? Since they are not the same, the neutral does not merge [with the valency of good and evil]; and since they are not different, they are not dispersed either. Since they are not merged, neutrality does not arise; and since they are not dispersed, neither does it perish.[430]

[18c2] Consider, too, from which of the twelve items the neutral thought has arisen, for whom it has arisen, and who is the one thinking [the neutral thought]. When one contemplates in such a way, one finds the neutral thought to be as empty as space. Yet a single neutral dharma also gives rise to the tenfold dharmadhātu and all the dharmas in it. Moreover, the neutral dharma is also identical to the dharma-nature.[431]

427. TCTL, T 25.588a.

428. Chan-jan (T 46.209b1–5) says: "If the mental features [of the neutral thought] are not made manifest, it is extremely difficult to focus on them as an object [for contemplation]. Should one contrast them with good and evil and delineate their similarities and differences, then neutrality can be identified and an object of contemplation established."

429. Chan-jan claims that Chih-i dispenses with the formula of the four temporal phases here and opts instead for a lateral contrast of neutrality and valency. Chan-jan (T 46.209b4–7) says: "Because its nature is indeterminate and the four phases [of mental activation] are not clearly manifest, we apply the investigation of the tetralemma exclusively to the opposition [between neutrality] and [the valency] of good and evil. If one were to work out the permutations to the full, there should also be sixteen possible propositions. That is to say, the arising of neutrality, nonarising of neutrality, both, and neither each has four propositions. Since the four phases are not used here, it is not necessary to extend the analysis to [the full] range of sixty-four propositions."

430. Chan-jan (T 46.209b) says: "The essential nature of the neutral thought and that of the good or evil thought are not different. In substance they are the same; in name, they differ. Thus we use the designation 'neither merged nor dispersed.' "

431. Chan-jan (T 46.209b16–17) says: "The first sentence represents the view

That the dharma-nature is eternally quiescent is the meaning of "calming"; that, though quiescent, it is eternally luminous is the meaning of "contemplation."

[18c6] One attains to the Buddha's way through the nonway of contemplating neutral thoughts. Neutral thoughts are themselves the dharmadhātu. Horizontally encompassing all dharmas and vertically including the six identities, each neutral thought is fully endowed with both the height and breadth [of Buddha dharma]. [The rest of the contemplation] may be inferred by analogy with the foregoing discussion of the contemplation of evil.

[18c8] Now if the samādhi of following one's own thought is explained in terms of the final good, this is the gradual sense [of calming and contemplation].[432] If the samādhi of following one's own thought is explained in terms of both good and evil, then this is the sudden sense [of calming and contemplation].[433] And if the samādhi of following one's own thought is explained in terms of the good that involves applying[434] [the manifold levels and forms of contemplation] as needed, then this is the variable sense [of calming and contemplation].

Concluding Deliberations

[18c10] The four forms of samādhi differ in explicit procedure (*fang-fa*) but are the same in their contemplation of principle (*li-kuan*).[435] Basically

---

of emptiness; the tenfold dharmadhātu, the view of provisionality; and dharma-nature, the middle."

432. Chan-jan (T 46.209b23–25) explains: "This idea of the 'final good' is defined in reference to the various evils. First one resorts to the conventional distinctions between good and evil, then progressively refines its meaning to the point where the good is identified solely with the perfect [teaching]. Because the perfect occupies the final position, this represents a gradualistic scheme."

433. Chan-jan (T 46.209b27–28) says: "The expression 'both good and evil' here means that every action is identified with the dharmadhātu of the three views, whether we are speaking of distinctively defined forms of evil or the good deeds of the six perfections."

434. According to Chan-jan (T 46.209c2–3), this is an expression used later in the MHCK (T 46.68b) as a name for the fourth of ten applications of the tetralemma. It means that the four lines of the tetralemma "may be applied fluidly" to the ordinary person, the two vehicles, bodhisattvas, and Buddhas (e.g., which represent the views of existence, inexistence, both, and neither, respectively).

435. Chan-jan (T 46.209c10–17) explains: "The opening lines of this passage briefly point out that the [four samādhis] differ in terms of [ritual] activity but are the same in [their focus upon] principle. It also places [the practice of] freely following one's thought in a position distinct from the other three [samādhis]. Why? To show that they differ in the degree to which they set in motion impediments to the way. Even so, however, in their discernment of principle they do not differ.

the procedures found in the foregoing three practices make liberal use of ancillary techniques designed to assist [realization of] the way (*chu-tao fa-men*). [In so doing] they also set in motion obstructions to the way.[436] As [the samādhi of] freely following one's thought is comparatively meager in the use of such procedures, it produces this situation to a lesser degree.

[18c13] Now, if one understands [a practice] solely in terms of the supportive role that its given procedures (*fang-fa*) are alleged to play, then its phenomenal [ritual] program (*shih-hsiang*) will prove ineffective [in prompting realization of the way].[437] But if one understands contemplation of principle (*li-kuan*), there will be no phenomenal feature (*shih-hsiang*) that will not penetrate [to realization]. Again, if one does not grasp the basic idea behind this contemplation of principle, even the assistance to the way promised by these phenomenal features will not be successful. However, once one understands contemplation of principle,

---

"Q: In constant sitting one contemplates the three circuits [of the obstacles], etc. In [the samādhi of] constant walking one contemplates the thirty-two marks of the Buddha; in the vaipulya, the visage of the lordly *vaipulya-dhāraṇī*; in the lotus [repentance], the white elephant of six tusks, etc. In following one's thought one contemplates good, evil, and nonvalent [deeds and thoughts]. Certainly the contemplations are each unique. Why do you say they are the same?

"A: These descriptions are all couched in terms of the phenomenal [ritual] program to which [contemplation itself] is applied. If one is able to 'discern the discerning,' there is nothing that stands apart from the one mind. Nor is there a moment when the principle that one contemplates is not identical to the three truths."

436. The line rendered as "they also set in motion obstructions to the way" (*tung chang-tao*) is somewhat ambiguous. There is good evidence from other works of Chih-i that it might also be read: "activating obstructions to the way." Thus the ritual programs of the previous three samādhis may either be understood to "create" obstructions (by encouraging naïve attachments to the phenomenal content of the rite) or to "activate" existing obstructions as a therapy for removing them. Chih-i's works on meditation (see *Tz'u-ti ch'an-men*, T 46.501a–508a; 491c; MHCK, T 46.49b, 102c, 111c22–112114c) frequently speak of the cathartic power (and role) of certain ascetic exercises and ritual orchestrations to "activate" (*tung*) latent karmic impediments, thereby causing them to "manifest" (*fa*) in the form of vexation, illness, visions, etc. Once manifested, they can also be effectively dealt with and removed, thereby bringing speedy progress on the path. The previous three samādhis, with their physical rigor, devotional color and fervor, and intense mental concentration are noted especially for this twin function of both "posing" and "removing" obstructions. It is with this latter sense in mind that *Kōgi* (2.47) interprets "factors that may obstruct the way" as karmic manifestations.

437. Chan-jan (T 46.209c18) says: "The line from 'if one simply,' etc., shows that principle is absolutely essential for the phenomenal program of the practice to be effective. The line that begins 'not understanding the import of contemplation of principle,' etc., explains how one must rely upon principle as the basis for the phenomenal aspects of the practice."

the samādhis associated with these phenomenal programs will be achieved effortlessly. Individuals who cultivate the way primarily on the basis of phenomenal content [i.e., the previous three forms of samādhi] will be able to apply themselves effectively while inside the sanctuary (*tao-ch'ang*) but will not be able to maintain this when they come out. In the case of the [samādhi] of freely following one's thought, however, there is no break [between the two]. It is only in the first three samādhis that explicit procedures are employed;[438] but the contemplation of principle (*li-kuan*) runs through all four.

[18c18] Q: Each of the previous three samādhis contains an exhortation to practice. Why does the fourth alone lack it?

[18c19] A: The nonway of the six obscurations is assuredly the way of liberation; but those whose faculties (*ken*) are dull and heavily beset with obstacles, upon hearing this, might misunderstand and founder [in the sea of afflictions].[439] If we were then to add an exhortation to practice, their misunderstanding would be all the more severe.

[18c20] In the region north of the Huai and Ho[440] rivers are people who cultivate the Mahāyāna emptiness but who dispense with all restraint and seize the snake [of desire].[441] I will tell you about them now. Their former teachers used wholesome dharmas as the basis for contemplation,

438. Chan-jan (T 46.209c22–23) says: "This is not to say that explicit procedures (*fang-fa*) are not necessary [in this samādhi of following one's thought]. It is just that explicit procedures are not prescribed as a fixed feature of this samādhi practice. Thus 'explicit procedures' is really a feature belonging to the other three [samādhis]."

439. Perform actions that would cause them to sink to lower destinies.

440. Chan-jan (T 46.210a3) says: "North of the Ho and north of the Huai there are people given to a depraved sense of emptiness who make the exaggerated claim that this is the Great Vehicle."

441. Chan-jan (T 46.210a4–6 and 19–22) states: " 'Restraint' means 'control,' because by the art [of proper handling] one controls or restrains the creature. Desire is likened to the serpent; the method of contemplation, the means of restraint. Practicing the contemplation of desire is like handling or grasping the snake. If one is not skilled in the use of the tetralemma, it is like having no means to properly restrain it. . . . If one takes up the staff of the wondrous contemplation, enters the forest of the six sense objects, meets the snake of desire, pins down its head of the four phases of thought, and seizes it with meditative discernment, then its venom will not produce [evil] deeds of the body and cause one to lose the pure and ever abiding dharma body."

The simile originates from the *Alagaddupama Sutta* in the *Madhyamāgama* (T 1.763b–764b). A certain monk named Ariṣṭa, having misunderstood the Buddha's teaching regarding the middle path, advocated indulgence of desire as the way. The Buddha likens him to one who sets out to capture a poisonous snake with no knowledge of the art of snake handling. He grasps the serpent by the middle, and it turns and bites him (see Horner, trans., *The Collection of the Middle Length Sayings*, 1.167–182).

but, as a long time passed without their penetrating to realization, they released their minds [from the precepts] and turned toward evil dharmas as objects of contemplation. Thereby they did succeed in gaining a meager taste of samādhi (*ting-hsin*) and tenuous understanding of emptiness.[442] But they neither took cognizance of their listeners' capacities (*ken*) and circumstances in life (*yüan*), nor did they penetrate to the real intent of the Buddha's [teaching]. They simply took this one dharma and taught it indiscriminately to everyone.

[18c24] Having expounded this dharma to others over a long period of time, one or two [of their disciples] have managed to gain some benefit. But this is like insects accidentally producing legible words by their random gnawing at a tree.[443] Taking it as proof, they claim their doctrine has been verified. They brand all other teachings as lies and ridicule those who observe the precepts and cultivate the good, saying, "That is not the way!" Expounding nothing but this pernicious doctrine to others, they cause a host of evils to be committed everywhere. Themselves blind and eyeless, unable to tell right from wrong, their spiritual capacities have become all the more obtuse and their afflictions even graver.[444]

[18c29] Because the words they hear conform so readily to their own desires and passions, [people everywhere] submit faithfully to this teaching and follow it obediently. They discard completely the moral prohibitions, and there is no wrong they won't commit. Thus their sins pile up as high as mountains. At length the common people are brought to despise [the moral precepts] as so many weeds. And, in response, the king of the land and his ministers move to exterminate the Buddha's dharma. This noxious tendency has penetrated deeply and even now has yet to be rectified.[445]

442. Chan-jan (T 46.210a24–27) says: "These former masters were both obtuse in spiritual capacity and heavily burdened by obstructions. Because they could not succeed at cultivation on the basis of the good, they gave up, gave in to evil, and [so produced] something resembling the contemplation of emptiness. This they construed to be an understanding of emptiness and acclaimed as profound realization. It represents failure in one's own practice. 'Not identifying the capacities of others,' etc., represents failure in training others."

443. *Kōgi* (2.50) says this happens where such a teacher accidentally manages to fit the teaching to the student, without understanding why it works, and the latter benefits from it.

444. Chan-jan (T 46.210b1–4) says: " 'Blind and eyeless,' etc., describes the failure of the disciples who erroneously accept this teaching. 'Blind' means to be without the eye [that knows the comprehensive classification of] the teachings. When cultivation of the good produces no result, it is called 'dull capacity.' When one frequently gives rise to desire, 'afflictions are heavy.' Following their desires and following their emotions, they 'commit a host of evils everywhere.' "

445. Chan-jan (T 46.210b7) remarks: "Because [this problem] was still present during the Sui dynasty, [Chih-i] says: 'It is yet to be rectified.' " Chih-i is likely

[19a2] The *Shih chi* says, "At the end of the Chou dynasty a certain person appeared with dishevelled hair and stripped naked, who did not observe the rules of ceremony. As a result, the barbarians of the west (i.e., the Ch'üan and Jung) invaded the country."[446] The few males of the ruling family who were not exterminated hung on like a thread, and the house of Chou gradually died out.

[19a4] To take another example, Juan Chi was a gifted person who "wore dishevelled hair and let his belt hang loose."[447] In later times the children and grandchildren of the aristocracy imitated him. They held that only by sharing mutual shame with servants and dogs could one achieve naturalness and called those who vied to uphold the norms of conduct "country bumpkins." These were portents of destruction for the Ssu-ma house [of the Western Chin dynasty].[448]

[19a7] The Northern Chou annihilation of Buddhism by Yü-wen

---

alluding to the famous Northern Chou persecution of Buddhism (574–577), which occurred just before the pro-Buddhist Sui dynasty conquered the north (581). For a thought-provoking discussion of the impact of this event on Chih-i's own religious outlook, see Satō, *Tendai daishi no kenkyū*, pp. 42–43; also, Kyōda, *Tendai daishi no shōgai*, pp. 113–120.

446. This passage is not in the *Shih chi* but in the *Tso chuan* (twenty-second year of the annals of the Duke of Hsi), which says: "Formerly when Emperor P'ing (770–720) had moved his residence to the east (Loyang), the grand prefect Hsin-yu came to the Yi River (in Honan) and saw there someone with dishevelled hair performing a sacrifice in an open field. The prefect said, 'Before a hundred years have passed, this country will, I fear, be occupied by the barbarians of the west. The rules of ceremony are already not being observed here.' Then in autumn (686 B.C., i.e., less than a hundred years later), the princes of the Ch'in and Chin transported the western barbarians of Lu Huan to the Yi River" (cf. Legge, *The Chinese Classics*, 5.181–182).

Chan-jan (T 46.210c4–6) says: "The naked man with dishevelled hair represents the depraved Buddhist masters. The true teaching may be likened to the person who took cognizance of the situation. Breaking the precepts is like 'neglect of the rules of decorum.' The objects of desire are like the Ch'üan-jung barbarians, and the destruction of right contemplation like the invasion of the Middle Kingdom. The true cause (i.e., path) not being totally cut off is analogous to the 'single thread.' "

447. From the *Chin shu* (Po-na edition) 49:1a–b. This man was one of the "seven sages of the bamboo grove," the celebrated Neo-Taoist group of the Three Kingdoms period who were famous for indulging in wine and eccentric behavior as a statement of social protest and personal freedom. See Holtzman, *Poetry and Politics: The Life and Works of Juan Chi (A.D. 210–263)*.

448. Chan-jan (T 46.210c25–211a3), explaining Chih-i, attributes the momentous loss of northern China to the barbarians at the end of the Western Chin (A.D. 311–316) to the neglect of military arts and traditional culture brought on by the licentious and undisciplined example of Juan Chi and the Seven Sages.

Yung[449] was also due to the demonic deeds of [the renegade monk] Yüan-sung.[450] These two men were the evil spirits behind the destruction of the Buddha's dharma, and they were also evil spirits for the times. This could hardly have any connection with the real meaning of "freely following one's thought." Why not? Because such things happen mainly when stupid people of this kind, completely lacking in insight and understanding, put blind faith in their teachers, admire and imitate their example, and conclude decisively that, "This is the way." Also, taking the easy path of following their emotions, they indulgently grasp after pleasure without ever thinking to correct their errant ways.[451]

[19a11] Take for example the famous beauty Hsi-shih. Once she was stricken with a mental illness and took such delight in grimacing and groaning that even the hundred hairs of her eyebrows all grew contorted. Yet it served only to enhance her beauty. The other women in the neighborhood, being ugly from birth, imitated her grimaces and groans but instead grew so loathsome in appearance that the poor moved far away and the wealthy closed their gates, fish in grottoes dove deeper yet, and birds fled into the heights.[452]

[19a14] The people we have spoken of earlier are similar to these ugly

449. The massive persecution of Buddhism in the north initiated by Emperor Wu of the Northern Chou in 574.

450. The renegade monk Wei Yüan-sung became renowned in later tradition as one of two main figures responsible for stirring up the furor that led to Emperor Wu's proscription of Buddhism (and Taoism) in 574. The second figure (mentioned by Chan-jan, T 46.211a19–23) is the Taoist priest Chang Pin. See Ch'en, *Buddhism in China*, pp. 184–194, for a summary of the events surrounding the Northern Chou persecution.

451. Chan-jan (T 46.211b21–25) summarizes: "Wei Yüan-sung is comparable to the evil dharma master, while Emperor Wu is comparable to the misled and foolish disciples. The text from the line 'Why not?' elucidates erroneous faith. For the person practicing samādhi it also applies. First, internally the person has no insight or understanding; second, he or she places [blind] faith in the teacher; and third, he or she esteems and imitates the teacher's example. Thus one should know that first you must train yourself in the teachings and only then put faith in the teacher. Otherwise you will just be indulging evil, thinking it to be the true way."

452. From *Chuang-tzu*, 38/14/42–44; cf. Watson, *The Basic Writings of Chuang Tzu*, pp. 160–161. For Chan-jan (T 46.211c25–212a7), the beautiful Hsi-shih illustrates the person of keen roots for whom contemplation while engaged in evil is timely and effective. The ugly women who imitate her represent the depraved practitioners. The poor who move far away signify practitioners of the Hīnayāna. The rich who shut their doors represent Mahāyāna devotees. The fish signify practitioners of worldly good; and the birds, practitioners of mundane meditation. All four types of people turn away from this depravity, just as the poor, the rich, fishes, and birds all turn away from an ugly spectacle.

women. Like mad dogs they chase after thunder[453] and create for themselves karma leading to hell. How pitiful they are; how painful to behold! Once they have tasted the pleasure of [indulging] desire, they can no longer stop themselves. They are like bluebottle flies, which stick [to their food] by their own spittle. This, in essence, is the fault of dissipation.

[19a17] The essential flaw of their teachers lies in their failure to assess their disciples' spiritual endowments (*ken-hsing*) and understand the design of the Buddha's [teaching]. The reason the Buddha taught that desire is the way is that, by taking into account what is suited to [different] salvific circumstances (*chi*), he knew some beings were so base and deficient in merit that they could never cultivate the way by means of the good. If such beings were left to their sins there would be no end to their transmigration; so the Buddha had them practice calming and contemplation in the very act of desire. It was because they were completely unable to control their craving that he created this teaching.

[19a21] It is analogous to parents who, seeing that their child has taken ill, know that no other medicine than yellow dragon potion will do.[454] Though it scores his teeth and makes him vomit, if the child takes the medicine, it will cure his sickness. The Buddha is like this as well: he fits his doctrine to the salvific circumstances (*chi*) of his listeners.

[19a23] A nimble horse needs to see but the shadow of the whip for him to follow the proper path.[455] That desire and the way are identical is, indeed, the true sense of the Buddha's teaching. But, for the benefit of those beings who are not suited to the practice of calming and contemplation amid evil, the Buddha also taught the [practice of] the good and called it the way. The Buddha thus has two doctrines [which he applies to fit the occasion]. Why, then, do you denounce good and cleave to evil? If things are really this way, then you yourselves are superior to the Buddha! Can you in all honesty make this claim publicly before the Buddha? It is true that there may be times when emergencies arise. Called to the service of the state, you may be unable to engage in the practice of the good. The Buddha under these circumstances allows calming and con-

453. Chan-jan (T 46.212a9–10) says: "Because of the madness of their craving they pursue the thunder of indulgence in evil."

454. A black, bitter medicine of the Chinese pharmacopia that is made from excrement and said to be efficacious against fevers and various serious diseases.

455. From the *Saṃyuktāgama* (*Tsa a-han ching*, T 2.234a–b). The simile distinguishes four kinds of trained horse, which are comparable to four capacities of practioner: the best horse will obey the will of the horseman upon seeing only the whip's shadow. The others have to be struck on their hair, or their skin, or be cut to their very bones, before responding. The best dharma practitioner merely has to hear and think of the suffering around him to develop complete aversion to the world. For the Pāli version contained in the *Catukka Nipāta* of the *Aṅguttara-nikāya*, see Woodward and Hare, trans., *Book of Gradual Sayings*, 2.118–120.

templation to be practiced in the midst of evil. But, at the moment, there is no crisis and no conscription. Why then do you employ in your teaching nothing but the medicine of milk, thereby poisoning the wisdom life of other people?[456]

[19b1] For this reason it says in the *Āgamas* that if a cowherd is familiar with a good crossing he can bring his herd to safety.[457] If there are problems with the good crossing and it cannot be used, then he has no choice but to use a bad crossing. Yet the bad crossing being fraught with perils, out of a hundred cattle he might fail to get a single one across.

[19b3] You are now without pressing affairs of state and are fortunate to be able to drive your cattle over a good crossing onto a good road. Why, then, do you mire both yourselves and others in the bad path? You destroy the Buddha's dharma, eclipse his majestic light, and enmesh animate beings in error. These are acts of the worst kind of spiritual friend[458]—one who fails to comprehend the true intent of the Buddha.

[19b5] Again, level and precipitious paths can both lead to the goal; the steeper one is used if there is some obstacle on the other. In the same way, [contemplation of] good as well as [contemplation of] evil will enable the practitioner to reach his end. After his salvific needs (*chi*) have been scrutinized [by the teacher], he may [as a last resort] enter [contemplation of] the obscurations.

456. From the *Nirvāṇa Sūtra*, T 12.617–618c. The sūtra distinguishes between the conventional deluded view of existence as permanent, pleasurable, endowed with self, and pure and these same qualities as they are understood according to the profound doctrines of the Mahāyāna. Those who would espouse the validity of these four qualities at the worldly level are compared to an incompetent doctor who indiscriminately uses milk to treat every illness. A wiser doctor arrives in the kingdom and persuades the king that this milk is poisonous, has the other doctor banished, and proceeds to prescribe a variety of medicines for the variety of diseases from which the subjects of the kingdom are suffering. Finally, however, the king himself grows ill and the medicine that the doctor prescribes turns out, to the king's great surprise, to be milk again. The second doctor was able to do this because, unlike the first doctor, he could discriminate between patients and give them the proper medicine for the occasion. Used by the ignorant doctor, the milk is like poison, for it did harm rather than good. Applied by the skilled doctor it is an effective medicine. The sūtra concludes by likening the ignorant doctor's occasional success to the worms who accidentally produce legible words through their random gnawing on the bark of a tree.

457. From the *Ekottarāgama* (*Tseng-i a-han ching*, T 2.794c, 795a). A slightly different version also appears in the *Saṃyuktāgama* (*Tsa a-han ching*, T 2.342c–343b). For an English translation of the Pāli version, see Woodward, trans., *The Book of the Gradual Sayings*, 5.224–227; and Horner, trans., *The Collection of the Middle Length Sayings*, 1.271–277.

458. The polar opposite of the "worthy or good friend" (*shan chih shih; kalyāṇamitra*) who helps one advance along the path.

[19b7] But if, by rejecting the good and keeping exclusively to the evil, you are indeed able to achieve your goal via the nonway, why then do you not walk through water or fire, or clamber over mountain precipices? Since, in fact, you are unable to proceed along such steep paths even in the worldly realm, how much less should you be able to understand the true way through proceeding on evil paths! How could this ever be done?

[19b9] Moreover, you are unable to take cognizance of peoples' differences in capacity (*ken*) and circumstance (*yüan*). Even a single person sometimes desires good, sometimes evil—preference is not necessarily fixed. Still more indeterminate are the preferences of countless numbers of people. Despite this, it is through the indulgence of desire alone that you strive to train them. The *Vimalakīrti Sūtra* says, "I think that śrāvakas do not take account of the capacities of people and for this reason should not expound the dharma to them."[459] Practitioners of the two vehicles do not take stock [of their listeners], and even misjudge their own salvific needs (*chi*). How much greater is your failure, blind, benighted, and eyeless teachers that you are! You yourselves violate the sūtras and fail to accord with both the spiritual circumstances (*chi*) of your listeners and true principle. How could your stupidity and delusion have suddenly come to such a pass?

[19b15] If a person should appear who, without identifying what is proper to the circumstances (*chi*) of his audience, practices and expounds this doctrine, then he is a corpse in the ocean of the disciplinary code and should be ostracized as the vinaya prescribes.[460] Do not let poisonous trees flourish in the landowner's courtyard.[461]

[19b17] Moreover, upon examining your evil conduct we find, in fact, that it is a selective kind of immorality. You say that desire is identical to the way and so are willing to debauch any and all women. But you cannot bring yourself to say that, since anger is also identical to the way, one should injure any and all men.[462] You love only the delicate and smooth touch [of a woman's body] and affirm it as the way, while you fear the painful feeling of being beaten and deny that it has any part in the way.

459. T 14.541a. Pūrṇa Maitrāyaṇīputra has just told how Vimalakīrti once reproved him for preaching to some new monks without first entering samādhi and determining the receptivity of their minds to the teaching.

460. According to the *Dharmagupta Vinaya* (*Ssu-fen lü*, T 22.567c), a monk who has broken the code is to be ostracized just as the ocean rejects a corpse. This ostracism (*pravrājana*) can take three forms: temporary expulsion, enforced silence, and permanent expulsion.

461. In the *Nirvāṇa Sūtra*, T 12.620c, the Buddha compares the proper expulsion of a sinful monk from the sangha to the act of a wealthy householder who removes poisonous trees from his property.

462. Craving and anger, together with stupidity, represent the basic afflictions of the three poisons.

One you do but not the other. You say that the way is in one and not in the other. Stupid and benighted as lacquer is black,[463] your biases lead only to defilement and harm, like a putrid corpse contaminating a beautiful garden.

[19b22] Our rebuttal to this obsessed and biased behavior is as given above. Sometimes if one threatens such people with water, fire, knives, or clubs, they will fall silent. Then again they might reply, "You don't understand that I am always able to enter these pleasures without getting defiled." These are self-deceptive and shameless words, which further reveal that these people do not grasp the meaning of the six identities.

[19b25] There is a reason why [such cautionary] remarks as these are appropriate. The first three methods of practice are very stringent and physically demanding; hence they require an "exhortation to practice." In this method of freely following one's own thought, one "softens one's light"[464] and enters into evil. From the very start it is easy to practice. Hence cautionary words are necessary. In the same way, when taking as medicine a large amount of yellow dragon potion, one ought to provide oneself with plain hot water to temper [its virulent side affects].[465]

[19b27] Q: When one uses the true contemplation of the middle way to unify one's mind, it is already sufficient the instant one puts it into practice. What further need is there for such complicated arrangements as the four forms of samādhi and application [of contemplation] to good, evil, and the twelve items? When the water is muddied, the pearl is concealed. When the wind blows heavily, waves beat on the surface.[466] How can [practices such as these] possibly contribute to the clarity and stillness of the water?

[19c1] A: Your attitude is like that of a pauper: upon acquiring just a little advantage he thinks it enough and does not set his sights on anything better. If one contemplates the mind using only one form of practice, what happens when you are confronted with all sorts of different mental states? Under such circumstances your own practice is bound to

463. Stupidity being the third of the three poisons, we can safely assume that the libertine would not affirm it as the way either.

464. From the *Lao-tzu*, chapter 4: "[The Tao] softens its light and mixes with the world." In the samādhi of freely following one's thought, one mixes unrestrainedly with the profane world instead of retricting oneself to a meditation chamber or ritual structure.

465. Chan-jan (T 46.213a7–8) says: "One must provide the teachings of the vinaya to temper [its virulence]."

466. Chan-jan (T 46.213a9–11), paraphrasing the question, says: " 'Water' stands for right contemplation, the 'pearl' for the essential nature of principle, and 'wind' for the various religious practices. When the wind is great, waves beat [on the surface]. Since the prescribed gestures of phenomenal [ritual] procedure cause contemplation to be muddied, of what use are the four forms of samādhi?"

suffer. Should you use [this method exclusively] to instruct others, the spiritual capacities (*ken-hsing*) of others are all unique. Since the afflictions of a single person are already countless,[467] how much more numerous are those of many people!

[19c5] Let us say there is a physician who gathers all kinds of medicines to treat a whole range of diseases. A patient comes along who suffers from one specific illness and needs but one particular medicine to cure him. [Looking about him,] he thinks it strange that the doctor should carry so many other medicines. Your question is like this.[468]

[19c6] The mental diseases that are the defilements are innumerable and boundless for even a single person, let alone for many. How can one generalize on the basis of just one individual? If someone wants to hear you expound on the four kinds of samādhi, and is made joyous by hearing this, then you ought to teach him in a broadly appealing manner—this is the worldly [siddhānta]. If, through hearing about the four forms of samādhi, he gradually engages in religious practice and is able to generate good dharmas, then give him a more detailed and complete exposition of the four—this is the individual [siddhānta]. Then again, if engaging in constantly seated samādhi proves appropriate for curing his evils, or the samādhi of freely following one's thought, [and one instructs the person accordingly,] then it is called the therapeutic [siddhānta]. When this person has, through the use of these four methods, achieved full awakening, it is the ultimate [siddhānta]. Even though it is for one person, four different expositions may be required. Why then should they not be used?

[19c14] If the four samādhis are expounded to many people at the same time, one of them may want to hear of the constantly seated samādhi and not the other three. Another may want to hear of the constantly walking samādhi and not the other three. To follow the preference of the majority is the worldly siddhānta. The other three siddhāntas may be understood accordingly.

[19c16] Moreover, any one among the [four] forms of samādhi contains the import of all four siddhānta. Taking, for example, the first two samādhis, if a practitioner wants to walk, then he should walk; but if he wants to sit, then he should sit.[469] If when he walks his good roots manifest, and he penetrates the totality of the dharma, he should at such a

467. Chan-jan (T 46.213a15–16) says: "Since it is like this in one's own practice, certainly it must apply for training others as well. In one's own practice there are differences according to whether one is at the beginning [of the path] or at its end. When it comes to the salvific circumstances (*chi*) of others, each is unique."

468. Chan-jan (T 46.213a16–17) says: "Even if we allow that a single method is sufficient for one's own practice, it would be a mistake to teach this one method to everyone."

469. Chan-jan (T 46.213a22) identifies this with the worldly siddhānta.

time continue to walk. If when he sits his mind becomes clear, joyous, and relaxed, he should at such a time continue to sit.[470] If his mind becomes torpid and dull during sitting, then to shake it off and rouse himself he should walk, while if he grows distracted or tired during walking, he should sit.[471] If during walking he becomes enraptured and utterly abstracted, then he should continue to walk; while if during sitting [his mind] becomes very bright and keen, he should then continue to sit.[472] The application of the four siddhāntas to the other three kinds of samādhi operates in the same way.[473]

[19c22] Q: The good is conducive to the ultimate principle and can therefore be used in the practice of calming and contemplation. But evil runs counter to principle. How can one [use evil as a basis for] the practice of calming and contemplation?

[19c23] A: In its discussion of spiritual endowment (*ken*) and karmic hindrance (*che*), the *Great Treatise* distinguishes four categories of people. First are those whose spritual capacities (*ken*) are keen and who are also free of hindrances (*che*).[474] Second are those of keen endowment but who also suffer from hindrances. Third are those of dull capacity but who are free of hindrances. Fourth are those of dull capacity who are also plagued by hindrances.[475]

[19c25] The first category is the highest. Among those individuals who lived at the time of the Buddha, Śāriputra is a good example.[476] If such

470. According to Chan-jan (T 46.213a22) this is the individual siddhānta.

471. Chan-jan (T 46.213a23) identifies this as the therapeutic siddhānta.

472. Chan-jan (T 46.213a23) identifies this as the ultimate siddhānta.

473. In fact, the first two of the four samādhis appear to have been discussed, leaving only two, not three.

474. The Chinese term *ken* is used to render two very different concepts—*indriya* or "faculties" (as in the sense faculties), and *mūla* or "roots" (as in wholesome karmic roots). Both meanings are likely operating here, since wholesome karmic roots may certainly manifest in the form of a keen mental proclivity for the way. TCTL uses the term *che* specifically in the sense of "impeded (*che*) by the fetters or afflictions." In MHCK it often appears in the binome *che-chang*, meaning hindrances or impediments that obstruct the way generated from past evil deeds (see T 46.91a–b).

475. TCTL, T 25.239a. The text describes in detail the Buddha's ability to know the varying capacities of his followers. The TCTL gives examples for the first three categories, though not for the fourth: Śāriputra and Maudgalyāyana typify the first group, Aṅgulimālīya the murderer illustrates the second, and Cūḍapanthaka, famous for his stupidity, the third. Chan-jan (T 46.213b8–9) identifies the fourth category with ordinary unenlightened people (*pṛthagjana*).

476. Chan-jan (T 46.213b11–13) explains: "The instant he heard the first three [of the noble] truths, he realized the first fruit. Seeing a person drop his burden he realized arhathood. In the *Lotus* assembly he was the first to receive prediction [of Buddhahood]."

people practice calming and contemplation within good dharmas, their energetic attention to wholesome dharmas will keep them free of karmic hindrances in the future and their constant practice of calming and contemplation will ensure that their spiritual capacities are keen. When one has mastered these two points[477] in the past, even the slightest effort at practice in the present will bring immediate response (*hsiang-ying*). From the stage of the identity of meditative practice, one will enter [the identity of] resemblance and, finally, true reality. If practitioners are unable to achieve this in the present, it is because they have not applied themselves to these two points in the past. Should they now apply themselves to [calming and contemplation] of the good, it will enable them to speedily enter [the identities] in the future.

[20a1] In the next category are those who have a keen capacity for attaining the way but who suffer heavy hindrances due to an accumulation of sins. During the time when the Buddha was in the world, King Ajātaśatru[478] and Aṅgulimālīya were examples of such people. Although their sins and obstructions were so grave that they should have been reborn in hell, still, by seeing the Buddha and hearing his exposition of the dharma, they were able to awaken and achieve sainthood. Their hindrances could not obstruct [their enlightenment] because of the keenness of their capacities. Those practitioners of today who engage in calming and contemplation while in the midst of evil are of this class. Because of the evil they do they will suffer karmic hindrances in the future; but because they practice calming and contemplation their spiritual capacities will be keen in their lives to come. Upon meeting with a good spiritual friend, they will penetrate the true way [the instant they see the shadow of] the whip. How can you say that evil dharmas contravene principle and are not suitable for practice of calming and contemplation?

[20a8] Next are those who have dull capacities but are free of hindrances. Cūḍapanthaka is an example of such a person from the time when the Buddha was in the world. Although he committed no trans-

477. The practice of calming and contemplation and the practice of good deeds.

478. Ajātaśatru committed the cardinal sins of killing his father, the kindly King Bimbisāra, as well as conspiring with the evil disciple Devadatta to do away with the Buddha. According to Chan-jan (T 46.213b17–26), upon the occasion of the preaching of the *Nirvāṇa Sūtra* (see T 12.717–728), Ajātaśatru's intrinsic capacity began to manifest in the form of shame, and his obstructions became activated in the form of boils that appeared all over his body. When he finally went before the Buddha to repent, he awakened the aspiration for enlightenment, achieved the stages of the ten faiths, and was healed.

For Aṅgulimālīya see note 379 above. He, according to Chan-jan (T 46.213b27), achieved the forbearance or conviction of the nonarising of the dharmas.

gressions of body, speech, or mind, his capacity by nature was exceedingly dull. It took him ninety days to learn to recite this one stanza for children: "The wise do not engage in evil acts of body, speech, or mind; ever watchful, they are not infatuated with objects of desire; nor do they assent to the profitless ascetic practices that prevail in the world."[479]

[20a12] Those who currently observe the monastic code and engage in the practice of good, but do not train in calming and contemplation, will suffer no hindrances in the future. However, they will find it exceedingly difficult to awaken to the way.

[20a13] In the final category are all those who both engage in evil and neglect the practice of calming and contemplation. Due to the latter, they fail to achieve the way. Their capacities are so dull that even repeating an explanation a thousand times still leaves them ignorant and uncomprehending. Then again, on account of committing numerous sins and evils, they suffer every kind of hindrance. They are like lepers, whose numbed bodies may be stabbed with needles to the very bone without their being aware of it. They beshroud themselves in nothing but evil.

[20a17] For these reasons, although the good is conducive to principle, the way derives primarily from calming and contemplation. For, though evil actions may contravene principle, keenness of capacity will eradicate the hindrances produced by them. Thus it is the way alone that is esteemed as noble. How could evil necessitate the abrogation of calming and contemplation?

[20a19] The *Nirvāṇa Sūtra* says, "One who is lax in observing the disciplinary code is not necessarily to be considered lax, but one who is lax in the dharma is rightly called lax."[480] The four categories yielded by the pairing of "laxity" and "strictness" [with "dharma" and "morality"] should be elucidated in the same way as were the meanings of "capacity" and "hindrances" above.[481]

479. TCTL, T 25.268a. See also the *Mūlasarvastivādin Vinaya*, T 23.796b. Despite his stupidity, learning this one verse enabled Cūḍapanthaka to astound his contemporaries with the attainment of magical powers and mastery of the dharma.

480. T 12.641b. MHCK inverts the order of the two clauses given in the sūtra. Here the Buddha has been explaining to Kāśyapa that a bodhisattva who in the service of protecting and promoting the dharma commits acts that contravene the disciplinary code, and who repents of his infractions, remains unstained by them.

481. See Chan-jan (T 46.214a28–b2) for specifics: those who are strict in the dharma (of the Mahāyāna) as well as in observance of the disciplinary codes will both be keen in the capacity to understand dharma and lack hindrances; those who are strict in keeping to the dharma but lax in the codes will have sharp capacities but be burdened with karmic hindrances; those who are lax in the dharma but strict in observing the codes will be weak in capacity but lack karmic

[20a21] Such is the meaning of the statement in a sūtra, "Better to be Devadatta than Udraka Rāmaputra."[482] One should practice by diligently listening to the dharma and pondering it, never pausing having once begun. [This supreme importance of the dharma] may be illustrated by the case of the drunken brāhmin who took the tonsure[483] or the actress who donned monastic robes.[484]

---

hindrances; and those who are lax in both dharma and the disciplinary codes will be both weak in capacity and burdened with karmic hindrances.

482. From the *Samyukta-abhidharma-hṛdaya Śāstra* (*Tsa a-p'i-t'an hsin lun*, T 28.949c). Devadatta, despite his misdeeds, recited Buddhist sūtras, as a result of which he was able to achieve liberation (as a pratyekabuddha) after his karma had been used up in hell.

Udraka Rāmaputra, one of the ascetic teachers of the Buddha, was deeply practiced in mundane meditative concentrations (i.e., the highest of the four *samāpattis*). This enabled him to be reborn in the heavens, but sins he committed out of anger at those who disturbed his meditation caused him shortly thereafter to suffer rebirth in the lower realms for many aeons. The TCTL (T 25.189a), which recounts his deeds in considerable detail, uses his story as an example of the erroneous thinking of those who make an absolute distinction between distraction and meditative concentration and become attached to the latter.

483. From TCTL, T 25.161b. A drunken brāhmin approached the Buddha and asked to be ordained as a monk. The Buddha accordingly had Ānanda shave the man's head and outfit him in monk's robes. When the brāhmin regained his sobriety, he was aghast at his own behavior, changed his mind about membership in the saṅgha, and hurriedly departed. Naturally the other monks were puzzled as to why the Buddha had ordained such a man in the first place, but Śākyamuni explained that for innumerable previous lives the fellow had not entertained the slightest thought of entering the religious path. Now his drunkenness had stimulated his first tentative leanings in that direction and begun the process that would, after many rebirths, eventuate in his attainment of enlightenment. Chan-jan, restating the point of the story, says (T 46.214b16–17): "A monk's breaking of the disciplinary code is still superior to a layman's keeping of the code, for keeping the lay prohibitions does not lead to liberation."

484. TCTL, T 25.161a–b. The Buddha declares here that, "Even though they break the code and fall into sin, those who have abandoned the secular life for the Buddha's dharma will, after the karmic retribution for their sins has been exhausted, obtain liberation." The example is then given of the nun Utpalavarṇā (Pāli, Uppalavaṇṇā). In a past life she was an actress, who one day put on a nun's habit just to amuse herself. As a consequence she actually became a nun in a later life. Still impure, however, she harbored pride in her own beauty and violated the rules of discipline, which caused her to go to hell when she died. Once her sins were expiated, she was reborn in the age of Buddha Śākyamuni, became a nun again, and attained the six superhuman powers and arhatship.

LESSER CHAPTER 3

Manifesting the Great Result

[20a24] In chapter three we explain how calming and contemplation is expounded for the purpose of illumining the pure and great result (*kuo-pao*)[1] [that is the true aim] of the bodhisattva. If practice should deviate from the middle way,[2] then [bodhisattvas] will experience recompense or results within the two extremes of [samsāra and nirvāṇa]; while if their practice should conform to the middle way, they will earn the supreme and wondrous result. Even if they have not yet emerged from the common [samsāra],[3] the flower recompense [that they earn in this current life][4] will still surpass what comes to those [in the Buddha Land] of the

1. The binome *kuo-pao*, translated as "result" or "recompense," can refer to the reciprocal effect or fruition of karma (in which case it is rendered "retribution" or "recompense") as well as to the fruition or result of the causal path of practice (in which case it is rendered as "result"). In this chapter the word primarily carries the latter sense of "result," as in the grand fruit of Buddhahood. As Chan-jan (T 46.214c20–21) says: " 'result or recompense' (*kuo-pao*) takes its meaning from the idea that the result comes in the form of recompense. [For example,] if one destroys nescience one obtains the patience of the nonarising of dharmas (*anutpattika-dharma-kṣānti*)."

2. Chan-jan (T 46.214c7–8) says: "To 'deviate from the middle way' means that [the bodhisattva] has simply not yet severed nescience and not yet realized the [truth of] the middle way. To dwell with the dharma-body at the stage of the first of the ten abodes is to 'conform' [with the middle way]." It means that the bodhisattva has not yet entered the key stage of the ten abodes or the identity of increments of the truth on the path of the perfect teaching.

3. The "common saṃsāra of fixed allotments" (*fen-tuan sheng-ssu*) represents the cycle of rebirth within the six destinies (i.e., three realms) to which the ordinary person is subject. It stands in contrast to the supernal saṃsāra, which is spontaneous rebirth by spiritual transformation in a pure land (i.e., a never-returner or arhat) or in saṃsāra as an enlightened bodhisattva intent on saving others.

4. The *Nirvāṇa Sūtra* (T 12.717a) distinguishes between recompense in the

Seven Expedients.[5] More exalted yet is the [Buddha Land of the] True Recompense.[6] The city of All Fragrances, with its seven levels and the sides of its bridges like paintings, are the features of this Buddha land.[7] These ideas will be set forth in detail in greater chapter 8.[8]

Q: The *Tz'u-ti ch'an-men* also explains "practice and realization" (*hsiu-*

---

present life (the "flower") and that in future lives (the "fruit"). The TCTL (T 25.140c), on the other hand, calls the recompense of happiness in this and future lives the "shadow" of the tree; the state of śrāvakas and pratyekabuddhas, the "flower"; and the state of a Buddha, the "fruit." Here the text appears to be following the *Nirvāṇa Sūtra.*

5. The Buddha land of the Seven Expedients is the second lowest of the four Buddha lands distinguisheded by Chih-i (see MHCK, chap. 1, note 108). These four lands include the Co-dwelling Land (inhabitated by both ordinary people and saints of the lesser vehicle), the Land of the Seven Expedients with Residue, the Land of Real Recompense without Obstacles, and the Land of Eternal Quiescence and Illumination. All four of these are called Buddha lands because the Buddha enters them all for the purpose of expounding the dharma to beings and leading them toward enlightenment.

As for the Land of Seven Expedients, the term "expedients" here refers to the seven kinds of beings who reach this land, not to methods or devices in the usual sense of the word. According to Chan-jan (T 46.215a12–13), the seven refer to humans, devas, śrāvakas, and pratyekabuddhas of the two vehicles, plus bodhisattvas in the shared, separate, and perfect teachings who have yet to acquire clear realization of the middle way. The third land—that of Real Recompense Without Obstacles—contains only bodhisattvas who have begun to sever nescience and have achieved the insight of the middle way (i.e., the ten stages of the separate teaching or ten abidings and identity of increments of the real in the perfect teaching). The fourth land is the abode of all Buddhas, the Secret Treasury. Chan-jan (T 46.214c3 and 214c17) states that the Buddha land won by the practitioner of this perfect and sudden calming and discerning is number three, the Land of Real Recompense without Obstacles.

6. This, according to the *Nirvāṇa Sūtra*, would mean recompense in future lives. Chan-jan states (T 46.214c21–23), and *Kōgi* agrees (2.82), that this recompense is represented by the third land.

7. From the famous tale of the bodhisattva Dharmodgata and his disciple Sadāpralāpa (the "Ever-Weeping") in the *Pañcaviṃśati* (see TCTL, T 25.734a–b). Dharmodgata dwells in the city (i.e., Buddha land) called All Fragrances (*Sarvagaṇḍha), to which Ever Weeping makes his way at the cost of great effort, in order to hear the dharma. The city is described in the sūtra as having seven levels, an appearance "as splendid as a painting," and "bridges leading into it, the sides of which are as broad and pure as the earth."

8. As we have noted in the introduction, greater chapters 8 (Result or Recompense), 9 (Generation of the Teachings), and 10 (Returning of the Purport) were never completed due to the fact that Chih-i's lectures on the MHCK were terminated after the material for chapter 7 (Contemplation Proper). This lesser chapter 3 on Result or Recompense corresponds to (and represents a brief presentation of) greater chapter 8.

cheng).[9] To what extent is it in agreement with the result or recompense discussed here?

A: In the *Tz'u-ti ch'an-men*, "practice" refers to the [habitual] discipline of cultivation, while "realization" means to experience [its result] in the form of a manifestation. Again, "practice" in this instance refers to the habitual or like-natured cause (*hsi-yin*), and "realization" refers to the like-natured effect (*hsi-kuo*).[10] Both of these can be earned during the current life. However, the result under discussion [in this chapter] is limited to future lives. In this respect it differs from the "realization" of the *Tz'u-ti ch'an-men*. The two vehicles have only the like-natured effect in the present life, and no result or recompense in future lives; but the Mahāyāna has them both.

9. Chapter 7 (i.e., the last five fascicles) of Chih-i's *Tz'u-ti ch'an-men* (T 46.508a–548c) discusses "cultivation and realization" (*hsiu-cheng*) with respect to the individual thematic meditations that make up the graduated path of calming and contemplation. Like the MHCK, *Tz'u-ti ch'an-men* was also intended to have three additional chapters—(8) result or recompense (*kuo-pao*), (9) generation of the teachings (*ch'i-chiao*), and (10) returning to the purport (*kuei-ch'ü*)—that were never completed. In referring to the *Tz'u-ti ch'an-men*, one wonders why the interlocutor here asks about "cultivation and realization" (chapter 7) rather than the chapter on "result and recompense" (chapter 8).

10. *Sabhāga-hetu* and *niṣyanda-phala* or "like-natured cause" and "like-natured effect" describe cases where the moral valency of a given effect (good, evil, or neutral) is tied directly to the presence of a distinct cause of the same valency. Each particular method of meditation described in the *Tz'u-ti ch'an-men* represents a thematically strict program designed to elicit a particular result of similar nature. Thus cultivation (*hsiu*) immediately prefigures the character of realization (*cheng*) as "like-natured cause" does "like-natured effect."

LESSER CHAPTER 4

Rending the Great Net

[20b4] In chapter 4 we explain how this calming-and-contemplation is expounded for the purpose of rending the great net [of doubt that arises from the diversity] of the sūtras and treatises.[1] If a person is skilled in the use of calming-and-contemplation to contemplate the mind, inner insight will become bright and discerning, and he or she will come to comprehend all the teachings, gradual as well as sudden. Just as if one were to break open a single mote of dust to reveal a billion rolls of sūtras, Buddhist teachings as extensive as sands of the Ganges will be realized within a single [moment of] thought.[2]

[20b7] Whoever, out of the desire to benefit others, would devise teachings that are properly attuned to peoples' salvific circumstances (*chi*)

1. The image of the "great net of doubt" and its "rending" originates from the *Lotus Sūtra*: Because of their attachment to the earlier provisional vehicles, the śrāvakas and other individuals of the assembly are thrown into confusion over the Buddha's intention to preach the one Buddha vehicle. By revealing that all prior teachings of the three vehicles are expedients and the one Buddha vehicle alone is real (i.e., the great message of the Expedient Devices chapter of the *Lotus Sūtra*), their "network of doubts" is "rent" and the arhats and śrāvakas are enlightened to the Buddha vehicle (see, for example, T 9.10c16–17; Hurvitz, p. 50.)

Chan-jan (T 46.215a6–b1) says: " 'Rending the great net' means to rend the net of doubt that is associated with [biased] attachment to the provisional teachings. The first part of the passage speaks of pervasively removing ones own doubts as well as those of others. For this reason it says, 'pervasively rends.' Furthermore, one must understand how all teachings—sudden as well as gradual—are produced from a single moment of thought. If one is not skilled in applying the inconceivable contemplation to discern the inconceivable realm within a single moment of mind, how could one ever rend the great doubt that comes from clinging to the teachings?"

2. From the *Avataṃsaka Sūtra*, T9.624a; also see *Ratnagotravibhāga*, T 31.827b.

must [strive to] conform to their abilities and preach dharma accordingly.[3] Even when one finally becomes a Buddha and [has the power to] train beings [by manifesting different likenesses], sometimes one will take the form of the King of the Dharma to expound the sudden and the gradual dharma, or take the form of a bodhisattva, a śrāvaka, god, māra, human, hungry ghost, or some other being from among the ten realms [of the dharmadhātu]. [But in doing so] one will always devise teachings and act in accordance with [those beings' needs].

[20b11] One may [adopt the expedient] of being questioned by the Buddha, whereupon one replies with extensive [explanations of the] sudden or gradual teachings. Or one may restrain one's own spiritual abilites and ask [leading questions of] the Buddha, so that the Buddha replies with a sudden or a gradual [turning of the] wheel of dharma. These ideas will be set forth in detail when we come to [greater] chapter 9 [on Generation of the Teachings]. They are also treated in brief in [greater chapter 4 on] the Encompassing of All Dharmas.[4]

3. Following Muranaka, p. 191.

4. Greater chapter 4 (T 46.29c–32a), along with greater chapter 2, is one of the two shortest chapters in the MHCK. It sets forth the contention that the "one practice" of calming and contemplation encompasses the whole of the Buddhist teaching within itself. The discussion has six sections: (1) the totality of principle encompassed in calming and contemplation, (2) all delusions encompassed, (3) all forms of wisdom encompassed, (4) all forms of practice encompassed, (5) all stages of attainment encompassed, and (6) all teachings encompassed in calming and contemplation. As we have noted in the introduction, Chih-i interrupted his lectures before he ever preached greater chapter 9 (Generation of the Teachings).

LESSER CHAPTER 5

Returning to the Great Abode

[20b13] In chapter 5 we explain how calming and contemplation is expounded in order to return the practitioner to the ultimate emptiness of all dharmas, "the great abode (*ta-ch'u*)."[1]

[20b14] It is easy for a sticky hand to adhere,[2] and hard to awaken from deep dreaming. Some people seal up a text and restrict its sense, declaring their own personal understanding of it to be right. They vie with others to seize tiles and pebbles, thinking they are baubles of lapis lazuli.[3] Even the most familiar things and explicit statements they fail to understand;[4] how could they not but err when it comes to the abstruse

1. *Kōgi* (2.89) says that practice and realization ultimately return one to where there are no distinctions to be made between cause (practice) and effect (realization), nor between self and other.

2. From the *Nirvāṇa Sūtra*, T 12.761a17–b5. See also the *Saṃyuktāgama*, T 2.173b–c, sūtra 620. The Pāli version, in the *Saṃyutta-nikāya*, 47.1.7, is the "Monkey sūtra" (*Makkata-sutta*), translated by Rhys-Davids and Woodward, *The Book of the Kindred Sayings*, 5.127–128. Commonplace individuals infected with attachment and biased views are compared to a foolish monkey, who cannot resist touching bird-lime or pitch which a hunter has set out as a trap. First one of the monkey's hands gets stuck to the pitch, and then as he tries to free himself, his other hand, both legs, and mouth become stuck as well. The hunter then appears, impales the poor animal on a pole, and carries him off for dinner. The monkey represents commonplace individuals (*pṛthagjana*) with no genuine insight into Buddha dharma; the hunter represents the māras, and the pitch represents willfulness or desire. In the *Nirvāṇa Sūtra* the analogy is set within an extended discussion of the common person's tendency—due to attachment and biased views—to misconstrue the teachings of the Buddhas and bodhisattvas concerning the nature of mind, cause and condition, and cause and effect.

3. From the *Nirvāṇa Sūtra*, T 12.617c.

4. Chan-jan (T 46.215b27–8) here criticizes: "There are also those who attain to the abstruse principle yet have no familiarity with ordinary discourse, like the

principle and hidden teaching? This is why it is necessary to discuss the returning of the purport (*chih-kuei*).

[20b17] "Returning of the purport"[5] signifies [the place where] the purport of a text leads, like the sea to which all streams flow, or the sky to which all flames point.[6] One must [learn to] distinguish the hidden and arrive at the abstruse without being stymied or waylaid anywhere.[7] Be like the wise minister who always fathoms the meaning of his king's veiled words.[8] Whatever you hear from [the Buddha's] preachings, know that inevitably it leads to the ground of omniscient wisdom.[9] Whoever grasps this point indeed comprehends the returning of the purport to the great abode (*chih-kuei ta-ch'u*). "Purport" means to orient oneself to the three virtuous qualities [of Buddhahood],[10] and "returning" means to direct others toward them as well: this is why it is called "the returning of the

dhyāna-masters of sudden enlightenment (*tun-wu ch'an-shih*) from the Tao-shu Monastery of K'uai-chi who are able to awaken to the profound principle but are utterly incognizant of commonplace matters (lit.: matters at hand)."

5. Chan-jan (T 46.215b29–c2) states: " 'Text' refers to the teaching; 'purport' refers to [its] meaning or import. To 'return' is to proceed toward. 'Returning of the purport' means the place where the import of the teaching leads."

6. Chan-jan (T 46.215c2–3) makes the similes explicit: "Water and fire are analogous to the teaching or dharma, their flowing and pointing are like the import of a given text or discourse, and the sea and sky represent the place [to which teaching and text] proceed."

7. Chan-jan (T 46.215c3–4) says: "If your understanding is versed in the secret or hidden teaching and comprehends the abstruse principle, then you will not dally in the exoteric teaching, nor become entangled in more commonplace principles."

8. Based on a parable in the *Nirvāṇa Sūtra*, T 12.662b. Here the Buddha is compared to a king who orders *saindhava* to be brought to him. The Sanskrit word *saindhava* is, however, ambiguous, being an adjective derived from the word *sindhu* ("river," "Indus River," "ocean," or "the province of Sind"), and so can mean "maritime," "a horse from Sind," "a person from Sind," "the salt which is so plentiful in Sind," "a container for water," etc. The sūtra lists four possible meanings: salt, jug, water, and horse. Only a wise minister will be able to guess which of the four the king wants at a particular time: salt if he wants to eat, a jug if he wants to imbibe, water if he wants to wash, and a horse if his fancy turns toward sport. Similarly, the wise disciple of the Buddha knows that when the Buddha declares the (Hīnayāna) doctrine that all dharmas are impermanent, bring suffering, lack selfhood, and are impure, he means, esoterically, that the nature of reality is actually permanence, pleasure, selfhood, and purity.

9. *Sarvajñābhūmi*. Either the ground or stage of the realization of omniscient wisdom of a Buddha—i.e., Buddhahood. The term appears in the *Lotus Sūtra* (see T 9.19a).

10. The dharma body, prajñā, and liberation, which, according to the *Nirvāṇa Sūtra* (T 12.616b8–14), represent the three changeless aspects of intrinsic Buddhahood or enlightenment.

purport." Again, "returning" means entering into the three qualities oneself, and "purport" means causing others to enter into them. It is to this end that the chapter is called "the returning of the purport."

The Three Meritorious Qualities of Buddhahood or Ultimate Reality

[20b23] Now we shall explain the "returning of the purport" again, both in general summary (*tsung*) and in detail (*pieh*). As for the summary explanation, the Buddhas appear in the world in order to bring about the one great event.[11] [To fulfill this end] they display a variety of corporeal forms, through which they lead beings to the realization of the [unchanging and markless] dharma body. Once these beings have perceived the dharma body, Buddhas and beings both revert to the dharma body. Again, the Buddhas also expound a variety of dharmas, by which they bring animate beings to complete mastery of a tathāgata's omniscient wisdom of all modes (*i-ch'ieh chung chih*).[12] Once in possession of this omniscience, both Buddhas and animate beings alike return to prajñā. Moreover, the Buddhas exhibit a variety of expedients, superhuman powers, and magical transformations, by which they liberate beings from their fetters. They do not enable only a single person to annihilate his bonds, for the bonds of all beings are destroyed by the annihilating power of the tathāgata. Once their bonds have been annihilated, both Buddhas and beings return to liberation. It says in the *Nirvāṇa Sūtra*, "Having placed all my children at rest in the secret treasury (*pi-mi tsang*),

11. An allusion to the following celebrated passage in the Expedient Devices Chapter of the *Lotus Sūtra* (T 9.7a21–28; Hurvitz, 30): "The Buddhas, the World-Honored Ones, for one great cause alone appear in the world. . . . The Buddhas, the World-Honored Ones appear in the world because they wish to cause the beings to hear of the Buddha's knowledge and insight and thus enable them to gain purity. They appear . . . to demonstrate the Buddha's knowledge and insight to beings. They appear . . . to cause beings to understand. They appear . . . to cause beings to enter into the path of the Buddha's knowledge and insight."

12. *Sarvākarajñatā*—the third and highest of three wisdoms distinguished in the *Pañcaviṃśati* and TCTL and frequently referred to by Hui-ssu and Chih-i as analogues to the three truths (see T 25.257c–260c; Lamotte, *Traité*, 4.1758–1759). Omniscient wisdom of all modes pertains only to Buddhas and nonretrogressing bodhisattvas who, in T'ien-t'ai parlance, have opened the Buddha-eye and achieved unmediated insight into the middle truth. The first wisdom—*sarvajña[tā]* or "omniscient wisdom"—represents insight into emptiness, and corresponds to the liberative wisdom of the two vehicles and novice bodhisattvas. The second wisdom—*mārga-jña[tā]* or "wisdom of the modalities of the path or destinies"—represents insight into the provisional truth, and corresponds to the wisdom of skillful use of expedients developed by bodhisattvas in the Mahāyāna.

I myself will also abide there before long."[13] These are the summary or general features of the "returning of the purport."

[20c3] Now, there is the detailed [explanation of] the three qualities: There are three kinds of Buddha-body: first is the physical body, second is the body of teachings [which serve as accesses to dharma], and third is the body of reality itself. The "returning" that takes place after the activity of teaching and training is over may be construed as follows: the physical body returns to liberation, the body of the teachings returns to prajñā, and the body of reality returns to the dharma body.

[20c6] We also speak of three kinds of prajñā: first is the wisdom that knows the modes of the paths or destinies (*tao chung chih*), second is omniscient wisdom (*i-ch'ieh chih*), and third is omniscient wisdom of all modes (*i-ch'ieh chung chih*).[14] The meaning of the "returning" that takes place after the teaching activity has desisted is that the wisdom of modes returns to liberation, omniscient wisdom returns to prajñā, and omniscient wisdom of all modes returns to the dharma body.

[20c8] There are also three kinds of liberation: first is liberation from the fetters (*fo*) of ordinary incognizance, second is liberation from the fetters of attachment to features [of doctrine], and third is liberation from the fetters of nescience.[15] With the termination of teaching activity and return [to the great abode], one reverts to liberation when the fetters of ordinary incognizance are released, returns to prajñā when the fetters of attachment to the features of doctrine are released, and reverts to the dharma body when the fetters of nescience are released. As such, when discussed in terms of specific attributes, "returning of the purport" still means returning to the secret treasury (*pi-mi chih-tsang*) of the three qualities [of Buddhahood or ultimate reality].

The Inconceivability of the Three Qualities

[20c12] Now the three meritorious qualities are in reality neither three nor one but are utterly inconceivable. Why?

If we say that the dharma body is simply the dharma body and that

13. T 12.616b8. The passage in the sūtra goes on to speak of the secret treasury as being endowed with the three meritorious qualities (dharma body, prajñā, liberation) in perfect interfusion. They are neither arrayed in vertical sequence nor arranged separately in horizontal relationship but exist in perfect equilibrium just as the three dots that make the letter "i" in the Siddham alphabet, or the three eyes on the brow of Maheśvara.

14. The three wisdoms described in note 12 above: *mārgajña[tā]*, *sarvajña[tā]*, and *sarvākarajña[tā]*, respectively.

15. The origin and identity of this particular set of three "fetters" is unclear. The commentaries offer no help: neither Chan-jan, *Kōgi*, *Shiki*, nor *Kōjutsu* comment on the passage.

alone, then that is not the [real] dharma body. Know therefore that the dharma body is a body, while, at the same time, it is not a body, both a body and not a body, and neither a body nor not a body. When one abides in the *śūraṅgama-samādhi*,[16] one manifests all manner of corporeal forms and images. As such, we use the term "body." Once their function has been accomplished, [these bodies] revert to liberation. Wisdom illuminates the fact that the myriad forms are no-form, which is why we use the expression "not a body." Once its function has been performed, it returns to prajñā. The body of ultimate reality is neither the corporeal body of material form and image nor the body of teaching [that provides access to dharma], which is why we use the expression "neither body nor nonbody." Once its function has been performed, it returns to the dharma body. "Returning" means arriving at the realization that these three bodies have neither the mark of sameness nor difference, and "purport" means expounding to others that these three bodies are neither the same nor different. In both cases one enters into the secret treasury, and this is why we use the expression "the returning of the purport."

[20c21] If we say that prajñā is simply prajñā and that alone, then this is not [real] prajñā. Know therefore that [real] prajñā is, at once, knowing, not-knowing, and neither of these. Prajñā at the level of the wisdom of modes has universal knowledge of the conventional world (*su*),[17] which is why we use the term "knowing." Once its activity is finished it returns to liberation. Prajñā at the level of omniscient wisdom has comprehensive knowledge of the true or real (*chen*), which is why we use the expression "not-knowing." Once its activity is finished it returns to prajñā. Prajñā at the level of total omniscience of all modes has universal knowledge of the middle, which is why we use the expression "neither knowing nor not-knowing." Once its activity is finished, it returns to the dharma body. "Returning" means attaining to the realization that these three [forms of] prajñā have neither the mark of sameness nor difference, and "purport" means expounding to others that these three forms of prajñā are

16. Extolled in the sūtra of the same name (T no. 642), this samādhi is also first in the list of 108 great samādhis of the Mahāyāna given in the TCTL (and *Pañcaviṃśati*), T 25.396b27 and 398c27. The latter describes it as a samādhi wherein the bodhisattva, "distinguishes the features of all samādhis, their relative endowments and their depth, just as a general knows the relative strengths of his soldiers. Also, a bodhisattva upon attaining this samādhi cannot be despoiled by any of the heavenly māras or māras of the afflictions, just as a wheel-turning king . . . ventures wherever he chooses without ever being overcome." In T'ien-t'ai it is equated with full realization of the truth of the middle way, the omniscient wisdom of all modes, the opening of the Buddha-eye, and entry into the first of the ten abodes (of the perfect teaching). See *Hsiao chih-kuan*, T 46.472c9–473a10.

17. *Kōgi* (2.95) says that it does not err in its cognition of (phenomenal) things.

neither the same nor different. Both together enter into the secret treasury, and this is why we use the expression "the returning of the purport."

[20c29] If we say that liberation is liberation and that alone, then it is not [real] liberation. Know therefore that [real] liberation is, at once, liberation, not liberation, as well as neither of these. Liberation at the level of purity of expedients[18] tames animate beings but is not soiled by them, which is why we use the term "liberation." Once its activity is finished it returns to liberation. Liberation at the level of perfect or complete purity does not perceive the mark of either a living being or liberation, which is why we use the expression "not-liberation." Once its activity is finished it returns to prajñā. In the case of liberation at the level of purity of intrinsic nature, there is "neither liberation nor no liberation." Once its activity is finished, it reverts to the dharma body. Whether we attain to realization ourselves or expound it for others, these three liberations have neither the mark of sameness nor difference. Both simultaneously enter into the secret treasury, and this is why we use the expression "returning of the purport."

The Three Qualities and the Three Obstacles

[21a7] Now the three meritorious qualities are neither "new" nor "old," yet they are at the same time new and old.[19] Why is this? When the three obstacles[20] impede the three qualities, nescience impedes the dharma

18. The first of three kinds of liberation, the other two being (b) liberation of perfect or complete purity, and (c) liberation of or as purity of intrinsic nature. They are discussed by Chih-i elsewhere in MHCK (T 46.140b), as well as in *Wei-mo ching hsüan-shu* (T 38.553c2) and *Chin-kuang-ming hsüan-i* (T 39.3b23–c1) as the "three nirvāṇas." Like MHCK here, all three instances treat them within the context of an extended discussion of the three meritorious qualities (dharma body, prajñā, and liberation).

19. Chan-jan (T 46.216a23–25) and *Kōgi* (2.96) both indicate that the "three obstacles" should be included along with the three qualities in this statement. The former says: "[Here] there is the generic discussion of the three meritorious qualities and the three obstacles, where the obstacles and qualties in their mutual opposition [are shown to be] not different, yet at the same time different. If one speaks of the obstacles and meritorious qualities from the perspective of principle (*li*), they are nondual and, likewise, devoid of [any distinction between] 'new' and 'old.' "

20. The three obstacles (*san-chang*) discussed here are not the better known *āvaraṇa-traya* or obstacles of the afflictions, karma, and reciprocity referred to with frequency elsewhere in MHCK, but the above-mentioned three "fetters" of incognizance, attachment to features, and nescience. Chan-jan (T 46.216b2) suggests that the three fetters be equated with the well-known T'ien-t'ai formulation of the "three delusions" (*san-huo*): the delusions (of the three realms) removed in the paths of vision and cultivation, the delusion that obscures multiplicity (and

body, attachment to the features of the teaching impedes prajñā, and incognizance impedes liberation. [Under these circumstances] we call the three obstacles "old" because they are preexisting, and we call the three qualities "new" because they only appear once the three obstacles have been eradicated. But [from the ultimate point of view] the three obstacles are identical to the three qualities, and the three qualities identical to the three obstacles. Because the three obstacles are themselves identical to the three qualities, the three obstacles are ultimately not old. And by the obverse, the three qualities are ultimately not new. Because they are new and yet not new, the practitioner is endowed with the three qualities at every stage [of the path], from the first arousing of the thought of enlightenment to the ultimate attainment of Buddhahood. And because they are old and yet at the same time not old, the three obstacles are [actively] countered and suppressed at every stage from the arousing of the thought of enlightenment to the ultimate attainment of Buddhahood. Because of being both new and not-new, both old and not-old, the three qualities exist as the inherent nature of principle (*li-hsing*). If one attains to the general (*tsung*) understanding that the three qualities are neither new nor old yet also are new and old, that they are neither the same as nor different from [the three obstacles], and one instructs others accordingly—then the purport of the teaching has indeed returned to the secret treasury (*chih kuei pi-mi tsang chung*).

[21a17] Now to explain [the three obstacles individually]: Nescience is called old because it is preexistent, while the dharma body, which is enlightenment or illumination (*vidyā*), is called new because it eradicates nescience. But [at the ultimate level] nescience is identical to enlightenment, and enlightenment identical to nescience. Because nescience is itself identical to enlightenment, nescience is not old (i.e., preexistent), while because of the obverse, enlightenment is not new. Attachment to the features [of the teaching] is called old because it is preexistent, while [the view of] marklessness is called new because it eradicates attachment to features. But [at the ultimate level], the presence of features is identical to featurelessness, and featurelessness is identical to the presence of features. Which could be new and which old? Incognizance is referred to as old because it is preexistent, while knowledge is called new because it eradicates incognizance. But [at the ultimate level] incognizance is itself identical to knowledge, and knowledge identical to incognizance. Which then could be new and which old?

[21a24] If one has attained to the realization that the new and old are neither the same nor different, whether they are considered in general

---

impedes the bodhisattva's powers of expediency), and root nescience (that obscures the truth of the middle). His interpretation seems to be based on *Fa-hua hsüan-i*, T 33.742b28–c18.

summary (*tsung*) or in specific detail (*pieh*), and if one teaches others accordingly, then this is what is called "the returning of the purport to the secret treasury." Pairs of antonyms like vertical and horizontal, analyzing (*k'ai*) and synthesizing (*ho*), beginning and end,[21] are all to be understood similarly.

The Meaning of "Purport" and "Returning"

[21a26] [The meaning of the binome] "returning (*kuei*) of the purport (*chih*)" is also to be understood in this way: "Purport," "nonpurport," "neither purport nor nonpurport," "returning," "nonreturning," "neither returning nor nonreturning"—each of these [can be understood to] enter into the secret treasury. This can be grasped by way of analogy with the foregoing discussion, for "purport" represents one's own practice, "nonpurport" the teaching of others,[22] and "neither purport nor nonpurport" the absence of both self and other.

[21a26] Such is the ultimate quiescence of the three qualities which represents the "returning of the purport." What words could possibly denote it? How is one to label it? Forced to give it a designation, we call it "the middle way," "reality," "the dharma body," "neither-quiescence-nor-luminosity."[23] Or we use such terms as "omniscient wisdom of all modes," the "great wisdom of perfect equality,"[24] the "prajñāpāramitā," "insight or contemplation (*kuan*)"; or we force on it such labels as "*śūraṅgama-samādhi*," "*mahāparinirvāṇa*," "the inconceivable liberation,"[25] or "calm (*chih*)."

[21b5] Know therefore that every aspect of the whole array of [doctri-

21. Chan-jan (T 46.216b4–5) says: "When listing [the three qualities] in textual passages, the dharma body must come first, then prajñā and, finally, liberation. This is what is meant by 'vertical.' But when one takes them, one by one, according to their meaning so that each is in turn elaborated or analyzed as three, then it is 'horizontal.' This is also what we mean by 'analyzing or elaborating.' That the three are merely one is what we mean by 'synthesizing.' Awakening the thought [of achieving enlightenment] is 'beginning,' and ultimate [realization of buddhahood] is 'end.' Or, the [preaching of the dharma at the] Deer Park is the 'beginning,' and [lying down between] the twin [sāla] trees is the 'end.' "

22. *Kōgi* (2.98) says "non-purport" because the teaching must be adapted to their deluded passions (rather than to the ultimate truth).

23. Analogues to "calming" and "contemplation" (*chih* and *kuan*) understood here as the result of practice rather than as tools to achieve this final state.

24. A term for the wisdom of a Buddha, found *inter alia* in the *Lotus Sūtra* (see T 9.32b29).

25. From the chapter of the same name in the *Vimalakīrti Sūtra* (T 14.546b–c). A bodhisattva who has won this liberation can put Mount Sumeru in a mustard seed, oceans in a single pore of his skin, hold the universe in his hand, and bend time itself to fit his purpose—for he has fully realized the voidness of all these things.

nal] features, discourses, and [displays of] superhuman power enters into the secret treasury.

[21b6] This "returning of the purport": What is it? Where is it? Who is it?[26] The path of speech is cut off.[27] The reach of discursive thought is annihilated.[28] Eternally quiescent, it is like open space. This is what we mean by the "returning of the purport." It will be set forth at length in [greater chapter] 10.[29]

26. *Kōgi* (2.100) says the first of these three questions wipes out names (subjective designations), the second wipes out substance (objective designates), and the third wipes out the subject (designator) himself (that which regards itself as existent). Nothing else is left.

27. *Sarva-vāda-caryā-uccheda.*

28. *Citta-pravṛtti-sthiti-nirodha.*

29. The lectures for chapter 10, as mentioned previously, were never completed.

Character Glossary

Chinese Terms

an 安
an-chao ch'an-shih 暗照禪師
an-cheng ch'an-shih 暗證禪師
an-hsin 安心
Chan-jan 湛然
ch'an (confession, repentance) 懺
ch'an (Zen, dhyana) 禪
ch'an-shou 懺首
ch'an-t'ang 禪堂
ch'ang 唱
ch'ang-chi-kuang-t'u 常寂光土
ch'ang-chu 常住
chao 照
chao-ch'ing fa (summoning) 召請法
che 遮
che-chang 遮障
che-k'ung 折空
chen 真
chen-hsin kuan 真心觀
chen-hsing 真行
chen ju-shih ti-tzu 真入室弟子
ch'en 塵
ch'en-sha huo 塵沙惑
cheng (true, correct) 正
cheng (realize) 證
cheng-chu ho-hsing 正助合行
cheng-chu shuang-hsing 正助雙行
cheng-hsiang 證相
cheng-nien 正念
cheng-shou 正受
cheng-te 證得
cheng-tsung 正宗
cheng-t'ung 正統
ch'eng-ming 稱名
chi (identity) 即
chi (salvific circumstance) 機
chi-chao 寂照
chi-chu 記主
chi-kuang yu-hsiang 寂光有相
chi k'ung chi chia chi chung 即空即假即中
chi-yüan (salvific circumstance) 繫緣
chi-yüan fa-chieh 繫緣法界
ch'i 起
ch'i chiao 起教
chia 假
chia-ming 假名
chiang 講
chiang-t'ang 講堂
chiao 教
chiao-chu 教主
chiao-kuan 教觀
chiao-wai pieh-ch'uan 教外別傳
chieh 解
chien 漸
chien-huo 見惑

chien-tz'u 漸次
chih (point to) 指
chih (awareness) 知
chih-hsin 至心
Chih-i 智顗
chih-kuan 止觀
chih-kuan ming-ching 止觀明靜
chih-kuei 旨歸
Chih-li 知禮
chih-shih seng 知事僧
Chih-yüan 智圓
chin-k'ou tsu-ch'eng 金口祖承
chin-shih tsu-ch'eng 近師祖承
ching 境
ching-hsing 經行
ching-shih 靜室
Ch'ing-chao 慶昭
ch'ing fo 請佛
ch'ing-hsin 輕心
ch'ing-kuei 清規
chu 助
chu-tao fa-men 助道法門
chu-tao fang-fa 助道方法
chu-tao kuan 助道觀
chu-tao shih fang-fa 助道事方法
chu-tao shih-hsiang fang-fa 助道事相方法
ch'u fa-hsin 初發心
ch'u-hsin 初心
chuan 轉
ch'uan-fa 傳法
chuang-yen tao-ch'ang 莊嚴道場
chung-hsing 中興
chung-tao 中道
chung tao ti-i-i ti 中道第一義諦
chü 具
ch'üan (provisional) 權
ch'üan (exhort) 勸
ch'üan-ch'ing 勸請
ch'üan-hsiu 勸修
chüeh-i san-mei 覺意三昧
fa 法
fa-chieh 法界
fa-hua ch'an-fa 法華懺法
fa-hua san-mei 法華三昧
fa-hua tsung 法華宗
fa-hua wen-chü 法華文句
fa-shen 法身
fa-shen yu-hsiang 法身有相
fa-ssu 法嗣
fa-t'ang 法堂
fa-tso 法座
fa-yüan 發願
fan-chao kuan-ch'a 反照觀察
fang-chang 方丈
fang-fa 方法
fang-pien 方便
fang-teng ch'an-fa 方等禪法
fen-chen chi 分真即
fen-cheng chi 分證即
fen-hsi k'ung 分析空
fen-tuan sheng-ssu 分段生死
fo 縛
fo fa-shih 佛法式
fo-li 佛立
fo-tien 佛殿
fu 伏
ho 合
hsi (analyze) 析
hsi (cease/pacify) 息
hsi-kuo 習果
hsi-t'an 悉檀
hsia-hua 下化
hsiang-chü 相具
hsiang-fa 像法
hsiang-hsiao 香餚
hsiang-hsiang wan-jan 相相宛然
hsiang-hsü 相續
hsiang-tai 相待
hsiang-ying 相應
hsiao 餚
hsiao-ts'ai 肴菜
hsien 賢
hsien-tao 先導
hsin-chieh 信解
hsin-chü 心具
hsin-yao 心要
hsing-e 性惡

hsing-tao 行道
hsiu-cheng 修證
hsü-mi-tso 須彌座
hsüan-i 玄義
hsüan-jao 旋遶
Hsüan-lang 玄朗
hui-hsiang 廻向
Hui-ssu 慧思
Hui-wen 慧文
i (different) 異
i (mind, intention) 意
i-ch'ieh chih 一切智
i-ch'ieh chung chih 一切動智
i chih-kuan 意止觀
i-chung hsüeh-hsi seng 依衆學習僧
i-hsin ching-chin 一心精進
i-hsing 一行
i-hsing san-mei 一行三昧
i-nien ling-chih 一念靈知
i-nien san-ch'ien 一念三千
i ta shih yin-yüan 一大事因緣
i-ti 一諦
jan-ai chih hsiang 染礙之相
Jen-yüeh 仁岳
ju-fa 如法
ju-shih 入室
k'ai 開
kan 感
kan fo chiang 感佛降
kan-ying 感應
kan-ying tao-chiao 感應道交
kao-tso 高座
kao-tsu 高祖
ken 根
ken-hsing 根性
k'ou-chüeh 口決
kuan 觀
kuan-chao 觀照
kuan-fa 觀法
kuan-hsin 觀心
kuan-hui 觀慧
kuan pu-k'o-ssu-i ching 觀不可思議境
Kuan-ting 觀頂
kuang 廣
kuei-chih 歸旨
kuo-pao 果報
lei 類
li 理
li-ch'an 禮懺
li ch'an-hui 禮懺悔
li-fo 禮佛
li-hsing 禮性
li-ken 利根
li-kuan 理觀
li-shih kuan-fa 歷事觀法
ling-chih 靈知
liu-chi 六即
liu-ken ch'an-hui 六根懺悔
liu-ken ch'ing-ching 六根請淨
liu-miao fa-men 六妙法門
liu-shih 六時
lüeh 略
man 滿
mi 迷
miao-chüeh 妙覺
miao-hsing 妙行
miao-li kuan 妙理觀
mien-ch'ien 面前
mo-ho t'an-ch'ih t'o-lo-ni 摩訶袒持陀羅尼
nei 內
ni 逆
ni-li shih-hsiang 逆理事相
ni-yüan 逆緣
nien-fo 念佛
nien-fo san-mei 念佛三昧
nien-ming 念名
pan 半
pan-chou san-mei 般舟三昧
p'an-chiao 判教
pao-kuo 報果
pao-shen 報身
pi-mi chih tsang 祕密之藏
pi-mi chih yao 祕密之要
pi-yao 祕要
pieh 別
pieh-chiao 別教

pieh-kuan 別觀
p'ien 偏
pu-ch'eng 不成
pu-chü 不具
pu ju fa 不如法
pu-k'o-ssu-i 不可思議
pu-ting 不定
p'u-hsien ch'an-fa 普賢懺法
p'u-hsien se-shen san-mei 普現色身三昧
p'u-t'i hsin 菩提心
san 散
san chang 三障
san kuan 三觀
san-mei 三昧
san tao 三道
san te 三德
san ti 三諦
san wai pieh i 三外別一
san-yeh kung-yang 三業供養
seng-t'ang 僧堂
shan-chia 山家
shan-wai 山外
shang-ch'iu 上求
shang-ch'iu hsia-hua 上求下化
she 庶
she fo kuei hsin 攝佛歸心
she hsin kuei fo 攝心歸佛
sheng (sage, saint) 聖
sheng (arise) 生
sheng-ch'i 生起
shih (reality) 實
shih (phenomenal) 事
shih ch'an-hui 事懺悔
shih ch'eng kuan-fa 十乘觀法
shih [kuan] ching 十[觀]境
shih hao 十號
shih-hsiang (reality) 實相
shih-hsiang (phenomenal features) 事相
shih-hsiang chu-tao fang-fa 事相助道方法
shih-hsiang kuan-fa 事相觀法
shih-i (phenomenal rites) 事儀
shih-i (ritual ceremony) 式儀
shou-tso 首座
shu 疏
shuang chao shuang wang 雙照雙亡
shuang shih shuang fei 雙是雙非
shun 順
shun-li shih-hsiang 順理事相
shun yüan 順緣
ssu chiao 四教
ssu-chü t'ui-chien pu-te 四句推檢不得
ssu chung san-mei 四種三昧
ssu-fa 嗣法
ssu hung-yüan 四引願
ssu huo 四惑
ssu sui 四隨
su 俗
sui-hsi 隨喜
sui-tzu-i 隨自意
sui-tzu-i san-mei 隨自意三昧
sung-ching 誦經
sung-wen fa-shih 誦文法師
ta-ch'u 大處
ta-i 大意
tai-che 侍者
t'an-fo chou-yüan 歎佛呪願
tao 道
tao-ch'ang 道場
tao-chi 道機
tao-chung-chih 道種智
tao-hsin 道心
te-fo 得佛
te fo-i 得佛意
te-hsüeh po-fu 德學博福
teng-chüeh 等覺
t'i 體
t'i-hu 醍醐
t'i-k'ung 體空
tien-tao 顛倒
T'ien-t'ai 天台
ting-hsin 定心
tou fa 逗法
tsang-chiao 藏教
tso-ch'an 坐禅

tsu 祖
Tsun-shih 遵式
tsung (line of teaching) 宗
tsung (general) 總
tsung-kuan 總觀
ts'ung chia ju k'ung 從假入空
Ts'ung-i 從義
ts'ung k'ung ch'u chia 從空出假
tu-wu 獨悟
tuan 斷
tui-chih 對治
tui-yang 對揚
t'ui 推
tun 頓
tun-ken 鈍根
tun-wu ch'an-shih 頓悟禪師
tung-chang 動障
tung chang-tao 動障道
t'ung 通
t'ung-chiao 通教
t'ung-hsing 同行
tzu-ch'eng 資成
Tzu-ch'ing 自慶
tzu-tsai 自在
tz'u-ti 次第
tz'u-ti ch'an-men 次第禪門
tz'u-ti hsing 次第行
wai 外
wai-hu 外護
wen-chü 文句
wen-tzu shih 文字師
wu fu-tz'u 五復次
wu-hsiang an-lo hsing 無相安樂行
wu hui (five penances) 五悔
wu li-i 無利益
wu-ming 無明
wu-shih pa-chiao 五時八教
wu-ti 無諦
yen-chung 嚴重
yin-ch'eng 因成
ying 應
ying-shen 應身
ying-yen-chi 應驗記
yu-hsiang an-le hsing 有相安樂行
yu-ti 有諦
yü 語
yü-lu 語錄
yüan (vow) 願
yüan (perfect) 圓
yüan-chiao 圓教
Yüan-ch'ing 源清
yüan-hsiang 緣相
yüan pu-chü 緣不具
yüan-tun 圓頓
yüan-tun chih-kuan 圓頓止觀
yüeh-hsing (identical practice) 約行

Japanese Terms

gaigi 外儀
gai naru keitai 外なる形態
kei-shiki 形式
naikan 內觀
shingi 身儀
shushō 修證
zen no hōben 禪の方便

Bibliography

Primary Sources

A-p'i-ta-mo chü-she lun 阿毘達磨俱舍論 (*Abhidharmakośa*), by Vasubandhu. Translated by Hsüan-tsang 玄奘. T vol. 29, no. 1558.

A-p'i-ta-mo p'i-p'o-sha lun 阿毘達磨毘婆沙論 (*Abhidharma-mahāvibhāṣa Śāstra*). Translated by Hsüan-tsang 玄奘. T vol. 27, no. 1545.

A-she-shih wang wen wu-ni ching 阿闍世王問五逆經. Translated by Fa-chü 法炬. T vol. 14, no. 508.

Chan-ch'a ching 占察經. See *Chan-ch'a shan-e yeh-pao ching*.

Chan-ch'a shan-e yeh-pao ching 占察善惡業報經. Translation attributed to Bodhidīpa. T vol. 17, no. 839.

Ch'an-men kuei-shih 禪門規式. Attributed to Pai-chang Huai-hai 百丈懷海. See *Ching-teh ch'uan-teng lu*, T 51.250c–251b.

Ch'ang a-han ching 長阿含經 (*Dīrghāgama*). Translated by Buddhayaśas and Chu Fo-nien 竺佛念. T vol. 1, no. 1.

Chao-lun 肇論, by Seng-chao 僧肇. T vol. 45, no. 1858.

Ch'eng-shih lun 成實論 (*Tattvasiddhi Śāstra*), by Harivarman. Translated by Kumārajīva. T vol. 32, no. 1646.

Ch'i fo pa p'u-sa so-shuo t'o-lo-ni shen-chou ching 七佛八菩薩所說陀羅尼神呪經. Translator unknown (Eastern Chin). T vol. 21, no. 1332.

Chia-yeh shan-ting ching 伽耶山頂經 (*Gayāśīrsa Sūtra*). Translated by Bodhiruci. T vol. 14, no. 465.

Ch'ien-shou-yen ta-pei hsin-chou hsing-fa 千手眼大悲心呪行法, by Chih-li 知禮. T vol. 46, no. 1950.

Chih-che ta-shih chuan lun 智者大師傳論, by Liang Su 梁肅. See *Fo-tsu t'ung-chi*, T 49.440a–c.

Chih-kuan fu-hsing ch'uan-hung chüeh 止觀輔行傳弘決, by Chan-jan 湛然. T vol. 46, no. 1912.

Chih-kuan i-li 止觀義例, by Chan-jan 湛然. T vol. 46, no. 1913.

Chih-kuan ta-i 止觀大意, by Chan-jan 湛然. T vol. 46, no. 1914.

Chin-kang pan-jo p'o-lo-mi ching 金剛般若波羅密經 (*Vajracchedika-prajñāpāramitā Sūtra*). Translated by Kumārajīva. T vol. 8, no. 235.

Chin-kang pan-jo p'o-lo-mi ching lun 金剛般若波羅蜜經論 (*Vajracchedika-prajñāpāramitā-sūtra Śāstra*), by Vasubandhu. Translated by Bodhiruci. T vol. 25, no. 1511.

Chin-kuang-ming ch'an-fa 金光明懺法, by Chih-i 智顗. See *Kuo-ch'ing pai-lu*, T 46.796a–b.

Ching-li fa 敬禮法, by Chih-i 智顗. See *Kuo-ch'ing pai-lu*, T 46.794a–795a.

Ching-teh ch'uan-teng lu 景德傳燈錄, by Tao-yüan 道原. T vol. 51, no. 2076.

Ching-t'u shih i lun 淨土十疑論. Attributed to Chih-i 智顗. T vol. 47, no. 1961.

Ch'ing kuan-shih-yin ch'an-fa 請觀世音懺法, by Chih-i 智顗. See *Kuo-ch'ing pai-lu*, T 46.795b–796a.

Ch'ing kuan-shih-yin hsiao-fu tu-hai t'o-lo-ni ching 請觀世音菩薩消伏毒害陀羅尼經. Translated by Nandin. T vol. 20, no. 1043.

Ch'ing kuan-yin ching 請觀音經. See *Ch'ing Kuan-yin hsiao-fu tu-hai t'o-lo-ni ching*.

Ch'ing kuan-yin ching shu 請觀音經疏, by Kuan-ting 灌頂. T vol. 39, no. 1800.

Chiu-ching i-sheng pao-hsing lun 究竟一乘寶性論 (*Ratnagotravibhāga*). Translated by Ratnamati. T vol. 31, no. 1611.

Chiu-mo-lo-shih fa-shih ta-i 鳩摩羅什法師大義, by Kumārajīva and Lu-shan Hui-yüan 廬山慧遠. T vol. 45, no. 1856.

Chu-fa wu-hsing ching 諸法無行經 (*Sarvadharma-pravṛtti-nirdeśa Sūtra*). Translated by Kumārajīva. T vol. 15, no. 650.

Chu Wei-mo-chieh ching 注維摩詰經, by Seng-chao 僧肇. T vol. 38, no. 1775.

Ch'u yao ching 出曜經 (*Udāna-varga*). Translated by Chu Fo-nien 竺佛念. T vol. 4, no. 212.

Chüeh-i san-mei 覺意三昧, by Chih-i 智顗. See *Shih mo-ho pan-jo p'o-lo-mi ching chüeh-i san-mei*.

Chung-lun 中論 (*Mūlamadhyamaka-[kārikā]-śāstra*), by Nāgārjuna (with commentary by *Piṅgala). Translated by Kumārajīva. T vol. 30, no. 1564.

Chung a-han ching 中阿含經 (*Madhyamāgama*). Translated by Saṅghadeva. T vol. 1, no 26.

Fa-hua ching 法華經. See *Miao-fa lien-hua ching*.

Fa-hua ching an-le-hsing i 法華經安樂行義, by Hui-ssu 慧思. T vol. 46, no. 1926.

Fa-hua ching shu 法華經疏, by Tao-sheng 道生. HTC vol. 150.

Fa-hua ching i-chi 法華經義記, by Fa-Yün 法雲. T vol. 33, no. 1715.

Fa-hua hsüan-i 法華玄義, by Chih-i 智顗. See *Miao-fa lien-hua ching hsüan-i*.

Fa-hua hsüan-i shih-ch'ien 法華玄義釋籤, by Chan-jan 湛然. T vol. 33, no. 1717.

Fa-hua san-ta-pu pu-chu 法華三大部補注, by Ts'ung-i 從義. HTC vols. 43–44.

Fa-hua san-mei ch'an-i 法華三昧懺儀, by Chih-i 智顗. T vol. 46, no. 1941.

Fa-hua shih-miao pu-erh men shih-chu-chih 法華十妙不二門示珠指, by Yüan-ch'ing 源清. HTC vol. 100.

Fa-hua wen-chü 法華文句, by Chih-i 智顗. See *Miao-fa lien-hua ching wen-chü*.

Fa-hua wen-chü chi 法華文句記, by Chan-jan 湛然. T vol. 34, no. 1719.

Fang-teng ch'an-fa 方等懺法, by Chih-i 智顗. See *Kuo-ch'ing pai-lu*, T 46.796b–798c.

Fang-teng san-mei hsing-fa 方等三昧行法, by Chih-i 智顗. T vol. 46, no. 1940.

Fang-teng t'o-lo-ni ching 方等陀羅尼經. See *Ta-fang-teng t'o-lo-ni ching*.

Fo-tsu t'ung-chi 佛祖統紀, by Chih-p'an 志磐. T vol. 49, no. 2035.

Fu fa-tsang yin-yüan chuan 付法藏因緣傳. Translated by Kekaya and T'an-yao 曇曜. T vol. 50, no. 2058.

Hsiang-fa chüeh-i ching 像法決疑經. T vol. 85, no. 2870.

Hsiao chih-kuan 小止觀, by Chih-i 智顗. See *Hsiu-hsi chih-kuan tso-ch'an fa-yao*.

Hsin ching 心經. See *Mo-ho pan-jo p'o-lo-mi ta-ming-chou ching* or *Pan-jo p'o-lo-mi-to hsin ching*.

Hsiu-hsi chih-kuan tso-ch'an fa-yao 修習止觀坐禪法要, by Chih-i 智顗. T vol. 46, no. 1915.

Hua-shou ching 華手經 (*Kuśalamūla-saṃparigraha Sūtra*). Translated by Kumārajīva. T vol. 16, no. 657.

Hua-yen ching 華嚴經. See *Ta-fang-kuang fo hua-yen ching*.

Hung-ming chi 弘明集. Compiled by Seng-yu 僧祐. T vol. 52, no. 2102.

Jen-wang ching 仁王經. See *Jen-wang pan-jo p'o-lo-mi ching*.

Jen-wang pan-jo p'o-lo-mi ching 仁王般若波羅蜜經. Translation attributed to Kumārajīva. T vol. 8, no. 245.

Ju-lai pi-mi tsang ching 如來祕密藏經 (**Tathāgata-guhya-garbha/kośa Sūtra*). Translator unknown. T vol. 17, no. 821.

Ju-lai tsang ching 如來藏經. See *Ta-fang-teng ju-lai tsang ching*.

Jui-ying ching 瑞應經. See *T'ai-tzu jui-ying pen-ch'i ching*.

Kannon sangenki 觀音纂玄記, by *Hōtan* 鳳潭 (1657–1738). MS. in Taishō University and Ryūkoku University libraries.

Kuan-ching jung-hsin chieh 觀經融心解, by Chih-li 知禮. See *Ssu-ming tsun-che chiao-hsing lu*, T 46.865c–868a.

Kuan-fo san-mei hai ching 觀佛三昧海經. Translated by Buddhabhadra. T vol. 15, no. 643.

Kuan-hsin lun 觀心論, by Chih-i 智顗. T vol. 46, no. 1920.

Kuan-hsin lun shu 觀心論疏, by Kuan-ting 灌頂. T vol. 36, no. 1921.

Kuan hsü-k'ung-tsang p'u-sa ching 觀虛空藏菩薩經. Translated by Dharmamitra. T vol. 13, no. 409.

Kuan p'u-hsien ching 觀普賢經. See *Kuan p'u-hsien p'u-sa hsing-fa ching*.

Kuan p'u-hsien p'u-sa hsing-fa ching 觀普賢菩薩行法經. Translated by Dharmamitra. T vol. 9, no. 277.

Kuan wu-liang-shou fo ching shu 觀無量壽佛經疏, attributed to Chih-i 智顗. T vol. 37, no. 1750.

Kuan wu-liang-shou fo ching shu 觀無量壽佛經疏, by Shan-tao 善導. T vol. 37, no. 1753.

Kuan wu-liang-shou fo ching shu miao-tsung ch'ao 觀無量壽仏經疏妙宗鈔, by Chih-li 知禮. T vol. 37, no. 1751.

Kuo-ch'ing pai-lu 国清百錄. Compiled by Kuan-ting 灌頂. T vol. 46, no. 1934.

Leng-chia ching 楞伽經 (*Laṅkāvatāra Sūtra*). See *Leng-chia a-pa-to-luo pao ching*.

Leng-chia a-pa-to-lo ching 楞伽阿跋多羅經 (*Laṅkāvatāra Sūtra*). Translated by Guṇabhadra. T vol. 16, no. 670.

Li chih-fa 立制法, by Chih-i 智顗. See *Kuo-ch'ing pai-lu*, T 46.793b–794a.

Liu-chi i 六即義, by Hsing-man 行滿. HTC vol. 100.

Liu miao-fa men 六妙法門, by Chih-i 智顗. T vol. 46, no. 1917.

Makashikan bugyō kōgi 摩訶止觀輔行講義, by Chikū 癡空. In *Makashikan* 摩訶止觀, 5 vols. *Bukkyō taikei* 仏教大系 no. 22–26. Edited by Bukkyō taikei kanseikai (Iwada Kyōen 岩田教圓, chief editor). 1919, 1923, 1933, 1934. Reprint. Tokyo: Nakayama shobō Busshorin, 1978.

Makashikan bugyō kōjutsu 摩訶止觀輔行講述, by Shūdatsu 守脫. In *Makashikan* 摩訶止觀, 5 vols. *Bukkyō taikei* 仏教大系 no. 22–26. Edited by Bukkyō taikei kanseikai (Iwada Kyōen 岩田教圓, chief editor). 1919, 1923, 1933, 1934. Reprint. Tokyo: Nakayama shobō Busshorin, 1978.

Makashikan bugyō kōroku 摩訶止觀輔行講錄, by Kōken 光謙 (1652–1739). MS. in Kyōto University, Kōya-san University, and Ryūkoku University libraries.

Mi-lo hsia-sheng ch'eng-fo ching 彌勒下生成佛經 (**Maitreya-vyākaraṇa Sūtra*). Translated by Kumārajīva. T vol. 14, no. 454.

Miao-fa lien hua ching 妙法蓮華經 (*Saddharmapuṇḍarīka Sūtra*). Translated by Kumārajīva. T vol. 9, no. 262.

Miao-fa lien-hua ching hsüan-i 妙法蓮華經玄義, by Chih-i 智顗. T vol. 36, no. 1716.

Miao-fa lien-hua ching wen-chü 妙法蓮華經文句, by Chih-i 智顗. T vol. 34, no. 1718.

Miao-sheng ting ching 妙勝定經. See *Tsui miao-sheng ting ching*.

Mo-ho chih-kuan 摩訶止觀, by Chih-i 智顗. T vol. 46, no. 1911.

Mo-ho chih-kuan fu-hsing sou-yao-chi 摩訶止觀輔行搜要記, by Chan-jan 湛然. HTC vol. 99.

Mo-ho pan-jo p'o-lo-mi ching 摩訶般若波羅蜜經 (*Pañcaviṃśati-sāhasrikā-prajñāpāramitā Sūtra*). Translated by Kumārajīva. T vol. 8, no. 223.

Mo-ho pan-jo p'o-lo-mi ta-ming-chou ching 摩訶般若波羅蜜大明呪經 (*Mahā-prajñāpāramitā-hṛdaya Sūtra*). Translated by Kumārajīva. T vol. 8, no. 250.

Mo-ho-seng-ch'i lü 摩訶僧祇律 (*Mahāsaṃghika Vinaya*). Translated by Buddhabhadra and Fa-hsien 法顯. T vol. 22, no. 1425.

Nieh-p'an ching 涅槃經 (*Nirvāṇa Sūtra*). See *Ta-pan nieh-p'an ching*.

Pa-p'o p'u-sa ching 拔陂菩薩經 (**Bhadrapāla-bodhisattva Sūtra or Pratyutpanna-buddha-sammukhāvasthita-samādhi Sūtra*). Translator unknown. T vol. 13, no. 419.

Pan-chou san-mei ching 般舟三昧經 (*Pratyutpanna-buddha-sammukhāvasthita-samādhi Sūtra*), 3 fascicles. Translated by Lokakṣema. T vol. 13, no. 418.

Pan-chou san-mei ching 般舟三昧經 (*Pratyutpanna-buddha-sammukhāvasthita-samādhi Sūtra*), 1 fascicle. Translated by Lokakṣema. T vol. 13, no. 417.

Pan-jo p'o-lo-mi-to hsin ching 般若波羅蜜多心經 (*Prajñāpāramitā-hṛdaya Sūtra*). Translated by Hsüan-tsang 玄奘. T vol. 8, no. 251.

Pao-hsing lun 寶性論. See *Chiu-ching i-sheng pao-hsing lun.*

Pei-hua ching 悲華經 (*Karunā-puṇḍarīka Sūtra*). Translated by Dharmakṣema. T vol. 3, no. 157.

Pieh li chung-chih 別立衆制, by Tsun-shih 遵式. See *T'ien-chu pieh-chi*, HTC 101.309b–311a.

P'u-hsien kuan ching 普賢觀經. See *Kuan p'u-hsien p'u-sa hsing-fa ching.*

P'u-li fa 普禮法, by Chih-i 智顗. See *Kuo-ch'ing pai-lu*, T 46.795a–b.

P'u-sa chieh ching 菩薩戒經. See *P'u-sa ti-ch'ih ching.*

P'u-sa ti-ch'ih ching 菩薩地持經 (*Bodhisattvabhūmi* section of the *Yogācārabhūmi Śāstra*), by Asaṅga. Translated by Dharmakṣema. T vol. 30, no. 1581.

P'u-sa ying-lo pen-yeh ching 菩薩瓔珞本業經. Translation attributed to Chu Fo-nien 竺佛念. T vol. 24, no. 1485.

San kuan i 三觀義, by Chih-i 智顗. HTC vol. 98.

San pao lun 三報論, by Lu-shan Hui-yüan 廬山慧遠. See *Hung-ming chi*, T 52.34b–34c.

Shan-chu-i t'ien so-wen ching 善住意天所問經 (*Susthitamati-devaputra-paripṛcchā Sūtra*). See *Sheng shan-chu-i t'ien-tzu so-wen ching.*

Shan-ting chih-kuan 删定止觀, by Liang Su 梁肅. HTC vol. 99.

Sheng-man ching 勝鬘經 (*Śrīmālādevī-siṃhanāda Sūtra*). See *Sheng-man shih-tzu-hou i-sheng ta-fang-pien fang-kuang ching.*

Sheng-man shih-tzu-hou i-sheng ta-fang-pien fang-kuang ching 勝鬘師子吼一乘大方便方廣經 (*Śrīmālādevī-siṃhanāda Sūtra*). Translated by Guṇabhadra. T vol. 12, no. 353.

Sheng shan-chu-i t'ien-tzu so-wen ching 聖善住意天子所問經 (*Susthitamati-devaputra-paripṛcchā Sūtra*). Translated by Vimuktajñāna and Prajñaruci. T vol. 12, no. 341.

Shih ch'an p'o-lo-mi tz'u-ti fa-men 釋禪波羅蜜次第法門, by Chih-i 智顗. T vol. 46, no. 1916.

Shih-chu p'i-p'o-sha lun 十住毘婆沙論 (**Daśabhūmika-vibhāṣa Śāstra*), attributed to Nagarjuna. Translated by Kumarajiva. T vol. 26, no. 1521.

Shih-men kuei-ching i 釋門歸敬儀, by Tao-hsüan 道宣. T vol. 45, no. 1896.

Shih mo-ho pan-jo p'o-lo-mi ching chüeh-i san-mei 釋摩訶般若波羅蜜經覺意三昧, by Chih-i. T vol. 46, no. 1922.

Shih pu-erh men 十不二門, by Chan-jan 湛然. T vol. 46, no. 1927.

Shih pu-erh men chih-yao ch'ao 十不二門指要鈔, by Chih-li 知禮. T vol. 46, no. 1928.

Shih pu-erh men shih-chu chih 十不二門示珠指, by Yüan-ch'ing 源淸. See *Fa-hua shih-miao pu-erh men shih-chu chih.*

Shih-sung lü 十誦律 (**Sarvāstavāda Vinaya*). Translated by Puṇyatara and Kumārajīva. T vol. 23, no. 1435.

Shih-ti ching lun 十地經論 (*Dasabhūmika-vyākhyāna*), by Vasubandhu. Translated by Bodhiruci. T vol. 26, no. 1522.

Shih-t'ieh yen-ch'ing ssu 使帖延慶寺, by Chih-li 知禮. See *Ssu-ming tsun-che chiao-hsing lu*, T 46.909a–910a.

Shikan bugyō shiki 止觀輔行私記, by Shōshin 證真. In *Makashikan* 摩訶止觀, 5 vols. *Bukkyō taikei* 仏教大系 no. 22–26. Edited by Bukkyō taikei kanseikai (Iwada Kyōen 岩田教圓, chief editor). 1919, 1923, 1933, 1934. Reprint. Tokyo: Nakayama shobō Busshorin, 1978.

Shou-leng-yen san-mei ching 首楞嚴三昧經 (*Śūraṅgama-samādhi Sūtra*). Translated by Kumārajīva. T vol. 15, no. 642.

Shou-leng-yen ching 首楞嚴經. See *Ta-fo-ting ju-lai mi-yin hsiu-cheng liao-i chu p'u-sa wan-hsing shou-leng-yen ching*.

Ssu chiao i 四教義, by Chih-i 智顗. T vol. 46, no. 1929.

Ssu-fen lü 四分律 (*Dharmagupta Vinaya*). Translated by Buddhayaśas and Chu Fo-nien 竺佛念. T vol. 22, no. 1428.

Ssu-i ching 思益經 (*Viśeṣacintabrahma-paripṛcchā Sūtra*). See *Ssu-i fan-t'ien so-wen ching*.

Ssu-i fan-t'ien so-wen ching 思益梵天所問經 (*Viśeṣacintabrahma-paripṛcchā Sūtra*). Translated by Kumārajīva. T vol. 15, no. 586.

Ssu-ming fa-chih tsun-che shih-lu 四明尊者實錄, by Tse-ch'üan 則全. See *Ssu-ming tsun-che chiao-hsing lu*, T 46.919b–920a.

Ssu-ming shih i shu 四明十義書, by Chih-li 知禮. T vol. 46, no. 1936.

Ssu-ming tsun-che chiao-hsing lu 四明尊者教行錄. Compiled by Tsung-hsiao 宗曉. T vol. 46, no. 1937.

Ssu nien-ch'u 四念處. Attributed to Chih-i 智顗. T vol. 46, no. 1918.

Sui T'ien-t'ai Chih-che ta-shih pieh-chuan 隋天台智者大師別傳, by Kuan-ting 灌頂. T vol. 50, no. 2050.

Sui-tzu-i san-mei 隨自意三昧, by Hui-ssu 慧思. HTC vol. 98.

Ta-chi ching 大集經 (*Mahāsaṃnipāta Sūtra*). See *Ta-fang-teng ta-chi ching*.

Ta-chih-tu lun 大智度論 (**Mahāprajñāpāramitā Śāstra*). Attributed to Nāgārjuna. Translated by Kumārajīva. T vol. 25, no. 1509.

Ta-fang-kuang fo hua-yen ching 大方廣佛華嚴經 (*Avataṃsaka Sūtra*). Translated by Buddhabhadra. T vol. 9, no. 278.

Ta-fang-pien fo pao-en ching 大方便佛報恩經. Translator unknown. T vol. 3, no. 156.

Ta-fang-teng ju-lai tsang ching 大方等如來藏經 (*Tathāgatagarbha Sūtra*). Translated by Buddhabhadra. T vol. 16, no. 666.

Ta-fang-teng ta-chi ching 大方等大集經 (*Mahāsaṃnipāta Sūtra*). Translated by Dharmakṣema. T vol. 13, no. 397.

Ta-fang-teng t'o-lo-ni ching 大方等陀羅尼經 (**Mahāvaipulya-dhāraṇī Sūtra*). Translated by Fa-chung 法衆. T vol. 21, no. 1339.

Ta-fo-ting ju-lai mi-yin hsiu-cheng liao-i chu p'u-sa wan-hsing shou-leng-yen ching 大佛頂如來密因修證了義諸菩薩萬行首楞嚴經. Translation attributed to Pan-tz'u-mi-ti 般刺蜜帝. T vol. 19, no. 945.

Ta-hua-yen ch'ang-che wen fo na-luo-yen li ching 大花嚴長者問佛那羅延力經. T vol. 14, no. 547.

Ta Hüan Hsüan ming pao-ying lun 答桓玄明報應論, by Lu-shan Hui-yüan 廬山慧遠. See *Hung-ming chi*, T52.33b–34a.

Ta-pan nieh-p'an ching 大般涅槃經 (*Nirvāṇa Sūtra*). Translated by Dharmakṣema. T vol. 12, no. 374.

Ta-pan nieh-p'an ching 大般涅槃經 (*Nirvāṇa Sūtra*). Translated (and emended) by Hui-yen 慧嚴. T vol. 12, 375.

Ta-pan nieh-p'an ching chi-chieh 大般涅槃經集解. Compiled by Pao-liang 寶亮. T vol. 37, no. 1763.

Ta pao-chi ching 大寶積經 (*Mahāratnakūṭa Sūtra*). Translated by Bodhiruci (T'ang). T vol. 11, no. 310.

Ta-p'in pan-jo ching 大品般若經 (*Pañcaviṃśati-sahasrikā-prajñāpāramitā Sūtra*). See *Mo-ho pan-jo p'o-lo-mi ching*.

Ta-sheng ch'i-hsin lun 大乘起信論. Attributed to Aśvaghoṣa. Translation attributed to Paramártha. T vol. 32, no. 1666.

Ta-sheng i chang 大乘義章, by Ching-ying Hui-yüan 淨影慧遠. T vol. 44, no. 1851.

T'ai-tzu jui-ying pen-ch'i ching 太子瑞應本起經. Translated by Chih-ch'ien 支謙. T vol. 3, no. 185.

T'ien-chu pieh-chi 天竺別集. Compiled by Hui-kuan 慧觀. HTC vol. 101.

T'ien-chu ssu shih-fang chu-ch'ih i 天竺寺十方住持儀, by Tsun-shih 遵式. See *T'ien-chu pieh-chi*, HTC 101.306b–309a.

T'ien-t'ai ch'an-lin ssu pei 天台禪林寺俾, by Liang Su 梁肅. See *Fo-tsu t'ung-chi*, T 49.438b–c.

T'ien-t'ai chiao sui-han mu-lu 天台教隨函目錄, by Tsun-shih 遵式. See *T'ien-chu pieh-chi*, HTC 101.263b–266b.

T'ien-t'ai chih-kuan t'ung-li 天台止觀統例, by Liang Su 梁肅. See *Fo-tsu t'ung-chi*, T 49.438c–440a.

T'ien-t'ai ssu-chiao i 天台四教儀, by Chegwan 諦觀. T vol. 46, no. 1931.

T'ien-t'ai tsu-ch'eng chi 天台祖承記, by Tsun-shih 遵式. See *T'ien-chu pieh-chi*, HTC 101.262b–263b.

Tsa a-han ching 雜阿含經 (*Samyuktāgama*). Translated by Guṇabhadra. T vol. 2, no. 99.

Tsa a-p'i-t'an hsin lun 雜阿毘曇心論 (*Samyuktābhidharma-hṛdaya Śāstra*), by Dharmatrāta. Translated by Saṅghavarman. T vol. 28, no. 1552.

Tseng-hsiu chiao-yüan ch'ing-kuei 增修教苑淸規, by Tzu-ch'ing 自慶. HTC vol. 101.

Tseng-i a-han ching 增一阿含經 (*Ekottarāgama*). Translated by Saṅghadeva. T vol. 2, no. 125.

Tsui miao-sheng ting ching 最妙勝定經. See Sekiguchi Shindai 關口真大, *Tendai shikan no kenkyu* 天台止觀の研究. Tokyo: Iwanami bunko, 1969.

Tz'u-ti ch'an-men 次第禪門, by Chih-i 智顗. See *Shih ch'an p'o-lo-mi tz'u-ti fa-men*.

Wei-mo-chieh so-shuo ching 維摩詰所說經 (*Vimalakīrti-nirdeśa Sūtra*). Translated by Kumārajīva. T vol. 14, no. 475.

Wei-mo ching hsüan-shu 維摩經玄疏, by Chih-i 智顗. T vol. 38, no. 1777.

Wei-ts'eng-yu yin-yüan ching 未曾有因緣經 (**Mahāmāyā Sūtra*). Translated by T'an-ching 曇景. T vol. 17, no. 754.

Wen-shu-shih-li so-shuo ching 文殊師利所説經 (*Saptaśatika-prajñāpāramitā Sūtra*). See *Wen-shu-shih-li so-shuo mo-ho pan-jo p'o-lo-mi ching*.

Wen-shu-shih-li so-shuo mo-ho pan-jo p'o-lo-mi ching 文殊師利所説摩訶般若波羅蜜經 (*Saptaśatika-prajñāpāramitā Sūtra*). Translated by Mandrasena. T vol. 8, no. 232.

Wen-shu-shih-li wen ching 文殊師利問經 (**Mañjuśrī-paripṛcchā Sūtra*). Translated by Saṅghabara. T vol. 14, no. 468.

Wen-shu shih-li wen p'u-ti ching 文殊師利問菩提經 (*Gayāśīrsa Sūtra*). Translated by Kumārajīva. T vol. 14, no. 464.

Wen-shu shuo ching 文殊説經 (*Saptaśatika-prajñāpāramitā Sūtra*). *Wen-shu-shih-li so-shuo mo-ho pan-jo p'o-lo-mi ching*.

Wen-shu wen ching 文殊問經 (**Mañjuśrī-paripṛcchā Sūtra*). See *Wen-shu-shih-li wen ching*.

Wu-fen lü 五分律 (*Mahīśāsaka Vinaya*). Translated by Buddhajīva and Chu Tao-sheng 竺道生. T vol. 22, no. 1421.

Wu-liang-i ching 無量義經. Translation attributed to Dharmagatayaśas. T vol. 9, no. 276.

Yang-chüeh-mo-lo ching 央掘魔羅經 (*Aṅgulimālika Sūtra*). Translated by Guṇabhadra. T vol. 2, no. 120.

Ying-lo ching 瓔珞經. See *P'u-sa ying-lo pen-yeh ching*.

Secondary Sources

Andō Toshio 安藤俊雄. "Tendai Chigi no jōdokyō 天台智顗の浄土教." In *Tendai shisō-shi* 天台思想史. By Andō Toshio 安藤俊雄. Kyoto: Hōzōkan, 1959, pp. 340–420.

———. *Tendai-gaku: konpon shisō to sono tenkai* 天台學:根本思想とその展開. Heirakuji shoten, 1968.

———. *Tendai-gaku ronshū: shikan to jōdo* 天台學論集:止觀と浄土. Kyoto: Heirakuji shoten, 1975.

———. *Tendai shisō-shi* 天台思想史. Kyoto: Hōzōkan, 1959.

———. *Tendai shōgu shisō ron* 天台性具思想論. Kyoto: Hōzōkan, 1973.

Bell, Catherine. *Ritual Theory, Ritual Practice*. New York: Oxford University Press, 1992.

Bielefeldt, Carl. "Chang-lu Tsung-tse's *Tso-ch'an i* and the 'Secret' of Zen Meditation." In *Traditions of Meditation in Chinese Buddhism*. Edited by Peter N. Gregory. Studies in East Asian Buddhism, no. 4. Honolulu: University of Hawaii Press, 1986.

———. *Dogen's Manuals of Zen Meditation*. Berkeley: University of California Press, 1988.

Buswell, Robert E., Jr., *The Formation of Ch'an Ideology in China and Korea*. Princeton: Princeton University Press, 1989.

———, ed. *Chinese Buddhist Apocrypha*. Honolulu: University of Hawaii Press, 1990.

Buswell, Robert E., Jr., and Robert M. Gimello, eds. *Paths to Liberation: The Mārga and Its Transformations in Buddhist Thought*. Kuroda Institute Studies in East Asian Buddhism no. 7. Honolulu: University of Hawaii Press, 1992.

Chan, Wing-tsit. "The Evolution of the Neo-Confucian Concept of *Li* as Principle." *Tsing-hua Journal of Chinese Studies* 4 (1964): 123–149.

Chappell, David. "From Dispute to Dual Cultivation: Pure Land Responses to Ch'an Critiques." In *Traditions of Meditation in Chinese Buddhism*. Edited by Peter N. Gregory. Studies in East Asian Buddhism no. 4. Honolulu: University of Hawaii Press, 1986.

———, ed. *Buddhist and Taoist Practice in Medieval Chinese Society*. Buddhist and Taoist Studies no. 2. Honolulu: University of Hawaii Press, 1987.

———, ed. *T'ien-t'ai Buddhism: An Outline of the Fourfold Teachings*. Tokyo: Daiichi shobō, 1983.

Ch'en, Kenneth K. S. *Buddhism in China: A Historical Survey*. Princeton: Princeton University Press, 1964.

Chūgoku Bukkyō kenkyū-kai 中國仏教研究會. *Makashikan inyō tenkyo sōran* 摩訶止觀弘用典拠総覧. Tokyo: Nakayama shobō Busshorin, 1987.

Collcutt, Martin. "The Early Ch'an Monastic Rule: *Ch'ing-kuei* and the Shaping of Early Ch'an Life." In *Early Ch'an in China and Tibet*. Edited by Whalen Lai and Lewis Lancaster. Berkeley Buddhist Studies Series no. 5. Berkeley, 1983.

Dayal, Har. *The Bodhisattva Doctrine in Buddhist Sanskrit Literature*. London: Kegan Paul, Trench, Trubner, 1932.

de Bary, William Theodore, ed. *The Buddhist Tradition in India, China, and Japan*. New York: Random House, 1969.

Donner, Neal. "Chih-i's Meditation on Evil." In *Buddhist and Taoist Practice in Medieval Chinese Society*. Edited by David Chappell. Buddhist and Taoist Studies no. 2. Honolulu: University of Hawaii Press, 1987.

———. "The Great Calming and Contemplation of Chih-i. Chapter One: The Synopsis." Ph.D. dissertation, University of British Columbia, 1976.

———. "The Mahāyānization of the Chinese Dhyāna Tradition." *Eastern Buddhist* 10, 2 (October 1977): 49–64.

———. "Sudden and Gradual Intimately Conjoined: Chih-i's T'ien-t'ai View." In *Sudden and Gradual Approaches to Enlightenment in Chinese Thought*. Edited by Peter N. Gregory. Studies in East Asian Buddhism no. 5. Honolulu: University of Hawaii Press, 1987.

Faure, Bernard. "The Concept of One Practice Samadhi in Early Ch'an." In *Traditions of Meditation in Chinese Buddhism*. Edited by Peter N. Gregory. Studies in East Asian Buddhism no. 4. Honolulu: University of Hawaii Press, 1986.

———. *The Rhetoric of Immediacy: A Cultural Critique of Chan/Zen Buddhism.* Princeton: Princeton University Press, 1991.

———. *La volonté d'orthodoxie dans le bouddhisme chinoise.* Paris: Centre National de la Recherche Scientifique, 1988.

Foulk, T. Griffith. "The 'Ch'an School' and Its Place in the Buddhist Monastic Tradition." Ph.D. dissertation, University of Michigan, 1987.

———. "Myth, Ritual, and Monastic Practice in Sung Ch'an Buddhism." In *Religion and Society in T'ang and Sung China.* Edited by Patricia B. Ebrey and Peter N. Gregory. Honolulu: University of Hawaii Press (in press).

Fujita, Kōtatsu. "One Vehicle or Three?" Translated by Leon Hurvitz. *Journal of Indian Philosophy* 3 (1975): 79–166.

Fukushima Kōsai 福島光哉. "Tendai ni okeru kan'ō no ronri 天台における感應の論理." *Indogaku Bukkyōgaku kenkyū* 印度學仏教學研究 18, 2 (1970): 253–256.

Gimello, Robert M. "Apophatic and Kataphatic Discourse in Mahayana: A Chinese View." *Philosophy East and West* 26, 2 (1976): 117–136.

———. "Chih-yen (602–668) and the Foundations of Hua-yen Buddhism." Ph.D. dissertation, Columbia University, 1976.

Gjertson, Donald Edward. "A Study and Translation of the 'Ming-pao chi': A T'ang Dynasty Collection of Buddhist Tales." Ph.D. diss., Stanford University, 1975.

———, trans. *Miraculous Retribution: A Study and Translation of T'ang Lin's Ming-pao chi.* Berkeley: Centers for South and Southeast Asian Studies, University of California at Berkeley, 1989.

Goddard, Dwight. *A Buddhist Bible.* Boston: 1938. Reprint. Beacon Press, 1966.

Gregory, Peter N. "Tsung-mi and the Single Word 'Awareness' (*chih*)." *Philosophy East and West* 35, 3 (1985): 249–269.

———. *Tsung-mi and the Sinification of Buddhism.* Princeton: Princeton University Press, 1991.

———, ed. *Sudden and Gradual: Approaches to Enlightenment in Chinese Thought.* Studies in East Asian Buddhism no. 5. Honolulu: University of Hawaii Press, 1983.

———, ed. *Traditions of Meditation in Chinese Buddhism.* Studies in East Asian Buddhism no. 4. Honolulu: University of Hawaii Press, 1986.

Grimes, Ronald. "Ritual Studies." In *The Encyclopedia of Religion.* Edited by Mircea Eliade et al. New York: Macmillan, 1991.

Groner, Paul. *Saichō: The Establishment of the Japanese Tendai School.* Berkeley Buddhist Studies Series no. 7. Berkeley, 1984.

Harrison, Paul. "Buddhānusmṛti in the Pratyutpanna-Buddha-Sammukhāvasthita-Samādhi-Sūtra." *Journal of Indian Philosophy* 6 (1978): 35–57.

———. *The Samadhi of Direct Encounter with the Buddhas of the Present: An Annotated English Translation of the Tibetan Version of the Pratyutpanna-Buddha-Sammukhāvasthita-Samādhi-Sutra.* Studia Philologica Buddhica Monograph no. 5. Tokyo: International Institute for Buddhist Studies, 1990.

Hayashi Zenshin 林善信. "Makashikan ni okeru shishu-zammai no ichi kōsatsu 摩訶止觀における四種三昧の一考察." *Indogaku Bukkyōgaku kenkyū* 印度學仏教學研究 25, 1 (1976): 208–210.

Hibi Nobumasa 日比宣正. *Tōdai Tendai-gaku kenkyū: Tan'nen no kyōgaku ni kansuru kōsatsu* 唐代天台學研究:湛然の教學に関する考察. Tokyo: Sankibō Busshorin, 1975.

———. *Tōdai Tendai-gaku kenkyū josetsu: Tan'nen no chosaku ni kansuru kenkyū* 唐代天台學研究序說:湛然の著作に関する研究. Tokyo: Sankibō Busshorin, 1966.

Hirabayashi Fumio 平林文雄. *San-tendai-godaizan-ki kōhon narabi ni kenkyū* 參天台五台山記:校本並に研究. Tokyo: Fukan shobō, 1978.

Hirai Shun'ei 平井俊榮. *Hokke-mongu no seiritsu ni kansuru kenkyū* 法華文句の成立にかんする研究. Tokyo: Shunjusha, 1985.

Horner, I. B., trans. *The Collection of the Middle Length Sayings (Majjhima-Nikāya)*. 3 vols. London: Pali Text Society, 1975–77.

Hurvitz, Leon. "Chih-i (538–597): An Introduction to the Life and Ideas of a Chinese Monk." *Mélanges Chinoises et Bouddhiques* 12 (1962): 1–372.

———, trans. *Scripture of the Lotus Blossom of the Fine Dharma (The Lotus Sūtra)*. New York: Columbia University Press, 1976.

Ikeda Rosan 池田魯參. *Makashikan kenkyū josetsu* 摩訶止觀研究序說. Tokyo: Daitō shuppansha, 1987.

———. "Shimei Chirei no shōgai to chojutsu 四明知禮の生活と著述." *Tōyō bunka kenkyūjo kiyō* 東洋文化研究所紀要 100 (1986): 195–247.

———. "Tendai kan'ō shisō no seiritsu igi 天台感應思想の成立意義." *Komazawa daigaku Bukkyōgakubu kenkyū kiyō* 駒沢大学仏教学部研究紀要 29 (1971): 93–112.

———. "Tendai shishu-zammai no shūyō 天台四種三昧の宗要." *Indogaku Bukkyōgaku kenkyū* 印度學仏教學研究 17, 2 (1969): 132–133.

Ishida Shūshi 石田充之, ed. *Shunjō risshi* 俊芿律師. Kamakura Bukkyō seiritsu no kenkyū 鎌倉仏教成立の研究. Kyoto: Hōzōkan, 1972.

Jan, Yün-hua. "Buddhist Historiography in Sung China." *Zeitschrift der deutschen morganlandischen Gesellschaft* 114 (1964): 360–381.

Kodera, Takashi James. *Dogen's Formative Years in China*. London: Routledge and Kegan Paul, 1980.

Lai, Whalen. "The *Chan-ch'a ching*: Religion and Magic in Medieval China." In *Chinese Buddhist Apocrypha*. Edited by Robert E. Buswell, Jr. Honolulu: University of Hawaii Press, 1990.

Lai, Whalen, and Lewis Lancaster, eds. *Early Ch'an in China and Tibet*. Berkeley Buddhist Studies Series no. 5. Berkeley, 1983.

Lamotte, Étienne, trans. *L'Enseignement de Vimalakīrti (Vimalakīrtinirdeśa)*. Louvain: Publications Universitaires and Leuven: Institut Orientaliste, 1962.

———, trans. *La traité de la grande vertue de sagesse*. 5 vols. Louvain: Bureaux du Museon, 1944, 1949, 1970, 1976, 1980.

Lau, D. C., trans. *Confucius: The Analects*. New York: Penguin Books, 1979.

Legge, James, trans. *The Chinese Classics*. 5 vols. Oxford: Clarendon Press, 1893.

Luk, Charles (Lu K'uan-yü). *Secrets of Chinese Meditation*. New York: Samuel Weiser, 1969.

McRae, John R. *The Northern School and the Formation of Early Ch'an Buddhism*. Studies in East Asian Buddhism no. 3. Honolulu: University of Hawaii Press, 1986.

———. "Shen-hui and the Teaching of Sudden Enlightenment in Early Ch'an Buddhism." *In Sudden and Gradual: Approaches to Enlightenment in Chinese Thought*. Edited by Peter N. Gregory. Studies in East Asian Buddhism no. 5. Honolulu: University of Hawaii Press, 1987.

Magnin, Paul. *La vie et l'oeuvre de Huisi (515–577)*. Paris: École Francaise d'Extreme-Orient, 1979.

Makita Tairyō 牧田諦亮. *Rikuchō Kanzeonōgenki no kenkyū* 六朝觀世音應驗記の研究. Kyoto: Heirakuji shoten, 1970.

Mochizuki Shinkō 望月信享. *Bukkyō daijiten* 仏教大事典. 10 vols. Tokyo: Sekai seiten kankō kyōkai, 1958–1963.

Mou Tsung-san 牟宗三. *Fo-hsing yü pan-jo* 佛性與般若. 2 vols. Taipei: Hsüeh-sheng shu-chü, 1982.

Muranaka Yūjō 村中祐生. *Makashikan* 摩訶止觀. Daijō Butten: Chūgoku-Nihon hen 大乘仏典：中國日本篇 no. 6. Tokyo: Chūō kōronsha, 1988.

Murti, T. R. V. *The Central Philosophy of Buddhism*. London: George Allen and Unwin, 1960.

Nakayama Shōkō 中山正晃. "Chō-Sō Tendai to jōdokyō—sono jissen-men ni tsuite 趙宋天台と浄土教ーその實践面について." *Indogaku Bukkyōgaku kenkyū* 印度學仏教學研究 34, 1 (1985): 206–211.

Nitta Masa'aki 新田雅章. "Chigi ni okeru bodaishin no seiritsu konkyo ni tsuite 智顗いおける菩提心の成立根拠について." *Indogaku Bukkyōgaku kenkyū* 印度學仏教學研究 16, 2 (1968): 271–277.

———. *Tendai jissō-ron no kenkyū* 天台實相論の研究. Kyoto: Heirakuji shoten, 1981.

———, trans. *Makashikan* 摩訶止觀. Butten kōza 仏典講座 no. 25. Daizō shuppansha, 1989.

Ōchō Enichi 横超慧日. *Chūgoku Bukkyō no kenkyū* 中國仏教の研究. Kyoto: Hōzōkan, 1958.

Oda Tokunō 織田得能. *Bukkyō daijiten* 仏教大辞典. Revised edition. Tokyo: Daitō shuppansha, 1977.

Ōkubo Ryōjun 大久保良順. "Tōdai ni okeru Tendai no denshō ni tsuite 唐代における天台の伝承について." *Nihon Bukkyō gakkai nempō* 日本仏教學會年報 17 (1952): 87–98.

Ōno Eijin 大野榮人. "Hōtōdaranikyō ni motozuku sembō 方等陀羅尼經にもとずく懺法." *Shūkyō kenkyū* 宗教研究 52, 2 (1968): 51–77.

———. "Hōtō-zammai-gyōhō no kenkyū 方等三昧行法の研究." *Indogaku Bukkyōgaku kenkyū* 印度學仏教學研究 27, 1 (1978): 254–259.

———. "Shishu-zammai no tenkyo to sono kōsatsu (jō): jōza-zammai to jōgyō-zammai 四種三昧の典拠とその考察:常坐三昧と常行三昧(上)." *Zen kenkyūjo kiyō* 禪研究所紀要 6 and 7 (1976): 271–305.

———. "Tendai Chigi no zammai shisō kō 天台智顗の三昧思想考." In *Bukkyō ni okeru zammai shisō* 仏教における三昧思想. Nihon Bukkyō gakkai. Kyoto: Heirakuji shoten, 1976.

Pruden, Leo M. "T'ien-t'ai." In *The Encyclopedia of Religion*. Edited by Mircea Eliade et al. New York: Macmillan, 1987.

Pulleyblank, Edwin G. "Neo-Confucianism and Neo-Legalism in T'ang Intellectual Life, 755–805." In *The Confucian Persuasion*. Edited by Arthur F. Wright. Stanford: Stanford University Press, 1969.

Ramanan, K. Venkata. *Nāgārjuna's Philosophy as Presented in the Mahā-Prajñā-Pāramitā-Śāstra*. New York: Samuel Weiser, 1966. Reprint, Delhi: Motilal Banarsidass, 1978.

Rappaport, Roy. "Ritual, Sanctity, and Cybernetics." *American Anthropologist* 73 (1971): 59–76.

Rhodes, Robert F. "An Annotated Translation of the *Ssu-chiao i* (On the Four Teachings)." *Ōtani daigaku Shinshū sōgō kenkyūjo nempō* 大谷大學真宗総合研究所年報 *(Shin Buddhist Comprehensive Research Institute Annual Memoirs)* 3 (1985): 27–101 and 4 (1986): 93–141.

———. "*Hokke-zammai-zangi kenkyū josetsu* 法華三昧懺儀研究序說." *Bukkyō seminaa* 仏教セミナー 45 (1987): 17–33.

Rhys Davids, Caroline A. F., and F. L. Woodward, trans. The *Book of the Kindred Sayings (Samyutta Nikāya) or Grouped Suttas*. 5 vols. London: Pali Text Society, 1950, 1952, 1954, 1956.

Rhys Davids, T. W., and Caroline A. F. Rhys Davids, trans. *Dialogues of the Buddha (Dīgha-Nikāya)*. 3 vols. Sacred Books of the Buddhists vol. 2–4. London: Pali Text Society, 1956, 1957, 1959.

Robinson, Richard. *Early Mādhyamika in India and China*. Madison: University of Wisconsin Press, 1967.

Satō Tetsuei 佐藤哲英. "Shō-o shisō no sōshōsha wa Chigi ka Kanjō ka 性悪思想の創唱者は智顗か灌頂か?" *Indogaku Bukkyōgaku kenkyū* 印度學仏教學研究 14, 2 (1966): 47–52.

———. "Tendai daishi ni okeru shishu-zammai no keisei katei 天台大師における四種三昧の形成過程." *Indogaku Bukkyōgaku kenkyū* 印度學仏教學研究 12, 2 (1964): 52–58.

———. *Tendai daishi no kenkyū* 天台大師の研究. Kyoto: Hyakka'en, 1961.

———. *Zoku Tendai daishi no kenkyū* 續天台大師の研究. Kyoto: Hyakka'en, 1981.

Schuster, Nancy. "Changing the Female Body: Wise Women and the Bodhisattva Career in Some *Mahāratnakūṭasūtras*." *Journal of the International Association of Buddhist Studies* 4, 1 (1981): 24–69.

Sekiguchi Shindai 関口真大. *Tendai kyōgaku no kenkyū* 天台教學の研究. Tokyo: Daitō shuppansha, 1978.

———. *Tendai shikan no kenkyū* 天台止觀の研究. Tokyo: Iwanami shoten, 1969.

———. *Tendai Shōshikan no kenkyu* 天台小止觀の研究. 1954. Reprint. Tokyo: Sankibō Busshorin, 1961.

———, ed. *Shikan no kenkyū* 止觀の研究. Tokyo: Iwanami shoten, 1975.

———, trans. *Makashikan: zen no shisō genri* 摩訶止觀:禪の思想原理. 2 vols. Tokyo: Iwanami shoten, 1964.

Sharf, Robert. "Occidentalism and the Zen of Japanese Nationalism." Paper presented for the panel on "Buddhism and Orientalism at the Turn of the Century," American Academy of Religion annual meeting, Kansas City, Nov. 1991.

Shimaji Taitō 島地大等. *Tendai kyōgaku-shi* 天台教學史. Tokyo: Ryūmonkan, 1977.

Shioiri Ryōdō 塩入良道. "Chō-Sō Tendai ni okeru jissen-men no kōsatsu 趙宋天台における実践面の考察." *Indogaku bukkyōgaku kenkyū* 印度學仏教學研究 11, 2 (1963): 79–85.

———. "Hokke-sembō to shikan 法華懺法と止觀." In *Shikan no kenkyū* 止觀の研究. Edited by Sekiguchi Shindai 関口真大. Tokyo: Iwanami shoten, 1975, pp. 307–335.

———. "Sange-sangai ronsō no hottan 山家山外論争の発端." *Bukkyō shisō-ron: Bukkyō naibun ni okeru tairon* 仏教思想論:仏教内分における対論. Chūgoku-Chibetto 中國チベット no. 4. Tokyo, 1981, pp. 141–174.

———. "Sembō no seiritsu to Chigi no tachiba 懺法の成立と智顗の立場." *Indogaku Bukkyōgaku kenkyū* 印度學仏教學研究 7, 1 (1959): 45–55.

———. "Shishu-zammai ni atsukawareta Chigi no sembō 四種三昧に扱われた智顗の懺法." *Indogaku Bukkyōgaku kenkyū* 印度學仏教學研究 8, 2 (1960): 269–274.

Smith, Jonathon. *Imagining Religion.* Chicago: University of Chicago Press, 1982.

———. *To Take Place: Toward Theory in Ritual.* Chicago: University of Chicago Press, 1987.

Stevenson, Daniel B. "The Four Kinds of Samadhi in Early T'ien-t'ai Buddhism." In *Traditions of Meditation in Chinese Buddhism.* Edited by Peter N. Gregory. Studies in East Asian Buddhism no. 4. Honolulu: University of Hawaii Press, 1986.

———. "The T'ien-t'ai Four Forms of Samadhi and Late North-South Dynasties, Sui, and Early T'ang Buddhist Devotionalism." Ph.D. dissertation, Columbia University, 1987.

Swanson, Paul L. "Chih-i's Interpretation of *jñeyāvaraṇa*: An Application of the Threefold Truth Concept." *Ōtani daigaku Shinshū sōgō kenkyūjo nempō* 大谷大學真宗総合研究所年報 (Annual Memoirs of the Otani University Shin Buddhist Comprehensive Research Institute) 1 (1983): 51–72.

———. *Foundations of T'ien-t'ai Philosophy: The Flowering of the Two Truths Theory in Chinese Buddhism.* Berkeley: Asian Humanities Press, 1989.

Taira Ryōshō 平了照. "Ryōzen dōchō ni tsuite 靈山同聽について." *Tendai gakuhō* 天台學報 14 (1966): 3–11.

Takao Giken 高雄義堅. *Sōdai Bukkyō-shi no kenkyū* 宋代仏教史の研究. Kyoto: Hyakka'en, 1975.

———. "Sōdai jōdokyō ni kansuru ichi kōsatsu 宋代浄土教に関する一考察." *Nihon Bukkyō gakkai nempō* 日本仏教學会年報 11 (1938): 30–41.

———. "Sō igo no jōdokyō 宋以後の浄土教." *Shina Bukkyo shigaku* 支那仏教史學 3, 3–4 (1940): 57–93.

Takemura Shōhō 武邑尚邦. *Jūjūbibasharon no kenkyū* 十住毘波沙論の研究. Kyoto: Hyakka'en, 1979.

Tambiah, Stanley J. "A Performative Approach to Ritual." *Proceedings of the British Academy* 65 (1979): 113–169.

T'ang Yung-t'ung 湯用彤. *Han Wei liang-Chin Nan-pei Ch'ao Fo-shiao shih* 漢魏兩晉南北朝佛教史. 2 vols. Taipei: Shang-wu yin-shu kuan, 1938.

Tsuda Sōkichi 津田左右. "Chigi no hokkezammai 智顗の法華三昧." *Tōyō gakuhō* 東洋學報 31, 1 (1927): 1–52.

Watson, Burton, trans. *The Complete Works of Chuang Tzu*. New York: Columbia University Press, 1968.

———, trans. *Hsün Tzu: Basic Writings*. New York: Columbia University Press, 1963.

Weinstein, Stanley. "Buddhism, Schools of: Chinese Buddhism." In *The Encyclopedia of Religion*. Edited by Mircea Eliade et al. New York: Macmillan, 1987.

———. *Buddhism under the T'ang*. Cambridge: Cambridge University Press, 1987.

———. "Imperial Patronage in the Formation of T'ang Buddhism." In *Perspectives on the T'ang*. Edited by Arthur Wright and Denis Twitchett. New Haven: Yale University Press, 1973.

Woodward, F. L., and E. M. Hare, trans. *The Book of Gradual Sayings (Anguttara-Nikaya) of More-Numbered Suttas*. 5 vols. London: Luzac & Co., 1960–1965.

Wright, Arthur F. *Buddhism in Chinese History*. Stanford: Stanford University Press, 1959.

———. "The Formation of Sui Ideology." In *Chinese Thought and Institutions*. Edited by John K. Fairbank. Chicago: University of Chicago Press, 1957.

———. *The Sui Dynasty: The Unification of China, A.D. 581–617*. New York: Alfred A. Knopf, 1978.

Yampolsky, Philip B. *The Platform Sutra of the Sixth Patriarch*. New York: Columbia University Press, 1967.

Index

About the Authors

Neal Donner received his Ph.D. from the University of British Columbia with a translation of the *Mo-ho chih-kuan.* His articles are published in *Sudden and Gradual: Approaches to Enlightenment in Chinese Thought,* edited by Peter N. Gregory, and in *Buddhist and Taoist Practice in Medieval Chinese Society,* edited by David W. Chappell.

Daniel B. Stevenson, currently professor of Chinese Buddhism in the Department of Religious Studies at the University of Kansas, received his Ph.D. from Columbia University with a dissertation on the Four Forms of Samādhi in the early T'ien-t'ai tradition. He has published a definitive study on the subject in *Traditions of Meditation in East Asian Buddhism,* edited by Peter N. Gregory, and is translating the ritual manuals of Chih-i.

HAWAII

Production Notes

Composition and paging were done by the printing division of Princeton University Press. Text design by Kenneth Miyamoto. The text typeface is Baskerville and the display typeface is Palatino. Offset presswork and binding were done by The Maple-Vail Book Manufacturing Group. Text paper is Writers RR Offset, basis 50.